For Phillip, who kept reminding me about how long I had been talking about writing this book

Contents at a Glance

Beginning 3D Game Development with Unity:

The World's Most Widely Used Multi-platform Game Engine

Sue Blackman

Apress®

Beginning 3D Game Development with Unity:
The World's Most Widely Used Multiplatform Game Engine

ISBN-13 (pbk): 978-1-4302-3422-7

ISBN-13 (electronic): 978-1-4302-3423-4

President and Publisher: Paul Manning
Lead Editor: Michelle Lowman
Technical Reviewer: Peter Laliberte and Robert Reed
Editorial Board: Steve Anglin, Mark Beckner, Ewan Buckingham, Gary Cornell, Jonathan Gennick, Jonathan Hassell, Michelle Lowman, James MarkhamMatthew Moodie, Jeff Olson, Jeffrey Pepper, Frank Pohlmann, Douglas Pundick, Ben Renow-Clarke, Dominic Shakeshaft, Matt Wade, Tom Welsh
Coordinating Editor: Anita Castro
Copy Editor: Mary Behr, Mary Ann Fugate, and Sharon Terdeman
Compositor: Richard Ables
Indexer: BIM Indexing & Proofreading Services
Artist: SPi Global
Cover Designer: Anna Ishchenko

Distributed to the book trade worldwide by Springer Science+Business Media, LLC., 233 Spring Street, 6th Floor, New York, NY 10013. Phone 1-800-SPRINGER, fax (201) 348-4505, e-mail orders-ny@springer-sbm.com, or visit www.springeronline.com.

For information on translations, please e-mail rights@apress.com, or visit www.apress.com.

Apress and friends of ED books may be purchased in bulk for academic, corporate, or promotional use. eBook versions and licenses are also available for most titles. For more information, reference our Special Bulk Sales–eBook Licensing web page at www.apress.com/bulk-sales.

The source code for this book is available to readers at www.apress.com. You will need to answer questions pertaining to this book in order to successfully download the code.

Contents

About the Author

 Sue Blackman is a 3D artist and interactive applications author and instructor based in southern California. She has taught 3ds Max and game classes for artists for well over ten years in top-rated community colleges and private schools, such as the Art Institute of California, and has been lead 3D artist on games for Activision through one of their subsidiaries. She has worked in the industry for several years to help train Fortune 1000 companies, such as Boeing, Raytheon, and Northrop Grumman, to create serious games and training applications with game-based formats. She has been involved with the commercial development of real-time 3D engines for nearly ten years. She is an avid tutorial writer and has created both tutorials, as a contributing author, and artwork for various 3ds Max books over the years, as well as training manuals for 3D authoring applications for serious games. She has also written for ACM Siggraph on serious games, one of her favorite topics. You can visit her web site at www.3dadventurous.com.

About the Technical Reviewers

 Peter Laliberte runs the web site burgzergarcade.com, which focuses on teaching game development with a strong emphasis on using Unity3d. He came over to Unity3d around two years ago after using Objective-C for iPhone development, and has never looked back. Besides using Unity3d, he is a skilled programmer in several languages, including C/C++, PHP, and Java. When he is not busy cooking up some crazy game mechanics, he enjoys spending time outdoors with his two-year-old son and wife.

 Robert Reed is currently enrolled at Collins College in Phoenix, Arizona, studying game design, and he is set to graduate in March 2011. He quickly learned JavaScript and Unity3d in about a year and loved working on this book.

Acknowledgments

Thanks go out to Gabriel Acosta and Jenny Wang, who helped brainstorm much of the game play for the book's project. I owe special thanks to Jenny for the start menu design and stele idea.

Thanks also to Bryan Taylor and Sean McCurry of Binary Sonata Studios for the temple music and camera match code, and to Daniel Butler for providing the voice (in three different variations) of the temple guardian.

Thank you all for taking time out from your own game projects to contribute to mine. Your assets, ideas, and enthusiasms were much appreciated.

Introduction

Why Write This Book

Real time 3D games have been around for well over ten years now. We've played them, created assets in the style of our favorites, and maybe even "mod"ed a few of them. But until recently, the cost of licensing one of the premier game engines has ranged from several hundred thousand to several million dollars per title (!), relegating the dream of creating your own 3D game to an unattainable fantasy.

Times have changed. 3D has become affordable not only in the movie industry, as seen by the number of titles featuring CG (computer graphics), but also in the game industry where we've seen a shift in casual games from 2D to a 3D format. With Unity's bold move to offer a robustly featured free version of their engine, a radical change in the pricing models of the high-end engines has rocked the industry. The cost of the engine is no longer a barrier to taking your game from a nebulous idea to a working prototype and even on to a marketable product.

Whether your interest is in casual games or you have more ambitious aims, if you have no previous scripting experience but are eager to bring your art assets and story to life, this may be just the book to get you underway. In today's modern game engines, the heavy programming is handled by the engine itself, so the logic and game play can be scripted by those with more creativity than traditional programming knowledge.

In this book, I will approach game creation and design decisions from a 3D artist's view, taking the logic and scripting in small pieces, while introducing artists, budding game designers, and novice programmers to real-time game engine concepts at the same time.

This book is written in a project-based format so you will not only end up with a playable game and scripting resources you can reuse for other games, but you will experience typical design decisions that need to be addressed throughout the process. You will create your game by starting with the basics and refining it as you add functionality; I will explain the logic behind certain choices and real-time game concepts as you go along.

The project for this book is based on a first person point and click adventure game, complete with inventory, state management, load/save functionality, and a strong emphasis on the visual aspects of game creation. Even if you are more of a first person shooter-type game enthusiast, you will be able to see how including entertaining or interesting tasks and features can enhance your favorite genre.

The aim of this project is to introduce you to a logical progression of design decisions and problem solving that will be of value well beyond the scope of the adventure game genre. It provides a framework and a methodology for creating and, more importantly, *finishing* your own game. You will be going beyond the basic Unity functionality and use of standard assets to investigate topics rarely covered in online tutorials or books. All of the necessary art assets to complete the project are provided.

Author's Note

In a recent game class, after working through a race game, a first person shooter, and a platform jumper, I decided that the last project would be a classic adventure game. Much to my surprise, the class got quite motivated with all of the design decisions and logic involved. As there were no existing tutorials at the time on this genre, we created the game from the ground up, borrowing scripts from the previous projects, creating several of our own, and drawing heavily on the knowledge base of the Unity community. This book grew out of that experience, both to fill a need and to share the adventure with others.

Classic Adventure Game

For this project you will be creating a variation on the classic point and click adventure game. The adventure genre, of which there are many variations, is an ideal starting place for artists and others with little or no scripting experience. The story, art assets, and animation are major components of this type of game, and the slower pace allows more freedom from script optimization as split-second player reaction time is not required.

One of the most enjoyable components of the adventure game is the collection and usage of an odd assortment of objects. Because of the importance of inventory and state management, several chapters are dedicated to their design and implementation. Neophyte Unity developers often ask how to implement these features in community forums, but they rarely receive answers due to the scope of the topic. By the end of this book, you will be armed with the scripts, concepts, and experience to be able to take the knowledge beyond this genre.

Interactive adventure games are also ideal for indie developers, and they appeal to a broad range of players. Tell Tale Games' *Tales of Monkey Island* was one of the top selling casual games of the year, proving once again their appeal, established by the original LucasArts series.

About the Unity Game Engine

Unity is the perfect choice for small studios, indie developers, and those of us who have always wanted to make our own games. Its large user base (over 400,000 as of April 2011) and extremely active user community allows everyone from newbies to seasoned veterans to get answers and share information quickly.

Unity provides an excellent entry point into game development, balancing features and functionality with price point. The free version of Unity allows people to experiment, learn, develop, and sell games before committing any of their hard-earned cash. Unity's very affordable, feature-packed Pro version is royalty free, allowing people to make and sell games with the very low overhead essential to the casual games market.

The market for multi-platform games—especially casual games for iPhone—is extremely popular at the moment, and Unity's commitment to cross platform delivery is well proven. Originally a Mac-based authoring application that could publish to Mac and Windows, Unity unveiled its Windows version in the spring of 2009. As expected, it has opened up opportunities for PC-based developers and artists. Since that time, Unity has continued to add support for iPhone, Android, iPad, and Wii and is developing support for Xbox 360 and PS3. The free Unity Web Player has surpassed 35 million installations.

Early adapters of the Unity engine tended to migrate from Flash and Director, making the scripting environment easily adoptable. While many Unity users have an ActionScript background in making Flash games, it is by no means a prerequisite. There is a lot of material for creating games in Unity, including first person shooters, racing games, platform jumpers, and the like. Even if your interest lies elsewhere, there are plenty of helpful tips and tricks to be gleaned from even the most unlikely sources. Don't be afraid to take advantage of the resources available on the Unity web site (www.Unity3D.com), the

Unity forum (forum.unity3d.com), the wiki (www.unifycommunity.com/wiki), UnityAnswers (answers.unity3d.com), and numerous private party web sites devoted to the Unity engine.

Unity documentation also contains a wealth of valuable information, but, as with any technology that has a unique vocabulary, it's sometimes hard to find just what you're looking for. Prefacing your query with Unity3D and searching the Internet is often the easiest way to find elusive concepts or functionality. You can make use of them via the Help menu, but it is often quicker to take advantage of the online version.

Will I have to learn to script?

You don't have to be a programmer to make your own game with Unity, but you *will* need to be able to understand enough of what the scripts do to know what can be tweaked to your advantage or decide if a particular script will suit your needs.

Most game play needs to be scripted in Unity, but there are hundreds of scripts already available that can be readily reused. Unity ships with several of the most useful. More can be found by searching the forum, Wiki, or UnityAnswers. Many forum members will even write bits of script for less adept users. In the Collaboration section of the forum, you can even find scripters looking to trade for art assets. By the end of this book, you should know enough to be able to take advantage of the wealth of material available from the Unity community.

Games, by their very definition, are about interaction; even with games that are largely controlled by physics, logic-driven cause and effect is what differentiates games from linear plot-driven passive media. Even the most "artist friendly" game engines need scripting to move beyond simple environmental walkthroughs. This book's aim is to familiarize you with scripting a few lines at a time, while providing visual feedback as often as possible. The assumption is that you have not yet decided to *learn* to script but are happy enough to participate in its creation in a more passive manner.

Scripting is More About Logic Than Syntax

While many people worry that learning a new language will be difficult and intimidating, think of it this way: most people under the age of 35 are quite fluent in texting, which is a valid subset of our native language. To a certain extent, it has its own vocabulary and syntax, and it is very similar to scripting languages in that it is more of a subset than an entirely new language.

The difference mainly lies in the method used to acquire the "language." In texting, as with our native language, one doesn't set out to study and *learn* the language. Instead, one absorbs, experiments, and eventually becomes competent through repeated contact, trial and error, and a host of other passive means rather than rote memorization and stressful examination. This book, because it's about the *logic* behind game design and creation, treats scripting as an immersive experience that is a sideline to the game development process. You are free to choose your own amount of involvement with the scripting. Whatever you choose, the main scripts developed in the book will enable you to create or expand upon the final output of the book, the game, with your own ideas and art assets.

That being said, there are only a few important concepts and a handful of keywords you need to know in order to get an idea of what's being done in a script. Fortunately, most scripters are quite good at including comments explaining what the code is doing, thus making complicated scripts much less daunting to investigate.

Scripts developed in this book will be provided on a per-chapter basis and the logic behind them explained in the chapters, but I hope that you will display classic adventurer curiosity and take advantage of the scripting explanations to do some experimenting on your own.

What About Math?

One of the most common things we hear people say in the 3D industry is, "If I'd known math was going to be so useful, I would have paid more attention in class." Be that as it may, most artists and designers are not going to want to invest any time in brushing up on their math skills. Don't worry! My primary goal is to help you create a game. Some of the functionality you will scavenge for your game is easy to use without even knowing how it works. Most of us are quite happy to drive cars without having extensive knowledge of the internal combustion engine. Don't be afraid to treat scripting the same way!

Assumptions and Prerequisites

This book assumes that you are at least somewhat familiar with 3D assets and 3D space, but it does have a short review of the concepts and plenty of tips and tricks throughout.

It assumes that you will not have had much scripting experience (if any at all) but that you'll be willing to work through it in order to bring your stories to life.

It assumes that, as of yet, you have little or no experience with using the Unity game engine.

It also assumes that you are fairly new to the game-making process but have a strong desire to create your own real-time 3D game.

Additionally, this book assumes that if you want to explore genres other than classic point and click adventure games, you will work through the book with a goal of thinking about how to apply the various techniques to get results related to the other genre. In the casual game market, combining elements of adventure games, first person shooters, and other genres is not only acceptable but makes for some very entertaining results.

What This Book Doesn't Cover

This book is not about conventional game design; it is more of a precursor, getting you into the habit of analyzing needs and weighing choices. Not only is creating a massive design document intimidating when you are the one who will have to implement everything, but it is likely to be unrealistic until you are more familiar with the engine and your own capabilities. You're going to build your game up a little bit at a time, prototyping ideas and functionality as you go along.

This is not a book on how to become a programmer, still less on programming best practices. The scripting in this book is designed to ease a non-programmer into the process by providing instant visual feedback as often as possible. While there are usually several ways to attain the same goal, the scripting choices made in this book are the easiest to read and understand from an artist or designer's point of view. In this book, scripting is presented in the way a native speaker learns his own language. He is surrounded by it, immersed in it, and allowed to tinker with it to slowly gain a basic working knowledge of it. Don't worry about remembering it all. Some things you will use throughout the project and others you will be encouraged to take note of for future reference.

Conventions Used in This Book

1. Instructions look like this.

Tips Follow this format.

Code looks like this.

Platform

This book was written using Unity 3.x in a Windows 7 and a Windows XP environment. Differences for shortcut keys and operating system file storage with Unity on a Mac will be noted throughout the book.

CHAPTER 1

Exploring the Genre

As mentioned in the introduction, the classic point and click adventure genre provides not only a forgiving environment in which to create a game, but it also allows you to explore tips, tricks, and techniques often ignored in other beginning Unity game books.

Coupled with the fact that it appeals to a wide range of players, including many that have never played a first person shooter type game, it becomes an ideal vehicle for the casual games market. And, given that so many people have their own idea for some variation of the genre, it appears to be a good place to start.

Historical Reference

"You are standing at the end of a road…"

The granddaddy of all adventure games is arguably *Adventure*, the text-based game originally design by Will Crowther in the mid 1970s. In an era where computer games were dominated by *Pong* and *PacMan*, the text-based game that catered to those with a dexterous mind rather than dexterous fingers was a revelation. In the earliest version, also known as *Colossal Cave*, Crowther set the scene for intrepid adventurers to explore a great underground cave system, collecting loot, and dealing with the occasional monster. It was reportedly fashioned after the Mammoth Cave system in Kentucky where Crowther had developed a vector-based map in conjunction with his own explorations and existing surveys. Figure 1-1 illustrates some of the collectable items from *Adventure*.

Figure 1-1. *A few of the collectables from Adventure*

The prose in the game was always beautifully descriptive and often highly entertaining due in part to the vocabulary and parsing of the user's input. Don Woods expanded the original a year or two later, adding the concept of a scoring system as well as introducing other characters from the realm of fantasy—both important ingredients for the fledgling genre. Other early enthusiasts went on to form their own software companies, notably the husband and wife team of Roberta and Ken Williams who founded the company that eventually became Sierra Entertainment, and Infocom, the company that defined the genre with its *Zork* series created by Marc Blank, Dave Lebling, Bruce Daniels, and Tim Anderson.

Infocom's *Zork* series, introduced us to the Great Underground Empire, the Flathead dynasty, and the coin of the realm, the zorkmid (Figure 1-2). They spawned several memorable lines such as "Your lamp is getting dim," "You can't get there from here" and many running jokes. Anyone who knows what a grue is can tell you that when your lamp goes out, you are in danger of being eaten by one. While many adventure game puzzles are mechanical, the Frobozz Magic [insert item name here] Company, a subsidiary of FrobozzCo, introduced various magical items.

Figure 1-2. *The famous zorkmid coin*

Common to most text adventure games is the means of navigation. Locations became "rooms" with exits in Cartesian directions such as North, East, South, West, Up, and Down that could be mapped out on paper as the player explored the environment (see Figure 1-3). Inventories were generally a must as well as the need to combine various objects to solve logic-based or mechanical puzzles to move forward in the game. So popular was the idea that the television series *MacGyver*, that aired in the mid to late 1980s and starred Richard Dean Anderson, drew heavily on many of the puzzles found in the earlier text adventure games.

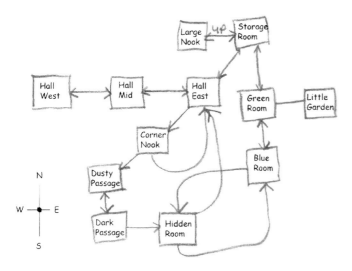

Figure 1-3. *A player's hand drawn map of a text-based adventure game*

Graphical Adventure

With the advent of computer graphics, the text-based adventure game genre waned as graphic quality and resolution slowly improved. Eventually, the text-based predecessor gave way to the still image format or graphical adventure genre, pioneered by Sierra Online's *King's Quest*, a host of LucasArts offerings, and Infocom's later *Zork* titles.

The graphical format spelled the end of players typing in their instructions or questions, relying instead on a short predefined list of verbs and mouse picks (see Figure 1-4). Gone was a large part of the charm of the early text adventures where one could type in just about anything to see if the authors had allowed for it, no matter how ridiculous or risqué.

Figure 1-4. *LucasArts' Indiana Jones and the Fate of Atlantis*

As far as creating material for the new genre, it now required more than just a writer and programmer. It introduced the artist as a major part of the production pipeline. As resolution increased, so did the art assets required. The graphical games typically had four levels or worlds in which to explore, collect useful objects, solve tasks, and gain treasures or points in pursuit of the final goal. Unlike levels in today's first person shooters where the player faces enemies that are increasingly more difficult to overcome in each successive level, the worlds in adventure games continue to be strongly differentiated by theme, visual style, color scheme, and music. The reward for gaining access to the various worlds is the discovery of new and intriguing environments, designed to stimulate the senses and draw the player into the fantasy.

In the early 1990s, Rand and Robyn Miller's *Myst* twisted the usual format to introduce the concept of using game play to reveal the story itself. Acquisition and inventory was practically non-existent, but interaction and task or puzzle solving was visually breathtaking for the times (Figure 1-5). As one of the first to incorporate 3D graphics instead of traditional artwork, they introduced another shift in the genre. Now, not only did one need artists to produce a game, a good number of them had to be able to create artwork in the fledgling 3D programs.

Figure 1-5. *Myst, one of the first adventure games to make use of 3D graphics. (Myst (TM) is the sole property of Cyan Worlds Inc. Copyright 1993, 2001. Cyan Worlds, Inc. All rights reserved. Used with permission)*

With the acquisition of Infocom by Activision in the late 1980s, *Zork Nemesis* made the jump to 3D graphics, but an attempt to shift the story and mood to the dark side was met with varied reception. The game was well received in its own right but had little to do with the original series. A later attempt with *Zork Grand Inquisitor* to return it to its roots fell short due in part to inconsistent graphics quality. A high point was the university level created by 3D artist Eni Oken (Figure 1-6).

Figure 1-6. *Activision's Zork Grand Inquisitor, featuring the 3D artwork of Eni Oken*

Sierra Online took the adventure game genre in other directions with *King's Quest*, where fantasy moved closer to classic fairy tale, and the *Gabriel Knight* series, which pursued the realm of the supernatural.

LucasArts Titles

Undoubtedly a force in the early days of the graphical adventure game genre was LucasArts. With an army of professional film personnel from which to draw, LucasArts titles gained a huge reputation for outstanding storytelling, topnotch graphics, and marvelous soundtracks. Of note is the *Monkey Island* series. As with several other titles such as *Sam and Max* and *Day of the Tentacle*, the entertainment is heavily driven by humor, references to pop culture, and a hearty sense of the ridiculous.

Monkey Island III, The Curse of Monkey Island was one of the last LucasArts titles to use traditional hand painted backdrops and cell animation (see Figure 1-7). Rather than looking dated, its style and execution continue to stand the test of time.

Figure 1-7. *LucasArts' Monkey Island III, The Curse of Monkey Island,1997 (COURTESY OF LUCASARTS, A DIVISION OF LUCASFILM ENTERTAINMENT COMPANY LTD.)*

Fast Forward to Real Time

The next paradigm shift in the game industry came with the introduction of real-time environments and navigation. By now, adventure game enthusiasts expected stunning high-end graphics such as those in *Myst*'s sequel, *Riven* (Figure 1-8). The difficulty of staying oriented in a beautiful pre-rendered world was still preferable to the low resolution, minimalistic environments of real-time navigation. While it allowed the graphical adventure genre to hold on a bit longer, the latest threat to the prerendered format's existence became economical. In the early 1990s, the big publishers found larger markets with real-time first person shooters such ID's *Doom* and its successor, *Quake*, at a fraction of the production cost.

Figure 1-8. *Cyan's Riven, the pinnacle of the pre-rendered adventure game (Riven (TM) is the sole property of Cyan Worlds Inc. Copyright 1997, 2003 Cyan Worlds, Inc. All rights reserved. Used with permission.)*

Now, over a decade later, graphics quality is finally beginning to approach pre-rendered standards and once again the adventure game genre is making a comeback, but not in the expected venue. As major publishers (as well as software companies) have grown larger, they are less inclined to spend money on developing games that will not sell millions of copies. Other genres that traditionally might sell only 70,000 to 150,000 units each slowly disappeared from the shelves, as did the stores and shelves themselves.

The two biggest factors in the revival of not only the adventure game genre, but other specialty genres, are the shift to online buying of products, enabling developers to bypass the big publishers, and the ease and affordability of the software required to author and produce games. The ensuing casual games market, blown wide open with the advent of the iPhone and other mobile platforms, has enabled small studios to enjoy success and motivated individuals to break into the industry as never before.

What draws people to this genre?

The repeated revival of the adventure game genre proves that there is a continuing need for this type of entertainment. While it would be fairly easy to copy its puzzle format without understanding the underlying principles, the resulting game would probably be less than satisfying. If, on the other hand, you take the time to start with a list of people's motivations for playing adventure games, it will take a lot of the guesswork out of the design process. Once identified, you will be surprised at how quickly the design and development will progress. We can surmise that the audience for adventure games is not looking for a way to let off steam, challenge themselves with physical dexterity, or develop an online persona for a social network. Let's do a bit of investigating to uncover the motivation.

As a broad generalization, it could be said that people play adventure games in order to escape to a world more interesting and stimulating than our own reality. While this observation is probably too generic to be of much use, it provides a starting point.

We may be seeking experiences that we don't have the time or money to pursue ourselves. *Monkey Island* becomes the Caribbean vacation that is always just out of reach. Rather than risking thousands of dollars hoping the real experience will provide the unexpected, we know that, with our help, Guybrush Threepwood will bumble through cultural faux pas, discover local points of interest, and land in plenty of sticky situations (see Figure 1-9).

Figure 1-9. *LucasArts' Monkey Island III (COURTESY OF LUCASARTS, A DIVISION OF LUCASFILM ENTERTAINMENT COMPANY LTD.)*

In games, we are also allowed virtual experience without physical or social accountability. Fox Network's *House, M.D.* series once touted House as the "doctor you love to hate." Far from hating House, most of us envy his lack of adherence to social norms. In adventure games, we are at liberty, and often required, to forego the social niceties in pursuit of the game's goal. Trespassing, grand theft, and a host of misdemeanors are often part and parcel of the required actions to complete the game (see Figure 1-10).

Figure 1-10. *The temptation of the forbidden: there must be something useful in there…*

Intellectual stimulus is another of the factors that appeals strongly to the adventure game enthusiast. Without a doubt, it is one of the main advantages that interactive games have over the passive media of films and TV. Recent studies have shown how important it is to exercise and challenge the brain in order to slow its aging process. That game companies such as Nintendo have been highly successful with their brain teasers, brain training, and brain fitness games validates peoples' need for cerebral exercise. Most of us are already aware that we will thrive in surroundings that provide problems that have attainable solutions as opposed to the brainless monotony of a boring environment. The classic adventure game is one means of filling this need.

The most difficult aspect of this part of the game design process is deciding how challenging the task will be to solve (Figure 1-11). Other than text-based clues and hints, we need to decide how many visual and/or audio hints ought to be included. Players will feel cheated if solutions are too easy but may quickly become frustrated if they are too hard. Fortunately, the Internet is generally full of cheats and walkthroughs for those who are more interested in moving the story forward than solving a particularly baffling task on their own. Aside from trying to decide what the *overall* difficulty should be for the target audience, we also need to strive to maintain a consistent level of difficulty with the tasks. We may opt to increase it gradually as the game nears its conclusion, or, better yet, carefully orchestrate it so that the pieces of the puzzle fall into place at the finale providing the player with that highly rewarding "ah ha!" moment.

Figure 1-11. *Levels of hints, visual and text-based.* **Top Left**: *"A nondescript, melon-sized rock."* **Top Right**: *"An interesting melon-sized rock with the faint remains of some sort of glyphs." **Bottom Left**: "A melon-sized rock with deeply etched glyphs. It appears to be covering something." **Bottom Right**: "A glyph-covered rock, the size of a melon, bathed in an eerie green light. A large iron key is just visible beneath it."*

Aside from the intellectual stimuli, we also enjoy having experiences without physical risk or discomfort. As with books, film, and television, we love to picture ourselves in dire situations of extreme climates and dangerous predicaments but have little desire to experience the reality of actual physical pain from horrendous temperatures or disabling injuries (see Figure 1-12).

Figure 1-12. *120 degrees Farenheit. Are we hot yet?*

Adventure game enthusiasts are not afraid of admitting to being couch or computer potatoes. Unlike fans of first person shooters, we have no illusions that complicated keyboard and mouse sequences will prove our own physical prowess. That doesn't mean that battling monsters to get to a particular place in the storyline is verboten; it merely means two or three attempts should provide the probability that allows us to be victorious and move on. When confronted by a chasm that may only be leaped by a superhuman, we should be able to do so with a simple mouse click (see Figure 1-13). The achievement of physical tasks should be aimed at making the story more interesting, rather than merely posing problems to be solved by dexterous use of keyboard, mouse, or other input devise.

Figure 1-13. *Make it so, number one…preferably with a single mouse click.*

Unlike first person shooters, where one is usually moving through the scene too fast to appreciate the surroundings, a big draw for the adventure genre is the visual richness of the environment itself. Although *Riven* raised the bar to almost impossible heights, real-time visual quality is finally getting close enough to be acceptable for realistic environments. Visual richness is not, however, limited to photorealism. Even in the cartoon styled games such as the later *Monkey Island* episodes, our suspension of disbelief is maintained by unfamiliar vegetation, whimsical buildings, and Rube Goldberg-type contraptions. As long as the environment is full of interesting content, the artistic style can be considered a separate component. Whether the game takes place in a location filled with objects from the art nouveau period, a fantasy steampunk tableau, or a war-torn post apocalyptic environment, filling the scenes with appropriate paraphernalia and motifs encourages the adventurer to explore and investigate the surroundings regardless of moving the game forward (see Figure 1-14).

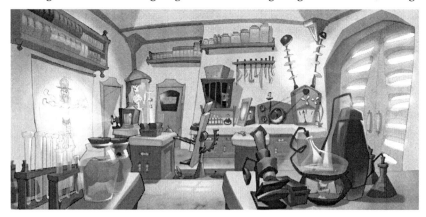

Figure 1-14. *Clutter, Tales of Monkey Island, TellTalesGames,2009.*

The story also tends to be of greater weight in adventure games as it can often be the only clue to solving several of the tasks or puzzles. A formal story-driven plot versus the goal being revealed as you advance through the game will also set the scene for the style of game play. Without a clear plot at the outset, successful short term goals move the game forward by being intriguing and challenging in their own right, drawing us into the game as we tinker with the intractable objects. Conversely, with plot driven games, we work through the game in anticipation of having all of the pieces finally fall into place in hopes of a clever twist on the expected results. It is no surprise that many games in this genre are based upon books or stories by conventional authors.

As with books and to a lesser extent films, associating with the main character is a good portion of why we enjoy playing any kind of immersive game. Additionally, the mechanism of controlling a character in the story, whether as first person or third person, draws us in even deeper. In the games where character interaction is minimal, we become the protagonist in first person format, being responsible for his actions and decisions as the story unfolds. Successful adventure games that rely heavily on interaction with characters of any type, on the other hand, tend to include and develop quirky regulars that appear throughout subsequent additions to the series. Anticipation of the entertainment value of these secondary characters, apart from the assumed conversations, greatly enriches the story.

Intriguing Locations and Entertaining Solutions

Now that we have a better idea of why people like playing games, let's consider the implications of these findings. Assuming you do not have a fifty artist team and two years to produce your game, you will need to make some smart design decisions to enable a good chance of success. Story line, concept art, interaction, and to some extent functionality can proceed independent of the game engine. At some point, however, you will find that technology, regardless of how many man-hours you have allotted for the art assets, will not allow for everything you can envision. The toughest part for the artist is deciding what can be sacrificed. At the design stage, with some forethought, you can make the process less painful as you visualize the intriguing locations and entertaining solutions (see Figure 1-15).

Figure 1-15. *I don't think we're in Kansas anymore. (Triberian Oasis, Sue Blackman, 2002)*

The movie *Avatar* has raised the bar on our expectations of virtual worlds. With the massive amount of geometry and special effects, even a single frame of that world took a reported thirty to fifty *hours* to render. In real time, we hope to have at least thirty frames *per second*. Obviously, something will need to be sacrificed.

Figure 1-16 depicts a world that, in 2003, was pre-render only with its 1.5 million polygons and special effects. Today, in real time, this scene easily achieves a high enough frame rate to be used as a game environment—even before optimization.

Figure 1-16. *What was once only possible in pre-rendered scenes may now be reproducable in real time (Swamp Scene, Sue Blackman, 2003)*

Visual quality in real time *can* be achieved with clever application of a lot of "smoke and mirrors," thanks to today's shaders and the graphics cards they are designed to communicate with. Unfortunately, the time and resources required to build large, stunning, photorealistic environments are generally not within reach of casual or budding game developers. Don't despair. Rather than falling short of the realism you are trying to achieve, you can sidestep the problem with a few easy-to-implement design decisions.

Defining a Style

By clearly defining a style for your environment, you can prevent people from expecting unattainable levels of realism. It can be as overt as using a cartoon, anime, or other well defined visual language, or it can be more subtle by placing the world itself in a fantasy or alien realm. Shortcomings in photorealism are much harder to detect when the mind has nothing with which to compare. When you decide upon a style, start by listing its most distinctive features for colors, motifs, lighting, and anything else that visually defines it. Whatever style you choose, be careful to keep continuity throughout the assets wherever appropriate. Just for fun, let's use the classic adventurer's companion, the lantern, to illustrate a few different styles. The two basic requirements of a lantern are it must be a light source and it must be readily portable.

New, but classic design (see Figure 1-17, left): This lantern could be bought at any hardware store or through any catalogue for any time in the past 150 years. Lacking wear and tear, this could indicate that this is your protagonist's first adventure and the world fairly contemporary. Colors should reflect the period chosen.

Dust and rust (see Figure 1-17, right): This is the same lantern after a century or so of neglect. This could be a chance encounter as your protagonist explores an unexpected find, or it could be part of a story set in a post-apocalyptic world where everything is rusted, decaying, or deteriorated. Colors would be muted, mostly grays and browns, and broken bits of technology would litter the scenes.

Figure 1-17. *Left: New, but classic design* **Right:** *Dust and rust*

Steampunk (see Figure 1-18, left): In the Mechanical Age, metals and fabricating were an art form and in high use. Motif was in the form of functional detail more than particular designs. This style can be cutting edge of its era, or it can be combined with a healthy dose of grunge for interesting environments. Colors are muted except for brass, copper, iron, and polished steel.

Fantasy, magic, and imagination (see Figure 1-18, right): Ornamentation and use of gold trim and colors such as magenta, cyan, and the like are prevalent in this style, Shapes tend to be flowing and whimsical. Mechanical details can be left out.

Figure 1-18. *Left:* Steampunk *Right:* Fantasy, magic, and imagination

"**Toon**" (see Figure 1-19, left): Primary or secondary colors and simplified or whimsical shapes define this style. With today's shaders, you can also combine "toon" style with realism for a hybrid style, as shown in this variation of the adventurer's lantern.

Alien (see Figure 1-19, right): Anything goes in this style so long as there is a reasonable connection to the physical constraints of the world. Think like a native and make use of what you "find." In this variation on the lantern, I distilled the two basic requirements—it must be a light source and readily portable—and then I built it with "native" materials.

Figure 1-19. *Left:* "Toon" *Right:* Alien

Compartmentalizing Environments

Any given game engine, in conjunction with the machine it is running on, can only draw so many objects on screen at any one time. Additionally, machines can only hold so many textures and meshes in memory at any one time. When asked why there are game levels, a room full of gamers will give any number of reasons—the primary one being as a measure of accomplishment. While that is a valid reason as far as game play and story goes, the real truth is that the technology becomes the limiting factor.

Although streaming data may become more prevalent in the future, at this time we will soon hit a limit as to how much geometry and textures can be loaded and in memory. Obviously, the amount will vary with the platform and graphics card (see Figure 1-20), so the first decision is the minimum platform your game should be able to run on. That will serve as a basis for determining how vast each level can be.

Figure 1-20. *Different platforms and technology*

While the hardware is a limiting factor for the entire level, the design will be key to determining how many objects will need to be drawn on screen *at any one time*. The trick is to design the environment so that major clusters of polygons/art assets are only visible at particular times. Think in terms of creating towns or areas of interaction inside box canyons (see Figure 1-21). The steepness and height of the walls will block the view of neighboring clusters of settlements or whatever the assets are. Twisting entries to the areas can block line of sight to other polygon-heavy areas.

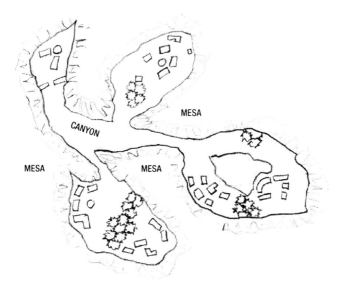

Figure 1-21. *Environment designs*

Designing buildings works in much the same way. Long straight vistas where everything must be rendered are far less economical than creating hallways and passages that block the view of all but the immediate area (see Figure 1-22). If you can effectively narrow visibility to smaller spaces, you are free to fill those spaces up with more objects to increase the visual sophistication of the area.

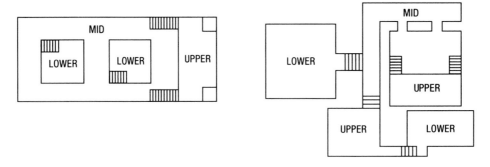

Figure 1-22. *Building designs*

Parallax

A cheap but effective way to increase the visual interest in a real-time environment is to take full advantage of the parallax effect. The parallax effect is where objects in the distance appear to move more slowly than those close to the camera or person's vantage point. With real-time navigation, using several different elevations for the ground or building, as well as multiple freestanding large objects, increases the perception of being in a 3D space and incrementally improves the user's visual experience of the environment. Put simply, parallax helps convince the brain that you are in a true 3D environment—without the help of 3D glasses! While it is difficult to see the effect with a series of still shots, study the positions of the foreground, midground, and background elements in relationship to each other as in Figure 1-23.

Figure 1-23. *Parallax:objects in the foreground appear to move faster than objects in the background as the view is panned right or left.*

Animation

In many cases, animation can make up for realism. An object that has less sophisticated materials and lower poly count than its pre-rendered counterpart can be far more believable with a well done animation. Be aware that the human brain is just as quick to pick up animations that "just don't look right" in mechanical sequences as it is with organic or character type animation. To be believable and compelling, they must be of the highest quality. Fortunately, top-notch animation generally takes up the same amount of resources as poorly executed animation.

Challenges, Tasks, and Puzzles

While the previously mentioned considerations are a good basis for generic game design in several different genres, this topic is much more specialized for the adventure genre where interaction and problem solving are among the key features.

Designing challenges that are gratifying to solve is not enough in itself because what is difficult and fulfilling for one person may be easy and trivial for someone else. The resulting sequence should be compelling, entertaining, and interesting whenever possible. Here we can also learn from the comedy of Peter Sellers or the suspense of Alfred Hitchcock: if the solution seems obvious, do something extra and use anticipation to your advantage. Add something unexpected to the mix. The *Monkey Island* series, now carried on by TellTale Games, has mastered the art. Many objects, once found, immediately suggest their purpose, but when used, tend to surprise the player with something unexpectedly entertaining in addition to the anticipated result.

As the aim is to reward the player for correct behavior or actions, it is also a good idea to avoid frustrating him. Allowing the player to think he has the correct solution worked out, then letting him down by having that interaction lead to more necessary tasks before success can be attained, is not particularly enjoyable. The recent Wallace & *Gromit* series, also by TellTale Games, is a good example. The style and music are true to the well loved short films, and the animation, modeling, and texturing of the art assets are top notch. Where the early games in the series fall short is that they constantly set the player up for failure, in compliance with the Wallace character in the films. When obvious interaction and solutions are constantly foiled, the player's interest in trying to solve the next version of the problem wanes. While we expect bumbling Wallace to muck things up, it's one thing watching the entertaining results in a movie or short film but quite another to be forced into his persona in a game and have to deal with the challenges within the limits of the original character. Cleverly, midway through the series, TellTale Games worked out the recipe to allow game play to reward the player while still remaining true to the Wallace character. This kind of research and analyzation shows why TellTale Games dominates the casual adventure game market.

For more enjoyable game play, then, the character can certainly bumble into sticky situations, but he should be able to get himself out with cleverness, ingenuity, and a dollop of luck. In short, avoid setting the player up for failure. If you plan on making it so that the obvious will not work, at least give the player hints beforehand.

What went wrong with the genre?

With a list of do's and don'ts for adventure games, you may be wondering what caused the drop in popularity from the era of its heyday in the early 1990s. The topic is certainly worth investigating before you plunge headlong into your own game.

In the early 1990s, the text based adventure had been relegated to its own place in history, being categorized as interactive fiction. The graphical adventure, pioneered by the cutting edge graphics of

Myst and *Riven*, became a feast for visual enjoyment. Predictably, producing such graphics was costly. Success invariably breeds inexpensive knock-offs and several studios jumped on the bandwagon, either to milk what they could from the genre, or because they also had ideas for similar games but not enough budget or expertise to pull it off.

Unfortunately, weak storylines and third rate graphics soon flooded the market with mediocre offerings. Wary consumers learned to beware of marketing that touted "stunning graphics" and "intriguing worlds." Users quickly learned not to waste money on a few of the more notorious publishers of formulaic, outsourced dross.

That is not to say there was nothing of quality produced after *Riven*. Of note are *The Longest Journey* and *Syberia*. Both contain strong story, interesting locations, good art assets, and interaction for tasks and puzzle solving. Other than the baker in a small French village having a Bronx accent in *Syberia*, and the required dialogue being a bit on the heavy side in *The Longest Journey*, the player finds it easy to keep his suspension of disbelief as the games progress.

In all fairness, as the genre moved from text-based to graphical, the move from user-typed input to canned dialog choices limited the interaction, causing the player to feel he was interacting in a nearly linear storyline. One of the best parts of the old text games was that you could try anything with objects. Authors of graphical adventures need to be very creative with the visual results of player interaction because it's not feasible to create animations for every interaction possibility. Where the possibilities for interacting with a rock (take, roll, kick, toss, crush, etc.) in a text-base game could produce a wide range of entertaining replies, in graphical games, the verbs for interaction are quickly distilled down to "take" and "use."

Another drawback appeared with the move to real time. The classic point and click in still rendered scenes was now complicated by the need for a less passive means of scene navigation. On one hand, the player was finally able to keep his bearings as he played through the world, but the down side was the navigation itself. The classic shooter navigation , WASD (keyboard controls for forward, strafe left, backward and strafe right) with mouse to look and turn, not only took skill and practice, but was developed for games where the navigation is fast, faster, jump, and shoot. Hybrid adventures such as LucasArts' *Grim Fandango* (see Figure 1-24) let you move a character around in a limited space, but it continued to use disjointed camera changes for each room.

Figure 1-24. *LucasArts' Grim Fandango (COURTESY OF LUCASARTS, A DIVISION OF LUCASFILM ENTERTAINMENT COMPANY LTD.)*

As the next logical step in the evolution of the adventure genre took the pre-rendered graphical format into real time, another major factor in the decline of the adventure game was the quality of the graphics. Throughout the early days of real-time games, the quality of the art assets was severely crippled by technical limitations. Studios, however, seeing the writing on the wall, adopted the new technology out of necessity; pre-rendered stills were going the way of the dinosaur. Adventure game aficionados did not readily accept the shift to the new technology. Even the most compelling story and interesting game play was not enough to overcome the technically-poor graphic quality of the time. Eventually, the technology improved and with it, visual graphic quality, but up until recently, the machines required to display the high-end graphics were the domain of hardcore gamers. Today, we are finally seeing main stream machines with reasonable graphics cards that are able to display and run games with graphics-rich environments, whether they are first person shooters or other genres.

Modern Successes of the Genre

Not surprisingly, the current reincarnation of the classic adventure game has followed the thought of choosing other than a photorealistic style, thereby allowing studios to concentrate on story, game play, and content that does not require the income of a small country to produce. Adventure games have become increasing popular with independent studios as they are able to cut out the extra overhead of the big publishers and do well without having to sell over a million copies to recoup their outlay.

Also instrumental in the continued interest in the adventure game genre is the burgeoning casual games market. Coupled with the latest trend in releasing chapters as opposed to entire traditional length games, production times and costs can be better managed, which allows developers to keep the cost to consumers in the realm of impulse purchases. The traditional format of four worlds translates perfectly into the chapter or installment format. That TellTales Games' *Tales of Monkey Island* was one of the most successful casual games of 2010 is a testament to the ongoing popularity of the genre.

What basic human characteristics make for fun?

Above all, we play games for entertainment. Unlike passively watching a movie on the television, an interactive game takes commitment. If it's not enjoyable or challenging, we'll turn it off and walk away. Even with the games that are more serious than tongue in cheek, the basic characteristics that make us human prompt us to behave in predictable patterns.

Ferengi Rules of Acquisition: Like the Ferengi of *Star Trek: The Next Generation*, we like to collect things, especially if they don't belong to us. Call it a survival trait from our distant past; if it isn't nailed down, our instinct is to collect it and stash it for a rainy day. Bumper stickers that read "He who dies with the most toys wins" echo the sentiment in a more modern day context (see Figure 1-25).

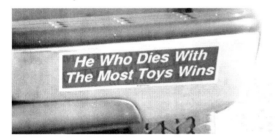

Figure 1-25. *Bumper sticker*

Naughty or nice: We like to fantasize about doing things deemed naughty or somewhat socially unacceptable. In games, we can act on our baser instincts without having to worry about the censure of our peers. Often, it is even a requirement to move the game forward (see Figure 1-26).

Figure 1-26. *But it's the only way to get past that security guard…*

Super powers: We like to fantasize about having physical prowess or skills that may involve danger or years of training, but unlike the gamers who play first person shooters, we feel no need to master complicated or dexterous key and mouse sequences to perform such feats (see Figure 1-27).

Figure 1-27. *Super powers: no platform-jumper skills are required here to rescue little Sparky.*

Consequences: We like to be able to see what happens when we hold that bomb or grenade too long, because in this type of genre, we expect the unexpected and entertaining to happen (see Figure 1-28).

Figure 1-28. *Consequences: we enjoy the unexpected.*

Why make your own?

Everyone has a story or game idea, and chances are if you find someone else to work with, their idea will be different than yours. Even if you establish yourself as the leader, conflicts will arise and the probability of splitting up increases (unless, of course, you are able to pay them a reasonable wage). Typically, first time authors are not in the position to be able to pay employees. With non-funded collaboration comes the likelihood that the game will never get finished if the team falls apart. By accepting that you will be solely responsible, you can get on with the creation and development. Even if your skills will take you only as far as a proof of concept, the completion of that version will establish your credibility. A working prototype proves both intent and the ability to see a project through.

In the past, game authoring engines were either fully featured commercial offerings such as the UnReal engine that was licensed on a per-game basis, or proprietary in-house engines that by necessity only did what the game required. With the advent of the casual game, you now have a multitude of engines available in which to author your own games. Because the low-end engines tend to be very specialized, they take most of the decision-making out of the process; you end up with a formulaic game that, when coupled with the included art assets, is far from satisfying.

Happily, you now have the choice of several offerings that provide a would-be author with many of the features that are standard in high-end engines with a price point and licensing format that is within the range of almost anyone. The Unity engine is ideal for a first serious effort at game creation in that it offers a lot of high-end features, has a free version and low cost Pro version, runs on either a Mac or a PC, and has the capability of authoring to several different platforms.

Multiple Roles

The biggest drawback to being the sole author of your first game is the need to wear three different hats during the process. The first, designing game play, story, and style, is within reach of most people, though perhaps more suited to the artistic type. The second, creation of art assets for the game, is clearly an artist task, but there are plenty of free assets to be found on the Web for the art-challenged. The problem for non-artists becomes creating continuity. The third component of game creation is the scripting. In high-end commercial engines, this was traditionally the realm of hardcore programmers, but today's authoring engines have redesigned the scripting process to allow the artist to readily use pre-scripted animations and component scripts to achieve their visions.

This book is specifically written with the goal of helping the artist or designer become familiar with the scripting process in order to produce a reasonably sophisticated game or proof of concept. With the examples and concepts you will discover in this book, it is hoped you can realize your dream, or at least take the first step in that direction.

The bottom line is that a lot of people talk about making games. Very few, however, actually do it. This book aims to remove barriers and lessen the learning curve so that you will have the opportunity to fulfill your ambition to create a game.

Two Logical Variations for Indies

Having established that the adventure game genre will be the vehicle for your game, you need to look at the two major variations in format and weight their pros and cons before you begin in earnest.

First Person

In this format, the player takes a first person role throughout the game.

Full freeplay: The biggest advantage of the first person format in a 3D world is that it allows the artist or programmer to fully benefit from time spent in creating the terrain and environs without a huge amount of asset creation. Being able to be up and exploring quickly in your own custom world is a gratifying quick win. The downside of being able to navigate anywhere in a scene is that the player *must* navigate to the key places, and traditional first person navigation was never designed for the fine control and non-gamer skill levels typical of the adventure game genre.

Character animation: Because you never see the first person in this type of game, it doesn't require the extensive character animation of the third person format. Character interaction is not even necessary in a typical first person format where the premise is usually some sort of deserted world. In addition to being able to get away without character animation, you can also avoid complicated dialog trees that usually are part and parcel of adding characters to a scene. If you opt for characters with no possible interaction, then you would need to provide basic AI to prevent the player from coming in contact with the characters.

Mechanical: Another typical component of the first person format is that the tasks or puzzles tend to be mechanical in nature. Mechanical animation is much easier for both artists and programmers to get right.

Character

The other candidate for your game is the third person format where the camera follows a character around the scene as the player controls the character's navigation and action. The main book project is based on the first person format, but it's worth weighing the differences between the two. In the final chapter, I will briefly look at the changes needed for third person.

Role playing and character development: This format allows role playing and identification with character that is an attractive part of many of the popular ongoing adventure game series. It also allows the author to create and flesh out supporting characters that can make appearances in future episodes, adding to the anticipation of the next installment.

Technical requirements: Unlike first person shooters where characters may be limited to a small set of behaviors (idle, walk, run, shoot, jump, die), the third person format requires extensive character animation to deal with all of the required object interaction and conversation scenarios. Along with the creation of dialog trees, you would also need to engage voice actors to record all of the dialogue. A way around this would be to follow the lead of the popular Japanese interactive novels where the conversation takes place in dialogue bubbles and the character assumes a neutral position instead of speaking. As this tends to distract from the task-oriented format of the classic adventure game, you won't be using that option either.

Camera considerations: Another side effect of using the third person format is increased camera handling complexity. In enclosed spaces, collision detection between camera and walls can be problematic. If the character can move in and out of buildings or other enclosed spaces, you need to decide whether to cut open the buildings or bring the camera closer to the character. A variation of the third person format allows the camera to follow the character within particular bounds while carefully restricting the character's range of movement. When the character collides with the boundary, a new camera for the next location is activated. The disadvantage with this is often a lack of continuity between locations, similar to the old pre-rendered still-shot format. An advantage is that this type of navigation allows for exceptionally easy occlusion culling of each of the camera areas, which means that the game can run efficiently on older machines or new mobile platforms.

Common to Both

There are a number of features that, as they help define the genre, are common to both approaches. It's a good idea to keep them in mind as you work through the process of creating your game.

Entertaining: Above all, the adventure game should be entertaining. Whether it comes from humorous interaction, intriguing animation sequences, or intellectual conundrums, game play and environment must draw the player in and keep him engaged.

Story/Goal: The game is not a Big Book of Puzzles. The tasks or puzzles should at least have a logical, mechanical, or physical tie to the world's defined properties (as in the case of magic being part of its description), and preferably tie in with the premise of the story.

Object interaction: Interaction with objects is one of the defining features in all aspects of the genre. Whether the player is allowed to gather objects or must only work with what is immediately at hand, the typical point and click functionality is a mainstay.

Object-to-object interactivity: A big part of the task-solving component of adventure games is the player's ability to combine multiple objects to attain the key that lets him solve a problem or repair a mechanism in order to move the game forward. While this is not always present in all adventure games, it is a common feature.

Inventory: Also not a requirement but a much loved component is the inventory system. In order to allow the player to collect everything that is not nailed down, the game must keep it all readily available for use. Sophisticated or large games should also provide a means of scrolling through the player's stash in case the on-screen representation of the contents of the inventory is limited.

Save/Restore: Unlike many of today's casual games, even the shorter chapter-style adventure games are rarely played from start to finish in one sitting. Players may devote an hour or so in an evening to playing the game, stopping when they are stuck and starting up again when their mind is fresh. Saving the game is a necessity when the game is expected to give the player several hours of enjoyment over a period of days or weeks.

Music and sound effects: As defined by the early graphical games, sound effects helped reinforce and enhance object interaction. Music not only sets the mood for the individual worlds or environments but is also commonly used as part of the solution to puzzles or tasks in game.

Action objects: Also common to the various derivations of the adventure genre is a means of identifying interactive objects. In the original text adventures, the interactive objects were always listed after the general room description. With the shift to graphical adventures, the player was often forced to search a still image pixel by pixel to find the available objects. Occasionally, they could be identified by their lack of anti-aliasing, but with advancing technology and higher resolution, it became common to change the cursor or highlight the cursor/action object when the mouse moved over it.

Design Considerations for First Person

To summarize, here is a final compilation of things you will need to be aware of as you develop the game in the book.

Directing/suggesting game play in an open world: When the world is open and large, as in a first person format, you will need to provide clues as to where important locations are found. Textures, geometry, lighting, animation, and text hints are all valid means of helping the player find key elements in an open, freely navigable world. Do not hide key objects without some sort of clue or you will create the real-time version of the old "pixel hunt" problem. A game should be entertaining, not tedious.

Paths created with textures or indicated by geometry are the most obvious means to lead the player to the right places. Geometry markers, visible from a distance, can also indicate potential places of interest. Do not cry wolf. Always include something of interest to reward the player for investigating something that draws his attention; even if it's not puzzle- or task-related, it could provide a clue for something else in the game.

Lighting and color can also catch the player's eye, encouraging him to explore a particular area. Keep to a planned color schemes so the introduction of a different color will draw the eye. A drastic change in lighting will also stand out and provide a visual clue that there is something important to look at. Visual cues can range from subtle to comic.

Audio is also a usable mechanism for drawing a player to a particular location. 3D sound not only has the ability to motivate a player to explore, it also helps direct him with the addition of stereo speaker sound systems.

Navigation considerations: Navigation in a 3D world is one of the biggest challenges. When coupled with the unknown skill level or game-playing experience of the player, the best bet is to make navigation as transparent as possible. For this game, you will allow both WASD for grognards (experienced gamers) and arrow navigation for the rest of the players. One of the issues you will need to compromise on will be the method of looking around a scene.

Because of the requisite need to click on objects as the main means of interaction, the classic mouselook isn't practical. Having the screen spinning wildly while you attempt to get a cursor over the correct object is counter-productive. You will require the user to either be moving or using an additional key or mouse button to look around.

You may also need to facilitate moving up to a particular object to observe the consequences of interaction with it. Navigating with arrow keys or WASD does not allow for analogue speed changes, so you will occasionally need to take over navigation to move a player into the optimal position. You could also use the same mechanism to allow people to examine objects at close range. The fantasy of physical prowess without needing the dexterous skill of shooters may also take a similar canned approach.

Object interaction: You will also need to decide how to make one object interact with another, both in-game and in inventory mode. Additionally, you will need to decide on the mechanism for controlling your inventory, such as how the user gets in and out of it, how it is extendable, and a few other issues.

As you can see, the adventure will be filled with interesting discoveries and unexpected decisions.

Developing the Story and Challenges

Even at its simplest, the game creation process is not trivial. As you work to create your first game, you may want to keep a few of these tips and tricks in mind:

- **Rule #1**. Don't waste your best ideas on your first game. Work out the technology, but consider your first project a learning experience.

- **Keep a log of the hours you spend on everything.** Break it down into researching, documenting, scripting, modeling, mapping, animating, and testing. This will give you a good idea of how long things take so you will eventually be able to make realistic time schedules, access co-workers or employees, and most importantly, meet milestones.

- **Don't bite off more than you can chew.** Most creative people tend to get carried away when they design things. When a project gets too big and complicated, its chances of reaching completion diminish drastically. Plan for levels of completeness to allow you to reach attainable goals. Instead of organizing your milestones into the separate game levels or worlds, organize the *entire game* into levels of completeness or sophistication. Think in terms of the base amount that must be accomplished first. Then add a list of extra features or improved assets you'd like to have if you had more time. And finally, have a list of refinements, features, and improvements you would add if time and money was no object. This way, you will always be able to fall back on a less sophisticated level and still have something to show for your efforts.

- **Entertaining or tedious?** Ask yourself this question before implementing an idea for a task or game play. As text adventures became more sophisticated, the player was required to eat and drink during his explorations or he would become faint and eventually die. While needing to keep you lamp full of lamp oil could make for an interesting turn in the game, failing to eat or drink was merely tedious.

- **Feasible?** It doesn't have to be real if it's logical and your world permits it. Just make sure the premise of the world and the population's culture is clearly defined.

- **The path of least resistance.** Good design choices can speed up production. The development of color schemes, design motifs, and local building materials early on will allow for faster design of individual assets as well as provide continuity of visual environment. For instance, if the local environment is short on wood and has long-established settlements where the culture symbolized their faith with an equilateral triangle, you might expect to see the majority of buildings made of stone and utilizing a triangular motif throughout. Wood might be reserved for precious objects. A particular plant indigenous to the area might figure largely in the production of cloth and the color might dominate the settlement. Aside from making design decisions much quicker, you will also find that you can reuse a good number of the assets throughout the environment. Even if the player is not informed of the underlying reasons, his subconscious will find the world more believable.

- **Bait and switch.** Don't be afraid to use stunt doubles for multiple tasks. It is often much quicker to create a duplicate for a different task than trying to complicate the original to perform both.

- **Assets: freebees, purchase, or build from scratch?** Weigh the costs in time and money carefully. If an object is so generic as to look the same no matter who creates it, consider using one that's readily available. Conversely, sometimes the time spent in preparing and repairing a purchased object outweighs its cost. If the object is unique to your game or world, then plan on creating it yourself; but sometimes new and unique mapping and a small bit of tweaking of an existing asset will do the job.

- **Technical considerations.** Decide at the start whether your game will require cutting edge technology, mid-range technology, or if it will be able to run on older hardware. If you are developing on faster, better equipped machines, test your progress regularly on a target machine until you get a feel for the frame rate and limitations required.

- **Available features.** Don't design with the hopes that a crucial bit of technology will be available by the time you need it, unless you have a viable substitute.

- **Design alternatives**. Be flexible in case the functionality you want is not feasible for the current software technology or your target machines. Don't waste time on trying to make high-end features work when you know frame rate or hardware will not properly support them.

- **Platform considerations.** Investigate the requirements and limitation of various platforms before you start designing your game. Be aware of the differences between platforms if you wish to develop for multiple deliveries.

- **Plan and test first.** Know where you are going and what you will need *before* you start out. Don't get bogged down in details until the basics have been sorted out and you have a clear understanding of what is needed.

- **Paper design.** Sketch ideas, environment maps, and other ideas before starting on the permanent 3D assets, environments, textures, and other art work.

- **Proxy objects.** Create proxies and stand-ins for mock-ups, tests, and early proof of concepts. Make sure of the functionality before spending time on the final assets. Inability to get a particular idea working may change the asset requirements drastically.

- **Consistency.** Research ideas for styles, worlds, and content. Choose a theme, define a world, a style, a mood, and color scheme, and then stick to it faithfully.

- **Beta testers.** Don't tell everyone about your clever ideas; you will need beta testers that come to it fresh. Don't stand over them and provide hints and instructions; watch to see what they do without knowing the critical path to follow.

- **Interactivity.** Create flow charts or other diagrams until you have mapped out exactly how each object should act and react before you start working on the actual functionality.

New to Real Time vs. Pre-Render

Even the most seasoned 3D artist will be confronted with a multitude of concepts, restrictions, and issues unique to real time when they first delve into creating their own game. While many of the words and phrases may already be familiar, dealing with them can be challenging. As an artist, the compromise between the asset in all its glory and the physical requirements to keep the game running at an acceptable frame rate can be extremely frustrating.

The most common misconception is that poly count is the main factor in frame rate. In reality, almost everything costs. Besides poly count, frame rate is also affected by the number of lights in a scene, the complexity of materials or shaders, the amount of memory taken up by both textures and meshes, physics, animations, particle systems, and just about everything else. Most of the concepts new (or at least more visible) to real time are used mainly to help improve frame rate.

This section provides a short description of many of these terms, but more importantly, explains why and how they work to increase frame rate.

DCC (Digital Content Creation applications): These programs include 3ds Max, Maya Cinema4D, Blender and many others. While a few have an associated real-time engine, most are geared toward creating assets for real-time applications or pre-rendered still shots or movies for their final output.

Frame rate: The human eye does not see much beyond thirty frames per second. In DCC applications, an animation, the finished product, is usually viewed at twenty-four or thirty frames per second, depending on whether it is for film or video. In DCC applications, when you animate an object, you keyframe according to the frame rate used by the target media. In real time, frame rate takes on a whole new meaning. Real-time engines render frames constantly during runtime. Depending on what is in the scene and visible, what is animating, using physics, being lit, or any of the other myriad factors, the frame rate will be *constantly changing*. Add processor speed and graphics card into the mix and you can easily see why keeping frame rate as fast as possible for the target audience becomes important.

In a studio situation where game development may be spread out over two years for a AAA title, if you start development on a cutting edge machine at the beginning of the project, that machine will probably be mainstream by release time. Indy developers, on the other hand, may have development times of two to six months per title and need to plan accordingly. Thirty frames per second is a good low-end range to aim for unless your game is more of a training application where 20 fps (frames per second) is generally acceptable. As a rule of thumb, if you have a fairly fast machine, you will probably want to set a low-end limit of 100 to 150 fps. If possible, you will want to try some benchmarking tests to solidify your frame rate targets on your working machine. Be aware of your target market and their typical hardware for your game from the start of the project.

Navigation: One of the big differences between DCC and real time is scene navigation. A big part of games is the method of controls used to move around a 3D environment. Far from being standardized after near twenty years of real-time games, in a room full of twenty budding game artists and designers, you will get at least twenty different opinions on the best controls for a game. Obviously, the type of game plays a big part in the choice, but additionally, the skill level of the player also dictates the choices. Many games allow the key controls to be re-mapped or assigned by the player, while others strive to make navigation as invisible to the user as possible by allowing a mixture of controls.

Collision: Another big concept in real time is that of collision. Once the user is allowed to travel wherever he or she wishes in a 3D world, physical constraints must be set to prevent players from traveling through walls yet allowing them to move over uneven terrain, stairs, and other obstacles. In a 3D engine, typically the constraints will be invisible primitive objects or they may be derived from the mesh object's geometry directly. The former are the most economical as far as frame rate goes. With complicated meshes, one often creates a lower poly stand-in for collision. Many game engines will do this for you.

Poly (short for polygon): This term is used in many different ways depending on the application. In real time, we are generally talking about a triangular face of a mesh object. Poly count refers to the number of polygons in a mesh object or in an entire scene. People new to the game development process almost always ask how many polys their characters should be. The answer is always dependent on whatever else is happening in the scene. If you have a scene with a lot of geometry that is drawn at the same time in every frame, the number would be a lot lower than if the character was always alone in a desert with a couple of rock formations. As before, the target machines the game will be running on will be a deciding factor as well.

Another important concept is how important the object is, or how close it will be viewed. If the object is secondary to the plot or game play, it probably doesn't warrant a high poly count. If the player will never see the object larger than 200 x 200 pixels worth of screen space, there's a good chance that high poly detail will be wasted resources, both in creation time and CPU usage.

Simple primitives vs. mesh objects: A primitive is an object that is parametrically defined by a set of parameters. A sphere, for example, can be described by its radius and height and width segments. A mesh object is defined by giving the exact location or offset of its vertices in relation to the object's transform axis. Most engines will have at least a few primitive objects for simple use cases. They are most useful for experimentation and occasionally, projectiles. While a primitive object is smaller on disk, once in the game, it will go into memory just as any mesh type object.

LOD or **Level of Detail** (Figure 1-29): If an object will be seen up close and needs lots of detail at some point in the game, but it will be far enough away at other times to needlessly tax the engine, one often uses an LOD stand-in. At a particular distance, the high poly object is hidden and the low poly stunt double is shown in its place to improve frame rate. With some engines, this may be handled by the engine itself creating the lower poly version and swapping out at a pre-determined distance. In other engines, or with important meshes, the artists will provide the LOD version or versions.

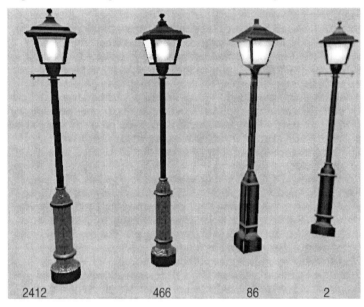

2412   466   86   2

Figure 1-29. *LOD example showing poly count of the different versions of an object*

The lowest poly version is often an alpha channel using image. In its static form, two planes containing the image are crossed to form an X configuration; occasionally, three planes are used. The image is always fully self illuminated. The dynamic version consists of a single plane containing the image that is always turned to face the camera. This technique is called billboarding (see Figure 1-30).

Figure 1-30. *X-trees and billboarded trees using the same image*

Distance culling: Related to LOD, distance culling means that at a particular distance, the object will no longer be drawn in the scene. When a high poly count object takes only a few pixels on screen, it is wasting resources. Typically, one might use a low poly stand in at a particular distance, then use distance cull to stop drawing the low poly stand-in at some point.

Fog (Figure 1-31): Besides being visually more interesting for an environment, fog works well with distance culling by allowing the objects to be culled sooner as they disappear into the fog. Fog can be of two types: vertex fog where the vertex color of an object is affected more as the object recedes, and pixel fog, which gives more consistent results but uses more resources.

Figure 1-31. *Left: No fog* **Right:** *Fog, vertex based*

Figure 1-32. *Fog with camera clipping*

Clipping planes (Figure 1-33): Cameras have near and far clipping planes. Objects are not rendered if they are closer than the near clipping plane or beyond the far clipping plane. When used in conjunction with fog, clipping planes present a quick and efficient means of limiting the rendering of objects in the scene (see Figure 1-32). If any part of an object's bounding box is within the view frustum (the part of the screen you see) and the camera clipping planes, then each face of the object has to go through the checking process to see if it will need to be rendered.

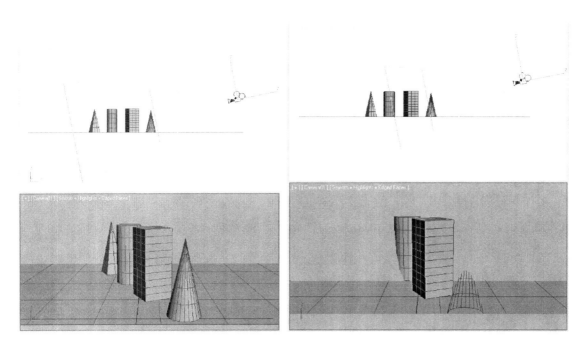

Figure 1-33. *Camera clipping planes*

Draw order (Figure 1-34): When a scene is rendered, objects are drawn into that scene one at a time. Depending on how an engine is set up, it may also draw certain types of objects before or after other objects. If the objects are drawn in the order they were added to the scene, it's possible that you will see alpha draw order issues. This happens when an object with partial transparency is drawn sooner than objects that lie behind it. During drawing, if an object is partially occluded, that part is not drawn. The check for occlusion does not check the opacity of all of the occluding objects; it's either occluded or not. To ensure that objects are drawn behind transparent objects, the semi-transparent objects are drawn last.

In some engines, the scene is parsed at start time to determine locations of semi-transparent objects so that it knows the order in which to draw them, therefore avoiding draw order issues. The downside of this method is when a semi-transparent object is animated out of its starting position, draw order may be adversely affected.

In engines that draw objects into the scene in a predictable order, you can have fun with draw order by creating an x-ray machine (see Figure 1-35). In other engines, you may be able to use special shaders to achieve the same effect.

Figure 1-34. *Draw order and opacity.* **Top Left:** *Window is drawn first; other objects are only drawn where they are not occluded.* **Top Right:** *Window is drawn last after all other objects have already been drawn.* **Mid Left:** *Floor is drawn after window.* **Mid Right:** *Lioness is drawn after window.* **Lower Left:** *Wall and lioness are drawn after window.* **Lower Right:** *Wall is drawn after window.*

Figure 1-35. *X-Ray machine using draw order*

Occlusion culling (Figure 1-36): Occlusion culling is another means of increasing frame rate by not rendering certain object in a scene. With automatic occlusion culling, data is created with the scene objects in order to be able to check large blocks of objects. In the example where towns or settlements were located in box canyons, you know that when you are in one canyon, the others by definition will be occluded. Rather than having to check objects one at a time to see if they are visible from a particular vantage point, the entire contents of the town can be skipped.

Good game design can make occlusion culling possible and help to increase frame rate. Manual occlusion culling can easily be done by organizing objects in groups or marking tags. When the player crosses in or out of zones, all objects that will not be seen can be turned off or on.

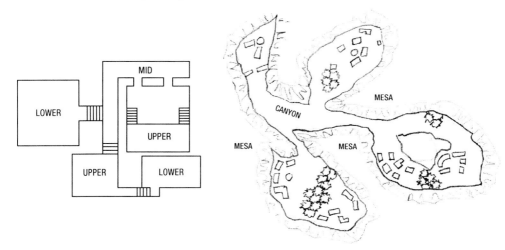

Figure 1-36. *Designing for occlusion culling*

Lighting: In 3D, basic, non-GI (global illumination) is performed on a per-vertex basis. Each vertex has what is called a vertex normal, a vector that determines how the face or triangle will be lit, (Figure 1-37). A ray is traced from the light to the vertex and the angle between the two, the Angle of Incidence, is used to calculate the percentage of that light received by that vertex. The light received by each vertex is averaged between each. The smaller the angle, the more light the vertex receives.

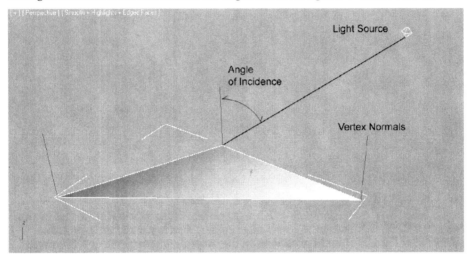

Figure 1-37. *Basic lighting on a single face*

Shared or averaged vertices (Figure 1-38): Whether adjacent faces share vertices or use an average of their vertex normals, the result will be a soft or smoothed result. When vertices are not shared or their normals averaged, a hard edge is perceived because the amount of light is calculated for each vertex. Most DCC applications hide the true number of vertices to make modeling easier. This is why the cube that had eight vertices when you modeled it is suddenly shown as having twenty four vertices after import into real-time engine.

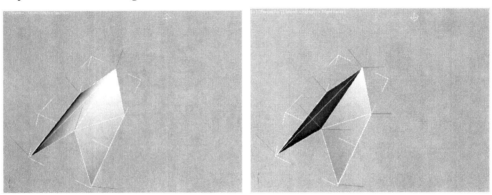

Figure 1-38. *Smoothed (shared vertices) vs. hard edges(not shared)*

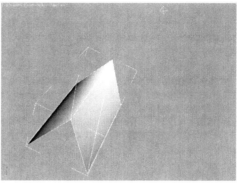

Figure 1-39. *Flipped edges: lighting averaged differently across faces*

Vertex vs. pixel lighting: The previous examples use what is called vertex lighting. It is the fastest type of lighting and is quite efficient with lower polygon models (see Figure 1-39). Unfortunately, with low poly models, the averaging of the light between vertices can leave splotchy, irregular results. As expected, higher poly count makes for more even lighting, but at the cost of needing to calculate lighting on more vertices. Pixel lights, on the other hand, perform more calculations on the mesh depending on its current on screen size. A close object receives more extra render time than the same mesh farther back in the scene.

Pixel lighting also allows for other affects such as shadows, cookies (projected masks), and normal maps—all at a cost, of course. While these features are assumed in DCC programs, they are each responsible for using additional resources and slowing frame rate in real time. In the Unity game engine, if a graphics card does not support pixel lights, the lights will automatically be dropped back down to vertex lights.

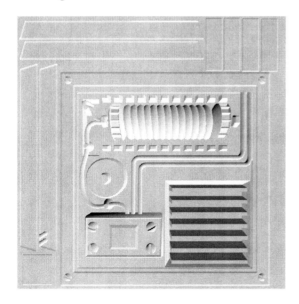

Figure 1-40. *Normal map: the distinctive colors represent the directional topology of the original mesh. The lighting pass is made from this information rather than the lower poly mesh's vertex normals.*

Normal mapping (Figure 1-40): Normal mapping works by simulating surface details on a mesh so that lighting can be performed as if the detail was actually in the mesh. While this doesn't save much in resources for rendering, the overhead of high poly meshes can be greatly reduced. The trade-off is in extra storage for the normal map which can be quite large if it represents a lot of detail. While most people are familiar with images of low-res monster heads with normal mapped detail, it is noteworthy to be aware that normal maps are quite good at providing detail for non-organic objects as well, as shown in Figure 1-41 and Figure 1-42.

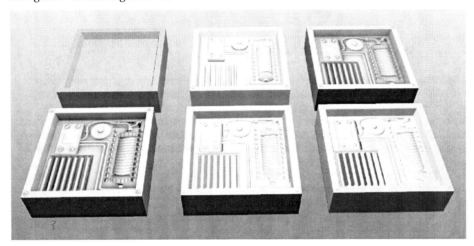

Figure 1-41. *Normal maps.* **Top Left**: *The low poly mesh.* **Top Middle**: *The high poly meshes.* **Top Right**: *The low poly mesh with the resulting lightmap.* **Bottom Left**: *The low poly mesh with the lightmap and a high res normal map.* **Bottom Middle**: *The low poly mesh with a low res normal map.* **Bottom Right**: *The low poly mesh with a high res normal map and no lightmap.*

Figure 1-42. *Normals lit left (upper image) and normals lit right (lower image). Note the lighting of the spring object at the right side of the box*

Shaders: In 3D, after you create a mesh object, you assign a material to it that contains all the properties needed to visually describe its surface properties. These can be color, texture or pattern, smoothness, reflectivity, emissive qualities, and many more. Traditionally, the render was handled generically and limited to only a handful of properties. As graphics cards have improved, they have taken over more of the tasks involved in describing the object's surface, so now you have specific bits of code called Shaders that tell the graphics card what to do for each material. Shaders, as with lights, can be written for vertex rendering or pixel rendering. As before, vertex shaders are more efficient than pixel shaders, while pixel shaders have much higher visual quality and are able to portray many more effects (Figure 1-43).

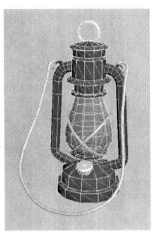

Figure 1-43. *Pixel lit materials(middle) are more sensitive to edge geometry than their vertex lit counterparts (right). Note how the edges are apparent in the vertex lit sample.*

Boundaries, real and invisible: An important design consideration for real-time games is how to stop the user from leaving the game area. Physically, you need only create invisible collision walls. Visually, there are several common methods of defining the player boundaries. The two most common outdoor solutions are to set the scene either on an island surrounded by water, in a plane, or in a valley surrounded by mountains. City environments may be blocked by walls, road blocks, and blind alleys. In games where the environment or story permits, swamps or mine fields could provide reasonable barricades.

Terrain generators: Most modern game engines contain terrain-generating modules. The author is allowed to paint the shape of the terrain, creating hills, valleys, lakes, and more with an internal displacement map. Actual geological data, in the form of a displacement map, can also be used. Once the mesh is in place, most engines allow the user to paint textures onto the terrain with various brush types. A mask is internally created for each texture and the result layered together to provide a rich and varied terrain.

Some terrain generators also provide the option to paint trees, foliage, and other meshes around the terrain. Trees and small scrubs or grasses can often be affected by wind and will generally contain an automatic LOD mechanism.

Dynamic tessellation (Figure 1-44): In addition to terrain generators, the resulting terrain mesh is often dynamically tessellated to provide more detail up close where the player is focused, and less farther away where higher detail can be an unnecessary waste of resources.

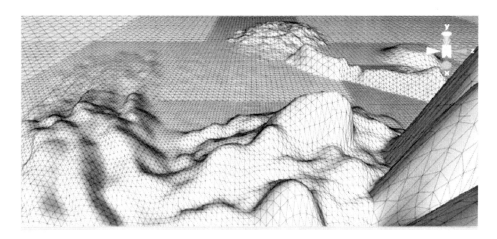

Figure 1-44. *Tessellation of a terrain mesh*

Chapter Summary

In this chapter, you reviewed the history of the adventure game from its roots as interactive text through the early graphical adventures and on into the 3D rendered era that eventually gave way to the real-time formats of today. Along the way, you identified the elements of the genre that persist through the changes in style and format. Intrepid adventurers want to play in worlds that are more interesting and stimulating than their own reality. With no special computer skills, they want to have the fantasy of physical prowess and experience while they collect everything that is not nailed down and solve intellectual conundrums without the baggage of social accountability.

You looked at design elements for developing your game from physical issues such as environmental layout to the conceptual considerations of what is fun to the technical specifications that ultimately influence your final decisions. Then you explored the pros and cons of the first person format versus the third person format and came up with a list of things to avoid as well as good practices for first time game creators.

And finally, you started to look at 3D from the perspective of real-time engines as opposed to pre-rendered DDC applications such as 3ds Max, Maya, Cinema4D, and Blender. You found that the frame rate required to run a successful game depends on a multitude of factors such as poly count, lighting types, materials, and culling of various types. The navigation so unique to real time, with its interaction with floor and wall collision, will present you with a variety of challenges that will be revealed as you continue through the book.

In the next section, you will get your feet wet in Unity, discovering (or reviewing) basic functionality of transforms, viewports, and asset management, followed by a short section on 3D in general.

■ ■ ■

Unity UI Basics—Getting Started

As you are probably pretty anxious to get started creating something in Unity, I'll keep the introduction to Unity's UI (user interface) rather brief. We will explore and investigate it more fully as the need arises, but for now let's get a basic feel for the layout and concepts. If you'd like to delve further into the UI before moving on, there is a very good section on getting started in the Unity help files.

Installing Unity and Starting Up

Download Unity from http://unity3d.com/unity/download/ and install it. When you run it for the first time, you'll need to register the product by following the prompts. Registration can be done quickly online even if the machine you've installed it on isn't connected to the Internet. If your machine is connected, you'll be taken directly to the registration page. A thirty-day trial of the Pro version is available from Unity3D. As we'll use many of the Pro features in the last few chapters, you may wish to try the Pro version at that time.

Figure 2-1. *The Unity icon*

To start Unity, you can click the icon (Figure 2-1) that was added to the desktop, or choose it from the Windows Start menu ➤ Programs ➤ Unity, and on the Mac, Applications ➤ Unity.

Loading or Creating a New Project or Scene

To work with Unity, you always start with a project.

■ **Tip** The folder you create or select for your project *is* the project. When you open a project, you select the folder, not any of its individual contents.

When you create a new project, a directory or folder is created with subfolders containing the required files. Be sure to note where the project is installed, or use the Browse button to select a different location. You will be asked to choose which asset packages you want to include with your project. Earlier versions of Unity had generic Pro and Standard packages as the choices. Now, however, the packages have been split into component parts so you can reduce clutter for specific game types. In the book, we'll use most of the packages so you can get a feel for what is available. Note that if you're using the free version, you can import the Pro packages, but you won't be able to use them.

1. Open Unity.

The Project Wizard dialog opens, prompting you to select a project.

2. Select the Create New Project tab, as shown in Figure 2-2.

▪ **Tip**   If Unity is already open, choose New Project from the File menu,

---

3. Click Browse and navigate to where you'll keep your Unity projects, then create a New Folder for the book project.

4. Name the folder BookProject.

5. Check all but the Toon and the Standard Assets (Mobile) packages and the Pro packages (if you are using free Unity).

Figure 2-2. *Project Wizard-Packages*

⬛ **Note**   This book will make optional use of several Pro features, but the project will not rely on them to get a finished result. Should you decide to upgrade to Unity Pro or try the thirty-day trial midway through the project, you can import the Pro packages easily through the Assets menu under Import Package.

---

6.   Click Create.

Unity closes and reopens to show your new project—BookProject.

Unity Pro ships with the updated "dark" UI, as shown in Figure 2-3. For this book, as many readers will be using the free version, screen shots will reflect the original, lighter version of the UI.

Figure 2-3. *Unity Dark Pro scheme, factory settings*

To choose between the two skins, you can access the Preferences dialog through the Edit menu, as shown in Figure 2-4.

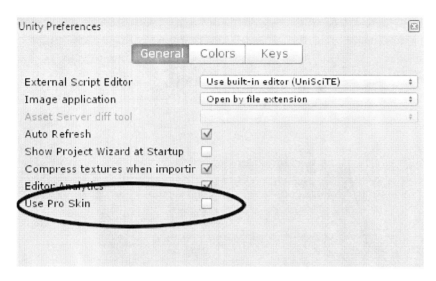

Figure 2-4. *The Unity Preferences dialog*

Notice there is a camera in the Hierarchy view and a Standard Assets folder in the Project view (see Figure 2-5). When you create a new project, a folder called Assets is created in your machine's file system, the contents of which are seen in the Project view.

▒ **Important!**   Once an asset has been added to your scene, *never* rearrange or organize it using the OS, i.e., Explorer (Windows) or Finder (Mac), as that will break internal paths and metadata in the scene.

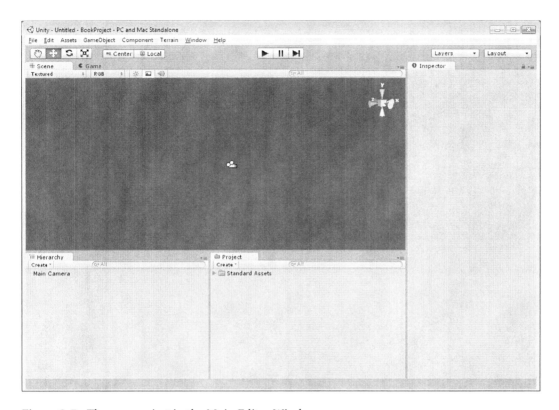

Figure 2-5. *The new project in the Main Editor Window*

Before we go any further, let's save the scene. Think of scenes as levels. A project can contain several scenes. Some may be actual levels, while others may be menus, splash screens, and so forth.

    7. From the File menu, choose Save Scene, and save the scene as TestScene1.

The new scene is saved in the Assets folder, one of the folders created when you start a new project. In Unity, it appears in the Project view with the Unity game icon next to its name, as shown in Figure 2-6. We will eventually give the scenes a subfolder of their own, but for now the scene is easily visible. When you open a project, you will often need to select a scene before anything shows up in the Hierarchy view.

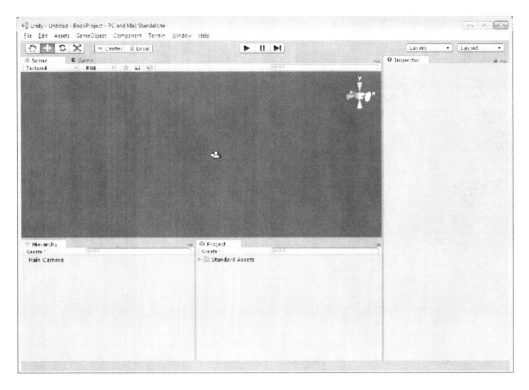

Figure 2-6. *The new scene*

The Layout

There are many ways to rearrange the layout of the Unity UI. For this book, we will use the standard 2 ×
3 layout, as shown in Figure 2-7, but you can use whatever is most comfortable for you. You can change
the layout by selecting from the Layout drop-down in the upper right area of the application window, as
shown in Figure 2-8.

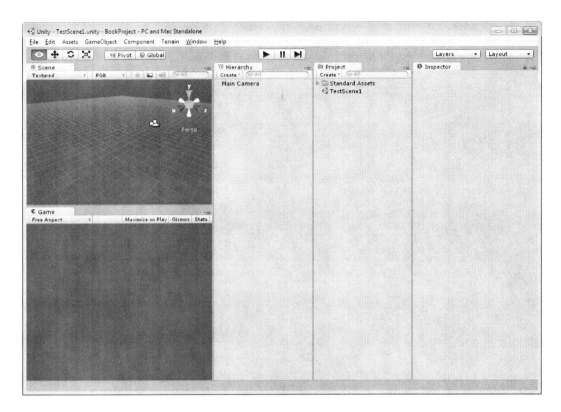

Figure 2-7. *Unity's UI—the 2 × 3 layout*

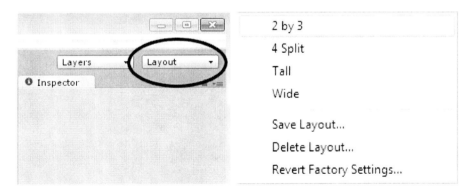

Figure 2-8. *The 2 × 3 Split layout*

Scene Window

The Scene window, shown in Figure 2-9, is where you build the visual aspects of your scene—where you plan and execute your ideas.

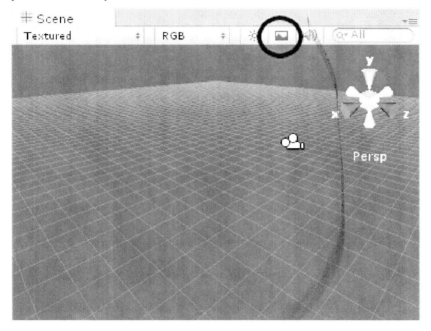

Figure 2-9. *The Scene window showing the camera icon and the grid*

░ **Tip**   To show the grid in the Scene view, toggle off the Game Overlay button (Figure 2-9).

Game Window

The Game window, shown in Figure 2-10, is where you test your game before building it in the runtime environment. You can't select objects in this view and, unlike the Scene view, it has no default lighting. You'll need to use the Main Camera to see objects in the Game window.

Figure 2-10. *The Game window*

Hierarchy View

The Hierarchy view, Figure 2-11, shows what's in the currently active scene. GameObjects that are dynamically added and removed from the scene during runtime will appear here when they are active in the scene.

Figure 2-11. *The Hierarchy view with the Main Camera*

53

Project View

The Project view, shown in Figure 2-12, contains all the assets available to the current project, as well as all scenes or levels available for the finished game or application. It is a mirror of the Asset folder in the directory where the project resides. Removing assets from this location deletes them from the hard drive! Removing assets from the directory in Explorer removes them from the Project view and could break the scene.

Figure 2-12. *The Project view*

Inspector

You use the Inspector view to access various properties and components for objects you've selected in either the Hierarchy or Project views. You can also access other scene-related information here. Select the only object that's in the scene now, the Main Camera, from the Hierarchy view, and then take a look at the Inspector, as shown in Figure 2-13.

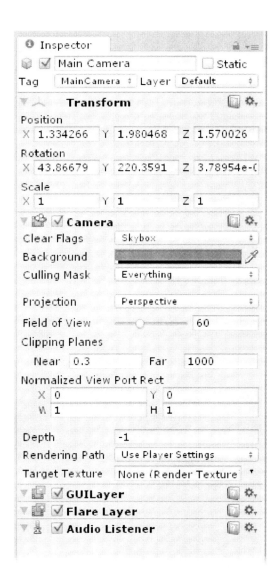

Figure 2-13. *The Inspector with the camera selected*

Toolbar

Below the menu bar is the toolbar (see Figure 2-14), which contains five different controls.

Figure 2-14. *The Toolbar*

The Transform tools, shown in Figure 2-15, provide functionality for navigating and transforming. The button on the far left, the pan tool, can also become orbit and zoom tools for navigating and adjusting the Scene view. You can click and drag to move the view around (to pan). To orbit around the current viewport center, hold the Alt key down while clicking and dragging. And to zoom, hold the Alt key (Windows) or the Cmd key (Mac), plus the right mouse button. There are other ways to perform these tasks, as you'll see when we add an object to the scene. But don't test the navigation until you have an object to work with.

Figure 2-15. *Scene navigation tools*

The remaining three buttons are for transforming objects in the scene in edit mode. The available transforms are move, rotate, and scale.

Objects can be transformed in different coordinate systems and from different pivot points. The next set of controls to the right of the Navigation tools, shown in Figure 2-16, let you toggle between the choices.

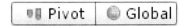

Figure 2-16. *Pivot point and coordinate system tools*

The center controls, those shown in Figure 2-17, are the play mode controls that allow you to see how the game will work in real-time, as if you were the player.

Figure 2-17. *The Play mode controls*

To the right of the play controls, you'll find the Layers drop-down (Figure 2-18). Layers are used in Unity for controlling which objects are rendered by which cameras or lit by which lights.

Figure 2-18. *The Layers control*

We have already tried the Layout drop-down (Figure 2-19) when we set it to use the 2 x 3 split layout. You can rearrange and customize most of Unity's UI. The Layers drop-down lets you quickly get back to several default or predefined layouts.

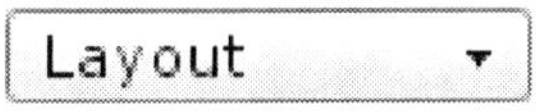

Layout ▼

Figure 2-19. *TheLayoutControlTheLayoutControl*

Menus

Along with the usual file-handling options, there are many concepts and features that are specific to Unity. Most are found in the menus, as shown in Figure 2-20. Menus items also show the keyboard shortcuts for those who prefer them.

File   Edit   Assets   GameObject   Component   Terrain   Window   Help

Figure 2-20. *The Unity Menus*

File

In the File menu, you can load, create, and save scenes and projects. It is also where you build your game as an executable or other deployment.

Edit

The Edit menu (Figure 2-21) contains the expected Cut, Copy, Paste, Duplicate, and Delete commands, as well as several runtime commands. The actual editing of assets, however, is done in the Inspector. Of particular value here are the keyboard shortcuts shown next to the commands.

There are several scene settings that are not accessed through the Hierarchy or Projects view. Besides the Render Settings, the Project Settings (Figure 2-21) are where you'll access many of your scenes' attributes. When you choose an option, the information will show up in the Inspector view.

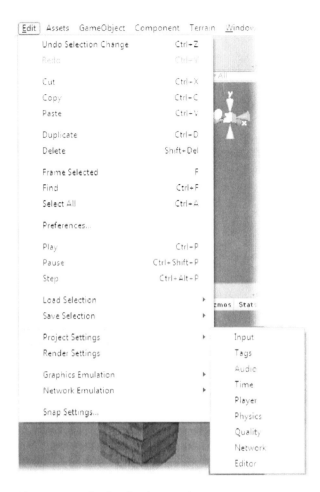

Figure 2-21. *Project Settings options*

Assets

In the Assets menu, you will find the Create submenu. This is where you can create the type of assets that generally can't be imported from DCC programs, such as non-mesh special effects, physics materials, and scripts. It is also the place to define custom fonts and organize the project with folders and prefabs. You can also reach this menu by right-clicking in the Project view.

GameObject

The GameObject menu lets you create an empty GameObject. The GameObject is the base container for objects, scripts, and other components in Unity. Like a group, it has its own transform and so is a logical means of organizing similar objects or meshes. At its simplest, a GameObject may contain only a simple script, collider, or other component, but GameObjects are invaluable when used as a parent group or folder to keep scene objects organized.

You can create various objects, such as lights, particle systems, GUI 2D objects, and Unity primitive objects from the Create Other submenu. As with primitives in render programs such as Max and Maya, these objects differ from imported meshes in that they are internally described as a set of parameters rather than a collection of points in space.

Component Menu

The Component menu gives you access to items associated with objects, such as sound, scripts, and colliders, as well as those that create or extend functionality with predefined behaviors or even editors. Components let you add physics characteristics to imported meshes, function-curve animation to objects, and all of the interactive intelligence that drives games and other more serious applications via scripts.

Terrain Menu

In the Terrain menu, you can define the base parameters of the terrain before using the terrain editor to generate the details and populate it with foliage, rocks and other features. This also where you'll go to import and export heightmaps for your terrain.

Window Menu

As you'd guess, this menu displays the commands for managing various windows and editors in Unity, along with the keyboard shortcuts.

Help Menu

The Help menu provides access to the various Unity help manuals, as well as to the massively supported Unity forum, release notes, and instructions for reporting bugs.

Creating Simple Objects

It always helps to have something in the scene when you're going to experiment with navigation in a 3D application. Though you will import most of the assets for your games, you'll find many uses for the primitive objects available in the Unity game engine.

1. From the Create Other item in the GameObject menu, select Cube, as in Figure 2-22.

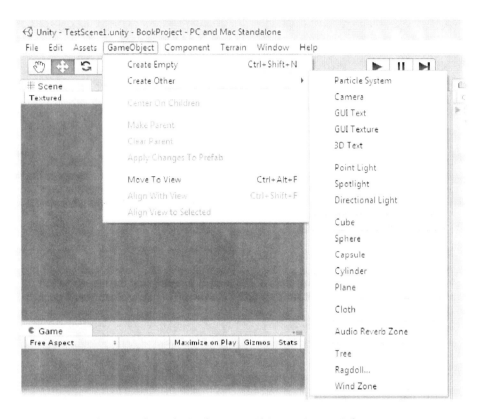

Figure 2-22. *Choosing the Cube in the GameObject ➤ Create Other menu*

A cube is created in the center of the Scene viewport. It may be little more than a speck at this point if you've played with the viewport navigation tools. You may also see it as a small dark square in the game window.

■ **Tip**   if you have not navigated the viewport yet, the Move button will be active in the Navigation toolbar and you will see the cube's transform gizmo.

---

2. Zoom in using the middle mouse roller or the Cmd button on the Mac; zoom in and out on the new cube in the Scene window, as shown in Figure 2-23.

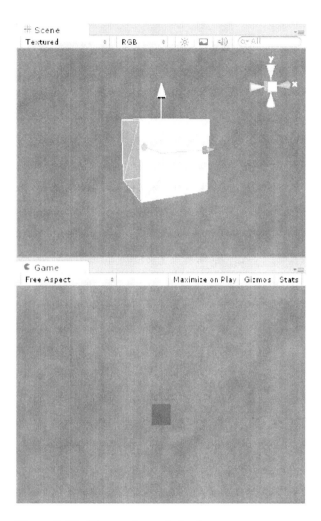

Figure 2-23. *The newly created cube*

To see the cube more clearly in the game window, you need to move the camera. Rather than fussing with moving and rotating the camera, though, let's set the camera to match the Scene view where we've already adjusted the preferred view of the cube.

    3.   Select the Main Camera in the Hierarchy view.

    4.   From the GameObject menu, choose Align with View.

The cube is now visible in the Game window and in the camera Preview inset in the Scene view (see Figure 2-24).

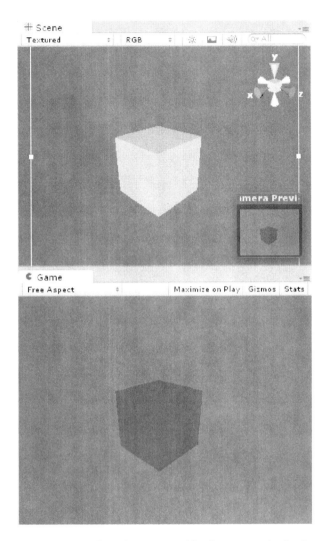

Figure 2-24. *The cube as viewed by the camera in the Game window*

When the Light button is off, the Scene window is lit with default lighting, a single light pointing straight into the viewport. This assures that the object in focus is always well lit.

5.   Toggle the default light off and the scene lighting on.

The cube is now lit only with the scene ambient light as in the Game window (Figure 2-25).

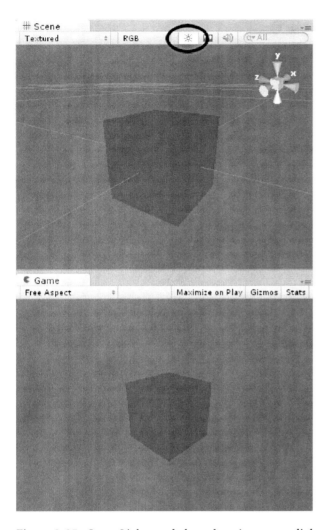

Figure 2-25. *Scene Light toggled on-there is no scene light yet*

Navigating the Scene viewport does not affect the camera. You can also zoom in and out by positioning the cursor in the viewport, holding the Alt key down, and holding the right mouse button down and moving the mouse back and forth. On a Mac, hold down the Cmd key while clicking and dragging to zoom.

Don't pan the viewport yet.

6. Deselect the camera by clicking in a blank area of the Hierarchy view.

7. Select the cube.

8. To orbit the viewport around the cube, position the cursor in the viewport, hold down the Alt key and the left mouse button and move the mouse around.

CHAPTER 2 ▨ UNITY UI BASICS—GETTING STARTED

The view pivots around the center of the viewport's focal point. The cube itself is not rotated as you can see by watching the cube in the Game Window.

You can pan the viewport clicking the Pan button and then holding the left mouse button down and dragging in the viewport. You can also position the cursor in the Scene window, hold the middle mouse roller down, and move the mouse.

9. Toggle the Scene lighting off so the cube is lit by the default lighting.

10. Pan the viewport so the cube is no longer centered.

11. Use the Alt key again and orbit to see how the view still orbits around its current center point, *not the cube* (Figure 2-26).

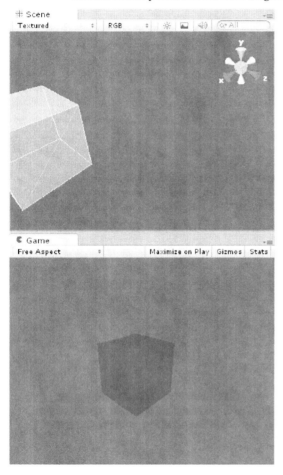

Figure 2-26. *The cube is no longer focused in the Scene view.Note that adjusting the view in the Scene window does not affect the camera's view as seen in the Game window.*

Selecting and Focus

One of the most important navigation concepts in Unity is that of quickly zooming in to specific objects or areas.

To focus the viewport back to the cube, or to "find" the cube, do the following:

1. Make sure the cube is selected in the Hierarchy view.

2. Put the cursor over the Scene window.

3. Press the F key on your keyboard.

The view shifts to center of the cube.

Also note that the edges of the selected object show in pale green. Using the View mode drop-down, shown in Figure 2-27, you can view scene objects in several other modes.

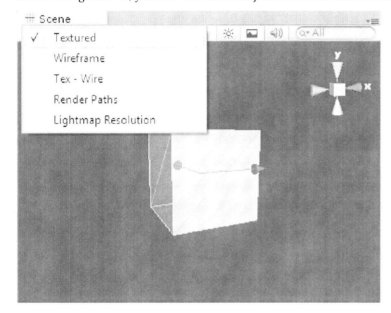

Figure 2-27. *The View mode drop-down*

4. Try the Wireframe mode.

The object shows only the object edges.

5. Try the Tex - Wire.

The Tex - Wire mode shows the solid object with the edges, but unlike the selected object in Texture mode, all of the scene objects will also be shown textured and edged.

6. Return the view mode to Textured.

Transforming objects

In 3D space, we use what is called the Cartesian coordinate system. If you come from Autodesk products, you will be used to Z representing "up" in the world. This derived from traditional drafting where the paper coordinates on the drafting table were X and Y, so Z became up. In Unity, Y is up, deriving from the early days of 2D monitor space where X is horizontal and Y is vertical. With the advent of 3D space on computers, Z was assigned to back or forward from the monitor. You will hear more about Z depth in real-time programs.

No matter which way is up, the directions are color coded, with red, green, blue, (RGB) corresponding to X, Y, Z.

Objects can be transformed (Move, Rotate, Scale) around the scene with the rest of the tools on the upper left toolbar (Figure 2-28).

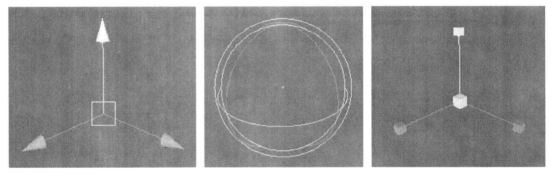

Figure 2-28. *Translate(Move), Rotate and Scale Tool gizmos*

1.   Select the cube from the Hierarchy view or by picking it in the Scene view.

2.   Select the Move button.

A Transform axis appears for the cube.

3.   Click and drag on any of the three axes.

The active direction turns yellow and the movement is confined to that arrow's direction. The object also moves in the Game window, as Figure 2-29 shows.

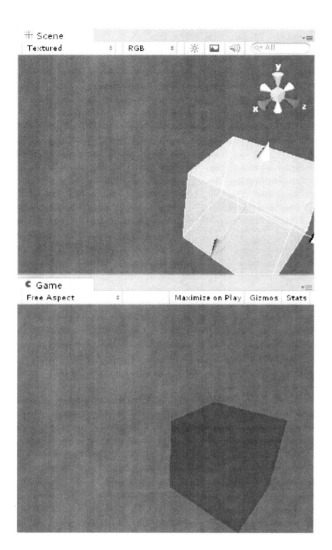

Figure 2-29. *The translated (moved) cube. Note that the camera has not moved, but the cube has, as is reflected in the Game window.*

4. Next choose the Rotate icon.

The gizmo consists of circles, once again color coded.

5. Click and drag the red, green, and blue circles to see what happens.

The gray outer circle will rotate the object to 2D screen coordinates no matter which way you orbit the view.

In the Inspector, you can set the object's transforms manually (see Figure 2-30).

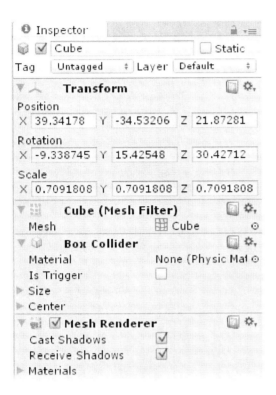

Figure 2-30. *Performing transforms on the cube as shown in the Inspector*

6. In the Transform section for the cube, set the Y Position to **0**, the X Position to 20, and the Z Position to **10**.

7. Use the F key to focus the view port to the cube's new position, but remember to position the cursor in the Scene window first.

■ **Tip**   In Unity, a single unit is generally considered to be one meter. As with most 3D apps, though, scale is really quite arbitrary. Still, you'll find that elements like lights and physics typically have default settings that will require quite a bit of tweaking if you stray too far from the norm.

The transforms are all floating point numbers; that is, they can have fractions as indicated by the decimal points.

You can also adjust the numbers by positioning the cursor over the axis label, pressing the left mouse button, and dragging.

8. Position the mouse over the Y Scale label and drag.

The cube is scaled on its Local axis and the values change accordingly in the Inspector.

The small center gray rectangle allows you to adjust more than one axis at the same time. With the Scale gizmo, it will cause the object to be uniformly scaled on all three axes.

9. Select the Scale tool.

10. Test the uniform scale by clicking and dragging within the small gray cube at the center of the Scale gizmo.

11. Set the X, Y, and Z Rotations and Positions to **0.**

12. Set the Scale X, Y, and Z to **1.**

13. Use the F key to focus the viewport again.

Snaps

Besides manually moving objects in the Scene view or adjusting their transforms in the Inspector, you can snap objects by incremental amounts or to each other by vertex.

1. From the bottom of the Edit menu, open the Snap settings dialog, shown in Figure 2-31.

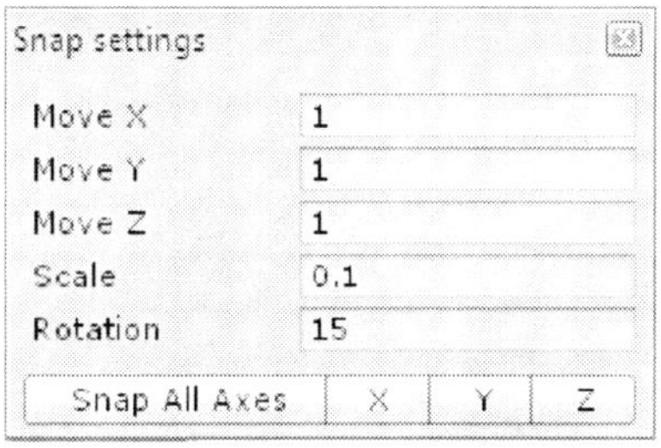

Snap settings	⬚
Move X	1
Move Y	1
Move Z	1
Scale	0.1
Rotation	15

Snap All Axes	X	Y	Z

Figure 2-31. *The Snap settings dialog*

Note that Move X, Move Y, and Move Z are all set to 1 and the Rotation snap is set to 15 degrees. To use the increment snap, hold down the Ctrl (Windows) or Cmd (Mac) key while transforming the object.

2. Select the cube.

3. Make sure the Transform tool is active.

4. Hold down the Ctrl or Cmd key and move the cube slowly in the Scene window.

Ever so subtly, the cube moves in 1 unit increments, as you can see by watching the Inspector.

5. Zoom out a bit using either Alt + the right mouse button or the scroll wheel on the mouse if you have one.

6. In the Snap settings dialog, change the Move amounts from 1 to 5.

7. With the Ctrl or Cmd key still down, move the cube again.

8. Set the Move amounts back to **1**.

This time the snap is more noticeable.

Rotation snaps can be very useful when changing an object's orientation. Rotation snaps work the same way as the position snaps.

1. Select the cube.

2. Make sure the Rotation tool is active

3. Hold down the Ctrl or Cmd key and rotate the cube slowly in the Scene window

The cube snaps in 15 degree increments.

4. Close the Snap settings dialog.

Vertex Snaps

As well as the increment snaps, you can also snap objects using their vertices as registration points. While this may not be terribly useful in an organic environment, it can be invaluable for snapping roads and tracks together.

1. Activate the Move tool.

2. Select the cube.

3. Use Ctrl + D to duplicate the cube.

4. Select one of the cubes and move it away from the other.

5. Hold down the V key (for Vertex) and slowly move the cursor over the repositioned cube.

The transform gizmo snaps to the cube's vertices as you move the cursor, as shown in Figure 2-32.

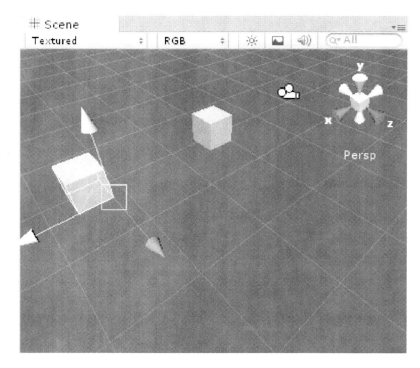

Figure 2-32. *The transform gizmo snapped to one of the cube's vertices*

6. Continuing to hold the V key down, press and hold the left mouse button and move the cube toward the other cube until it snaps to the desired vertex on the other cube.

7. Delete the extra cube by using the Delete key on the keyboard or right-clicking on the cube in the Hierarchy view and selecting Delete from the menu.

For more information on positioning objects with the snaps, see "Positioning GameObjects" in the manual.

Scene Gizmo

So far we have adjusted the viewport and transformed the object in a Perspective viewport. While this is useful when you know the exact location, or don't need to be exact at all, it can be challenging and slow to continually rotate the view and adjust the object with more accuracy. The Scene Gizmo icon, shown in Figure 2-33, lets you switch between Perspective and Orthographic views. Orthographic views (Front, Back, Top, Bottom), because they have no perspective, allow you to judge position and scalar relationships.

Figure 2-33. *Scene Gizmo*

1. Click the Y cone on the Scene Gizmo icon.

You are now in a Top viewport.
At this point, the screen-space transform gizmos make more sense.

2. Select the cube and activate the Rotate tool.

3. Rotate the cube about twenty or thirty degrees or so with the outer circle until it is no longer in an orthographic orientation.

4. Activate the Move tool.

5. Change the coordinate system from Global to Local (see Figure 2-34).

Figure 2-34. *Global to Local Coordinate system and object pivot to object center toggles*

The local coordinate system allows you to transform the object in relation to its own local coordinates as opposed the fixed scene or World coordinates. You may also wish to use the object Center instead of the object's creation Pivot, shown in Figure 2-34.

6. Now move the box in its local X direction.

7. Set the cube's rotations back to **0** in the Inspector.

You may have noticed a small grey square in the middle of the Move gizmo; it allows 2-axis movement and is very useful in orthographic views.

Non-Snap Alignment

To align an object with another, we can once again use the options in the GameObject menu.

1. Click the gray center box of the Scene Gizmo to get back to a perspective viewport.

2. Select the cube and use the F key to focus or find it.

3. From the GameObject menu, choose Create Other ➤ Create a Sphere.

4. Activate the Scale tool.

5. Scale the sphere using the center yellow cube on the gizmo to uniformly scale it so it shows through the cube (see Figure 2-35).

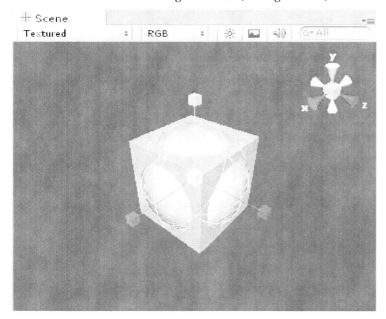

Figure 2-35. *The sphere is created in the same position as the cube.*

The sphere is created in the same spot as the cube.
To align existing objects, you can use the third alignment option from the GameObject menu.

1. Select the Move tool.

2. Move the sphere away from the cube.

3. Select the cube and focus the view to it.

4. Select the sphere.

5. From the GameObjects menu, select Move to View.

The sphere is positioned at the cube once again, because the cube was focused to the center of the view.

6. Delete the sphere by selecting it in the Hierarchy view, then pressing the Delete key, or by selecting Delete from the Edit menu, or by pressing Shift + Delete.

CHAPTER 2   UNITY UI BASICS—GETTING STARTED

Lights

In the Game window, the cube is dark, lit only by ambient scene lighting, but in the Scene window it is lit. When you pressed the Lighting button at the top of the window, it toggled off the built-in lighting so you can see the scene lighting. Since there are no lights in the viewport yet, it went dark, just as in the Game window.

1. Focus the Scene view on the cube again and zoom out a bit.

2. From the GameObject menu, choose Create Other ➤ Create a Directional Light.

Directional lights emit parallel rays no matter where they are in the scene.

3. Move the light up and out of the way of the cube.

4. Rotate it in the Scene window until the cube is lit nicely in the Game window, as shown in Figure 2-36.

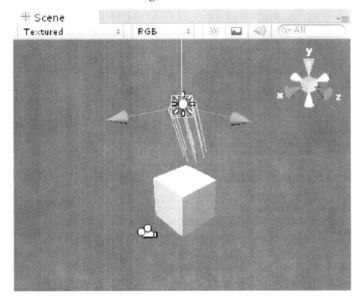

Figure 2-36. *The Directional light oriented to light the cube*

5. Using Alt + the left mouse button to drag, orbit the viewport so you are facing the unlit side of the cube, as shown in Figure 2-37.

74

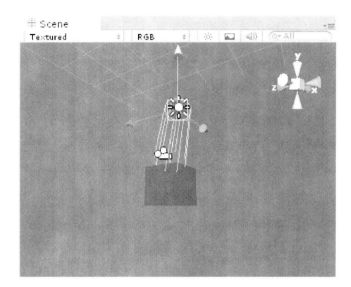

Figure 2-37. *The unlit side of the cube*

The details disappear.

6. Toggle the scene lighting back off with the light icon (Figure 2-38).

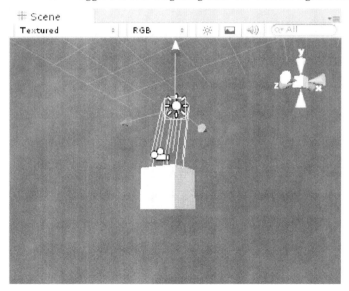

Figure 2-38. *Scene light toggled off (default turned on)*

The default lighting shines directly into the viewport, ensuring objects are easy to see regardless of viewpoint in the Scene window.

As you create your scene, you will probably toggle the Scene lighting off and on regularly.

Now is a good time to take a peek at the Inspector, shown in Figure 2-39.

Figure 2-39. *Light selected in the Inspector*

7. With the light selected, uncheck then check the box next to the light component's label.

The light turns off then on.

8. Click on the color swatch next to the Color label.

The Color dialog opens, as shown in Figure 2-40.

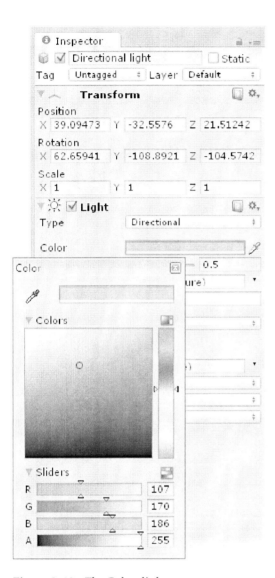

Figure 2-40. *The Color dialog*

9. Click and drag in the Colors image and watch the light's color on the cube change.

10. Choose something subtle.

11. Close the dialog.

Let's add a material to the cube to replace the default.

1. In the Inspector, select the Cube.

2. In the Mesh Renderer section, click to open the Materials list (see Figure 2-41).

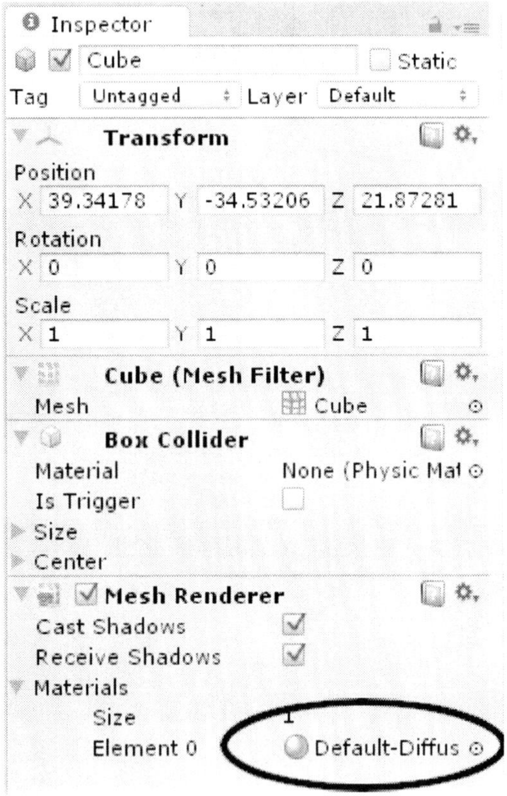

Figure 2-41. *The cube's default material*

With the exception of one or two, the ready-made materials from the standard assets package are all specialty materials, so we will create our own. First let's create a new folder to keep them organized.

3. From the Assets menu, choose Create ➤ Folder, (Figure 2-42).

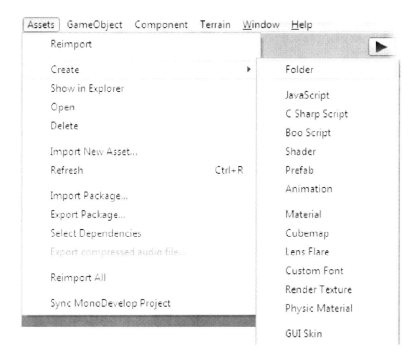

Figure 2-42. *Creating a new folder*

4. Rename the folder **My Materials**.

▪ **Tip** As you create new assets for a game, it becomes important to stay organized and keep the Project view uncluttered. We will be creating several folders for that purpose throughout the book.

You can access the same menu directly in the Projects view.

5. Right-click on the new Materials folder and from the same Create submenu, choose Material (Figure 2-43).

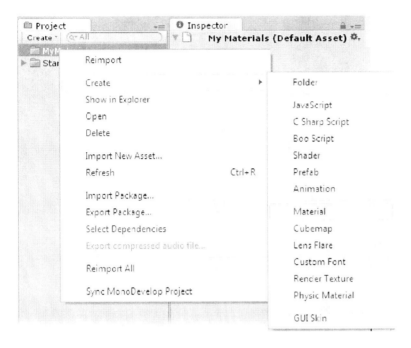

Figure 2-43. *Creating a new material*

A New Material entry appears in the Inspector.

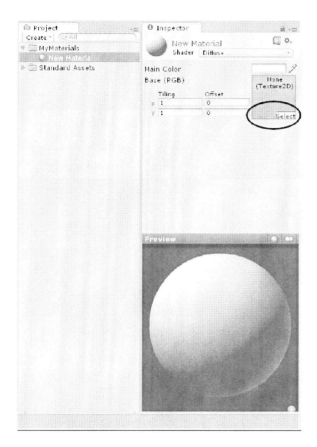

Figure 2-44. *The new material in the Project view and in the Inspector*

6. Name the new material **TestBark**.

7. Drag and drop the material from the folder onto the cube in the Scene window.

8. In the Texture thumbnail window (not the Preview window), pick the Select button (Figure 2-44) and, with the preview slider all the way to the left in the Asset Selector (Figure 2-45), choose PalmBark.

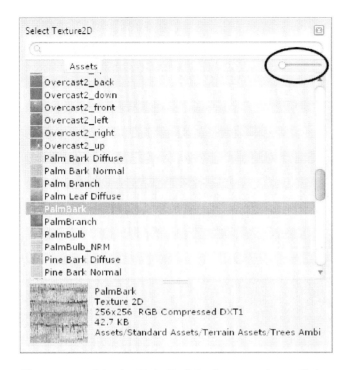

Figure 2-45. *Selecting PalmBark in the asset selector dialog*

▨ **Tip**   The Asset Selector is one way to load images, animation clips, and sound clips into components, shaders, or other parameters in your scene. It has the advantage of filtering for only the correct asset type, but the disadvantage is that it shows *all* available assets of that type. Later in the project we will also drag assets directly from the Project view into the target parameters.

The cube now has a more interesting texture.
The default shader is a simple Diffuse shader.

9.   Click the down arrow and select the Specular shader.

10.   Try adjusting the Shininess slider.

Note the texture is retained as you experiment with different shaders.
Now that our simple test scene has a few objects in it, we should save it.

11.   From the File menu, select Save Scene, then repeat to Save Project.

░ **Tip**   While it is not always necessary to save the project as well as the scene, it is a safe habit to get into, so we will continue to do so throughout the book.

3D Objects

This book is generally aimed toward artists looking to become familiar with the Unity engine and game engine concepts in general. However, as a review for those already familiar with 3D as well as a short primer for those with a 2D art background, we will look at 3D from a slightly different viewpoint to see how several concepts relate to real-time and game-associated issues.

Most people these days are quite familiar with the end product of 3D through film or games. Many have watched several "Making Of" documentaries and already have a basic knowledge of many of the concepts. As we have already introduced and experimented with transforms and viewport navigation in the previous sections, let's look at the objects themselves.

Meshes

While outwardly they appear no different from the primitive objects we've been using as test subjects so far, meshes are stored quite differently. Instead of being stored as a list of parameters used to create a 3D object, meshes are stored as a collection of points in space. As such, they can take on an endless variety of shapes, but tend to take up a lot of hard drive space. In memory, both types of objects take up the same amount of space, so storage, and download time, become more important issues when deciding if it is easier to create simple meshes in Unity, or import them as collapsed meshes.

Sub-Objects of a Mesh

Unity does not provide easy access to the sub-objects of a mesh, but you can affect them through scripting so it is worth looking into what makes a mesh.

- **Vertex:** A vertex is the smallest sub-object, a point in space. Since vertices are little more than locations, they are not drawn. They can, however, contain information about color, opacity, and lighting, for example.

- **Edges:** Edges are the straight lines between vertices. It is worth noting that in most 3D applications, the rendered result does not contain true curved lines or surfaces; rather they are approximations of curves created by a large number of smaller straight lines.

- **Faces:** The face, also referred to as a triangle (see Figure 2-46), is the smallest renderable part of a mesh. It is defined by three vertices, the edges that connect them, and the surface between them. A face also has what is called a Normal to tell the engine on which side to render the face. Unless you're using a shader that specifically indicates that a face should be rendered on both sides, a face is drawn only on one side.

Figure 2-46. *Anatomy of a Face*

Faces are often treated differently in DCC applications. In 3ds Max, for example, you can work with backfaces "turned on," but at render time and export time, they are not calculated. In Maya, the default actually creates backfaces that render and export. This increases the amount of information contained in a mesh as well as taking extra time to cull out the hidden faces at render time—a step to be avoided in real-time engines. A good practice is to get in the habit of turning off backfaces when you are modeling assets for your game.

The face normal is not to be confused with the vertex normal. Vertex normals are used to calculate the light a face will receive. A vector is traced from the light to the vertex normal, and the angle of incidence, the angle between the two, is used to calculate the amount of light received at that vertex. The smaller the angle of incidence, the higher percentage of the light it receives. A vertex with a light directly over its normal would have an angle of incidence of 0 degrees and would receive the full amount of light.

Occasionally, you'll see faces with either the face normal flipped or the vertex normals flipped, giving very odd results, as shown in Figure 2-47. CAD data used for meshes often has no face normal information at all; as it tends to be always drawn double-sided, when normals are created for it, they are often mixed up.

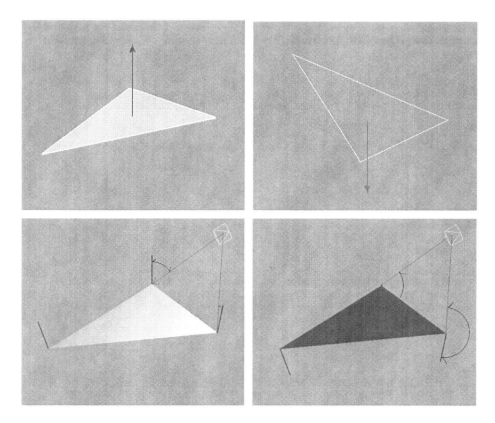

Figure 2-47. *Faces and their face normals and vertex normals*

- Top row: The face normal determines which side the face is drawn on.
  - Left: Face normal.
  - Right: Face normal pointing down (the face is not drawn).
- Bottom row: The vertex normals and angles of incidence. Note the large angle of incidence on the face with its vertex normals pointing the wrong direction.
  - Left: Face normal and vertex normals pointing up.
  - Right: Face normal pointing up, but vertex normals pointing down.

Mapping

Whenever an object uses a texture or image as part of its material, it needs mapping coordinates to tell the renderer how to apply the image to the object's faces. At its simplest, mapping can be as straightforward as a planar projection or as complicated as multiple UV unwraps.

Mapping coordinates are referred to as U, V, and W, where U represents one side of the map and V represents the other edge, as in Figure 2-48. W is the axis of a face normal and is of use when rotating the map about that axis.

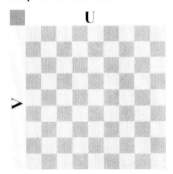

Figure 2-48. *UVW coordinates*

The four most common mapping types are planar, box, cylindrical, and spherical, as shown in Figure 2-49.

Figure 2-49. *The four most common mapping types*

- **Planar:** The image is projected from the chosen direction, through the mesh.

- **Box:** Planar projections of the image are put on each side of the object in a cube fashion.

- **Cylindrical:** The image is wrapped into a cylinder and projected inward and outward onto the mesh. This mapping type requires a map that tiles at the edges so the seam won't be noticeable, or that the position of the seam is never seen.

- **Spherical:** The image is wrapped into a cylinder, and then gathered at top and bottom. This also requires seamless tiling.

An object can have a combination of mapping types as with the sign shown in Figure 2-50. The posts are cylindrical, the sign is box-mapped, and the finials are spherical.

Figure 2-50. *Compound mapping on an object*

- Top left: The sign's geometry.

- Top right: The sign with box, cylindrical, and spherical mapping.

- Bottom left: The mapped sign with a single texture.

- Bottom right: The mapped sign with multiple textures.

When a single texture is painted for an object, as opposed to using separate materials for its sub-objects, it is considered unwrapped. The mapping is arranged (packed) to fit within a specific aspect ratio, usually one to one, a square, and the pieces hand-painted to achieve a more customized texture. The tricky part about unwrapping is the compromise between less distortion but hard to paint (lots of small pieces) and more distortion but easier to paint (large pieces), as shown in Figure 2-51.

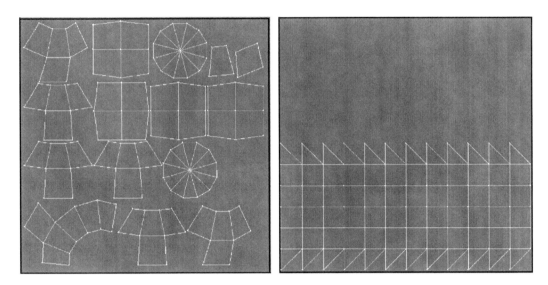

Figure 2-51. *Unwrap compromise with a sphere*

The downside is that you generally forfeit resolution in favor of custom detail. The upside is that for one-off objects, a single material is far easier to manage in the game engine. Additionally, in Unity, separate objects are internally combined or *batched* when they use the same material and are below a certain vertex count for more efficient handling.

When the object is structural rather than organic, you can save the hand-painting step by rendering the conventional mapping and materials into the unwrap map, as shown in Figure 2-52. This can be touched up or altered in your painting program or used as is.

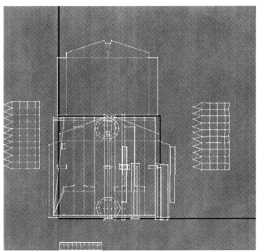
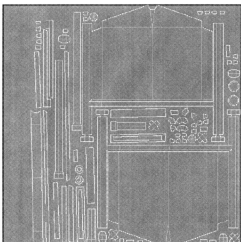

Figure 2-52. *The sign, mapping before, mapping unwrapped, packed and rendered out using the pre-existing materials and mapping*

Typically, you also include lighting information in "one-off" objects. This is known as *baked lighting*. It can be actual scene lighting, or serve as grunge or *ambient occlusion* (the darkness in nooks and crannies), as shown in Figure 2-53.

Figure 2-53. *The sign with lighting baked in as well, fully self-illuminated, no lighting*

One problem with lightmaps is that you can't have any pieces overlapping. This means that parts of the mesh that are identical or mirrored now have to be separated. The pieces all must be shrunk to fit once again within the map, causing a loss of resolution.

One solution to this problem is to use two sets of UV maps—one for the diffuse texture and one for the lightmap, (see Figure 2-54). Although this does take a bit more time to render, it allows for much higher resolution of the diffuse textures as they can be tiled and/or overlapped. The lightmap, usually much smaller as it doesn't need the same amount of detail, is added in at render time. Typically, buildings and other structures with large areas of the same physical material are handled this way, where a large lightmap will service an entire structure and a single detailed texture map is tiled across all. It is also quite useful for terrains, where parts of the baked shadow map are swapped out at runtime for real-time shadows, and also for games and configurators that let the player customize textures in the game or application.

Figure 2-54. *A structure using separate diffuse and lightmaps and the resulting combination of the tiled diffuse modulated with the lightmap.*

Materials

Materials are generally different in real-time engines than in their DCC counterparts. At best, simple materials with a diffuse texture will import intact. Plan on spending time rebuilding materials with their shader counterparts, once they're in the engine. Most game engines have a particular process for best practices when dealing with imported textures.

Modern engines have shaders for many uses so you can use your textures and masks to duplicate the more complex materials from your DCC application.

Summary

In this chapter, you got your first look at using Unity. You started by creating a new project, then took a quick look at each of the five main views: Scene view where you edit and arrange your assets; Hierarchy view where the assets in the current scene are listed; Project view where all of the assets available to the project reside; the Game window where you can see and interact as the player; and the Inspector, where you can access asset parameters, components, and scene or project settings. The most important takeaway from this section is that you should never rearrange the contents of the project's Assets folder from the operating system's file manager.

Next you took a brief look at some of the menus to get an idea of what they contain, noting especially the Help menu with its link to the Unity Forum, the Unity Answers.

You created your first object, a simple cube, in Unity and used it as a test subject to explore viewport navigation, object finding or focusing, and object transforms (move, rotate, and scale). You were able to create a directional light and also match a camera to the Scene view so you could view your test object in the Game window. You found that selected objects displayed their parameters and other information in the Inspector and that you could modify their transforms more accurately by changing their values in the Inspector. And finally, you learned how to create a new folder in the Project view and create a new material asset to go inside it.

Having gotten a start (or perhaps a review) on exploring the 3D space of viewports, objects, and transforms, you delved a bit deeper into concepts uniquely 3D and looked at the sub-objects that comprise a 3D mesh. You saw how light is calculated and what gives a mesh a soft or smooth look as opposed to a hard edge. You then looked at the mapping of 3D objects, starting with simple mapping types and working your way up to fully unwrapped and light-mapped treatments, and the logic of when to use each. To finish, you found that most materials will probably require a bit of attention to get the best results after importing your meshes.

In the next chapter, we will take a look at scripting in Unity. We will start by creating very simple scripts to make our objects perform on cue, then deconstruct a couple of Unity's most useful standard asset scripts to start getting a feel for the syntax.

CHAPTER 3

■ ■ ■

Scripting: Getting Your Feet Wet

The heart of interactivity is scripting. In Unity, everything needs to be scripted. Fortunately, there are ready-made scripts from a multitude of sources. Unity ships with a large collection of useful scripts to get you up and running. The Help section is full of examples and snippets of script; it also includes a full Scripting section. The Unity3D Wiki, Unity Forum, and Unity Answers are other good sources. Another useful place to find what you need is in the tutorials that you can download from the Unity web site. Most of the tutorial resources do a very good job of explaining what the code does. Note that while Unity scripts can be written in JavaScript, C#, and Boo, most official Unity tutorials and help examples are written in JavaScript, so I will follow suit in this book.

While the purpose of this book is not necessarily to *teach* you to script, you will be able to do more if you can at least learn to read through the scripts and have a basic understanding of what each part does. Many scripts are well commented, but others are not, so I will examine key parts as you develop your game functionality, adding to your knowledge as painlessly as possible. Keep in mind that scripting is as much about *logic* as it is about *syntax*—and logic is what drives interaction.

What is a Script?

Think of a script as a set of instructions. Let's say you're going to your great Aunt Mildred's farm house for a party this weekend. You might use Google or MapQuest to get the directions and print them out, taking advantage of the easy-to-follow instructions. You volunteered to bring chips and a dip to the gathering, so you might also make a note to yourself at the top of the directions to remember to stop by the supermarket and get the items. Your sister tells you to park your car on the far side of the barn so there will be room for everyone. Your brother warns that if you drive your motorcycle instead of your car, you should bring a cover to put over it to keep the chickens from trying to roost on it. Realizing that you are likely to forget something, you add the extra instructions to the back of the driving directions so *everything pertaining to the party will be in one place.* If you have written your notes on different pieces of paper, you might staple them all together and write "Aunt Mildred's Party" across the top.

Scripts, then, can contain any amount of information and instruction. It will be up to you to keep your scripts organized so the game engine will know how and when to use the information.

Another scripting challenge is deciding where to put the scripts. With some scripts, like the instructions to open and close a door, the choice will be easy; in this case the script can go on any door in the scene that needs to be functional. Likewise, the script that causes an alligator to rush out and snap at the player's character will more than likely belong on the alligator. Other scripts, however, may not be associated with anything in particular, such as a script that changes day into night. It may control the state of several objects in the scene, but it may be dependent on time, rather than player interaction, to know when to execute the instructions. In this case, you would probably make an empty GameObject for the express purpose of holding that particular script and name it accordingly.

In Unity, objects can be manipulated by any number of scripts in the scene. A script can reside on the GameObject it will manipulate, or, as in the case of a light switch, it could trigger an action on a different object such as a light. While an object could conceivably have a single script containing all of the information and functionality it needs, the script would tend to be too specialized and not very re-usable. Think of it like a teenage girl's outfit. For a particular outfit, she could keep her dress, shoes, purse, scarf, and hat all in one place. But in doing so, she loses the flexibility to mix and match accessories with other outfits. Good generic scripts are like accessories—they may be used and reused over and over. By having smaller scripts to do specific tasks, what you lose in ease of access is often more than made up for in portability.

Before your head starts spinning from too much scripting theory, let's simplify the process and just start building some simple scripts.

Components of a Script

Scripts consist of four main types of components: *variables, functions, equations,* and *comments.* Variables hold values that can be anything from numbers to text. Functions do something, generally with variables and equations. Comments are ignored when the code is executed, allowing you to make notes about what the code is or should be doing or even to temporarily disable the code.

Functions

Functions in Unity can be roughly grouped in three types: game related (system, input, network), object specific, and user defined.

If you are reopening Unity for this chapter, open the scene you were working on in Chapter 2, TestScene1.

1. Click on TestScene1 in the Project view.

2. Create a New Folder in the Project view.

3. Name the new folder My Scripts.

4. With the new folder selected, right-click it to bring up the contents of the right click menu. Select JavaScript from the Create sub-menu

---

■ **Rule**   Any time you are asked to create a new script for this book, assume that it will be a JavaScript script.

A new script called NewBehaviorScript is added to your folder. You can see its contents in the Inspector (see Figure 3-1), but you can't edit it from there.

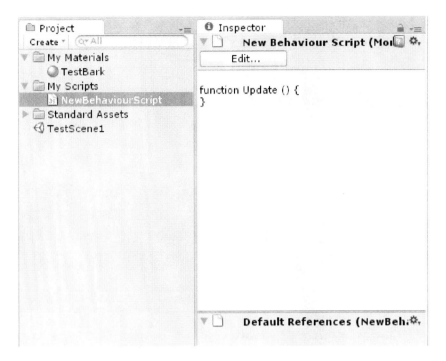

Figure 3-1. *The new script*

■ **Tip**   Always rename the newly created script before editing it.

---

5.   Change its name by clicking on the name in the Project view and waiting for it to go into rename mode.

6.   Name this script SimpleRotate and press Enter to finish.

7.   To open the UniSciTE script editor (Unitron on the Mac), either double-click the name in the Project view or click the Edit button at the top of the Inspector.

■ **Tip**   If you are using Unity on a Mac, the scripting editor is the Unitron editor. Colors and fonts will appear somewhat different.

Figure 3-2. *The new script opened in the scripting editor*

As you can see in Figure 3-2, the new script already has some code in it—an empty *Update* function.

```
function Update () {

}
```

Anatomy of a Function

- What it is: `function`. It is in lower case and bold in Unity's UniSciTE script editor. A function carries out a set of instructions.

- Its name: `Update`. Function names are *always capitalized.*

- Arguments: `()`. Information that gets passed to the function when it is called. In this case, there is nothing being passed, so the parentheses remain empty.

- Content: `{}`. The content, or instructions, goes inside the curly brackets. There are no instructions as of yet in this function.

The `Update` function is one of the most important functions in any game engine. This system function is checked at least *every frame* during runtime to see if anything needs to be executed. It can make a `Transform` such as a rotation continuously loop, check to see if a particular condition is met, and many other things.

1. Position the cursor after the open curly bracket and press Enter a few times to make room for some code.

2. From inside the function (inside the curly brackets), tab over and add the following:

```
transform.Rotate(0,5,0);
```

■ **Tip** Indenting or tabbing over is not a required part of the syntax, but it will make it easier to read your scripts as you add more functionality.

The parts of this line of code mean the following:

- `transform` is part of a set of definitions that control how an object can behave.

- `Rotate` is the Rotate function (note that its first letter is in caps) for a specific operation from the transform class.

- `(0,5,0)` refers to the X, Y, and Z rotations parameters that are needed by the Rotate function.

- `;` indicates the end of the operation or line.

This line of code also employs *dot notation* (see Figure 3-3), which is the way to access functions and variables (parameters) available to various objects and operations.

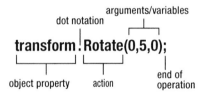

Figure 3-3. *Dot notation*

Because the script will be put on your cube, you assume that the object that will be rotated is the object that the script resides on so you don't need to preface the line with the object itself.

Since your little bit of code is inside the `Update` function, the object will be rotated 5 degrees each frame.

3. Save the script by pressing the Save icon or through the File menu ➤ Save

The script is updated in the Inspector as soon as you change focus to the Unity application.

4. Minimize (don't close) the script editor, and then drag the script from the Project view onto the Cube, either in the Hierarchy view or in the Scene window.

5. Select the Cube in the Hierarchy view and look for the `SimpleRotate` script in the Inspector.

It will be right above the material (which is always listed last), as shown in Figure 3-4.

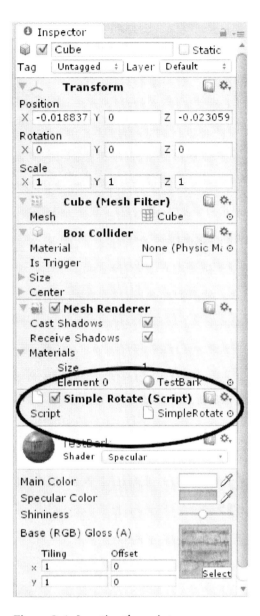

Figure 3-4. *Locating the script*

6. Click the Play button at the top of the editor.

The editor goes darker and the cube spins in both the Scene and the Game windows, as shown in Figure 3-5.

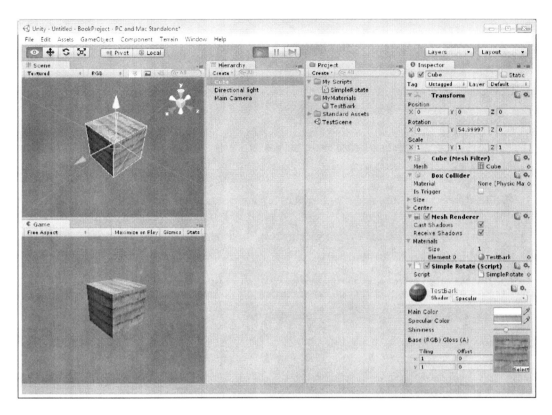

Figure 3-5. *Game mode dark*

7. Maximize the script editor again and change the 5 to a 1, like so:

```
transform.Rotate(0,1,0);
```

8. Save the change and click on the editor again to resume focus.

The cube rotates slower.

9. Click the Play button again to stop play mode.

Because the rotation is set to occur every frame, everyone will see a different speed depending on frame rate of their machine.

The next important concept in Unity scripting is Time.deltaTime. Time.deltaTime allows you to animate things on a per second basis rather than per frame, so animations will be consistent across machines and their varying frame rates. Time.deltaTime is a variable that returns the amount of time that has passed since the last call to the Update function.

10. Change the line to read

```
transform.Rotate(0,5 * Time.deltaTime,0);
```

Now instead of rotating 5 degrees *per frame*, it will rotate 5 degrees *per second*.

11. Click Play.

The speed is radically different.

12. Change the degrees from 5 to about 50 and save again to see a nice effect.

■ **Tip**   Remember to save the script after each change to see its effects.

Let's add a Translate (move) and see what happens if your syntax is not correct. Note the lowercase *t* on *translate*.

1. Add the following inside the Update function just below the Rotate line:

```
transform.translate(2 * Time.deltaTime,0,0);
```

As soon as you save your addition, an error immediately pops up in the status line below the Game window (see Figure 3-6). You can click on it to open the console, (see Figure 3-7).

① Assets/My Scripts/SimpleRotate.js(5,19): BCE0019: 'translate' is not a member of 'UnityEngine.Transform'. Did you mean 'Translate'?

Figure 3-6. *The error reported on the status line*

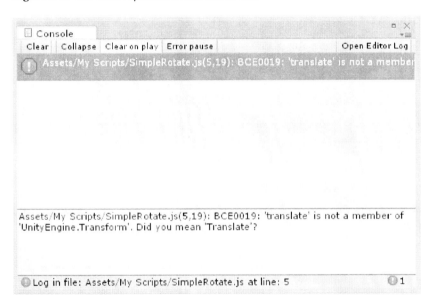

Figure 3-7. *The console and error message*

In this case, the error was easily recognized and a suggestion was made.

2. Change the lowercase t to uppercase T and resave.

The error message goes away, as you can see in Figure 3-8.

Figure 3-8. *The error corrected*

3. Close the console.

4. Save the changes and click Play.

The script now tells the cube to move at 2 meters per second, but the cube may or may not behave as you expected. Apparently, the rotate is evaluated first, and the move/translate is evaluated second on the cube's local axis.

If you want the cube to rotate while traveling in a straight line in the X direction, you can to enlist the help of a GameObject. In Unity, the GameObject is used to order functionality, organize assets in the scene, and other useful purposes. You will often see it referred to as the GO.

Before you set up the GameObject, separate your two operations into different scripts.

1. Click the Play button to stop playback.

2. From the Edit menu in the script editor, choose Save As and name the clone SimpleMove.js.

Because SimpleRotate was renamed, you will need to re-open the original in the script editor. You will now see both scripts in the Project view, so you can open it from there.

3. Open the SimpleRotate.js script.

You should now have a tab for each script in the editor, as you can see in Figure 3-9.

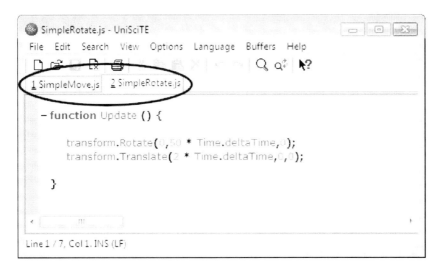

Figure 3-9. *The two scripts in the editor*

1. In the SimpleRotate.js script, add two backslashes to the beginning of the line with the translate operation, as follows:

```
//transform.Translate(2 * Time.deltaTime,0,0);
```

The line should turn green and appear in a different font indicating that it has been *commented out* and should be ignored.

■ **Tip**   You just used the comment mechanism to prevent code from being executed while you experiment. You will also be using it to make actual comments about what the code does. This makes it easier for you to remember what the code should do; comments also make it easier for another user to understand the code.

---

2. Repeat the process for the SimpleMove.js script, commenting out the rotate operation like so:

```
//transform.Rotate(0,50 * Time.deltaTime,0);
```

3. Be sure to save the changes for both scripts.

4. Minimize the script editor.

5. Back in the regular editor, from the GameObject menu, select CreateEmpty.

6. Name the new GameObject Cube Parent, as shown in Figure 3-10.

Figure 3-10. *The new GameObject, Cube Parent*

 7. Drag and drop the Cube onto the Cube Parent in the Hierarchy view.

 8. Drag and drop the SimpleMove.js script from the Project view onto the Cube
Parent object in the Hierarchy view.

The SimpleMove script appears in the Inspector when you select the Cube Parent (see Figure 3-11).

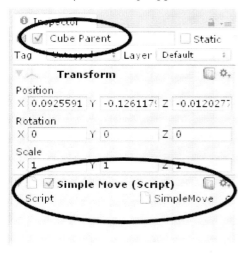

Figure 3-11. *The Cube Parent and the Simple Move script in the Inspector*

 9. Click Play.

The cube rotates slowly as it heads off in its local X direction. You may need to zoom out in the
Scene view to see the action more clearly.

Variables

Until now, most of the changes have been made to scripts, which need to be saved before they can be
tested. As you have just made several changes to the scene, now would be a good time to save it.

1. Use Ctrl+S to save or Save from the File menu.

About now you may be feeling a bit intimidated about handling animations by *hardcoding* them into the game. Don't worry! You will using different methods to animate the actual game objects; scripting the transforms just provides obvious feedback for your first efforts at scripting.

Let's look next at variables. Variables provide a means to keep track of states, values, text, and more. Variables are a mechanism for storing information. In Unity, those variables can be exposed to the Inspector so you no longer have to open a script to make changes. This also lets you to keep the scripts generic so the same script can be used on several different objects while allowing for custom settings for each.

As it stands right now, when you want to change the speed of the Cube's rotation, you need to change the number inside the rotate operation. Let's switch it over to a variable.

Tip   Give your variables meaningful names, but keep them short. You can—and should—add comments for a fuller explanation.

Rule   Variable names may not start with a numeric digit or certain special characters and may not include spaces. Also, there are several reserved words you should not use as names. While not strictly necessary, it is good scripting practice to start each variable name with a lower case character. When words in the variable name are capitalized, a space will appear in the Inspector.

---

2. Change the code in the SimpleRotate script to the following:

```
var myDegrees = 50;

function Update () {

    transform.Rotate(0,myDegrees * Time.deltaTime,0);

}
```

3. Save the script.

4. Click on the Cube Parent to open the group and gain access to its child, Cube.

5. Select the Cube and look in the Inspector to see the new variable exposed (see Figure 3-12).

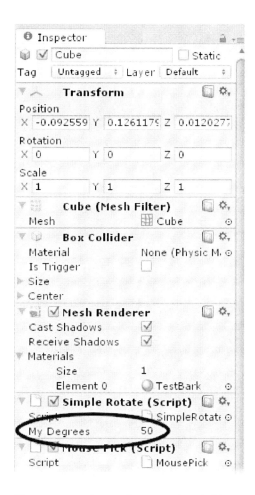

Figure 3-12. *The newly exposed variable, My Degrees*

Note that where a character in the variable name was capitalized, there is now a space in the name, making it easier to read in the Inspector. The first character has also been capitalized.

6. Click Play and note that nothing looks any different.

7. In the SimpleMove script, change the 2 to 0.5 to slow down the move animation so the cube is visible in the scene window for a longer period of time.

8. Save the script and select the Cube if it is not already selected.

9. Click Play.

10. In the Inspector, not the script editor, change the My Degrees parameter from 50 to 200.

The cube spins faster.

11. Click Play again to stop the game.

Note that the value has been reset to 50.

 Rule   In Unity, any changes made in the Inspector during runtime **will be lost.** While this allows you to experiment and get direct feedback without breaking anything, it also means you must return to Edit mode before you can make permanent changes.

---

12. In the script editor for the `SimpleRotate` script, change the variable's value to 100 and save the script

Note that the original value of 50 remains in the Inspector.

13. Click Play.

The rotation uses the slower value from the Inspector. The value in the Inspector always overrides the value initialized in the script itself.

 Rule   Once a variable has been exposed to the Inspector, it will always override the original value in the script where the variable was declared and/or initialized.

---

14. Stop playback.

15. Now that you are no longer in Play mode, change the value of your parameter in the Inspector to 200**.**

16. Click Play.

The rotation is fast as expected.

17. Save your scene and your project.

 Caution   If you set the rotation on an object too fast, it may strobe or appear to go slower or even backwards on slower machines that can't deliver a fast frame rate.

There are a few other things you ought to know about variables. As mentioned, there are a few different types. In the rotate script when you declared myDegrees to equal 50, it automatically interpreted the number to be of type `int` (integer, a whole number). If you had used 50.0, it would have assumed a `float` (floating point, a fractional number). Many variables are only declared for their type, waiting to have their values assigned or initialized at a later time. Let's add a couple of new variables to the SimpleMove script.

1. At the top of the SimpleMove script, add the following:

```
var mySpeed : float;
var someString : String = "This is a test";
var someSetting : boolean = true;
var someObject : GameObject;
```

2. Save the script and select the Cube Parent to see the new additions in the Inspector (see Figure 3-13).

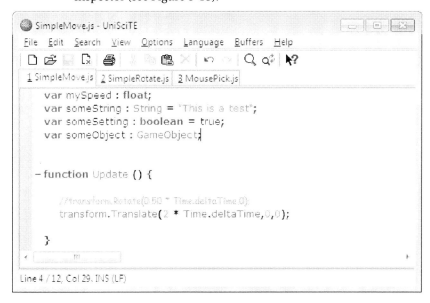

Figure 3-13. *The newly added variables*

Let's get a closer look.

- **var** mySpeed : **float**; declares a variable of type float, but doesn't initialize a value.

- **var** someString : String = "This is a test"; declares and initializes a variable of type String. Strings are always surrounded by quotation marks and appear purple in the UniSciTe script editor.

▪ **Caution** If you copy and paste the quotation marks from a word processor, the characters may be different than the editor expects. If you get an error, try retyping them manually in the editor.

107

- **var** someSetting : **boolean** = true; declares a variable of type Boolean (true or false) and initializes it as true. In the Inspector, a Boolean variable is depicted as a checkbox.

░ **Tip**   As long as the value of the variable is an obvious type, declaring the type is optional. If you do declare the type, you save the engine from trying to decide automatically what the type should be. For mobile platforms, such as iOS or Android, you *must* declare type. For this book, I will use both methods so you will get used to seeing it done both ways.

Note that all of the variables start with *var*. In Unity, *var* is assumed to be a *public* variable. In other words, it will be exposed to the Inspector.

3. Try changing someSetting to private var instead of just var.

4. Save the script.

5. Pick in the editor to change the focus and update the Inspector.

The someSetting parameter no longer appears in the Inspector.

- **var** someObject : GameObject; Along with the usual types seen in most programming languages, Unity lets you define a variable as being something as broad as a top level GameObject, down to as specific as its transform or other property, or even object type (such as Camera or Light).

For a script to have access to another object's variables and functions, it must be declared as the value of a variable. However, because an object's name is just one of its properties, the object must be accessed in a more abstract manner.

6. Try dragging the light or the camera in your scene from the Hierarchy view into the Some Object parameter in the Inspector

Once assigned, the script has access to that object's parameters and those of its children and components.

There is no need to handle parents or children with this method as there is a built-in way to gain access.

7. Save your scene and project.

Picking an Object in the Game

While you are digesting your first taste of scripting, let's stop a moment to consider one of the big differences between first person shooters and classic point and click adventure games. In the former, interaction is generally proximity based: you bump into an elevator button with your weapon and the doors open; you get within range of an enemy and it turns and starts firing upon you; or you shoot a pile of crates with a missile launcher and the missile, with the help of physics, scatters the unfortunate crates.

In classic point and click adventure games, generally, the cursor becomes the means of interaction rather than collisions, physics, and ray casting.

1.   Open the scripting Help (Help ➤ Scripting Reference).

2.   Do a search for "On Mouse Down."

You will see 57 matches. Glancing through them, you can see that the second one is the most likely candidate.

3.   Click on MonoBehavior.OnMouseDown

Let's create a new JavaScript for it. You could add it to one of the existing scripts, but you may decide to move it around.

4.   Select the MyScripts folder, right click and create a new JavaScript.

5.   Name the new script MousePick and open it in the script editor.

6.   You don't need the Update function for this script, so rename it OnMouseDown after the function you found in the Scripting Reference.

The sample in the help shows the code loading a new scene, but you just need to see if the pick registers. Unlike the Update function, the OnMouseDown function is only called when that event occurs.

A typical way to check for the expected functionality is to have the program print a message to the console. In the scripting help, do a search for "print to console." A quick glance through the offered results suggests that Debug.Log will log a message to the console. Pick it to see what the syntax looks like. It should be fairly straightforward. Also take note of MonoBehaviour.print for later use as it produces the same results as Debug.Log.

7.   Add the following line inside the OnMouseDown function:

```
Debug.Log("This object was picked");
```

8.   Save the script.

Note that the description says the function "is called when the user has pressed the mouse button while over the GUIElement or Collider." You don't have any GUI (Graphical User Interface) elements in your simple scene, so you need a Collider.

9.   Select the Cube.

In the Inspector, you will see that it already has a Collider.

▒ **Tip**   Primitive objects created in Unity are assigned a Collider component on creation.

To make the cube easier to pick, you will disable the SimpleMove script on the Cube Parent so it doesn't escape the Game view.

10.   Select the Cube Parent.

11.   Uncheck the SimpleMove script so it is no longer enabled (see Figure 3-14).

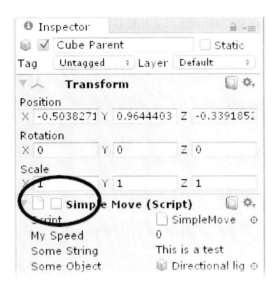

Figure 3-14. *The disabled SimpleMove*

12. Now drag and drop the MousePick script onto the Cube in the Hierarchy view.

13. Click Play and pick the Cube.

The message appears on the status line (see Figure 3-15).

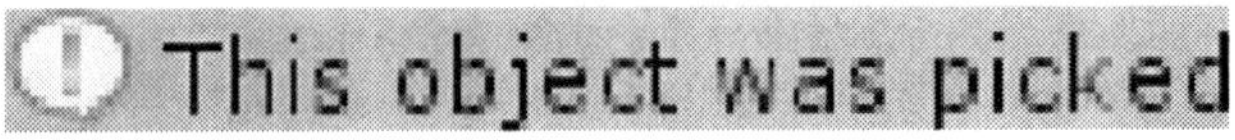

This object was picked

Figure 3-15. *The Debug.Log message on the status line*

■ **Tip**   If nothing happens when you pick the cube, make sure you put the MousePick script on the Cube, not on the Cube Parent as it does not have a Collider.

---

14. Open the Console by clicking on the status line.

Each time you click on the Cube, the message is output to the console (see Figure 3-16).

```
 Console                                                        □ ×
 Clear   Collapse   Clear on play   Error pause       Open Editor Log
         This object was picked
         UnityEngine.Debug:Log(Object)
    !    This object was picked
         UnityEngine.Debug:Log(Object)
    !    This object was picked
         UnityEngine.Debug:Log(Object)
    !    This object was picked
         UnityEngine.Debug:Log(Object)
    !    This object was picked
         UnityEngine.Debug:Log(Object)
    !    This object was picked
         UnityEngine.Debug:Log(Object)
```

This object was picked
UnityEngine.Debug:Log(Object)
MousePick:OnMouseDown() (at Assets/My Scripts/MousePick.js:4)
UnityEngine.SendMouseEvents:DoSendMouseEvents()

Assert in file: Assets/My Scripts/MousePick.js at line: 4

Figure 3-16. *The console after picking the object several times*

Objects don't have to be visible or rendered to be pickable. This allows you to get very creative in a game environment.

15. Select the Cube and note where it is in the Game window.

16. In the Inspector, uncheck Mesh Renderer to disable it.

The cube disappears from the Game window. In the Scene window, though, you can still see the green bounding box of the cube (see Figure 3-17).

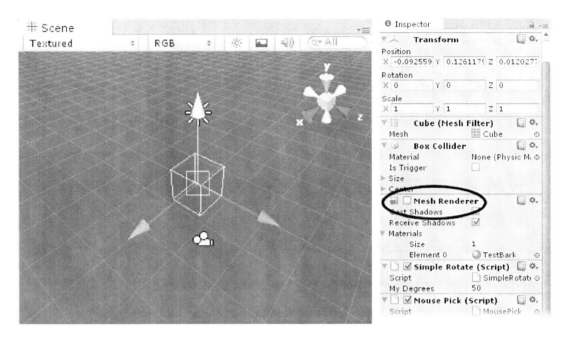

Figure 3-17. *The Cube's disabled MeshRenderer*

    17.   Pick the area in the Game window where the cube used to be.

A pick is still registered in the console (see Figure 3-18).

This object was picked

Figure 3-18. *The invisible (not rendered) Cube, still pickable*

18. Turn the MeshRenderer back on.

19. This time, deactivate the entire object by unchecking the checkbox at the top of the Inspector (see Figure 3-19).

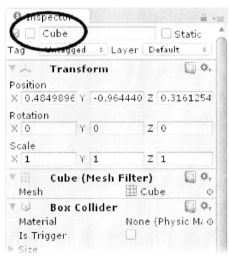

Figure 3-19. *The deactivated Cube in the Inspector*

Note that the Collider no longer shows in the Scene window and the object is grayed out in the Hierarchy (see Figure 3-20).

Figure 3-20. *The deactivated Cube grayed out in the Hierarchy*

20.   Try to pick where the cube should be in the Game window.

Nothing happens.

21.   Stop playback and close the console.

22.   Save your scene and the project.

Counting Mouse Picks

In your point and click adventure game, some objects will need to be picked more than once to advance the object to its next state or behavior. This time you will add a variable to keep track of how many times the object has been picked.

1.   Open the MousePick script in the script editor.

2.   At the top of the MousePick script, add the following line:

private var pickNum = 0;

Next, you need to add a line inside the OnMouseDown function to increment the pickNum every time the function is called.

3.   Add the following line above the Debug.Log line:

pickNum = pickNum + 1; // increment the number of times the object was picked

Note the use of the comment to remind you what the line does; everything after the // is ignored. You can also get the Debug.Log to report the number to you. Go ahead and start using the print syntax to achieve the same output. Note that print is not capitalized. Also note that to add a variable to the message, you need to separate the strings (the text within the quotation marks) with plusses.

4.   Rewrite the Debug.Log line as follows:

print("This object was picked " + pickNum + " times.");

5. Save the script.

6. Click Play and start picking the cube.

The message updates each time to show the latest number of clicks (see Figure 3-21).

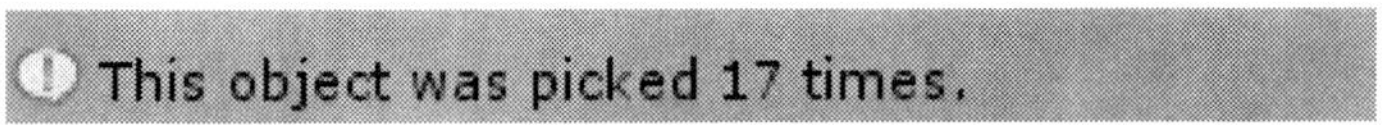

Figure 3-21. *The status line reporting the number of mouse picks*

Sometimes you may see an abbreviated syntax for incrementing a variable. The `pickNum = pickNum + 1;` could also be written as `pickNum += 1;`

7. Substitute the abbreviated version for the original, as follows:

```
pickNum += 1; // increment the number of times the object was picked
```

8. Save the script.

9. Click Play and test.

The results are the same.

Conditionals and State

The key to engaging interaction is being able to specify conditions under which various alternative scenarios play out. Even in a traditional shooter game, an object may need to be hit a certain number of times before it switches to its destroyed state. Each time it is hit, the program must check to see if certain conditions have been met before it knows what to trigger. Each of these conditions can also be thought of as a *state*.

In a classic point and click game, state becomes even more important. Typically, almost everything you can interact with needs to be aware of its state. When you click on a door, it has to know if it is locked or unlocked, closed or open, before the correct response can be triggered.

Continuing with your simple cube, let's set up a basic two-state system to turn the rotation off and on. Because you want to control the rotation, you will add an `OnMouseDown` function to the rotation script.

You will use a private var so it will not be exposed to the Inspector. Theoretically, you could use a Boolean type for your variable since it only has two states (on/off or true/false) to use less memory. However, because many action objects will have more than two states, it's better to start thinking of states in terms of numbers, so use integers.

1. Open the `SimpleRotate` script.

2. Add the following variable and its comment at the top of the script:

```
private var rotationState = 1; // this variable keeps track of the state of the rotation↵
- whether it is off or on- 1 is on, 0 is off
```

▒ **Tip** The order that variables and functions are listed in the script is not crucial, but one generally organizes regular variables at the top (because they will appear in the Inspector), followed by private vars. Because the book is not showing the entire script each time it gives an instruction, you will generally be told to add new code above or below existing code. The finished scripts for each chapter can be downloaded from the book's page on the Apress web site.

---

3. Add the following function beneath the `Update` function:

```
function OnMouseDown () {

        if (rotationState == 1) {

                rotationState = 0;

        }

        else if (rotationState == 0) {

                rotationState = 1;

        }

        print("State = " + rotationState);
}
```

4. Save the altered script as `SimpleRotateToggle.js`

▒ **Tip** When using Save As to save a script to the computer, be sure to add the *js* extension so the script editor will know how to format it and the engine will know how to read it.

Rather than removing the existing `SimpleRotate` script component and adding the new version, you can re-assign the script in the Inspector. This method has the advantage of retaining variable values that have been assigned in the Inspector.

1. Open the Cube Parent in the Hierarchy view and select the Cube.
2. Click on the Browse icon next to the loaded script in the Inspector (see Figure 3-22).

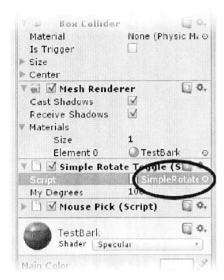

Figure 3-22. *Replacing an existing script component*

The Asset browser lists the scripts available for your project (see Figure 3-23).

Figure 3-23. *The available scripts*

3. Select the `SimpleRotateToggle` script.

The `SimpleRotate` script is replaced, but the MyDegrees setting remains intact.

Deconstructing the Conditional

if (rotationState == 1)

Within the parenthesis is the expression whose condition must be met in order to do what is inside the curly brackets. Of note is the double equal sign; this is the *equivalency operator* and it checks to see if the variable `rotationState` currently holds the value of 1. If so, inside the curly brackets, it updates the value of `rotationState` to 0 so now `rotationState = 0` (the single equal sign being the *assignment operator*). Otherwise, you get `else if (rotationState == 0)`, the rotationState is currently 0, so set it to 1, `rotationState = 1`. After the state has been identified and updated, you will have it printed out to the console, as in `print("State = " + rotationState)`.

If you were to click Play and test the functionality right now, you would have to open the console to see the results because the message output by the `MousePick` script is being output after your state message. Instead of opening the console, you can disable the print line in the `MousePick` script.

1. Open the `MousePick` script and comment out the `print` line out by prefacing it with two backslashes, like so:

```
// print("State = " + rotationState);
```

2. Save the script.

3. Click Play and test the functionality.

The state toggles between 1 and 0 as you pick the cube. Now that you know that the state tracking mechanism works, turn the rotation off and on.

4. Open the `SimpleRotateToggle` script.

5. In the `Update` function, change the code to the following:

```
function Update () {

    if (rotationState == 1) {
        transform.Rotate(0, myDegrees * Time.deltaTime, 0);
    }

}
```

6. Save the script.

7. Click Play and test the functionality.

The cube starts and stops its rotation nicely depending on what state it is in.

8. Save the scene and the project.

Order of Evaluation

In scripting, the order of evaluation is generally the same as in mathematical equations. Multiplication and division are evaluated first, then addition and subtraction, and finally, comparisons (and/or). Contents of parentheses are evaluated from the inner-most nested to the outer most.

Chapter Summary

In this chapter you got your first taste of controlling a 3D object with scripting in Unity's implementation of JavaScript. You found out that scripts have *functions* for carrying out instructions, use *variables* to allow for both storing and changing values, and that *comments* can both disable instructions as well as provide a commentary about what the script is doing.

You learned about the `Update` function, a system function that is called every frame during runtime, and that objects can be transformed (move, rotate, scale) on a per second basis rather than per frame by using `Time.deltaTime`. You also found that the order of evaluation between moves and rotates can be controlled by parenting objects.

You discovered that case (capitalization) is generally critical in the scripting syntax, but that sometimes the error message in the console will help by suggesting the correct case for the offending command. You also discovered that you could tell the console to print out information on the state of your variables, whether the code is being read in a particular function or other uses.

To pick an object in the scene, you found that it needed to have a Collider to be able to register the pick, but that the object did not actually need to be drawn by the Mesh Renderer. If you deactivated an object in the Inspector, it was no longer available for use in the scene.

Variables, you found, can be of different *types:* integers, character strings, Booleans, and floats, to name a few. By using an addition operation to increment the value of an integer type variable, you could count how many times an object has been picked. This lead to the introduction of two of the most important concepts in game development: *state* and the *conditional.* You learned that different sets of instructions could be carried out depending on the results of the expression being evaluated or the state it represented.

Functions introduced:

- Update (a system type function)

- OnMouseDown (an event type function)

- print (a generic function used with other sets of instructions within other functions)

Methods (object level functions):

- transform.Rotate(x,y,z)

- transform.Translate(x,y,z)

CHAPTER 4

Terrain Generation:
Creating a Test Environment

One thing common with many game engines is a terrain editor. Not only can you sculpt your idea into being, but you can populate it with foliage from grass to bushes to trees via paint textures.

In Unity's full-fledged terrain editor, many things are handled for you, such as LOD (level of detail), distance culling, and animations. While this makes it extremely easy to get up and running around a terrain, as with anything that does a lot of the work for you, it also comes with limitations. For more in-depth information on the tree generator, go to the Reference Manual ➤ Terrain Engine Guide.

In this chapter, you will create a basic terrain to test more functionality than is strictly necessary for a classic point and click adventure game. During the process of developing the functionality and logic sequences for your game, you will quickly discover the need to keep everything in a fairly small area. Having to travel halfway across the terrain to find an object will get old fast. For that reason, you only need a smallish area to work in until everything not related directly to the topography is up and running.

Note   You may import terrains created in DCC (digital content creation applications such as 3ds Max, Maya, Blender, etc.) programs to use as the ground, but you will not be able to paint trees, grasses, and other detail meshes that respond to wind and scene lighting. A compromise would be to create a height map from your external terrain, and then load it into a Unity terrain instead of painting the topography.

As long as you are still in test mode, go ahead and create a new scene from the Files menu.

1. Open Unity if you have not already done so.

It should open the BookProject project by default unless you have opened other projects since the last time you saved it. If it does not open the BookProject, from the File menu, choose Open Project and select it from the Open Project tab. You may also use the version available in the Chapter 4 folder from the book's downloadable package.

2. If the project opened with TestScene1 loaded, go to File ➤ New Scene.

3. From File ➤ Save Scene, save it as TerrainTest.

4. In the Project view, create a new folder and name it Scenes.

Tip   During the project you will be creating and importing many assets. You will soon be buried under folder upon folder, so it is good practice to stay organized. Even those of us who are inclined to be organizationally impaired will soon be forced to admit that it is an important requirement of making even smaller games. As Unity's file system is based on dependencies, you must always remember to implement your housekeeping chores inside the Project view and never out in the OS's Finder or Explorer. Drag both the TestScene1 and TerrainTest scenes into the new folder.

---

5.   From the Terrain menu, select Create Terrain, as shown in Figure 4-1.

Figure 4-1. *Create Terrain in the Terrain menu*

You will see that a Terrain object has been added to the scene in both the Hierarchy and the Project views with one of its corners at 0,0,0, as shown in Figure 4-2.

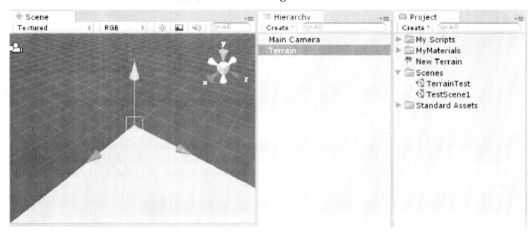

Figure 4-2. *The new terrain object with its corner at 0,0,0*

In the Inspector, with the Terrain object selected, you will see its properties and the tools available for refining it, as shown in Figure 4-3.

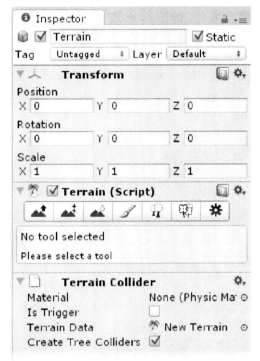

Figure 4-3. *The Terrain Tools in the Inspector*

6. Make sure you are using Default rather than Scene lighting in the Scene window.

Tip Scene lighting can be toggled off and on using the button at the top of the scene view. It's a sure bet that you will often find yourself toggling this critter off and on throughout the project depending on the objects with which you are working.

Before experimenting with the tools, you need to set the other parameters of the terrain.

1. From the Terrain menu, select Set Heightmap resolution, as shown in Figure 4-4.

Set Heightmap resolution	
Please note that modifying the resolution will clear the heightmap, detail map or splatmap.	
Terrain Width	2000
Terrain Height	600
Terrain Length	2000
Heightmap Resolution	513
Detail Resolution	1024
Detail Resolution Per Patch	16
Control Texture Resolution	512
Base Texture Resolution	1024

Set Resolution

Figure 4-4. *The Set Heightmap Resolution dialog*

 2.   Take heed of the "Modifying the resolution will clear the height map, detail map or splat map" warning.

If you start creating your terrain, then decide to change its resolution, you will lose much of your modifications.

 Tip   A *splat map* is another name for the Terrain texture map/mask. Once you have started painting your terrain, you will be able to see that it is basically a gray-scale mask on drugs; it uses RGBA, and each color channel is used to mask a different texture.

---

 3.   Set the Terrain Width and Length to 500 meters and the Height to 200 meters.

This size is still overkill for what you will need during the development process, but it will allow for lots of practice with the terrain tools. Don't stress over making it perfect.

 4.   Click the Set Resolution button.

Because you can sculpt the terrain up or down, you will need to set the base height to allow for maximum depth where you may want to paint the terrain lower (see Figure 4-5).

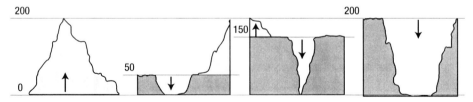

Figure 4-5. *Terrain base height shifted to allow painting of depressions for lakes, crevasses, etc.*

5. From the Terrain menu, select Flatten Heightmap.

6. Set the Height to 50 to give you 25 percent of your terrain's total height below
    sea level.

7. Click Flatten.

The terrain drops out of sight in the Scene window.

Before you sculpt, take a few minutes to experiment with the navigation tools; there are subtle
differences in how they work with terrains because of the scale involved.

1. Select the Terrain in the Hierarchy view.

2. Position the cursor so it is *not* over the terrain in the Scene window and press
    the F key.

The viewport is zoomed all the way out so you can see the extents of the terrain object, as shown in
Figure 4-6.

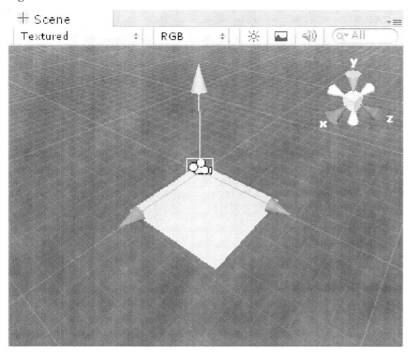

Figure 4-6. *The full terrain found or focused in the Scene view*

3. Position the cursor *over* the terrain near the right hand edge and press the F
    key

The view is zoomed to a more specific location, as you can see in Figure 4-7.

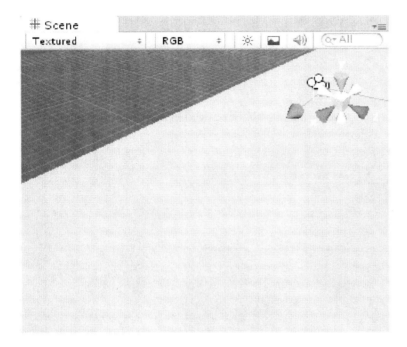

Figure 4-7. *Zooming to a specific area on the terrain*

Flythrough Scene Navigation

You can also do flythrough navigation. This becomes useful when creating terrains because it allows you to travel through the scene in the direction you are looking as if you were a bird or even a caped superhero.

1. Click and hold the right mouse button.

2. Use the WASD keys to move left/right forward/backward.

3. Use the Q and E keys to move up and down.

4. Hold the shift key down to move faster.

Topography

Time to do some damage to your terrain!

1. Zoom out so more of the terrain is visible.

2. In the Inspector, choose the first tool: Raise/Lower Terrain .

Note the use instructions immediately beneath the Terrain Tools toolbar when you select a tool; it may be cryptic at first, but once you get underway it will start making sense.

3. Select a Brush.

4. Click and drag or use your favorite pressure pen to create mountains around the terrain, as shown in Figure 4-8.

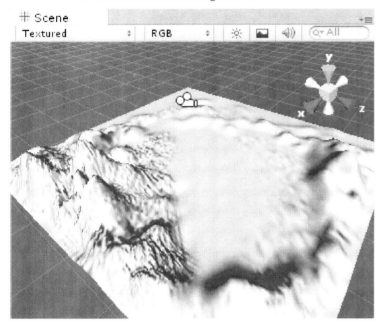

Figure 4-8. *Mountains created on the terrain*

■ **Tip**   You can undo the last action with Ctrl+Z. Unity allows a large number of undos, but as with any program, you should not rely on going back too far. Inevitably, the action you want to get rid of will be one more than the limit.

Note that as you paint, if you have zoomed out to see the entire terrain, you will see the terrain at its highest resolution in an area around the cursor. One of the great benefits of using Unity's Terrain system is that it has a built-in LOD (Level of Detail) mechanism. As soon as you let go, the terrain reverts to its LOD resolution for the far distance (see Figure 4-9). While this can be frustrating, remember that it is just terrain, and the scale is such that once in game, it is likely not going to be crucial. You will be able to adjust the LOD distance later should you wish in the Terrain Settings Detail Distance.

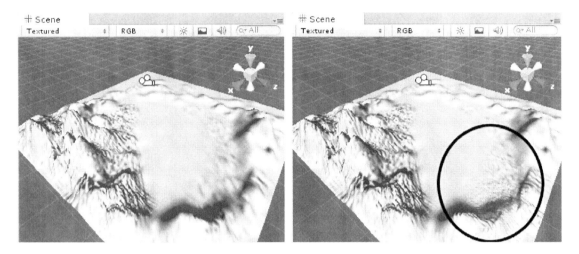

Figure 4-9. *True LOD resolution on the left and the temporary higher resolution or detail where you are painting on the right*

For now, just experiment with the Brush, Brush Size, and Opacity (strength). The brush size will be depicted as blue in the Scene window.

■ **Tip** With this tool, you may paint over existing topography to increase it up to the maximum set in the Set Resolution dialog (in your case, 200).

---

5. Hold the shift key down while painting to push the ground down, as shown in Figure 4-10.

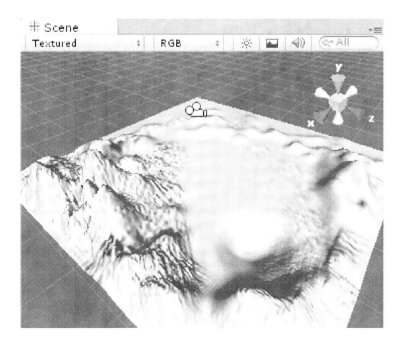

Figure 4-10. *A depression made in the terrain by holding the shift key down while painting*

Because you set the Flatten Height to 50, that is as deep as it will go down when you paint. You will deal with the hard edge later. You may also use the shift key to lower mountain peaks that are too high, but there is a better tool for that coming up.

The next tool to try is the Paint Height tool. This tool *specifies* a height to work to so the amount you set dictates whether you will be painting up or down. The most important thing about this tool is that it allows you to create flat areas at specific heights such as building pads, plateaus, mesas, sink holes, or anything else where the surface is superficially flat.

Remember that your default height is set to 50, so the height you set here will determine whether the painting adds or subtracts to the terrain.

6. Select the Paint Height tool .

7. Set the Height to 40 and paint in a default flat area until the hole bottoms out at 40.

8. Now set the Height to 60 and paint an area so the height tops out at 60 (see Figure 4-11).

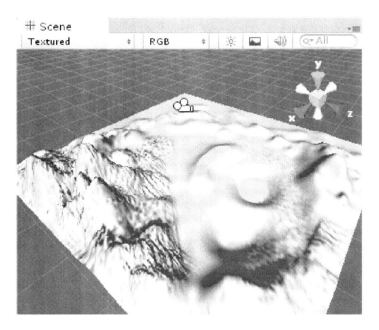

Figure 4-11. *The Paint Height results from 40 (right) and 60 (left)*

If you want to be extremely clever, write down the height of areas you plan to place structures upon at some point. This way, instead of manually moving the object up and down until it looks sort of okay, you can type in the Y position in the Inspector and move on. As anyone who has worked with 3D for any length of time can tell you, deciding when an object is "on the ground" can be challenging. If you are using Unity Pro with dynamic shadows, the task is somewhat easier, but shadows are not a silver bullet. Numbers are still your friend.

To get rid of the nasty looking sharp edges where the tools have bottomed out or caused a crease, you can use the next tool in the collection. Smooth Height relaxes the terrain to give it a more natural look or adds a bit of weathering to your jagged mountains.

9. Zoom in to the area where you painted the Height.

10. Select the Smooth Height tool .

11. Smooth the hard edges left over from the Paint Height tool (see Figure 4-12).

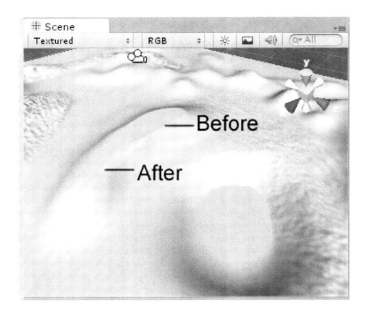

Figure 4-12. *The half-smoothed topology*

12. Experiment with the three Height tools until you are comfortable with your efforts. Remember that this is just a temporary terrain.

13. Save your scene and project.

Paint Texture

With the topography in place, it's time to put some textures on the terrain so it looks less like something from a government survey site (see Figure 4-13).

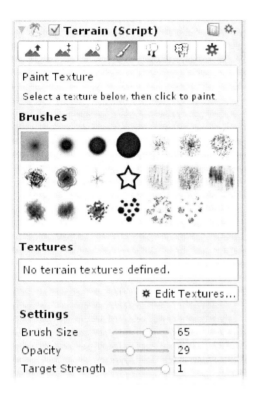

Figure 4-13. *Paint Texture and Edit Textures buttons*

1. Click the Paint Texture button [brush icon].

Before you can start painting the terrain, you will need to set up some textures. The first texture you load will fill the entire terrain, so choose a texture that will make the most sense as a base texture.

2. To load textures for painting, click the Edit Textures button and choose Add Texture (see Figure 4-14).

Add Texture...

Edit Texture...

Remove Texture

Figure 4-14. *Add Texture*

A dialog box appears and you are prompted to select a texture. You can do this by either clicking the browser icon to the right of Splat and choosing from the asset list (double-click it), or you can drag and drop a texture into it directly from the Project view. To finish the addition, you must pick the Add button at the bottom of the dialog (see Figure 4-15 and 4-16).

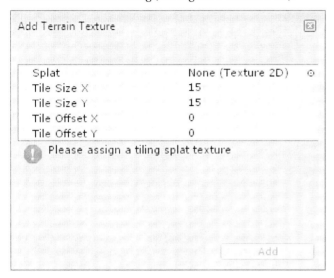

Figure 4-15. *Add Terrain Texture dialog*

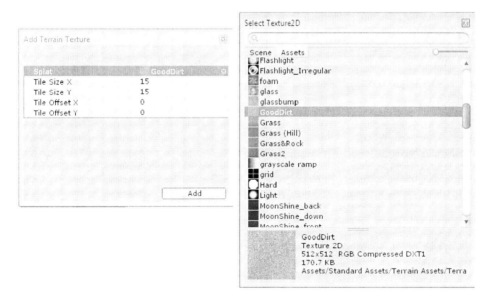

Figure 4-16. *Adding a texture*

133

Tiling parameters indicate the size of the tiling, not the number of tiles. Smaller numbers will increase the number of tiles while larger numbers will decrease the tiling. At this point, you probably have no idea of the scale, so you may adjust the tiling parameters later by clicking Edit Texture then selecting Edit Textures.

3. Add a couple more textures to your palette. The active texture has a blue highlight, as shown in Figure 4-17.

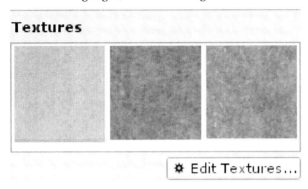

Figure 4-17. *More textures for the terrain: GoodDirt, Grass(Hill), Grass&Rock*

4. Using the various Brushes, paint the textures onto the terrain, as shown in Figure 4-18.

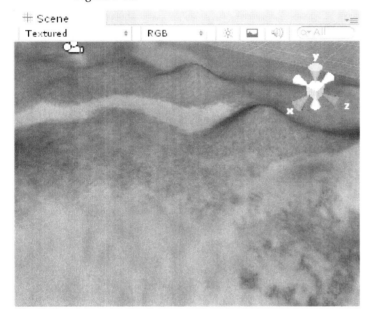

Figure 4-18. *The terrain painted*

As with any of the other terrain tools, you can access and adjust or change any of your terrain elements whenever you wish.

Tip   Remember you can zoom to an area by moving the cursor to the spot you want, then pressing the F key.

To view the splat map created while you painted the various textures onto the terrain, you can look at the Terrain asset in the Project view.

5.   Save the scene to make the Splat map show in the Project view.

6.   Open the Terrain asset in the Project view.

7.   Select the SplatAlpha 0 object.

The splat map shows in the inspector (see Figure 4-19). Note that it uses the Red, Green, Blue, and Alpha channels as a mask for the various textures.

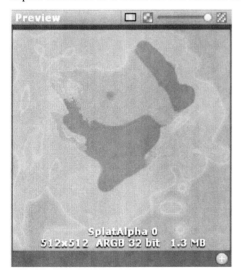

Figure 4-19. *The terrain's SplatMap in the Inspector*

Trees

An important part of the terrain editor is the Place Trees tool. While you could create and place your own trees, using the terrain editor to populate your scene provides several advantages. As you might expect, it also has some limitations.

> **Pros:** Trees generated by the terrain editor may be set to animate to sway in the breeze. They also have automatic LOD; at a certain distance the full mesh tree is

swapped out for a billboarded plane with the tree's image, and at a far distance, the billboard object is not drawn at all, or *distance culled.* These distances can be set in the Inspector for the Place Trees tool, but more importantly, the engine will automatically reduce the distances to insure acceptable frame rate on slower machines. *Shadowing* is automatically generated for the trees. If the tree is on the shadowed side of a mountain, the trunk and leaves will be darkened.

Cons: Trees used for the Place Trees tool should not be over 2,000 polygons. Anything larger may not load properly in the terrain editor. Trees can't use more than two materials. The materials used are limited to two specialty shaders. If you don't use the Nature-Ambient Occlusion shaders in their materials, the lighting and the billboard will not be generated. In sparse areas, the transition between LOD models may be too noticeable.

■ **Rules** Imported trees used for the terrain editor should be no more than 2,000 polygons, can have no more than two materials, and those materials must use the Nature-Soft Occlusion shaders.

---

1. Select the Place Trees tool  shown in Figure 4-20.

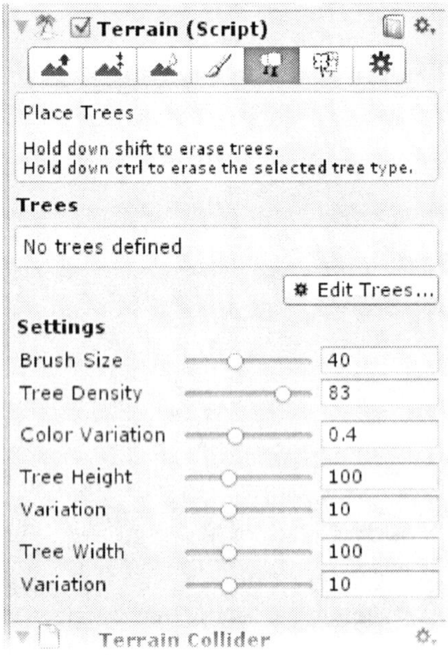

Figure 4-20. *The Place Trees tool*

Trees must be loaded before they can be used, just as textures must be loaded as well.

2. Click the Edit Trees button and choose Add Tree (see Figure 4-21).

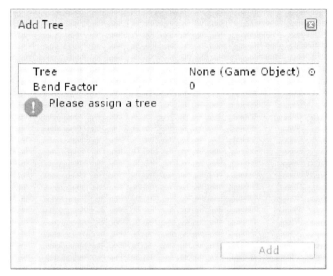

Figure 4-21. *The Add Tree dialog*

3. In the dialog, click the Browser icon and select the Palm tree asset (see Figure 4-22) but do not click Add yet.

Figure 4-22. *The Palm tree asset*

Bend Factor is the parameter that animates the trees in the environment. Be aware that a little goes a long way. To see your trees bend at runtime you will need to add a WindZone object. You will be using WindZones later in the project, but feel free to experiment with one now.

4. Set the Bend Factor to 0.5.

5. Click Add.

6. Paint some trees on the terrain, experimenting with the various parameters, as shown in Figure 4-23.

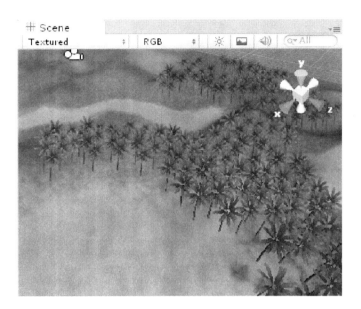

Figure 4-23. *The palms trees added to the terrain*

7. Navigate the viewport until you are close enough to see the mesh trees rather than just their billboarded LOD versions, as shown in Figure 4-24.

Figure 4-24. *A closer view of the palm trees*

To get a better view of the trees in the Game window, you need to do a few more things. Just as with the first cube experiments, you need to match the camera to the view you want, then you need to add a directional light. Additionally, because this is a real outdoor environment, you ought to add a sky.

1. Select the Main Camera.

2. From the GameObject menu, choose Align with View.

The camera matches the Scene view and the view appears in the Game window.

3. From the GameObject menu ➤ Create Other, create a Directional light.

4. Rotate the light until the palm trees are well lit, as shown in Figure 4-25.

Figure 4-25. *The trees lit and seen in the Game window*

5. Toggle the coordinate system to Global rather than Local and move the light up out of the way.

■ **Tip**   You will find that it will be necessary to toggle the Scene lighting off and on throughout the project, depending what you are doing.

Now that you can see the trees more clearly in the Game window, you may notice that the trees are very rough looking. In the default settings of Good Editor Quality, anti-aliasing is turned off.

ANTI-ALIASING

When an object is drawn against an existing background or other objects, its edges will appear jagged. In render-type DCC applications, anti-aliasing is done on an object basis with a variety of anti-aliasing algorithms depending on the desired effect and style.

In real time, however, where speed is of the utmost importance, that type of anti-aliasing is too slow. Instead, it is performed by what is known as super-sampling where the scene is rendered out 2, 4, 6, or 8 times (depending on the capabilities of the graphics card) the size of the render window, then sized down to the final dimensions. The scaling produces a reasonable softening of the edges in a fraction of the time of traditional anti-aliasing.

Non-anti-aliased edges (the "jaggies") on the left and traditional anti-aliasing (fuzzy) on the right

Super-sampling(sharp but smooth)

6. From the Edit menu ➤ Project Settings, select Quality.

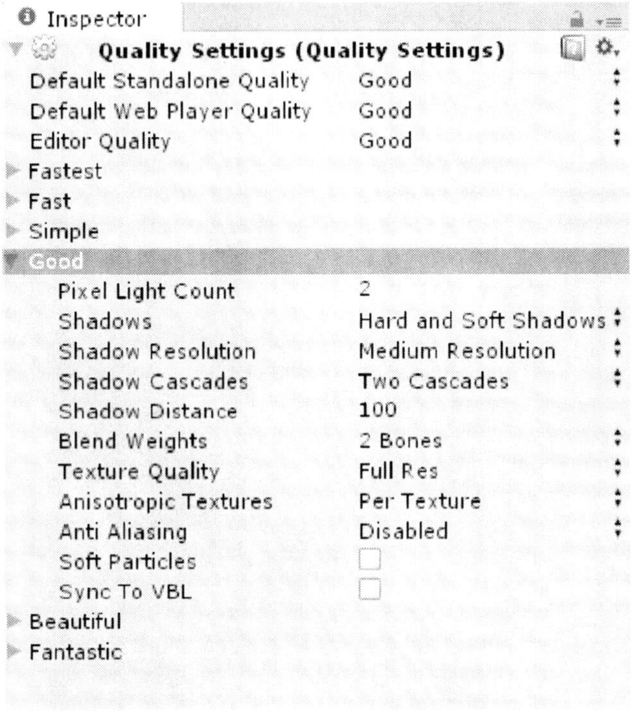

Figure 4-26. *The Quality settings*

7. Open the Good preset, as shown in Figure 4-26.

Note that anti-aliasing is turned off in this preset.

8. If your graphics card is fairly good, change the editor quality to Beautiful or Fantastic to see the difference, as shown in Figure 4-27.

Tip You can set the Default Standalone Qualities here, but the player will have the option to change them when first starting the game. Unity will automatically drop down to a setting that is supported by the player's graphics card.

Figure 4-27. *The scene with Fantastic quality turned on in the editor*

Sky

As long as you are taking a brief side track to improve the overall look of things, let's add a sky to the scene. Skies can be added to regular geometry as in the case of a skydome or, in Unity, you can employ a shader that uses a six-sided cubic map to do the job, as shown in Figure 4-28.

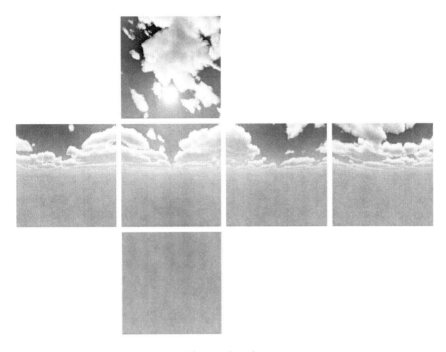

Figure 4-28. *The six images used for a cubic sky map*

A traditional skydome would have the advantage of working on systems that do not have much shader support, but because it generally uses simple spherical mapping, it's prone to distortion at the top. Take care to use an image that avoids the problem as much as possible. Skydomes also have the disadvantage of finite geometry. If they are too close, you will see where they intersect the regular scene geometry. If they are too far, they extend the camera clipping plane and increase the possibility of Z order fighting where two surfaces are too close to each other.

Because you are creating your game to play on traditional computers, you will go ahead and use the built-in shader type sky for your scene. Unity has two shader options for skies: one uses six separate maps and one that is able to use some preformatted cube maps. If you are using an external cube map, it may need to be broken into the six images using the RenderFX/Skybox. The advantage of component parts means you can make adjustments to size and quality via the import settings.

1. In the Project view, open the Standard Assets folder and open the Skyboxes folder.

2. Select the skybox info text asset and quickly read through it.

It gives information about skyboxes in Unity.

3. Click on each of the materials (sphere icons) to look at the choices.

4. Expand the Textures folder and open the Sunny3 folder.

This is where the images used to generate the materials reside and where you would go to re-import them using different settings.

5. Select the Sunny3 Skybox material, as shown in Figure 4-29.

Each of its component images are shown.

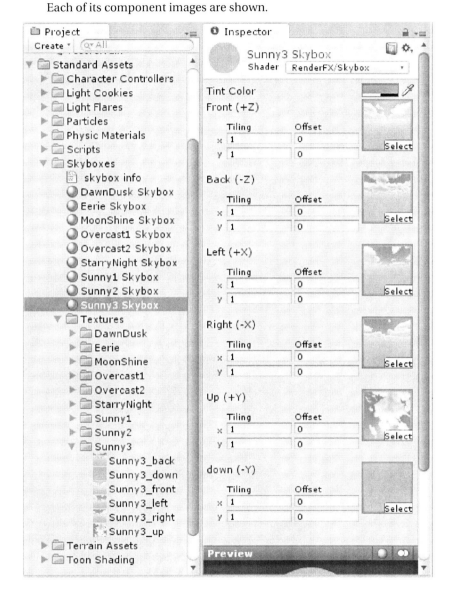

Figure 4-29. *The Sunny3 Skybox material in the Inspector*

To load a skybox into your scene, you will access Render Settings from the Edit menu.

Tip   You can also load a skybox into a camera directly in the Component/Rendering menu.

6. From the Edit menu, select Render Settings.

7. Drag the Sunny3 Skybox texture into the Skybox Material slot, or pick the asset browser icon to the far right and select it from the list (see Figure 4-30).

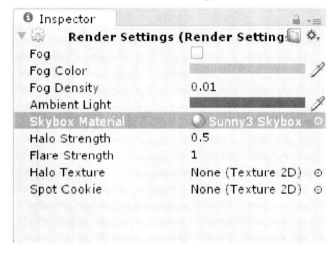

Figure 4-30. *The Sunny3 Skybox loaded into the Render Settings's Skybox Material setting*

Figure 4-31. *The skybox in the Game view*

■ **Tip**   You can turn the skybox on in the Scene view by toggling on the Game Overlay icon next to the Scene Lighting toggle. It will also turn on GUI objects, so it is usually left off once the scene has more content.

Back to the Trees

Now that your environment is looking better, you can continue with the Terrain editor.

1.   Select the Terrain object in the Hierarchy view once again.

2.   In the Inspector, select the Place Tree tool again.

3.   Select the Palm tree and choose Edit Trees to change the Bend Factor.

As with the Edit Texture, edits affect parameters on all existing elements.

■ **Tip**   Changes made to the Terrain editor during runtime will not be lost when you stop playback, so you can freely adjust parameters animation while getting instant feedback. Parameters such as scale will need to be changed in Edit mode to see the effects.

Once loaded, the billboard version of the tree (an image with an Alpha Channel) will show in the editor. The currently active tree's alpha area will appear gray and the selected tree outlined in blue when it is selected for use.

4.   Paint the palm tree around your test terrain and experiment with the various parameters.

■ **Tip**   In case you got a bit heavy handed with the brush, you can erase trees by holding down the shift key. Any tree, regardless of the currently selected tree will be removed. Holding down the Ctrl key will selectively remove the currently selected tree.

Packages

You are probably getting tired of palm trees by now. Let's see how to go about re-using assets from another scene.

Importing trees for use with the terrain involves more than just bringing in a textured mesh. Unity makes good use of what are called *prefabs*, prefabricated game objects that can contain all kinds of information, sub-objects, scripts, and other components. In the case of trees, they will need the special Nature shaders, and, if thicker than saplings, will probably need Colliders.

You've seen Colliders used before to "catch" mouse events. The more obvious use for Colliders, of course, is to prevent the player from going through what should be solid objects. To that end, larger trees will need Collider components.

1.   Select the Palm tree in the Project view, as shown in Figure 4-32.

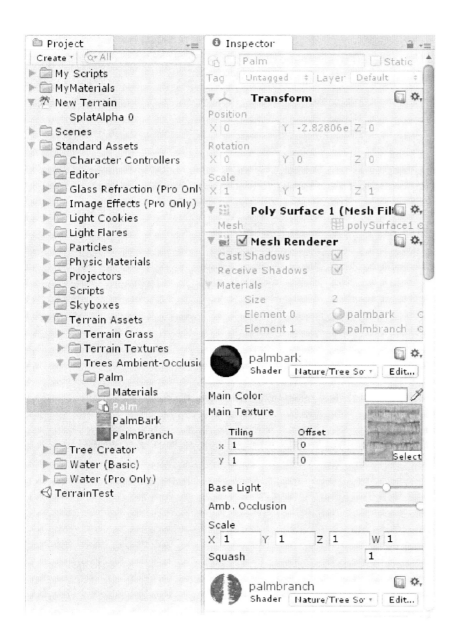

Figure 4-32. *The palm tree prefab in the Project view*

If you scroll through its components in the Inspector, you will see that it does not have a Collider. At runtime, you would be able to move through it. Testing for collision does use resources, so not all trees will or should have colliders. In the case of the palm trees, it will be less frustrating for the player if you let him go through them.

■ **Tip**   An empty prefab is represented by a white cube. As soon as you add scripts or meshes to it, the cube becomes blue.

If you use Import Asset to import a tree, only the GameObject (the parent group), the mesh, and the materials and textures will come. The textures will need to be re-assigned and the shaders changed to the Nature shaders.

By copying the whole folder into the scene's Assets folder via the OS (Explorer for Windows) there will be less to repair, but you'll certainly lose some connections. The safest way to transfer assets from one scene to the other is to save them as packages.

Packages are collections of assets that, for the most part, can be imported into a project without losing important connections or dependencies. In the following section, you will be making use of an asset package created for this book. You may also wish to experiment with an asset package available for download from the Unity3D web site, TerrainAssets.unitypackage. This package contains several useful textures, trees, and other terrain-related assets.

■ **Tip**   Check out `http://unity3d.com/support/resources/assets/` for Unity assets.

---

2. From the Assets menu, select Import Package.

3. Navigate to the Book Assets folder and select ExtraTerrainAssets.unitypackage.

4. Click Open.

The package is decompressed and you are presented with a dialog that allows you to select the assets you wish. They should all be checked by default, as shown in Figure 4-33.

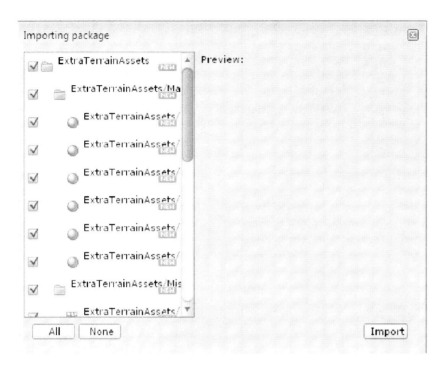

Figure 4-33. *The Importing Package dialog*

5. Click Import.

6. A new folder with the name of the package's original folder name is added to the Project view.

7. Open the ExtraTerrainAssets folder.

8. Open the Trees Ambient-Occlusion folder.

■ **Tip** In order for trees to cast and receive shadows, they must be in a folder named Trees Ambient-Occlusion and make use of the Nature shaders.

---

9. Select the BanyanOld prefab, as shown in Figure 4-34.

Figure 4-34. *Banyan prefab*

Note that it does not yet have a Collider. Since it is probably larger than a meter in diameter in real life, you really ought to prevent the player from going through it. Before you add the collider, you should make sure the import scale was correct. Let's load the new tree into the Terrain Editor and try it out to see how the scale looks.

1. Select the Terrain object in the Hierarchy view.

2. Activate the Place Trees tool in the Inspector.

3. Click Edit Trees and Add Tree.

4. Select the BanyanOld.

5. Choose an empty area near the palm trees (so you will be able to judge the scale) and paint some banyan trees on the terrain.

6. If you see no results, zoom in very close to the ground where you painted the trees.

As you paint the banyan, you may see tiny specks on the ground where you expected a great spreading tree (see Figure 4-35). You probably pictured them bigger!

Figure 4-35. *Tiny trees*

On import, meshes are scaled to the last used Scale value and these will probably need their scale adjusted.

7. Select the Banyan Tree mesh in the Project view.

If the Scale Factor is 0.1, change its value to at least 1 and click the Apply button just above the Preview window near the bottom of the panel, as shown in Figure 4-36. The banyans grow dramatically.

Tip In a perfect world, you may be able to control the scale the imported assets are using in the original DCC program so that they always come in the same. It is probably more realistic to assume you will end up scrounging assets from several different sources and will need to adjust the Scale Factor. Fortunately, Unity is very good with scale adjustments, even skinned meshes.

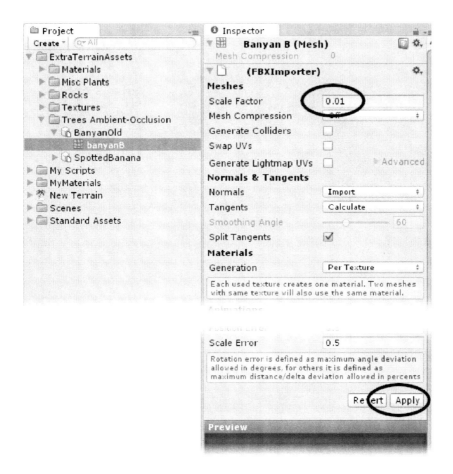

Figure 4-36. *The Apply button*

8. Rotate the view to exam the newly scaled trees.

Depending on your view, you may notice the billboarded versions are still small. Any time you make changes to assets used in the terrain editor, you need to update them to make sure the automatically generated features are updated as well.

9. In the Terrain menu, select Refresh Tree and Detail Prototypes.

▨ **Tip**   Refresh Tree and Detail Prototypes updates light maps, LOD billboards, materials, etc.

---

10. Use Ctrl and paint to remove the newly enlarged trees.

Before repainting the trees, you need to add the colliders. With the exception of the materials, imported assets cannot be directly affected in the Project view. To add a collider, you will need to instantiate a copy of the tree directly into the scene, add the collider, and then use it to create a prefab which can then be used in the Terrain editor.

1. Select BanyanOld in the Project view from the ExtraTerrainAssets folder's Trees Ambient-Occlusion folder.

2. Drag it into the Hierarchy view.

3. Use the F key to find it in the Scene view.

4. From the Component menu ➤ Physics, select Capsule Collider, as shown in Figure 4-37.

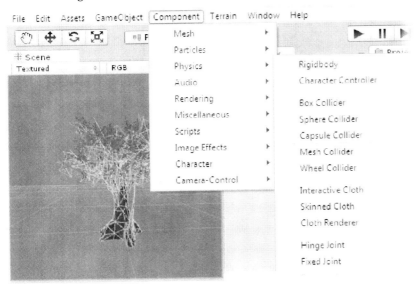

Figure 4-37. *Adding a Capsule Collider*

5. Click Add at the dialog that warns about losing the prefab, as shown in Figure 4-38.

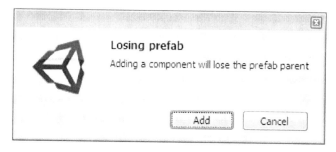

Figure 4-38. *The Losing Prefab dialog*

A collider is added to the tree encompassing the entire tree.

6. In the Inspector, set the collider's radius to about 2, and adjust the Center parameters to align the collider with the trunk and smaller trunk extension, as shown in Figure 4-39.

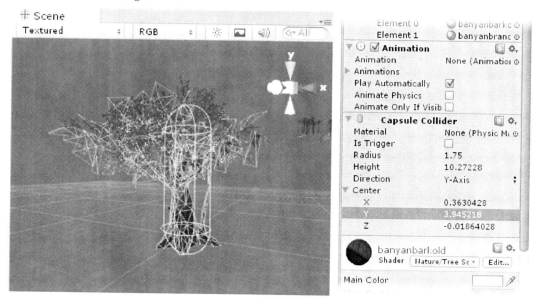

Figure 4-39. *The adjusted Collider in the Scene view and Inspector*

The tree is now ready to be "prefabbed."

7. Select the ExtraTerrainAssets folder.

8. Create a new folder in it and name it Prefabs.

9. Select the new folder.

10. Right-click folder, select Create ➤ Prefab, as shown in Figure 4-40.

■ **Tip** Alternatively, you can access the Create sub-menu from the Assets menu.

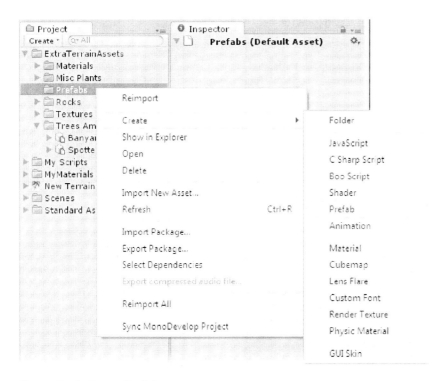

Figure 4-40. *Create Prefab*

11. Name it BanyanTree.

12. Drag the BanyanOld object from the Hierarchy into the new prefab.

Once the prefab has been created, you can delete the altered original from the Hierarchy view. The prefab does not need to be in the Trees Ambient-Occlusion folder because it references the original BanyanOld from there. The white cube icon for the prefab turns blue once an asset is added to it.

13. Select the BanyanOld in the Hierarchy view and delete it.

14. Select the Main Camera.

15. From the GameObject menu, use Align View to Selected to get back to where you were last planting trees.

16. Select the Terrain and activate the Place Tree tool in the Inspector.

Now that you have a replacement tree with a collider, you need to delete the currently loaded version of the Banyan.

17. Select the currently load banyan.

18. From the Edit Trees menu, select Remove Tree.

The previously painted banyans are removed.

19. From Edit Tree, select Add Tree and load the new BanyanTree prefab.

20. Adjust the Density and repaint them where you want them.

The bark appears quite dark on the banyans. Even considering that their dense foliage would be blocking a lot of light, you may wish to lighten the material a bit.

21. Select the BanyanBarkOld material in the Hierarchy view.

22. Experiment with the Base Light and Ambient Occlusion sliders (see Figure 4-41).

23. In the Terrain menu, select Refresh Tree and Detail Prototypes after each adjustment if you are not seeing the results.

Figure 4-41. *The lightened bark*

Before you continue with the terrain tools, you will want to change the scale on the other objects in the package. As they were all created and exported with the same scale, they will all need to be set to 1.0.

24. Adjust the scale on the other imported meshes to 1.0.

Now that the tree is the correct size, you can set up the collider for it.

■ **Tip** If the trees need to be a little larger and you do not wish to adjust the import size further, you can increase the Tree Height in the Place Trees settings.

Sometimes it's quicker to remove trees from a densely populated area than to paint them manually. You can populate your entire terrain all at once to make things quicker. To mass place trees, from the Terrain menu, select Mass Place Trees. You may set the amount of trees. All trees currently loaded in the editor will be used, but you can't specify the percentages. Once populated, you can remove trees from unwanted areas by using the shift key.

Unity also has a Tree Generator that you will use later in the book to create a special tree for your final scene.

Paint Details

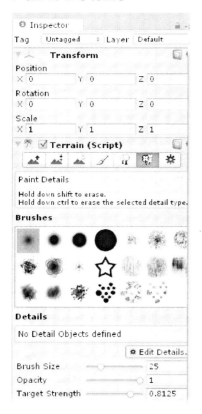

Figure 4-42. *Paint details*

This section lets you paint grasses, scrubs, rocks and other details (see Figure 4-42). There are two main types of details: grasses and meshes. Grasses are simple planes that are billboarded (they always face the camera) and can be set to animate to sway in the breeze. When you set up grasses, you will select only an alpha channel-using texture.

1. Select the Paint Details tool .

2. Pick Edit Details and Add Grass Texture (Figure 4-43).

| Add Grass Texture |
| Add Detail Mesh |
| Edit |
| Remove |

Figure 4-43. *Add Texture*

3. Select Grass, as shown in Figure 4-44.

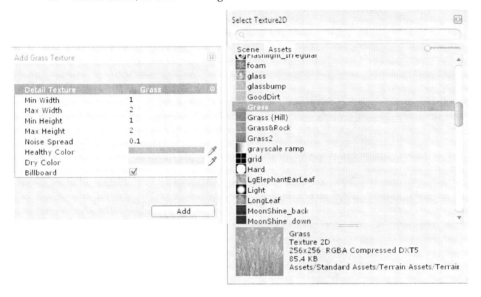

Figure 4-44. *The Grass asset*

4. Paint the grass around the scene, as shown in Figure 4-45.

160

Figure 4-45. *Grass added to the terrain*

Note the color variation provided by the Dry Color and Healthy Color textures.

Tip   Take care when painting grasses and detail meshes. If you are too far away when you are painting, the grass will automatically be distant culled so you may not see the results of your work until you zoom in closer, at which point you may find you have a lot more than you planned.

Unlike trees that have a Bend Factor, it is assumed that grass will bend and sway in the wind. Bend Factor isn't what makes the trees sway back and forth, it just dictates how stiff or bendy the tree is. Wind speed, along with several other parameters, can be found in the Terrain Settings tool.

The remaining Detail type is a mesh object. This is where you will add 3D meshes such as rocks and mesh plants. The detail meshes are like grasses in that they have color ranges with Healthy and Dry. They can also be animated to move in the wind with Render Type. Grass will let them be affected by wind, Vertex Lit will keep them static. Noise Spread is the size variation.

1. Add the SpottedBanana as a detail mesh and set it to Grass Render Mode so it will sway in the wind.

2. Try adjusting the Height to positive and negative numbers.

3. Remove some of the saturation from the Healthy Color texture.

4. Turn the Opacity and Strength down.

5. Be sure to select the Spotted Banana in the Details palette before you start to paint.

6. Carefully click to place the plants, as shown in Figure 4-46.

You will probably need to adjust the material's Base Light and Ambient Occlusion. Remember to Refresh Tree and Detail Prototypes after each adjustment to see the results.

Figure 4-46. *A few more plants*

Next, add the rock as a static mesh in Details. Remember to change its Scale Factor to 1 from the FBXImporter section before you add the rock to the terrain editor.

1. Click Edit Details and select Add Detail Mesh this time (Figure 4-47).

2. Add the Rock by dragging it from the Rocks folder or selecting it from the browser.

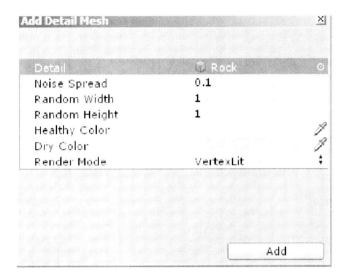

Figure 4-47. *The Rock asset*

3. Change the Healthy and Dry Colors to something more subtle.

4. Since rocks shouldn't sway in the wind, set the Render Type to Vertex Lit.

5. Adjust the Noise Spread to get a nice size variation on the rocks.

You may be tempted to populate you terrain with boulders using detail meshes.

6. Try increasing the height of your rocks, then zooming in and out (Figure 4-48).

Unlike the trees, detail meshes are not replaced with lower poly replacements at distance; they are merely distance culled.

7. Remove the boulders.

8. Edit the Noise Spread to something smaller. As with the other terrain assets, you will need to select the icon in the Inspector, select the Edit button, and choose Edit from the list of options.

Figure 4-48. *A good size for rocks that will be distance culled*

For large plants, you may be better off adding the mesh to the tree section. Do be aware that only one billboard tree image is made from the mesh, and trees all face the same direction, so asymmetrical meshes will not work well in sparsely populated areas. Also, detail meshes may not have colliders. As with all painted terrain assets, they will disappear at the culling distance so think carefully when deciding what to place manually and what to paint.

Creating Your Own Terrain Assets

Assuming you may want to try your hand at creating your own terrain assets, there are a few things to keep in mind. As mentioned before, trees and plants require the Nature shaders, Tree Soft Occlusion Bark, and Tree Soft Occlusion Leaves to receive shadows and color tints. The shadowing color on trees is created with vertex color, as are the Healthy/Dry variations, and is added to the color set by the texture and shader Main Color.

Besides keeping the tree under 2,000 faces, it must also use no more than two materials. Careful unwrapping and texturing can do much to make up for this limitation. The banyan tree, using a derivation from the TerrainAssets package, has a texture with full leaves, a bare branch, and a vine of some sort all using the alpha channel.

If you create your assets in 3DS Max or another application that uses Z as up rather than Y, you will need to orient the objects so they appear up in the top viewport (see Figure 4-49).

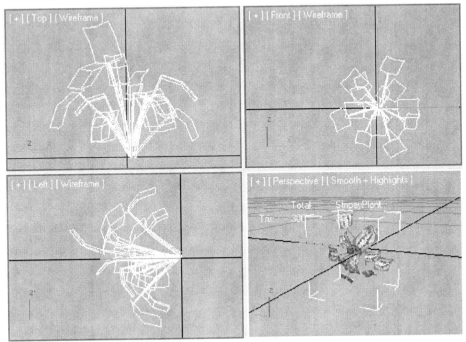

Figure 4-49. *Orientation in 3DS Max*

Unlike the regular imports that are able to convert their native orientation, terrain assets must be correct before import. To insure the transform is baked in, create a plane in the top viewport, attach (from the Edit Mesh modifier) the terrain asset to it, then remove the plane with sub-object element, as shown in Figure 4-50.

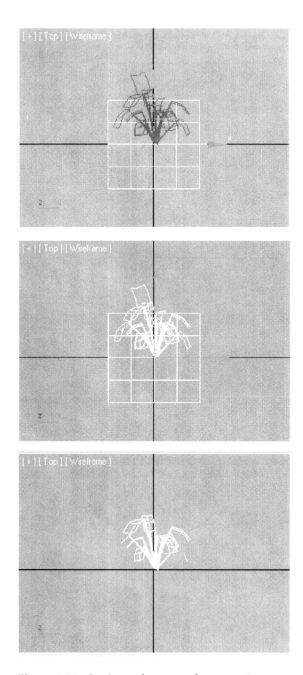

Figure 4-50. *Getting a clean transform matrix*

1. Create a plane in the Top viewport.

2. Collapse the plane to an editable mesh and attach the plant to it.

3. In sub-object element, select the plane and delete it.

4. Name the object and export.

▪ **Tip** Unity will create a material for the mesh on import using the name of the Diffuse texture. If no texture is used, it will create a generic material using the name of the file and the object name.

Export vs. Use Native Format

If you are not using a versioning software such as SVN or Unity's Asset Server, you may prefer to export as FBX format so you always have access to earlier versions of your files and can use the FBX file on any machine without having the original application installed.

Versioning software allows you to save directly to the Unity project, but keeps previous versions in case you need to revert to an earlier version.

Terrain Settings

The last icon on the Terrain Editor deals with Terrain settings. This the place where you can change distances for LOD and distance culling for trees and details as well as adjust wind strength.

1. Select the Terrain object.

2. Select the Terrain Settings tool in the Inspector .

3. Click Play.

4. Adjust the wind settings, speed, size, and bending until it looks good.

You may wish to change some of the larger plants to Vertex Lit instead of Grass to prevent them from bending.

▪ **Caution!** Detail Meshes that are Vertex Lit will *not* be able to use their alpha channels!

Figure 4-51. *The same plant as a tree (upper left), a Vertex Lit Detail Mesh (upper right), and a Grass Detail Mesh (lower)*

In Figure 4-51, the image in the upper left shows the Tree version being affected by scene lighting and with its own Bend settings. As you can see in the image in the upper right, the Vertex Lit Detail Mesh will not use alpha channel opacity. It is not affected by scene lighting except as a generalized vertex tinting: if the plant is in shadow, the vertex tint is darkened. Finally, the image in the lower middle shows the Grass Detail Mesh. It is not affected by scene lighting except as a generalized vertex tinting; if the plant is in shadow, the vertex tint is darkened.

Tree Bending is set individually for each loaded tree type. Detail Mesh Grass bending is controlled generically in the Terrain Settings.

■ **Tip**   Terrain adjustment made during Play mode will be retained. You will need to use undo to remove unwanted adjustments may during Play mode.

Shadows

Next, let's bake some shadows into the terrain. Since terrains can be quite large, generating lightmaps for them can take a lot of time and use a lot of texture memory. *Baked* shadows can add a lot of definition to your scene but don't allow for objects that are dynamic or will animate. Dynamic shadows will track animated objects but lack the subtlety that can be obtained with large numbers of carefully set lights and global illumination (where light bounces are calculated).

If you are using Unity Pro, you can have the best of both. You can bake the shadows into the terrain and have dynamic shadows as well with the dual lightmap system. Two lightmaps are created; one with all shadows included, Far, and one with only the indirect lighting shadows, Near. Within a specified range, the Shadow Distance, the Near map is used and realtime shadows calculated. Beyond that range, the Far shadow map is used (see Figure 4-52).

Figure 4-52. *No shadows (left) and dynamic, realtime shadows (right)*

In your test scene, you have only one light, the Directional light, and its Lightmapping parameter is set to Auto, so you should be good to go. Let's start with a brief look at the Lightmapping dialog.

1. Select the Terrain object.

2. From the Window menu, select Lightmapping, as shown in Figure 4-53.

169

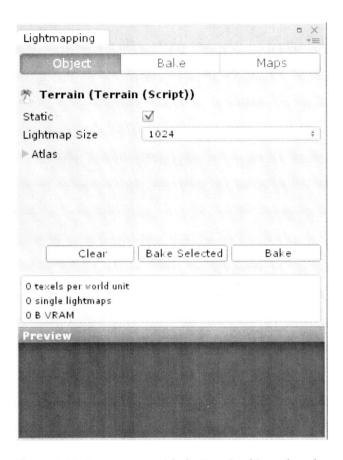

Figure 4-53. *Beast startup with the Terrain object selected*

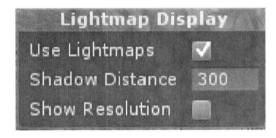

Figure 4-54. *The Lightmap Display in the lower right corner of the Scene window; the default Shadow distance will vary according to your Quality settings.*

The first thing of note is the Static check box. Because this is a terrain and will not be animating, it is automatically set to Static. Later, when you import assets that are not used with the Terrain editor, you will need to remember to set the objects as Static or not, depending on whether they will be animating. Only Static objects will be included in lightmapping

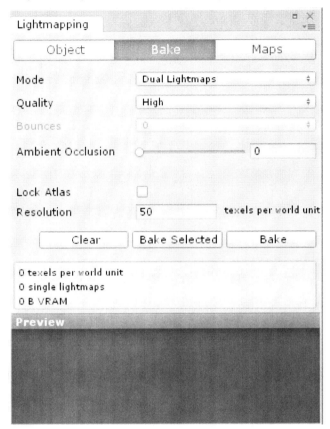

Figure 4-55. *Beast in the free version of Unity. No Bounces or Global Illumination options*

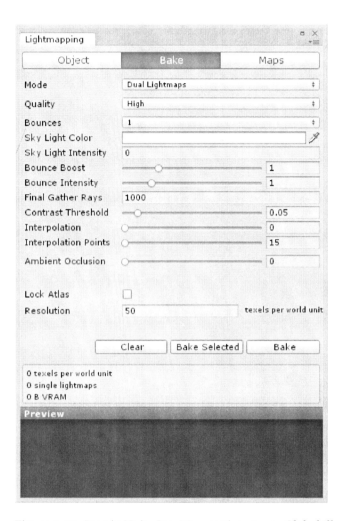

Figure 4-56. *Beas in Unity Pro. More settings to use Global Illumination*

Let's start by baking out a couple of different sized lightmaps just to see the difference. Since you will be adding objects to the scene throughout the development of a game, the lightmap will need regular updating, so there is no need to spend much time on it at this stage.

1. If you are using Unity Pro, set the Bounces to 0.

2. Set Mode to Single Lightmaps if you are using Unity Indie.

3. With the Terrain selected, pick the Bake Selected button.

The status line, bottom, far right, will show the progress as the light is baked. A thumbnail of the resulting map (or maps) is shown in the Preview window.

4. Note the time it took to render the map[s] and the memory it[they] will use, as shown in Figure 4-57.

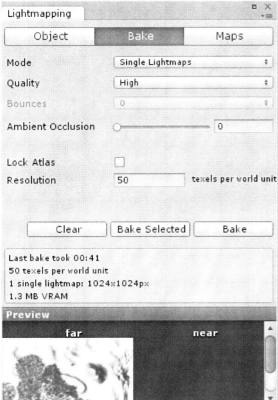

Figure 4-57. *The first bake of the Terrain*

For comparison, you will bake the same settings to a smaller map size. The default size for the Terrain is 1024; try one at 256 to see the difference.

1. From the Object tab, change the Lightmap Size to 256.

2. Press Bake Selected.

Figure 4-58. *The results of the two map sizes, 256 (left) and 1024 (right)*

As you can see in Figure 4-58, the smaller map produces soft indistinct shadows. Note that the smaller map takes up 85.3KB instead of 1.3MB.

3. If you are using Unity Pro, set the Bounces back to the default of 1 Bounce and render the 1024 map size again.

There may be a slight lightening of the shadows from light that could bounce back off the tree trunks, but at this point, it is not worth the extra render time (see Figure 4-59). Bounced light will become more important with the addition of structures. For this book, since it is not assumed that everyone will have Unity Pro, the structures will contain pre-baked lightmaps.

Figure 4-59. *Terrain with baked shadows*

You may be tempted to try the Ambient Occlusion settings. Ambient Occlusion, located in the Bake tab, is calculated apart from any scene lights. It mimics the affect of nooks and crannies being occluded from light (see Figure 4-60). Generally, only objects with convex or occluded areas will benefit greatly from this option and it adds considerable time to calculate. Unity terrains rarely fall under this category, so skip it for now.

Figure 4-60. *An object that will benefit from ambient occlusion (left) and one that will not (right).*

Fog

As a final touch for your test scene, you can add a bit of fog for some environmental perspective. Fog is fairly cheap and will help promote the feel of a moist tropical jungle.

1. From the Edit menu, select Render Settings.

2. Check Fog, as shown in Figure 4-61.

3. Change the fog color to a greenish blue to simulate light filtering through the forest with high humidity, as shown in Figure 4-62.

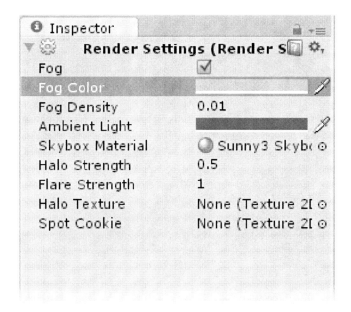

Figure 4-61. *Render Settings with Fog activated*

Figure 4-62. *The fog in the Game window*

Before you move on, you will need to create a large flat area somewhere in the environment for your game's future structures.

1. Set the Paint Height tool's Height setting to 50.

2. Create an area approximately 50 units/meters in diameter somewhere on the terrain.

3. Clear most of the trees from the area. Use the shift key to remove the trees in Place Tree mode.

Chapter Summary

In this chapter, you learned how to use Unity's built-in terrain editor to create the basis for your outdoor environment. Using the Raise/Lower Height, Paint Height, and Smooth Height tools, you were able to sculpt mountains, lakes, and valleys, as well as create building pads and other areas of interest. You learned that focusing on a terrain object is different than regular objects, but that the Flythrough mode of scene navigation is quite useful.

You were able to paint multiple textures on the terrain using the variety of brushes available in the editor. You also learned how to add grass and mesh objects with the option to sway in the wind. Trees were added the same way, but you discovered that to prevent the player from going right through the trunks, you needed to create a prefab containing a Collider. You discovered how to import packages of prepared assets and learned a few tips for creating your own terrain assets. Finally, you learned how to bake shadows into the terrain at a few different settings and then added a bit of fog for some environmental perspective.

In the next chapter, you will learn how to navigate through your environment and start customizing the existing scripts to fit the needs of your adventure game.

▪ **Tip**   You can find more on terrain creation with Unity's Terrain Toolkit. This a free tool provided by Unity that you can use to rapidly create terrains. A video tutorial provides a brief but helpful introduction on how to use it. Go to `http://unity3d.com/support/resources/unity-extensions/terrain-toolkit`.

CHAPTER 5

■ ■ ■

Navigation and Functionality

So far we have explored the terrain in the Scene view with zoom, pan, orbit, and flythrough navigation. Every environment artist's dream is to be able to experience her creation firsthand. And while "holodeck" technology is not quite here yet, being able to travel through your environment in first-person mode for the first time is, for many of us, one of the best parts of making real-time games. To make your environment into an actual game environment, you will need to be able to travel around inside the world, responding to terrain topography and large objects during runtime. Only by doing this can you tell if scale, layout, color scheme and all the rest of the design have come together to create the mood you intend. Even though what you're creating here is just a temporary test scene, the effect is the basis for every entertainment author's goal—suspension of disbelief.

Navigation

Happily, Unity provides a prefab for a First Person shooter-type Controller. It consists of a Capsule Collider to provide physical interaction with the scene, a camera to provide the viewpoint, and scripts to allow the user to control them through keyboard and mouse.

Anyone who has ever played 3D games, even of the same genre, is well aware that there are many different means of controlling the character or the first person. Moreover, if you get a group of twenty people together in the same room and ask them what the best controls are, you would most likely get a different answer from every person, depending on the game he is currently playing or his all-time favorite game.

We will, of course, be tweaking a bit of the first person controller as we develop our game, but it is extremely useful to be able to jump right in and travel around the scene right off the bat.

1.   Open the Project as we left it in the previous chapter.

2.   Set the Scene view to the clearing area you prepared in the last chapter, as shown in Figure 5-1.

Figure 5-1. *The clearing*

3. From the Character Controllers folder in the Standard Assets directory, drag the First Person Controller into the Scene view.

Because the First Person Controller is a prefab, its text appears blue in the Hierarchy view instead of the usual black (Figure 5-2).

■ **Tip**   You can add an object into the scene in a couple of different ways. Previously, we focused the view and added the object to the Hierarchy so it appears at the focus spot. This time, we added the object directly into the scene. If you know the object's position will need to be changed, you can just drag it directly into the Scene view and get on with the repositioning. Since you'll be aligning it to the view anyway, it becomes six of one, half dozen of the other as to which method to use.

Figure 5-2. *The new First Person Controller in the Hierarchy view*

4. From the GameObject menu, choose Align with View to move it near the existing view.

5. Use the Scene Gizmo to select the Top view (Y) and select the First Person Controller in the Hierarchy view.

6. Zoom out to see the area better.

7. Select the Move tool.

8. Using the gray rectangle from the transform gizmo, position the prefab over the clearing you made in your terrain (Figure 5-3).

Figure 5-3. *The First Person Controller and its camera in the Top viewport*

▪ **Tip**　The First Person Controller contains its own camera that overrides the existing Main Camera object, so you will now see its view in the Game view.

Since the default height was set to 50, the prefab may be beneath the terrain surface if you modified it in that area.

9. Use the F key to focus the view on the First Person Controller prefab.

10. Click the center white cube of the Scene Gizmo to put the Scene view back to a perspective view.

11. Move it up or down in the viewport by dragging its Y arrow up until you can see the ground in the Game view.

12. Use F to focus the First Person Controller prefab again.

13. Adjust its height until the capsule is *slightly above* ground level (Figure 5-4).

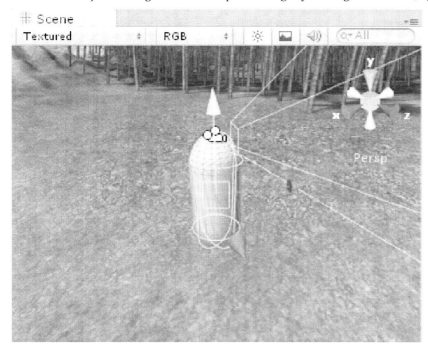

Figure 5-4. *The First Person Controller in the Scene view*

Before you head off to experience your scene in first person mode, let's take a quick look at what the prefab contains.

1. Select the First Person Controller in the Hierarchy view and click the arrow to the left of the name to open the group (or GameObject), as shown in Figure 5-5).

Figure 5-5. *The contents of the First Person Controller*

It has two children—something called Graphics, and a Main Camera.

Graphics, as you probably guessed, contains the mesh for the capsule. If you check and uncheck Mesh Renderer in the Inspector (Figure 5-6), you can see that it affects whether or not the capsule is drawn in the Scene window. Note that neither cast nor receive shadows is checked. If you are using Unity Pro, you will be able to see what happens if they are checked.

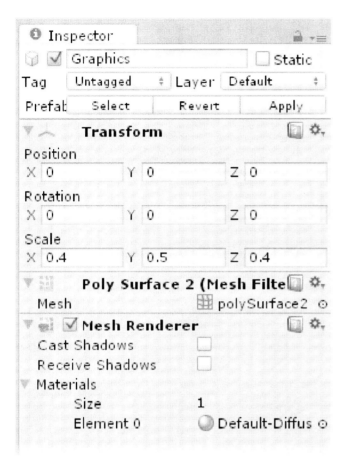

Figure 5-6. *The Graphics object in the Inspector*

Because the camera object is *inside* the capsule and you are looking out through the back side of the mesh's faces, you will not see it in the game window. Remember that faces are only drawn on the side that their normals are pointing—in this case, the outside of the capsule.

    2.   Click Play.

You may notice that the Console status line is telling you there are two Audio Listeners in the scene. (See Figure 5-7.)

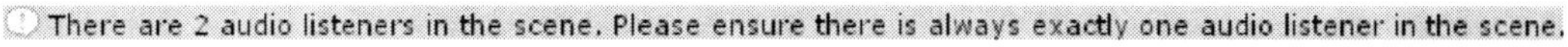

There are 2 audio listeners in the scene. Please ensure there is always exactly one audio listener in the scene.

Figure 5-7. *The status line warning*

    3.   Stop the scene by clicking the Play button again.

As you may surmise, this has to do with enabling audio, but you should have only one per scene. Because every scene must have at least one camera, the default camera comes supplied with that component, as does the Main Camera present in the First Person Controller.

Eventually you'll need to add and animate other cameras to show the player when and where some particularly important event happens, but for now just remember to delete the default Main Camera whenever you add the First Person Controller prefab.

4. Select the original scene Main Camera, right-click, and delete it.

The remaining MainCamera object will be referenced *by name* by various other objects throughout this project, as well as by any other games that use the scripts you'll be creating. Do not rename this object!

5. Click Play.

6. Move around the scene using W to go forward, S to go backward, A to strafe left and D to strafe right.

7. Move the mouse around to look up and down or to turn left or right.

8. Use the spacebar to jump.

9. Try running into one of the banyan trees.

10. The collider prevents you from going through it.

If you experimented with tiling on the terrain textures, you may want to select the Terrain object and change the tiling on some of them. Remember, a smaller number increases the tiling, making the image smaller on the terrain.

11. Select the First Person Controller in the Inspector.

12. You will find three scripts and one component.

13. Take a look at the variables exposed to the Character Motor script (see Figure 5-8).

As long as you are in Play mode, you can make changes to speed, jump speed, and gravity that will not be permanent.

■ **Tip** To remove focus from the Game window, click outside of it before trying to access other parts of the editor—this will stop the view from spinning wildly.

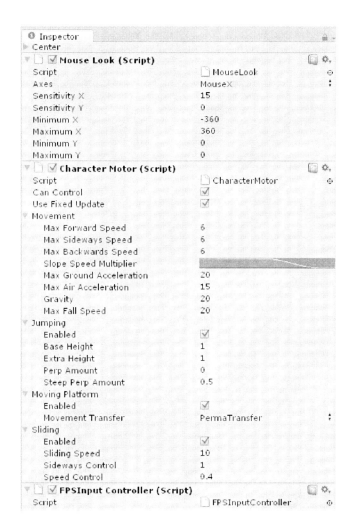

Figure 5-8. *The Character Motor script and its parameters*

Opening the script in the editor is somewhat overwhelming. Fortunately, you can just accept that it does lots of nice things to help you travel around the scene and leave it at that. Movement and Jumping are pretty self-explanatory, even if a few of the parameters are not. Sliding is whether the character sticks or slides back down steep slopes when jumping. Moving Platform is a new addition to the First Person Controller system that we will experiment with a bit later.

The First Person Controller is basically a first person shooter-type control, with some attributes that will be useful and some that will not. The quickest way to find out what controls what is to turn off scripts and see what happens—or in this case, no longer happens.

1. Select the First Person Controller.

2. Try disabling the Mouse Look script to see what it affects. You'll find that you can still go forward and sideways, but you can't turn left or right; you can only strafe with the left and right arrows or A and D keys.

You can still look up and down, however. A bit of investigation shows that the Main Camera also has a Mouse Look script, but that its rotation Axes is set to work on the X axis rather than the Y axis as is the one on the main group or GameObject (see Figure 5-9). This means that to turn to look, the whole object is turned. When the object goes forward, it will always go in the direction it is facing. When it has to look up or down, only the camera is rotated, leaving the forward direction correct.

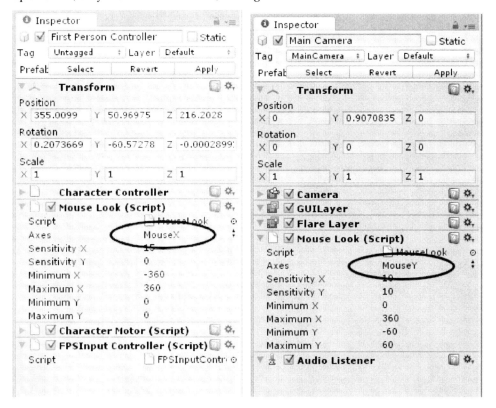

Figure 5-9. *The* MouseLook *script on the First Person Controller, left, and the* MouseLook *on the Main Camera*

3. Turn off the Mouse Look script on the camera.

4. Test the restricted functionality.

Now you can only go forward, backward, or sideways. On the positive side, we now have full use of the cursor for our point and click adventure.

5. Stop Play mode.

Arrow Navigation and Input

Typically, people who are not avid shooter type game players are more comfortable using the arrow keys to travel and turn. Ideally, you want to cater to both types of users as transparently as possible. To do so, you need to do a bit of tinkering with the Input system.

Unity's Input system lets you assign different input types to a named functionality. This enables two important things: it lets you reference the name of a behavior rather than specifically calling each key or mouse control the behavior can use, and it lets users change or remap the keys according to their preferred configuration. Because we will be making the two control types work together, we will not allow the user to remap the keys. We can, however, still make use of the naming benefits when we set up the functionality for our game.

Let's see how the remapping works. Jump has only a positive key assigned—the spacebar, or *space*. It's easy to temporarily change this input assignment.

1.   From Edit ➤ Project Settings, choose Input.

2.   Click the down arrow next to Axes to see the assignments.

There are currently 17 presets.

3.   In the Jump preset, select the Positive Button's entry field (Figure 5-10).

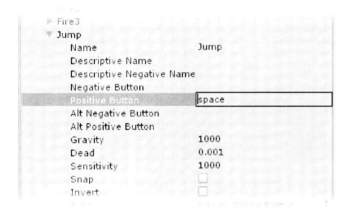

Figure 5-10. *Remapping the Jump key*

4. Change space to a different key (in lowercase).

5. Click Play and test.

The jump function now works from the newly assigned key. This means you can eventually let the user remap or assign the keys without having to change any of your scripts.

6. Stop Play mode and change the Positive Button back to space.

■ **Tip**   See Appendix B for the names of the keyboard keys to use in scripts.

Let's get started altering the default First Person Controller navigation.

The first thing to do is turn off strafing for the left and right arrows, leaving that capability strictly to the A and D keys.

7. Open the first Horizontal and Vertical sets (there are duplicates of both further down the list), as shown in Figure 5-11.

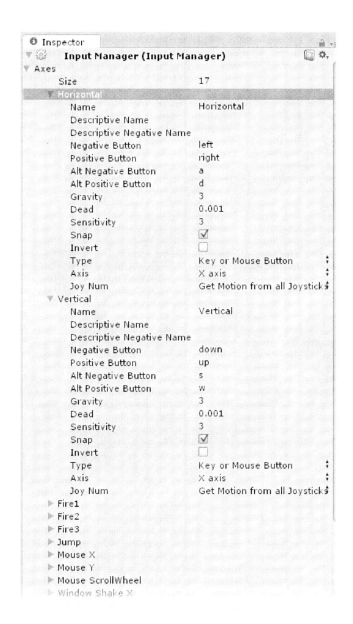

Figure 5-11. *The Input Manager, Horizontal, and Vertical opened in the Inspector*

A good portion of the parameter assignments are handled internally so you can safely ignore them. Of interest to us are the button assignments: Positive, Negative, Alt Positive, and Alt Negative. Horizontal and Vertical are misleading if you're used to a 3D world. Vertical is not up and down as you'd assume, but forward and backward. Horizontal is a strafe (move sideways) left or right. At first glance, they don't make much sense in our 3D world, but if you picture early 2D games played on screen, you can see how the left and right arrows would move the cursor left and right on the *horizontal* X axis and the up and down arrows would move it up and down on the *vertical* Y axis. Tip the whole thing down to make the ground plane and you can see why some 3D packages use Z as the up axis and why Unity calls its axes Vertical and Horizontal (see Figure 5-12).

Figure 5-12. *The origin of Unity navigation terminology. Left: The overhead view of a world where Vertical(on the monitor) moves you forward through the scene. Right: The directions tilted down to use in a 3D world.*

The Vertical preset is perfect for our use, using either the W and S keys or the up and down arrows to move forward or backward. The Horizontal needs a bit of modifying to disable the left and right arrow keys.

8. In Horizontal, delete the *left* and *right* entries for both the Positive Button and the Negative Button (Figure 5-13).

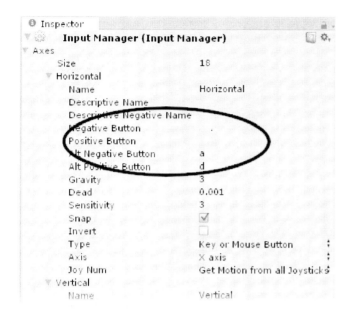

Figure 5-13. *Left and right removed from the Horizontal preset*

9.   Click Play and test the left and right arrows.

The arrows no longer strafe.

10.   Stop Play mode.

11.   At the top of the Inspector, change the Size to **18.**

A duplicate of the last preset, Jump, is created.

12.   Open the new preset and change its Name to **Turn**.

13.   Change its Negative Button to **left** and its positive button to **right**.

14.   Change its Sensitivity to **3**.

Now you need to see if the engine will recognize input from the new preset. The most logical place to test your new input preset is in the FPS Input Controller script.

15.   Select the FPS Input Controller script in the Project view ➤ Standard Assets ➤ Character Controllers ➤ Sources ➤ Scripts. Use Ctrl + D (Cmd + D on the Mac) to duplicate the script.

16.   Rename it to FPAdventurerInputController.js.

17.   Double-click it to open it in the editor.

18.   From the View menu in the script editor, turn on Line Numbers.

Note that if you are using Windows and the UniSciTE editor, you can turn on line numbers via the script editor's View menu, but to have them show for each script you will need to do the following:

19. Open the folder where you installed Unity.

20. Browse the subfolder Unity/Editor/Data/Tools/UniScITE/ and open ScITEGlobal.properties with a text editor such as Wordpad or Notepad.

The second section in ScITEGlobal.properties is called #Sizes and Visibility in edit pane. Remove the # at the beginning of the line that says #line.margin.visible = 1 so it is no longer commented out.

21. Close UniScITE and open it again; the line numbers will now be visible by default.

At line 4, you'll see a new function called Awake. It is a system function and is one of the very first to be evaluated when a game is started. Objects are created first, then scripts. Once the scripts exist, Awake is the first function to be called. We will look at it in some of the later chapters.

Lines 38 and 39 (36 and 37 in the Unitron editor on the Mac) are an oddity; they begin with an @ and don't end with a semi-colon. These lines are not JavaScript and their functions differ.

- The first one, @script RequireComponent checks to make sure a certain component is attached to the GameObject. If that component is missing, the RequireComponent attribute will add it if it is missing.

- The second one, @script AddComponentMenu adds this script to the Component menu so you can easily access it when you want to add it to a new GameObject.

Fortunately, by definition, the whole purpose of @script lines is to do things for us so we don't have to worry about them.

A familiar item in the script should be the Update function at line 9. Most of the script's contents, however, seem to be dealing with more vector math than you probably care to analyze. Traditionally, most books start with an in-depth analysis of the navigation scripts. Since the newer character controller scripts are three or four times larger and more complicated than their predecessors and this book is written more for artists, we will accept its functionality as is and be grateful for it.

■ **Important Concept**   You don't necessarily have to understand something to use it. People who get bogged down trying to understand every little detail rarely finish their first game. Don't expect the game to be perfect; you can always revisit it and make improvements as your understanding grows. In this project, we will be constantly improving and refining the scripts and functionality.

There should be a few more bits that catch your eye as being vaguely familiar. Since you were just tweaking the Input settings, Input.GetAxis("Horizontal") and Input.GetAxis("Vertical") should stand out. While you shouldn't interfere with either of these, they should provide a clue as to how to check for input from our new preset, Turn.

Let's start with something simple.

1. Under the **var** directionVector = **new** Vector3 line, add the following:

```
if (Input.GetAxis("Turn")) print ("turning");
```

■ **Tip**   You can also use Debug.Log instead of print. It has the advantage of giving you more information, and that will make more sense as you get more familiar with scripting.

---

2. Save the new script via the Editor's Save button or through the File menu.

3. Select the First Person Controller in the Hierarchy view.

4. In the Inspector, with the First Person Controller selected, click the browse icon next to the FPSInput Controller script and select our new version of it, FPAdventurerController.

■ **Tip**   Replacing a script this way preserves the current values exposed in the Inspector as long as the variable names have stayed the same.

Because you are changing the First Person Controller prefab in the Hierarchy, you'll get a warning about losing the prefab connection.

5. Press Continue.

Eventually you'll make your own prefab, once everything is set up, so you can reuse it in any of your games.

6. Click Play.

7. Click in the Game window and then try the arrow keys.

As soon as you press either the left or right key, the "turning" message appears in the status line. You haven't yet told the first person controller to turn, but at least you know it reads your code.

You can get a bit more information from Input.GetAxis. It returns a value between -1 and 1 as you press the two arrow keys.

8. Change that line to the following:

```
if (Input.GetAxis("Turn")) print ("turning " + Input.GetAxis("Turn"));
```

9. Save the script.

10. Click in the Game window and test the keys again.

The left arrow returns a value less than 0 and the right arrow returns a value greater than 0. This tells us which direction to turn. We will add the turn functionality next, but instead of adding it to the Update function, which is frame-dependent, we will use another system function, the FixedUpdate function. The FixedUpdate function is called at fixed intervals rather than every frame. While this function is primarily used for physics operations, it is handy for other functionality that needs to be consistent across different systems and throughout the game. This way, the turn speed should be about the same on an old machine as on the latest cutting-edge gaming system.

11. Delete the **if** (Input.GetAxis("Turn")) line you added to the script.

We are ready for the real functionality now (caution: scary math follows).

12. Add the following function above the // Require a character controller line at the bottom of the script:

```
//this is for the arrow turn functionality
function FixedUpdate () {

    if (Input.GetAxis("Turn")) {     // the left or right arrow key is being pressed
        // the rotation = direction * speed * sensitivity
        var rotation : float = ( Input.GetAxis("Turn") ) * rotationSpeed * rotationSensitivity ;
        // add the rotation to the current orientation amount
        rotation = rotation + transform.eulerAngles.y ;
        // convert degrees to quaternion for the up axis, Y
        transform.localRotation = Quaternion.AngleAxis ( rotation, Vector3.up ) ;

    }
}
```

13. Near the top of the script, just beneath the motor variable declaration, add the two variables needed to go along with the arrow turn code:

```
//add these for arrow turn
var rotationSpeed : float = 20.0;
private var rotationSensitivity = 0.1 ; // This makes rotationSpeed more managable
```

14. Save the script.

Tip   When you are having trouble making a bit of code work, you can often get the help you need on the Unity forums. If you have more complex issues and not enough time to work them out on your own, you might consider trading art assets for code. One of the great things about the Unity forums is the Collaboration section. To get the rotation functionality nailed down quickly for a few key features of our game, I enlisted the help of the team at Binary Sonata Studios. Thanks guys!

---

15. Click in the Game window and test the keys again.

The left and right arrow keys now allow you to turn left and right in the scene.

16. Stop Play mode.

17. Save the scene and save the project.

Rotation math can be very complicated. Euler angles allow us to change rotations on X, Y, and Z axes independently, but they are subject to gimbal lock, which is when the camera is watching a target and must flip to continue. In Figure 5-14, the character on the left can watch the sphere as it goes around him by rotating around his vertical axis with no problems. The figure on the right rotates his head on a horizontal axis, but when the sphere goes overhead, he must turn 180 degrees on his vertical axis to continue watching it once it has passed overhead. With Euler angles if a rotation involves multiple axes, it needs to be handled one axis at a time. Deciding which axis to solve first is often problematic.

Quaternions (complex numbers used to represent rotations) are not subject to gimbal lock, but are more confusing to use without a good background in vector math (which is akin to voodoo for many of us). Quaternions use vectors to point in a given direction so they can always rotate the objects on all axes simultaneously to get to the desired new vector with efficiency and stability.

On top of all of this, objects have both local (object space) and global (world space) rotation possibilities. To further complicate matters, transforms can be permanently changed, as in the editor, or temporarily changed as in game animations.

When you see `transform.rotation` in a Unity script, it is referring to quaternions. When you see `transform.eulerAngles`, it is dealing with degrees. The numbers we see in the Inspector's Transform component for rotation show us `localEulerAngles`. Internally, Unity uses quaternions, but in scripting, you will see both used.

Bottom line: Feel free to accept the navigation code as is (with no shame) so we can continue with the game.

If you are still curious about rotation, try looking up "Quaternions and spatial rotation" in Wikipedia. While you are there, check out 'gimbal' to see the origin of the term and a nice example of one in action.

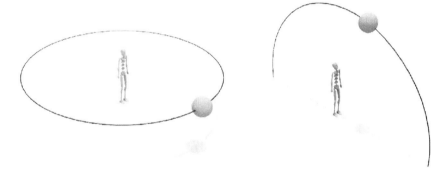

Figure 5-14. *An depiction of gimbal lock*

Adding the Mouse Look Back

Before we change the existing `MouseLook` script, we need to define the required functionality. At the top of the list is preventing it from working all the time. There's nothing worse than having the view spinning wildly as you try to position the cursor on an object in the scene. The first thing the script will need is a conditional to tell it when it can be used. We will start with the basics and add to them.

1.   Stop Play mode.

2.   Select the `MouseLook` script in the Project view ➤ Standard Assets ➤ Character Controllers>Sources ➤ Scripts.

3.   Duplicate the script using Ctrl +D (Cmd + D on the Mac).

4.   Rename it `MouseLookRestricted`.

Note the `.cs` extension. The MouseLook script looks a bit different as it is written in C# instead of JavaScript. The syntax is close enough in many cases for making minor adjustments. All of the rest of the scripts we create or deal with in this project are JavaScript.

5. Replace the MouseLook script for both the First Person Controller and the Main Camera with the new MouseLookRestricted (see Figure 5-15).

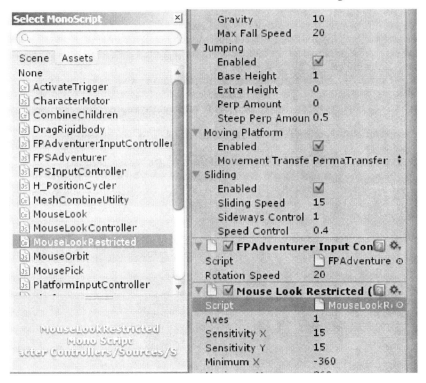

Figure 5-15. *Substituting the MouseLookRestricted.cs for the MouseLook.cs*

Double-check to make sure the Main Camera is using the Mouse Y axis and the First Person Controller is using the Mouse X axis (Figure 5-16).

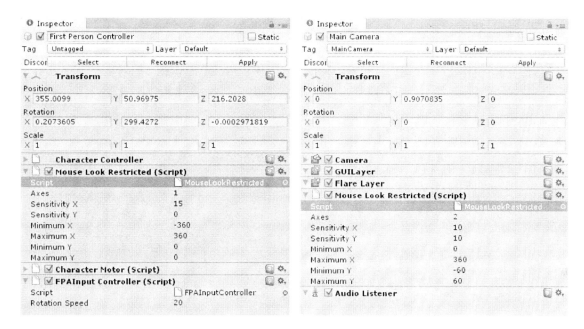

Figure 5-16. *The correct axes for the First Person Controller and Main Camera*

6. Open the MouseLookRestricted script in the script editor.

7. Inside the Update function (void Update ()), just beneath the open curly bracket, add the condition so it looks like this:

```
void Update ()
{
// only do mouse look if right mouse button is down
if (Input.GetMouseButton ( 1 ) ) {
```

You can use curly brackets inline, as with the line containing the **if** conditional, or on a different line altogether, such as with the void Update () line. Feel free to use whichever makes the script easier to read. The important point to remember is that, just as with parentheses, if you have an open one, you must have a closed one to match.

■ **Tip**   If you are using Windows and the UniSciTE editor, you can find the closing curly bracket that goes with an opening bracket by highlighting the opening bracket. It turns blue as does its mate and the line that spans the lines between the two. Unitron, the editor for the Mac doesn't have this same functionality.

In this case, we are putting the entire contents of the Update function within the conditional so the closing curly bracket will go right above the Update function's closing curly bracket.

8. Add the closing curly bracket up one line from the curly bracket that closes the Update function (the only thing left below that in the script is a short *Start* function).

The final four lines of the Update function are as follows:

```
transform.localEulerAngles = new Vector3(-rotationY, transform.localEulerAngles.y, 0);
  }
  } // add this to close the conditional
}
```

9. Save the script and test. You may get an error on the status line, as shown in Figure 5-17.

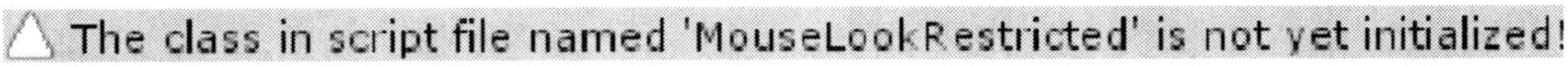

⚠ The class in script file named 'MouseLookRestricted' is not yet initialized!

Figure 5-17. *One of many possible errors reported in the console*

The status line tells us that the renamed script is not yet initialized, that the namespace global::' already contains a definition…. Or if you are using a Mac, you may see "The class defined in script file named 'MouseLookRestricted' does not match the file name!" A quick look through the script shows that the script is referred to by name somewhere around lines 17 and 18.

10. Change those lines to reflect the new name:

```
[AddComponentMenu("Camera-Control/Mouse Look Restricted")]
public class MouseLookRestricted : MonoBehaviour {
```

11. Save the script.

The console should clear itself of error messages.
Line 17 is interesting in that it shows how scripts can add to the Component menu for easy access.

12. From the Component menu ➤ Camera-Control, observe the new entry, Mouse Look Restricted, shown in Figure 5-18.

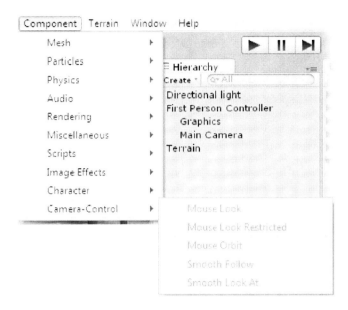

Figure 5-18. *The new menu item*

13. Stop Play mode.

14. Click Play and test.

■ **Tip** If you do a search in the Scripting Reference for Input.GetMouseButton, you will see that it "Returns whether the given mouse button is held down. /button/ values are 0 for left button, 1 for right button, 2 for the middle button."

You should now be able to mouse look when the right mouse button is held down…unless you *don't have a right mouse button*!

If you are developing on a Mac or just want your executable to run on either a Mac or a PC, you'll need to add another option for the conditional. This time we'll select a key that must be held down to enable mouse look.

To do this, we will need to introduce the or operator in the condition that must be met. The or operator uses two pipe characters, **| |** (the shift character of the \ key).

15. Change the **if** line to include a check for the left Shift key:

```
if (Input.GetMouseButton ( 1 ) || Input.GetKey ("left shift") ) {
```

Note that the key name is all lowercase characters. The Scripting Reference indicates that Input.GetKey() "Returns true while the user holds down the key identified by name." In contrast, Input.GetKeyDown() "Returns true during the frame the user starts pressing down the key identified by name." This function represents a single event and therefore is not the one we want to use.

203

16. Save the script and test.

Now mouse-button-impaired users can also take advantage of mouse look.

░ **Tip**   See Appendix B for the names of the keyboard keys for use in scripts or search for Input Manager in the Unity Manual.

If the user tries to use the right Shift key instead of left Shift, he will find that it doesn't work. We should probably add the right Shift to round out the choices.

17. Add the right Shift option:

```
if (Input.GetMouseButton (1) || Input.GetKey ("left shift") ||
    Input.GetKey ("right shift")){
```

18. Save the script and test.

By now you're probably getting some idea about controlling input. A nice touch for WASD users would be to allow automatic mouse look while *navigating the scene*. You know when the player is navigating the scene because of the keys mapped out for this. To cover all of the possibilities, the conditional would look something like this:

```
if (Input.GetKey ("up") || Input.GetKey ("down") ||Input.GetKey  ("d") ||
    Input.GetKey ("s") || Input.GetKey ("w") || Input.GetKey ("a") || Input.GetKey
    ("left shift") || Input.GetKey ("right shift") || Input.GetMouseButton ( 1 ) ) {
```

Though this will certainly work as expected, it hardcodes the keys that must be used, some of which already have virtual counterparts in the Input Manager.

We have used Input.GetAxis() to get movement from our virtual buttons, but we will need something that returns a Boolean value (true or false) to check to see if our virtual buttons are being held down. That will be Input.GetButton(), which "Returns true while the virtual button identified by buttonName is held down."

Now you can simplify the condition by using the virtual buttons.

19. Change the **if** line to the following:

```
if (Input.GetMouseButton ( 1 ) || Input.GetKey ("left shift") ||
    Input.GetKey ("right shift") || Input.GetButton("Horizontal") ||
    Input.GetButton("Vertical") ) {
```

░ **Tip**   Make sure there is a ‖ between each of the conditions or you will get several errors.

---

20. Save the script and test.

Now when the player is navigating the scene, the mouse look works automatically as with regular shooter controls, but as soon as the player stops, the cursor can be moved around the scene without the world spinning dizzily.

At this point, it may have occurred to you that if you could create a virtual button for any keys that need to held down when the user is not navigating, you could simplify things even more and consider yourself quite clever in the process. Let's create a new virtual button called ML Enable (Mouse Look Enable).

21. Stop Play mode.

■ **Tip**   As we experimented with the code in the MouseLookRestricted script, we were able to keep Unity in Play mode because saving the script recompiled it and the changes were picked up immediately in the Update function. If we had added changes to the Start function, we would have needed to restart Unity after each save so the new content could be used. Awake and Start are evaluated only at startup.

---

22. From Edit ➤ Project Settings, select Input.

23. Increase the array size to **19.**

24. Open the new Turn duplicate and name it ML Enable.

25. Add the shift keys and mouse-button buttons into the Positive, Negative, and Alt Negative Button fields (Figure 5-19).

26. Set the Descriptive Name to Enable Mouse Look.

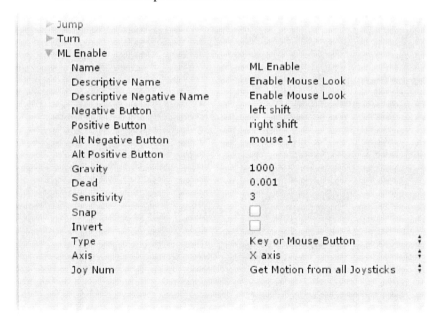

Figure 5-19. *The new ML Enabled virtual button*

Since the settings were inherited from the previous entry, yours may be different if you tweaked any of them.

Now you can simplify the **if** conditional in the MouseLookRestricted script.

27. Change the line to the following:

```
if (Input.GetButton ("ML Enable") || Input.GetButton("Horizontal") ||
    Input.GetButton("Vertical") ) {
```

28. Save the script.

29. Click Play and test.

The functionality should remain the same.

As a final refinement, you can allow mouse look *only on the X axis* when the left or right arrows are pressed so the player can mouse look up and down. The tricky part about this functionality is that the same script is used on the camera for X-axis rotation *and* on the First Person Controller for the Y-axis rotation. Since the left and right arrow keys rotate the first person on the Y axis, you need to avoid multiple, possibly conflicting, input on the Y.

The script uses a variable named axes that lets the author choose the axis to rotate. Of the three choices, RotationAxes.MouseXAndY, RotationAxes.MouseX, and RotationAxes.MouseY, the only one that does not allow Y to rotate is RotationAxes.MouseX. The condition that must be met if the mouse look is allowed will be if either Turn virtual button is pressed *and* the value of the axes variable is RotationAxes.MouseX. To ensure that the entire condition is evaluated together, we will wrap it in parentheses. The *and* in the conditional is written as a double ampersand, &&.

30. Finally, change the **if** line to the following:

```
if (Input. GetButton ("ML Enable") || Input.GetButton("Horizontal") ||
    Input.GetButton("Vertical") ||
    (Input.GetButton("Turn") && axes == RotationAxes.MouseY) ) {
```

31. Save the script.

32. Click Play and test the functionality.

The navigation for the game is now ready to use.

Now that you've altered a few scripts, you should start organizing your scripts for the game before they get out of hand.

33. Create a new folder in the Project view.

34. Name it **Adventure Scripts**.

35. From the Standard Assets ➤ Character Controllers ➤ Sources ➤ Scripts folder, move the FPAdventurerInputController.js script into the new folder.

The MouseLookRestricted script is C# rather than JavaScript and needs to be left where it is. Unity compiles scripts according to where they are located, which can affect access to the scripts by other scripts. JavaScript is more forgiving so you can move the other scripts where you please. All of the rest of the scripts you'll deal with or create are JavaScript.

36. Save the scene and save the project.

Since you added Input presets, remembering to save the project as well as the scene is important.

At this point, you need to make an executive decision—a design decision. The other navigation inputs are handled only if the Collider is on the ground. If you want the player to be able to turn only while on the ground, you need to add your code inside the if (grounded) conditional. If, however, you want the player to be able to "turn his head," or even "twist his body around" while in midair, the code should not be inside the conditional. Since the purpose of the game is entertainment, let's go with the latter.

Fun with Platforms

As a reward for getting through the navigation code, let's have a bit of fun using one of the features of the Character Motor script—the Platform functionality. Unless you are an experienced platform-jumper player, the thought of trying to navigate several fast moving platforms may be intimidating. For this adventure game, however, you might want to make use of platforms that aren't challenging to use but add interest to navigating the environment. Many graphical adventure games of the prerendered era featured rendered sequences where the player was taken on wild rides through tunnels or on skyways.

1. Select the First Person Controller.

2. Set its Y Rotation to **270** in the Inspector.

3. Select the Main Camera from the First Person Controller object.

4. Use Align View to Selected to set the Scene window.

5. Create a Cube and name it Platform.

6. Change its Scale to **2** on the X, **0.3** on the Y, and **6** on the Z (Figure 5-20).

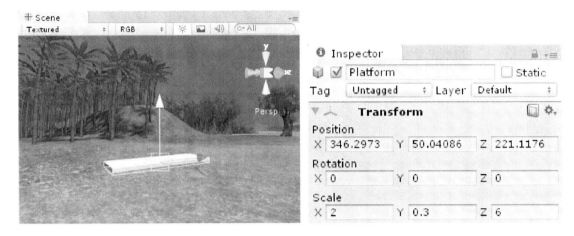

Figure 5-20. *The new Platform settings*

7. Move it down so it just intersects with the ground.

8. Add a material such as TestBark to it (Figure 5-21).

Figure 5-21. *The new platform*

Next you need to build a simple script to move the platform. You could feed numbers into it, but it will be easier to set up if you just create a couple of target objects to move between. I have borrowed the code from a script in the 2D platform tutorial on the Unity site.

9. Select the Adventure Scripts folder.

10. Create a new JavaScript in it.

11. Name the script PlatformMover.

12. Open the script in the editor.

13. Replace the default Update function with the following:

```
var targetA : GameObject;
var targetB : GameObject;

var speed : float = 0.1;

function FixedUpdate () {
        var weight = Mathf.Cos(Time.time * speed * 2 * Mathf.PI) * 0.5 + 0.5;
        transform.position = targetA.transform.position * weight +
                    targetB.transform.position * (1-weight);
}
```

▓ **Tip**   Just in case the math for that last bit of code made your head hurt, you should know it originated from the 2D Platformer tutorial on the Unity website. As recommended at the start, you can find all manner of useful code in tutorials for all different genres. Don't be afraid to copy, paste, and tweak—you never know what will prove useful in your game!

---

14. Save the script.

Plan Ahead

In the early stages of prototyping your game or even just testing techniques for functionality, it is tempting to go with the simplest solution. When you are dealing with animating objects, however, it is well worth a couple of extra steps to create a GameObject to hold the mesh and then put the animation on it instead of the mesh. This gives you the freedom to swap out early proxy objects with the final versions or add more objects to the group without having to redo the animation or triggers.

1. Focus the scene on the Platform by double-clicking the Platform in the Hierarchy view.

2. Create an Empty GameObject; it should be created in the same place as the Platform.

If the GameObject is not in the same place (especially the Y axis), you can just copy the x, y, and z coordinates from the Platform's Transform component at the top of the Inspector to the new Empty GameObject's x, y and z.

3. Name it Platform Group.

4. Drag the `PlatformMover` script from the Project view onto the Platform Group object.

5. Drag the Platform into the Platform Group.

This script uses two target objects for their transforms. The variables that will hold them are defined as type `GameObject`. After you create a couple of targets, you'll need to drag the target objects onto the variables' value fields in the Inspector (Figure 5-22).

Figure 5-22. *The Target A and B variables in the Inspector, waiting for GameObjects*

The `Speed` variable allows you to adjust the speed with which the platform will move between the targets.

Because you want the speed to be consistent regardless of framerate or computers, you'll use the `FixedUpdate` function.

Inside the `FixedUpdate` function, a `cosine` function is used in conjunction with the speed and target positions to move the platform between the targets (see Figure 5-23).

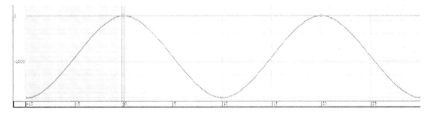

Figure 5- 23. *A cosine function curve. With time on the horizontal and position on the vertical, you can see how the platform slows to a stop before reversing direction.*

Theoretically, all you need to use for your target objects is a couple of empty GameObjects. The problem is that it would be difficult to get them positioned correctly without any geometry. As an alternative, you can clone the original platform, position it, and then remove its renderer and collider components.

6. Select the Platform object.

7. Use Ctrl + D (Cmd + D on the Mac) to make a duplicate of it.

8. Name it **PlatformMesh** and drag it out of the Platform Group.

9. Locate its Box Collider component in the Inspector.

10. Right-click on the component label and choose Remove Component as shown in Figure 5-24.

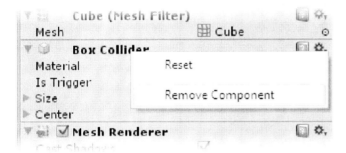

Figure 5-24. *Remove Component*

11. In the Mesh Renderer component, uncheck Cast Shadows and Receive Shadows (Figure 5-25).

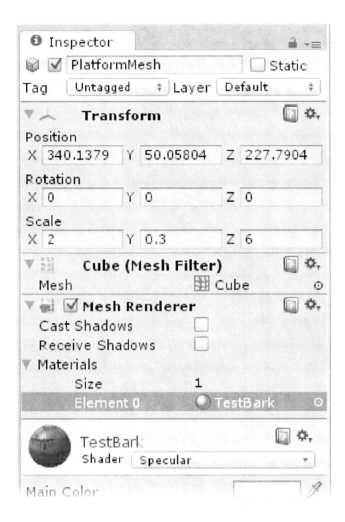

Figure 5-25. *The Platform mesh cleared of nonessential components*

It might seem logical to remove the material by setting its size to 0, but rather than reverting to the Default-Diffuse material, you can assign <none> to it and have it turn a violent shade of fuchsia/magenta. As you'll be turning off the renderer after placement, the current material won't be costing any extra overhead.

At this point, you could clone the platform and finish the platform functionality, but in the spirit of getting in the habit of using an important Unity concept, let's create a prefab for extended use.

1. Create a new folder.

2. Name it Adventure Prefabs.

3. Select the new folder.

4. Right-click on top of it and create a new prefab.

5. Name the prefab Platform Target.

6. Drag the PlatformMesh object from the Hierarchy view onto the Platform Target prefab in the Project view.

The PlatformMesh is now an instance of the Platform Target prefab and its white cube icon has turned blue.

7. Rename the PlatformMesh to Target A.

Since it is already in the same place as the original platform, you can leave it in place and use it as one of the target positions.

8. Drag the Platform Target prefab from the Project view into the Hierarchy view.

9. Rename it Target B.

10. In the Scene view, move Target B away from the platform in the Z direction. See Figure 5-26.

Figure 5-26. *The two target platforms (A is in place over the original platform)*

11. Select the Platform Group object.

12. Drag Target A and Target B from the Hierarchy view onto their target parameters in the Inspector as shown in Figure 5-27.

Figure 5-27. *The PlatformMover script with both targets loaded*

13. Save the scene and save the project.

14. Click Play.

The PlatformGroup moves smoothly between the two targets (Figure 5-28).

Figure 5-28. *The Platform in action*

Having positioned them, we can now turn off their MeshRenderers so they will not be rendered in the scene. One of the beauties of the prefab is that by turning off its Mesh Renderer, it will be turned off in both of its children.

1. Stop Play mode.

2. Select the PlatformTarget prefab in the Project view.

3. Uncheck the Mesh Renderer component (see Figure 5-29).

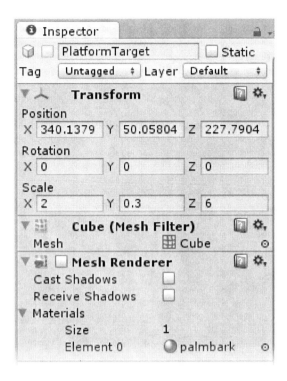

Figure 5-29. *Turning of the Mesh Renderer*

The two target platforms are no longer rendered in the scene.

    4.   Click Play.

    5.   Drive the First Person Controller onto the platform.

If your platform is low enough to drive onto, the First Person Controller gets taken for a ride. If not, use the spacebar to jump up onto your platform, or lower it so the First Person Controller can climb aboard (Figure 5-30).

Figure 5-30. *Going for a ride*

The default platform functionality is only a starting point for serious platform jumpers. We don't need more than the basics for our game, so we just need to be aware of what it can and can't do. Let's investigate.

6. Drive off the platform and position the First Person Controller in the path of the platform.

Depending on your platform height, the platform may push the First Person Controller out of the way or it may just go through it, occasionally picking it up and taking it for a ride. The important thing to note here is that the results are not consistent. You should investigate functionality fully so you know its pros and cons before deciding to add it to your game and spending time on asset creation.

Let's see what happens if the platform is taller.

7. Select the Platform object and change its Y Scale to **1**.

Half of the platform goes lower, but there's still have about half a meter above ground.

8. Move into the path of the moving platform again.

This time, the platform passes through the First Person Controller every time, as in Figure 5-31.

Figure 5-31. *The taller platform ignores the First Person Controller*

9. As the platform approaches again, press the spacebar to jump on to it as it gets close.

You should now be riding the platform again.

If you drive at the taller platform, the First Person Controller *might* be stopped, but unless it is in motion, collision is not detected. While there are things you can do to overcome this effect, they are generally costly and are not within the scope of our adventure game.

If you *do* want to use a moving platform in your game, you'll need to set up a system to prevent the player from getting near the platform while it is in motion. This could be a toll gate or barricade that the player can only enter at certain times. It could require the player to insert a token into a receptacle to activate the platform. You'd also need a means of preventing the player from jumping off the platform, which, of course, you'd need to disable to let him off and on at the correct times. All of this is possible and would indeed increase player enjoyment of the game, but you should always be aware of the work involved.

10. Change the platform Y Scale back to **0.3**.

11. Stop Play mode.

12. Select the PlatformTarget object in the Project view and turn its Mesh Renderer back on.

13. Select the Target B object and move it up about ten meters in the Scene view.

14. Turn off the PlatformTarget's Mesh Renderer.

15. Click Play.

16. Take a ride on the lifting platform (Figure 5-32).

Figure 5-32. *View from the top*

The First Person Controller is carried up to the new vantage point.

17. While you are up near the top, drive off the platform.

The First Person Controller falls gracefully to the ground.

Clearly we will need to design carefully to deal with the various aspects of the functionality. While you might be happy to let the player jump off the funicular while it is in motion, you'll want to prevent him from landing where it will be able to pass through him on the way back down. As this is a more complicated problem to solve, we will leave it for now and tackle walls.

18. Stop Play mode.

19. Save your scene and save the project.

Collision Walls

In travelling around your terrain, you've had firsthand experience with the topography of both the terrain, and the moving platform. You've also had a run in or two with the collider on the banyan tree. We need colliders on anything we don't want the player to be able to pass through. Unity can generate Mesh Colliders for imported meshes, such as buildings, and offers several primitive colliders as well for more efficient collision detection.

As with the platform, walls in Unity have some peculiarities that need to be investigated.

1. Select the First Person Controller.

2. Use Align View to Selected from the GameObject menu.

3. Create a cube and position it in front of the First Person Controller.

4. Name it **Wall**.

5. Set its Scale parameters to **0.3** for X, **5** for Y and **6** for Z.

6. Move the wall up in the Y direction so only a small bit intersects the ground.

7. Move it away from the platform.

8. Rotate it about **5** degrees on the Y so it does not face the viewport exactly and the First Person Controller will approach it at a slight angle.

9. Drag the TestBark material onto it.

10. Zoom back in the viewport until you can see above it quite a bit. See Figure 5-33.

Figure 5-33. *The wall object and adjusted Scene view*

The Green bounding box you see in the Scene view is the Collider that was automatically generated when the cube was created. In the Inspector, you'll see that it is a simple Box Collider.

  11.   Click Play and drive into the wall.

The First Person Controller is stopped.

  12.   Use the spacebar to jump as you try to move forward.

It does not get you any farther.

  13.   Stop Play mode.

  14.   In the Inspector, rotate the wall to **20** degrees on its Z axis.

  15.   Click Play and drive at the wall again.

The First Person Controller may *slide* left or right along the wall as you continue to try to go forward, but it does not climb the wall.

  16.   Once again, use the spacebar to jump while trying to move forward.

This time, you can easily scale the wall and go over the top if you move at a bit of an angle.

While this may be quite entertaining, it means that your players can probably get to places you'd prefer they do not. You could turn off jumping altogether in the Motor script, but it is does make navigation more interesting when allowed.

17. Stop Play mode.

18. Select the First Person Controller.

19. In the Inspector, in the Jumping section of the Character Motor component, set the Base Height to **0.5** and the Extra Height to **0**.

20. Click Play and attempt to climb or jump the wall again.

It is more difficult, but tenacious gamers may discover that moving sideways a bit as they jump and move forward will eventually allow them to reach the top.

⬛ **Tip**   Always assume that if something can be done, it will be done, regardless of how pointless it seems to you as the author of the game.

So far we know that a player will not be able to scale a fully perpendicular wall. Anything with even a small amount of slope, however, is subject to abuse. Because Unity does not differentiate between floor and wall collision surfaces, we will need a way to prevent unwanted climbing of some buildings or other artifacts. Rather than getting deep into the Character Motor code and worrying about up vectors and the like, we will take the artist's way out and simply block access with a nonrendering planar object.

1. Stop Play mode.

2. Again, in the Character Motor component, temporarily set the Base Height to **3** and the Extra Height back to **1**.

3. Create a Plane object and position it about three-quarters of the way up the wall.

4. Adjust its size and position to make it an effective barrier, as shown in Figure 5-34.

Figure 5-34. *The plane in position as a ceiling*

5. Click Play and test the new barricade.

The First Person Controller still gets through it.

6. Select the plane.

7. Rotate the Scene view until you can see underneath the plane...

Figure 5-35. *The underside of the plane*

And nothing shows!

In the Inspector you'll see that the plane has a Mesh Collider. Since there are no faces on the backside of the plane, no collision detection is taking place. The other collider types (Box, Sphere, and Capsule) use only the primitive shape of their collider and are not dependent on the object mesh for collision.

It would seem you could solve the problem by flipping the plane over.

8. Set the plane's X rotation to **180**, as shown in Figure 5-36.

Figure 5-36. *The plane flipped upside down—note the orientation of the transform gizmo*

    9.   Click Play and try to jump over the wall again.

This time the First Person Controller hits the ceiling and falls back down.

Since you can now see the plane from the underside, we need to either turn off its Mesh Renderer or remove that component altogether.

    10.   Stop Play mode.

    11.   Select the Plane.

    12.   Right-click over the Mesh Renderer component and Remove it.

The plane is no longer drawn in the Game window, but the Mesh Collider is drawn in the Scene view (see Figure 5-37).

Figure 5-37. *The Plane's Mesh Collider showing now that the Mesh Renderer was removed*

Another experiment worth trying is to see what happens to the First Person Controller when the platform rises through it.

13. Move the plane so it is in the path of the rising platform.

14. Click Play and jump onto the platform.

When the First Person Controller gets to the plane, it is pushed down through the platform. Apparently, the First Person Controller is inheriting the movement from the platform and collision detection against the plane is registered.

A final test might provide the means for keeping the player from jumping off a moving platform.

15. Set the Z rotation of the plane to **90** degrees in the Inspector (Figure 5-38).

Figure 5-38. *The Plane as an invisible wall*

16. Click Play and try to drive through the invisible plane.

You will find that you can pass through it from the back side but not the front side.

If you surround the platform with planes for collision, you could allow the player to get onto the platform, but not off, thereby preventing him from jumping off midway.

The problem then becomes how to let him disembark when he reaches the plane's destination.

17. Stop Play mode.

18. Select the plane.

19. In the Inspector, in the object's Mesh Collider component, check Is Trigger.

20. Click Play.

21. Now try going through the plane from both sides.

The collider no longer acts as a barrier.

■ **Tip** The Is Trigger feature does not update automatically from the Inspector during play mode.

Let's create a simple script to toggle the IsTrigger variable off and on with a key press. Before assuming a particular functionality will work, you should always test first.

22. Select the Adventure Scripts folder.

23. Create a new JavaScript.

24. Name it `ToggleIsTrigger`.

25. Open it in the script editor.

In this script, we will watch for a key down in the `Update` function. When one is detected, we will call another function that we will create—a user-defined function. If you think that you'll use a particular procedure over and over and call it from different places or objects, it may be worth putting in its own function. An example might be a three-way light switch. Three separate switches can toggle the light off and on, but only the light contains the code to handle the functionality. Each of the switches would call the light's on/off function. In the case of the `IsTrigger` toggle, you might test it with a key press, but later you might need to press a button to toggle it or even let it be triggered by some other event. Let's name the function `ToggleTrigger`.

26. Change the `Update` function as follows:

```
function Update () {

    // call the ToggleTrigger function if the player presses the t key
    if (Input.GetKeyDown ("t")) ToggleTrigger();

}
```

■ **Tip**   When a method or object-specific function returns a Boolean value, true or false, there is no need use the `==` operator. In the conditional you just wrote, the `if(Input.GetKeyDown("t"))` could also be written as `if(Input.GetKeyDown("t") == true)` and produce the same results.

Now let's create the `ToggleTrigger` function. You'll need to check the state of the collider's `isTrigger` variable and then reset it depending on the result. At its simplest, you could write it in just a few lines.

27. Add the following somewhere below the `Update` function:

```
function ToggleTrigger () {

    if (collider.isTrigger == true) collider.isTrigger = false;
    else collider.isTrigger = true;

}
```

When you are first testing code and functionality, it's worth adding some `print` statements so you can see what's happening. Note that the `if` conditional doesn't require curly brackets as long as only one command is given if the condition evaluates to true (the if), or only one is specified when the condition does not evaluate to true (the else).

Think of the `if` and `else` as hands that can each hold only one object. The curly brackets are like a shopping bags—the hands still hold a single object (the shopping bag), but the bag can contain lots of objects.

28. Change the `ToggleTrigger` function to include a couple of `print` statements:

```
function ToggleTrigger () {

        if (collider.isTrigger == true) {
                collider.isTrigger = false;
                print ("Closed");
                }
        else {
                collider.isTrigger = true;
                print ("Opened");
                }
}
```

29. Save the script.

■ **Tip**   Function names always start with a capital letter. Like variable names, function names may not contain spaces, start with numbers or special characters, or be reserved words. To make the names easier to read, you will often see underscores instead of spaces, or the first letter of each word capitalized.

---

30. Drag the `ToggleIsTrigger` script onto the `Plane` object.

31. Click Play.

32. Select the Plane and watch its Is Trigger parameter in the Inspector.

33. Press it to toggle the Is Trigger off and on. Try driving forward and backward through the invisible plane.

You should be able to drive through from both sides when Is Trigger is turned on, but only from the back side if Is Trigger is off.

So far we have used the IsTrigger parameter for one of its side effects—to turn off physical collision. Its *designed* purpose is to allow an object, such as the First Person Controller, to trigger an event or action by passing into or out of a (frequently) non-rendered object containing a collider.

Going back to our hypothetical light example, picture a long hallway with sensor lights. Each light has a zone that when entered turns the light on and when exited turns the light off. The zones are Box colliders and you can use the `OnTriggerEnter` and `OnTriggerExit` functions to trap the events and send the message to the light.

Without going to the trouble of creating collision walls for the platform, you can still get a feel for how you can use a collider to manipulate the `isTrigger` parameter of other colliders. Let's set up a GameObject that will turn the `isTrigger` parameter of the plane off and on when the platform enters and exits its collider.

34. Stop Play mode.

35. Deactivate the Wall object by unchecking the box at the top of the Inspector (Figure 5-39).

CHAPTER 5 ■ NAVIGATION AND FUNCTIONALITY

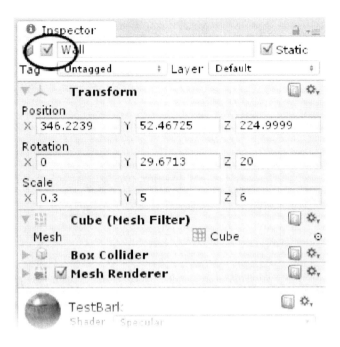

Figure 5-39. *The activate checkbox for the Wall object*

■ **Tip** Deactivating an object not only prevents it from being drawn in the scene, it also disables its collider and any other components. Note that the object's name is grayed out in the Hierarchy. You will make good use of the Active property of GameObjects when you start adding interactive objects as the game progresses.

---

36. Select the PlatformTarget in the Project view and turn on the Mesh Renderer.

37. Create an Empty GameObject.

38. Name it **TheTrigger**.

39. With TheTrigger still selected, choose Physics from the Components menu and add a Box Collider.

40. Scale the collider by using the X,Y, and Z Size parameters in the Box Collider component in the Inspector.

41. Position the collider so it is high enough off the ground to prevent the First Person Controller from running into it and so it is stretched between the two platform targets as shown in Figure 5-40.

Figure 5-40. *The Trigger's collider sized and positioned*

Make sure to check the collider in a Top view for alignment and position (Figure 5-41).

Figure 5-41. *The Top view of the collider*

    42. Make sure TheTrigger is selected so you can see the collider in the Scene view.

    43. Click Play.

    44. Move the First Person Controller onto the moving platform.

    The First Person Controller is pushed off the platform as the platform moves into the collider (Figure 5-42).

Figure 5-42. *First Person Controller being pushed off the platform*

45. Stop Play mode.

46. Check the Is Trigger parameter in the Inspector.

47. Click Play and test.

The First Person Controller no longer gets pushed off the platform (Figure 5-43).

Figure 5-43. *The First Person Controller is no longer affected by the collider.*

Now we need to create a script that that sends a message to the plane to tell it to toggle its Is Trigger parameter.

1. Stop Play mode.

2. Select the Adventure Scripts folder.

3. Create a new JavaScript.

4. Name it `SendMessageOnTrigger`.

5. Open it in the editor.

6. Delete the default `Update` function and add the following:

```
var sendToObject  : GameObject;

function OnTriggerEnter (object : Collider) {

        sendToObject.SendMessage("ToggleTrigger");

}
```

Let's see what is happening with this function.

The variable `sendToObject` is defined as a `GameObject` type, but the value is not yet provided. `SendToObject` will be the object that contains the script with the `ToggleTrigger` function you need to call.

Just as with the platform targets, you will need to drag and drop the actual object into it in the Inspector. The reason you can't specify the object when you declare the variable is that variables are read into the system *before* any of the scene objects are loaded and therefore do not yet exist.

The `OnTriggerEnter` function is an event-type function that is called when another object's collider first enters its collider. With the argument `object : Collider`, the colliding object is returned in case you need to do any condition-checking with it. The local variable `object` is declared as a `Collider` type. It gets its *value*, the colliding object's collider, when the event happens. Because it is a local variable, it is destroyed as soon as the function is finished, thereby freeing memory. You don't need to use the word **var** because it is understood that the argument is a variable.

The guts of the function, `SendToObject.SendMessage("ToggleTrigger")`, looks through the `sendToObject`'s scripts for one with a function named `ToggleTrigger`. When it finds one, it calls that script.

7. Stop Play mode.

8. Save the script.

9. Drag it onto TheTrigger.

10. Drag the Plane object onto its Send To Object parameter in the Inspector.

11. Click Play and watch the status line to see when the plane is "opened" or "closed."

Nothing appears to be happening.

12. Drive the First Person Controller onto the platform and let it go for a ride.

Now the status line reports when the plane's Is Trigger parameter is being toggled.

The Scripting Reference for `OnTriggerEnter` tells us that "*trigger events are only sent if one of the colliders also has a rigidbody attached.*" You can't see it, but the First Person Controller has its own simplified version of a rigidbody. To make the platform trigger the `OnTriggerEnter` event, you will need to add a rigidbody component to it.

13. Stop Play mode.

14. Select the Platform Group object.

15. From the Component menu ➤ Physics, select Rigidbody.

16. Click Play.

The intersection with TheTrigger is now registering, but the platform is sinking lower and lower (Figure 5-44).

Figure 5-44. *The sinking platform*

17. Stop Play mode.

18. Uncheck the Rigidbody's Use Gravity parameter in the Inspector.

19. Click Play.

The Platform triggers the intersection event but may be wobbling a bit.
Let's not forget to test it with the First Person Controller.

20. Drive the First Person Controller to the platform and jump aboard.

The platform skews wildly and the First Person Controller eventually falls off (Figure 5-45). There seems to be a small problem….

Figure 5-45. *Before freezing rotation on the Platform's Rigidbody component*

21. Stop Play mode.

22. In the Rigidbody component, check Freeze Rotation.

23. Click Play and take the First Person Controller for a ride on the platform again.

Everything works as expected now.

24. Select the PlatformTarget prefab in the Project view and deactivate its Mesh Renderer.

Now that you've had a first look at triggering events, let's get back to the script. The script toggles the plane's Is Trigger parameter only when the collider is entered. If you were indeed using the script to affect collision walls around the platform, you would want the exit event to toggle the plane's Is Trigger as well. As you might guess, there is an OnTriggerExit function.

1. Copy the OnTriggerEnter function and paste it below the original.

2. Change Enter in the name to Exit.

3. Save the script.

4. Watch the status line.

The message from the Plane's ToggleTrigger function shows that it is now being called when the platform enters the collider *and* exits it.

Let's not forget our First Person Controller.

Jump the First Person Controller onto the platform and watch the status line.

Now both objects, the First Person Controller and the platform, trigger the function call, so the messages changes quickly or don't appear to change at all. If you open the Console, you'll see that the function is working (Figure 5-46). (The console can be opened through the Window menu or by the keyboard shortcut found there.) It is now over-working in fact. This is where the argument that reports the colliding object comes in handy.

Figure 5-46. *The triggering objects being reported in the Console*

5. Inside both OnTrigger functions, just above the sendToObject.SendMessage line, add the following line:

```
print (object.name); // this is the name of the object triggered the event
```

6. Save the script and watch the results in the console.

Object Names

The most important concept to understand here is that an object's name *does not represent the object.* The *name* is only another parameter of the object. This is another reason why you can't type an object name as the value of a variable. The name is of type String. It is just a string of characters and does not represent the actual object.

For the script, you need to determine if the colliding object is the one you are interested in. In a shooter type game, you're less interested in the colliding object specifically and more interested in generalities. If the object is a projectile, it needs to send a message to whatever it hit to take damage points or even to be destroyed. For this adventure game, you need to be more specific. Let's add a variable that holds the only object we want to trigger the send message. You may be thinking that the Platform Group is the collider since that was what we added the rigidbody to, but a check of the console printout shows us that the Platform itself is what has the collider and was passed in as an argument (another good reason to print out the colliding objects).

1. Add the following variable beneath the **var** sendToObject line at the top of the script:

```
var correctObject: GameObject; //this is the only object we allow to trigger the event
```

2. Save the script.

3. Drag the Platform object onto the Correct Object parameter in the Inspector (Figure 5-47).

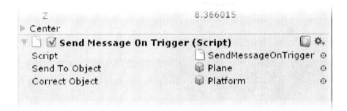

Figure 5-47. *The loaded parameters*

4. Change the sendToObject.SendMessage line in both OnTrigger functions to the following to add the conditional:

```
if(object == correctObject.collider) sendToObject.SendMessage("ToggleTrigger");
```

Now the only time the ToggleTrigger function will be called is when the argument (a collider object) that is passed in on intersection matches the collider component of the object you specified as the correct object (see Figure 5-48).

Figure 5-48. *The filtered collider—only the Platform calls the* `ToggleTrigger` *function*

(Opened or Closed is printed.)

As a final bit of functionality, let's see about making our little `SendMessageOnTrigger` script more generic.

The function being called is referred to by its name, a character string. Strings are easy to recognize because they are always enclosed in quotation marks. If you create a variable to hold the name of the function, you'll be able to use this script on other objects triggering other functions.

5. Add the following variable below the two existing variables at the top of the script:

```
var targetFunction : String; // the name of the function to call
```

6. Replace the "ToggleTrigger" with `targetFunction` in both of the `OnTrigger` functions.

7. Save the script.

8. After the Inspector has updated to show the new `targetFunction` variable, click in the blank space below the Platform entry to activate the text field.

9. Type in ToggleTrigger (see Figure 5-49).

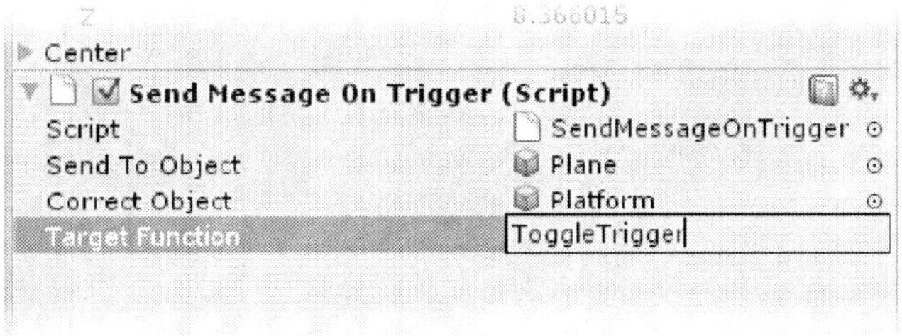

Figure 5-49. *The text entry for the Target Function*

▪ **Tip** Note that ToggleTrigger doesn't need quotation marks as it is in a text field that already expects a character string entry.

---

10. Comment out or delete the two print statements.

The final SendMessageOnTrigger script should look like this:

```
var sendToObject : GameObject;
var correctObject : GameObject; //this is the only object we want to trigger the event
var targetFunction : String; // the name of the function to call

function OnTriggerEnter (object : Collider) {

        //print (object.name); // this is the name of the object triggered the event
        if(object == correctObject.collider) sendToObject.SendMessage(targetFunction);

}

function OnTriggerExit (object : Collider) {

        //print (object.name); // this is the name of the object triggered the event
        if(object == correctObject.collider) sendToObject.SendMessage(targetFunction);

}
```

11. Click Play and see that the functionality remains the same.

12. Save the scene and save the project.

Your First Build

Now that you can travel around the environment and interact with some of it, you may as well try your first *build*. Because the project already contains three scenes, you'll need to specify which one you want.

1. From the File menu, select Build Settings (Figure 5-50).

Figure 5-50. *The Build Settings window*

2. Click the Add Current button at the lower right of the Scenes In Build window (Figure 5-51).

3. If there are any other scenes there that are checked, uncheck them.

4. Select your Target Platform as Windows or Mac.

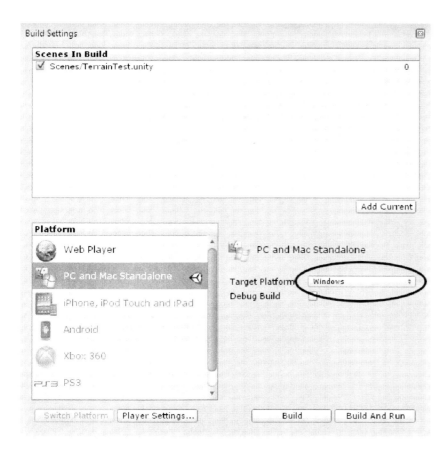

Figure 5-51. *The Build Settings window with the current scene loaded*

5. Click Build and Run.

You will be prompted to give a file name and location.

6. Name your scene Chapter5Navigation.exe.

As indicated by the button name, the game will be built and then immediately run.

The first thing you'll see is the configuration window (Figure 5-52), where the user can choose screen resolution and see or change the keyboard and mouse mapping. You will learn how to suppress this dialog to prevent the player from setting up conflicting keyboard controls.

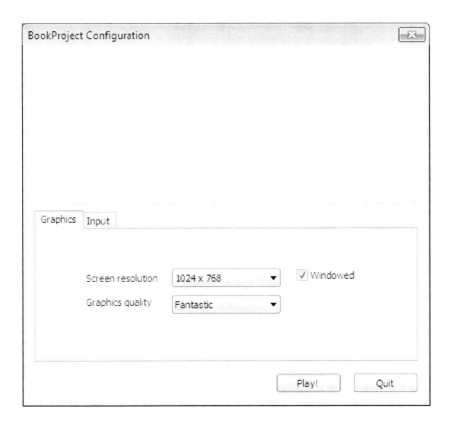

Figure 5-52. *The configuration window in Windows. (It will be slightly different on a Mac).*

7.   Click on the Input tab.

A pruned-down version of the Input Manager appears with all of the key assignments (see Figure 5-53).

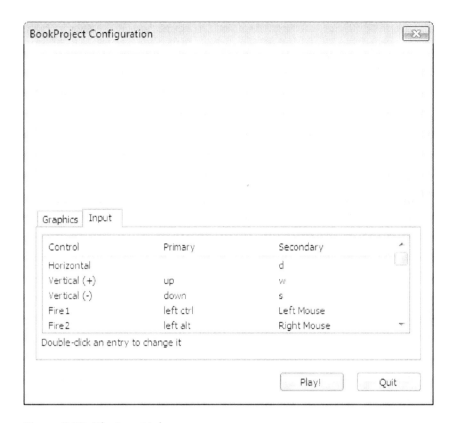

Figure 5-53. *The Input tab*

When creating a Unity .exe for Windows deployment, you will have the .exe file and a folder of the same name that contains the data (see Figure 5-54). If you wish to share your file at that stage, you will need to distribute both the folder and the .exe. For Mac deployment, you'll get one package with everything in it.

Figure 5-54. *The files associated with the runtime application in Windows*

8. Click Play and test the scene (Figure 5-55).

Don't forget the invisible wall—the platform will toggle it off and on, or you can use the **t** key.

Figure 5-55. *The scene running as an* .exe

Defining Boundaries

You may have discovered that you can fall off the edge of the world. Even with steep mountains around the edges, you can still use the jump technique to climb to the top and then jump off. If you think about what you've learned about collisions walls, you know you need something perfectly perpendicular to foil those pesky jumpers and climbers. You've seen a planar object used to provide a collision wall, but you've no doubt noticed that there's no Plane Collider, so you can assume it's not very economical. The best choice is a Box Collider for each side.

1. Use the Scene Gizmo to get to a Top view of the scene.

2. Zoom out in the Scene window until you can see the edges of the terrain, as shown in Figure 5-56.

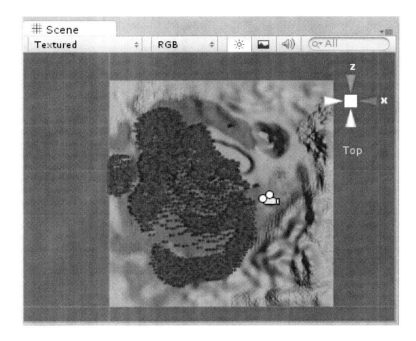

Figure 5-56. *The edges of the known world*

3. Create an Empty GameObject.

4. Name it **Terrain Boundaries**.

5. Create another Empty GameObject.

6. Name it **Boundary1**.

7. Add a Box Collider to Boundary1.

8. Adjust the Collider's Size to create a thin wall at the edge of the terrain.

9. Drag it into the Terrain Boundaries object (Figure 5-57).

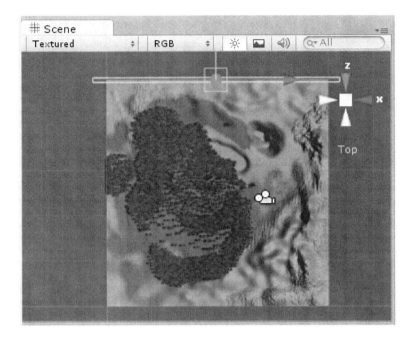

Figure 5-57. *One of the boundaries*

10. Clone Boundary1 to create the remaining three sides (Figure 5-58).

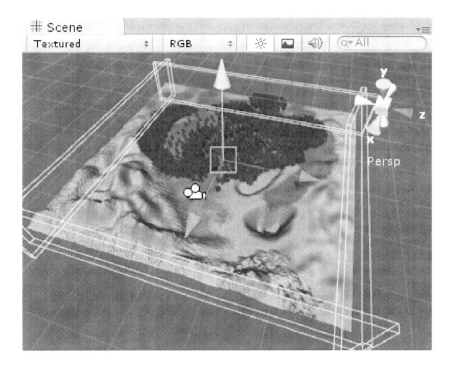

Figure 5-58. *The scene boundaries*

11. Save the scene and save the project.

Summary

In this chapter, you added player navigation to your test terrain by starting with the First Person Controller prefab and making a few changes. With the help of the Input Manager, you modified the shooter-type controls, WASD, to allow less-experienced gamers to use the arrow keys to turn instead of strafe. After turning on line numbers in the script editor, you added the code for arrow turning in the FPSInputController script to create your own version of the script, the FPAdventurerController. Since the arrow turns needed to be framerate-independent, you added that code to the FixedUpdate function rather than the regular Update function, as FixedUpdate is checked at set intervals rather than every frame.

In your version of the MouseLook script, MouseLookRestricted, you restricted mouse look to require the shift keys, the right mouse button, or any of the regular navigation keys. The restriction on the mouse look functionality will enable your player to interact with or pick objects in the scene without having the view spin wildly as he tries to put the cursor over a particular object.

By using the concept of the virtual buttons created in the Input Manager, you were able to use Input.GetButton after creating your own virtual buttons instead of hardcoding each individual key or mouse button with Input.GetKey and Input.GetMouseButton. You used the logical and, &&, and the logical or, ||, to expand your conditional statements to check for multiple conditionals.

From another component of the First Person Controller, the CharacterMotor script, you found where you could fine-tune navigation speeds and functionality. As one of the options was to enable platform functionality, you experimented with a simple moving platform to explore its capabilities and limitations. You discovered that your platform didn't exhibit consistent-enough behavior to use without a lot of extra thought and design.

With the platform targets, you learned to create prefabs for objects that would have multiple instances in a scene to allow for more economical handling. You found you could remove or disable components such as the Mesh Renderer or Colliders to streamline the functionality of your objects.

This introduced the concept of collision walls to block the player from going through objects. You discovered that a fully perpendicular wall will stop the First Person Controller from getting through an object with a collider, but that if the wall was not perpendicular, the player could possibly use the jump action to climb the wall. Rather than delving into mathematical calculations to prevent this, you found that a simple plane object with its Mesh Collider would effectively block the action.

During your experiments with the plane object, you found that a collider's Is Trigger parameter would let you pass through an object and even trigger an event as long as one of the objects, or its children, also contained a rigidbody component. With the help of the `SendMessage` function, you learned how to call functions when intersection was caught by the `OnTriggerEnter` and `OnTriggerExit` event functions. By using the `String` variable type, you were able to make your code more generic by letting a variable store the name of the user-defined function you created. You also found that a GameObject's name was merely a parameter of the object, of type String, and did not represent the GameObject itself. Finally, you built your first `.exe` of the scene, only to discover you still needed to create collision walls around the perimeter of the terrain.

In the next chapter, we will be developing our cursor functionality so we can have full control over its behavior. Cursors, after all, are key to the point and click adventure genre.

■ ■ ■

CHAPTER 6

Cursor Control

Cursor Visibility

In point and click games, cursors are a large part of the user experience. Besides showing the user where the cursor pick point is, they often give the user clues as to when they are over an action object and even the type of interaction expected. But when you are navigating about the scene, seeing the cursor flashing off and on tends to squelch the "suspension of disbelief." As long as you know when the navigation is happening, you probably ought to take the opportunity to hide the cursor.

One of the more confusing problems when first learning to script in Unity is knowing where to put the bit of code shown in the Scripting Reference or other sample source for testing. Since the cursor is not related to a particular object in the scene, the code to control it could go in any script's Update function as it needs to be checked every frame. For this test, you will create an empty GameObject to hold your small test script.

1. Open the TerrainTest scene in Unity that you created in the previous chapter.

2. Save the scene as CursorControl in the Scenes folder.

3. Deactivate the Plane, the Wall, and TheTrigger at the top of the Inspector.

4. Save the scene.

5. Create an empty GameObject.

6. Name it ScriptHolder.

7. In the My Scripts folder, create a new JavaScript.

8. Name it HideCursor.

9. Open it in the script editor.

It is time for a design decision. You know you don't want the cursor to appear when the player is navigating the scene so you need to check for the virtual buttons involved in navigation: Horizontal, Vertical, and Turn. If any of them are being pressed, the cursor should be hidden. The decision is whether to have it show during mouse look while the player is stationary. Since looking is a type of navigation, let's include the virtual ML Enable button in the conditional (but you may leave it out if you wish).

10. To hide the operating system cursor, add the following lines inside the Update function:

```
if (Input.GetButton("Horizontal") || Input.GetButton("Vertical") ||
```

```
   Input.GetButton("Turn") || Input.GetButton("ML Enable") ){
    // a navigation key is being pressed, so hide the cursor
   Screen.showCursor = false;
   }
```

11. Just above the last curly bracket of the Update function, add:

```
else {
// no navigation keys are being pressed, so show the cursor again
Screen.showCursor = true;
}
```

12. Save the script.

░ **Note**   In your conditional, you have used `Input.GetButton` because it returns a true or false value when the virtual button or key is down. You could also use `Input.GetAxis` even though it returns numbers, which are less intuitive. If you eventually plan on creating apps for iPhone or iPad, `Input.GetAxis` is the one to use as it has no mouse button functionality!

---

13. Drag it onto the `ScriptHolder` object in the Hierarchy view.

14. Click Play and test navigation.

The cursor may or may not disappear as expected. If not, it should in maximize mode.

15. Turn off Play mode.

16. At the top of the Game window, turn on Maximize on Play, circled in Figure 6-1.

Figure 6-1. *Maximize on Play*

    17. Now click Play.

The Game view window is maximized (Figure 6-2) and now the cursor behaves as expected: it disappears when you are moving.

Figure 6-2. *The maximized game window*

> 18. Turn off Play mode and turn off Maximize on Play.

Let's see what happens when the First Person Controller is riding on the platform.

> 19. Click Play again.

> 20. Drive the First Person Controller onto the platform.

The cursor is visible while the First Person Controller is passively riding the platform. On the off chance you want to have an action object that the player must interact with while enroute, such as picking an orchid off a rocky cliff face or stealing an egg out of a bird's nest, you can consider it acceptable.

> 21. Stop playback.

> 22. Save your scene and project.

Custom Cursors

As mentioned, a big part of point and click adventurer games is the cursor. In the first person variety, when navigation stops, the user is free to scan the objects in the view or frustum to see if any objects are action objects.

Tip The viewing *frustum* is the area of the 3D world that can be seen within the game's viewport at runtime or in Play mode. If the player turns and an object is no longer visible in the scene, it is considered "out of the frustum." The state of an object in respect to the frustum is important in that any manner of things can be done to improve frame rate such as stopping calculations on looping animations.

For your purposes, you will consider an action object something that can be put into inventory or will animate when picked; it's something that is a critical part of the game/story.

Typically, to identify an action object, the cursor might change color or appearance. In more stylized games, the action object itself might change color or tint. Once the cursor picks an object, it will usually either be turned off while the object animates, or, if the object is an inventory object, it (or a 2D icon representing it) could become the cursor. One of the fun features of adventure games is finding out which items can be combined to make a third, more useful object.

In Unity, 2D sprites and GUI (graphical user interface) objects are handled quite differently than 3D mesh objects. Unity's camera layering system will allow you to overlay mesh objects onto your 3D world space, but the mesh objects will rarely appear scaled to fit the objects with which you wish to interact depending on the player's location in the scene. Using 2D textures as cursors will involve a little work but provide a great amount of flexibility.

Cameras have a built-in GUI layer that automatically draws 2D objects into 2D screen space, layered on top of the 3D world. UnityGUI is a purely scripted means of drawing 2D objects onto the screen; it's handy for menus and controls but is less intuitive for artists. For now, you'll experiment with a tangible object that can be seen and manipulated from the Hierarchy view.

GUI Layer

1. In the Project view, create a new folder.

2. Name it Adventure Textures.

3. From the Assets menu, select Import New Asset.

4. From the downloadable code Book Assets folder ➤ Textures folder, select GamePointer.tif (Figure 6-3).

5. Select the image in the Project view.

Figure 6-3. *The GamePointer image in the Inspector*

Texture Importer

The Texture Importer comes with several handy presets as well as the Advanced option for full control. Let's take a quick look at it just to see the possibilities.

1. In the Texture Type drop-down at the top of the Texture Importer, select Advanced.

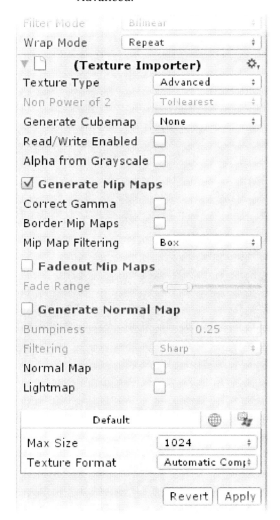

Figure 6-4. *The advanced parameters*

Take a look at the parameters in the Inspector (Figure 6-4). Since the texture will only be used as a cursor in 2D screen space, it doesn't need to be Mip mapped. This will save memory.

MIP MAPPING

Mip mapping is when an image is copied and reduced in size and clarity to provide blurrier images at greater distances. This reduces the nasty flickering as the view is changed. As an example, picture a black and white checker texture. As the texture gets farther back into 3D space, there are less and less pixels to represent the black checkers and the white checkers. At some point it is a tossup as to whether the pixel will be black or white. In one frame, it may be black, but in the next, it may be white. This causes a flickering known as *artifacting*. By scaling the image down by powers of two, the successive images are blurrier and blurrier, eliminating or greatly reducing artifacting.

Mip Maps for a checker texture at 256, 128, 64, and 32.

You may also notice in the Preview window that the image is shown as an RGBA Compressed DXT5 image. Unity converts image formats to the .dds format, so feel free to use larger file size images such as .tif, .psd, and others.

■ **Tip** Unity automatically updates images when changes are made to them so you may indulge yourself and leave them in a layered format in the Assets folder.

Fortunately, your needs for the GamePointer image are simple, so you can use a preset.

2. From the Texture Type dropdown, select GUI.

3. Just above the Preview window, click Apply.

The image is ready to use (Figure 6-5).

Figure 6-5. *The texture as GUI import type*

4. With the image still selected in the Project view, from the GameObject menu ➤ Create Other, select GUI Texture (Figure 6-6).

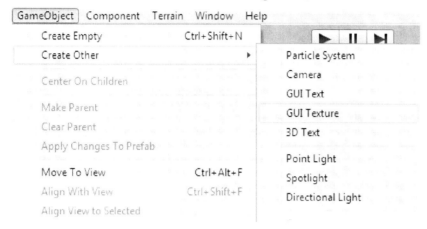

Figure 6-6. *New GUI Texture*

The image appears in the middle of the Game view (Figure 6-7).

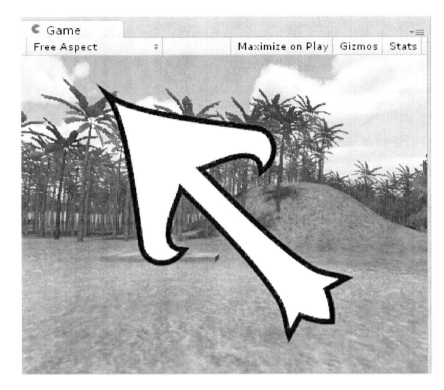

Figure 6-7. *The new GUI Texture in the Game window*

When created by selecting the texture first, the new GUI Texture object is given the name of the texture.

5.   If you choose to use your own texture, rename the new GUI Texture object GamePointer.

The GamePointer object will be referenced by name by various other objects throughout this book's project and any other games where you use the scripts you're creating here. You may not rename this object.

■ **Tip**   When an image is selected before the GUI Texture gameobject is created, the sprite or screen blit will be made the exact size of the image and will be given the image's name as well.

A bit of history: The term *blit* originated as an acronym (Berryman Logical Image Technique) whereby copying a rectangle on the screen and *blitting* it into another position on a computer screen was an early means of 2D animation.

---

6.   Click in the Game view to move the focus to that window.

7.   Press the spacebar to toggle the view to maximum.

Note that the GUI Texture remains the same size.

8.   Toggle the view back and adjust the Game view window size by hovering the cursor over the edge until you get a resize icon, then drag the window smaller (Figure 6-8).

The pointer image remains the same size.

Figure 6-8. *The squashed Game window*

Before you can decide how big the GUI Texture object should be, you need to decide on the size of the window when the game is published. As you may remember from the Configuration window that popped up before your test game was played, the user can be allowed to change the screen size. As you may guessed, because 2D UI objects do not scale to keep their size relative to the screen size, allowing the user to change it would mean a lot of extra scripting on your part. While you may choose to go that route eventually, for now you'll look into constraining the resolution and preventing the player from making changes.

⬛ **Note**   Near the end of the project you'll see that you can force screen mode and screen size in the Player Settings, but this gives you a good way to learn about the Screen functions that are useful throughout the project, so let's experiment with them.

If you do a search for resolution in the scripting help, you will see several useful resolution related topics. Let's start with Screen.SetResolution.

The code and description looks pretty straightforward. You feed it an X and a Y dimension and use a Boolean true/false to tell it to use full screen or not. The question is the usual if you are new to scripting and/or Unity: where to use the code and what function to put it under.

Since this is something that should be handled at the start when the game is loaded, let's create an object just for holding scene settings.

1. From the GameObject menu, create a new Empty GameObject.

2. Name it Control Center.

3. In the Adventure Scripts folder, create a new JavaScript and name it GameManager.

4. Open it in the editor.

The GameManager object will be referenced by name by various other objects throughout this project and any other games where you use these scripts. You may not rename this object.

So far, you have put code in the Update function so it will be evaluated every frame or the FixedUpdate function when it needs to be evaluated at a constant rate. For the starting settings, however, you need to look at two new functions: the Awake function and the Start function.

The Awake function is used to initialize any variables or scene states before the game starts but after all objects have been created. It is always called before the Start function. The Start function is where you can pass variables to scripts that will need them. As with Update, any script can have its own Awake and Start functions, so theoretically, you could set the size of the game window anywhere. Logically, you will want to be able to find the scene settings script or scripts quickly, hence the creation of the GameManager script.

A published exe file will allow the user to change the screen resolution on startup. If you have a HUD or other GUI elements that could be impacted by view resolution, you may need to add code to internally compensate for screen resolution. For now, however, you'll just force a resolution override. You may wish to comment it out after you have tested it. Unity defaults to using pixel size and location with its GUI elements but allows you to position parent groups from the sides or center, so this may not impact the visual layout of your GUI as the screen is resized.

1. In the GameManager script, change the Update function to an Awake function.

2. Add the following line inside its curly brackets so it looks as follows:

```
function Awake () {

    Screen.SetResolution (1024, 768, false);

}
```

3. Save the script.

4. Drag it onto the Control Center object.

5. At the top of the Game view, click the left-most button.

6. Choose Standalone (1024 × 768), one of the options in Figure 6-9.

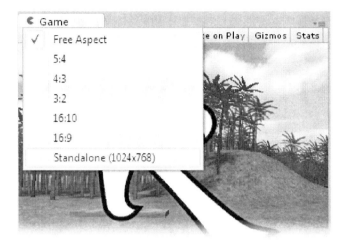

Figure 6-9. *Game view settings*

7. Toggle Maximize on Play (Figure 6-10).

8. Click Play.

Figure 6-10. *The window at game resolution and/or aspect ratio*

Now you can see how big the cursor will appear. In your case, it happily occupies a large portion of your game window. Obviously, you need to make some adjustments.

9. Stop playback.

10. Select the GamePointer GUI Texture object from the Hierarchy view.

11. In the Pixel Inset section, change its size from 256 × 256 to 32 × 32.

12. Change its X and Y offsets to -16 (half of its new size).

Figure 6-11. *The resized GUI Texture object*

As you can see in Figure 6-11, allowing some program (like a game engine) to scale an image down may give less than desirable results: note that the edges are jagged and nasty looking.

1. Select the Adventure Textures folder in the Project view.

2. From the Assets menu, select Import New Asset.

3. Import GamePointerSm from the Book Assets ➤ Textures folder.

4. In the Inspector, change its Texture Type to GUI.

5. Click Apply (you will be prompted to do so if you forget).

6. Select the GamePointer in the Hierarchy view.

7. Drag the GamePointerSm texture onto the Texture field or use the Browse icon next to the currently loaded GamePointer texture to select it from the Asset browser.

The new cursor image does not appear jagged as its shrunken predecessor did (Figure 6-12).

Figure 6-12. *The smaller version of the GamePointer texture*

BASE 2

If you are at all familiar with game texture assets, you may recognize that most are in powers of two. This is because computer memory is arranged in base two sized blocks. Images in pixel sizes that are powers of two fill the block entirely. An example would be an image that is 256×256 pixels. If that image was just one pixel larger in each direction, it would use up a 512 × 512 sized block—nearly four times as much memory! Therefore, whenever possible, the final image should be made in sizes such as 2, 4, 8, 16, 32, 64, 128, 256, 512, 1024, 2048, etc.

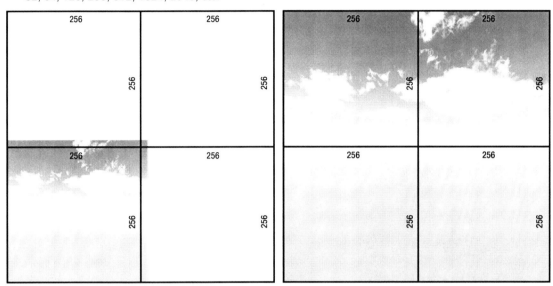

Memory usage

The image on the left takes up the same amount of memory as the image on the right. As soon as the image is even one pixel larger than the base two size, it uses the next chunk of memory.

Now that you've made some decisions for the start of the game, you can probably see how you could allow the user to change both the screen resolution and mode at any time during the game, should you wish to. Just remember that it require a lot of math on your part any time you add 2D elements of any type.

8. Set the Game window back to Free Aspect.

9. Turn off Maximize on Play.

10. Save your scene and project.

Tip   you can see the GUI objects in the Scene view by toggling on the Game Overlay button.

Color Cues

Now that you have shrunk your cursor into an acceptable size, let's try a few experiments on the cursor texture or image.

1. Select the GamePointer object in the Hierarchy view.

2. In the Inspector, find the Color parameter in the GUITexture section and click on the color swatch to bring up the Color dialog.

3. Change the color while watching the results in the Game view (Figure 6-13).

Figure 6-13. *Changing the cursor color*

4. When you find a color you like, write down its RGBA numbers for later use, then return the color to white.

Cursor Position

In Unity, in order to use a custom texture as a cursor, you need to turn off the OS (operating system) cursor, then track its position and feed it to your custom GUI Texture. Since there are several tasks that must be managed with your cursor, it makes sense to create a script for that very purpose.

1. Create a new JavaScript in your Adventure Scripts folder.

2. Name it CustomCursor.

3. Open it in the script editor.

Getting and assigning a cursor position is obviously something that needs to be done at least every frame, so it belongs inside the Update function. You will also add offsets to put the actual pointer in the correct position.

4. Add the following code inside the Update function so it looks as follows:

```
function Update () {
    // gets the current cursor position as a Vector2 type variable
    var pos = Input.mousePosition;

    // feed its x and y positions back into the GUI Texture object's parameters
    guiTexture.pixelInset.x = pos.x;
    guiTexture.pixelInset.y = pos.y - 32; // offset to top
}
```

5. Save the script.

6. Drag it onto the GamePointer object.

7. Click Play and move the cursor to the middle of the Game view.

Your brand new cursor will not appear if your game window is small!

8. Move the cursor to the bottom left of the view.

The custom cursor now comes to the center of the viewport. It looks like you've got an offset issue.

9. Stop playback.

10. In the Inspector, look at the values for the GamePointer's X and Y Transforms.

They are both 0.5, which explains the large offset.

11. Set them both to 0.0 to line the custom cursor up with the OS cursor.

Tip   GUI transforms are shown as a percentage of screen; full width and height is 1.0.

---

12. Click Play and test again.

If curiosity has gotten the best of you and you have tweaked the X and Y Pixel Inset, you will have discovered that it reflects the screen position offset from the transforms. Rather than doing a bunch of math, let's add the offset to the positioning code in the script. If you are using your own cursor image, you may need to adjust the offset on the Y position or add an offset to the X position.

13. Make any adjustments necessary to the offsets in the script.

14. Save the script.

Now the custom cursor should match the OS cursor position better. Don't worry if things are not exact. You'll eventually add a color cue to let players know when they are over an action object; this will also allow you to get creative with cursor icons as the player picks up various action objects for use.

15. Toggle on Maximize on Play.

16. Click Play again.

17. Move the cursor about the viewport, watching the Pixel Inset values change in the Inspector.

18. Stop Play mode.

Managing a GUITexture Cursor

You will see that the OS cursor disappears when you are navigating the scene, but your new custom cursor does not. Thinking back, you may remember that you added code to your ScriptHolder script to hide and show the OS cursor.

With the advent of your spiffy new custom cursor, you'll need to change things a bit. First off, since you will no longer need the OS cursor at all, you ought to turn it off at the very start of the scene. The most logical place to take care of that task is probably the GameManager script you made for the Control Center object, as it's the brains of your game.

1. Open the GameManager script in the editor.

So far it only has an Awake function. You will be doing several things at startup eventually, and many will depend on all objects being loaded and read, so this time you will put your code in a Start function.

2. Add the following code to the script below the Awake function:

```
function Start () {

    Screen.showCursor = false; // hide the os cursor

}
```

3. Save the script.

You can now remove the ScriptHolder since you will no longer be using the OS cursor.

4. Select the ScriptHolder object and delete it from the scene or move it into the MyScripts folder.

Next, you need to create a script similar to the HideCursor script and have it hide and show your custom cursor instead of the OS cursor. Because it is a GUITexture object, you need to see what will turn it off and on. In the earlier test scene, you discovered that you could prevent objects from being drawn on screen by disabling a mesh object's Mesh Renderer.

Take a moment to refresh your memory.

5. Select the Platform Target prefab in the Project folder.

6. Check and uncheck its Mesh Renderer in the Inspector view.

The target platforms are revealed and then hidden in the Scene view.

7. Select the GamePointer in the Hierarchy view.

In the Inspector, there's a check box next to the GUITexture label.

8. Uncheck it and click Play.

You will need to click the Game view to change the focus to see whether it is there or not. It is not showing.

9. Check it to enable the GUITexture and once again click in the Game view.

The custom cursor is once again being drawn, so it looks like you have a means of turning the GamePointer object off and on. You just need to know how to write it.

1. Stop Play mode.

2. Turn the GUITexture component on again.

3. In the Scripting docs, do a search for GUITexture.

4. Choose the first in the list: GUITexture.

Under the Inherited Variables list, the first thing you see is enabled. Using dot notation, write something like

```
guiTexture.enabled = false;
```
Since the GUITexture it is referring to needs to be the GUI object you want turned off, let's add the line to a script that is already on the GamePointer object: the CustomCursor script.

5. Open the CustomCursor script in the editor.

6. Add a Start function to put the line in as follows:

```
function Start () {

        guiTexture.enabled = false;   // disable the GUITexture object at start up

}
```

░ **Tip**   Function order in the script generally doesn't matter but it's traditional to list the functions in the order that they are used. After the script's variables, an Awake function would be first, then the Start function, followed by the Update, the FixedUpdate, and then event-based and user-defined functions.

This should turn it off when the scene is started.

7. Save the script.

8. Click play and watch the Inspector. The checkbox is unchecked as the game starts.

9. Just to make sure, click in the Game view to see if it is there or not.

It's not showing, so you are good to go.

Object-to-Object Communication

Now comes the tricky part and one of the most crucial concepts to understand in Unity: how to access one object's variables from another object's scripts. This will enable all of the individual objects to access generic settings, allow events on one object to trigger events on other objects, and generally tie all the game information together.

As mentioned, you can gain access to parents and children of GameObjects without too much trouble, but in order to allow "unrelated" objects to communicate, you must "introduce" them to each other first.

Hardcoding the objects into each other's code will require the object to exist in the scene; otherwise, you will get an error. Your game will have a few objects that must be named correctly in order for them to be accessed this way. Hopefully you have been heeding the warning about which object names you may not change. In this section, you will set up the functionality to keep track of whether the player is currently navigating through the scene or not in the GameManager script. This way the action objects can access it whenever their scripts are activated.

While you could just duplicate the check-for-navigation keys being pressed in each script that needs that information, having the same condition checked in multiple scripts every frame (remember, it's inside an Update function) is a waste of resources and could slow frame rate. As it turns out, you've already done that twice (once for the HideCursor and once for the MouseLookRestricted, so you really ought to only calculate it once, if possible, and have whatever scripts need it access it from a single location.

FRAME RATE

When asked what affects frame rate (the number of frames per second that the engine can output) most people are quick to reply "poly count" (the number of polygons in the scene). While this is certainly a major contributor, in reality almost everything contributes: the number of scripts being evaluated, the objects that are animating, the physics solutions being calculated, the GUI elements being rendered and monitored, the amount of textures stored in memory, the number of polygons within the view frustum at any one time, the network communications being sent back and forth, the shadows and shaders being calculated, and just about everything else. Unity's Profiler is a great help in finding where resources are bottlenecking and can help you streamline your code for games that need high frame rates or need to run well on mobile platforms where resources are more limited.

As you get deeper into your game creation, you will find other tasks and variables that will need to be accessed by multiple scripts, so you may as well use your GameManager script for that purpose.

GLOBAL VARIABLES

Some of you may already be familiar with the concept of global variables. Global variables in Unity are, at best, only global to the object they are on. While this makes it necessary for you to do a lot more work to access the variables from other objects, it makes it possible for the game to make better use of multiple processors and multi-threading.

1. Open the GameManager script.

At the top, create a new variable that will keep track of whether the player is navigating through the scene (i.e. pressing one of the navigation keys). Because it's only for internal use, let's make it private.

2. Add the following at the top of the script:

```
private var navigating : boolean;    // flag for navigation state
```

3. Below the Start function, add an Update function and add the code that checks for the keys being pressed.

```
function Update () {

    if (Input.GetButton("ML Enable") || Input.GetButton("Horizontal") ||
        Input.GetButton("Vertical") || Input.GetButton("Turn")) {
        navigating = true;
    }
    else {
        navigating = false;
    }

}
```

Tip   Flags are merely variables whose values are watched for use in conditionals. A variable named doorLocked could be considered a flag; if doorLocked is true, the user will not be able to interact with the doorknob to open the door. If doorLocked is false, not only could the user open it, but other events (such as randomly spawned monsters coming through the door) could be generated as well.

Flags can track more than simple true/false states. A sidewalk café might need a flag for the weather. If it is sunny and hot, the variable weather = 0; if it is raining, weather = 1; and if it is overcast, weather =2. If weather < 2, the umbrellas need to be put out. The weather constantly changes.

The conditional for navigating in the MouseLookRestricted script is slightly different so you can leave it as is. You do, however, need to tell the GamePointer object when to be visible according to the state of the navigating variable in the GameManager script. To change a variable on another object, the object doing so must be aware of the other object first.

1. Open GameManager script.

2. Below the navigating variable declaration, add a variable to hold the GamePointer object:

```
private var gamePointer : GameObject;
```

Tip   It generally doesn't matter in what order one declares variables, but it's usually easier to read if the variables that are exposed in the Inspector are listed before the private vars.

This line defines a variable called gamePointer of type GameObject. This gives you a means of introducing the GamePointer object to the Control Center gameObject so you can gain access its parameters.

Tip   Different scripts may use the same variable name but it does not follow that the variables share the same value. To do so, one or both must update the other.

Vars and private vars can share the same name as variables in other scripts. Even when they contain the same information, because they live in different scripts, they are not the same entity. Think of it as two people named John Smith. They both have the same name but live in different houses. John Smith on Maple Lane constantly checks with John Smith on 6th Street to see if he is in his house or out traveling about. Depending on the latter's status, the former will take appropriate action.

As you found out in an earlier chapter, you can't refer to an object by name when declaring a variable. You *could*, however, drag and drop an object into the value field for the variable in the Inspector. While this may seem like an easy solution, when you start adding action objects to the game, it will quickly get tedious dragging the same objects over and over. Because you won't be loading it in the Inspector, you can use a private variable for its type.

It turns out that once the GameObjects have been loaded, you can find them by name. Having already created a variable to hold the GamePointer object, you can assign it in the Start function when you find it.

3. Add the lines to the Start function below the Screen.showCursor line to complete the "introduction." It should looks as follows:

```
function Start () {

    Screen.showCursor = false; // hide the os cursor
    // assign the actual GamePointer object to the gamePointer variable
    gamePointer = GameObject.Find("GamePointer");

}
```

Now you can turn off the GUITexture on the GamePointer object directly from the GameManager script on the Control object.

4. In the Update function, below the navigating = true line, add the following:

```
gamePointer.guiTexture.enabled = false; // turn off the pointer
```

5. In the Update function, below the navigating = false line, add the following:

```
gamePointer.guiTexture.enabled = true; // turn on the pointer
```

6.   Save the script.

7.   Click Play and test.

The custom cursor now behaves as the original OS cursor did.

8.   Save the scene and the project.

Mouse Over Cursor Changes

Before you start working on mouse over events, you need to have an understanding of how mouse over works. The most important concept is that rather than the cursor constantly firing rays into the scene and then evaluating what it's over, an object can report when the cursor is over it. While it is safe to say you will only want a limited number of objects to trigger the mouse over event, it will be well worth your while to make one generic reusable script that will handle interactions. Since this script will get larger as you progress through the functionality of your game, let's start by defining some of your own functions in order to keep things tidier.

Your first order of business is to work out the mechanics of your cursor color change. By definition, if you're going to change the color, you will need to define the default color so you'll know what to return it to. As long as you're in the design process, you may as well plan on letting the author (and possibly the player, at some point) choose the mouse over color rather than hardcode it in. Since that should be an option in the game, let's add it to the GameManager script.

1.   Open the GameManager script.

2.   At the top of the script add:

```
var mouseOverColor = Color.green;
```

3.   Save the script.

Note the use of a pre-packaged color, Color.green. If you do a search through the scripting help for color and select the top choice, Color, you will see the other class variables.

Now you can easily change the color manually in the Inspector to the color of your choice at any time.

You may decide to use your own cursor image and that image may be more than just black and white. The best choice for the default color is white, so let's consider white the default color, as it will not interfere with the texture's image.

Your next task is to take the assigned color and create some user defined functions: one to change the color and one to change the color back.

1.   Open the CustomCursor script.

At the top, you need to gain access to the Control Center's GameManager script. Since the CustomCursor script is only used once, you'll set up a variable that you can drag the Control Center into manually by declaring its type without assigning a value in the script.

2.   Add the following:

```
var controlCenter : GameObject;
private var mouseOverColor : Color;
```

For both of the variables, you are just making space for the value by declaring the type it is.

3. Save the script.

4. Stop Play mode.

5. Select the `GamePointer` object.

6. Assign the `Control Center` object to the new `Control Center` variable in the Inspector.

By the time the `Start` function is called, all objects have been loaded, so that is when and where you need to place the color—before game play starts.

7. In the `CustomCursor`'s `Start` function, below the `guiTexture` line, add the following :

```
mouseOverColor= controlCenter.GetComponent(GameManager).mouseOverColor;
```

8. Save the script.

Let's take a closer look at this last addition. You are assigning the value of a variable that lives on another object's script to a variable of the same name on this object's script. When you disabled or enabled the `GamePointer`'s `GUITexture` component, all you had to do was tell it the object, the component, and the inherited variable. Both the `GUITexture` component and its enabled variable were already defined as being part of a `GUITexture` object. When the component is a script, a generic something you have written and added to the object ourselves, you have to identify it much as you did a `GameObject` when you found it by name. For scripts, use GetComponent(SomeScript). Unlike the `Find` function, you don't use quotation marks around the script's name, presumably because you are getting the script and not its name. Once you have the script component, you can use dot notation to get or assign the value of one of its variables, in this case its `mouseOverColor` variable.

Now that the `CustomCursor` script knows what color to use for mouse over, you need to create your own function that can be called from other objects to change the cursor color when the mouse goes over and off the object. As you have seen before, user-defined functions look the same as the system and event functions, except that you can choose their names. You'll call this function `CursorColorChange`. It will be a simple toggle to switch back and forth between the default white color and the specified mouse over color.

Let's also look at a new concept, that of passing an argument or value to a variable. You used this with the `OnTriggerEnter` function when it reported the object that intersected with it, but this time you'll be in charge of passing the argument as well as receiving it. Start by putting the name of the variable or argument and its type inside the function's parenthesis.

For the argument, you'll tell the function what state the cursor is in when you call the function so it will know which color to set it to.

1. In the `CustomCursor` script, add the following function below the `Update` function:

```
function CursorColorChange (colorize: boolean) {

    if (colorize)  guiTexture.color = mouseOverColor;

    else  guiTexture.color = Color.white;
}
```

2. Save the script.

In using a Boolean type for the value you pass in to your function, you don't really need to think of it as true or false; it's just as useful to think of it as 0 or 1. The cursor is either white or the mouse over color, one of two states. Let's consider the default color, white, to be state 0 and the mouse over color to be state 1. Reading through the function, if it was passed a false (0), it will change the color to the mouse over color; otherwise (else), it was passed a true (1), so it will turn it back to white.

You have had no control over the functions you have previously used; Awake and Start are called when you first start the game and Update and FixedUpdate are called every frame. A user-defined function, in contrast, can be called whenever you wish.

You will be calling the CursorColorChange function from inside a couple of system functions, OnMouseEnter and OnMouseExit. But you first need to make a very generic script to put on every action object.

1. In the Adventurer Scripts folder, create a new JavaScript.

2. Name it Interactor and open it in the script editor.

3. Delete the default Update function.

This script will need to talk to the GamePointer object to call the function you just created, so add the following lines to the new script:

```
// Gain access to these objects
var gamePointer : GameObject;

function OnMouseEnter () {

    gamePointer.SendMessage("CursorColorChange", true); // colorize the pointer
}
```

4. Save the script.

OnMouseEnter and OnMouseExit are similar to the OnTriggerEnter and OnTriggerExit functions you used in the previous chapter. They are all event type functions. As with their OnTrigger cousins, the OnMouse functions also require that the object has a Collider before they will work.

When you used the SendMessage function or method in the previous chapter, the only thing you sent was the name of the function you wanted to call. This time, separated by a comma, you send the argument that your function is expecting: type Boolean.

▓ **Tip**   User-defined function can hold as many arguments as needed. SendMessage, however, can only send a single message.

Before you can see the fruits of all your labor, you'll need to create a test object to mouse over.

1. Stop playback.

2. From the GameObject menu ➤ Create Other, select Sphere.

3. Move the sphere in the Scene view until you can see it in the Game view (Figure 6-14).

Figure 6-14. *The sphere in view*

4. Drag the Interactor script onto the Sphere.

5. Select the Sphere.

6. Drag the GamePointer from the Hierarchy view onto the Game Pointer parameter in the Inspector

7. Click Play and test the functionality.

The cursor changes color as it moves over the sphere. Next, you'll revert the color when the cursor moves off the object.

8. Add the following code to the Interactor script beneath the OnMouseEnter function:

```
function OnMouseExit () {

    gamePointer.SendMessage("CursorColorChange", false); // turn the pointer white

}
```

9. Save the script.

This function, as you would expect, is called when the cursor passes off the action object. Since your CursorColorChange function can handle either state, you send it a false this time to tell it to carry out the else clause.

10. Click Play and test the mouse over functionality.

Everything works as expected (Figure 6-15).

Figure 6-15. *The mouse over color change*

░ **Tip** You may experience cursor flickering between the custom cursor and the OS cursor. This will not happen when the Game view is maximized.

Now comes the fun part.

1. From the GameObject menu, create a Cube and a cylinder near the Sphere.

2. Drag and drop the Interactor script onto each of the new objects.

3. Select the Cube and drag and drop the GamePointer from the Hierarchy view to the Game Pointer parameter in the Inspector.

4. Repeat for the Cylinder.

5. Click Play and test the mouse over functionality with the new objects (Figure 6-16).

Figure 6-16. *The three action objects*

While the other scripts you have built will be reusable in future games, the Interactor script is a generic script that will be applied to every action item in your scene.

By exposing variables to the Inspector, you can customize the events associated with the individual action object without changing the actual Interactor script. An example of this is an informative (or entertaining) message on mouse over where the message differs for each object ("It is a solid looking cube, approximately one meter square" or "It is a featureless sphere suspended in thin air"). Eventually, the Interactor script will contain the functionality to deal with all types of interaction, no matter what action object it resides on.

Because the same script is on all three objects, when you make a change to it, all objects using it are updated.

6. Back in the Game view, move backwards from the objects you have added until they are only a few pixels in the viewport.

7. Stop and test the mouse over functionality.

It still works (Figure 6-17), which is probably not something you want to happen.

Figure 6-17. *Mouse over triggered from far, far away…*

Distance Check

In the early days of point and click adventures, the game was based on a series of beautifully rendered high resolution still shots (Cyan's Riven) or hand painted toon-style backgrounds (LucasArts' Curse of Money Island). Hotspots (the area on the image where the item was in the picture) were created manually for each still shot.

In real-time 3D, the action object itself becomes the hotspot whether it is near or far. As you have discovered, this opens up the possibility of opening doors or picking up buckets while several hundred meters away. While this could be part of the design in a game, to prevent your player from triggering things he can't even see, you'll limit the distance within which the player can interact with an object.

First, you'll need to get the distance the First Person Controller is from the action object, and then you'll check to see if it is within mouse over range. If it isn't within range, you need to skip the mouse over functionality.

Let's start by creating a function that will calculate the distance from the object to the camera. This is a very typical user-defined function; it can be found an almost any game with enemies that can turn to face you (and shoot if you are within range). The nice thing is that you need not understand the math that makes the script work to reap the benefit.

⬛ **Tip**   It pays to read through tutorials for other game genres (even if they don't interest you) because they may contain intriguing functionality that you can use in your game.

---

1.   In the Interactor script, add the following user-defined function:

```
function DistanceFromCamera () {

    // get the direction the camera is heading so you only process stuff in the line of sight
    var heading : Vector3 = transform.position - cam.transform.position;
    //calculate the distance from the camera to the object
    var distance : float = Vector3.Dot(heading, cam.transform.forward);
    return distance;
}
```

⬛ **Note**   In this function you see the use of a `Vector3` type variable. It expects a three-part value such as (X,Y,Z) or (R,G,B). A `Vector2` might expect (X,Y) and a `Vector4` might expect (R,G,B,A).

There's something else that's new in this function: it *returns* a value. When you see how the function is called, you will notice that the value returned by the function is being assigned directly to a variable.

Before you can get this working, however, you will need to define cam, the camera it is referencing. Rather than having to drag and drop it into the script every time you add it to a new action object, you can let Unity search the scene and find it for you—as you did with the `GamePointer` object in the `GameManager` script earlier. As long as you need only do that once in the `Start` function, you won't be slowing the rest of the game down. Avoid using this technique in the `Update` function, however.

2.   Add the following private variable beneath the gamePointer variable declaration:

```
private var cam : GameObject;
```

3.   Then add the following Start function above the mouse over functions:

```
function Start () {

    // search the scene for an object named "Main Camera" and assign it to the cam var
    cam = GameObject.Find("Main Camera");

}
```

■ **Note**   You may wonder why you didn't use this method to "introduce" some of other objects into script instead of declaring then using drag and drop. The catch with this method is that the name of the object you are looking for is hardcoded into the script. In the case of your game, so far either would work. Since you will eventually be replacing the GUITexture object, the drag and drop method will be less code to remove, so it was used to specify the GamePointer object.

Before you add some scripting to make use of your distance calculating function, you need to look into something you have not yet come across in your scripts. The last line inside the DistanceFromCamera function says **return** distance. The variable distance was declared and assigned a value in the previous line, so that is nothing new. But the word **return** is bold, indicating it is a reserved word.

Variables declared inside functions are *local* to that particular function. They are not accessible outside the function and are cleared on completion of the function. So in order to be able to access the distance variable, it would either have to be declared out with the regular script variables or its value passed out to whoever called the function in the first place.

On its own, *return* simply tells you to leave the function (and that will be useful very shortly). But when coupled with a variable, it sends the value of that variable back to where the function was called.

Right now you want to check the distance from the camera before you allow the cursor color change to happen.

1.   Add the following lines of code above the gamePointer.SendMessage line inside the OnMouseEnter function:

```
if (DistanceFromCamera() > 7) return;
```

You call the function with DistanceFromCamera() and it returns the distance it calculated in the function. You then immediately check to see if that returned value or distance is less than 7 meters. If not, this return bumps you out of the OnMouseEnter function before the color change function can be called. If it's evaluated as less than 7 meters, the rest of the contents of the OnMouseEnter function are carried out and your cursor's color is changed.

You may decide that 7 meters is not the optimal distance for the mouse over to work. Rather than digging through the code each time to change it, it would make sense to create a variable hold the distance you want to declare. Creating a variable near the top of the script will make it easier to change as you add more functionality to your script, but if you expose it to the Inspector, it will also allow you to change the distance on an individual action object basis, which could possibly be beneficial.

2.   Add the following line up at the top, above the other public variables:

```
// Pick and Mouseover Info
private var triggerDistance = 7.0; // distance the camera must be to the↩
 object before mouse over
```

3.   Change the previous line to use the variable instead of the hardcoded value:

```
if (DistanceFromCamera() > triggerDistance) return;
```

You may decide that manually changing the trigger distance is a tedious way to hone in on the optimal distance.

If you temporarily have the distance print out to the console, you can decide very quickly what it ought to be.

    4.   Add the following line above the **if** clause in the OnMouseEnter function:

```
print (DistanceFromCamera());
```

    5.   Save the Script.

    6.   Click Play.

    7.   Experiment with the trigger distance, changing it inside the script.

▪ **Tip**   If your distance check seems to be rounding off the number in the conditional, check to make sure set the distance to 7.0 (a float) rather than 7 (an integer) or type cast the variable as a float to begin with (always a good practice), like so:

```
private var triggerDistance : float = 7.0;
```

---

    8.   When you are happy with it (Figure 6-18), change the triggerDistance var so it is no longer private.

Figure 6-18. *Slightly too far away to trigger the pointer color change*

9. Remove or comment out the print line.

10. Save the script again.

11. Save your scene and project.

■ **Tip**   As soon as you change a value in the Inspector, it will always override the value initialized in the script. If you change the value in the script and want to reset the value in the Inspector, you can change the variable to private, then change it back again. This will effectively reset the default value in the Inspector.

Quick Publish

At this point you may be getting itchy to see how everything runs, so let's take a few minutes to build an .exe and try it out.

Because you are now using a different scene, CursorControl, you will need to Add Current in the Scenes to Build and uncheck TerrainTest.

1. Save the scene and the project.

2. From the File menu, select Build Settings.

3. Click Add Current.

4. Uncheck the other scenes in the Scenes in Build window (Figure 6-19).

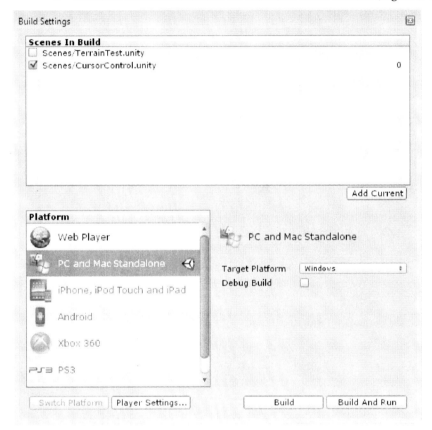

Figure 6-19. *Scenes in Build window*

5. Click Build And Run and save this exe as CursorControl.exe

6. Test the build.

With the cursor responding to objects in the scene, your little scene is starting to look like a real game (and you're no longer tripping over the OS cursor).

7. Close the Build Settings dialog.

Next you'll go over the top and get the action object's materials changing.

Object Reaction to Mouse Over

Another means of action object identification, often seen in more stylized point and click adventures such as the Tales of Monkey Island, is to have the object itself change color. This method is particularly advantageous on mobile devices such as phones where the screen is small as it provides an additional visual cue.

At its simplest, you can tint the basic material by changing its Main Color.

1. Drag and drop the Test Bark material onto the sphere and the cube in either the Scene view or the Hierarchy view. Do not drag it onto the cylinder.

2. Select the material in the Project view.

3. Open the Color dialog for the material's Main Color and change it to a nice highlight color such as the one you used to color the cursor on mouse over.

Even in a well lit area, only the part of the object that is receiving light reflects the change well (Figure 6-20). If the texture was fairly dark, it might not show much at all, making it less than useful for a visual cue.

Figure 6-20. *Main Color darkening the material*

4. With the material selected, press Ctrl + D to make a duplicate of the material.

5. Drag and drop the duplicate material onto the sphere.

6. Change the Shader from Specular to Vertex Lit.

If your sphere was under some trees and you are using shadows, you will notice that the sphere no longer receives them.

▨ **Tip** There are a few Shaders that use vertex lighting. They do not receive shadows.

For your purposes, it really doesn't matter if it receives shadows or not—you want something that will make it stand out from the 3D scene, as in Figure 6-22.

7. Click on the Emissive color swatch to bring up the Color dialog (Figure 6-21). Experiment with the color.

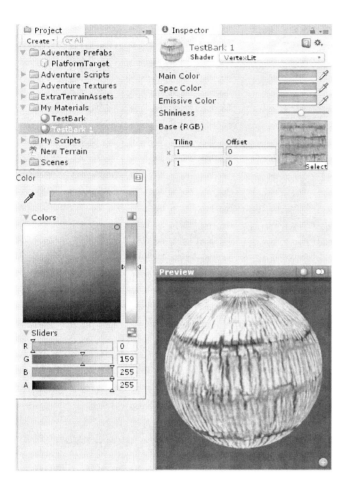

Figure 6-21. *Emissive color increased on the Vertex Lit Shader*

Figure 6-22. *The Vertex Lit material standing out in the scene*

As long as at least one component (R, G, or B) is at least 128, the shading on the sphere becomes negligible and the sphere stands out nicely from the rest of the 3D scene.

Realistically, the texture map must still be lighter rather than darker. The places that are black can't be lightened, but this will at least give you a starting point.

Any time you change a unique value that will need to be re-instated at a later time, you must save it. For your cursor color change, you knew that it would always need to go back to white so you could just hardcode Color.white into your code.

With your material change, you'll need to save the material for each object individually. Fortunately, you have a script, Interactor, that can hold variable values unique to each action object that uses it. Once stored in a variable, you can use it whenever you want. The ideal place to get the material is in the Start function, before game play starts. As before, to have the variable accessible throughout the Interactor script, you need to declare it first. This one should be private so it can't be changed by mistake during authoring. Notice its type: Material.

1. Open the Interactor script.

2. Add the following lines beneath the //Gain Access to section:

```
//Misc vars
private var originalMaterial : Material;
```

Before you can reference an object's material, you need to see where it resides.

3. Select the sphere in the Hierarchy view.

In the Inspector, you can see that Material is a property of the Mesh Renderer component, and the Mesh Renderer is a component of the sphere (Figure 6-23).

Figure 6-23. *The TestBark1 material in the Sphere's Mesh Renderer component*

To make sure it is saving the right material, you will temporarily tell it to print out the material for you right after it stores the material in the variable you created for it.

4. In the Start function, under the cam line, add the following:

```
originalMaterial = GetComponent(MeshRenderer).material; // load the material into var
print (originalMaterial);
```

5. Save the script and Click Play.

The message tells you that it is UnityEngine.Material (Figure 6-24). If you search the scripting reference for the material class, you will find that one of the inherited variables of material is its name. As with objects, the material name is a parameter of material itself.

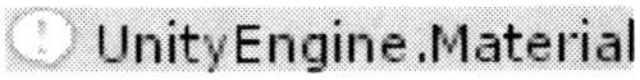

UnityEngine.Material

Figure 6-24. *The material, not its name reported on the status line*

6. Change the line to read :

```
print (originalMaterial.name);
```

7. Save the script and click Play.

Now the name of the material is returned as expected (Figure 6-25).

⊙ **TestBark 1 (Instance)**

Figure 6-25. *The material name*

The next thing to think about is the mouse over material. You might think you'll need to make one for each action object, but the only thing that is different is the texture. If you dynamically change the texture of the mouse over material, you can re-use a generic material each time. Unlike the pointer, you don't need to change the texture used by the mouse over material back to its original as it will be replaced by the next action object's texture. You will, however, need to store the texture in a variable for quick use.

If you again check the material class in the scripting reference, you see it has something called mainTexture. If you click on that, it takes you to the Material.mainTexture page that shows its usage. The first example shows how to assign a texture to it. You need to do the opposite: get the texture it currently holds.

1. In the //Misc vars section, add the following line to create a variable to hold the action object's texture:

private var aoTexture : Texture;

As you may have guessed, you can't simply refer to the texture by name. You need to find the texture.

2. In the Start function, immediately following the line where you get the material and just above the print line, assign the texture to your new variable:

```
// search the scene for an object named "main Camera" and assign it to the variable cam
cam = GameObject.Find("Main Camera");
originalMaterial = GetComponent(MeshRenderer).material; // load the material into var
aoTexture =  originalMaterial.mainTexture; // assign the materials texture
print (originalMaterial.name);
```

And now let's have it tell you what that texture's name is by changing the print line. While you're at it, you may as well have it tell you the name of the object the script is on as well.

3. Change the print line to the following:

```
print (name + ":  "  + aoTexture.name);
```

■ **Note**   You could also have used the syntax **this**.name to return the name of the object the script is on, but when it is omitted, it is assumed to be the object that the script is on.

---

4. Save the script.

5. Click Play and check the Status line.

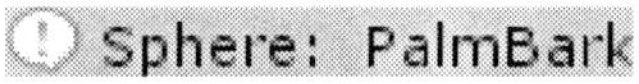

Sphere: PalmBark

Figure 6-26. *The material's mainTexture*

    6.   Open the Console by clicking on the Status line.

The texture name, not the material name, is reported this time (Figure 6-26).

Since you did not assign a material to the Cylinder, you will see a NullReferenceException error in amongst the object names with their textures (Figure 6-27).

Figure 6-27. *The Null Reference Exception error message*

If you couldn't stop yourself and went ahead and added materials to all of your test objects, go ahead and create another object and leave it using the default material.

    7.   Click Play and then check the console for the error message.

    8.   Double-click the line with the error.

It will briefly highlight the offending object in the Hierarchy view, Figure 6-28. In your case, it is the cylinder because the default material contains no texture.

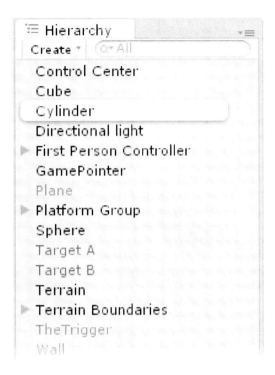

Figure 6-28. *The offending object*

Tip   Since the code you are working with is in the `Start` function, you will need to stop playback and start it each time you make a change in the code to see the latest results in the console. Code in the `Awake` and `Start` functions is only evaluated when the scene first starts up.

---

9.   Select the cylinder in the Hierarchy view and look at the default material in the Inspector.

Note that it has no texture assigned to it. So when the code tries to assign the nonexistent texture, it fails because it is trying to reference *null* or nothing.

Since it is entirely possible that an object may have a color only and no texture, you should check to make sure a texture exists before you try to assign it to your aoTexture variable.

10.   Change the aoTexture and print lines of code so they now look like the following, encapsulated in a conditional:

```
if (originalMaterial.mainTexture) { // if a texture exists, do…
    aoTexture = originalMaterial.mainTexture;
    print (name + ":  " + aoTexture.name);
```

}

11. Save the script.

12. Click Play and check the console.

The error no longer occurs (Figure 6-29). Your texture checker works to prevent the error.

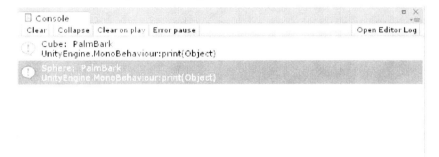

Figure 6-29. *Error resolved*

Tip   Quite often when the error involves an entity that does not exist, you can put the part that is causing the error into a conditional. If it exists, it returns true and the instructions can be carried out. If it returns false, it does not exist and the instructions are bypassed.

---

13. Comment out the print line:

```
//print (name + ":  "  + aoTexture.name);
```

14. Save the script.

15. Stop Play mode.

Now you're ready to create the mouse over material itself.

1.   Duplicate the Test Bark 1 material and name it MouseOverMaterial.

Next, you need to get your material into the scene before it is actually applied to an object's mesh renderer. The logical place to do this is in the GameManager script—a place where you will be storing all sorts of things for the game.

2.   Open the GameManager script from the Control Center object in the Hierarchy view.

3.   Add the following line near the top:

```
var mouseOverMaterial : Material;
```

4.   Save the script.

5. Select the Control Center.

6. Drag the `MouseOverMaterial` onto the newly exposed variable in the Inspector (Figure 6-30).

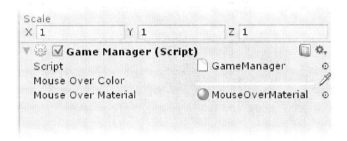

Figure 6-30. *The MouseOverMaterial loaded*

You now have a means of accessing the material, even though it is not yet used in an object's Mesh Renderer in the scene.

In the `Interactor` script, go ahead and access the `Control Center` object as it will eventually hold a lot of other information that you'll need to utilize.

1. Open the `Interactor` script.

2. Under the `//Gain access to` section, add the following:

```
var controlCenter : GameObject;
```

3. And create a private variable to hold the mouse over material under the `//Misc` section:

```
private var mouseOverMaterial : Material;
```

4. Inside the `Start` function, below the `cam` line add:

```
controlCenter = GameObject.Find("Control Center");
mouseOverMaterial = controlCenter.GetComponent(GameManager).mouseOverMaterial;
```

Let' see if it works. The trigger for the material change will be the mouse over, so the next code you add will be inside the `OnMouseEnter` function. Remember that the first condition will exit you out of the function if you are not close enough to "see" the action object.

5. In the `OnMouseEnter` function, add the following code beneath the `gamePointer` line:

```
renderer.material = mouseOverMaterial; // swap the material
```

You may be wondering why you use `renderer.material` rather than `MeshRenderer.material`. The latter is a property of a component whereas the former is a property of the object.

6. Save the script.

7. Select the TestBark1 material.

8. Change it back to a Specular shader.

9. Set its Main Color back to white or light grey.

10. Load a different texture, LongLeaf, into it using the *Select* button on the Base thumbnail image (Figure 6-31).

Figure 6-31. *The Select button to load a new texture into the material*

The interesting thing here is the Shininess/Gloss mask (Figure 6-32). The leaf texture contains an alpha channel for opacity, but when the texture is used in the Specular shader, it functions as a mask for shininess: Base (RGB) Gloss (A).

Figure 6-32. *The new texture, LongLeaf, in the material and in the scene. Note the shininess masking.*

11. Rename the material as TestLeaf.

12. Select the original TestBark material.

13. Set its Main Color back to light grey or white.

14. Click Play and test the mouse over.

Figure 6-33. *Preliminary mouse over material changes*

Each of the action objects (those with the `Interactor` script) changes to the `MouseOverMaterial` (Figure 6-33). The only problem is that they don't yet adopt the individual object's texture. They also do not revert back, but you haven't dealt with that yet.

Additionally, you'll need to plan for materials whose textures may be too dark to show well with your default mouse over material or don't even have a texture.

Let's deal with textureless materials first. You already know when a material is lacking a texture from the conditional you created in the `Start` function. You'll need to add a variable or flag that will keep that bit of information for later use.

1. In the `Interactor` script, in the `//Misc` vars section, add the private variable to hold it:

private var useTexture : **boolean;**

2. Inside the `Start` function, inside the `if` clause where you have already ascertained there is a texture, add the following line to tell you to use the texture:

useTexture = true;

3. Just below the `if` section, beneath its closing curly bracket, add the `else`:

else useTexture = false;

The Start function should now look as follows:

```
function Start () {

    // search the scene for an object named "main Camera" and assign it to the var cam
    cam = GameObject.Find("Main Camera");

    controlCenter = GameObject.Find("Control Center");
    mouseOverMaterial = controlCenter.GetComponent(GameManager).mouseOverMaterial;

    originalMaterial = GetComponent(MeshRenderer).material; // load the material into var
    if (originalMaterial.mainTexture) { // if a texture exists, do...
        aoTexture =  originalMaterial.mainTexture;
        useTexture = true;
        //print (name + ":  " + aoTexture.name);
    }
  else useTexture = false;

}
```

4. Save the script.

Now let's add the texture changing code inside the OnMouseEnter function, right before you switch the material.

5. Immediately above the renderer.material line, add the following:

```
if (useTexture) mouseOverMaterial.mainTexture = aoTexture;

else mouseOverMaterial.mainTexture = null;
```

6. Save the script.

Now you get to see if it works.

7. Click play and test the functionality.

Figure 6-34. *The MouseOverMaterial displaying the proper texture for the action object it is over*

Now when the mouse moves over the cylinder or whatever other action object has no texture, the mouse over material uses the blank or null texture (Figure 6-34).

Before you panic about all the objects changing after each new mouse over, remember that you haven't added anything to OnMouseExit yet. Let's take care of that next; it should be pretty straightforward. The only thing you need to do is restore the original material.

1. In the OnMouseExit function, add the following line of code beneath the gamePointer line:

```
renderer.material = originalMaterial;
```

2. Save the script.

3. Click Play and test.

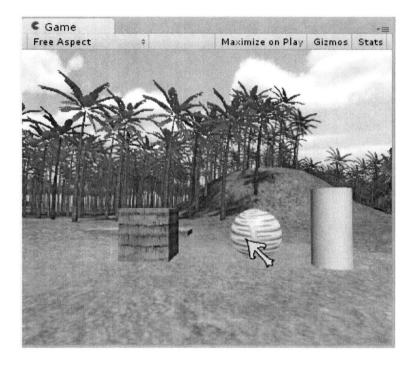

Figure 6-35. *The materials reverting properly after mouse over*

The three materials revert nicely after each mouse exit (Figure 6-35). Feel free to tone down the MouseOverMaterial.

4. Save the scene and the project.

One of the biggest challenges with designing interactivity, especially when you want the functionality to be reusable, is to make sure you have thought of all possibilities and have included the logic to keep everything working smoothly. While it might be tempting to ignore the last mouse over scenario, you can be sure it will crop up when you least expect it and cause trouble.

So the last solution is to be able to deal with a material whose texture is too dark, whose Main Color figures largely in the mix, or maybe just requires something totally different (in case it uses a specialty shader). The ideal solution, if you lump all of these problems together, is to allow the author to assign a custom material to use in place of the default MouseOverMaterial. It will require a variable and a conditional and then you should be safe.

1. Open the Interactor script.

2. Create a variable in the //Misc vars section, as follows:

var overrideMaterial : Material;

In the OnMouseEnter function, you'll wrap the existing code into an else clause following the if clause that checks to see if there has been an override material assigned.

3. Change the if (useTexture) code here

```
if (useTexture) mouseOverMaterial.mainTexture = aoTexture;

else mouseOverMaterial.mainTexture = null;
```

to this

```
if (overrideMaterial) mouseOverMaterial = overrideMaterial;

else {

    if (useTexture) mouseOverMaterial.mainTexture = aoTexture;

    else mouseOverMaterial.mainTexture = null;
}
```

Tip   When the condition only needs one expression or line, curly brackets are not required, but some people prefer to use them. You will see them used both ways throughout this project.

---

4. Save the script.

5. Click Play and test.

There should be no change because you have not assigned any override materials.

6. Stop Play mode.

7. Add a Capsule object to the scene (Figure 6-36).

8. Drag and drop any material to it.

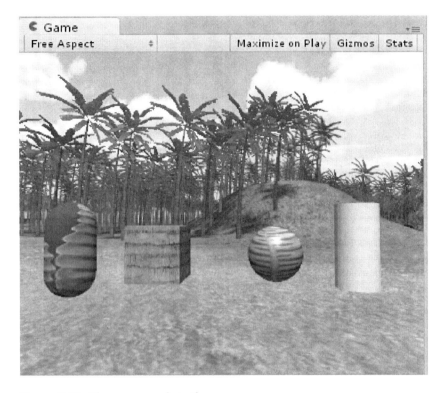

Figure 6-36. *The new capsule in the scene*

9. Select the My Materials folder.

10. Right click and create a new Material.

11. Name it Overrider.

12. Change its Shader to VertexLit and make it look different than the regular mouse over material by changing its Emissive color to a nice magenta.

13. Add a texture such as BanyanBarkOld to it.

You need to add the `Interactor` script to the new object before you can test your custom override material.

14. Drag and drop the `Interactor` script onto the capsule.

15. Select the capsule.

16. Drag and drop the `GamePointer` onto the Game Pointer parameter.

17. Drag and drop the Control Center onto the Control Center parameter.

18. Drag and drop the Overrider material onto Override Material parameter.

19. Click Play again and test the objects (Figure 6-37).

Figure 6-37. *The override material on the capsule*

The capsule's mouse over material has the custom override material assigned to it.

20. Save the scene and save the project.

Making the New Functionality Optional

By now you are probably thinking that the cursor and the action object changing colors is a bit of overkill. Okay, maybe that is an understatement. Let's take a moment to think about it. Ideally, you would, as an author, decide from the outset which visual cues to use on an individual game basis. In accordance with that way of thinking, you shall make the use of each an option.

As you have probably guessed by now, this will involve a couple of checkboxes and some more conditionals. The variables for the checkboxes will need to go on the GameManager script where all of the action objects can access them.

1. Open the GameManager script and add the following:

```
var useMOCursorChange : boolean = true;
var useMOMaterialChange : boolean = false;
```

Feel free to organize them with respect to their related variables.

2. Save the script.

305

3. Back in the Interactor script, under the //misc vars section, add the same variables as private variables, but don't assign any values.

```
private var useMOCursorChange : boolean;
private var useMOMaterialChange : boolean;
```

4. Assign the values in the Start function with:

```
useMOCursorChange = controlCenter.GetComponent(GameManager).useMOCursorChange;

useMOMaterialChange = controlCenter.GetComponent(GameManager).useMOMaterialChange;
```

Now each action object will contact the GameManager and get the correct settings when the game starts.

5. In the OnMouseEnter function, change the gamePointer .SendMessage line to the following:

```
if (useMOCursorChange) gamePointer.SendMessage("CursorColorChange", true); // turn the⏎
 pointer back to white
```

Now the pointer color will only change if the use flag is true.

6. Repeat for the OnMouseExit function.

```
if (useMOCursorChange) gamePointer.SendMessage("CursorColorChange", false); // turn the⏎
 pointer white
```

7. For the material change, in the OnMouseEnter function, select all of the code for the material change starting with the **if** (overrideMaterial) line and ending with the renderer.material line (six lines of actual code).

8. Click the tab key to tab it over.

9. Above it, add the following line:

```
if (useMOMaterialChange) {
```

10. And just below its last line, add the closing curly bracket.

```
}
```

Tip Tabbing the contents of curly brackets isn't required, but it does make the contents easier to read.

---

11. Save the script.

12. Click Play and test.

The scene starts with object material change turned off (Figure 6-38).

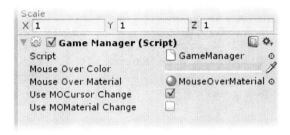

Figure 6-38. *The two new options in the GameManager*

13. Stop playback.

14. Turn on the Use MOMaterial Change option in the ControlCenter's Game Manager script.

15. Click Play.

The material change is activated.

16. Uncheck the option while still in Play mode.

The action objects continue to exhibit material change.

If you remember, the flags are set in the Start function. Therefore, when they are changed during runtime in the GameManager, the Interactor script has no knowledge of it. Eventually, when you tackle the user options menu, you'll need to send a message to update the state of the flags in the Interactors.

Preventing Mouse Over Functionality While Navigating

You probably have not yet navigated around the scene after setting the material color change on mouse over. Now would be a good time to do so as you have yet another unexpected issue to deal with (yep, turns out that's a regular occurrence during game development).

1. Make sure the Use MOMaterial Change option is on.

2. Click Play.

3. Drive towards and away from one of the action objects with the pointer in the approximate area.

As you get within range, the object changes color. While this is exactly what you set it up to do, it becomes apparent that you may not want it to do so during navigation. The cursor was not a problem because it was set to hide while the player is navigating the scene. The action object obviously needs to remain visible. You can, however, use the same mechanism to bump it out of the mouse over function as you did to hide the cursor.

You'll still need access to the navigating variable from the GameManager script. The Interactor script holds the mouse over functionality for its own action object, so you need to add the navigation checking code to it. Since you've already accessed and introduced the ControlCenter object in the Start function, you need only add one line of code to see if the player is navigating the scene, and, if so, bump him out of the function with return before anything is done. Because this condition overrules the distance check, you need to put it above that line. There's no sense in checking distance if you're moving, as the mouse over functionality will be bypassed anyway.

4. Open the `Interactor` script.

5. Inside the `OnMouseEnter` function, above the existing code, add the following:

```
// if navigating [is true], exit the function now
if (controlCenter.GetComponent(GameManager).navigating) return;
```

6. Save the script.

7. Click Play and test the navigation.

The action objects should no longer change color on mouse over unless you are not navigating the scene. That's much better.

8. Stop Play mode.

9. Uncheck Use MOMaterial Change.

10. Save the scene and the project.

Now you're ready to start using the real thing instead of proxy test objects.

Chapter Summary

In this chapter, you experimented with cursor control, finding that you could hide the operating system's cursor with a simple `Screen.showCursor = false`. After creating a variable called `Navigating` that checked your virtual buttons to see if any were active, you were able turn the cursor off while moving and back on as soon as you stopped.

To allow for more artistic license, you substituted a `GUITexture` object as a cursor with the help of the Texture Importer presets. You learned that GUI objects in Unity are not sized relevant to screen size and so explored forcing screen resolution via scripting.

By getting the OS cursor's position with `Input.mousePosition`, you were able to set your own cursor's Pixel Inset values with `guiTexture.pixelInset.x` and `guiTexture.pixelInset.y`.

You then started designing a script that would hold and manage the master game information and be able to communicate with other object's scripts. You found that after creating a variable to hold a `gameObject`, you could either drag one into it in the Inspector or use `GameObject.Find` in the `Start` function to locate the object you wanted to communicate with. Names, you discovered, are only properties of objects, materials, and components and representatives of their objects. The same variable names used in different scripts don't store the same values unless you specifically update them.

With the introduction of `OnMouseEnter` and `OnMouseExit`, you were able to instigate color changes for your cursor as it passed over and off your action objects, and later, with the use of `renderer.material`, materials also to provide the player with visual clues for interactive objects. By using `GetComponent`, you found you could access variables from the script components you created, allowing you to keep important data on a single script that could be accessed by all.

Finally, after allowing for totally custom override materials on a per object basis, you discovered that there was such a thing as too much visual prompting and made both cursor and material changes on mouse over optional.

In the next chapter, you'll work with imported objects and their animations and start to get them acting like actual game assets.

Action Objects

Importing Assets

Having made a good start on the cursor, let's move on to animating our action objects. Obviously, the handful of primitive objects available in Unity won't go very far for creating games, so you'll need to look into one of the more challenging aspects of game creation—importing assets built in other programs. As anyone familiar with creating games or other 3D content can tell you, every game engine or 3D application handles the import process differently. Some handle it more gracefully than others, but there are always going to be issues and gotchas. The idea is to try to understand the reasoning behind the implementation and develop guidelines for your own particular needs.

Unity was designed primarily to create first person shooters, where imports are most likely characters or static buildings and other structures. A classic point and click adventure game, on the other hand, features the animation of a multitude of different objects, many of which animate together to play out complicated sequences as a reward for the player's cleverness in hitting upon the correct solution.

You will start by learning how to handle imported animations as there are always going to be sequences that are better off imported. Then you'll delve into Unity's Animation view and try a few animations directly in Unity.

Since it is a pretty fair bet you'll be creating your objects in a Digital Content Creation (DCC) program such as 3ds Max, Maya, C4D or Blender, we will start with importing and see if we can work out a 'best practices' process. For this book, we are using assets created in 3ds Max and exported in FBX format. As the FBX format seems to change on a regular basis, we are pretty much aiming at a moving target.

As with any asset in Unity, once the asset has been imported or added to the Assets folder through the OS, you must only move the file around inside the Project view (expect to be reminded of this regularly—it is crucial!). If you delete it from the Asset folder, it will be *deleted for good*. Always have a reference scene in your program's native format stored elsewhere on your hard drive that you can go back to should you forget and nuke something by mistake.

Unity supports the file types of 3ds Max, Maya, C4D, and Blender by converting them internally into FBX format once they are in the Asset folder. You can still work on them and resave them, and they will be automatically updated on scene load. If you are creating assets for someone else, you should get in the habit of saving as FBX so they have maximum portability. Once the assets are in the folder, you'll find a number of settings worth looking at. The most important ones are Scale Factor, which you've already seen, Generate Colliders, and those in the Animation section.

You'll be importing two types of objects—non-animated objects and pre-animated objects. You can think of the former as *static* objects, like structures and large environmental objects, but the latter can be structural as well as animated. Couple this with the fact that you can add animations to objects once they've been imported into Unity, and the line becomes blurred. Both small objects and large objects, whether you can interact with them or not, may have colliders. To make things even more flexible, you can turn off an imported object's animation to conserve resources.

Unity attempts to create materials similar to what the object had in the DCC app, but since there are few correlations between regular materials and shaders, you can pretty well count on redoing them all. That being the case, keep materials as basic as possible as you'll almost always need to rebuild after import to take advantage of anything other than the apparently default Diffuse shader. And before you go getting all excited about using Diffuse Parallax Reflective Bump shaders on everything, remember that *everything* affects frame rate—use the fancy stuff sparingly.

Tip   If Unity can't find the textures at the time of import, it will create generic Diffuse materials and you'll have to set them all up manually once you've loaded the textures. When saving a new DCC file directly to the Asset folder, it's safest to load the textures first so the materials will be generated with them when the meshes are loaded.

TIPS FOR CREATING YOUR OWN ASSETS

- Name all objects.

- Use naming conventions for your textures. Unity will create only a base Diffuse texture for your objects on import; you will need to add bump, shininess, height and other specialty maps.

- When a material has a Diffuse texture, the material generated in Unity will use that as its name (so you may even decide that making a bogus texture just to get the name associated with the material on the imported object is worth the trouble).

- Name all materials. Unity will preface the material names with the file name if they don't have Diffuse textures.

- Two objects using the same material in your DCC app will also share the material in Unity.

- Collapse max objects to editable mesh, not editable poly to prevent edge errors. FBX does not support turned edges so your model could change on export.

- Expect to go back and make adjustments to smoothing and vertices. Realtime renderers and navigation will show errors and mistakes that you may miss in your DCC app.

- When exporting the FBX, make sure to check Animations if you have them; Y is up in Unity (you can keep the original Z from Max if you wish with the latest FBX exporters); and note the scale—it can be changed in Unity, but it is worth noting.

- Keep complex animation hierarchies in orthogonal orientation until after importing into Unity. Unity doesn't support non-orthogonal rotation matrices.

- Unity does not currently support vertex animation, e.g., morph targets. Any animation that affects objects on a vertex basis must be done with bones.

- Be sure to have keys for all used transforms and objects at the start and end of each behavior or time segment.

- Time segments for behaviors may *not* overlap unless the various objects can use the same named time segment or clip.

- Make sure you are using the latest FBX exporters whenever possible as the results may vary when importing files made with older versions.

- If you are using 3ds Max, you can use the Resource Collector to copy your textures into the Assets folder before you export the FBX.

Importing

OK, enough doom and gloom! Let's do some import tests and see if we can get a handle on importing in general.

1. Open the CursorControl scene.

2. Save it as ImportedAnimations.

3. Locate the Book Assets folder in the code that you can download from the Apress Web site. Navigate to the right book page and you'll find a link there!

4. Copy the Animation Tests folder into the Assets folder in your project folder via Explorer (Window) or Finder (Mac).

The folder has both the FBX files and the textures in it, so it should import nicely.

Unity will take a few moments to process the assets, adding internal IDs and mapping out connections between the meshes and their materials as well as generating Unity-specific parameters for the Inspector. As always, once the assets are in the project, you must only move, rename, or perform any similar operations *inside* the Project view.

When Unity finishes loading, you should see the new Animation Tests folder in the Project view.

5. Open the new Animation Tests folder and inspect the contents, as shown in Figure 7-1.

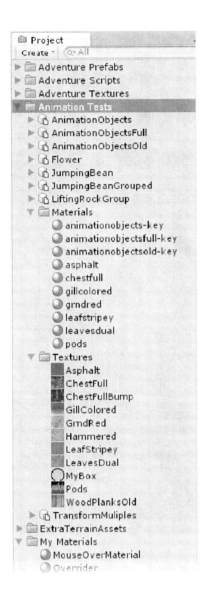

Figure 7-1. *The contents of the Animation Tests folder*

Unity has made a prefab to hold each FBX file, using the preexisting Textures folder, and generated a Materials folder with the materials for each object.

6.   Open the AnimationObjectsOld prefab (Figure 7-2).

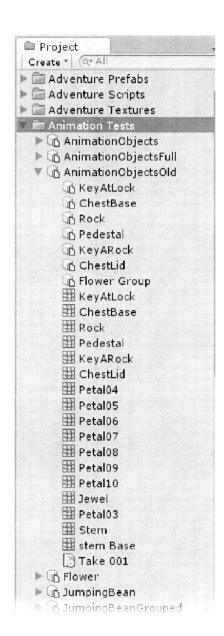

Figure 7-2. *The contents of AnimationObjectsOld*

Inside the prefab for the individual files, you'll find a GameObject/prefab for each individual mesh to hold its properties, as well as something called Take001. You'll also see a list of all of the meshes separately.

7. In the Inspector, close the FBXImporter section so there's room to see each object in a Preview window (Figure 7-3).

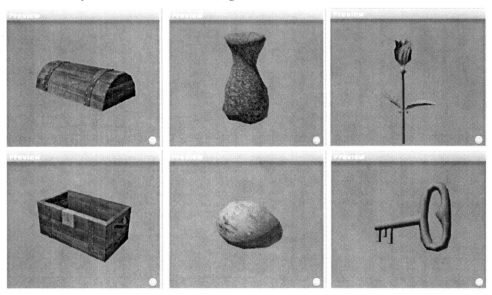

Figure 7-3. *The objects from the AnimationObjectsOld scene*

8. Click and drag the objects in the Preview window to rotate the view and inspect them.

9. Click on one of the mesh objects ⊞ to see it in the Preview window (Figure 7-4).

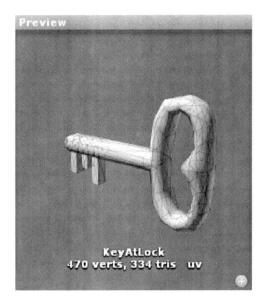

Figure 7-4. *One of the meshes from the scene*

The mesh is shown with edges, and the vertex and triangle ("tris") count is shown.

■ **Tip** Clicking on the mesh's GameObject counterparts will open the files in your default FBX app. You may not rename the imported objects in the Project folder.

Before you bring the imported objects into the scene, you'll want to deactivate your test primitives. You can do this by deactivating the group you put them in.

1. Create an Empty GameObject.

2. Name it Test Action Objects.

3. Move the primitive objects (Sphere, Cube, etc) and the deactivated objects (they are grayed out) into the Test Action Objects group.

4. Select the Test Action Objects group in the Hierarchy view.

5. In the Inspector, uncheck the box next to the object name at the top of the view.

6. At the prompt, choose Deactivate Children.

Now you'll be able to concentrate on the imported objects.

7. Drag the AnimationObjectsOld prefab into the Scene view, somewhere near the First Person Controller.

8. Move and rotate the group until you can see it in the Scene view. See Figure 7-5.

9. Do *not* move the objects individually!

Figure 7-5. *The imported objects in the scene*

Unfortunately, the objects seem to have had some of their transforms mixed up on import. The flower, rock, and key-at-lock have wandered off, as shown in Figure 7-5. The flower should be on the pedestal, the key-at-lock should be on the front side of the chest, and the rock should be on top of the key as in Figure 7-6.

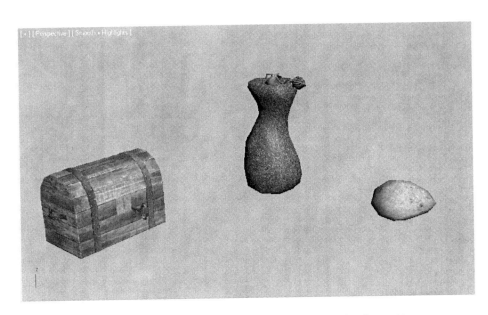

Figure 7-6. *The objects as they were in 3DS Max(the key is under the rock)*

When transforms include layers of animation, linkages, and groups, they can get quite complex and may not fare so well during import. The flower in this file has bones, a skinned mesh, separate objects linked to the bones, *and* it was animated with a combination of IK (invert kinematics), FK, and look-at controllers. While most objects with animations you import will no doubt be simpler than this rig, it is worth investigating.

Exporters, like the FBX exporter, collapse procedural animations like path constraints, look-at constraints, and IK onto the objects as basic position, rotation, and scales; in other words, transforms. Moving object pivot points can add even more layers of complexity.

With this scene, grouping all of the scene's objects before exporting as an FBX fixed the transform issue. Keep that trick in mind in case you have similar issues when working with your own assets.

10. Delete AnimationObjectsOld from the Hierarchy view.

11. Delete the prefab from the Project view.

12. Drag AnimationObjectsFull into the Scene window.

The rock, plant, and key-at-lock are now in the correct positions (Figure 7-7).

Figure 7-7. *Grouping the objects before the FBX export*

While your own imported meshes are likely to have a consistent scale, you may occasionally come across scenes where that's not the case. Scaling 3D objects in Unity is simple. The unit of measure in Unity is a meter, which is approximately three feet. The cube in your current test scene is one meter and can therefore give us a good idea about the scale of the newly imported objects.

1. Drag the cube out of the Test Action Objects group.

2. Reactivate the cube.

3. Move the cube near the chest to assess the scale (see Figure 7-8).

Figure 7-8. *Imported objects and cube for scale comparison*

If the cube is one cubic meter, the chest is about the size of a compact car. It looks like the imported objects could stand to be much smaller. One of the advantages of bringing these objects in as a group is that they can be quickly scaled all at once.

4. Select the AnimationObjectsFull prefab in the Project view.

5. In the Inspector, open the FBXImporter section and change the Scale Factor to **0.0035** (see Figure 7-9).

6. Click Apply near the bottom of the panel, just above the Preview window.

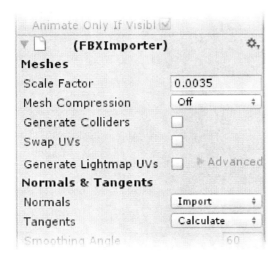

Figure 7-9. *Changing Scale Factor settings in FBX Importer*

7. Readjust the group's position in the Scene view.

8. Deactivate the cube and put it back into the Test Action Objects group.

With something more recognizable in the scene, the ground texture looks a bit large. Now is a good time to briefly revisit the Terrain editor.

1. Select the Terrain GameObject, the Paint Terrain tool, and the ground textures

2. From Edit Texture, edit the ground textures and reduce the Tiling size to about 8, then Apply the change. Figure 7-10 shows the ground before and after editing.

Figure 7-10. *The ground with the default 15×15 scale (left) and the new 8×8 scale (right)*

■ **Tip**   In a fast-paced game, the large tiling would be less obvious, but in a classic point and click, the player is more likely to be focused on the immediate surroundings and will notice poorly scaled textures.

---

3. Toggle on Scene Lighting in the Scene view and move and rotate the group or the First Person Controller until the imported objects can be clearly seen in the Game view.

4. Click Play and observe the animations.

The rock moves aside to reveal a key. A key gets inserted in the lock at the chest. The chest lid opens, and then closes. The key is removed. The flower revives and then the jewel at its center spins.

5. Drive up to the objects and look around them.

Either the objects need to be bigger, or we need to adjust the camera.

In games, scale is not always exact. Often you'll need to increase the scale of an object to make it more playable. In our case, however, it turns out the camera field of view is more suited to a first person shooter that requires more peripheral vision than for an adventure game where small objects need to be noticed.

1. Open the First Person Controller.

2. Select the Main Camera.

3. In the Inspector, change the camera's Field of View to **32**.

4. Examine the objects again.

As Figure 7-11 shows, now you can get a good view of the objects when you are close.

Figure 7-11. *Reduced Field of View on the First Person Controller's camera*

5. Stop Play mode.

6. Make the change to the camera permanent for now.

After you've finished with your test objects and have more of the scene completed, you'll probably want to adjust the camera's Field of View again, but while you are setting things up, you may as well make it easy to access the objects.

7. Adjust AnimationObjectsFull in the Scene view so it is visible in the newly adjusted Game window.

8. Select the Main Camera.

9. Set its X Rotation to **12** to get a better view of the objects when they animate (Figure 7-12).

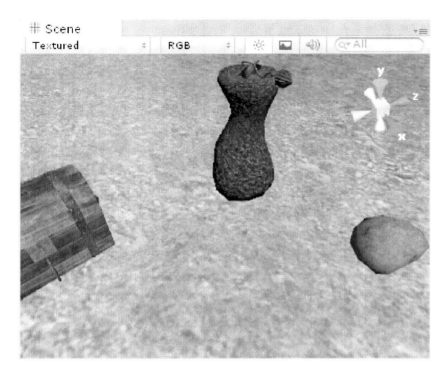

Figure 7-12. *The objects ready to view*

FBX Importer

Once you start putting script components on imported objects, you've already added to the Scene/Hierarchy. You will lose the prefab connection so it's a good idea to set up all of the Animation parameters at import time. You will still be able to do things like scale from the FBXImporter, but changing the Generation type or setting up animation clips at a later stage will often mean updating the scene objects manually.

Unity offers several options for importing assets with animation. Understanding the different options will help you decide how to prepare your FBX files. Regardless of which import setting you choose, you should write down the frames used by each object's behaviors so you can define the clips.

■ **Tip** For more information on mesh importing, see the Reference Manual ➤ Components ➤ Asset Components ➤ Meshes.

Table 7-1 shows the time segments in the AnimationObjectsFull object.

Table 7-1. *Object Behaviors in the Animation*

Object, Behavior	Start Frame	End Frame
g-rock move	1	30
g-key insert	31	60
g-chest open	61	90
g-chest close	91	110
g-key remove	121	150
g-flower revive	151	275
g-flower idle	276	350

Note that none of the behaviors overlap in the timeline. If they did overlap, all objects at that position on the timeline would animate at the same time, which defeats the purpose of being able to call them individually. The order of the behaviors is not important, only the fact that they occupy discrete sections of the time line.

■ **Tip**   In scenes with multiple objects imported, name clips with the object name first and the behavior second, such as chest open, chest close, chest rattle.

1.   Click Play and watch the animations.

2.   Stop Play mode.

3.   Select the AnimationObjectsFull object in the Project view and expand it.

4.   In the Inspector, find the Animations section of the FBXImporter (Figure 7-13).

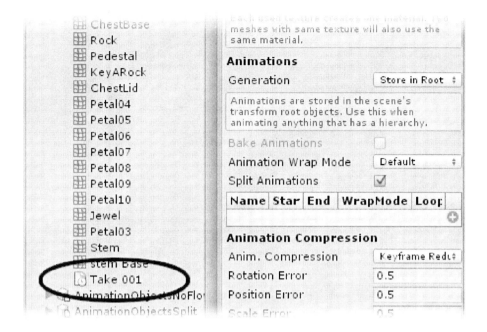

Figure 7-13. *The default animation import, Store in Root*

5. From the Generation parameter, select Don't Import (Figure 7-14).

6. Click Apply.

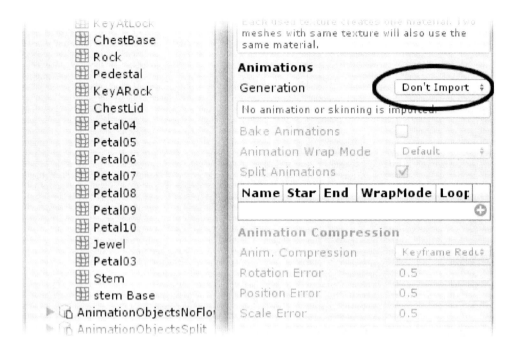

Figure 7-14. *Take001 is no longer listed.*

As you can see, Take001—which represented the animation— no longer appears in the Project view.

    7.   Click Play

The animations no longer exist.

Just as it says, animation is not imported for the scene. Use this setting for things like buildings, landscaping objects, and other static or non-animating objects.

Before we try the next option, let's take a closer look at the Flower Group in the AnimationObjectsFull.

    1.   Expand the Flower Group in the Hierarchy view by holding down the Alt key when you click on it (Figure 7-15).

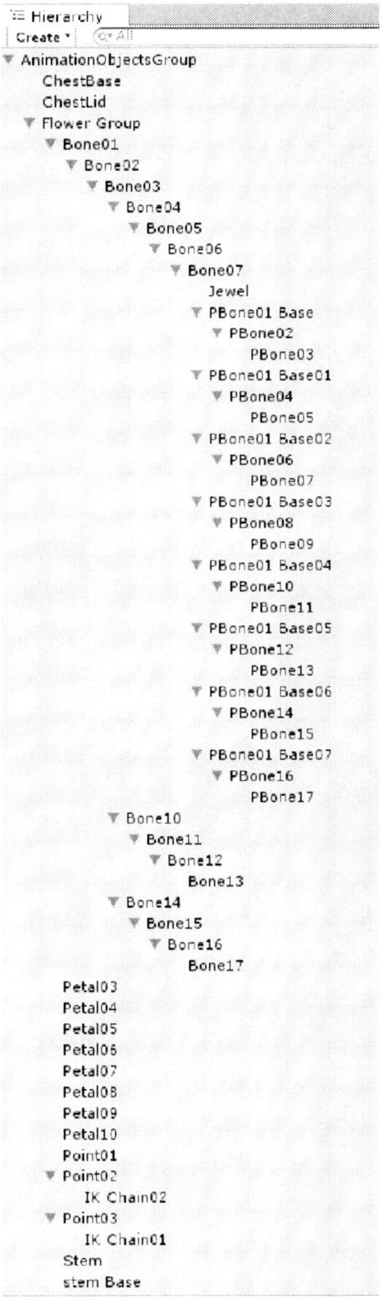

Figure 7-15. *The Flower Group expanded*

2. The Flower Group contains all of the bones that were used to animate the stem, leaves, and petals—they're all separate objects.

■ **Tip**   To expand a parent's hierarchy all at once, hold the Alt key while clicking on the parent object.

---

3. Select AnimationObjectsFull again in the Project view.

4. From the Generation parameter, select Store in Nodes.

5. Click Apply.

This puts the animations onto *each* individual object and creates animation clips for each.

6. Take a moment to look at the contents of AnimationObjectsFull in the Project view.

It has apparently added a Take 001 clip for each individual object. If we had split the take into several different clips, the full complement of clips would be listed for each object as well—not a good idea with our flower group.

7. Click on some of the bones in the Hierarchy view.

Each has an Animation component, such as the one in Figure 7-16.

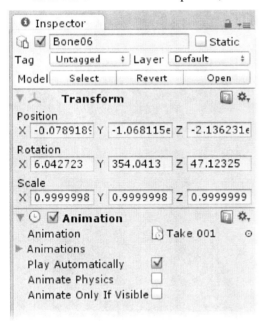

Figure 7-16. *One of the bones' Animation component*

Store in Original Roots sounds like a better choice here. On Import, Unity tries to determine the scene's parent nodes and puts the clips on them, but not their children.

8. Select AnimationObjectsFull again in the Project view.

9. Select Store in Original Roots.

10. Click Apply.

The number of animation clips is reduced to one in the Project view, but the individual bones still have Animation components. Unfortunately, the actual clips are not listed in the Animations arrays. Loading them in manually may not create a usable connection either.

Let's try the final and default option.

11. Select AnimationObjectsFull again in the Project view.

12. Select Store in Root.

13. Click Apply.

There is only one animation clip created for the entire AnimationObjectsFull, and only the parent GameObject in the Hierarchy view has an Animation component.

This is typically the choice you will make for *individual* imported characters or other complex animated hierarchies. This generation type calls *all* objects in the hierarchy for each specific *clip* or *time segment*. In the case of a character, you'd have a time segment or clip for idle, walk, run, jump, etc.

In our test import, we can still use this generation type because each of the objects has its behaviors animated at different time segments along the time line.

14. In the Animation Clip list, click the + to generate a new clip, as shown in Figure 7-17.

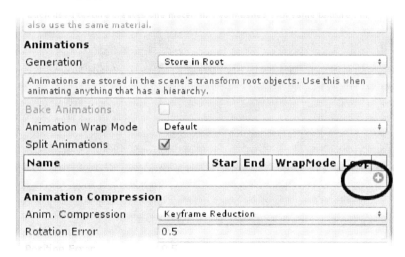

Figure 7-17. *The add button for the animation clips*

15. Click the + and use the information in Table 7-1 to fill out the rest of the clips.

16. Change the WrapMode on the g-flower idle clip to Loop (Figure 7-18).

Use this when animating anything that has a hierarchy.

Bake Animations	☐				
Animation Wrap Mode	Default			⇕	

Split Animations ☑

Name	Star	End	WrapMode	Loop	
g-rock move	1	30	Default ⇕	☐	⊖
g-key insert	31	60	Default ⇕	☐	⊖
g-chest open	61	90	Default ⇕	☐	⊖
g-chest close	91	110	Default ⇕	☐	⊖
g-key remove	121	150	Default ⇕	☐	⊖
g-flower revive	151	275	Default ⇕	☐	⊖
g-flower idle	276	350	Loop ⇕	☑	⊖
					⊕

Animation Compression

Anim. Compression	Keyframe Reduction ⇕
Rotation Error	0.5
Position Error	0.5
Scale Error	0.5

Rotation error is defined as maximum angle deviation allowed

Figure 7-18. *The animation clips named and specified*

17. Click Apply.

Note the clips now replacing the original Take 001 clip in the Project view (Figure 7-19).

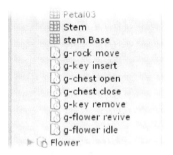

Petal03
Stem
stem Base
g-rock move
g-key insert
g-chest open
g-chest close
g-key remove
g-flower revive
g-flower idle
▶ Flower

Figure 7-19. *The newly defined clips in the Project view*

18. Select AnimationObjectsFull in the Hierarchy view to see its Animation component (Figure 7-20).

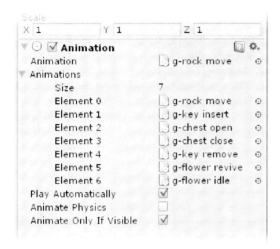

Figure 7-20. *The AnimationObjectsFull's Animation component*

19. Select the AnimationObjectsFull object.

20. Click Play and watch the default animation, the rock.

21. Experiment with loading different animations in the Animation parameter.

Note the Animations parameter. This is an array holding each of the available clips we generated in the FBX Importer. As long as the object is still a prefab, it will be updated should we change names or add or remove clips. Once we break the prefab by adding script components, you'll need to manually update this section. It is always best to make sure the animations' timelines are correct before setting up the animation clips. If the times don't change, the animations can be refined and improved with no extra work required when the file is updated.

We will go into more detail about animations after we have dealt with a few other import parameters.

22. Save the scene and save the project

More Control over Individual Objects

Up to now, we have been dealing with a scene and its animations as a *whole*. Let's try a few more import tests so we can experiment with animations more fully. When you need full scripting control of individual objects, you use Store in Nodes. Since the Flower has too many nodes to handle individually, it has been removed from the next test file.

1. Select the AnimationObjects prefab in the Project view.

2. Set the Scale Factor to match the other version's scale, **0.0035**.

3. Set the Generation to Store in Nodes.

4. Add the clips indicated in Table 7-2.

Table 7-2. *Animation Clips*

Object, Behavior	Start Frame	End Frame
rock move	1	30
key insert	31	60
chest open	61	90
chest close	91	110
key remove	121	150

░ **Tip**   Animation clips, unlike most things in Unity, are accessed by name. Unity allows almost anything to have duplicate names. If you need to differentiate between objects, components, or other assets, be sure to give their clips unique names.

5.   Click Apply

Unfortunately, the full complement of behaviors clips is created for each object with the same names, as Figure 7-21 shows.

Figure 7-21. *Multiple clips generated with Store in Nodes*

This version of the scene also follows the rule of no overlapping behaviors or clips.

6. Find AnimationObjectsFull in the Scene view.

7. Deactivate the entire AnimationObjectsFull in the Hierarchy view.

8. Drag the AnimationObjects prefab into the Scene view.

9. Click Play.

All of the objects animate only as far as the first clip, which means only the rock actually does anything. Unlike the objects in AnimationObjectsFull, however, they each have their own Animation component.

10. Compare ChestLid in AnimationObjectsFull and AnimationObjects.

In AnimationObjects, ChestLid has an Animation component (Figure 7-22, left), whereas in AnimationObjectsFull (Figure 7-22, right) it does not.

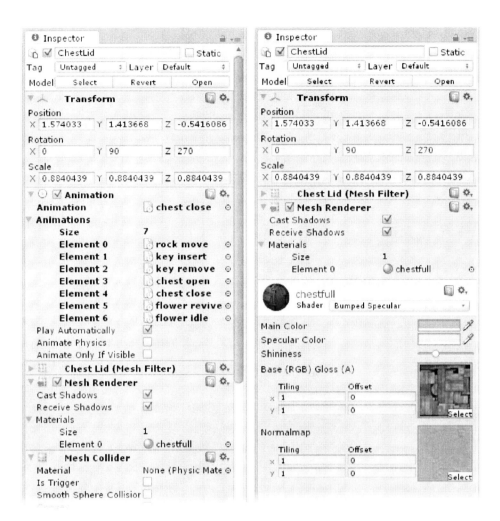

Figure 7-22. *ChestLid components from the two files*

11. Stop Play mode.

12. Select AnimationObjects in the Hierarchy view.

13. Uncheck Play Automatically.

14. Repeat for its children, Rock, and KeyAtLock.

15. Click Play.

Nothing animates. The location on the time line is too early for the ChestLid.

16. Stop Play mode.

17. Select the ChestLid.

18. Try to change the Animation to chest close.

You will notice there are several chest close animations listed. To find the correct clip, do the following:

19. Select the chest close clip in the Animations array drop-down.

When you first click it, the matching clip will highlight in the Project view.

20. Select the highlighted clip and drag it into the Animation field.

21. Click Play.

The lid slams shut.

22. Stop Play mode.

Individual Transforms

So far, we've only positioned objects by moving the entire group they came in with. Let's see what happens if we try to move a child of one of the imported groups.

1. Deactivate AnimationObjects and its children.

2. Activate AnimationObjectsFull and its children.

3. In the Hierarchy view, select its Rock and move it closer to the chest.

4. Select the AnimationObjectsFull object again.

5. Set its default Animation to g-rock move.

6. Click Play.

The rock jumps back to its original position in relation to its parent group or GameObject before animating.

7. Stop Play mode.

8. Click Undo from the Edit menu until the rock is back to its original position.

This is a key concept in Unity. Animated objects that are imported in a single file *may not be transformed individually*. This means you can only move, rotate, or scale the objects by transforming the *entire group*.

9. Try moving or scaling the pedestal.

10. Click Play.

Nothing happens because it has no animation.

11. Undo.

At this point, after seeing all the issues, you may be wondering why in the world you would even want to import several objects in a single file. One obvious scenario is something like a building that has operational doors with possibly complex animations. Trying to bring the doors in from individual files and making sure they are positioned *exactly* right could be challenging if anything was moved. And while you will learn how to animate simple behaviors in Unity, something like the compound movements of an airplane door and its complex mechanism are best left to DCC applications. You'd probably also use this approach with a mechanical construction, where all the different parts and gears need to animate since their positions relative to each other must be exact.

Most important for our point and click genre is that we need to control sequences of events so we can move the game forward. Take the example of a nice bull's eye target. The straw bales on which the target is mounted may have a particular area that when a projectile finds it, could trigger a series of catastrophic and/or amusing events. Relying on the user to find this "sweet spot" by chance with physics in charge of the action could mean the player never hits it. In this case, you would need a "canned" animation of the projectile hitting the correct spot and the ensuing animation of what could be several objects. If the author had to arrange each object manually, the sequence might not work. By bringing the objects in together in one file, with the sequence already animated, you are assured that the player will be able to move forward through the game. This is not to say you couldn't combine the two types of actions, randomly calling the canned version at predetermined points (to avoid frustrating those of us who seem to be incapable of hitting the broad side of a barn), but it is necessary to at least substitute the baked sequence at some predetermined time.

12. Delete AnimationObjectsFull and its children from the Hierarchy view.

13. Delete AnimationObjectsFull in the Project view.

14. Activate the *AnimationObjects* and its children.

15. Save the scene and save the project.

Complex Hierarchies

Because the flower has its own complicated bone system as well as FK (forward kinematics) animation, and because no other object in the scene will be affecting it, it makes sense to put it in its own file. We included the flower because it covers a lot of nonstandard issues you might come up against when you start designing your own action objects. And face it, complex animation is generally more intriguing for the player to watch. As there are a few things to beware of even with a single import, we will take a few minutes to become familiar with them. Although the flower will not be hopping around the scene trying to eat unsuspecting players, it is controlled much as a character is in that the Animation component is on the root or parent. All child animations are controlled from there.

1. Select the Flower prefab in the Project view.

2. Set its Scale Factor to **0.01**.

3. Set the Generation to Store in Root

4. Add the clips shown in Table 7-3.

Table 7-3. *Flower Behaviors*

Object, Behavior	Start Frame	End Frame
flower revive	1	124
flower idle	125	200

5. Click Apply.

6. Drag the Flower into the scene and move it around.

7. Click Play.

8. Save the scene and save the project.

It stays right where you drag it!

Parenting

The Flower behaves itself when transformed because, by its very nature, it is a *group* containing its various child elements. When an animated object has a parent, it can be positioned around the scene at will because the parent's transform is added to the child's. When an animated object does *not* have a parent, you need to create one for it before it can be positioned. The JumpingBean file contains a single animated object. In the JumpingBeanGrouped file, the bean has been added to a group *before* exporting.

1. Select the JumpingBean object in the Animation Tests folder in the Project view.

2. Set its Scale Factor to **0.01**.

3. Repeat the steps for the JumpingBeanGrouped object.

4. Drag both beans into the scene, remembering which is which.

5. Click Play.

As Figure 7-23 shows, the grouped bean animates as expected, but the regular bean disappears. It actually pops back to about 0,0,0, its origin in the Max file, but it may as well have left the scene entirely for all the good it does us.

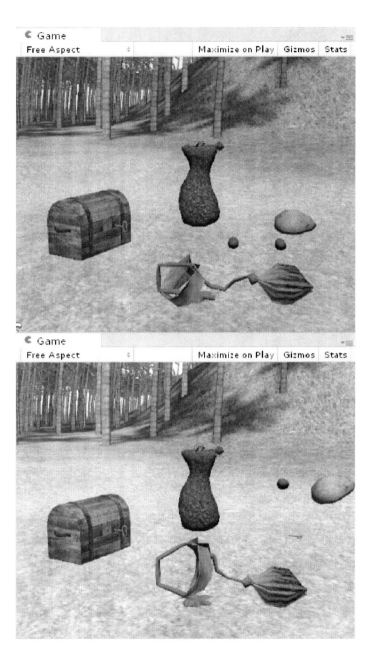

Figure 7-23. *The two beans at rest and in action; the non-grouped bean is MIA.*

You may not always have access to the original files or to a means of editing them when imported animated objects are in need of a parent. Don't despair, you can still create a parent GameObject in Unity to avoid the transform issue.

   6.   Delete the JumpingBean in the Hierarchy view.

   7.   Create a new Empty GameObject.

   8.   Name it BeanParent.

   9.   Set its Position to 0,0,0 in the Inspector.

   10. Drag a new JumpingBean into the Hierarchy, *not* into the Scene view.

Note that its Transforms are nearly 0,0,0.

   11. In the Hierarchy view, drag the JumpingBean into the BeanParent GameObject.

It is now parented so it should be safe to transform in the scene.

   12. Select the BeanParent as in Figure 7-24.

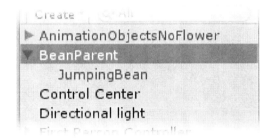

Figure 7-24. *The new bean group*

   13. From the GameObject menu, use Move to View to bring the BeanParent near the other test objects.

   14. Move it close to where it was before so you can watch it animate, being careful to move *only* the parent object.

   15. Click Play.

Both beans now animate as expected (Figure 7-25).

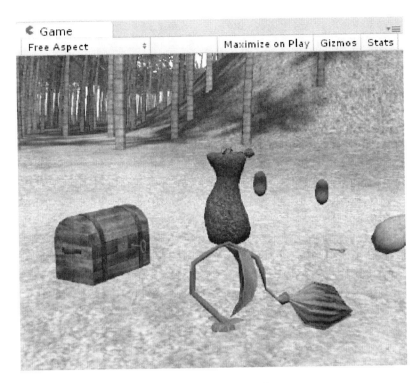

Figure 7-25. *Both beans animating as expected*

■ **Tip**   If an imported object disappears when you click play, it probably needs to be parented before it can be transformed in the scene. Use the technique of parenting to an empty GameObject at 0,0,0 before transforming.

---

16. Stop Play mode.
17. Delete all of the beans from both the Hierarchy and the Project Project view.

Setting up Materials

As mentioned earlier, Unity imports materials only on a very limited basis and most of our action objects, at least, deserve better than the default material. This means you'll definitely need to spend some time customizing and improving the defaults that are created on import. Unity uses shaders exclusively so you'll be able to get a lot of rather nice effects once you understand how they can be manipulated.

Let's look, then, to see how the objects came in. Since the textures were brought in at the same time, most of the objects will have had a default material created from their Diffuse texture. The default material uses a simple Diffuse shader that has only a Base texture and a Main Color that can be used to tint the texture map.

Let's go through the imported objects one at a time and "doctor" them up a bit.

The Keys

The two keys, a couple of wrought iron types, originally had only a bump map. Because they had no diffuse, Unity created a generic Diffuse texture, using the original material's diffuse color, the file name and the original material name, "Key." As we imported the four files with the keys in them, Unity generated four different materials. When we deleted two of those files from the Project view, the extra materials remained (Figure 7-26). Unfortunately, if you delete the material and then update or reimport the file, the material will be generated again. If you rename it, the file using that particular version of it will retain its connection to it.

Figure 7-26. *Duplicate key materials*

Tip Even if an object does not use a texture for its Diffuse channel, consider assigning a simple image with the name of the material to keep importing cleaner.

---

1. Delete the animationobjectsfull-key key material.

2. Delete the animationobjectsold-key key material.

3. Rename the animationobjects-key key material to Key.

4. Assign it to the keys in the scene

In 3ds Max, where the meshes were made, the bump uses a texture called Hammered.jpg. In Unity's shaders, we will use a Normal Map instead.

5. Select the Hammered texture from the Textures folder.

6. Check it out in the Preview window in the Inspector (Figure 7-27).

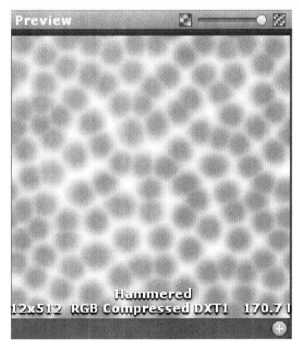

Figure 7-27. *The Hammered texture in the Preview window*

The texture has already been converted to a DXT1 texture format and Mip Maps have been generated for it. Unity converts all non-dds formatted texture to dds on import.

Unity can automatically turn it into a normal map for us so we will duplicate it first.

7. Use Ctrl + D (or Command +D) to duplicate the texture.

8. Select Hammered 1.

9. In the Texture Importer, change the Texture Type to Normal map.

10. Click Apply.

The map is now the distinctive Cyan/Magenta colors of a normal map, as shown in Figure 7-28.

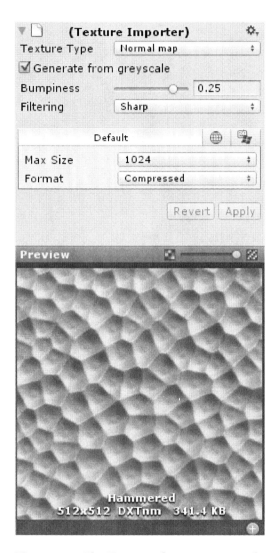

Figure 7-28. *The Hammered texture converted to a Normal map*

11. Rename the texture to reflect its new function: HammeredBump.

12. Select the *Key* material.

13. Change its shader to Bumped Specular.

14. Leave the Base map as None and drag and drop the HammeredBump onto its Normalmap thumbnail (Figure 7-29).

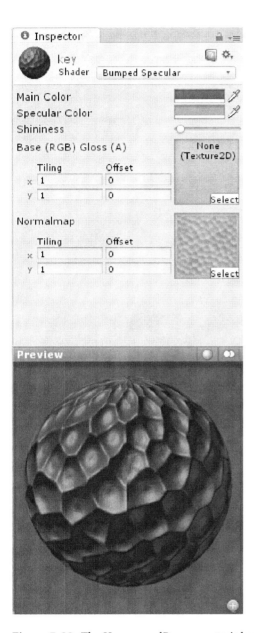

Figure 7-29. *The HammeredBump material using the Bumped Specular shader*

Normal maps are a means of creating virtual geometry for lighting calculations. When you start with actual geometry, the vertex normal for each vertex is recorded as a particular color on an image or texture. The texture map needs to be big enough to allocate at least one pixel for each vertex for full effect. In a game, the lighting calculations still take time to calculate, but the object itself has fewer vertices and takes up less overhead. As long as the normal map is not too big, the trade-off of polygons vs. texture memory is usually advantageous, providing the target platform has a graphics chip or card that can support it.

The bump probably looks too extreme.

15. Select the HammeredBump texture again from the Textures folder and drop its Bumpiness value to **0.1**.

16. Click Apply.

The material should look much improved.

17. Now select one of the keys in the Project view to check the end result in the Preview window, as in Figure 7-30.

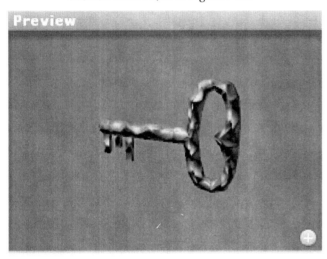

Figure 7-30. *One of the keys with the doctored material*

The texture needs to be tiled more to fit the mesh better.

18. Change both the x and the y Tiling to **5**, as in Figure 7-31.

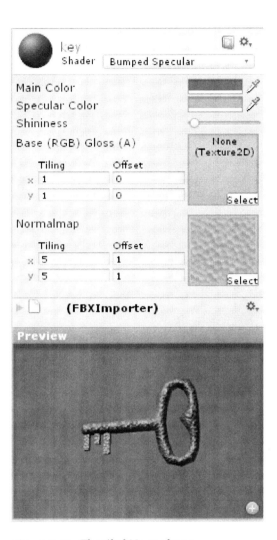

Figure 7-31. *The tiled Normalmap*

The material looks good in the preview, but we should check it in the scene.

19. Click Play and drive over to the key at the rock after it has been revealed (Figure 7-32).

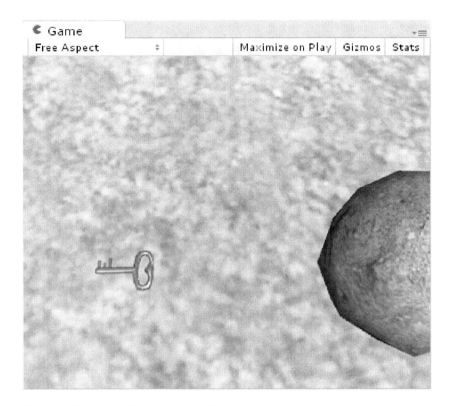

Figure 7-32. *One of the keys in the Game window at runtime*

The key doesn't stand out much. You may want to darken the Main Color or reduce the Shininess. In Unity Pro, with dynamic shadows turned on, you could have different issues. That's why it's important to test art assets in a game before they are finalized. For the key, you may decide gold or brass would be a better choice.

20. Experiment with the key material's settings until you are happy with the effect.

21. Make note of the new settings and make them permanent after you stop Play mode.

The Chest

The chest base and lid share a texture map, ChestFull. However, since the texture represents three different "materials" (wood, leather, and metal), you will also want to use a glossiness map along with a normal map to differentiate each beyond the diffuse color of the texture.

With shaders in Unity, it is not unusual to put other types of 8-bit maps in the alpha channel. Each shader will show what, if anything, the alpha channel is being used for.

1. Select the ChestFull material.

Even when the object's material comes in with a texture, you'll note that the Main Color defaults to mid-gray. This color gets added to the texture map, allowing you to tint it on an individual basis. If your texture looks too dark in the scene, you can change the Main Color to white.

Inspection of the default Diffuse shader shows the Base texture using RGB.

2.   Select the Bumped Diffuse and look at its parameters.

The Base is again RGB. The Normalmap is also RGB. If you are used to using grayscale bump maps, this will remind you that Unity Shaders use RGB Normal maps. Using a grayscale bump map instead of a normal map will produce odd lighting results.

■ **Tip**   Wait to convert your grayscale bump maps to normal maps in Unity so you can easily adjust their bumpiness strength.

---

3.   Select the next shader down, the Bumped Specular, for the ChestFull material.

This shader has a new parameter, Shininess, that will let you affect the specular highlight of the material. More importantly, it uses the alpha channel of the Base texture as a specular mask.

4.   Set the Shininess about half way along the slider to tighten the highlight.

5.   Now drag in the Preview window so you can see the difference in the "materials" as the view rotates around the sample sphere.

The straps are somewhat glossy, but the metal parts are more so.

6.   Select the ChestFull texture in the Project view.

7.   In the Inspector, toggle the diffuse/alpha button at the top of the Preview window to see the alpha channel of the texture.

This alpha channel was designed to be used as a bump and shininess map rather than an alpha mask. You may notice that there's a check box to Generate Alpha from Greyscale. That operation is permanent! If an alpha channel already exists (as with the ChestFull texture), it will be overwritten. If you want to experiment, make a duplicate of the texture first.

Figure 7-33 shows the superior contrast of the custom shininess map (center) compared with an automatically generated version. It will also be a better choice for generating a normal map.

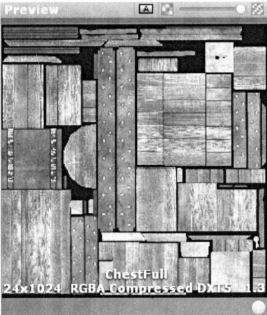

Figure 7-33. *The Diffuse texture, its custom alpha channel, and an alpha channel generated in Unity using its grayscale version*

8. Select the ChestFullBump texture.

9. Change its Texture Type to Normal map and click Apply (Figure 7-34).

10. Set the Bumpiness to about **0.05** and click Apply.

1024×1024 is a bit of overkill for one small chest.

11. Set its Max Size to **512** and click Apply.

Figure 7-34. *The ChestFullBump as a Normal map*

12. Select the ChestFull material again.

13. Drag and drop the newly generated normal map into its Normalmap thumbnail.

14. Click Play and navigate around the chest.

You may decide that the 1024×1024 diffuse/shininess map can be reduced as well. Once an asset is in the game environment, you'll have a better idea of how big of a texture map it rates. In this case, the 512 version is slightly blurrier on the wood section, but still provides good definition for the straps and hobnails, so it would be a worthwhile conservation of texture memory. On mobile platform such as iPhone or Android, you'll need to keep texture sizes fairly small to stay within their total texture limits.

Flower

Let's look at a last material. The flower is a bit different from the other objects in that it has multiple materials on one of its objects.

1. Activate the Flower in the Hierarchy view.

2. Open the Flower object in the Project view.

3. Select the Stem prefab.

In the Inspector, you will see that there are two materials listed for it, *leafstripey* and *leavesdual*.

4. Select the Stem from the Flower in the Hierarchy view and open the Materials array to view its contents.

The array has two elements, the two materials, as shown in Figure 7-35.

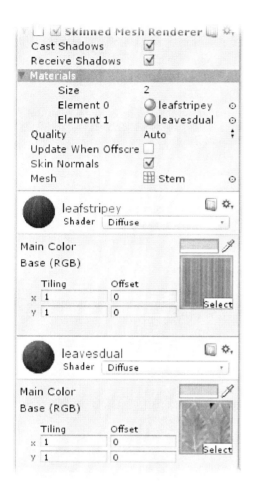

Figure 7-35. *The Stem Materials array*

▓ **Tip**   Arrays always start counting their elements at 0. An array of 2 has element 0 and element 1.

If you wanted the flower to be an action object, that is, one you'd need to click on, it would be better to use a single unwrap map to make the textures for the leaves *and* petals. Since you are only going to trigger its animation from an action object for now, you don't need to worry about it.

> **Tip** Assets with unwrap textures are generally easier to handle in games, but the trade-off is the possibility of using more texture memory to get the same resolution, or settling for a reduction in quality.

The jewel in the center of the flower presents some nice texture possibilities. Since the Jewel object is deep in the bone hierarchy, you will need to expand the Flower object to gain access to it.

Remember to hold down the Alt key when you open the group in the Hierarchy view.

5. Locate the Jewel just below Bone07 and select it.

It is using a material called Pods.

6. Change the shader to Particles/Additive (Soft).

7. Click Play to see the results when the flower opens up (see Figure 7-36).

Figure 7-36. *The Jewel's new shader*

In the Particles shaders, black is treated as transparent.

8.   Try experimenting with other Particles shaders.

Note that the changes to shaders are not lost when you stop Play Mode.
The Rock uses the RedGround texture.

9.   Change the grndred's shader to Bumped Diffuse.

10. Use Crtl+D to duplicate the Asphalt texture and turn the clone into a normal map.

11. Add the new normal map to the grndred shader.

12. Try experimenting with different shaders.

13. Save the scene and save the project.

Shadows

Now that you've used the materials to make the imported objects look much better, you are probably thinking some shadows would help to make them look like they belong in the scene and aren't just "photoshopped" in. In Unity Pro you can set the main light to cast soft shadows and everything will look much nicer—at the cost of some frame rate, of course.

Let's address shadows in Pro first as it is more a matter of tweaking the shadow strength. Depending on where your light source is, you may need to adjust the shadow parameters.

1.   Select the Directional light

In the Inspector, you can see the shadow parameters. Strength controls how dark or dense the shadow is.

2.   Select the Directional Light from the Hierarchy view.

3.   Adjust the Strength until the dynamic shadows match the baked shadows.

Take a look at Figure 7-37. On the left, we used dual lightmaps with Lightmapping set to Auto for the directional light. In the Project's Quality settings, we set the Shadow Distance to 45. The realtime shadows blend into the lightmap shadows 45 meters out from the Main Camera. On the right, we turned off the Use Lightmaps parameter (open the Lightmapper and uncheck the option in the Scene view) to show where the realtime shadows blend with the lightmapped shadows.

Figure 7-37. *Shadows in Unity Pro*

If you are using Unity Pro and have shadows, you may want to investigate Shadows further in the reference manual. You'll find some very nice examples of "Cascades" and see how they can improve the look of your shadows. You can find the Cascades setting in the Quality Settings.

Static Objects

If you don't have Unity Pro, you have a couple of choices—no shadows or fake shadows. If the objects never move, they can be marked as Static and shadows will be baked for them. But for animating objects, leaving a shadow behind as the object animates away from its original position is going to look pretty silly. In our example, some objects, such as the flower and chest lid, are probably fine with no shadows. Others, such as the rock, will need some help. Shadows, in any form, will cost. If they are baked in, they cost texture memory. If they are dynamic, they cost processor time. If we fake dynamic shadows with Unity's Blob Shadow preset—a light with a negative strength—they also cost processor time, but not as much.

Using shadows increases the quality of a scene, removes visual ambiguity, and, along with specular highlights, helps define a 3D shape. To put it bluntly, things just look better with shadows, but dealing with shadows in realtime is vastly different than in DCC programs.

To generate baked secondary shadows in Unity, the object must be marked as Static.

1.   Select the ChestBase.

2.   In the Inspector, at the top right, check Static (Figure 7-38).

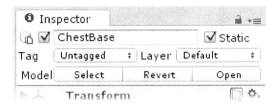

Figure 7-38. *Selecting the Static parameter in the Inspector*

The Pedestal does not animate either.

3.   Set the Pedestal to Static as well.

The next time you bake out the terrain lighting, the shadows will be added.

Blob shadows are often used for generic character shadows when you're creating games for low-end platforms. Objects like the rock are good candidates for a blob shadow if they're in an animated group.

If you don't see a Projectors folder in the Standard Assets folder (Figure 7-39), you'll need to bring it in.

4.   From the Assets menu, select Import Package.

5.   Navigate to where Unity is installed.

6.   Go to Editor ➤ Standard Packages ➤ Projectors.unityPackage.

7.   Select all and Import.

Figure 7-39. *The Projectors folder*

8. Select the LiftingRockGroup from the Animations Tests in the Project view.

9. Change its Scale Factor to **0.01** and click Apply.

10. Drag it into the Scene view.

11. Deactivate the Flower and its children so you have a good view of the rock.

12. From the Projectors folder, drag a Blob Shadow Projector into the Scene view.

13. Position it over the LiftingRockGroup and move it up or down until the "shadow" looks about the right size (Figure 7-40).

Figure 7-40. *Positioning the blob shadow*

Right now, the projector light projects on the top of the rock group. With a character, you'd use layers to prevent the blob shadow from projecting on the character itself. You can use the same technique on the rock or any of the action objects. For the test subject, let's adjust the clipping plane until the shadow looks correct and then create a layer so we can exclude the rock itself from receiving the shadow. We'll also look at a non-layer alternative.

14. In the Inspector, change the Blob Shadow Projector's Projector component's Aspect Ratio to **1.4**.

15. Change the Far Clip Plane to about **15**.

16. At the top of the Inspector, click the Layer drop-down and select Add Layer.

17. To the right of User Layer 11, activate the text field and name the layer NoBlob.

18. Select the Blob Shadow Projector again in the Hierarchy layer.

19. Click the drop-down for Ignore Layers and select the NoBlob layer.

20. Select the Rock.

21. At the top of the Inspector, click the Layer drop-down and select the NoBlob layer.

The rock is now ignored by the Blob Shadow Projector so only the ground receives the fake shadow, as shown in Figure 7-41.

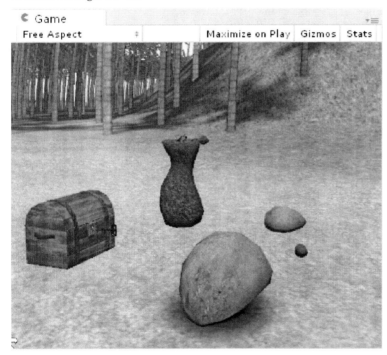

Figure 7-41. *Adjusting the Projector settings to fix the shadow*

22. When it looks about right, drag the Blob Shadow Projector onto the Rock Group.

23. Click Continue at the Losing Prefab warning.

24. Click Play and watch the Rock and its "shadow" (Figure 7-42).

25. Stop Play mode.

■ **Tip**   If you decide to use blob shadows and are using the NoBlob layer to exclude them from the projector lights, you will need to include the NoBlob layer in lights and cameras once you start changing their culling masks. We will delve deeper into Layers later on in the project as we set up an inventory system.

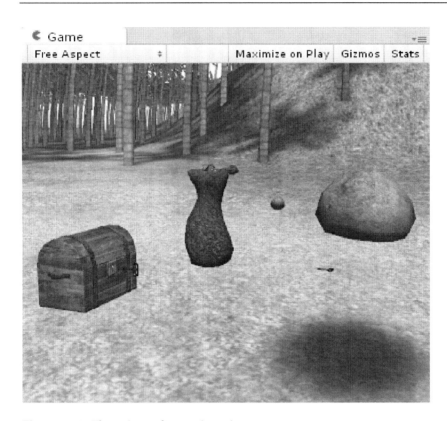

Figure 7-42. *The animated group in action*

If you don't wish to complicate the scene by adding a layer, you can spend a bit more time tweaking and adjust the Blob Shadow Projector's Near Clip Plane. It is a bit more work for each object, but you won't need to worry about lights and cameras later in the project.

1. Select the Rock and set its Layer back to Default.

2. Select the Blob Shadow Projector and set the Ignore Layers back to Nothing.

3. Change the Near Clip Plane to about **2.73** or until the top of the bean is no longer darkened.

4. Click Play and watch the rock move again.

5. Stop Play mode.

6. Deactivate the LiftingRockGroup and move it into the Test Action Objects group.

7. Save the scene and save the project.

■ **Tip**   Changing Ignore Layers tends to generate an error about deleted objects. You can clear the error message from the console, though, so it doesn't seem to actually affect anything. This could be the reason the Projectors package is not listed on new project choices.

Colliders

Before we get back to animations, let's do a quick scene check and navigate around our new objects.

1. Click Play and try going over the chest.

If the chest is centered in the Scene view, you will see the First Person Controller's capsule drive right through it.

Figure 7-43. *The chest doesn't have a collider*

2. Drag the Cube, Capsule and Sphere out of the Test Action Objects group and activate them.

3. Move them away from the other objects if necessary.

4. Click Play.

5. Try going through the objects we created in Unity.

These objects cause the first person to either go around or go over.

6. Click on each of the Unity objects and look in the Inspector for colliders.

You will see Box, Capsule, and Sphere colliders. When you create an object in Unity, the appropriate Collider component is automatically added. Colliders serve two main purposes. They provide a means of collision detection with the mesh in a physical manner, and they can also act just as a means to trigger an event or reaction.

Note the Is Trigger parameter present in each Collider component. As we saw briefly in the previous chapter, by using a trigger, you can define areas that turn lights off or on, activate enemies, load a new level, or start almost any other type of action that can happen in a given volume of space *without stopping* the First Person Controller.

Providing collision detection is, by far, the more common use for Colliders.

In the Component menu, under the Physics submenu, you will see three more collider types. The Wheel and Raycast Colliders are mainly used for vehicles in physics simulations, and so we will not be using them. The Mesh Collider, however, is a mainstay for imported objects.

If the task of adding colliders to every object you import for your game seems daunting, don't panic. One of the import options is to create Mesh Colliders for every object on import automatically.

1. Stop Play mode.

2. Deactivate the Cube, Capsule, and Sphere and move them back into the Test Action Objects group.

3. Select the AnimationObjects prefab in the Project view.

In the FBXImporter section, the third parameter down lets you have Unity generate colliders for you. Like scale, once configured in a scene, the collider setting will be automatically applied to subsequent imports.

4. Check Generate Colliders and then click Apply.

5. Try driving into the objects now.

A quick look through the imported objects will show that a Mesh Collider has been added to each, as shown in Figure 7-44. To change any of the settings, you'll need to select the objects that have been added to the Scene.

Figure 7-44. *The generated Mesh Collider*

Mesh colliders are the most expensive of the shapes to use as they calculate collision on a face basis from the actual geometry rather than a simple primitive. Many imported meshes can have their colliders reassigned for better efficiency.

Let's go through our objects one at a time, and assess their needs. The most important thing to note is that in a classic point and click adventure game, you will generally need prebaked animations to insure the correct results from user interaction. With the exception of the occasional task that requires some sort of munitions, our main focus will be with object interaction that is not physics-based. In our test setup, at any rate, none of our objects will be controlled by physics, so their needs are fairly simple. The benefit is that you can conserve resources by making some intelligent choices.

Starting at the bottom of the list in the Hierarchy view for the AnimationObjects, the rock can easily use a sphere type of collider.

1. Open the AnimationObjects group in the Hierarchy.

2. Select the Rock and add a Sphere Collider from the Components ➤ Physics submenu.

You will see a message warning that you will lose the prefab.

3. Click Add.

Next, you'll see a dialog that wants to know if it should Replace the existing collider, or Add, or Cancel.

4. Click Replace.

If you inspect the new collider in the Scene view, you may find it is a bit high (see Figure 7-45).

Figure 7-45. *The Sphere Collider on the rock*

5. From the Sphere Collider component, adjust its Z Center and Radius if necessary.

Next, look at the Pedestal object. The Mesh Collider follows the mesh exactly, including some concave areas. Concave mesh collision is the most expensive of the lot. Since we don't need that much accuracy for this static mesh, you could check the Convex Only check box. At this point, however, it looks suspiciously similar to the Capsule Collider, so we may as well use that instead.

6. Replace the Mesh Collider with a Capsule Collider.

7. Since the pedestal was imported with it Z axis up, move the Z center down and then adjust the radius of the collider if necessary.

■ **Tip**   You may occasionally find that complex meshes fail to generate a viable collider at all. If this happens and you can't use one of the standard colliders, consider creating a low poly stand-in for the Mesh Collider to use. Simply remove or turn off its Mesh Renderer.

---

8. Next, select the KeyAtLock.

It is small enough not to even bother with a collider for the sake of *collision*, but we do need to be able to pick it. That's the other reason to use a collider—to be pickable with the cursor, an object *must* have a collider.

9. Check Is Trigger.

You are probably zoomed in quite close at this point. If you zoom back a bit, you'll realize that the key presents a pretty small target for a mouse pick. It would make much more sense to exchange its mesh collider for a Box Collider.

10. Replace the Mesh Collider with the Box Collider (Figure 7-46) and check Is Trigger.

11. You may also wish the increase the Box Collider's size to make picking easier.

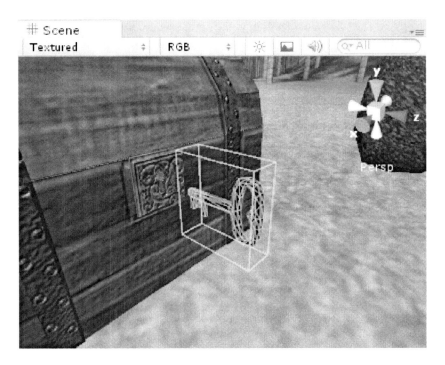

Figure 7-46. *A Box Collider on the KeyAtLock*

12. Select the rock and temporarily turn off its mesh renderer so you can see the key underneath it.

The KeyAtRock is a duplicate of the KeyAtLock, so you can repeat the previous steps for it. If you can't see it, raise it up until it sits above the ground (it doesn't yet have an animation so it's safe to do this). Remember to turn the rock's Mesh Renderer back on.

Let's deal with the Chest Lid next. A quick test with the automatically generated Mesh Collider shows that it is too high to "walk" over, so there's really no reason to use an expensive Mesh Collider.

13. Replace the Mesh Collider with a simple Box Collider (remember to stop Play mode before adding the collider).

14. Select the ChestBase.

You are probably thinking you'll use a Box Collider for this object. It certainly doesn't need the complexity of the handles or keyhole for a straight collision object. There is, however, another issue to factor in.

15. Temporarily turn off the ChestLid's Mesh Renderer.

16. Now look down inside the box.

If you use a Box Collider, it will intercept any picks aimed at objects placed within the box. Moreover, you can have only one of each kind of collider on each object, so you would need to create four GameObjects and parent them to the ChestBase, and then create and position a Box Collider for each to coincide with the ChestBase sides.

Given these issues, it's easier to simply use the generated Mesh Collider for the ChestBase.

The last collider you need to add is one for the lockplate. This one is for the sole purpose of receiving a pick, so be sure to check Is Trigger.

17. Create an Empty GameObject.

18. Name it LockPlate.

19. Add a Box Collider to it.

20. Make it stick out farther than the front of the chest so it will receive the pick first.

21. Drag it into the AnimationObjects group.

22. Turn on the ChestLid's Mesh Renderer.

Now all of the objects have colliders, as shown in Figure 7-47.

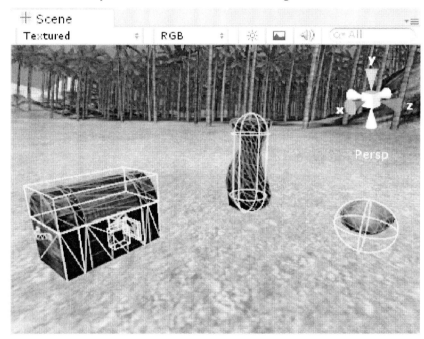

Figure 7-47. *The chest objects with their colliders*

23. Save the scene and save the project.

Animation

Now that you've got some objects with animations, you need a nice generic script to activate the clip of your choice.

So that you can see when you cause the animation to play, you'll call the script from the OnMouseDown function. You will need to turn off the Play Automatically setting on the objects you'll be testing. But first, let's decide which objects to test.

The simplest route is to use the animated objects in AnimationObjects. Because they were imported to Store in Original Root, you can access them directly rather than through their parent.

Testing will be easier if the camera is in the right place on start up.

1. Arrange the Scene window so you have easy access to the Chest, KeyAtChest, and Rock.

2. Select the First Person Controller in the Hierarchy view and use Align with View on the GameObject menu to move the start up position.

3. Make any other adjustments that are necessary, including the X Rotation of the Main Camera.

4. Select the ChestLid object in the Hierarchy view and uncheck Play Automatically in its Animation component.

5. For the KeyAtLock, uncheck Play Automatically.

6. In the Animations array, click on Element 1, key insert, to locate the clip in the Project view.

The correct clip will be highlighted in yellow in the Project view, as shown in Figure 7-48.

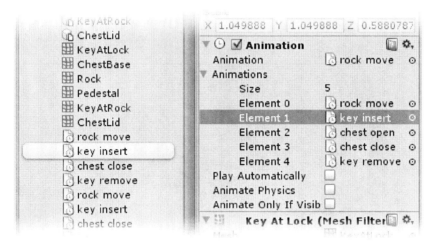

Figure 7-48. *Locating the correct Animation Clip*

7. Drag the correct clip into the default Animation parameter.

8. For the Rock, uncheck Play Automatically.

9. With our clips loaded as the default animations, let's create a simple script to trigger the clips.

10. Create a new JavaScript file in the MyScripts folder and name it `AniTest`.

11. Open the file in the editor.

You can cause an object's default animation to play by using `animation.Play()`. Let's use the `OnMouseDown` function so we can see the results when we pick it.

12. Change the `Update` function to an `OnMouseDown` function.

13. Add the following code inside the function:

```
function OnMouseDown () {

    print(name + " picked");
    animation.Play();

}
```

14. Save the script.

15. Drag and drop the script onto the Rock, the ChestLid, and the KeyAtLock.

16. Click Play.

17. Pick each of the three objects.

The ChestLid still has the *chest close* animation clip. Let's get a bit more practice finding clips.

18. Stop Play mode

19. Select ChestLid in the Hierarchy view

20. In the Inspector, open the Animations array list and pick Element 2, chest open, so it's highlighted in the Project view.

21. Drag the correct chest open clip into its Animation parameter.

22. Click Play and pick the ChestLid.

The lid opens correctly.

Currently, you're calling the default animation for each object. That's fine for the rock, which has only one behavior, but for the key and the chest lid, you'll eventually need a way to call the particular clip you want. Anything other than the default animation needs to be called by *name*. The name is a character string and so needs quotation marks around it, for example, `animation.Play("idle")`.

The problem with hardcoding the name in the command is that the script is no longer generic. Fortunately, you can declare a public variable of type `AnimationClip` and fill it in on an individual object basis.

1. Add the following line to the top of the `AniTest` script:

```
var aniClip : AnimationClip;
```

You might be misled into thinking you have only to put the `aniClip` variable inside the parenthesis to get it to work. If, however, you surmise that a clip has a lot of properties besides its name (duration, whether it is currently playing, and so forth), you may have already guessed at the solution.

2. Change the `print` and `animation.Play` lines to:

```
print(name + " picked for " + aniClip.name);
animation.Play(aniClip.name);
```

3. Save the script to expose the new variable in the Inspector.

4. Before you click Play, you will need to load the appropriate clip into each of the three objects' `aniClip` variable.

Let's take a moment to see what happens should you forget.

5. Click Play and pick the Rock.

Figure 7-49 shows the console displaying an error message on the status line.

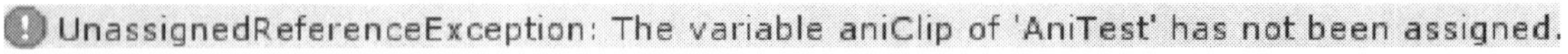

🔴 UnassignedReferenceException: The variable aniClip of 'AniTest' has not been assigned.

Figure 7-49. *Error message for a variable that needs to be assigned*

6. Stop Play mode.

7. Go ahead and assign the appropriate clips to the three objects by locating the correct clips in the Project view (click on them in the Animations arrays) and dragging them onto `aniClip`'s value field.

8. Click Play and test.

The objects animate as expected.

1. Stop Play mode.

2. Select the ChestLid.

3. Use the same method to find the correct clip and drag its chest open clip onto the `aniClip` parameter.

4. Repeat with KeyAtLock to make sure you can trigger both behaviors.

5. Click Play and test.

6. Stop Play mode.

As long as we have broken the prefab, let's go ahead and remove the unused Animation components on the Pedestal, ChestBase, and KeyAtRock.

7. Select ChestBase.

8. Right-click on the Animation component's label and select Remove Component.

9. Repeat for the other two non-animated objects.

This will keep things tidier as well as lowering overhead.

10. Save the scene and save the project.

Accessing Store in Root

Let's see how to call the animation clips on the file that was imported using the Store in Root option—the Flower.

1. Select the Flower in the Hierarchy view.

2. Activate it and its children.

░ **Tip**   From time to time, you may find it necessary to add new animations to your objects. If you have already broken the prefab, the new animations will not be automatically added to the animation clip array. To add clips, increase the Size of the Animations array and load the new clips in from the drop-down list.

---

3. Turn off Play Automatically.

4. Add the `AniTest` script to the parent GameObject, Flower.

5. Agree to lose the Prefab by choosing Continue.

6. Set the `AniClip` variable to flower revive.

7. Click Play and pick the Flower.

Nothing happens, not even a message to indicate the pick was received. This is because there are no colliders on the object to receive a pick.

8. Select the Flower in the Project view and check Generate Colliders.

9. Click Apply.

10. Click Play and try to pick the Flower.

Nothing happens.

11. Inspect the Flower child meshes.

There are no colliders.

12. Stop Play mode.

13. Select the Stem.

14. Add a Mesh Collider and the `AniTest` script.

15. Click Play and test.

Nothing happens. We didn't load a clip, but we still should expect the pick report in the console. Skinned meshes, apparently, need to be handled differently. This is not surprising when you think back to the platform problem. As soon as it was animated, it needed a RigidBody to process collisions. The platform was a single animating object, whereas the Stem is a mesh whose subobject faces all animate independently in response to the bones that control them. We need to pin down the picking process.

1. Stop Play mode.

2. Remove the Mesh Collider and the AniTest script from the Stem.

3. Select the Flower parent.

4. Add a Box Collider to it and adjust its size and alignment as in Figure 7-50.

Figure 7-50. *The Box Collider on the skinned mesh hierarchy of the Flower*

The AniTest script is already on it and set up so we are good to go.

5. Click Play and test

This time the Flower animates.
Let's see if we can trigger the looping flower idle clip by picking the Jewel.
Because the Jewel is a separate, non-skinned mesh, we should be able to add a collider and a script to it.

1. Stop Play mode.

2. Expand the Flower in the Hierarchy until you can find the Jewel.

Apparently Generate Colliders does work on non-skinned meshes in our Flower object's hierarchy. Although the Jewel is a fairly simple mesh, it will still give our players a bigger target if we change it to a primitive collider.

3. Add a Sphere Collider.

4. Click Play.

5. Pick the Flower and observe the collider in the Scene window to assure yourself that it will scale with the Jewel (Figure 7-51).

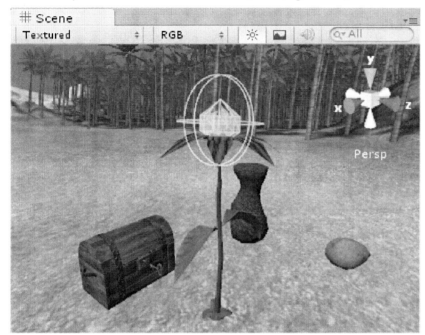

Figure 7-51. *The Jewel's scaled Sphere Collider on the revived Flower*

6. Stop Play mode.

7. Add the AniTest script.

8. Set the AniClip parameter to flower idle.

9. Click Play, pick the Flower, then pick the Jewel.

The console reports the message shown in Figure 7-52.

MissingComponentException: There is no 'Animation' attached to the "Jewel" game object, but a script is trying to access it.

Figure 7-52. *The missing-animation message*

You know that the animation is actually on the parent object, Flower, so you need to find out how to access it.

First you need to make a variable for it.

1. Open the AniTest script in the editor.

2. Add the following private variable to the AniTest script:

```
var parent : GameObject;
```

3. Save the script.

If you were using Store in Root for the AnimationObjects group, it would be easy because the parent of each of the objects is AnimationObjects. You could simply "introduce" the parent in a Start function so the rest of the script could access it, like this:

```
function Start () {

        parent = this.transform.parent.gameObject;

}
```

To find an object's parent, you need to access it through the object's transform component. The **this** is optional, but it helps remind us what object we are talking about.

To tell the engine whose animation clip to play, you would prefix animation.Play with parent., as follows:

```
parent.animation.Play(aniClip.name);
```

The problem with the Jewel is that its immediate parent, Bone07, does not have an Animation component either and you will get a Null Reference Exception message, meaning it couldn't find what you told it to look for.

In this case, the simplest solution is to just assign the Flower as the parent in the Inspector.

1. Stop Play mode.

2. Select the Jewel.

3. Drag the Flower onto the Parent parameter in the Inspector.

The problem now is that the other objects will no longer work. You could make two different scripts, but then you'd have to be careful about which one went on each object. Instead, you can add a condition to tell the script which object's animation to call.

4. Change the contents of the OnMouseDown function as follows:

```
function OnMouseDown () {

        // if there is an animation on this script's object...
        if (animation) animation.Play(aniClip.name);

        // else there wasn't, so it must be on the parent
        else parent.animation.Play(aniClip.name);
}
```

5. Save the script.

6. Click Play.

7. Pick the Flower and then the Jewel.

The Jewel was designed to have a continuous rotation. Let's set it to Loop.

8. Stop Play mode.

9. Select the Flower in the Project view.

10. Set the Wrap Mode to Loop and Check Loop (Figure 7-53).

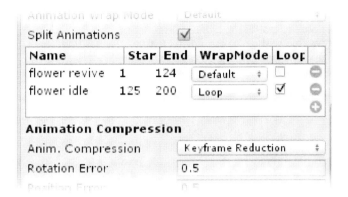

Figure 7-53. *The Flower's idle animation set to Loop*

11. Click Apply.

12. Click Play and try picking the various objects.

You now have access to the different types of imported animations from the individual objects or elements of complicated hierarchies.

13. Save the scene and save the project.

Adding Sound F/X

Game play will almost always be more immersive with the addition of sound effects to go along with the animations. Okay, let's admit it—sound effects make almost any animation vastly more entertaining. Audio cues are also a way to give the player subtle (or not so subtle) hints. Traditionally, many adventure games even featured an entire world or level that was almost exclusively audio-based. we have provided a few sound files for this project, but you are encouraged to find more to use as we go along.

Unlike textures in Unity, sound-file conversion to a more efficient format is optional. After a sound file is added to the Asset folder, you can decide on compression, format, and load format.

1. Copy the TestSounds folder into the Asset folder from the BookAssets folder.

Note that all of the sound clips have an extension of .ogg. Ogg Vorbis is an open source format with compression similar to mpegs. Unity can use other formats such as .aif, .wav, and .mp3, but it's recommended that you convert longer sound files to .ogg either in Unity or prior to importing. Free plug-ins are available for most sound-editing applications that don't already support Ogg Vorbis.

Let's look at one of the sound files and explore the options.

There are three components required to bring sound into your scene.

The first essential component is the Audio Listener. This may sound familiar as we had a warning at the start of the navigation section about having too many of these. The Audio Listener acts as a master switch to enable sound in a scene. As there should only be one Audio Listener in a scene, Unity automatically adds the component to any camera that is created. Because a scene must have at least one camera, this insures that there will always be a listener. Remember to delete extra Audio Listeners when you create additional cameras.

The second requirement for adding sound to your scene is the Audio Source component. This component is added to GameObjects throughout the scene when the sound needs to be emitted from specific locations. When the sound clips are mono as opposed to stereo, the sound can be what is called 3D sound. The sound is sent to the speakers according to the player's position in relation to the Audio Source. For sounds that are ambient in nature, such as background music, or environmental, such as wind or bird songs, you should put the Audio Source component on the main camera or first person controller.

The third requirement is the sound file itself, which must be loaded into the Audio Source component. You will be adding a bit of code to the AniTest script to trigger the sound effect at the same time as the animation when the object is picked.

Let's start with the chest lid.

1. Select the ChestLid and from the Components menu choose Audio ➤ Audio Source

2. Drag and drop the ChestOpen audio clip from the Test Sounds folder in the Project view or use the drop-down arrow and select it from the list (Figure 7-54).

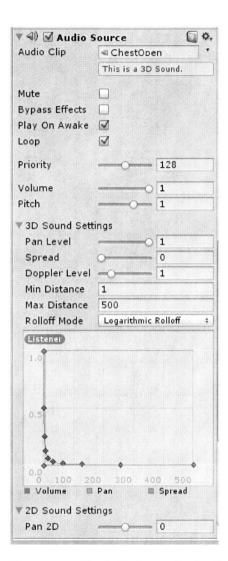

Figure 7-54. *The Audio Source for the ChestLid in the Inspector*

Until we get the Rolloff Factor, we will let the clip play On Awake (when we start the game).

3. Check Loop so you'll be able to test the various parameters.

4. Click Play and use the arrow keys to look from side to side to get the effect of the 3D sound.

5. Now move back and forth to see if the Max Distance is acceptable.

6. Experiment with the Pitch, Volume, and other parameters.

7. Turn off Play mode and make your preferred changes permanent.

8. Turn off Play On Awake and Loop.

9. Open the `AniTest` script.

10. Add the following to the `OnMouseDown` function, beneath the existing code:

```
audio.Play(); // play the default audio clip
```

11. Save the script and click Play.

12. Click the chest lid to test the sound effects.

13. Click the rock.

You get the usual MissingComponentException error shown in Figure 7-55.

⊘ MissingComponentException: There is no 'AudioSource' attached to the "Rock" game object, but a script is trying to access it.

Figure 7-55. *Missing Audio Source error message*

14. Stop Play mode and add an Audio Source component to the rock.

15. Uncheck Play On Awake.

16. Click Play and pick the rock again.

The clip is not yet assigned, but at least you don't get an error message.
To avoid the missing component message, you can add a condition to make sure the component exists before trying to call its `Play` function.

17. Change the audio line as follows:

```
//check to make sure an Audio Source component exists before playing
if (GetComponent(AudioSource)) audio.Play();
```

18. Save the script.

19. Click Play.

20. Pick the key at lock.

No error message is generated.

21. Stop Play mode.

22. Add an Audio Source to the KeyAtLock and load the LoudClick sound clip into it.

23. Uncheck Play On Awake

24. Load the plopsm sound into the rock's Audio Source component.

25. Uncheck Play On Awake.

26. Click Play and test the two new sound effects.

In both cases, the sound needs to play nearer the end of the animation rather than at first pick. Once again this is a factor that will be specific to each object so you will need to add another public variable that can be overridden in the Inspector.

27. At the top of the script, add the following variable:

```
var audioDelay : float = 0.0;
```

By assigning the float value 0.0, you have a default delay for all objects.

In JavaScript, you can add a delay with the yield statement. To set the yield time, the syntax is yield WaitForSeconds(3.0), which would cause the script to wait for three seconds before processing the lines of code that follow. In your script, you'll use the variable named audioDelay.

28. Rearrange the audio line as follows:

```
if (GetComponent(AudioSource)) {
    yield new WaitForSeconds(audioDelay);
    audio.Play();
}
```

Note that you need to add the curly brackets since more than one expression must be carried out when the condition is met.

CURLY BRACKETS

As you look at code from various sources, you will notice different ways to use curly brackets. In the simple conditional statements, as long as there is only one instruction, you can leave them off if you wish. Think of curly brackets as shopping bags. If one hand holds the *if* and the other holds the *else*, you can have only one of each. If each hand holds a shopping bag, you can use it to hold one or several commands. The following are all equivalent:

```
//sample 1, the strippy version
if (someCondition)  DoThisNext();
else DoTheOtherThing();

//sample 2, some people prefer always seeing the curly brackets
if (someCondition)  {DoThisNext();}
else {DoTheOtherThing();}

//sample 3, we use this layout a lot when we plan on adding more instructions later
if (someCondition)  {
    DoThisNext();
}
else {
    DoTheOtherThing();
}

//sample 4, another layout for the curly brackets and indents
if (someCondition)
    {
    DoThisNext();
    }
```

```
else
    {
    DoTheOtherThing();
    }
```

---

29. Save the script.

30. In the Inspector, change the delay variable to about **0.75** for the rock and key.

31. Click Play and check the animations and their sound effects.

32. Save your scene and save the project.

The final `AniTest` script looks as follows:

```
var aniClip : AnimationClip;
var parent : GameObject;
var audioDelay : float = 0.0;

function OnMouseDown () {

    // if there is an animation on this script's object…
    if (animation) animation.Play(aniClip.name);

    // else there wasn't, so it must be on the parent
    else parent.animation.Play(aniClip.name);

    //check to make sure an Audio Source component exists before playing
    if (GetComponent(AudioSource)) {
        yield new WaitForSeconds(audioDelay);
        audio.Play();
    }

}
```

Setting up a Two-State Animation

You've probably been wondering when we were going to get around to closing the chest lid. We already have the animation; we just need to work out the logic and the mechanics.

You've already seen a sample of state management with the `SimpleRotate` script you created earlier. In that script, a variable called `rotState` tracked whether the object should rotate or not. You'll use a similar flag or variable now to track whether the chest lid is open or closed so you know which animation clip to call.

In Shooter-type games, state more often than not takes care of itself as objects are simply destroyed or put into a permanent disabled mode. In point and click adventure games, it's not unusual for objects to move between states repeatedly. While some states could possibly be set up to work on a physical basis, others can't.

States such as are required by locked doors, for example, have no physical manifestation and so require management.

To test the two-state samples, you'll use a Boolean variable to indicate which state the object is in. You'll also need to allow for the second state's animation *and* audio delay, as it will very likely be different. In the case of a door or lid, the audio clip will need to be different as well.

Let's start by changing the aniClip and audioDelay variables to private and making two new exposed variables for each. You will also need private variables to keep track of the state of the lid (or key) and to hold the correct audio clip for the current state.

1. Duplicate the AniTest script.

2. Rename it to AniTwoState.

3. Open it in the editor.

4. Change the variables to the following:

```
var aniClip0 : AnimationClip;
var aniClip1 : AnimationClip;
var audioClip0 : AudioClip;
var audioClip1 : AudioClip;
var audioDelay0 : float = 0.0;
var audioDelay1 : float = 0.0;

private var parent : GameObject;
private var aniClip : AnimationClip;
private var fXClip : AudioClip;
private var audioDelay : float;
private var objState : boolean = true;  // true is the beginning state, false is the ↵
second state
```

■ **Tip**   Always comment state variables so you (or someone else) can see what each state represents.

Because the original variable names have been left intact, you can handle the state in the OnMouseDown function before you actually call the animation and sound.

5. Add the following inside, at the top of the OnMouseDown function above the existing code so it will be handled first:

```
if (objState) {      // if objState is true ~ open/1
   objState = false;  // so change its state to closed
   aniClip = aniClip0;  // set the new clips and delay
   fXClip = audioClip0;
   audioDelay = audioDelay0;
}
 else  {  // the objState must be false ~ closed / 0
   objState = true;  // so change its state to opened
   aniClip = aniClip1;  // set the new clips and delay
   fXClip = audioClip1;

   audioDelay = audioDelay1;
```

}

Because you are going to play different audio clips for the same Audio Source, you need to use something slightly different. This allows you to use the same Audio Source for *any* sounds you want associated with the object using the script. The animation code stays the same.

6. The last line that used to read audio.Play() should now say:

```
audio.PlayOneShot(fXClip); // play the substitute sound file
```

7. Save the newly remodeled script.

8. Select the ChestLid.

9. In the Inspector, load the AniTwoState script instead of AniTest.

So far, so good. Just one little problem—you no longer have a generic animation script. Not to worry. You just have to add a little logic and make a few changes to make it work for single- *and* two-state objects. While you could have the script check for the presence of a second animation or audio, it might provide false information if one was loaded for future use or for any other reason. Let's just make a simple check box for two-state objects.

10. Add the following line to the top of the public variables:

```
var twoStates : boolean = false; // default for single state objects
```

The Boolean type creates a check box in the listener. We will set its default to false for one-state objects like the rock.

11. Add the following line above the conditional that checks for state:

```
if (twoStates == false) objState = true; // if twoStates is false…
```

Or, you could use the logical *not*, the exclamation point !:

```
if (!twoStates) objState = true;   // if twoStates is not true
```

Either line sets the one-state object to a fictional state 1 so it always animates "into" state 0.

12. Save the script.

13. Replace the original aniTest script with the more robust two-state version on the ChestLid, assigning the appropriate values as needed.

14. Be sure to check Two States for the ChestLid.

15. Click Play and try it out.

16. Replace the original aniTest script with the more robust two-state version on the Rock, assigning the appropriate values as needed.

17. Click Play and try it out.

18. Check to make sure the chest lid still works and the rock does not throw an error.

▪ **Tip**   When adding new functionality to a script, be sure to test the original to make sure it still works as well. If you wait until you have made multiple changes, problem-solving will become a nightmare.

---

19. Change the KeyAtLock to the new script as well, assigning the appropriate values as needed.

20. Be sure to check Two States for the KeyAtLock.

21. Click Play and test the various objects for both sound and animation.

22. Save your scene and save your project.

Using Unity's Animation view

Sometimes you may find it easier to add simple keyframe animations in Unity directly. You've experimented with adding animations in the Update function, but that's much more suited to continuous action. As soon as you want to do something where the speed of the animation slows down, speeds up, varies, or just slows to a stop, there's a lot of math involved.

A better solution is to use Unity's built-in Animation view to create your own keyframe animations. Let's use it to lift the key from under the rock. First you need to hide the rock while you are animating the key.

1. Select the rock and disable it from the top of the Inspector.

2. Next, select the KeyAtRock.

Tip If a mesh disappears for no apparent reason, check its Mesh Filter component. If it is missing, browse to find it again.

---

3. Change its Mesh Collider to Box Collider.

4. From the Component menu, under Miscellaneous, add an Animation component as shown in Figure 7-56.

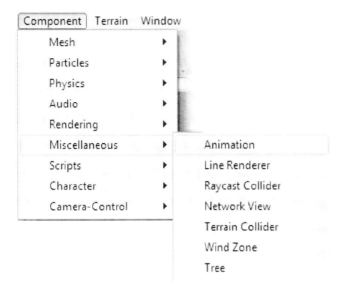

Figure 7-56. *Adding an Animation component*

In case you think it looks familiar, you're right—it's the same Animation component that's added on import. In fact, if you never got around to removing the one generated on import, you'll have gotten an error message about not being able to have two of the same components.

    5.   From the Window menu, select Animation or use Ctrl+6 on your keyboard to bring up the Animation editor, shown in Figure 7-57.

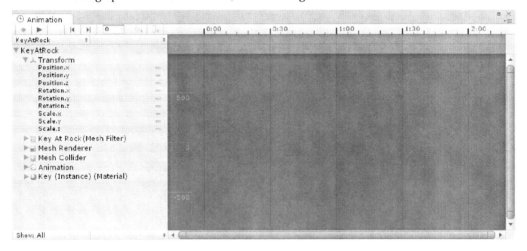

Figure 7-57. *The Animation editor*

Because it was selected, the Animation view comes up with the KeyAtRock featured. The key and all its components are listed, indicating that almost anything can be animated. This is important to note because there are a lot of things you may wish to animate that will not export with the FBX format.

The components and materials are listed as in the Inspector, and can also be expanded and contracted using the usual triangles or arrows.

Just as the imported animations came in as clips, a clip is what you'll create in the Animation view.

6.   Click the empty selection box to the right of the one with the object's name.

7.   Choose [Create New Clip]—your only choice at this point (see Figure 7-58).

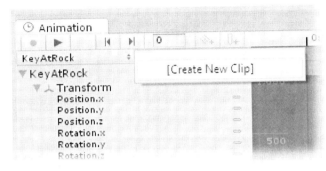

Figure 7-58. *Creating a new clip*

You will be prompted to name and save the clip in the Assets folder.

8.   Create a new folder inside the Assets folder and name it Animation Clips.

9.   Name the new clip key up.

Tip   If you haven't yet added an Animation component, one would now be added automatically.

---

10.   Reselect the KeyAtRock if need be.

The new clip shows up as Element 0 in its Animations array.

It also appears in what used to be the blank selection box in the Animation view, as shown in Figure 7-59.

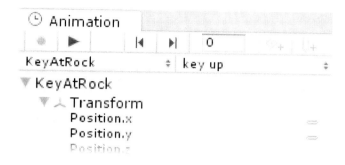

Figure 7-59. The new clip in the Animation view

> 11. Next, to begin animating, toggle on the Animation mode button—the red dot on the left, as shown in Figure 7-60.

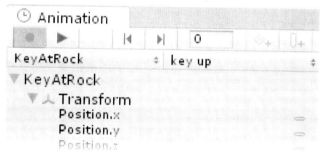

Figure 7-60. Animation mode

You now have an animation clip and you are ready to animate the key object to move up the Y axis. There are several ways to approach this. Let's try adding a new curve first.

> 1. Move the mouse over the small bar at the far right of the Position.y property.

The bar changes to show a drop-down (see Figure 7-61).

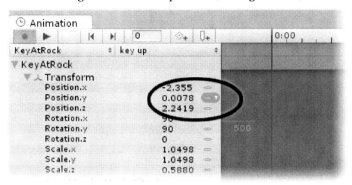

Figure 7-61. *The icon after the mouseover*

2.   Click the icon to bring up the menu (see Figure 7-62).

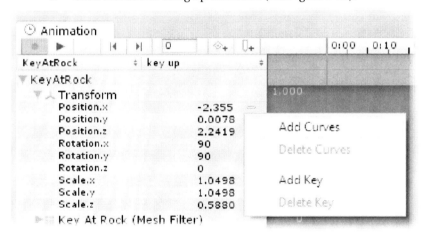

Figure 7-62. *The menu after clicking the icon*

3.   Click Add Curves.

Keyframes are created at frame 0 for Position.x, Position.y, and Position.z, establishing the key object's starting position in the animation (Figure 7-63).

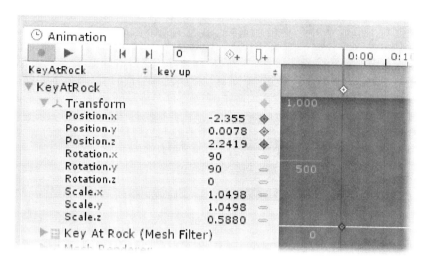

Figure 7-63. *The keys added via Add Curve*

The starting values of the object's transforms are now shown to the left of the Key Indicator column and color-coded markers are shown for the Position transform properties.

A vertical red line appears at frame 0 in the timeline. The frame is also shown to the right of the play controls.

4. Position your cursor over the red line on top of the timeline.

5. Click and drag to move it to time 1:00, watching the frame numbers change as you move the bar.

At 1:00, you can see that Unity's Animation editor uses sixty frames per second (see Figure 7-64).

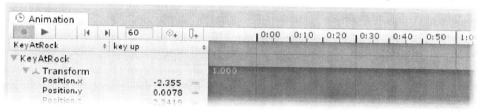

Figure 7-64. *60 frames at 1:00 (second)*

Let's go ahead and animate KeyAtRock by moving it in record mode. We are at frame 60 and Animation mode is on.

6. In the Scene view, move KeyAtRock up about a meter.

The new y position is reflected in both the Inspector and the value next to the Key Indicator. The green (y) line generated appears flat, however, so let's check to make sure something happened.

7. Drag the time bar back to frame 0 and observe the key's position as you do so. It does indeed animate.

You can also press the Play button in the Animation view to the right of the record button. This has the additional benefit of zooming in on the animation's range as soon as you click the Animate mode button again, so you can now see the y position's curve.

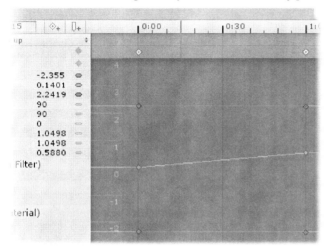

Figure 7-65. *A closer look at the new Position.y curve*

░ **Tip**   Navigating the Animation view uses the same controls as navigating the Scene view; you can focus or find selected tracks with the F key, and use the mouse and Alt key to zoom and pan. With no components selected, the F key will zoom out to the extents of all components, materials, and transforms. If you select a parameter, but none of its keys, the full animation curve will be zoomed to.

We can see by the straight line that the default animation curve for only two keys in Unity is constant; that is, the speed does not vary over the extent of the animation. While this is good for looping animations, it makes for very boring finite animation.

1. Right click over the Position.y key at frame 0 to bring up the key tangent options, shown in Figure 7-66.

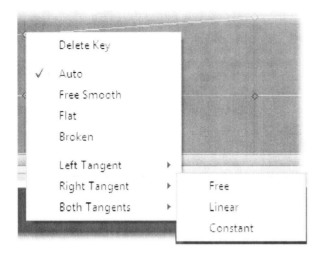

Figure 7-66. *The Key tangents in the right click menu*

The first key goes only to the right, so from Right Tangent, select Free to get a Bezier handle to manipulate.

2.   Click and drag down so the right handle is horizontal.

3.   Select the key at frame 60 and change its left tangent to Free.

4.   Move its handle down until it is horizontal as well.

5.   Deselect the key and select the Position.y track.

6.   Press the F key to zoom to the entire Position.y curve (Figure 7-67).

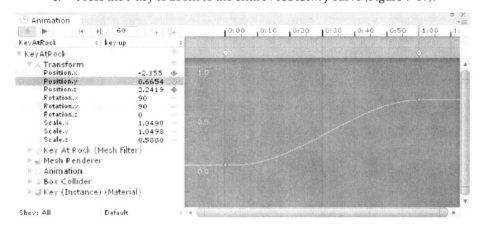

Figure 7-67. *The zoomed Position.y curve*

We now have a classic ease in/ ease out animation—it starts slow, speeds up, and then slows down again.

Click the Animation view's Play button and observe the improved animation.

READING ANIMATION CURVES

If you find reading animation curves confusing, learning the rules will help—and there are really only a few rules to remember. Time is always on the horizontal and the parameter that is being changed is on the vertical. Therefore, a line that is steep represents fast change over a short amount of time. Since a flat line represents *no change* over time, a shallow curve is slow. If the curve is straight, the rate of change is constant. Finally, if the curve changes direction, the value of the animating parameter is reversed—whether direction, rotation, opacity, etc.

fig. 1

fig. 2

fig. 3

fig. 4

fig. 5

fig. 6

fig. 7

fig. 8

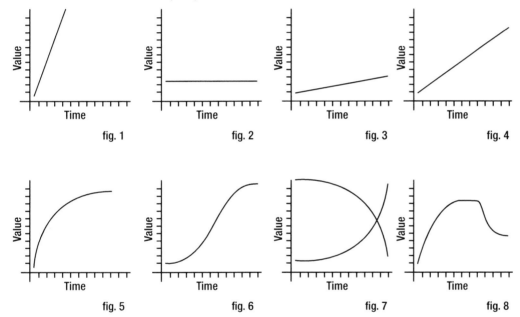

Some function curves:

fig.1- Steep = Fast

fig.2- Flat = Stopped or no change

fig.3- Shallow = Slow

fig.4- Straight = Constant rate

fig.5- Fast at start, slow at end

fig.6- Slow at start, then fast, then slow at end—classic *ease in/ease out*

fig.7- Two slow at start, fast at end curves

fig.7- Fast, then slow to dead stop, then fast back in the opposite direction (or value), then slow at end

Let's stop for a moment and add the `AniTwoState` script to the key.

1. Toggle off Animation mode in the Animation view and close the view for now.

2. In the Inspector, load the key up clip as the default animation and uncheck Play Automatically.

3. Drag the `AniTwoState` script onto the KeyAtRock.

4. Add the key up clip to the `AniClip 0` parameter.

5. Click Play and pick the key.

It animates as expected.

6. Stop Play mode and reactivate the rock.

7. Click Play and test again.

This time you must move the rock to get to the key.

Eventually, the key will go into inventory, so you shouldn't just leave it hanging in midair. You could have it pop out of existence by scaling it down to almost nothing at the last part of its animation, but you can better use the opportunity to experiment with something other than a transform. Let's have the key fade to transparent instead.

Unlike most DCC apps where you can animate the visibility of an object as one of its properties, in Unity, you need to use its *material* to affect a fade in or fade out.

Before you fade out the key, let's think about timing. One second was pretty fast for the key to move. If you add a fade out, it may happen too quickly to be visually effective. If you increase the y position animation to take place over two seconds, you can use the extra second to fade it out.

1. Stop Play mode and deactivate the rock again.

2. With KeyAtRock selected, open the Animation view.

3. Toggle on Animation mode.

4. Select the y position key at frame 60 in the Keyframe Line (just below the time line) and move it to time 2:00, frame 120.

■ **Tip**   To expose more frames before you move the key, use the arrows in the lower right corner of the Animation view.

---

5. Click the Play button in the Animation view to see the difference.

The animation time looks much more reasonable.

1. Stop Play mode.

Now you want to make the key fade out via its material, so the next thing to do is get a better look at what you need.

2.   Expand the Key material track at the bottom of the list.

You might also need to widen the left-side panel.

3.   Position the cursor over right-side edge where it meets the curves area and drag the edge over to expose the entire text for the material.

You will see that the material is shown as an instance. At this point, you may remember that KeyAtLock uses the same material. Fortunately, when we animate the opacity on the material for one key, it will not affect other objects using the same material.

4.   Select the KeyAtRock object.

5.   Open the Animation view and expand the material track again.

6.   Select the Color.a parameter and right click the Key Indicator marker and choose Add Curve.

A key is added at frame 0 with a value of 1, fully opaque.
The key should start fading at frame 60, 1 second, so you will need to add a key at that point.

7.   Move the time bar to that position and click the Add Keyframes button next to the frame indicator box (see Figure 7-68).

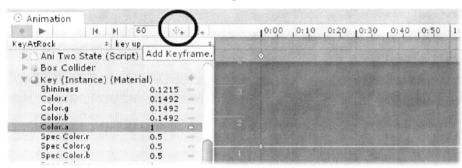

Figure 7-68. *Adding a Keyframe*

8.   Repeat at frame 120, seconds 2:00.

9.   While at frame 120, click to edit the value to the right of the Key Indicator, changing it from 1 (fully opaque) to 0 (fully transparent), as shown in Figure 7-69.

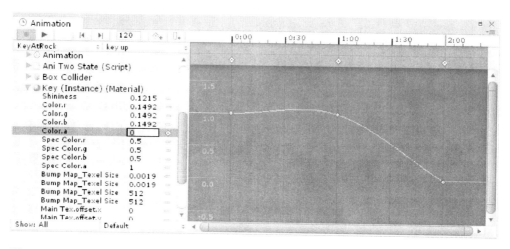

Figure 7-69. *A value of 0 at the last key*

Focusing in on the Color.a curve shows that the addition of a second key changes the default curve to a Smooth curve, the keys' tangents are interpolated smoothly from one to the next. However, the material needs to retain the value 1 until it reaches frame 60.

10. In the curve area, select the key at frame 0.

11. Right-click and change its right tangent to Constant.

12. Select the key at frame 1:00.

13. Set its left tangent to Constant.

The line straightens out nicely.

14. Adjust the rest of the curve with free tangents to get an ease in/ease out curve (Figure 7-70).

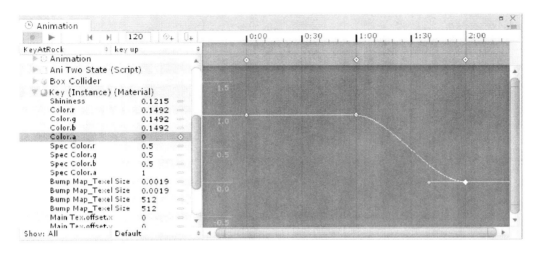

Figure 7-70. *The adjusted alpha channel curve*

> 15.   Drag the time bar to see the results.

Nothing seems to be happening. The numbers are correct—1 is fully opaque and 0 is fully transparent.

It turns out that even though you're animating the alpha *parameter*, you actually need to use a *shader* that is able to animate it as well.

1.   Select the Key material in the Project view.

2.   Change its shader to the Bumped Specular from the Transparent section.

3.   Select the KeyAtRock again so it shows in the Animation view.

4.   Zoom in closely in the Scene view so you will be able to see if it fades out.

5.   Turn on the record button and scrub the time bar again.

This time the key fades out as expected.

6.   Activate the Rock again.

7.   Save the scene and the project.

Changing Imported Animations

Now that you've added the fade out to the KeyAtRock, it has probably occurred to you that you should take a look at KeyAtLock next. It came in with imported animations, but the animations can also be viewed in the Animation view. Turns out they can't be edited, though. You need to reactivate the rock, so let's take a look at it first.

1.   Reactivate the Rock and open the Animation view.

2.   Click on the Transform track to see all of the transform curves, as shown in Figure 7-71.

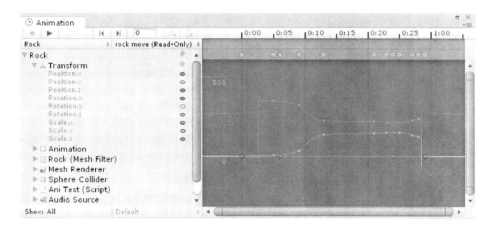

Figure 7-71. *The Rock's imported animation*

3. Try moving one of the keys.

Not only does nothing move, you can't even select a key in the first place.

If you click the clips list, you'll see that all of the clips are set to Read-Only.

To add animation to or edit an existing animation, you must make a copy of the Animation clip. While that sounds like a lot of extra work, it makes sense when you remember that the original clip belongs to the imported asset. The copy will be a duplicate but will not destroy the original.

4. Select the KeyAtLock in the Hierarchy view.

5. Locate its correct key insert clip in the Project view.

6. Use Crtl+D to duplicate it.

The duplicate will be created in the root of the Animation Tests folder.

7. Find the copy and append its name with "_copy."

8. Move the copy into the Animation Clips folder.

9. Replace the original with the copy in the KeyAtLock's Animation component for Element 1.

10. Replace the original with the copy in the `AniTwoState` script as well.

11. In the Animation view, select the KeyAtLock and the key insert_Copy clip (Figure 7-72).

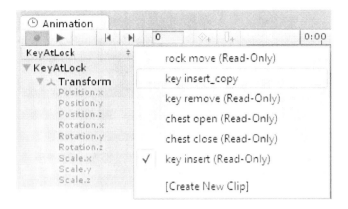

Figure 7-72. *Selecting the key insert_Copy clip*

12. Use the F key in the curve area to view the existing animation tracks.

13. Toggle on Animation mode.

14. Scrub the time bar to see when the key gets inserted into the lock.

It appears to be all the way in by frame 15, half a second in.
It would be much nicer if it had a full second to fade in before it was inserted.

■ **Tip** The imported animation was created using 30 frames per second, so the animation clip continues to use the same number of frames per second.

---

1. Expand the Key material and select the Color.a parameter

With the KeyAtRock, you used Add Keyframe to add a key to an existing curve. You can also use it to create a new curve on a selected track or tracks.

2. Move the time bar to frame 0 and click the Add Keyframe button to set the first key.

3. Save the scene and save the project.

4. At the bottom left of the view, toggle Show All to Show: Animated

Once you have a curve, you can use the filter Show: Animated to make things simpler to find.

5. Select all of the animated parameters in both Transform and Material.

6. Use F to make sure you see all the keys.

7. In the Keyframe line (just below the time line, click and drag to select all of the keys—they will turn blue, as shown in Figure 7-73.

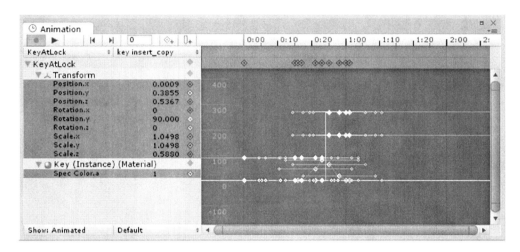

Figure 7-73. *Keys filtered for animated only, selected and ready to move*

8. Position the cursor over the key at frame 0 and move them to the right 30 frames.

9. Move the time indicator back to frame 0.

10. Click Add Key to set a new key at frame 0 as a placeholder.

11. Next select only the transforms, then right-click and change their right tangent to Constant.

12. Select only the Color.a track.

13. Use F to find the new curve.

14. Select the key at 0 and change its value from **1** to **0.**

15. Use the horizontal slider at the bottom of the Animation view to see the full timeline for the key.

16. Scrub the time indicator to see the results (Figure 7-74).

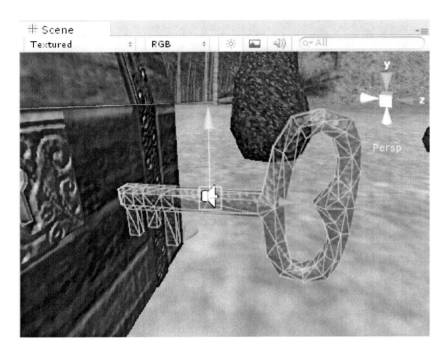

Figure 7-74. *The KeyAtLock fading in before starting to insert itself*

There seems to be a long gap between fade and move in. Animations tend to look more fluid when they overlap.

1. Select the Position.z transform and focus on it.

2. Select the second and third keys from the left in the KeyFame line and move them to the left so that they start at frame 15 (Figure 7-75).

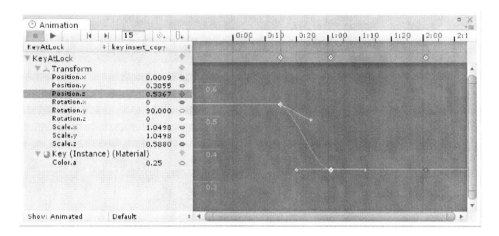

Figure 7-75. Overlapping transform and fade by shifting transform keys left

3. Close the editor.

4. If you haven't already done so, in the Inspector, swap out the AniTest Script for the AniTwoState script.

5. Add the new animation clip, insert key_Copy; the audio clip, LoudClick; and, because we shifted the whole animation over by one second, set the delay 0 to 1.75.

6. Click Play and pick the Key.

Unless you deliberately design it, you probably don't want to have a key floating in midair waiting to be picked. Furthermore, even if an object's Mesh Render is turned off, it is still pickable, so it stands to reason that even when its material is transparent, it can still be picked. Add to that the fact that you wouldn't know where to pick if it was invisible, and you'll quickly realize that the only logical way to activate the animation is to trigger it by picking another object.

The problem that raises is that all of your code is currently in the OnMouseDown function for the object it animates. Before you tackle a nice generic animation script, let's find out how to manually trigger another object's animation so you can handle those intriguing multi-object sequences.

7. Stop Play mode.

8. Save the scene and save the project.

Triggering Another Object's Animations

Until now, you've clicked directly on the object you want to animate. At some point, you'll need to be able to trigger one object's animation or change its state by clicking on another. The most typical example of this is a light switch. Pick the switch and light goes on, the switch itself toggles up, and maybe even the material changes to illuminate a lampshade. In a classic point and click adventure, anything could be triggered by interacting with any action object.

1. Create a new JavaScript in the MyScripts folder and name it `AniTrigger`.

2. Open it in the editor.

Before you add code, you need to think about what you'll need to access. You will need both the object to be triggered and the animation clip. This will require a couple of public variables so you can assign the correct objects and clips.

3. Add the following variables:

```
var aniObject : GameObject;
var aniClip : AnimationClip;
```

4. Change the `Update` function to `OnMouseDown` and add :

```
function OnMouseDown () {

    aniObject.animation.Play(aniClip.name);

}
```

5. Save the script.

6. Drag the new script onto the Pedestal object.

The pedestal already has a collider so you can't go through it, so it should be good to go. Let's trigger the flower's animation by picking on the pedestal.

Select the *Flower* GameObject in the Hierarchy view and check that it has the animation clips on its Animation component.

7. Reselect the Pedestal and drag the Flower onto the `AniObject` parameter.

8. Choose the *flower revive* clip from the `AniClip` drop-down list.

9. Use the F key to focus the Scene view to the Pedestal.

10. Make sure the Flower is positioned so you can see it when it animates without having to look around the scene.

11. Click Play and test the triggering by picking the Pedestal.

Just for fun, you can tell it to play a second, looping clip after the first is finished.

12. Add a second `aniClip` variable to hold the Flower's idle animation:

```
var aniClip2 : AnimationClip; // this will be called after the first is finished
```

13. And beneath the animation line inside the `OnMouseDown` function, add the following:

```
// wait the length of the first animation before you play the second
yield new WaitForSeconds (aniClip.length);
aniObject.animation.Play(aniClip2.name); // this one is set to loop
```

14. Save the script.

15. Stop Play mode.

16. Load the *flower idle* clip into the `AniClip2` parameter on the Pedestal.

17. Click Play and pick the Pedestal.

The flower animates through its revive clip, then loops its idle clip.

18. Open the `AniTwoState` script in the editor.

Ignoring the second clip for the time being, if you look at the code for *triggering* the animation, you can see that it's not much different from the code you're already using to call the parent object in the `AniTwoState` script. You are naming the object that contains the animation. If you don't name the object, it is assumed that the object is the one that the code resides on. But you can also refer to the object as `this`. So if you were to make a variable to hold the object with the animation, it could be assigned the `aniObject` (to trigger), the `parent` (found internally), or the object the script is on (`this`).

19. Add the variable for the triggered object:

```
var aniObject : GameObject; // if assigned this object's animation will be triggered
```
As it stands, this checks whether the object has an animation each time it is clicked before you decide which animation to call. In a point and click game, time is generally not of the essence so the slight overhead is not really an issue. For efficiency's sake, however, it makes more sense to find out which object needs its animation called only once if it does not change. The place for that is the `Start` function. This is where you will now determine and assign the target object. Let's call the new variable `aniTarget` and add it as a `private var`.

20. You will no longer be needing the `parent` variable, so you can rename it to `aniTarget`:

```
private var aniTarget : GameObject; // this will hold the final object
```
In the `Start` function, you check first for a trigger object since this will override the other objects.

1. Create the `Start` function as follows:

```
function Start () {

   if (aniObject) aniTarget = aniObject; // if one was assigned, it is the target- it must↩
contain an animation

   else aniTarget = this.gameObject; // else the target is the object this script is on

}
```
Next you check to see if the assigned target object has an animation. If it doesn't, you will use its parent's animation. You don't need to worry about the triggered object as you will have loaded the object that contains the animation anyway. From here on out, refer to `aniTarget` when calling animations, audio, etc.

2. Add the following to the `Start` function:

```
//  if the target does NOT(!) have an animation, use its parent instead
if (!aniTarget.animation) aniTarget = transform.parent.gameObject;
```
And now, down in the `OnMouseDown` function, the `if` and `else` lines that call the animation can be combined into one.

3. Replace:

```
// if there is an animation on this script's object…
if (animation) animation.Play(aniClip.name);
```

```
    // else there wasn't, so it must be on the parent
    else parent.animation.Play(aniClip.name);
```
with:
```
//play the specified animation on the specified object
aniTarget.animation.Play(aniClip.name);
```
And, finally, because of the location of the 3D sound, the audio should be part of the object whose animation is being played.

4.   Change the audio section to use the target object—whatever it may be:

```
if (aniTarget.GetComponent(AudioSource)) {
    yield new WaitForSeconds (audioDelay);
    aniTarget.audio.PlayOneShot(fXClip);
}
```

5.   Save the script.

6.   Click Play and test the ChestLid, the Rock, and the Key under the rock to make sure they still work with the new code.

7.   Stop Play mode.

Let's switch the Pedestal over to the revamped AniTwoState script.

1.   Select the Pedestal.

2.   Fill in the state 0 animation clip with flower revive.

3.   Load the synthup audio clip into the state 0 audio clip.

4.   Click Play and test the Pedestal.

The sound does not yet play because the code needs to use the Audio Source on the animating object, not the picked object.

1.   Stop Play mode.

2.   Add an Audio Source component to the Flower.

3.   Click Play and test again.

4.   Stop Play mode and add a **1** second audio delay on the Pedestal's Audio Delay **0** parameter.

5.   Click Play and test.

6.   Save the scene and save the project.

Now that your little scene is starting to act like an adventure game, you can see how much thought has to go into each object's animation sequence and how complicated things can get when you create complex sequences.

Limitations

While our nice generic script now works under several different conditions, it is still somewhat limited. At present, it has at *least* the following shortcomings:

- Handles only two states: The chest lid currently has two states, but with the lock, it needs at least three—closed and locked, closed and unlocked, and open. If you added a latch that sticks up when the chest is locked when the lid is open, it could prevent the lid from closing properly, adding an open and locked and a partially closed state for a grand total of five states.

- Triggers only one animation/audio: As you saw with the flower, there was an initial animation that needed to be followed by a looping clip.

- Triggers only one object's animation/audio: The hypothetical light switch illustrates this one most clearly. The switch needs to animate. The light needs to be activated. And the materials on the bulb and the lampshade need to be animated to change their appropriate parameters.

- Doesn't manage visibility for objects that fade: This is really a couple of separate issues. Setting the material's opacity to 0 prevents you from seeing an object, but it is still being rendered, costing frame rate. This is negligible on a one-to-one basis, but still worth considering. You could disable the Mesh Renderer, but that would require specific code as it is not an animation clip. The other problem is that even if an object is not rendered, its collider is still active, allowing the possibility of running into invisible walls. There is no way to disable a collider. It is possible to toggle on its IsTrigger parameter, but that would still allow a stray pick to activate it, not to mention that you are back to non-clip animations. You could handle it automatically—if the opacity is 0, disable the GameObject, but that will fail in cases where the GameObject exists for the sole purpose of providing something with which to interact. Ideally, you'd want to be able to enable or disable the entire GameObject.

- Isn't able to call other scripts or functions for special events: This is what you need to insure maximum flexibility and functionality in your generic animation script. You need to be able to instantiate things like particle systems and other non-keyframeable events by having access to bits of code as either scripts or functions.

Clearly, there are a lot of things yet to think about as you start to create a master script for handling your action objects (the objects that drive the game and story). The trick is going to be keeping it generic enough to use on all of the different types of objects without giving up the flexibility to reuse the code throughout the game and in future games. Besides triggering animations and sound effects, you will need a means of keeping track of the state the objects are in before and after they have been triggered. You need to manage the state objects go into the next time they are picked, especially when it varies according to which object is picking it. This, and the mechanics of how you design it, is what is known as state management, our next chapter's topic.

Summary

In this chapter, you began to investigate animation—both importing pre-animated objects and using Unity's Animation editor.

When importing animated assets, you learned how to correct scale and choose the most appropriate Generation type for the files. If a complex hierarchy of objects needed to be animated as one, you found that Store in Root was the best choice. For files with multiple objects that need to retain their transforms in relationship to each other, Store in Nodes was the choice that gives the most scripting access. Single animated objects, you found, need to be parented before you can adjust placement in a scene.

You learned how to split the Take 001 animation clip into individual behaviors and that named clips must not overlap in the timeline if you want to access them through scripting. To access clips on objects using Store in Root, you had to specify the parent as the individual objects had no Animation components.

On importing objects, we found that Unity creates generic materials using the original material's Diffuse texture map as the name. If no texture map was used for the material, the Unity material was named for the file and appended with the original material name.

After importing, you discovered you could use different shaders to improve the look of the materials. One of the most important concepts was that of using the alpha channel component of a texture as something other than an alpha channel mask. You also found that you could have Unity generate normal maps, but that you needed to duplicate the original texture before doing so. Additionally, you found that Unity converts all texture maps to dds format internally.

You examined colliders, learning to replace resource-heavy Mesh Colliders with their more efficient primitive counterparts. With the addition of OnMouseDown(), you found that to pick an object in the scene, the object needs a collider. For mouse picks, using the IsTrigger option on objects that were too small to worry about collision was a good choice.

With the introduction of animation.Play(), you found out how to call the default animations, but soon learned that you could call specific animation clips by name using the same function. On adding an Audio Source component, you could call sound effects with audio.Play() in the same manner, though calling by name used audio.PlayOneShot() to better advantage.

As the AniTwoState script got more robust, you learned you could check for a component's existence with GetComponent() before trying to use it and thus avoid Null Reference Object errors. By the time you dealt with identifying parents with the Animation component, you found it was easy to adapt the script to call an object's animations by picking a different object, a key concept for adventure games.

Using Unity's Animation editor, you learned how to create and add animation clips after import for non-animated objects. You also found you could add or edit imported animation clips, but only after making copies of them first.

Finally, you saw the shortcomings in the AniTwoState script's functionality with respect to future needs for the point and click adventure game project and found it somewhat lacking even after all of the modifications made to it.

CHAPTER 8

■ ■ ■

Managing State

In classic point and click adventure games, one of the most entertaining and challenging goals is to collect anything and everything that is not nailed down and then try to figure out where it needs to be used. To make things even more interesting, many games require you to combine inventory items before they will be able to perform the necessary task. It may be as mechanically logical as combining a hammer head with a wooden handle to make a usable tool, or as challenging as adding the correct ingredients to a brew. In the former, you might consider the combination object a totally new object that needs to be activated in the scene. In the latter, however, you might need to change its state each time an ingredient is added. Even something as simple as a door can have two states: open and closed. While some states, such as with the door, physically prevent access to a location or crucial object, others, such as a lock on the same door, have no physical manifestation. If the door's state is *locked*, interaction with it might produce a rattle, but if its state is *unlocked*, it will open when picked, putting it into a third state, *open*. Once you consider adding save and restore functionality to the game, the need for a means to track state becomes even more important.

Thus far in your journey into the realm of developing the mechanisms for interaction for your game you have used only a default pointer when clicking on your action objects. While changing the cursor to represent a particular object is a simple action of reassigning the texture, the manner in which the *picked* object responds may be vastly different. This sets you up for a dizzying amount of interaction possibilities when you stop to consider that *each* possibility must be considered. Besides tracking the state of objects, you must also have a list of objects with which they can interact, as well as the expected response from that interaction. Neglecting to check every possible interaction is one of the most common mistakes made by neophyte game developers. For that matter, even seasoned professionals are likely to miss a few as the game develops and undergoes the inevitable design changes. Even when you *think* you have every possibility covered, you will find that people will do the most unlikely (to your way of thinking anyway) things in your game, or worse, *to* your game.

BETA TESTERS

Beta testers are invaluable when developing adventure type games. Besides providing strong feedback on the logic, difficulty, and entertainment value of the puzzles or tasks in your game, they are masters at trying improbable actions and combinations of actions. When dealing with volunteer beta testers, there are a few important things to remember. Don't tell them any more about the game than what's available in the game's introduction. Don't stand over their shoulders prompting them to the correct paths or actions. If you must watch, keep your mouth closed (yes, that will be difficult) and your hands tightly clasped behind your back. Remember, their first run-through will be the most valuable. After they have played through as far as the game allows, you can ask for feedback. What may seem totally obvious to you may need more clues and vice versa.

Identifying the Possibilities

With the impressive number of options for interactivity with your objects, cursors, and inventory in mind, you can now see the need to be able to keep track of each and every one as they are activated, retired, combined, or taken by the player. Tracking and managing each object's state is crucial to this type of genre not only during game play, but also to enable the player to save and load the game at any time.

State management is a means or system used to handle conditionals on a large scale and in a fully generic manner. Before you delve into actually managing state, you will need to find a way of identifying and defining states and their associated actions (animations, audio and special effects, etc.) that you can apply to *any and all* of your action objects. To enable you to devise such a system, you will be adding a few more action objects to your collection: a crowbar, a message, a jewel, and a vial of restorative elixir. These action objects have different needs that you can test against as you develop your state management system.

To define the requirements for each, you'll create a plot involving the objects (and several future objects) and then generate the walk-through for your game.

Introducing the Plot

You find yourself in a tropical forest next to a couple of large stone structures. Investigation of the immediate area reveals a wooden chest, a crowbar, and a rock that looks somewhat out of place. Looking under the rock, you find the key that will unlock the chest. Inside the chest you find a message written by the last adventurer that passed this way. It mentions something about metal weapons being put into a maze that resets itself and how adding a little gold can disguise a weapon. You take the crowbar, message, and key. Moving on, you discover one of the structures must be the maze mentioned in the note. An eerie light and equally eerie sound are triggered as you enter the maze. Finding nothing, you continue to explore the area and discover an odd-looking glyph at the side of a shrine. Upon placing the glyph in the matching depression of an odd-looking stone drawer, you find the eerie sound and light are repeated when you close the drawer.

Next, you try to enter the temple but are told you must bring an offering to gain entrance. Further search reveals another shrine with a stone chest that contains a vial of liquid. Pouring the liquid on the wilted plant you discovered at yet another shrine reveals a fabulous jewel that looks to be perfect for an offering. With jewel in hand, you are able to pass through the light play between the stone cats and enter the temple. The voice mentions something about weapons, but you are too busy heading into the temple to listen. You quickly discover a passage up and find a golden ornament that looks like it will slip onto a rod of some sort. Taking it, you head downstairs, travel through the inner chamber, and discover a couple of storage rooms below. In one, touching a small iron sphere produces a hologram of a blasted tree with something golden in the opening at its base. Losing interest in it, you head over to the other room and find a couple of musty grain sacks. Prodding one of them, you find it so tough you think you will need a weapon to split it open. Checking your inventory, you discover your crowbar is missing. Thinking back, you remember the advice from the message.

You head back out of the temple and search the maze. After several false turns, you find your crowbar. Staring at it, you have an idea…sure enough, the golden sleeve fits snugly over it. Entering the temple once again, you rush down to the storage room and give the old sack a good whack with the adorned crowbar. It splits open to reveal a bumpy golden fruit the size of a large gourd. You take the fruit, wondering at its purpose, and wander slowly back up through the temple's main chamber. On reaching the main passage, you discover an opened door that you are sure was not there before. It provides access down into a damp passageway. You head down it to see what it reveals.

After passing out of a tiny damp room, you find yourself in a large cavern. Heading toward to beacon-like stele in the middle of the cavern's shallow lake, you find yourself suddenly transported to a strange twilight world. You head for its only feature, a collection of standing stones on a low mound. Within the stones you find the blasted trunk from the hologram and the mission suddenly becomes clear. You take the golden fruit from your pack and place it carefully in the opening at the base of the trunk and wait for something momentous to happen. The fruit begins to glow and suddenly, with a clap of thunder, a new Tree of Life (at least you assume that's what it is) appears. Apparently, however, you have one last task remaining. Using the adorned crowbar, you tap the tree to bring down a new fruit that will need to be hidden against the next time of need, but that's another story.

Walk-through

The next thing you will need is a walk-through or critical path to start breaking the requirements into bite-sized pieces. Obviously the game need not be totally linear, but there will be sections that require objectives to be met in order to gain access to the next solution.

1. Pick the rock so it moves aside to reveal a key.

2. Take the key.

3. Use the key with the lockplate on the chest to unlock the lid.

4. Open the lid.

5. Take the message from the chest.

6. Open inventory and read the message. It contains hints for getting a weapon into the temple by ornamenting it with gold. It also warns of an evil maze where confiscated weapons are hidden.

7. Take the crowbar you find near the chest.

8. Close the lid (optional).

9. Lock the chest (optional).

10. Take the key (optional).

11. Investigate the large stone maze. An eerie sound and green light coincide with your entry and exit from the maze.

12. Locate the shrine with the oddly shaped drawer.

13. Locate the music glyph on its left side.

14. Place the glyph in the depression in the drawer.

15. Click the drawer. When it closes and opens, you hear the same eerie sound and an equally eerie greenish light.

If you go back to the maze, you will see that its configuration has changed!

16. Locate the shrine with the stone chest.

17. Open its lid and take the vial of elixir.

18. Locate the shrine with the wilted plant.

19. Use the elixir on the wilted plant.

20. Take the jewel that is revealed when the plant revives.

21. Hold the jewel as you enter the temple. It will be accepted as an offering, but your crowbar will be confiscated as it is deemed a weapon.

22. Locate the passageway that leads up to the balcony inside the temple.

23. Take the golden sleeve from the offering bowl.

24. Go downstairs and find the two storage rooms.

25. In one room, pick the odd metal sphere on the ground. It produces a hologram of something golden in the trunk of a blasted tree.

26. In the other room, find a couple of old grain sacks. Clicking on them suggests that they are old and tough and you will need a weapon to open them.

27. When you check your inventory for your crowbar, you notice it's gone!

28. Exit the temple and go to the maze to find the relocated crowbar (as per the hint in the message).

29. Combine the golden sleeve with the crowbar either in the scene or in inventory after you take the crowbar.

30. Go back into the temple. This time you get in without losing the crowbar because it's encased in gold.

31. Use the ornamented crowbar to whack the old grain sack. A golden topi fruit slides out as the sack rips open, spilling its grain.

32. Take the golden fruit.

33. Head back up into the main temple passageway. A new door has opened revealing a passage leading down into a small damp room.

34. Go through the room into a vast underground cavern.

35. Head toward the stele in the center of the shallow lake.

36. You are transported to a new level whose only feature is a ring of standing stones.

37. Upon reaching the standing stones, you find a blasted tree trunk just like the one in the hologram.

38. Place the golden topi fruit inside the opening at its base. After many special effects, you see a new Tree of Life has replaced the blasted trunk.

39. You are instructed to take a new topi fruit and [presumably] hide it against the next time of need.

40. As soon as you take a new fruit, you have won the game and the credits roll.

Having the basic story and walk-through, you need to identify the action items. As with any adventure game, not all action items can be put into inventory. In your list, an asterisk indicates objects that can be put into inventory.

Action Items

Rock

*Key at rock/Key at lock

Lockplate

*Message

*Music glyph

Wilted plant

*Jewel

Chest lid (wooden chest)

Stone chest lid

*Crowbar

*Vial of elixir

Chest inside (this is an invisible but pickable object)

Temple Guardian entity (no mesh, but represented by particle system)

*Golden sleeve

Iron sphere

Grain sack

*Golden topi fruit

Tree Opening ((this is an invisible, but pickable object)

In case you are feeling overwhelmed at this point, don't worry; you will add the action objects to your scene a few at a time. If, on the other hand, you are thinking this is a paltry sort of mini-adventure game, there are plenty of props, assets, and possibilities for making the game more complicated once you get the mechanics worked out.

With your list of action objects in hand, you need to start thinking about how you are going to manage their states. For example, the crowbar and golden sleeve are separate objects. Once combined, do they become a new object or is the new object the old crowbar in a new state? What about the lockplate of the chest? Its states are strictly virtual, but it changes the states of the key and chest lid as you interact with it.

Rather than attack each object as it will be used in the final version of the game, you will be experimenting with different options for some of the sequences. By starting simple and working your way up to more complex interaction, you will be able to develop the thought process necessary for designing and engineering the more complex sequences. Keep this in mind as you try different methods of visually mapping out the interactions and resulting state changes. Treat these experiments as early tests.

Stunt Doubles

Before you go any further, let's look into the concept of *stunt doubles*. Just as in the movies where a stunt man performs the dangerous or skilled actions, you can use stunt doubles to reduce the complexity of many of your interactions. This allows you to swap out entirely different meshes, use UI textures for inventory or cursor objects, or avoid having to reposition and re-orient keyframed objects. Obviously, there's some overhead involved in duplicating meshes, but until you're comfortable handling complex state management, it will simplify the process by reducing the number of states an individual object can have.

The most obvious example of a stunt double in your test cases is the key that is used to unlock the chest. You have a Key at Rock and a Key at Lock. This way you can keep objects whose animations are dependent on the location and orientation of other objects from getting moved out of alignment by mistake.

Another extremely useful reason for stunt doubles is to allow you to use GUI texture images of the objects as cursors or in inventory. By treating them as separate objects instead of a particular state of a single object, you are free to pick and choose how you handle each. In the case of the key, you can easily go between the two mesh objects and a texture for inventory and cursor. You will also be using naming conventions to help with the handling of these assets.

■ **Rule**   All textures used for cursors and inventory representations of an object will be appended with "Icon."

And finally, if a stunt double is in the correct place from the start of the game, you needn't worry about moving and rotating it to various locations during runtime. You will eventually introduce the concept of *waypoints* (positions where objects can be moved to during the game), but for now having duplicate meshes will not impact your frame rate much since the meshes you use will be relatively small.

Developing a Flow Chart

The most familiar vehicle for tracking the possibilities of interaction is the flow chart. Let's take each object individually and create a flow chart for simplified version of the walk-through. To help keep things straight, you will use the phrase "in hand" to refer to an object that is the current pointer if it is other than the default pointer. Not necessarily all interaction will be user picked (e.g. the temple guardian that blocks entry into the temple and confiscates weapons).

■ **Tip**   For those who have avoided flow charts whenever possible, the symbols are simple: an ellipse initializes or starts an action, a diamond queries the action for a yes or no response to clarify, and a box contains the result of the action.

Your first run at the objects' flow charts might look something like Figure 8-1.

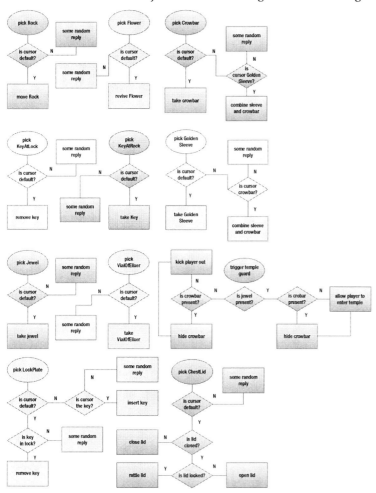

Figure 8-1. *Simple flow charts for some of the action objects*

Before you can go any further, you need to take off your game designer hat and put on a game developer hat. Essentially, you need to break down the components of an interaction in preparation for handling the mechanics of making all the right things happen.

Let's start by filling in the missing pieces. First and foremost is that each action object must be tested against *each and every* other object that can come in contact with it. This could be the entire list of possible inventory objects/cursors. There may be an occasional object that will have been left behind in order to reach the current location or level, but even that should be noted.

At this point, if there *is* a response to interaction with the incorrect object, whether audio or specific text, you can just abbreviate it with "snappy reply" instead of "generic reply."

The second run at the flow chart for the chest lid will look something like Figure 8-2.

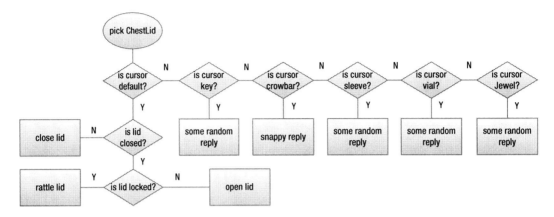

Figure 8-2. *Flow chart for all possible action object interaction with the chest lid*

As you can see, things are starting to get messy. Soon you will need a more structured means of defining possible interactions and their responses for each action object.

Separating State Metadata Transition Action

Looking at the flow chart, you can see that you're dealing with two types of things: object states and how they transition from one state to another. For example, the chest lid could have three states: locked; unlocked and closed; and unlocked and open. In going from state zero (unlocked) to state one (unlocked and closed), there's no animation involved. Going from state one (unlocked and closed) to state two (unlocked and open) will require an animation to visually transition between those two states or to make the lid hinge open.

The states themselves will eventually contain the metadata (information) for all of the actions associated with moving the object into that state.

You will use a simple description for each state while you work out the interactions. Eventually, the state will be represented by a number and the description of the state part of the metadata for that state.

Defining Interaction and State

When the interacting object is the correct one, you will need to tell the action object to move to a new state. States can be as obvious as the chest lid's *open* to the Key at Rock's *no longer visible in the scene* to the rock's *no longer pickable*. And, as mentioned previously, an object could currently be a cursor or be in inventory and could move between those states.

With the first example (the lid's open, closed, and locked states), the states are specific and unique to that object and most related to its animations.

⬛ **Note**   For this book, actions associated with a state are the events that happen to put the object *into* that state. So the action associated with the chest lid's open state will be the Open Lid animation.

Visualizing State Transitions

Before you can truly assess how many states each object will need, you will need a means of confirming the states you envision for them. Flow charts are useful for keeping track of possible interactions, but aren't great at showing state transitions.

Most of us are able to keep simple interactions straight in our heads. Visualizing something complex, however, can be extremely challenging. Unlike real life logic where the state itself takes care of the physical properties, you not only have to manage the object itself, but you may have to trigger several other actions or property changes on separate objects. Unlike with the flow charts, you won't cover each and every possible interaction—just those of the key elements; the flow chart has allowed you to weed out any non-essentials. In these visualizations, your aim is to define movement between states to make sure you have considered each object and its dependencies with relation to the other object. In these illustrations, an arrow leaving a state indicates a pick or other initiation of action on the object (see Figure 8-3).

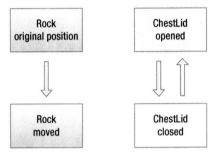

Figure 8-3. *Simple two-state examples*

In the first example, the rock has a single option for interaction: it can only be moved and not replaced. The chest lid, on the other hand, can move back and forth between its open and closed states.

Physically, the chest lid has just two states, open and closed. In your game, however, they are partially controlled by an outside source, the lock. But every time you queried the lid's closed state, you would also have to query the lock state. That means you would have to hardcode the condition and results for each object on an *individual* basis, losing the possibility of making a generic script to control all of the action objects. For example, when the player picks the chest lid, you first need to query the lid for its state (open or closed); if closed, you would have to query the lockplate to see if it was locked or unlocked.

As an alternative, you can create a different state for *each possibility* and allow outside objects to change that state. In Figure 8-4, you can see how the lock state can change the lid state and vice versa where you specify that the lock state can't be changed when the lid is open. Hang onto your hat; this is where things start to get complicated!

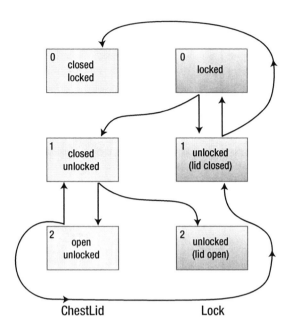

Figure 8-4. *Dual object interaction states*

If you now extend that model to include the KeyAtLock and its states, you discover that each object's states must be *multiplied* by the others' to cover each possibility. In the final version, you will have the key as a cursor and pick the lockplate to insert it. You will then pick the lock to unlock the chest. If the lid is closed, you can re-pick the key to lock it again; then re-picking the lockplate will take the key back out of the lock and put it into inventory or as cursor. The possible combinations will look something Figure 8-5.

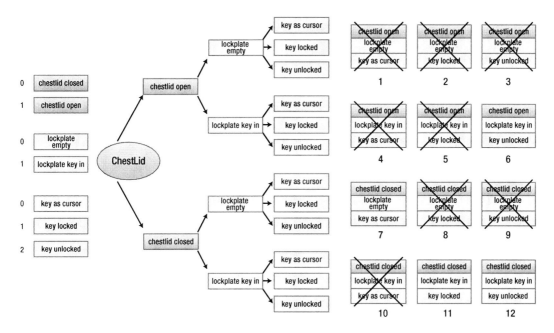

Figure 8-5. *All possible combinations for the ChestLid with the lockplate and key*

After you discard anything that *cannot* happen (lid open with locked key, etc.) you are left with four possibilities. For the lid itself, there are basically only three states: closed and locked; closed and unlocked; and open and unlocked.

Continuing with the chest/lock example, you have decided that when the lid is open, the player can't lock the lock. With this illustration, you add the lockplate that will allow you to insert and remove the key. In that case, the lockplate and key get a fourth state: unavailable. By mapping it out as you did with the ChestLid, you can also see that the other two objects need only have a total of four states each; the other states will never get accessed (Figure 8-6).

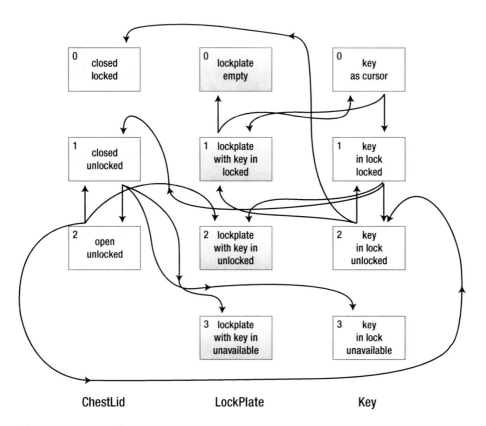

Figure 8-6. *Dependency states*

■ **Note**   While there may be multiple ways to put an object into a state, there may be no more than one possible way out by direct interaction with it—and that will most likely affect other objects as well. Arrows leading out of a state are the result of interaction with the object at that state.

If you think you have it down, try this next example with dependency states as in Figure 8-6. The scenario is a hand-powered radio containing three action objects: the power generator handle or crank, the telescoping antenna, and the contact switch. In order to be able to call out for help, you must have two rotation cranks on the handle and have the antenna fully deployed (a single action). The antenna toggles between its stowed and deployed state. The power from the handle being cranked does not dissipate. If you don't have enough power or an extended antenna, you will get a different result when you pick the Call for help button. Figure 8-7 shows the interactions.

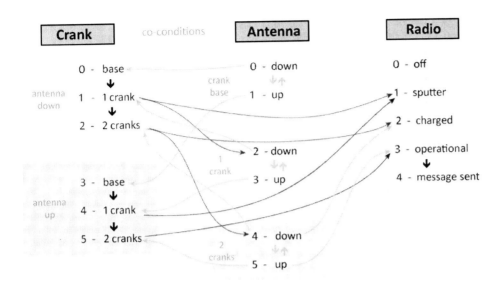

Figure 8-7. *Complex interaction between three objects*

One could, of course, require the user dial the right channel, interact with the voice on the other end, or a number of other conditions. Taken to the extreme, you can see how the point and click adventure genre can be extended to become real world training and assessment simulations.

If your head is hurting right about now, you aren't alone. Just for fun, try to explain in detail the steps needed to get to the other side of a closed door...to an alien being...who has tentacles. Now you need to specify all kinds of actions and objects that you regularly take for granted. Your brain manages logic sequences all the time without your even being aware of it.

If you're able to get your head around the dependency states diagrams without your brain overheating, you may consider yourself a high level adept at understanding the intricacies of state diagramming. If not, don't despair; you will be building a few get-out-of-jail-free mechanisms to allow you to cheat a bit later on when you start writing the script that controls the action.

For now, let's look at yet another way to visualize your states and transitions. Note that the chest/lock/key sequence is probably the most complicated you will deal with. Everything else will seem like a no-brainer in comparison.

State Diagram

With a state transition diagram, you can add in the actions that need to be performed. This is the opportunity to think through each response fully. It may involve animations, audio, messages, triggering of auxiliary objects' states, instantiating prefabs for special effects, or any number of events. If it is related to the pick or interaction, it should be listed.

Since it will be a while before you have inventory and cursors working, you will temporarily redefine the lid/lock sequence. The ChestLid is closed (ChestLid, state 0), the lid is locked, and the KeyAtLock is ready to be inserted into the lock (key, state 0). Click the KeyAtLock and it inserts the key and unlocks the lock (KeyAtLock to state 1, ChestLid to state 1). The ChestLid can then be opened (ChestLid to state 2). When the lid is opened, the key can't be picked (key to state 3). If the ChestLid is closed (ChestLid, state

1), picking the key will lock the chest (ChestLid to state 0), and the key removed (KeyAtLock to state 0). Figure 8-8 shows the options.

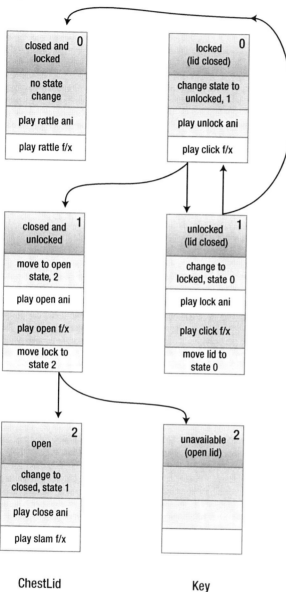

Figure 8-8. *State diagram (key as cursor not shown)*

And at this point, the good news is that you can remove the arrows since the instructions now tell you all you need to know and fill in the state numbers. This goes a long way towards making things easier to read, as you can see in Figure 8-9.

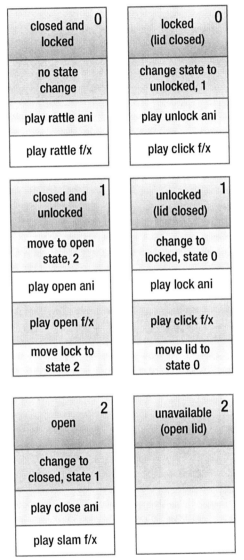

closed and locked **0**	locked (lid closed) **0**
no state change	change state to unlocked, 1
play rattle ani	play unlock ani
play rattle f/x	play click f/x

closed and unlocked **1**	unlocked (lid closed) **1**
move to open state, 2	change to locked, state 0
play open ani	play lock ani
play open f/x	play click f/x
move lock to state 2	move lid to state 0

open **2**	unavailable (open lid) **2**
change to closed, state 1	
play close ani	
play slam f/x	

Figure 8-9. *State diagram simplified*

Having disposed of those pesky arrows, you can develop a table using the information (see Table 8-1). Remember, the animations, sound effects, etc. associated with a state are used to put the object *into* that state.

Table 8-1. *Simple Tables*

Current State	Current Description	New State	Animation Sound F/X	Affect other objects ➤ State
Object: ChestLid				
0	closed and locked	0	rattle lid Rattle	none
1	closed and unlocked	2	open lid ChestOpen	disable KeyAtLock, state 2
2	open (unlocked)	1	lid close DoorClose	enable KeyAtLock, state 1
Object: KeyAtLock				
0	ready to insert	1	key insert LoudClick	move ChestLid to state 1
1	inserted and locked	0	key remove LoudClick	move ChestLid to state 0
2	unavailable (lid is open)	NA	NA	NA

Evaluating the Results

At this point, you have the information you need to set events in motion. For your master system, you will need to decide in which order you will check all of the possibilities. Although this could be somewhat arbitrary, you will start with the object that was picked.

1. You need to know *which* object was picked.

2. You will need to determine the object's present state.

3. You need to know what the current cursor object that picked it was.

Once you have *that* information, you can check the following:

4. What state the object goes into, and do all of the associated actions (animations, sound effects, custom scripts, etc.)

5. If there are any other objects affected and if so, the states they will go into so you can do all the associated actions.

The first is easy. You have access to that already.

The second is also easy. You will check the object's metadata (the fancy name for its variables that store its pertinent information) to see its current state.

The third is a little trickier. You only have one game pointer, but you will be swapping out the textures to create the illusion of a different cursor. If you are clever, you can use naming conventions for the texture that will use the name of the action object it represents (more on that in the next chapter). For now, assume that you can readily retrieve that information. With it, you will know which animation, audio clip, and custom scripts to call.

Any auxiliary objects are put into the state specified and are, in effect, processed exactly like the original object.

Lookup Table

Once you know what the possible states will be, you can put the state transitions information into a more comprehensive table. The actual events required for each object's states will be fully contained within its own metadata, so you need only refer to the state in the lookup table. The metadata will be processed after the correct case is found.

For each action object, the table will list its states, the possible interacting objects or trigger objects, the new states the various trigger objects will put the object into, and any other objects that need to be put into a different state (see Tables 8-2 thru 8-6). Note that for the auxiliary objects you can assume that the trigger is *none*, or the *default* cursor. You will eventually create a separate table to handle all of the events associated with transition from one state to another, so these tables don't include that data.

Table 8-2. *Object ChestLid*

Current State—Description	Trigger Object	New State	Aux. Object	New State	Aux. Object	New State
0 closed/locked	default	0				
1 closed/unlocked	default	2	KeyAtLock	1		
2 unlocked/open	default	1	KeyAtLock	2		

Table 8-3. *Object KeyAtLock*

Current State—Description	Trigger Object	New State	Aux. Object	New State	Aux. Object	New State
0 ready to insert	default	1	ChestLid	1		
1 in lock, unlocked	default	0	ChestLid	0		
2 unavailable	NA					

Table 8-4. *Object Rock*

Current State—Description	Trigger Object	New State	Aux. Object	New State	Aux. Object	New State
0 covering key	default	1				
1 moved, unavailable	NA					

Table 8-5. *Object Flower*

Current State—Description	Trigger Object	New State	Aux. Object	New State	Aux. Object	New State
0 wilted	default	1				
1 revived, unavailable	NA					

Table 8-6. *Object KeyAtRock*

Current State—Description	Trigger Object	New State	Aux. Object	New State	Aux. Object	New State
0 on ground	default	1				
1 picked up, unavailable	NA					

And although you don't have non-default cursor functionality yet, let's set up the Lockplate so you will have a way to test your parsing code. As well as defining the Key Icon object as a cursor or interacting object, you will need to put it from "as cursor" (state 2) to "not in scene" (state 0) as soon as it is used. When the KeyAtLock is removed, Key Icon goes into "in inventory" (state 1). The cursor and inventory functionality will need to be added before you actually see any results, but at least you can make sure the messages will be read (see Table 8-7).

Table 8-7. *Object Lockplate*

Current State—Description	Trigger Object	New State	Aux. Object	New State	Aux. Object	New State
0 empty	default	0				
	Key Icon	1	KeyAtLock	1	Key Icon	0
1 key in lock, locked	default	0	KeyAtLock	0	Key Icon	2
2 key in lock, unlocked, unavailable	NA					

Now that you've got the data into a table, let's look at how it will be evaluated using the plan mapped out in the previous section.

The object is what holds the information in the first place, so you can leave its name out of the table itself. The first check will be for the object's current state in column one. It will tell you which entry (and eventually which array) to look in.

So far, you have dealt only with the most obvious object/object interaction. As a seasoned adventurer, you know there are times when one needs to resort to pairing each inventory object with a particular object to elicit a response that provides a clue for solving its functionality. To that end, you need to add a case for not only the critical object but any other objects that could be used.

Since the default cursor will usually be the correct interaction or *trigger object*, you will check for it first. In your table and in your code, you will identify it as "default." After checking for the default cursor, the next object to be listed should be the "correct" non-default cursor if there is one or trigger object if it's not a cursor. Following that, list each cursor/object that should return a specific reply. An example might be if you tried to pick the chest lid with the crowbar in hand (as cursor) where the lid would do nothing but you might get a snappy reply like "Chest bashing will get you nowhere."

The trigger object will either be the cursor, or in some cases, a physical intersection with the triggering object, and that will determine which scenario for that particular state gets carried out. For that reason, the trigger object will be your second column—the second case or condition to be checked for a match.

The third column will be the new state that the object is moved into as a result of the interaction. Only the actual number of the state will be used in the array, but you may want to remind yourself what it is by adding a short description in the table.

Following the first two columns, the remainder will be evaluated in pairs. They will allow you to trigger any other objects that may need *their* states changed, animating, instantiating or any other special cases. The auxiliary object/new state pairs are optional but you may add as many as necessary.

To reiterate,

1. The *object* is picked or triggered by another means.

2. Its [current] *state* is determined and the correct table or array accessed.

3. The *trigger*[ing] *object* is identified and the matching row of the table or element of the array is located.

4. The object is then processed to move into the *new state*.

5. If they exist, the rest of the objects, *auxiliary objects*, will be processed into their *new states* using their own lookup tables.

You will need to fill out a table for each action object's possible states once you have determined and defined those states.

You have now created a lookup table to find out what each object should do when triggered by any other object. This, along with the metadata arrays you will create in the next chapter, will allow you to specify everything that needs to be done when a specific condition is met or identified. On a small scale, any table will do; for more ambitious projects, you may want to manage the lookup tables in the spreadsheet program of your choice.

Parsing a String

At this point, you need to make a design decision that has to do with the way Unity exposes arrays in the Inspector. Your lookup table is essentially a multi-dimension array. You can't gain access to that kind of array directly through the Inspector.

■ **Tip**   Unity's unique implementation of JavaScript has a special kind of array that can be visible in the Inspector and, unlike regular JavaScript arrays, can have its number of elements dynamically changed at any time. The downside is that there are several things you can do to regular arrays that can't be done with Unity arrays. Fortunately, you can change one type to the other when needed.

You do, however, have a means of parsing a string (such as this sentence) and breaking it into component parts according to a specified character. This allows you to store data in one large string, as a single element of the array, and then evaluate it on need. While this is not a method you would want to use in a shooter type game where response speed is crucial, it will not cause any problems in your slow-paced point and click game.

Parsing takes a string of characters and goes through them one at time (or however many you stipulate) to check for specific cases. In your case, you will be looking for commas. Additionally, you have a means to break the contents of the strings between the commas into elements of an internal array for identification and processing.

With your parsing technique in mind, the table data for the ChestLid will eventually be written into your array as follows:

- ChestLid:

    State 0: default,0

    State 1: default,2,KeyAtLock,1

    State 2: default,1,KeyAtLock,2

- KeyAtLock:

    State 0: default,0,ChestLid,1

    State 1: default,2,ChestLid,0

- Rock:

    State 0: default,1

- Flower:

    State 0: default,1

- Lockplate:

    State 0: default,0

    State 0: Key Icon,1,KeyAtLock,1,Key Icon,0

    State 1: default,0,KeyAtLock,0,Key Icon,2

░ **Note** There is no space after the commas. Since this is a typical typo to make, you will write the parsor so that it will ignore spaces after at least the first comma.

The states where the object is not available for interaction are not listed for processing. You will create a variable for each of three possible states an object could be in (0,1,2). Later, you can increase the number, but for now let's keep it simple. You will call your variables lookupState_0, lookupState_1, and lookupState_2.

Each variable/metadata will represent an array. The first element will represent the condition where there is no special cursor interacting with the object, the default. All of your test objects will have an element 0.

Additional elements will represent the cursors/interacting objects that produce some sort of non-generic response. Instead of "default," you will have the name of the triggering object, which in most cases will be a cursor but not the default cursor. In your test case, the only object to have an element 1 is the Lockplate. Eventually, when picked with Key Icon as the cursor, the KeyAtLock will unhide and insert itself into the lock.

When you were experimenting with importing objects and setting up colliders, you created a collider for the lockplate. Because you want to interact with *only* the lockplate, you need to create a separate object to receive the pick events rather than leave it on the ChestBase object. One could determine which of the ChestBase's colliders received a pick, but it will be simpler to make a new gameObject for it.

1. Select the ChestBase.

2. Remove the Box Collider component in the Inspector.

3. Use F to find or focus in on the ChestBase in the Scene view.

4. Create a new Empty GameObject.

5. Name it Lockplate.

6. Add a Box Collider to it.

7. Adjust the Box Colliders Size parameters and the new gameObject's transform until it covers the ChestBase's lockplate area.

8. Make sure the collider protrudes from the ChestBase so it will receive a pick first.

The Object Lookup Script

As with the Interactor script you started building in the cursor control chapter, you will be adding functionality throughout the development of your game to your next script. Inside it, you will store the instructions that will tell your game what to do when an object is picked or triggered.

Let's begin by creating a new script in the Adventure Scripts folder.

1. Create a new JavaScript.

2. Name it ObjectLookup.

3. Open it in the script editor.

4. Delete the Update function for now.

5. At the top of the new script, add the three variables and declare their types as Unity built-in arrays of type String:

```
// make a Unity array for the three possible states of the object, each will have:
// cursor, new state, other object, its state, another object, its state, etc...
// use 'default' for the default cursor name
var lookupState0 : String[];  //declare an array of string type content
var lookupState1 : String[];  //declare an array of string type content
var lookupState2 : String[];  //declare an array of string type content
```

6. Save the script.

The brackets tell you that the variables are arrays, and String tells you what type of variables are in the arrays. With the Unity arrays, because they can be exposed in the Inspector, the engine must know what type of input to expect. You do not need to tell it how many elements to expect as that can be changed in the Inspector.

The next array is a regular JavaScript array of type Array. You will initialize it to hold three elements so it will be easy to assign the corresponding Unity built-in arrays to each. The state variable will be used to tell it which element of the array you want to access.

7. Add the following variables beneath the `lookUpState` variables:

```
// make a regular array of type Array with three elements to process the selected⏎
 element's contents
private var stateArray = new Array [3];

var state : int; // a variable to hold the element number to process
```

8. Save the script.

9. Add the new script to the `Lockplate` object.

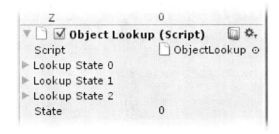

Figure 8-10. *The new array parameters in the Inspector on the LockPlate object*

According to your state table (Figure 8-10), the Lockplate has three states: no key (state 0), key inserted (state 1), and a Lockplate unavailable (state 2). When the lid is up, the key can't be removed by clicking on the Lockplate.

At state 0 (no key in the lock), eventually if you click it with the key (Key Icon) as cursor, the KeyAtLock unhides and inserts itself into the lock and the Lockplate goes to state 1.

If you click it with anything else, you will eventually get a generic message about not being able to use the trigger object that way with the lock.

At state 1 (with the key in the lock but not yet turned/unlocked and the chest still locked), if you pick it with the default cursor, the lock plate goes back to state 0 and the KeyAtLock goes back to state 0. In other words, if the key is still in locked position, it can be removed from the Lockplate.

At state 2 (with the key in the lock, having been turned/unlocked), the Lockplate is unavailable and does not change state.

10. Select the Lockplate.

11. Open each of the three Lookup State parameters.

Because they are arrays, the first thing you will see is a parameter called Size. It is created automatically and internally so you will only see it in the Inspector.

You can fill out arrays two different ways. If you fill in the Size first, you will get that number of elements. Remember that arrays always start with element 0 as their first element.

The other way to fill them out is to set the Size as 1, fill in the information, then change the size. When this method is used, the contents are copied into the added elements. This will be quite useful when you start adding text to go along with states.

To begin, let's use the first method. This way, you'll know at the outset how many possibilities you need to account for.

1. In the Inspector, set the Size for Lookup State 0 to 3.

2. Three elements are generated (Figure 8-11).

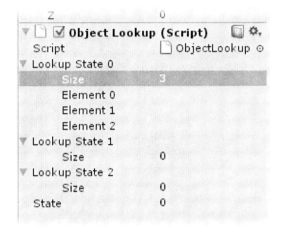

Figure 8-11. *Lookup State 0's three new elements*

Nothing is immediately obvious about where to enter the data.

3. Click below the Size's 3 to force the field into edit mode and enter Element 0's information (Figure 8-12).

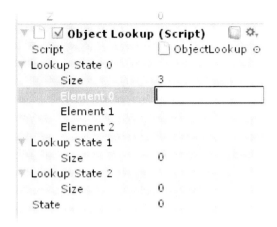

Figure 8-12. *Ready to enter data*

4. Add the cursor default and the state it goes into (or in this case, remains in), 1, separated by a comma, like so: default,0.

5. In Element 1, add: Key Icon,1,KeyAtLock,1.

Looking at the data for the Lockplate, you can see that there is no element 3. The only interaction to produce results with the Lockplate is being picked by either the default cursor or the Key Icon cursor.

6. Change Lookup State 0's Size to 2.

The extra Element field goes away.

7. Set the other two arrays to Size 1 and fill in their data as follows (your results should look like Figure 8-13):

> State 0: default,0
>
> State 0: Key Icon,1,KeyAtLock,1,Key Icon,0
>
> State 1: default,0,KeyAtLock,0,Key Icon,2
>
> State 2: default,2

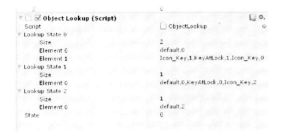

Figure 8-13. *The Lockplate's state information loaded*

■ **Tip**   Be sure there are no spaces after your commas. Should you leave a space after a comma, the parsing code will never find a match because it would be looking for a name beginning with a space. Later on you will add code to ignore a single space. You can resize the width of the views by hovering the cursor over the borders and dragging.

Before you can parse your Unity arrays, you need to load them into their JavaScript counterparts. Because they are not read into memory until the game is started, you need to wait until the Start function before making those assignments.

1.   Add a Start function and the array assignments to the ObjectLookup script.

```
function Start () {

    // load the Unity string arrays into the JavaScript array elements
    stateArray[0] = lookupState0;
    stateArray[1] = lookupState1;
    stateArray[2] = lookupState2;

}
```

2.   Save the script.

On startup, you will load the Unity arrays into the elements of your regular JavaScript arrays so they can be easily processed. Note the numbers inside the brackets. This time you are referring to a particular element of the array variable, StateArray, that you defined earlier. You are loading the contents of LookupState0 into StateArray's element 0, the contents of LookupState1 into StateArray's element 1, and the contents of LookupState2 into StateArray's element 2. Since the LookupState variables hold arrays in their own right, you are essentially creating an array of arrays.

The next part gets a bit tricky. You will manually tell it which array to parse via the state variable. Then you will go through that string chopping it up at each comma and putting the results into yet another array for final processing.

1.   Start the OnMouseDown function as follows:

```
function OnMouseDown () {
```

```
print ("Results for state " + state );

for (var contents : String in stateArray[state]) {
//split the contents into a temporary array
var readString : String[] = contents.Split(",".Chars[0]);
}
// now read the first two split out pieces (elements) back out
print ("elements in array for state " + state + " = " + readString.length);
print ("Cursor = " + readString[0]);
print ("New state = " + readString[1]);
```

Inside an OnMouseDown function, you use a for loop to parse, or go through, the contents (a String type), one character at a time. Every time you encounter a comma, you put the characters since the last comma, into an array named readString.

USING STRINGS IN ARRAYS TO STORE MULTIPLE TYPES OF INFORMATION

Still Confused? Perhaps a less abstract example using your format would be a primary school. Your initial array will be a string containing the teacher's name, the number of years they have taught, then each child in the class followed by their gender. You would have an array for each grade containing an element for each teacher that teaches that grade. It would look something like the following:

Kindergarten:

- Element 0   Miss Smith,2,Eric,M,Alice,F,Leroy,M,Ryan,M,Sandy,F

- Element 1   Miss Phillips,3,Tommy,M,Jill,F,Mary Alice,F,Alex F.,M,Alex S.,M

First Grade:

- Element 0   Mrs. Whitney,30,Tiffany,F,Joey,M,Timmy,M,Terry,F,Greg,M

- Element 1   Mr. Garcia,5,Fred,M,Brittany,F,Garret,M,Louise,F

Second Grade:

- Element 0   Mr. Johnston,Abby,F,Kai,M,Henry,M,Jeremy,M,Lucrecia,F,Sumy,F

Let's process Kindergarten, element 1, or kindergarten[1] into the readString array. The contents of kindergarten[1], a string of "Miss Phillips,3,Tommy,M,Jill,F,Mary Alice,F,Alex F.,M,Alex S.,M" become new elements of readString each time you encounter a comma.

The contents of the readString array are represented as ("Miss Phillips","3","Tommy","M","Jill","F","Mary Alice","F","Alex F.",:M","Alex S.","M"). Because each element is a string, it must be enclosed by quotation marks. Elements in an array are separated by commas. In your original string, you could just as easily use an asterisk for the split character, but an array must use commas.

Now that you have an array, you can quickly get the data you need. Element 0 contains the teacher's name. Element 1 contains the number of years the teacher has taught, and, starting at element 2, the even numbered elements are the names of the children in the class, and the element number + 1 will tell you their gender.

In code, it would look as follows:

```
kindergarten[1] = ("Miss Phillips","3","Tommy","M","Jill","F","Mary Alice","F",↵
"Alex F.",:M","Alex S.","M")
readString = ("Miss Phillips","3","Tommy","M","Jill","F","Mary Alice","F",↵
"Alex F.",:M","Alex S.","M")
readString[0] = "Miss Phillips"
readString[1] = "3"
readString[2] = "Tommy"
readString[3] = "M"
readString[4] = "Jill"
readString[5] = "F"
readString[6] = "Mary Alice"
readString[7] = "F"
readString[8] = "Alex F."
readString[9] = "M"
readString[8] = "Alex S."
readString[9] = "M"
```

Let's continue with your `ObjectLookup` script's `OnMouseDown` function.

2.   Add the following beneath the previous code:

```
//now read through the remainder in pairs
//iterate through the array starting at element 2 and incrementing by 2
//as long as the counting variable i is less than the length of the array
for (var i = 2; i < readString.length; i= i + 2) {
   print ("auxiliary object = " + readString[i]);
   print (readString[i] +  "'s new state = " + readString[i+1]);
}
} // close the OnMouseDown function
```

3.   Save the script.

To test, you will start with the simplest state, 2, and work your way backwards.

1.   In the Inspector, set the state variable to 2.

2.   Click Play.

3.   Pick the Lockplate in the Game window.

4.   Look at the results in the Console.

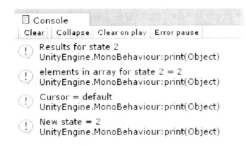

Figure 8-14. *Results of state 2*

5. Stop Play mode.

6. Change the State to 1.

7. Click Play and pick the Lockplate.

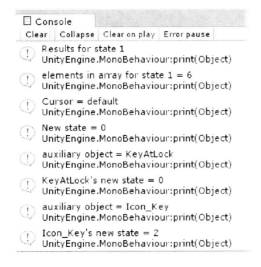

Figure 8-15. *Results of state 1*

8. Stop Play mode.

9. Change the State to 0.

10. Click Play and pick the Lockplate.

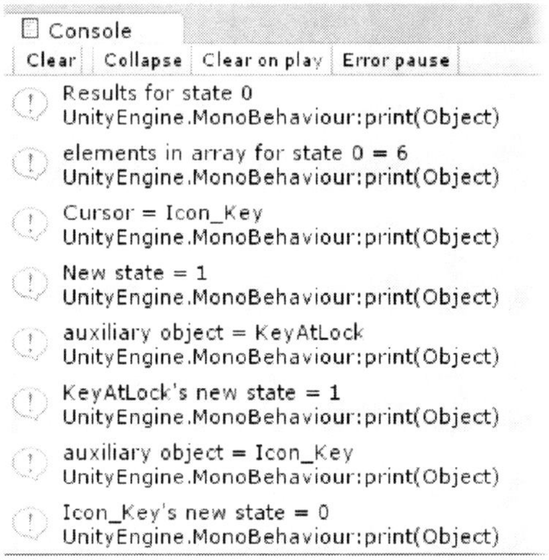

```
□ Console
Clear   Collapse   Clear on play   Error pause
(!)  Results for state 0
     UnityEngine.MonoBehaviour:print(Object)
(!)  elements in array for state 0 = 6
     UnityEngine.MonoBehaviour:print(Object)
(!)  Cursor = Icon_Key
     UnityEngine.MonoBehaviour:print(Object)
(!)  New state = 1
     UnityEngine.MonoBehaviour:print(Object)
(!)  auxiliary object = KeyAtLock
     UnityEngine.MonoBehaviour:print(Object)
(!)  KeyAtLock's new state = 1
     UnityEngine.MonoBehaviour:print(Object)
(!)  auxiliary object = Icon_Key
     UnityEngine.MonoBehaviour:print(Object)
(!)  Icon_Key's new state = 0
     UnityEngine.MonoBehaviour:print(Object)
```

Figure 8-16. *Results of state 0*

For state 0 you only see the contents of the second element (Figure 8-16). That is because you do not ask for a printout until all elements of the `stateArrays` have been processed. When you start using this code for the actual game functionality, you will search for a match for the cursor or trigging object, and, once found, the data gets processed and you look no further.

Thus you now have a means of storing and retrieving metadata that you can add directly into the Inspector for each action object. This is by no means the only way to manage and access the metadata, but rather a compromise between "easy to enter" and "easy to read." Ideally, one would want to look into creating custom UI dialogs that mimic the state tables.

▪ **Tip**   As some of your data entries will be rather long, you may wish to use a text editor to type your data, then copy and paste it into Unity. This will make it easier to check for errors.

So far you have only allowed for basic changing states that will be defined in the objects' metadata. While this may serve you well in the majority of cases, you should know that things like particle systems, projectiles systems, and special effects may be *instantiated* from prefabs during runtime. For these and a few other cases, you will need to create a custom script to handle anything outside of normal imported mesh animations.

■ **Tip**   Instantiation is used for things like particles systems and projectiles that are created from a prefab (template) during the game and have a limited lifespan (they are destroyed as soon as they have served their purpose).

Let's consider the oddball cases where there isn't even an object until one is instantiated, let alone an action object. It turns out there is another benefit of being able to parse a string—it allows you to use naming conventions to increase functionality. You can preface the object name with characters that will allow you to handle special cases.

As you go through the contents of each state's abbreviated set of instructions, you can contact any object to play its animation, instantiate a prefab to cause a special effect, trip a flag that will bypass animations to change the state only, or handle visibility on non-action objects. You will be using the following naming conventions for special cases:

- **a0_** will trigger an animation on an auxiliary object.

- **s0_** will send a message to call a function called "DoTheJob" on any script on this object.

- **b0_** will change state only on the object.

- **p0_** will instantiate a prefab of this name.

The underscore means that you are dealing with a special case. The first character, a letter, tells you which case, and the number allows you to specify specific cases within a case.

With that in mind, you may wish to trigger a particle system as the Flower revives. Here is the table and array for the Flower using the p0_ flag to indicate that a prefab of the name that follows the flag needs to be instantiated:

- Flower:

    State 0: default,1,p0_Sparkles

You will check for the *third* character, the underscore, to ascertain that it is a special case. This means that you have set aside these three characters as reserved. You can't use the underscore as the first third characters in *any* regular object names.

The b0_ flag will be useful for objects like the chest lid. In the lid's state 0, you can pick it and it will rattle but not change states. The problem comes when it is in state 1 (closed and locked) and the player removes the key. The action that removes the key (whether it is the key or the lockplate that is picked) moves the ChestLid into state 0. Since it is already set to rattle to go into state 0, it would rattle when the key was removed, which makes no sense. By using the b0_ flag, you can tell it to bypass the animation and just change the state. This allows you to avoid creating an extra state to manage the occurrence and is slightly more intuitive when working out the action. If you use the KeyAtLock scenario, its data would look as follows:

- KeyAtLock:

    State 0: default,0,ChestLid,1

    State 1: default,2,b0_ChestLid,0

You will not be implementing the flag system until the basic functionality is working, but it's nice to know you will be able to account for other than simple animation and sound F/X from your action object interaction. The beauty of the system is that it is extensible. If you devise an action sequence that is not covered with what you already have, you can merely define a new case and tailor its functionality to suit.

Action Related Messages

Besides calling animations and sound files for the action object, you will want to display a message describing the action. In the old days of pure text games, these messages were necessary to describe what had just happened in a non-visual world. Additionally, they could also be quite entertaining. You will make use of the text message both to entertain and to make sure the player hasn't missed some key factor of the action that was just played out.

Because you will want to display messages corresponding to a specific object/trigger-object interaction, which in most cases will be the cursor and may or may not invoke a state change, these interaction messages will be handled separately from the object's regular metadata. Since the messages are related to the action, you will keep them in the ObjectLookUp script with the rest of the state transition instructions.

░ **Rule**   The Reply arrays must be identical in size to the Lookup arrays. If the instructions say element 2, the reply that goes with them must also be in element 2.

---

1. Open the ObjectLookUp script.

2. Add the message array variables following the lookupState variable declarations:

```
var repliesState0 : String[];
var repliesState1 : String[];
var repliesState2 : String[];

var genericReplies : String[]; // Add one reply for each state
```

Note you've also added an array for more generic replies. Since it's also tied in with the states, it must have one reply for each state only.

Just as with the stateArray to hold the built-in arrays from the Inspector, you need to create a JavaScript array to hold the replies for each state.

3. Add the following line below the **private var** stateArray line:

```
// make a regular array holding three elements to hold the replies for each state
private var replyArray = new Array [3];
```

4. And finally, load the reply arrays into regular JavaScript arrays inside the Start function below the stateArray assignments:

```
// load the Unity string arrays into the JavaScript array elements
replyArray[0] = repliesState0;
```

```
replyArray[1] = repliesState1;
replyArray[2] = repliesState2;
```

■ **Tip**   For more information on JavaScript arrays versus Unity built-in arrays, consult the Scripting Reference for array.

> 5. Save the script.
>
> 6. Save the scene and save the project.

You will start filling in messages as you get the action objects up and running.

Chapter Summary

In this chapter you started looking deeper into object state and how to manage it. By introducing a plot for your game and a list of action objects, you were able to see the need for mapping out the actions and reactions of object/player interaction. You explored several different means of visualizing what states objects would need, which objects could interact with others, and what actions would be initialized upon interaction.

You found that flow charts could be valuable to map out simple interaction and state, but once you allowed objects to influence or change each other's states, those models quickly became unwieldy.

Simple state diagrams provided a means of listing state, associated actions, and animations as well as how objects transitioned from one state to the next. By the time you tested state diagrams against multiple interacting objects, they were also starting to get complicated.

The next step was to take the state diagram information and populate a table with it. At that point, you were getting a clearer idea of the data you had to work with and the critical path needed to process it. To simplify, you decided to handle the state transitions independent of their associated actions.

You defined the possible states available to an object, listed the possible triggering objects (usually a cursor, default or otherwise), and any auxiliary objects and the states they would be put into as a result of the primary interaction.

To store, manipulate, and manage the transition information, you created the first version of your ObjectLookup script. You found you could enter your pertinent data as a string into the built-in arrays available to the Inspector and then feed the contents into normal JavaScript arrays for further processing. That allowed you to parse the string and separate the contents of the string into individual elements of a new array in anticipation of future need. You were also learned how to introduce flags into your parsed data that allow for custom functionality at some point, giving you the flexibility to go far beyond simple action/reaction in this or future games.

In the next chapter, you will organize your action object's metadata so that all you will need to do is pass the object into the correct state and it will handle all the details.

CHAPTER 9

Object Metadata

In the previous chapter you set up the beginnings of your state management system. The ObjectLookup script, using the object's current state and the cursor or other object that interacted with it, will tell you what state the object goes into and the states that any auxiliary objects go into as well. The bulk of the information, animations, audio clips, descriptions, etc. will be stored on the individual object as metadata in the Interactor script. Each action object will need to know all of the information associated with each of its possible states as well as its current state.

The most important variable you will add to your object is for its *current state*. The current state, however, needs to be initialized. Even if you assumed that all objects started out in their state 0 (which they won't), you still need an easy way to test interactions without having to go through all of the steps (state changes) to get to the one you want. By creating an initial state variable, you will have the flexibility to start objects at whichever state you wish. This is the starting point for processing interaction with the object.

1. Open the Interactor script

2. Add the following above the //Misc vars section:

```
//state dependent variables
var initialState : int = 0; // in case you need other than state 0
```

You have initialized the state to 0 as that will usually be defined as an object's initial state in your game.

Tip While type declaration is not strictly necessary for your project, it will be for some platforms such as the iPhone. It is also slightly faster if the engine doesn't have to figure it out from the value you are using to initializing the variable.

A third consideration concerns issues with float type variables. If you don't state the type and forget to add a ".0" to your number, it will be set as an integer, possibly causing all sorts of odd results.

In this project, you will continue to use both methods because you will see it done both ways in other scripts. If, however, you want to be diligent about developing good habits, include type each time you declare a new variable.

State-Related Metadata

The individual states will need descriptive names, short and long descriptions (a *verbose* option) for mouse overs, as well as the animations, delays, sound effects, and action text associated with each. You can refer to an object's state by number and will then have a means to access to the information or *metadata* associated with it.

By declaring them as Unity's built-in arrays, you gain the advantages of being able to change their size at will and have them exposed to the Inspector so you can load each object's information into your generic script.

- *Name*: A descriptive name such as "Open Chest Lid."

- *Location:* The state of being of the object (visible, pickable, etc.)

- *Visibility Type:* How to handle visibility for this state.

- *Description (verbose)*: For example, "It is a beautifully constructed chest lid laying open for all to see."

- *Animation:* The animation that will play when the object goes into this state.

- *Animation Delay*: The time delay associated with the animation.

- *Audio*: The sound effect associated with the animation.

- *Audio Delay*: The delay associated with the sound effect.

- *Loop Animation*: The animation that will play after the initial animation.

- *Loop Audio*: The sound effect associated with the looping animation.

Instead of listing the metadata under each *state*, you will list the data by state under each *parameter* to make it easier to visualize when you actually add the information at a later time (see Table 9-1).

Table 9-1. *Two Ways to Organize the Data*

State 0	Location
• Location	• State 0
• Name	• State 1
• Description	• State 2
• Animation	Name
State 1	• State 0
• Location	• State 1
• Name	• State 2
• Description	Description
• Animation	• State 0
State 2	• State 1
• Location	• State 2
• Name	Animation
• Description	• State 0
• Animation	• State 1
	• State 2

Let's go ahead and add the variables for the object metadata.

1. Open the `Interactor` script.

2. Add the following public variables at the top of the script, like so:

```
//Object metadata
var location : int[];      // see notes
var visbility : int[];     // see notes
var objectName : String[];  // name/label of the object in this state
var description : String[];  // description of the object in this state
var animationClip : AnimationClip[];    // the animation that will play when picked
var animationDelay : float[];    // the time delay before the animation plays
var soundClip : AudioClip[];     // the sound that gets played when picked
var audioDelay : float[];     //the time delay before the sound gets played
var loopAnimation : AnimationClip[]; //animation that loops after main animation
var loopSoundFX : AudioClip[]; // sound that goes with it
var postLoop : boolean = false;  // flag to know if it has a looping animation to follow
var animates : boolean = true; // var to know if it animates at all
```

3. Save the script.

By keeping all of an object's critical information on the object itself, it is generally easier to maintain. In other words, it's easier to modify, easier to understand, and easier to make modular. Each object state contains its own specific metadata.

The remaining state examples are similar in that they are Boolean in nature: they are either true or false. Moreover, an object can only be in one of those states at any one time. It becomes apparent that you can easily differentiate the scene/location related states from the object-specific states and see that they should be kept in a separate variable. Unlike the object states, you can go ahead and define your scene states and associate them with numbers.

State of Being/Location

You added a variable called `location` along with the other state-related variables. It will tell you the abstract state of the object in the scene: whether it can be picked, if it's in inventory or being used as a cursor, if it's currently visible, and other esoteric information not especially related to its physical state. For want of a better term (as you are already using the term "state") you have called it "location." You will assign a number to represent each of the possibilities, as follows:

> 0: Object is in scene and active.
>
> 1: Object is in Inventory.
>
> 2: Object is Cursor.
>
> 3: Object is not pickable (in scene and inactive).
>
> 4: Object is no longer in scene.

You may want to print these out to have at hand while you work on the object's metadata.

■ **Tip**   When using numbers to represent states, it pays to think carefully about the order in which they are numbered.

In the Scene states assignments, you can quickly check to see whether anything should happen on mouse pick from the object's state via this code:

```
If (sceneLocation > 1) return; // object is not pickable so leave the function/method
```

It also allows you to easily filter through the action objects to see which need to be drawn in inventory, made visible on scene loads, and other useful things.

You will refer to this scene/location-related state as *location*.

Visibility Type

Another parameter that is assigned numbers to represent its options is `visibility`. When an object's location state changes, you need to know how and when to handle the change in visibility if one is needed. Rather than going to the trouble of duplicating animations and keyframing them for, say, fade-ins or fade-outs, you can set up the action once in code so any object with a transparency shader can be handled automatically. Hand in hand with fading is turning off the mesh render or perhaps the entire object by disabling or enabling it; remember, an object that is not drawn will still have an active collider.

> 0: Immediate change at start of animation.
>
> 1: Change visibility at end of animation.
>
> 2: Show at start, hide at end.

3: Hide at start, show at end.

4: Immediate change at start with fades.

5: Change visibility at end of animation, with fades.

6: Show at start, hide at end, with fades.

7: Hide at start, show at end, with fades.

As you can see, the system leaves you the option of defining any other combination you may need by adding more numbers to the definition.

If you remember what you learned when adding the fade-out to the KeyAtRock, you will realize that you can reduce the possibilities by checking for a transparent shader that will tell you when to use fades with the visibility changes. If it uses a Transparent shader, it fades in or out of its visibility type. The visibility type becomes simply

0: N/A

1: Show at start.

2: Hide at start.

3: Show at start, hide at end.

4: Hide at end.

░ **Tip**   Other shaders can use the alpha channel through their textures, but only with the Transparency shaders can you change or animate it with the Color's alpha parameter.

Game Notes

About now you are probably starting to get worried about remembering the rules and conventions you are setting up to make your game both powerful and extensible. It's time to introduce a handy method to store and access this information.

Besides adding comments in your scripts, you will find it crucial to have a brief document for notes on your game that is attached to the game itself. Unity's script editor is capable of reading and writing to several different file types including a simple text file. You will create a file whose sole purpose is an easy access repository for anything relate to your rules and conventions. This will allow you to concentrate on the interactivity without constantly trying to remember where all the bits and pieces were introduced.

1.   Open the script editor.

2.   From File, click New.

3.   Make sure you are saving the new file to the Adventure Scripts folder and name it GameNotes.txt.

4.   Add the definitions for both the *location* and *visibility types*.

5.   Save the text asset.

▪ **Tip**   You will be adding lots of information to your GameNotes text asset as you go. If you find yourself having to go back and look something else up, feel free to include it in the notes.

Current State

Having added the state definition arrays to the Interactor script, you will need to add variables to let the object keep track of its *current* state and all of the parameters that go with it so that when an object is processed to go into a particular state, you can re-use the code regardless of which state's metadata is being accessed.

1. Open the Interactor script.

2. At the top of the script, in the //state dependent variables section, add the following:

```
private var currentState : int = 0; // this will get updated in Start
private var currentLocation : int;  // see notes
private var currentVisibility : int; //see notes
private var currentObjectName : String; // short description
private var currentObjectDescription : String; // full description
private var currentSound : AudioClip;
private var currentAudioDelay : float = 0.0;
private var currentAnimationClip : AnimationClip;
private var currentAnimationDelay : float = 0.0;
private var currentAniLength : float;  // get length to calculate delays
private var currentLoopAnimation : AnimationClip;
private var currentLoopSound : AudioClip;
```

3. Save the script.

Note that there is no delay on the loop sound and animation. You will be adding the animation delay to the animation length to calculate when to start the loop animation and sound if it exists.

Mouse Pick Revisited

As you may recall when you were experimenting with animations, you created a series of scripts. You will now start incorporating some of their features into your Interactor script as well as a few other variables that will make your scripting more efficient and solve issues that may crop up.

Let's start by switching your test objects over to the script you are developing for the actual game.

1. Save the current scene as Interaction1 in the Scenes folder

2. Delete the deactivated objects, the Test Action Objects group, from the Hierarchy view.

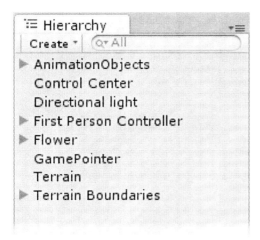

Figure 9-1. *The remaining objects in the newly renamed scene*

3. Remove the AniTest and AniTwoState scripts from the objects in the scene.

4. Add the Interactor script to the Rock, the Pedestal, and the KeyAtRock.

5. Select the First Person Controller's location so you can see the new action objects in the Game view.

6. Drag the GamePointer object onto the Game Pointer parameter for the Rock, the Pedestal, and the KeyAtRock in the Inspector in the Interactor script component.

The Control Center object is "found" in the Start function so you can make it a private variable so you won't have to drag it onto every action object you make. The GamePointer will eventually be swapped out so you will just use it as is for now.

7. Open the Interactor script.

8. Change the **var** controlCenter : GameObject line to:

private var controlCenter : GameObject;

9. Save the script.

You will need to factor in mouse pick logic before you worry about the actual animations, so you need not rush to fill out all of the new metadata arrays just yet. You have OnMouseEnter and OnMouseExit; now you need to add the OnMouseDown for your pick events.

10. Add an OnMouseDown function beneath the OnMouseExit function.

```
function OnMouseDown () {

    print    ("we have mouse down on " + this.name);

}
```

11. Back up at the top, under the //Pick and Mouseover Info section, add the following variables:

```
private var picked = false;  // so you can temporarily prevent mouse over action
private var mousedown : boolean; // so you know when this is true
private var processing = false; //so you can suspend mouse over actions, etc
```

12. Save the script.

As per the comments, these variables will help you refine the existing functionality as you go forward.

To get the full effect, you will need to turn on all of the mouse over options.

13. In the Control Center object's Game Manager script in the Inspector, turn on both the material and cursor color change options.

14. Click Play and mouse over, then click on one of your action objects.

If you got a response from the pick but saw no mouse over response, you will need to increase the Trigger Distance.

1. Stop Play mode.

2. Set the Trigger Distance to about 12 on the action objects.

3. Click Play and test again.

You realize that the color changes are likely to interfere with the visual experience, so it makes sense to turn them off as soon as you have a mouse pick. You've already got it in the OnMouseExit function, so you can just copy and paste.

4. Add the following lines to the OnMouseDown function:

```
// turn the object back to original if it is being used
if(useMOMaterialChange) renderer.material = originalMaterial;
```

To refresh your memory, save the object's original material in the Start function so you know what to switch it back to.

5. Save the script.

6. Click Play and do a test pick.

7. Add the following to the OnMouseDown function to turn off the cursor color change:

```
// *** send a message turn the cursor color back to original if it is being used
if(useMOCursorChange) {
    gamePointer.GetComponent(CustomCursor).SendMessage("CursorColorChange",false);
}
```

This one is a little trickier. Because you are changing the pointer GUI object, you need to first access its CustomCursor script, then call the function in that script to change the cursor back to its false state (in this case, a white diffuse color). Feel free to take a quick look at it in the Inspector. The three asterisks will allow you to quickly find the code at a later time.

8. Save the script.

9. Click Play and pick an object again.

The functionality is much nicer, but you need to try something else before you can move on.

1. Use the Clear button in the console to clear the existing messages.

2. Back away—far away—from the objects and mouse over, then mouse down/pick the object.

While the mouse over functionality was bypassed, the pick wasn't.

Once again, copy and paste the distance checking line from the OnMouseEnter into the OnMouseDown function. Make sure you add it *before* the print function so you know if it worked.

3. Add the following at the top of the OnMouseDown function:

```
// exit if you are not within range
if (DistanceFromCamera() > triggerDistance) return;
```

4. Save the script.

5. Click play and back out of mouse over range, and then pick the object.

Nothing happens.

6. Move within range again and pick to make sure it still works.

░ **Tip**   When adding functionality, it is always a good idea to make sure the original functionality still works before you no longer remember the changes you made.

After experimenting with picking the objects, you may have come to the conclusion that your Trigger Distance is really too far for picking. If you decrease it, the mouse over distance may be too close. The solution is to make two checks. By adding an offset distance, you can still get mouse over but without messing up Trigger Distance. As an additional benefit, you can control just which prompts will be activated when you implement the text message.

Because you have allowed the author to override the Trigger Distance for an object in the Inspector, it makes sense to add the offset rather than hardcode a separate value for the total distance. This way, when you adjust the Trigger Distance, the offset will still be the same distance from it, wherever that may be.

1. Add the following variable beneath the TriggerDistance variable in the //Pick and Mouse over info section:

```
var moOffset : float = 10.0;   // additional distance to allow mouse over to be seen
```

2. Change the **if** (DistanceFromCamera line in the OnMouseEnter function to include the offset:

```
// exit if you are not within range
if (DistanceFromCamera() > triggerDistance + moOffset) return;
```

3. Save the script.

447

Be sure to test the distance and the offset thoroughly before you put the Interactor script on other objects. If you forget and need to change all of the defaults, you can change the variable to private, save the script, and then change the variable back to public again.

4. Click Play and test the distance checking (Figure 9-2).

Figure 9-2. *Mouse over, but no mouse pick between range and range+offset*

You may have noticed the viewport jump when you first move forward in the scene. At one point you changed the Main Camera's X rotation to 12 so you had a starting view looking down on the action objects. If you wish to set it back to 0, feel free to do so after stopping Play mode.

5. Stop Play mode.

6. Save the scene and save the project.

Adding Metadata

Now would be a good time to start adding metadata to a couple of your objects. Let's go with the simpler state objects, the Rock and the KeyAtRock. The rock is obvious: it only moves to a second location. The key isn't quite as simple, though it does only have two states: on the ground and out of the scene. Remember, its stunt double is an entirely different object with states of its own. The same can be said of cursors.

Before you start filling out metadata for your new action objects, take a moment to get a bit more efficient. Locating the correct animation clips is probably beginning to feel like a shell game, but now that you have an Animation Clips folder, you can make things easier for yourself. While you can't move the correct clips into it individually (the entire Animations prefab would get moved), you can duplicate the correct clips and move them into the folder for easier access. As long as you are going to have to reassign the clips anyway, you may as well duplicate them now. Append their names with "_Copy" as you did the key insert clip.

1. Locate, duplicate, and rename each of the animated objects in the AnimationObjects folder.

2. Move the copies into the Animation Clips folder (Figure 9-3).

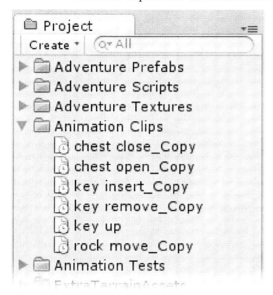

Figure 9-3. *The easier-to-access animation clip copies*

3. Assign the new clips to the correct element in each object's Animation array, as per Figure 9-4.

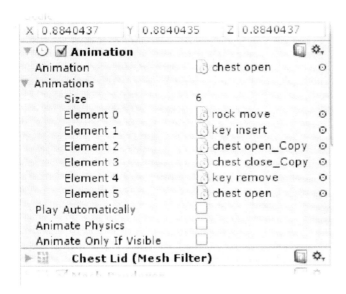

Figure 9-4. *The new animation clip copies for the ChestLid loaded into its Animation array*

■ **Tip**   When you substitute a new clip for one assigned to the default Animation, it will move the original to the end of the array. Since you are no longer going to be using the default animation for your action objects, you don't need to update the default.

---

4.   Open the Interactor for the Rock.

5.   With the exception of the two Loop arrays, set the size of each array to 2.

The Loop functionality has a checkbox telling you when to use it, so you don't have to worry about error messages about elements in those arrays that don't exist.

6.   Fill in the metadata information as shown in Table 9-2.

Table 9-2. *Metadata for the Rock and the KeyAtRock*

Rock			KeyAtRock		
Location			Location		
	Size	2		Size	2
	Element 0	0		Element 0	0
	Element 1	3		Element 1	4
Visibility Type			Visibility Type		
	Size	2		Size	2
	Element 0	0		Element 0	0
	Element 1	0		Element 1	2
Object Name			Object Name		
	Size	2		Size	2
	Element 0	Large Rock		Element 0	Old Key
	Element 1	Displaced Rock		Element 1	
Description			Description		
	Size	2		Size	2
	Element 0	It is a large rock on the ground		Element 0	It is an old iron key on the ground
	Element 1	It is a large rock that's been moved		Element 1	
Animation Clip			Animation Clip		
	Size	2		Size	2
	Element 0	none		Element 0	none
	Element 1	rock move _Copy		Element 1	key up
Animation Delay			Animation Delay		
	Size	2		Size	2
	Element 0	0		Element 0	0
	Element 1	0		Element 1	0

Rock			KeyAtRock		
Sound Clip			Sound FX		
	Size	2		Size	2
	Element 0	none		Element 0	none
	Element 1	plopsm		Element 1	none
Audio Delay			Audio Delay		
	Size	2		Size	2
	Element 0	0		Element 0	0
	Element 1	0		Element 1	0
Loop Animation			Loop Animation		
	Size	0		Size	0
Loop Sound FX			Loop Sound FX		
	Size	0		Size	0
Post Loop			Post Loop		

7. Fill in the metadata for the KeyAtRock as per Figure 9-4.

Review the location and visibility definitions in the GameNotes text asset to understand the number assignments.

The important thing to remember about your metadata is that it contains the actions needed to put an object *into* its target state. Therefore, if the key is in state 0 (on the ground) when you pick it, the animation to lift it up is in the state it goes *into*, state 1.

8. Save your scene and project.

Chapter Summary

In this chapter you started fleshing out your Interactor script to be able to hold all of the object's pertinent information, its metadata. By storing everything you need to know about the object in whatever state it is in, you are, in effect, create a *smart object*. Using arrays, you can now store the object's short and long descriptions, location, animation, audio, and other properties you wish to access by state.

You learned that you can keep the definitions and logic behind the setup stored in a text asset for quick access in the scene.

In the next chapter, you'll start to use the metadata by displaying your action object's description metadata on screen as you explore the Unity GUI controls.

■ ■ ■

CHAPTER 10

Message Text

One of the most common features of a classic point and click adventure game is the text prompt or message that identifies an action object as you mouse over. In our game, we will display the name and description of the object on mouseover when a player is within range, as well as a message informing him if he tries to pick the object and isn't close enough.

UnityGUI text design is patterned after the concept of cascading style sheets (CSS). You define colors and fonts for a particular style and all of the GUI elements inherit those properties with GUISkin. This makes for a consistent look and feel throughout. It also means the GUI elements involved are treated quite differently from 3D objects.

In Unity, there are two types of GUI elements. Of the objects that can be created through the GameObject menu, you have already used the GUI Texture. The GameObject varieties of text and texture objects are handled individually and exist in the game hierarchy. They are not affected by the GUI Skin specifications.

The second type of GUI elements, Unity GUI, *must be scripted to exist*. Now that you are a bit more comfortable with scripting, you'll be using the Unity GUI to create and handle text and to eventually convert the cursor. The Unity GUI consists of a GUI Skin and GUI Styles.

GUI Skin

The first step in getting text on screen is to create a GUI Skin. This gives us the default look and feel for the various types of GUI elements, should we need to use them.

1. Open the book project and load the Interaction1 scene.

2. Right-click in the Project view and choose GUI Skin from the bottom of the Create submenu.

3. Rename it **Game GUISkin**.

Take a few minutes to look through the parameters for the various elements in the Inspector. The GUISkin is a collection of predefined GUIStyles or templates that dictate the look and much of the behavior (by way of its name) of each element.

To see what the various control elements look like, see the Reference Manual ➤ GUI Scripting Guide ➤ GUI Basics.

For this game, you'll be using only a simple Label element for the onscreen text.

4. Open the **Label** element.

5. Under Normal, adjust the Text Color to something that will show up in your scene (see Figure 10-1).

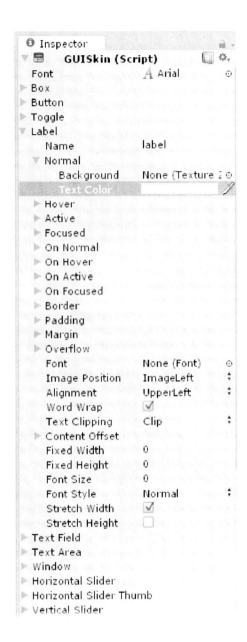

Figure 10-1. *GUISkin with Label selected in the Inspector*

At the top of the Inspector, you'll probably see that the default font is Arial. We will leave it as is for now. The font indicated here is the default font used by your operating system.

As previously mentioned, the GUI elements exist only in scripts, which means you'll need a GameObject to put the script on. There are a couple of choices at this point. You could create a new empty GameObject to hold the script, giving it a name that would remind you where you put it. The downside of this is that you'd need to add it to the list of objects that need to be accessed by each action object.

An alternative is to put the script on an object that is already being accessed by the action objects. This cuts down a bit on the overhead and clutter. The important thing is to give the script a nice descriptive name so you can locate it quickly. As it happens, you have an ideal candidate—the Control Center object. It already holds the GameManager script, which is a pretty good place to manage the text.

1. Select the Control Center object.

2. Open its GameManager script.

3. Create the following function beneath the Update function:

```
function OnGUI () {

   GUI.Label (Rect (0,0,100,50), "This is the text string for a Label Control");
}
```

The OnGUI function is the GUI equivalent of the Update function—it is called at least once every frame and is another of the system functions.

4. Save the script.

Nothing shows in the Game window. GUI elements show only during runtime. Since the function is continually being called, you can make changes, save the script, then return focus to the Game window to see the results without restarting the scene.

5. Click Play.

6. Look up toward the sky if it is hard to see in your environment.

The text appears in the upper left corner of the Game window (Figure 10-2).

Figure 10-2. *The Label's text in the upper left corner of the viewport*

The code (Rect (0,0,100,50) defines the pixel location and boundary the text must fit into. The Rect type uses a four-element array that defines the x and y screen location and the width and height, Rect (x_pos, y_pos, width, height).

7. Change the line to read:

```
GUI.Label (Rect (10,10,500,20), "This is the text string for a Label Control");
```

8. Save the file then click in the Game window to change focus and see the result.

The text no longer needs to wrap, as shown in Figure 10-3.

Figure 10-3. *The new location and bounds for the text*

9. Stop Play mode and click the Maximize on Play toggle on the Game view.

10. Click Play.

The text is still the same size. As with the GUI Texture object, it is a constant pixel size that does not scale with the window.

11. Stop Play mode.

OS Font Support

Unity will use the operating system's default font, Arial, until you provide something else. Using the OS default font makes the file size smaller, but carries a small risk that the text could appear different on different systems. For this game, let's start with Arial.

To change the size of the text, you need to access the font assigned to the GUI Skin. Because you haven't yet introduced a font, you can't yet change the font size.

1. Stop Play mode.

2. Via the OS, from the BookAssets folder, drag the Fonts folder into the project's Assets folder.

3. From the newly added Fonts folder, select the font, Arial.

457

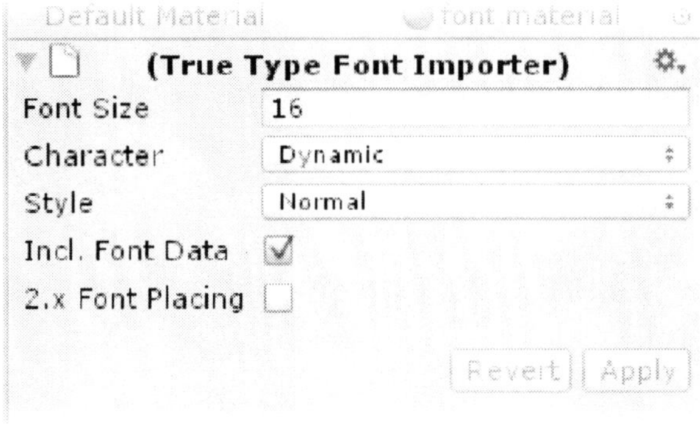

Figure 10-4. *The Arial font in the Inspector*

The most important thing to understand about fonts in Unity is that they can have only *one* size unless they are set to *Dynamic* (see (Figure 10-4). If the font isn't dynamic, for *each* font size, you will need to make a duplicate font and use either a duplicate GUISkin or a custom GUIStyle. Dynamic fonts allow you to override the size for separate templates or GUI styles.

4. Use Ctrl+D (Cmd + D on a Mac) to duplicate the Arial font.

5. Name it **arial2**.

6. Change its Font Size to **25**.

7. Keep its Character set to Dynamic and click Apply.

When using a font in most 3D engines for 2D text, a bitmap of the full alphabet and characters is generated for *each* font *and* size specified. When you specify Dynamic in Unity, the bitmap generated by the operating system is used, saving download time and texture memory during runtime. The downside is that if you specify a font that is not present on the operating system, a fallback font will be used in its place. Even when using generic fonts such as Arial, there may be slight differences among systems. We will investigate this further when we experiment with different fonts later on in the project. Dynamic fonts are currently supported only on desktop platforms (i.e., Mac and Windows).

8. Open the Fonts folder in the Project view.

9. Open the arial2 font and look at its font material and font texture in the Preview window.

You won't see anything there right now because the alphabet is being generated by the operating system.

10. Change the Character to ASCII default set and click Apply.

Both a texture and a material are generated for the font, as shown in Figure 10-5. It's worth noting that you can also choose all uppercase or all lowercase to reduce the size of the texture map.

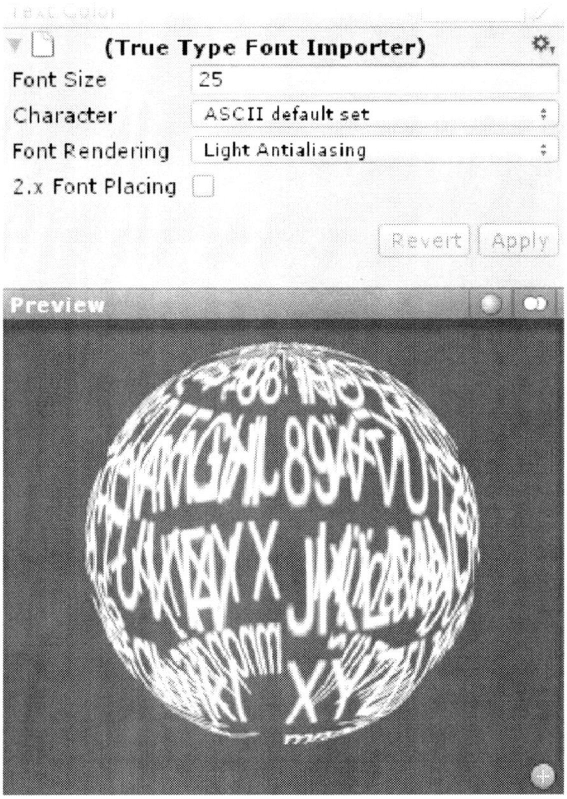

Figure 10-5. *Font material and texture generated for non-dynamic character type*

> 11. Select the Game GUISkin and load the duplicate font, arial2, at the top of the Inspector.
>
> 12. Click Play.
>
> 13. Stop Play mode.

Nothing happens because until you tell Unity otherwise, you are still using the default styles. You'll do that in the script that draws the GUI elements in its OnGUI function.

> 1. Open the GameManager script.
>
> 2. At the top of the script, add the variable:

```
var customSkin : GUISkin;
```

> 3. Then, in the OnGUI function, above the GUI.Label line, add:

```
GUI.skin = customSkin;
```

> 4. Save the script.

5. Stop Play mode and select the Control Center object.

6. Drag the Game GUISkin into the new Custom Skin parameter.

7. Click Play and observe the result (Figure 10-6).

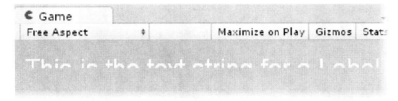

Figure 10-6. *The GUISkin in use*

The changes we made to the font and GUISkin now appear, but at Font Size 25, the font gets cropped.

8. Change the GUI.Label line as follows:

```
GUI.Label (Rect (10,10,500,40), "This is the text string for a Label Control");
```

9. Save the script.

10. Click in the Game window to return focus to it and observe the change (Figure 10-7).

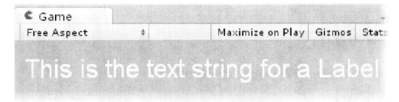

Figure 10-7. *The rectangle resized to fit the text*

The text color may get lost against the background. Let's use a Box element instead to make the text easier to read.

1. Comment out the GUI.Label line

2. Add the following beneath the GUI.Label line:

```
GUI.Box (Rect (0,40,500,50), " This is the text string for a Box Control ");
```

3. Save the script and observe the changes (see Figure 10-8).

4. Change the rectangle's parameters to fit your text.

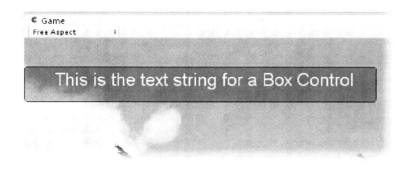

Figure 10-8. *The Box control*

The box itself uses an internal image, Box, which is scaled, keeping its outline intact. We can make our own version that behaves the same way, but first let's look at the default version in the Preview to check its size, opacity, and other parameters. Note that the text in the Box control is centered, as opposed to the Label's default—left-justified.

5. Select the Game GUISkin in the Project view.

6. In the Inspector, click the Box drop-down arrow.

7. Open the Normal section.

8. Double-click the Box in the Background field to show it in the Preview window.

9. Click the Alpha/Color toggle to see what its alpha channel looks like (Figure 10-9).

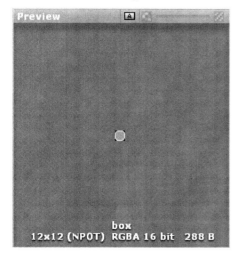

Figure 10-9. *The Alpha channel of the Box texture used on the Box GUI control*

The tiny 12 × 12 pixel texture shows a mostly rounded-corner box. The corners are set not to stretch in the Box template's settings, so the box image looks correct at any size.

■ **Warning**   Before you experiment with different textures in the GUISkin, you should know that if the texture does not show up in the asset browser, you won't be able to get it back without creating a new GUISkin. It is therefore a good idea to visit the Unity forum at http://forum.unity3d.com/threads/7173-Official-skins?p=84065 and download the source files for the internal textures.

In the Textures folder provided as part of this book's download, you will see a texture called MyBox. It is a variation on the default box, but it has the advantage of remaining a .png file so you can alter it. Let's load it into the skin.

1. Select the Game GUISkin again.

2. Click the down arrow to browse the texture assets for the Background field again.

3. Choose MyBox.

4. Click Play if you are not already in play mode to see the changes (Figure 10-10).

5. Experiment with the Text Color and other parameters until you are happy with the result.

Figure 10-10. *Experimenting with the Box control's settings*

Note that the box transparency is a function of the MyBox texture's alpha channel.

Now that we have gained a bit of control over the visual aspects of the text, let's look into alignment of the box itself.

If you are not planning on limiting the screen resolution, the user will be able to choose a resolution at run time. If you remember that GUI elements retain their pixel size regardless of screen resolution, it becomes clear that you need access to the screen size in order to center the text messages. Fortunately, you can use Screen.width, Screen.height, and a bit of math inside the command to get what you want. Let's go ahead and move the Box control to the bottom center of the screen.

6. Change the two GUI control lines as follows:

```
GUI.Label (Rect (Screen.width/2 - 250, 10, 500,35), " This is the text string for a⤸
  Label Control");
```

```
GUI.Box (Rect (Screen.width/2 - 250, Screen.height - 37, 500,35), " This is the text⤸
  string for a Box Control ");
```

7. Save the script.

8. Turn on Maximize on Play in the Game window.

9. Click Play and observe the changes.

The Box control text centers no matter what the screen size is, but the Label control text looks to be left-justified.

10. Select the Game GUISkin and change the Label's Alignment to Upper Center (Figure 10-11).

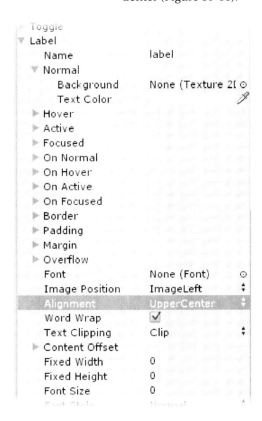

Figure 10-11. *The Label template's Alignment property*

You will be displaying three types of text messages. The first is the short description of the object that will be called currentObjectName in the metadata. You may decide the text for the short description label should be different. Instead of duplicating the GUISkin and changing it inside the OnGUI function at runtime, you can create a GUI Style that can override the regular skin's version of *any* control.

1. Add the following line near the top of the GameManager script:

```
var customGUIStyle : GUIStyle; // override the skin
```

2. Save the script and stop Play mode.

3. Select the Control Center object and look for the new Custom GUIStyle variable in the Inspector.

4. Expand the new variable as shown in Figure 10-12.

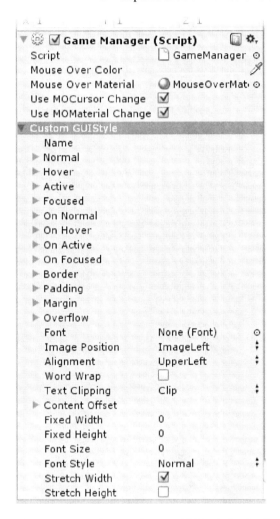

Figure 10-12. *The new Custom GUIStyle in the GameManager script*

Because the variable is of GUIStyle type, it automatically generates all of the parameters needed to create a new *style* or template of GUI control.

5. Change the Text Color in the Normal section to a paler shade of your regular label text.

6. Set the Alignment to Upper Center.

7. Duplicate the Label line and make the following changes:

```
GUI.Label (Rect (Screen.width/2 - 250, Screen.height - 65, 500,35),↵
  "Short Name", customGUIStyle);
```

Note the new GUIStyle variable is added as the *last* argument inside the parentheses. This is how the GUIStyle overrides the GUISkin specified at the top of the OnGUI function.

8. Save the script and click Play.

The new override version of the label behaves nicely, as shown in Figure 10-13.

Figure 10-13. *The new custom version of the Label control*

For those with no experience in web design and 2D text layout, the concept of CSS may be a bit nebulous. Unity's GUISkin and GUIStyle can be confusing if you have no background in this type of text design and layout. A GUISkin is a collection of styles. Each has the same list of parameters, but depending on the control it is named for, it may not use all of them. The Label, for example, never uses Hover, Active, Focused, or Normal, or many of the several other settings listed under it.

When we use GUI.Label, the defined preset for a Label control knows what kind of behavior is associated with the control and makes use only of the style's parameters that are applicable to a label. A custom GUIStyle, as you probably noticed, has the same settings as the rest of the prefabs, but it is not associated with any particular control *until it is added as an override*. At that time, only the applicable settings are used. You could, then, use the same GUIStyle for several different control types. If you set it up to look like a button and override a Label control, the label would look like button but still have the behavior of a label. If you override a Box control with it, it will look like a button and act like a box. If you override a Horizontal Slider with it, it will *not* look like a button because a Horizontal Slider does not use the same settings from the list as a button. This allows you to make custom GUIStyles for any control you need, but it comes with a lot of overhead since a good portion of the settings are never used.

Next you need a means of turning the text off and on.

1. While in Play mode, try turning the Main Camera's GUILayer off.

Nothing happens. Apparently UnityGUI is not affected by the GUI layer, as are the GUIText and GUITexture components of GameObjects. You'll need to devise another means of turning them off and on.

2. Stop Play mode.

Text Visibility

If you remember, the OnGUI function is similar to the Update function in that it is called at least every frame and that's where are code must be to create the GUI controls. Much as you did with the first scripting tests, you need to set a *flag* to tell the engine whether or not to draw the text. Let's start with a simple test to make sure we're on the right track.

1. Open the GameManager script.

2. Add the following variable near the top of the script:

```
var useText : boolean = true; // flag to suppress or allow all text
```

3. Then add the conditional to check for it, so the script now looks as follows:

```
function OnGUI () {

   GUI.skin = customSkin;

   if (useText){
      GUI.Label (Rect (Screen.width/2 - 250, 10, 500,35), " This is the text string↵
for a Label Control");
      GUI.Label (Rect (Screen.width/2 - 250, Screen.height - 65, 500,35), "Short Name",↵
customGUIStyle);
      GUI.Box (Rect (Screen.width/2 - 250, Screen.height - 37, 500,35), " This is the↵
text string for a Box Control ");
         }
}
```

4. Save the script.

5. Click Play.

6. Select the Control Center object and try turning the useText parameter off and on.

The controls now turn *all* GUI text off and on. This gives you a means of turning *all text* off and on for the game when you allow players to customize their game experience.

Because the text needs to show and hide with mouseovers, you need two types of flags. The *show* flag will be used for turning the text off and on during regular game play, and the *use* flag will globally control whether the text is being used at all. Show flags will be handled by the script so they will always be private variables.

As the variable name useText indicates, you'll use this flag to tell whether to show any text at all. But you also need a variable to let you know when the text should actually be seen during the course of the game. This means that when the object the cursor is over sends a message to the pointer object to change color, it should *also* tell the GameManager script to change a showText variable there as well. You should assign a false to this variable because the text should only show when the cursor is over an action object.

1. Add the showText variable beneath the useText variable declaration:

```
var showText : boolean= false; // flag to toggle text during play
```

And now you can embed the showText conditional within the useText conditional.

2. Add the showText conditional so the OnGUI function looks like this:

```
function OnGUI () {

  GUI.skin = customSkin;

  if (useText){  //global toggle
      if (showText){ //local toggle
     GUI.Label (Rect (Screen.width/2 - 250, 10, 500,35), " This is the text string↵
for a Label Control");
     GUI.Box (Rect (Screen.width/2 - 250, Screen.height - 37, 500,35), " This is↵
the text string for a Box Control ");
     GUI.Label (Rect (Screen.width/2 - 250, Screen.height - 65, 500,35), "Short name",↵
customGUIStyle);
      }
   }
}
```

3. Save the script.

4. Click Play

The text no longer appears in the game window.

Next let's hook up the cursor visibility and the text visibility.

You've seen how to send messages (i.e., call functions) from other objects with the GamePointer color change in the Interactor. Now let's try something different. You can set the value of a variable directly if you have access to the object it's on and know the script name. To control text visibility, you change the showText variable's value. With dot notation, you can access it as soon as you locate the object and the script. Because the mouseover check is done on the object, you need to look at the Interactor script.

1. Open the Interactor script.

In the Start function, you can see that the Control Center object has already been introduced, so you are good to go.

2. Inside the OnMouseEnter function, above the if (useMOMaterialChange) line, add the following:

```
//activate the text visibility on mouseover
controlCenter.GetComponent(GameManager).showText = true;
```

3. Inside the OnMouseExit function, above the if (useMOMaterialChange) line, add the following:

```
//deactivate the text visibility on mouseover
controlCenter.GetComponent(GameManager).showText = false;
```

4. Save the script.

5. Click Play and test the functionality.

6. Be sure to move out of range and check it as well.

So far things look pretty good, but you need to do more thorough testing.

1. Move close enough so that the text box is over part of the action objects.

2. Try to mouse over them.

The text flickers badly (Figure 10-14).

Figure 10-14. *The Box control, behaving as a Box control, blocks mouseovers.*

Let's take a moment to figure out what is happening. On mouseover, the text is displayed. The problem comes with the Box control because it blocks mouseover activity behind it. That triggers a mouse off, which turns off the control, which in turn unblocks it and causes another mouseover…and so on. Fortunately, it is not the graphic of the box that is the problem, it is the internal functionality of a Box GUI control.

3. Open the GameManager script.

4. Add another variable for a custom GUIStyle:

```
var boxStyleLabel : GUIStyle; // make a label that looks like a box
```

5. Save the script.

6. Stop Play mode.

7. Select the Control Center object.

468

8. In the Normal section of the new custom GUIStyle parameter, load the MyBox texture into the Background field.

9. Set Alignment to Upper Center.

10. Change the GUI.Box line as follows:

```
GUI.Label (Rect (Screen.width/2 - 250, Screen.height - 37, 500,35), "This is the text↵
 string for a fake Box Control", boxStyleLabel);
```

11. Save the script.

12. Click Play and mouseover the action objects.

The entire box texture is stretched to fit the specified rectangle (Figure 10-15).

Figure 10-15. *The MyBox texture stretched to fit the rectangle's dimensions*

1. From the Project view, select the Game GUISkin.

2. Compare its Box control's parameters with our Box Style Label's parameters.

Close inspection shows that the Box control uses a value of 6 in the Border parameters to avoid stretching the whole texture (the texture happens to be 12 × 12 pixels) and 4 in the Padding to prevent the text from getting too close to the edge of the texture.

3. Stop Play mode.

4. Change the Box Style Label parameters to match.

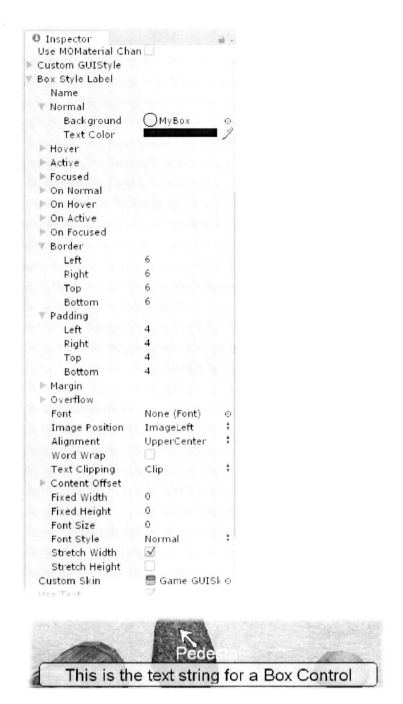

Figure 10-16. *Setting the Label's Border and Padding to match the Box control*

5. Save your scene and project.

It is time to think about feeding the object metadata into the text. You may want to add the Interactor script to the rest of the action objects at this time and fill out the object name and description arrays. The flower is a special case as it uses a *Skinned* Mesh Renderer instead of a regular Mesh Renderer, so for the time being, you will need to disable its Interactor.

Using the Object Metadata

Before accessing the action object's metadata, there are a few more things to do. In keeping with the rest of the optional functionality, you'll want to include the short and long descriptions. At this time, you also need to make an executive decision on what exactly the user will be able to turn off and on. Presently, the user can toggle mouseover cursor color, mouseover object color (material), and GUI text. The next options to consider are long and short descriptions of the object the mouse is over and the message that will appear when the object is activated, the *action* message.

If useText is on, let's assume the player wants to see the short description and the action text. If useLongDesc is on, let's include the long description as well.

1. Open the GameManager script from the Control Center and add the following variables near the top:

```
var useLongDesc : boolean = true;
private var showShortDesc : boolean = true;
private var showLongDesc : boolean = true;
private var showActionMsg : boolean = true;
```

As this will be feeding new text into the GUI controls every time the player mouses over and mouses off objects, you should also clear the text in case some objects don't yet have their data filled in.

2. Add the following near the top:

```
private var shortDesc : String = "";
private var longDesc : String = "";
private var actionMsg : String = "";
```

Now, you can make changes to the OnGUI function to add the individual conditions and also use the variables instead of static text.

3. Change the OnGUI functions as follows:

```
function OnGUI () {

  GUI.skin = customSkin;

  if (useText){  //global toggle
     if (showText){ //local toggle
     if (showActionMsg) GUI.Label (Rect (Screen.width/2 - 250, 10, 500,35), actionMsg);
     if (useLongDesc) {
         if (showLongDesc) GUI.Label (Rect (Screen.width/2 - 250, Screen.height - 37,↵
500,35), longDesc);
         }
     if (showShortDesc) GUI.Label (Rect (Screen.width/2 - 250, Screen.height - 65,↵
500,35), shortDesc, customGUIStyle);
     }
```

```
        }
    }
}
```

4.   Save the script.

If you test the functionality now, you should see nothing but the box texture on mouseover because the current values for the text are all "", empty strings. Let's head back to the `Interactor` script and have it send out the information we need.

1.   Open the `Interactor` script.

2.   In the `OnMouseEnter` function, under the `controlCenter.GetComponent(GameManager).showText = true` line, add:

```
//send the correct text to the GameManager for display
controlCenter.GetComponent(GameManager). shortDesc= objectName[0];
controlCenter.GetComponent(GameManager).longDesc = description[0];
```

Until you have your code loading the current state's metadata values, you can just use the first element's values. Remember the first element in an array is element 0.

The `actionMsg`, in case you are wondering, resides in the `ObjectLookUp` script. We will finish it when we hook up the state management results.

You no longer need a mouseover material change now that the text is going to tell you about the object.

3.   Select the Control Center object.

4.   Uncheck Use MO Color Change.

5.   Click Play and test the functionality.

If you got an "Array index is out of range." error message, it probably means the array size for the object name and object description is still 0, as with the Pedestal. If you disable the `Interactor` script on an object, you'll still get mouseover events happening and errors generated.

6.   Add the `Interactor` script to the ChestLid.

7.   Fill out metadata in the `Interactor` component for the Pedestal and ChestLid as shown in Table 10-1.

Table 10-1. *Metadata for the Pedestal and ChestLid*

Pedestal			ChestLid		
Location			Location		
	Size	1		Size	2
	Element 0	0		Element 0	0
				Element 1	0
Visibility Type			Visibility Type		
	Size	1		Size	2
	Element 0	0		Element 0	0
				Element 1	0
Object Name			Object Name		
	Size	1		Size	2
	Element 0	Pedestal		Element 0	Chest Lid
				Element 1	Open Chest Lid
Description			Description		
	Size	1		Size	2
	Element 0	It is an extremely ugly stone		Element 0	It is closed chest lid
pedestal				Element 1	It is an open chest lid
Animation Clip			Animation Clip		
	Size	0		Size	2
				Element 0	chest close_Copy
				Element 1	chest open_Copy
Animation Delay			Animation Delay		
	Size	0		Size	2
				Element 0	0
				Element 1	0
Sound Clip			Sound FX		
	Size	1		Size	2
	Element 0	none		Element 0	DoorClose
				Element 1	ChestOpen
Audio Delay			Audio Delay		
	Size	1		Size	2
	Element 0	0		Element 0	0
				Element 1	0.75
Loop Animation			Loop Animation		
	Size	0		Size	0
Loop Sound FX			Loop Sound FX		
	Size	0		Size	0
Post Loop			Post Loop		

8. Drag the GamePointer into the GamePointer for both.

Since there is no animation on the Pedestal, you can uncheck the Animates parameter.

9. Select the Pedestal and uncheck the Animates in the Interactor component.

It might be nice if the long message was shown only when within the pick distance. It is a few more lines of code, but aesthetically worth the trouble.

10. In the Interactor script, in the OnMouseEnter function, beneath the lines you just added to send the correct text to the GameManager for display, add the following:

```
// automatic bypass flag
if(DistanceFromCamera() <= triggerDistance) {
      controlCenter.GetComponent(GameManager).inRange =true;}
else  controlCenter.GetComponent(GameManager).inRange =false;
```

These lines set a flag we will call inRange in the GameManager that will bypass the long description if the inRange variable is false.

11. Save the Interactor script.

12. Open the GameManager script.

13. Add the following private variable near the top:

```
private var inRange : boolean; // distance flag for long desc
```

14. In the OnGUI function, in the showLongDesc conditional, add the "and", &&, so *both* conditions must be met in order for the long description to be shown:

```
if (showLongDesc && inRange) GUI.Label (Rect (Screen.width/2 - 250, Screen.height - 37,↵
500,35), longDesc);
```

15. Save the script.

16. Click Play and test the functionality (see Figure 10-17).

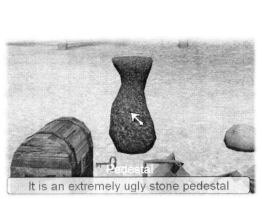

Figure 10-17. *The pedestal in range (left) and outside of picking distance (right)*

Now when the player is beyond pick range, the long description will not show.

    17.   Save the scene and save the project.

Handling the Action

You now have metadata information being displayed as text, mouseover prompts working well, pick events being registered, and a lookup table in place. It is time to see about using the lookup information to trigger the correct events.

The pick event is in the Interactor script, but the state transition information is in the ObjectLookup script. Processing the pick will require a pretty important function that will need information from both scripts.

Theoretically, it would have been simpler to combine the two scripts, but both have a lot of data that must be filled in, and it's easier to manage the input in two separate scripts. Therefore, the script that parses the lookup information will reside in the ObjectLookUp script, but will initially get called from the Interactor script, which already holds the OnMouseDown code.

Thinking back to the way we've set up the state management, it's clear we need three key ingredients before we can process an interaction. We need the object that has been picked. We need the object's current state, and we need the current cursor. More precisely, we need the cursor's current *texture*—which will have been named according to our naming conventions (appended with " Icon").

Let's go ahead and finish the cursor script to set that up for future needs.

    1.   Open the CustomCursor script.

    2.   Near the top, add the following line to create a variable to hold the current cursor's texture and the default texture:

```
var defaultCursor : Texture; // load in the texture for the default cursor
private var currentCursor : Texture; // the current texture on the cursor
```

3. Inside the Start function, add the following line to get and store the texture :

```
defaultCursor = guiTexture.texture; // from the default cursor at start up
currentCursor = defaultCursor;
```

At some point, you'll need a mechanism to change the texture to a new texture when the cursor changes.

4. Create the following function near the bottom of the script:

```
function SwapCursor (newCursor : Texture) {

    gameObject.guiTexture.texture = newCursor; //change the object's texture
    currentCursor = newCursor; // update the variable that holds the texture
    gameObject.guiTexture.enabled = false; //
}
```

In this function, you pass the new texture in as an argument of type Texture, change the cursor object texture to use it, update the current cursor variable, and temporarily hide the cursor.

5. Add a function to change the cursor back to the default:

```
function ResetCursor () {

    gameObject.guiTexture.texture = defaultCursor; //change back to default texture
    currentCursor = defaultCursor; // update the variable that holds the texture
}
```

This one was simpler since we already know what texture should be on the default cursor.

6. Save the script.

Next let's set up the code in the Interactor's OnMouseDown function to call the function named LookUpState, through which you'll pass the three key ingredients, the picked object, its current state, and the cursor that picked it. Since both scripts are on the same object, they can talk to each other with GetComponent.

1. Open the Interactor script.

2. Inside the OnMouseDown function, beneath the existing code, add the following:

```
//send the picked object, its current state, and the cursor [texture] that picked it
// to the LookUpState function for processing
GetComponent(ObjectLookup).LookUpState(this.gameObject, currentState, ↵
 gamePointer.GetComponent(CustomCursor).currentCursor.name);
```

Note that the cursor is not really the cursor *object*, but the *texture* that it is currently using.

Ingredient 1 is the object that was picked, **this**.gameObject.

Ingredient 2 is its current state, currentState.

Ingredient 3 is the gamePointer's *texture's* name, gamePointer.GetComponent(*CustomCursor*).*currentCursor.name*.

If you look at the CustomCursor script, you'll see that the variable currentCursor is of type Texture. Texture.name returns the name of the image or texture. The cursor will always be the same object but the texture will change, so it is the texture we will check for.

3. Comment out the print statement:

```
// print ("we have mouse down on " + this.name);
```

    4.   Save the script.

And now, so you don't get an error trying to call a function that does not yet exist, let's start to build our LookUpState function in the ObjectLookup script.

    1.   Open the ObjectLookup script.

    2.   Delete the entire OnMouseDown function used to test the array parsing.

When you create a function that receives arguments, it is usually a good idea to check to see if it is receiving them before going any further. Let's add a print statement for each just to make sure they are functioning.

    3.   Add the following framework for our LookUpState function:

```
//look up the state of the object to see what needs to happen
function LookUpState (object : GameObject, currentState: int, picker : String) {

    print ("Object: " + object.name);
    print ("State: " + currentState);
    print ("Picker: " + picker);

}
```

    4.   Add the ObjectLookUp script to the ChestLid, the Rock and the Pedestal.

    5.   Set the Size of their Lookup State 0 arrays to **1**.

    6.   Set the Element 0 data to **default,1,A**.

    7.   Use **B** for the ChestLid and **C** for the Pedestal.

    8.   Click Play and test the output for each.

The console reports the three arguments that were passed to the LookUpState function, as shown in Figure 10-18.

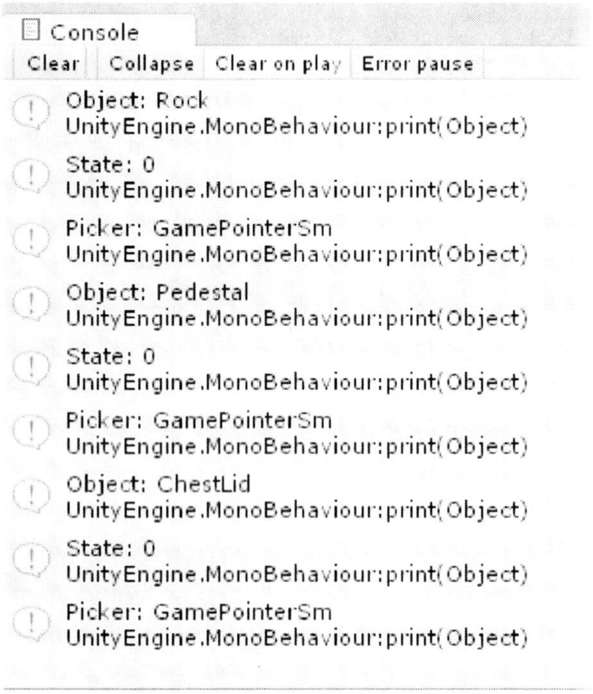

Figure 10-18. *The LookUpState function's received arguments on picking the three action objects*

Having confirmed that the correct information has been passed into the function, let's see if we can use it to read the metadata to which it pertains.

1. Open the ObjectLookUp function.

2. Select and comment out the top group of print statements with **Block Comment** or **Uncomment** from the script Editor's Edit menu.

3. Add the following code under the print statements and above the closing curly bracket:

```
for(var contents : String in stateArray[currentState]) {

// split the contents into a temporary array
var readString : String[] = contents.Split(",".Chars[0]);

    print (readString[0]);
    print (readString[1]);
    print (readString[2]);
```

```
} // end for loop
```

4. Save the script.

5. Click Play and pick your three test objects.

The console should print out the contents of the elements in the State 0 arrays, as shown in Figure 10-19.

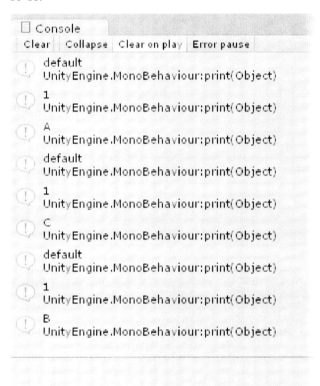

Figure 10-19. *The parsed contents of element 0 from the three object's Lookup State 0 arrays*

As you can see, as long as you fill out the arrays properly, the first split element, readString[0], will be what you need to check the current cursor against for a match. The texture name for the default cursor could be anything, so first check, and if it is the default cursor, substitute "default" for its actual texture name. This will allow us to use any name for the default texture's name. The icon texture names, however, will fall under our naming conventions.

1. Add the following directly above the original print statements:

```
// check the passed-in cursor texture to see if it is the default cursor; rename it if so.
if (picker == gamePointer.GetComponent(CustomCursor).defaultCursor.name) var↵
 matchCursor : String  = "default";
```

else matchCursor = picker;

As the comment says, if the name of the picker's texture matches the default cursor's texture name, make a variable, matchCursor, to use in its place. You'll use it to see if you have a match in the contents of readString[0]. Right now, of course, all of the objects will have a match, but you can easily change one to test.

Before you can access the gamePointer, you need to introduce it. And as long as you are adding code for it, you can add the Control Center as well, as it always needs to be kept abreast of interesting developments.

2. Add the following variables near the top of the ObjectLookup script:

```
//Gain access to
private var gamePointer: GameObject;  // the cursor
private var controlCenter : GameObject; //where the GUI is updated
```

3. And then "find" them in the Start function; you can add them above the array assignments:

```
gamePointer = gameObject.Find("GamePointer"); //find the cursor by object name
controlCenter = gameObject.Find("Control Center"); //find the control center by name
```

Now you can check for a match with the *current* cursor.

4. Delete the three print(readString… statements.

5. Add the following code in their place:

```
// if there is a match for the cursor…
if(readString[0] == matchCursor) {
    print ("we have a match with cursor: "+ matchCursor + " on " + object.name);
}
else print("no match for the " + object.name);
```

6. Save the script.

7. Click Play and pick the sample objects.

The console reports the matches as expected (see Figure 10-20).

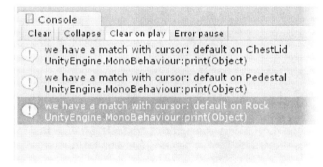

Figure 10-20. *A match for each*

To be on the safe side, let's change one of the defaults to something else to make sure we don't get a match.

1. Stop Play mode.

2. Select the Pedestal.

3. Change its Lookup State 0's Element 0 data to: **Key Icon,1,E.**

4. Click Play and test the three objects again.

As shown in Figure 10-21, the Pedestal reports no match.

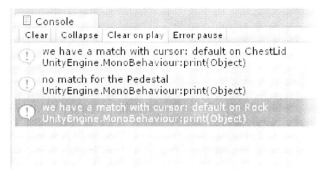

Figure 10-21. *No match on the Pedestal*

Getting Real

Now let's use the real states and change them when they are picked (yes, we're getting closer!). After adding the next batch of code, we will create the ProcessObject function it calls.

1. Open the ObjectLookup script.

2. In the LookupState function, add the following lines beneath the print ("we have a match… line:

```
//change the object's state to the new state by calling its ProcessObject function
var nextState : int = parseInt(readString [1]); //convert the string to an integer
object.SendMessage("ProcessObject", nextState); //send the new state to the object
```

3. Comment out the print ("we have a match… line.

4. Save the script.

If no match was found, you need to look at the next element in the state array and eventually loop though the available states.

Now let's build the ProcessObject function in the Interactor script to perform the required tasks to put the object into the new state.

5. Open the Interactor script.

6. Somewhere beneath the `DistanceFromCamera` function, start the following function:

```
function ProcessObject (newState : int) {
```

```
currentState = newState; // update the state
```
The first thing that happens is updating the "current" variables to reflect the new state just passed into the function.

7. Add the following:

```
//load new states' metadata
currentObjectName = objectName[currentState];
currentObjectDescription = description[currentState];
```

Managing Audio

Next we will update the current sound and use `AudioSource.PlayClipAtPoint()`. This is often used for projectiles. When they collide with an object, an Audio Source component is created, the sound is played at *that object's* position, after which the Audio Source component is deleted. Because our mouse pick is essentially interacting with our object's collider, we can keep the scene view and Inspector from being cluttered with permanent audio sources on each of the action objects.

1. Continuing with the `Interactor` script, add the following to handle sound effects:

```
// process audio
currentSound = soundClip[currentState];
currentAudioDelay = audioDelay [currentState];
//create an audio source and play a sound if there is one, at the location of the
//picked object, the audio source is deleted after playing
if(currentSound) { // if there is a sound,
    if (currentAudioDelay == 0) // if no delay, go ahead and play it
        AudioSource.PlayClipAtPoint(currentSound,transform.position,soundFXVolume);
    else { // else set up a timer to play after the delay
        timeLimit1= Time.time + currentAudioDelay; // add the delay to the current time
        timer1 = true; // start the timer (in Update function)
    }
}
```
The tricky bit here is the delay on the sound clip. The problem is that if you use `yield`, it delays everything that comes after it, not just the playing of the audio clip. The rock, for example, needs a delay of 0.75 for its audio clip, but with `yield`, the 0.75 delay would happen, the sound clip would play, and then the next batch of code would process the animation.

To solve the problem, you can create a virtual timer. Start by creating two new variables.

2. Just above the `Start` function, add the following:

```
//Timer variables
private var timer1 : boolean = false; // timer 1 on or off, it is off by default
private var timeLimit1 : float; // amount of time the timer runs for
```

3. Next, below the `Start` function, create an `Update` function with the timer code:

```
function Update () {
  //timer1
  if (timer1 && Time.time > timeLimit1) {
    AudioSource.PlayClipAtPoint(currentSound,transform.position,soundFXVolume);
    timer1 = false; // turn off the timer
  }
}
```

4. Save the script.

Setting timeLimit1 and turning on timer1 causes the Update function to check to see when the time limit has been reached or passed. If it has been reached, the current audio clip is played and the timer1 flag is turned off. Theoretically, you could have done without the timer1 variable, but then, instead of checking for a simple true/false value, the current Time.time would have to be retrieved and then checked against the last known value of timeLimit1. As this happens *every frame* or more regardless of whether the timer is running, the more efficient version is the one to choose.

With the audio clip in general, note that although an object doesn't have to have a sound associated with a particular state, you must ensure the soundFX array has been assigned the correct number of elements, even if those elements are left holding None, or you will get an error when trying to assign a nonexistent element to the currentSound variable.

Eventually you'll allow the player to adjust the volume of the audio as well as several other user preferences. Generally the audio is separated into voice, ambient or background sounds, and object or action sound effects. Let's take a couple of minutes to add variables for each to the GameManager, where we are storing the other user preference variables.

1. Open the GameManager script.

2. Add the following variables near the top:

```
//sound volumes
var soundFXVolume : float = 1.0; // sound effects volume
var ambientSoundVolume : float = 1.0; // ambient background sounds volume
var backgroundMusicVolume : float = 1.0; // so we don't have to force our music on⏎
 the player
var voiceVolume : float = 1.0; // in case we have character voices
```

3. Save the script.

4. Open the Interactor once again.

5. In the //Misc vars section, add the following:

```
private var soundFXVolume : float; // we will get this from GameManager
```

6. In the Start function, just below the mouseOverMaterial = line, add the following:

```
soundFXVolume= controlCenter.GetComponent(GameManager).soundFXVolume;
```

7. Save the script.

Now we can remove the existing audio components because PlayClipAtPoint creates and deletes one on the object on the fly.

8. Remove the Audio Source component from the action objects.

Processing Animation

The next bit of metadata to be processed is the animation. Unlike with sound, there is a variable that tells you whether or not it needs to be processed, `animates`. If it *does* animate, you update the current animation clips and delays.

We then wait for the delay and then check to make sure the object with the animation exists, if so, we play the current clip, wait until it is finished (since we can get its length), and play the post loop animation if there is one.

Before you write the animation instructions, think back to one of our earlier test cases. While experimenting with the flower, we discovered that with a hierarchy such as a skinned mesh or other linkage, the Mesh Renderer and animations may not be on the same object. Since you stipulated that the `Interactor` and `ObjectLookUp` scripts must be put on the component holding the renderer, you need to allow for a parent object that holds the animations. Just as you did in one of the early test scripts, you can use a variable to hold the object that contains the animations.

1. Continuing in the `Interactor` script, under the *//gain access to* section, add the following variable:

```
var aniObject : GameObject; // for use when the animation is on the parent
```

2. Inside the `Start` function, before the closing curly bracket, assign the regular object as `aniObject` if one was not assigned via the Inspector:

```
// find out if a parent animator object was assigned, if not, assign the object itself
if (aniObject == null) aniObject = gameObject;
```

And now, using the new generic variable, you can handle the animations.

3. In the `ProcessObject` function, add the following to process the animation[s] after the audio section:

```
if(animates) {
    // assign the current clip and delay for the new state
    currentAnimationClip = animationClip[currentState];
    currentAnimationDelay = animationDelay[currentState];
    //pause before playing the animation if required
    yield new WaitForSeconds(currentAnimationDelay);
    if (aniObject != null) { // if there is an animation- it is not null,
        aniObject.animation.Play(currentAnimationClip.name);
        aniLength = currentAnimationClip.length;// get its length

        // wait the length of the animation, then play looped animation if there was one
        yield new WaitForSeconds(aniLength);
        if (postLoop) aniObject.animation.Play(loopAnimation[currentState].name);
    }
} // close if(animates)
```

4. And, finally, close the `ProcessObject` function:

```
} // close ProcessObject function
```

5. Save the script and make sure you have no errors.

Now that we are getting close to using the initial state for testing, let's move that variable up to the top of the script so it will be first in the `Interactor` component. Let's also move the current state variable beneath it so we can watch for the state changes.

1. Open the `Interactor` script.

2. Move the **var** `initialState : ` **int** ` = 0; // in case you need other than state 0` line up to the top of the `Interactor` script

3. Move the **private var** `currentState : ` **int** ` = 0; // this will get updated in Start` line up beneath it.

4. Save the script.

And now you can update a few of the action objects so you can continue to test the code.

5. Add the `ObjectLookUp` script to KeyAtRock.

6. Update the metadata and states for KeyAtRock (see Figure 10-22):

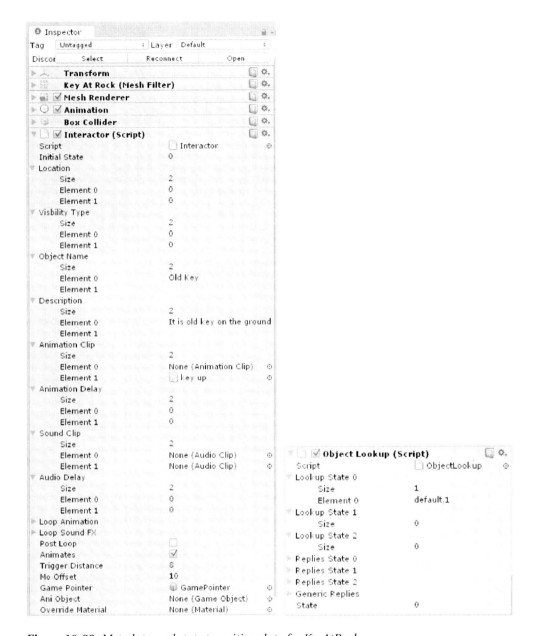

Figure 10-22. *Metadata and state transition data for KeyAtRock*

7. Update the metadata and states for the ChestLid as shown in Figure 10-23.

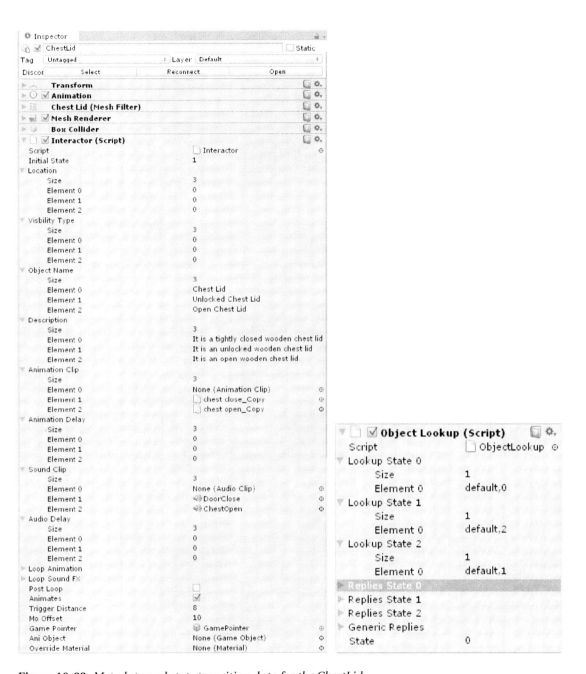

Figure 10-23. *Metadata and state transition data for the ChestLid*

8. Set the ChestLid's Initial State to **1** (unlocked, closed)

The ChestLid's state 0 does not have an animation associated with it yet and the code doesn't check to make sure the animation exists before trying to play it, so it throws an error. Not to mention, the lid wouldn't open anyway. By starting the ChestLid at state 1, you can open and close it, showing that the code is working as designed so far. The next section makes use of the `initialState` variable.

Loading the Start-Up Values

Before testing the new functionality, there are a couple of things to add. When you first set up the text messages, you just hardcoded the objects to send their state 0 value. Now that we are getting the states to update, you need to fix that, as well as load a value into the names and descriptions in the `Start` function.

1. Open the `Interactor` script.

2. At the bottom of the `Start` function, add the following lines:

```
// load the initial values
currentState = initialState; // this allows override of starting state only
currentObjectName = objectName[currentState];
currentObjectDescription = description[currentState];
```

3. In the `OnMouseEnter` function, change the `objectName[0]` and `description[0]` to `currentObjectName` and `currentDescription` as follows:

```
//send the correct text to the GameManager for display
controlCenter.GetComponent(GameManager).shortDesc= currentObjectName ;
controlCenter.GetComponent(GameManager).longDesc = currentObjectDescription;
```

4. Save the script.

And, finally, let's see if it all works…

5. Click Play and test the action objects that have both the `Interactor` and `ObjectLookup` scripts

If you get "Array index out of range" errors, you probably haven't finished filling out the metadata in the `Interactor` script for the object specified in the error message.

6. Stop Play mode.

There are several little problems, but you can see we are making progress—the chest lid opens and closes, the rock moves to reveal the key under it, the key rises up when picked, and the pedestal still sits there looking ugly.

Let's try a few more experiments before fixing the small issues.

Let's have some fun with the pedestal.

1. Fill out the Pedestal's metadata and state transition data as shown in Figure 10-24.

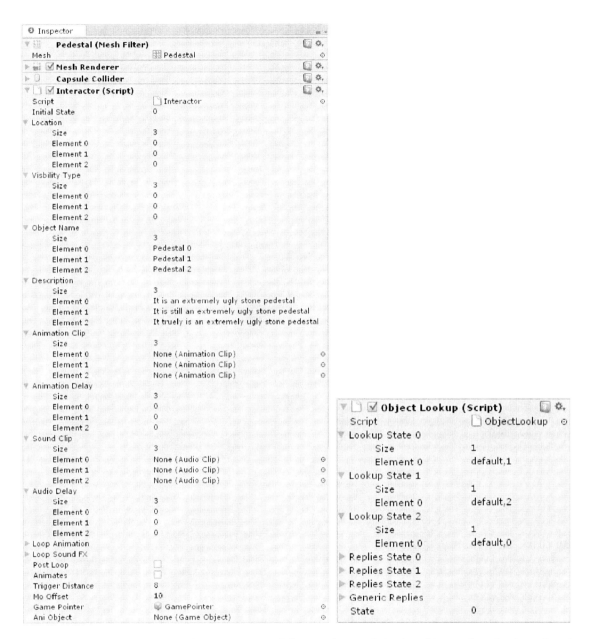

Figure 10-24. *The metadata in the Interactor and the transition info in the ObjectLookup for the Pedestal*

2. Click Play and watch the pedestal cycle through its states as you pick it.

3. Pick the other action objects.

Everything seems to be working according to the data in the `Interactor` and `ObjectLookUp` scripts. However, things seem to be a bit messy. It would make sense to turn off the cursor and the identification text while the object is animating and keep them off throughout the animation. This would allow the user to watch the animation and read the action text without interference.

4. Open the `Interactor` script.

5. In the `OnMouseDown` function, below the **if**`(useMOCursorChange)` conditional's closing curly bracket, add the following:

```
//deactivate the text messages
controlCenter.GetComponent(GameManager).showText = false;
```

6. Save the script.

7. Click Play and test.

Now you have a clear view of the objects animating.

Once you get the action text displaying from the mouse pick, you'll need a way to know when to turn it off and allow mouseovers to start working again.

You can make another timer like the one for the audio delay, but this one will need to be a bit more sophisticated to allow for animations of different lengths. Let's start by creating a couple of variables.

1. In the Interactor, add the following variables to the `//Timer` variables section:

```
private var timer2 : boolean = false; // timer 2 on or off
private var timeLimit2 : float; // amount of time the timer runs for
```

2. In the `Update` function, add the following:

```
// timer 2- animation processing delay
if(timer2 && Time.time > timeLimit2){
  processing = false;
  timer2 = false;
  print ("time's up");
}
```

Here's the tricky part. Our state look-up table allows any number of objects to be triggered from a single pick. Each object will be processed in its own `Interactor`'s `ProcessObject` function. If you start the timer inside the `ProcessObject` function, you could have multiple timers running at once that are set to turn off the action message upon completion.

The logical place to turn on the timer is in the `OnMouseDown` function where the player picks the action object. The problem with turning it on there is that you don't yet know how long to leave it on. Because you will be able to either turn it off or lengthen the time it's on, let's just go ahead and set it for two seconds to start.

3. In the `OnMouseDown` function, below the ...`showText=` `false` line you just added, add the following:

```
// start a timer to turn processing
timeLimit2 = Time.time + 2.0;
timer2 = true;
```

4. Save the script.

5. Click Play and test.

The console tells you when the time is up. Once you get the action message up and working, you can refine the timing, but for now let's look at the mouseovers again. If the cursor is still over an action object after the current two-second timer setting, you don't get mouseover messages unless you move off the object, then move back on. It would be nice if the mouseover reappeared shortly after the animation was finished.

Rather than resorting to an OnMouseOver, which is checked every frame, and instead of the current OnMouseEnter, you can make use of something we discovered earlier in the chapter. If you think back to the GUI.Box and the flickering issue it caused, you may begin to see how you can use what seemed an annoying property of the box control. This box control blocked mouseovers when it was on screen, but as soon as it was turned off, *it generated a new mouseover event*. All you need to do is flash a screen-sized GUI.Box on screen and the mouseover will be reinstated. Better yet, the new state's text will have already been updated.

1. Open the GameManager script

2. Add the following right after the inRange variable declaration:

```
private var resetMO : boolean = false; // flag to reset mouseover after pick
```

3. In the OnGUI function, after the **if** (useText){ conditional's closing curly bracket, add the following:

```
//reset mouseovers
if (resetMO) GUI.Box (Rect (0, 0, Screen.width,Screen.height),"");
```

Now let's add a little function to turn the flag off and on. Update and OnGUI functions can't contain yield statements since they are called every frame, so you'll need to create your own function to be able to get the timing right.

4. Add the following function to the bottom of the GameManager script:

```
function ResetMouseOver () {
    yield new WaitForSeconds(0.5); // pause after the action message
    resetMO = true; // turn on the GUI.Box element
    yield; // wait one frame
    resetMO = false;  // turn the GUI.Box off again
}
```

5. Save the script.

You'll call the function when the timer is up.

6. Open the Interactor script.

7. In the Update function, after the print ("time's up") line, add the following:

```
controlCenter.GetComponent(GameManager).ResetMouseOver();
```

8. Save the script.

9. Click Play and pick the Pedestal to test.

The mouseover text reappears as we wished, but there's a slight flicker as the full-screen GUI.Box flashes on screen for one frame. Right now it is using the default Box skin from the Game GUISkin. If you override it with a style that doesn't use a texture for the Normal parameter's Background, you should be able to eliminate the flicker. It so happens that we created just such a style for the override on the short description, the customGUIStyle.

1. Open the GameManager script again.

2. Change the **if** (resetMO) GUI.Box line to the following:

if (resetMO) GUI.Box (Rect (0, 0, Screen.width,Screen.height),"",customGUIStyle);

3. Save the script.

4. Click Play and test.

There is no more flickering and the text appears on cue.

More on Fonts and Text

You are probably thinking it would be easier to test if there was something to read after a pick.

1. In the Inspector, in the ObjectLookup component, set your Reply State arrays to match the size of their Look Up State counterparts

This is where we can have some fun. You might, for example, add something like this for the rock: "You grunt with effort as you move the rock aside, barely missing your foot as it thuds into place."

▪ **Tip** The Inspector is not an ideal place to type a lot of text into your arrays. It makes more sense to keep a text file with the information from which you could copy and paste.

You can also undock the Inspector view by clicking and dragging on the tab at its top. The quickest way to put it back is to set the layout back to 2 × 3.

2. Add a nice description of the animation or an imaginary action for each action object for the functionality tests, as shown Figure 10-25.

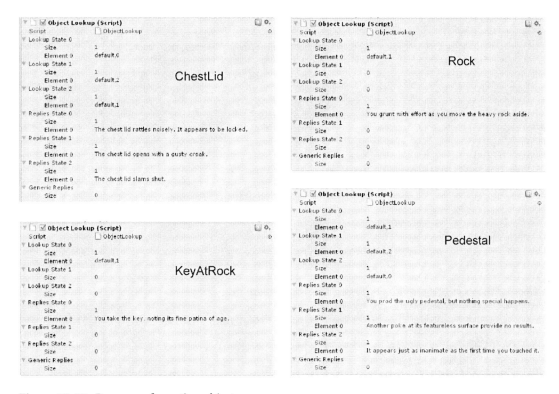

Figure 10-25. *Responses for action objects*

Let's finish adjusting the action text in the `GameManager`. You can have it display in the same spot as the description text, but you may need to make some changes in order to fit a nice, chatty account of the events.

> 3. Open the `GameManager` script.

The action message line is already there, but it is inside the `if`(`showText`) block, as well as in its own `showActionMsg` conditional. While you are working out how you want it to look, let's use a text string in a duplicate GUI element instead of the actual message.

> 4. Add the following test line inside the `OnGUI` function, just below the `GUI.skin` line:

```
GUI.Label (Rect (Screen.width/2 - 300, Screen.height - 47, 600, 32), "This is a↩
 really long and complicated bit of text, so we can test the text on screen size.");
```

> 5. Remove the `boxStyleLabel` from the `showLongDesc` line so it uses the regular Game GUISkin again

```
if (showLongDesc && inRange) GUI.Label (Rect (Screen.width/2 - 250, Screen.height - 37,↩
 500,35), longDesc);
```

> 6. Save the script.

7. Click Play.

8. Select the Game GUISkin in the Project view and open the Label preset.

---

9. Try adjusting the *Font Size*

Nothing happens because arial2 is not set to Dynamic (Figure 10-26).

Figure 10-26. *Arial2 is not dynamic so the font size doesn't change.*

10. Change the Overflow Font to **Arial** and adjust the Font Size to **16**

This time the font size changes, as shown in Figure 10-27.

Figure 10-27. *With Arial, the font size changes.*

11. Adjust the size so that all of the text shows.

12. Now mouse over one of the action objects.

The long description text has *also* been scaled (Figure 10-28). The short description text uses a custom GUIStyle and is not affected.

Figure 10-28. *All Game GUISkin font sizes are affected.*

13. Back in the Inspector, increase the Font Size to **24**.

The text is clipped at the end of the line, as shown in Figure 10-29.

Figure 10-29. *The text is clipped at the end of the line.*

    14. Experiment with the Font Style.

Arial has versions for italic, bold and bold italic included.

    15. Set the Font Style back to Normal.

    16. Uncheck Word Wrap.

The text is centered but clipped at both ends of the line (Figure 10-30).

Figure 10-30. *The text is now clipped at both ends of the line.*

    17. Change Text Clipping to Overflow.

The text extends over both sides of its rectangular (the Rect dimensions) bounds (Figure 10-31).

Figure 10-31. *The text extending beyond its bounds*

    18. Check Word Wrap and adjust the Font Size to **22**.

The text reverts to its originally specified size and wraps to a second line instead of being clipped or overflowing the rectangle (Figure 10-32).

Figure 10-32. *The text wrapping to a second line*

    19. Load the *WIZZARD* font into the Overflow Font. Figure 10-33 shows the result.

Figure 10-33. *The WIZZARD font*

20. Try adjusting the Font Style.

The *Wizzard* font changes accordingly.
Note that changes to the GUISkin during runtime are retained.

21. Drag and drop a TrueType font of your own choosing into the Fonts folder if you wish.

22. In the GameManager script, adjust the Rect size and placement to suit the font you chose,

23. Copy these Rect settings into the actionMsg line:

```
if(showActionMsg) GUI.Label (Rect (Screen.width/2 - 300, Screen.height - 75, 600, 32),↩
actionMsg);
```

24. Delete the test line.

25. Save the script.

At some point, you may have seen the warning message shown in Figure 10-34 in the status line.

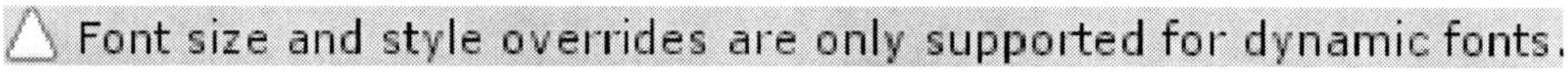

Figure 10-34. *The warning message*

1. Check to make sure the fonts you are using are all set to Dynamic.

2. Stop Play mode.

3. Save the scene and save the project.

Activating the Action Message

Now that you've learned a bit more about fonts, you can see about activating the action message and the other tasks that go with that.

1. Open the ObjectLookup script.

If you look at the **for**(var contents, etc... block of code in the LookUpState function, you'll remember that it loops through each of the elements of the state you sent it, looking for a match for the cursor in each element. The problem with that type of for loop is that it doesn't have an obvious way to know where it is in the process. You can easily add a local (to the LookUpState function) variable to keep track.

2. Inside the LookUpState function, at the top, add the following:

```
var element : int = 0; // variable to track the element number for a match
```
In the Start function, you may recall, we loaded the Unity built-in repliesState arrays into a single JavaScript array named replyArray. The arguments passed into the LookUpState function tell which state we need. The element where the match was found is used to find the corresponding element in the replies. Take a few moments to digest the logic behind what is happening if you need to.

    3.   Underneath the print ("we have a match... statement, add the following:

```
print (replyArray[currentState][element]);//print reply that corresponds to the↵
  matched stateArray
```

    4.   Below the **else** print("no match... line and above the for loop's closing curly bracket, increment the counter:

```
element ++; //increment the element counter by 1
```

    5.   Make sure you've added the correct number of elements to the ReplyArrays to correspond to the number of elements in the stateArrays.

    6.   Save the script.

    7.   Try picking the rock and the chest lid.

> ⊙ You grunt with effort as you move the heavy rock aside.

Figure 10-35. *The reply from picking the rock in the console*

The correct action text appears in the console (Figure 10-35), so now you can send it off to the other scripts for processing and tell GameManager to show the action text.

    8.   Replace your print statement so it sends the data to the GameManager instead of printing to the console:

```
//send the correct text message off to the GameManager
controlCenter.GetComponent(GameManager).actionMsg= replyArray[currentState][element];
```

    9.   Save the script.

    10. Open the Interactor script.

    11. In the ProcessObject function, above the // process audio section, add the following:

```
//tell the GameManager to show the action text
controlCenter.GetComponent(GameManager).showActionMsg=true;
```

    12. Save the script.

    13. Click Play and test the pick.

At this point, you can see that there's a problem. The OnMouseDown function has a line that tells the showText flag to be false, so the text is hidden as soon as the player picks an object.

    1.   Open the GameManager script and inspect the OnGUI function.

The problem is that the actionMsg line is inside the showText conditional and is turned off along with the short and long mouseover description text. Fortunately, this is an easy problem to fix. Keeping in mind that it still needs to be under the control of the global useText flag, you can move it below the useText line and above the showText line. In this case, it might have been better to name showText to showMoText (for mouseover).

2. Move the actionMsg text line so the OnGUI function looks like this:

```
function OnGUI () {

   GUI.skin = customSkin;

   if (useText){  //global toggle
      if (showActionMsg) GUI.Label (Rect (Screen.width/2 - 300, Screen.height - 47,↵
600, 35), actionMsg);
      if (showText){ //local toggle
         if (useLongDesc) {
         if (showLongDesc && inRange) GUI.Label (Rect (Screen.width/2 - 250,↵
Screen.height - 37, 500,35), longDesc);
         }
         if (showShortDesc) GUI.Label (Rect (Screen.width/2 - 250, Screen.height - 65,↵
500,35), shortDesc, customGUIStyle);
      }
   }

   //reset mouseovers
   if (resetMO) GUI.Box (Rect (0, 0, Screen.width,Screen.height),"",customGUIStyle);
}
```

3. Save the script.

4. Click Play and test.

Now the action message appears when the object is picked and the mouseover text disappears. But, as Figure 10-36 shows, if you are still hovering over an action object when the time is up, the mouseover text is drawn on top of it.

Figure 10-36. *The action message and mouseover text showing at the same time*

498

So, finally, you need to tell GameManager when to turn the action text off. Fortunately, this just happens to correspond with the time you set the processing flag to be false again in the timer script created in the Interactor's Update function.

1.   Open the Interactor script.

2.   Add the following line inside the Update function beneath the processing = false line:

```
//tell the GameManager to hide the action text
controlCenter.GetComponent(GameManager).showActionMsg=false;
```

3.   Save the script.

4.   Click Play and test the action objects.

▪ **Tip**   If you get an ArgumentOutOfRangeException, it means you have not yet defined the size of the Reply Arrays for that object.

Because the objects are still clustered rather close together, you may have discovered that mouseover text from another object could be drawn on top of the action text before it finishes displaying. You can easily add another condition to the GameManager to prevent this from happening.

1.   Open the GameManager.

2.   Change the **if**(showText) conditional to read:

```
if(showText && !showActionMsg) {
```
Now the two descriptions will not show if the action text is still showing.

3.   Save the script and test.

Now the mouseovers don't show up until the object has been picked in the scene. This suggests that the showActionMsg flag is initialized as true, thereby blocking the mouseover text display.

4.   Open the GameManager script.

5.   Change the showActionMsg flag to false:

```
private var showActionMsg = false;
```

6.   Save the script and test again.

This time all behaves as expected.

The messages behave well except for one minor issue. If you pick an object, then move quickly over to another and pick it, its action message disappears too quickly. While it seems unlikely at this point that you'd have two action objects this close together, it is important to work out how to solve this little problem. The first step is to figure out what's happening.

When Object 1 is picked, a timer is started in its Interactor script's Update function to allow processing time. When Object 2 is picked, its action message text replaces Object 1's text and another timer is started in *its* Interactor script's Update function. The problem is that they are *both* going to tell the GameManager to turn off the action message text. Object 1 will finish sooner and will tell the

GameManager to turn the text off before Object 2's timer is finished, thus shortening player reading time. The challenge is to devise a means of knowing if another object is already using the action message text.

To do that, you need to tell GameManager which object has activated the actionMsg text and, more importantly, which object is trying to deactivate it. If the two are not one and the same, the message should not be deactivated. Let's start by creating a variable in GameManager to hold the name of the currently active actionMsg.

1. Open the GameManager script.

2. Add the following variable below the rest of the text vars:

```
private var actionObject : String; // the name of the last action object to turn on the↵
 actionMsg
```

The script will update the variable each time something turns on the actionMsg and will consult it before turning the actionMsg off.

3. Save the script.

4. Open the Interactor script.

5. In the OnMouseDown function, add the following line beneath the // start a timer to turn processing section:

```
//tell the GameManager which object just started the timer2
controlCenter.GetComponent(GameManager).actionObject  = this.name;
```

6. Inside the Update function, change the timer2 section as follows:

```
// timer 2- animation processing delay
if(timer2 && Time.time > timeLimit2){
   processing = false;
   //tell the GameManager to hide the action text
   if (controlCenter.GetComponent(GameManager).actionObject  == this.name) {
      //tell the GameManager to hide the action text
      controlCenter.GetComponent(GameManager).showActionMsg=false;
   }
   timer2 = false;
   //print ("time's up");
   controlCenter.GetComponent(GameManager).ResetMouseOver();
}
```

7. Save the script.

8. Click Play and test.

The messages are now working smoothly.

Dynamic Read Time

The timing seems reasonable for reading a short action message, but it's perhaps too rushed for something longer. Fortunately, we have a means of finding out the length of a [character] string, though we won't know what the action message *is* until the pick has been processed in the ObjectLookup's LookUpState function.

Since the action messages are stored on the ObjectLookup component, we may as well process the time needed to read the message there. If you simply assume any reply over 25 characters gets two more seconds, you could add the code right after you find out which reply is being used. However, a better idea is to create a little function that will handle all of the work and is more flexible. Start by assigning the reply to a variable rather than accessing it twice; this makes the code easier to read.

1. Open the ObjectLookup script.

2. In the LookUpState function, change the following lines:

```
//send the correct text message off to the GameManager
controlCenter.GetComponent(GameManager).actionMsg= replyArray[currentState][element];
```

to:

```
//send the correct text message off to the GameManager
var actionMsg : String = replyArray[currentState][element];
controlCenter.GetComponent(GameManager).actionMsg= actionMsg;
TimeAdjuster(actionMsg); //send the message off to adjust processing time
```

The last line calls the TimeAdjuster function and passes it the reply string. You need to pass the actionMsg variable because it is local to the LookUpState function and does not exist outside of that. Let's create the TimeAdjuster function next. We will start by having it report the length of the replies.

3. Below the LookUpState function, add the TimeAdjuster function:

```
// function to calculate extra processining time to read action message
function TimeAdjuster(actionMsg : String) {

        var stringLength: int  =  actionMsg.length;
        print (stringLength);

}
```

4. Save the script.

5. Click Play and test to see how long the various messages are.

The replies probably vary between 25 and 60 characters including spaces.

You are already allowing two seconds to read the text when you start timer2 in the Interactor script. If you decide that the player can read about 20 characters per second (remember, it will be the first time he sees the message), you can divide the message by 20 to see how long it should take. You can then take the existing two seconds off the result to see how much you should add. Better yet, let's give the player half a second to focus on the text before he starts reading. So let's divide the string length by 20 and then reduce the result by 1.5 to get the amount of time to add to the default amount of 2.

1. Change the print line in the TimeAdjuster function as follows:

```
print (stringLength / 20.0 -1.5); //the length divided by 20 minus 1.5 to start reading
```

2. Save the script and test.

The amount printed out in the console looks like a good amount to add to the timer, unless it is less than 0.

3. Change the print line as follows:

```
  var addTime = stringLength / 20.0 -1.5; //calculate the amount of time to add
```

```
   if (addTime >= 0) GetComponent("Interactor").timeLimit2 =⏎
GetComponent("Interactor").timeLimit2 + addTime;
```

4. Save the script.

5. Click Play and test.

In case you are scratching your head about how this works with the timer itself, here's a brief rundown:

1. When the object is picked, the variable `timeLimit2` is set by getting the current time, `Time.time`, and adding 2 seconds to it.

2. The timer is started when `timeLimit2` is greater than `Time.time` (which it is by 2 seconds the instant it's set).

3. Meanwhile, the pick gets processed over in the `ObjectLookUp` where we add a bit more time to the `timeLimit2` variable.

4. `Time.time`, the current time, finally catches up and surpasses the `timeLimit2` value and the code in the timer now runs.

Note that you must specify the component both to access `timeLimit2` and to add to it.

1. Save the script.

2. Adjust the time as desired.

3. Save the scene and save the project.

A Final Refinement

With the mechanics in place for all of the messaging, you now have the opportunity to add a nice touch with little extra trouble. When a player is close enough to an object to get the short description but not yet close enough to pick the object, it would be nice to tell him that he is not close enough to interact with the object. You need only slip a bit of code into the `OnMouseDown` function.

The logic is as follows: If the pick is made between the `triggerDistance` and the `triggerDistance` + `moOffset`, the script will display a message using the `actionMsg` text for a couple of seconds, and then turn off the message and exit the `OnMouseDown` function.

1. Open the `Interactor` script.

2. Inside the `OnMouseDown` function, change the **if** `(DistanceFromCamera() > triggerDistance)` **return** line to include the offset distance:

```
// exit if we are not within the range plus offset
if (DistanceFromCamera() > triggerDistance + moOffset) return;
```

3. Directly beneath that line, add the following:

```
// if the player is within mouseover but not picking distance...
if (DistanceFromCamera()  > triggerDistance ) {
   var tempMsg : String = "You are too far from the " + objectName[currentState].ToLower() + "
to interact with it";
```

502

```
//send the GameManager the action text
controlCenter.GetComponent(GameManager).actionMsg = tempMsg;
//tell the GameManager to show the action text
controlCenter.GetComponent(GameManager).showActionMsg = true;
//wait two seconds then turn off the action text and then leave the function
yield new WaitForSeconds(2.0);
controlCenter.GetComponent(GameManager).showActionMsg = false;
return;
}
```

The script already knows you are within `triggerDistance + moOffset` (or you would have exited the function in the first distance check), so you need only check to see if you are farther than the trigger distance. If the condition is met, the code creates a string using the object's current state short description, sends it to the GameManager as an `actionMsg` text, and turns the `actionMsg` on. Next, the function uses a simple `yield` command to wait a couple of seconds, and then tells the `GameManager` to turn the `actionMsg` text off. You then exit the function so nothing further is done with the pick. Note the use of the `ToLower()` function to convert the object's current short description name to lowercase for use inside a sentence.

4. Save the script.

Before you start navigating around the scene again, you need to reset the camera rotations.

1. Stop Play mode.

2. Select the Main Camera and set its X Rotation to **0**.

3. Select the First Person Controller and set its X Rotation to **0**.

4. Click Play.

5. Back away from the action objects just far enough to stop the mouseover description and pick an object.

The new message tells you you're not close enough for a pick.

Figure 10-37. *Telling a player he is too far to pick*

6. Save the scene and save the project.

We've now got the basics of a simple, interactive adventure game blocked in. Inventory, of course, would make it a *lot* more interesting so we'll tackle that next.

Summary

In this chapter, you were introduced to the Unity GUI as a means of adding 2D text on screen to display mouseover and message text. You discovered the GUISkin, which provides a way of creating GUI elements with a consistent look and feel, and later, the GUIStyle, which is a means of overriding the skin in particular places. You experimented with the parameters for the GUI controls, and found you could make label controls look like box controls while still acting like labels. After you learned that the GUI elements exist only through scripting, you found that Rect parameters define the position and region a control will occupy.

You learned that dynamic fonts from the OS use less texture memory, but include the risk of dropping back to a default if the font you specify doesn't exist on the player's system. When using the alternative to dynamic fonts, the ASCII default sets, you discovered that a duplicate font must be created for each font for each size you need, and that a texture containing the entire set of characters is created for each.

Being able to draw text onscreen led to the next logical step—tapping the action object's metadata for the correct messages for both mouseover and action message. It seemed best to break the distance to the object into two zones. The outer zone provides the mouseover short description and doesn't allow for picked objects. The inner zone provides a long descriptions and allows the action objects to be picked.

Once the correct messages were working, you started hooking the animations and audio clips to the pick using the Lookup information to determine which state the objects needed to go into, and then using the object's metadata to handle the appropriate actions.

And, finally, you learned to use a virtual timer to control how long the action text is left on screen for the player to read according to the length of the message.

In the next chapter, you will start to develop an inventory system and allow for different cursors as the player collects various action objects for use through the game.

■ ■ ■

CHAPTER 11

Inventory Logic

In shooter-type games where the cursor is hidden during game play, when the user needs to access and interact with menus or other option information, it's usually handled by stopping game play and loading in an entirely different level for that express purpose. This bypasses the need to suspend navigation, reinstate the cursor, and a number of other issues, many of which you have already solved in previous chapters.

In a classic point and click adventure, interacting with the inventory is one of the most important features. That being the case, the inventory mode will be a layer that lives over the regular scene and can be brought up with a minimum of interference. Although you'll briefly look into a technique for creating an off-screen collection of 3D objects, you will be using 2D textures for the cursors and inventory representations for your game.

1. Open the Interaction1 scene in the project.

2. Use Save Scene As to save it as Inventory in the Scenes folder.

3. Save the project.

Layers

In order to manage the inventory without resorting to a different level, you will need to make use of Unity's Layers. Layers are mostly used by cameras and lights to define which objects get rendered or lit. They give you a way to define a collection of objects for processing. For cameras, you can think of the layers as you would compositing. Each layer can be turned off and on, but just as importantly, you can easily control the layering order.

Let's go ahead and create a few layers so you can start organizing things in preparation for the inventory.

1. Select the GamePointer object.

2. At the top of the Inspector, click on the Layer drop-down and choose Add Layer.

3. Click on User Layer 8 and click in the field area to the right of it to put it into edit mode.

4. Name the layer Pointer, as shown in Figure 11-1.

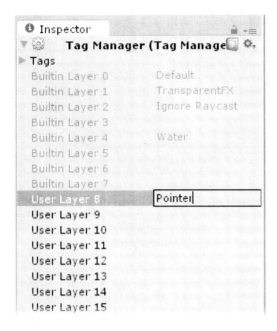

Figure 11-1. *The new Pointer layer*

5. While you are there, select the next layer, User Layer 9, and name it Inventory.

You will need to refer to these layers by number in specific instances, so you may want to note the numbers that correspond to the names you have assigned to each.

By giving the pointer its own layer, you will always be able to keep it on top of the scene and the inventory overlay.

Next, you need to add a couple of new cameras to the scene.

1. From the GameObject menu, choose Create Other and create a new Camera.

2. Name it Camera Inventory and remove its Audio Listener component.

3. In its Camera component, click the Clear Flags drop-down and select Depth Only.

4. Under Culling Mask, click Nothing.

5. Open Culling Mask again and choose the Inventory layer, as shown in Figure 11-2.

Figure 11-2. *Camera settings for Camera Inventory*

As of yet, you have nothing assigned to this layer, so you once again see the main camera's view in the Game view window.

1. Select the original Main Camera (on the First Person Controller).

2. In its Camera component, make note of its Depth setting, 0.

3. Select the Camera Inventory again.

4. Since it will be drawn after (in front of) the main camera's view, set the Depth to 1.

5. Create another new camera and name it Camera Pointer.

6. Remove its Audio Listener.

7. Set its Clear Flags to Depth Only.

8. Set its Culling mask to Nothing, then to Pointer.

9. Give it a Depth of 2 to put it on top of everything else.

The Depth parameter orders the draw order of the camera layers. The layers get drawn from lowest number to highest number. The main camera has a Depth of 0 so it is drawn first. The next item drawn is the Inventory camera with a Depth number of 1, and on top of all is the Pointer layer with a Depth of 2.

The text should draw on top of both the 3D scene and the 2D inventory. Rather than make a layer for the text, you can chose to use the UnityGUI. It automatically draws on top of all layers and is not affected by the cameras' GUI Layer. You will eventually convert the pointer, but for now, it gives you a good means to explore layering.

The only thing you have readily available for your new layers is the pointer.

10. Select the GamePointer object.

507

11. In the Inspector, click the Layer drop-down where it currently says Default.

Your new layers have been added to the list.

1. Select the Pointer layer.

Now it's time to give your new layers a test run.

2. Click Play and check up on your cursor in the Game view.

3. Select the Camera Pointer and turn off its GUILayer component.

4. Return to the Game view and click on it to change the focus.

The pointer object is still being drawn.

5. Stop Play mode and select the Main Camera.

6. In the Inspector, in its Camera component, under Culling Mask, select Nothing, then add the Default and TransparentFX layers.

7. Click Play.

8. Select the Camera Pointer and turn off its GUILayer component again.

9. This time the pointer is not drawn. Stop Play mode.

While you will be using 2D images for the inventory objects, let's see how you could use 3D objects in inventory instead of 2D texture objects. With layers, you could place a duplicate set of 3D objects in a nice clear spot in the scene for the inventory. It doesn't necessarily *need* to be in a clear area because of layers, but that will make it easier to edit.

1. Select the Camera Inventory in the Hierarchy view.

2. In the Scene view, switch to the Z orthographic view by using the scene gizmo.

3. Move the camera well below the lowest point of the terrain.

4. From GameObjects menu, choose Align View to Selected to see what the camera sees.

5. Create a new Cube and rename it to CubeInv.

6. In the Inspector, change its layer to Inventory.

7. Change the Scene view to the X view and move the cube away from the camera until it appears in the Game window.

It should appear in the Game view in front of the regular scene objects, as shown in Figure 11-3.

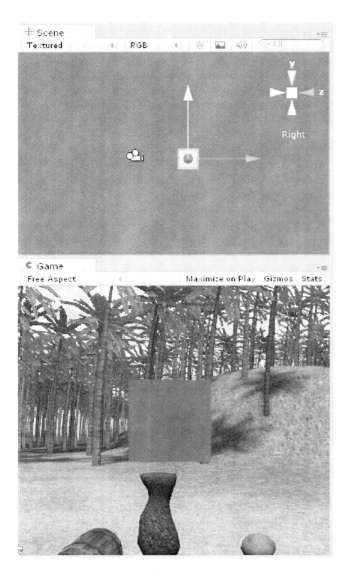

Figure 11-3. *The cube in the Inventory layer seen by the Camera Inventory*

8. Add the SimpleRotateToggle script from the MyScripts folder to the Cube.

9. Click Play and Pick the cube.

The functionality remains the same even with different layers.

10. Try navigating the scene.

The cube remains in the same place in relation to the 2D screen space, as shown in Figure 11-4.

509

Figure 11-4. *The cube happily rotating in front of wherever you go in the scene*

11. Delete the cube.

If you were tempted to drag the Interactor script onto the cube, you probably realized at some point that the distance to camera is checking with the main camera, not the inventory camera so you could never be close enough to pick the cube.

Now that layers have provided you with a good way to organize the inventory, let's start building its framework.

Converting the Cursor

When you were building your text message functionality, you may have realized the cursor, a GUI Texture object, shows up *under* the UnityGUI script-generated text. At a high resolution, the player's cursor may rarely cross paths with the text. You could even have it fade out if it was in the bottom section of the viewport where the text is drawn. As usual, there are several ways to solve the problem.

While it sounds scary, converting your pointer to a UnityGUI control will actually be fairly simple. You can cut and paste most of your existing code from the CustomCursor script and add it to the GameManager script since that is where the other UnityGUI controls are.

Tip UnityGUI controls are drawn in order of evaluation so your pointer will need to go last inside the OnGUI function. If it was on a different script, it may or may not get drawn on top of the text.

---

1. Open the GameManager script and the CustomCursor script,

2. Copy and paste the following lines from the CustomCursor script to the GameManager script, near the top with the other variables:

```
var defaultCursor : Texture; // texture for the default cursor
private var currentCursor : Texture; // texture for other cursors
```

3. Add the following line beneath the newly added variables:

```
private var showMOCursorChange : boolean; //flag for changing the cursor color
```

Previously, you used a function to change the GamePointer's color. Now that you are controlling the cursor through the OnGUI function, you need a flag to trigger the change.

4. To the GameManager script, add a variable to tell the OnGUI function when to draw the cursor:

```
private var showPointer : boolean; // flag for pointer visibility
```

There will be several lines pertaining to the gameObject pointer that you no longer need.

5. *Remove* the following line from the variables:

```
private var gamePointer : GameObject;
```

For a texture to be used as a screen blit with the UnityGUI, you need to use the DrawTexture control. It is similar to the previous controls, but instead of text, it takes a texture for its argument. It is also not part of the GUISkin.

6. Inside the OnGUI function, below the text handling code, add the following:

```
if (showPointer && !navigating) {

    var pos = Input.mousePosition; //get the location of the cursor
    if(useMOCursorChange && showMOCursorChange ) GUI.color = mouseOverColor;
    else GUI.color = Color.white;
    GUI.DrawTexture (Rect(pos.x, Screen.height - pos.y, 32,32), currentCursor);

}
```

GUI.color will tint the cursor and any following GUI controls, so it is crucial to put it where it will not affect the text.

Now that you will be handing the cursor visibility in the OnGUI function, you can remove the cursor code from the Update function where you are watching for navigation.

7. Change the two gamePointer lines so the Update function is as follows:

```
function Update () {

    if (Input.GetButton("ML Enable") || Input.GetButton("Horizontal") ||
        Input.GetButton("Vertical") || Input.GetButton("Turn")){
        navigating = true;
```

```
    }
    else {
        navigating = false;
    }
}
```

8. Because you need to initialize a couple of the cursor related variables, add the following to the Start function:

```
showPointer = true; // enable the pointer at start up
currentCursor = defaultCursor;
```

9. From the Start function, *remove* the following lines:

```
// assign the actual GamePointer object to the gamePointer variable
gamePointer = GameObject.Find("GamePointer");
```

10. Save the script.

You should have no errors from any references to the old GamePointer object.

1. Select the Control Center object.

2. In the Inspector, drag and drop the GamePointerSm texture from the Project view's Adventure Textures folder onto the Default Cursor variable.

Since you are now handling the cursor color change in the GameManager script, you can remove a couple of lines from the Interactor script.

3. Open the Interactor script.

4. Delete the following line from the //Gain access to these objects section:

```
var gamePointer : GameObject;
```

5. Locate the following line in the OnMouseEnter function:

```
if(useMOCursorChange) gamePointer.GetComponent(CustomCursor)↩
sendMessage("CursorColorChange",true)
```

6. Change it to the following:

```
controlCenter.GetComponent(GameManager).showMOCursorChange = true; // colorize↩
 the pointer
```

7. Locate its counterpart in the OnMouseExit function:

```
if(useMOCursorChange) gamePointer.GetComponent(CustomCursor)↩
sendMessage("CursorColorChange",false)
```

8. And change it to the following:

```
controlCenter.GetComponent(GameManager).showMOCursorChange = false; // return the↩
 pointer to default color
```

9. Locate the following lines in the OnMouseDown function:

```
//   *** send a message turn the cursor color back to original if it is being used
if(useMOCursorChange) {
```

```
    gamePointer.GetComponent(CustomCursor).SendMessage("CursorColorChange",false);
}
```

10. Change them to the following:

```
controlCenter.GetComponent(GameManager).showMOCursorChange = false; // return the↵
 pointer to default color
```

At the bottom of the OnMouseDown function, you are passing the picked object, its current state, and the current cursor's name property, which was in reality the name of its current texture. Even though you are now using a GUI control to draw the cursor, you still need to pass its current texture by name.

Looking at the changes you made, you will remember that you did add a variable for the currentCursor, a Texture type variable, and it is assigned in the Start function. You should be able to use almost the same code to refer to it.

1. In the GetComponent(ObjectLookup).LookUpState line, change gamePointer.GetComponent(CustomCursor).currentCursor.name to controlCenter.GetComponent(GameManager).currentCursor.name so it looks as follows:

```
//send the picked object, its current state, and the cursor [texture] that picked it
// to the LookUpState function for processing
GetComponent(ObjectLookup).LookUpState(this.gameObject,currentState↵
 ,controlCenter.GetComponent(GameManager).currentCursor.name );
```

2. From the Search menu in the script editor, use Find to see that all references to the GamePointer have been taken care of.

3. Save the script.

4. Click Play and test the new cursor.

The mouseover functionality is up and running again and now is drawn on top of the text messages! Let's check the ObjectLookup script next.

5. Open the ObjectLookup script.

6. Delete the following line:

```
private var gamePointer: GameObject;   // the cursor
```

7. In the Start function, delete:

```
gamePointer = gameObject.Find("GamePointer"); //find the cursor by object name
```

8. Near the top of the LookUpState function, change the if (picker == gamePointer line to the following:

```
if (picker == controlCenter.GetComponent(GameManager).defaultCursor.name )↵
 var matchCursor = "default";
```

9. Save the script.

Now that your cursor has been updated, you may as well make a few more refinements to its functionality.

A Few More Refinements

This is a good time to add a bit of code to hide the cursor while an animation is playing.

1. Open the `Interactor` script.

2. Near the bottom of the `OnMouseDown` function, just above the `//send the picked object` line, add the following:

```
// hide the cursor while processing the pick
controlCenter.GetComponent(GameManager).showPointer = false;
```

To make sure it gets turned on again when the processing is finished, you need to check your timer2.

3. In the `Update` function, right after the `processing = false` line, add the following:

```
controlCenter.GetComponent(GameManager).showPointer = true;
```

4. Save the script.

Just in case a match wasn't found for the cursor and the object never got processed, you need to turn the cursor in the `ObjectLookup` script as well.

5. Open the `ObjectLookup` script.

6. In the `LookUpState` function, change the `else print("no match for` line to the following:

```
else {
   print("no match for the " + object.name);
   controlCenter.GetComponent(GameManager).showPointer = true;
 }
```

7. Save the script.

As a last small refinement to your cursor, you might decide that if the user mouses off an object, even during processing, he ought to get the mouse back—or at least after a slight pause.

8. Back in the `Interactor` script, in the `OnMouseExit` function, add the following code below the existing lines:

```
yield new WaitForSeconds (0.5);
controlCenter.GetComponent(GameManager).showPointer = true;
```

9. Save the script.

10. Click Play and give the functionality a thorough test.

In the previous chapter, you worked out a way to determine the processing time for an object that was picked. You used it to keep the action message on screen long enough to read. Another use for it is to prevent mouseovers and mouse picks while the object is being processed. Start with the `OnMouseOver` function.

1. Open the Interactor script.

2. At the top of the OnMouseEnter function, add the following line:

```
if(processing) return; // curently processing this object, leave the function
```

And to make sure the current location gets updated with the state, you will need to add to the ProcessObject function.

3. At the top of the OnMouseDown function, add the following line:

```
if(processing) return; // curently processing this object, leave the function
```

If you are diligent, you may discover that you can move the rock, pick the pedestal, and then return to picking the rock and keep the last action message from the pedestal showing. Apparently the rock is being processed even though it has moved from its state 0 to its state 1 where the player is no longer able to interact with it. If you filled out the Location field for the rock correctly, it should contain a 3 (in scene but not longer pickable) in its Element 1.

4. Open the Interactor script.

5. At the top of the OnMouseDown function, add the following line:

```
if(currentLocation == 3) return; // object is no longer active in scene
```

And to make sure the current location gets updated with the state, you will need to add to the ProcessObject function.

6. In the ProcessObject function, in the //load new states' metadata section, add the following line:

```
currentLocation = location[currentState];
```

7. Save the script.

8. Click Play and test again.

The mouseover indicates that it is a rock that has been moved, but you can no longer pick it. You need to add the conditional to the OnMouseEnter function as well.

9. At the top of the OnMouseEnter function, add the following line:

```
if(currentLocation == 3) return; // object is no longer active in scene
```

10. Save the script.

11. Click Play and test again.

This time the player is no longer mislead into thinking the object is still interactive. At some point you may allow the rock to be picked and deliver a message in its moved state, but if you did so now, it would *animate into* that state again, which would be far worse than any of its earlier faux pas.

Hopefully, you have sorted out the extra pointer functionality glitches and cleared any remaining GamePointer code from your script. The final test is to delete the GamePointer object and test. If there are no errors, you should be good to go.

1. Delete the GamePointer object from the Hierarchy view.

2. Move the CustomCursor script to the MyScripts folder.

3. Click Play and make sure there are no errors reported due to the missing
    `GamePointer`.

░ **Tip**   While changing out the script for the GUI control cursor may have seemed like a bit of a waste, it allowed you to do two important things. Firstly, it allowed you to learn to manipulate the cursor as a tangible object by attaching its functionality to a script in an object oriented manner early on in the project. Secondly, making the change to a better solution introduced you to the concept of not being afraid to make changes. Sometimes the change will be prompted by discovery of a better method of implementation because the learning process is always ongoing. Other times the change may be prompted by version changes in the software where the benefits of migrating to the next version may outweigh the work involved in rewriting serious chunks of code.

---

4. Save the scene and save the project.

Inventory Screen

At this point, you need to make an executive decision. You have used the UnityGUI to create and handle your text and pointer. While it makes continuity of style throughout the game easier, it has the major drawback that there is nothing tangible to work with in the Hierarchy view. As this book is written more for those of you with an art background than a programming background, you will choose to use the object-based GUI Texture option for the inventory's construction so it will not be so abstract. This also allows you to continue using metadata and state lookups as with the 3D objects. Let's get building.

Rather than take up the entire screen, the inventory will allow the regular scene to show in the background to keep the feeling of "game" going. For this, you will need a texture upon which you can arrange the icons representing your collection of loot, tools, and objects of questionable purpose.

1. Copy the Inventory Assets folder from the BookAssets folder into the project's
    Assets Folder.

2. Open the folder and examine its contents.

You should see the following textures:

      ArrowLeft

      ArrowRight

      Crowbar Icon

      Crowbar with Sleeve Icon

      Earth Glyph Icon

      Golden Sleeve Icon

      InventoryIcon

      InventoryPanel

Iron Key Icon

Jewel Icon

Key Glyph Icon

Light Glyph Icon

Music Glyph Icon

Plant Glyph Icon

Topi Fruit Icon Vial of Elixir Icon

White

3.   Select the InventoryPanel texture in the Project view.

4.   In the Inspector, set the Texture Type to GUI.

5.   Click Apply.

This automatically removes things like MIP Mapping and other high resource, unneeded options.

6.   From the GameObject menu ➤ Create Other, select GUI Texture.

A new semi-transparent 2D object appears in the in the scene and in the Hierarchy view, as shown in Figure 11-5.

Figure 11-5. *The InventoryPanel GUI texture object in the Game view*

7.   Select the Main Camera.

8. Try toggling its GUI layer off and on.

Theoretically, you could control the inventory without the use of other cameras and layers since you are using GUI Textures for it. However, taking into consideration that you may opt to experiment with 3D inventory objects at some point, you will go ahead and make use of your camera layer as planned.

9. Select the InventoryPanel in the Hierarchy view.

10. In the Inspector, change its Layer to Inventory.

11. If the panel disappears in the Game view, select the Camera Inventory and make sure it is turned on at the top of the Inspector.

12. Try toggling the Game Overlay icon in the Scene window on and off to briefly see the panel in that view.

13. Try rescaling the game window to observe the placement and centering the panel has by default.

14. Click Play and see how it affects your current game functionality.

At present, there is no effect. Mouseovers and picks are still recognized. You may be thinking that this would have been a logical time to use the Box UnityGUI control that blocks interaction with the 3D objects underneath it. On the other hand, if you had Maximize on Play toggled on, you would realize that objects outside the panel would act as usual.

The first thing you will need to do, then, is come up with a means of knowing when the inventory is showing, or more expressly, when you are in Inventory mode. As usual, you can create a variable to hold that information. At this point, however, you need to decide where to put your variable. Let's start by adding it to the GameManager script since that is where you are storing most of the other variables that need to be accessed by other scripts.

1. Open the GameManager script.

2. Add the following private variable:

private var iMode = false; // flag for whether inventory mode is off or on

3. Save the script.

Since you will need to add a lot of functionality to manage the inventory, go ahead and create a script for it.

4. Create a new JavaScript in the Adventure Scripts folder and name it InventoryManager.

5. Open the new script.

First off, it will need to use the iMode variable. You can expose this one to the Inspector so you can test it easier.

6. Add the following to the top of the script:

var iMode = false; // local flag for whether inventory mode is off or on
private var controlCenter : GameObject;

7. Next, create a Start function and add it as follows:

function Start () {

518

```
    camera.enabled = false;
    controlCenter = GameObject.Find("Control Center");// access the control center
    iMode = controlCenter.GetComponent(GameManager).iMode;
}
```

To start testing the inventory mode, you will use the i key to toggle it off and on since this is a fairly standard key to use regardless of genre. Key presses are checked for constantly, so this code will go into the Update function. And since there will be several things to take care of, you can make it call a function that you can add to as you go.

1.   In the Update function, add the following code:

```
if (Input.GetKeyDown("i")) ToggleMode(); // call the function if i key is pressed
```

Since you are using layers, all you have to do is disable the camera to turn the visual part of the inventory off. You also need to inform the GameManager script of state changes in iMode.

2.   Create the ToggleMode function as follows:

```
// toggle inventory visibility
function ToggleMode () {

  if (iMode) { // if you are in inventory mode, turn it off
      camera.enabled = false;// turn off the camera

      iMode = false; // change the flag
      controlCenter.GetComponent(GameManager).iMode = false; // inform the manager
  }
  else { // else it was off so turn it on
      camera.enabled = true;// turn on the camera

      iMode = true; // change the flag
      controlCenter.GetComponent(GameManager).iMode = true; // inform the manager
  }

}
```

3.   Save the script.

If you don't specify a particular camera, the camera *must* be on the gameObject that contains the script, or, in your case, the script will be on the camera.

4.   Add the InventoryManager script to the Camera Inventory object.

5.   Turn the Camera component of the Camera Inventory object off (the panel will disappear from the Game window).

6.   Click Play and press the i key on the keyboard a few times to check the functionality.

A bit farther down the way, you will also give the player an icon on screen to get in and out of Inventory mode, but for now let's concentrate on the additional requirements for the functionality.

1. Try navigating the scene with the inventory panel showing, picking and mousing over the action objects.

As you can see, there are several things you need to prevent while in inventory. Let's start with the most obvious, scene navigation.

2. While in Play mode, try turning off various components of the First Person Controller gameObject to see what will be required.

3. Stop Play mode.

After a bit of experimentation, you will have found that you need to disable the First Person Controller but not its children, as you still need the main camera to render the 3D scene. But you also need to turn off the MouseLookRestricted script on the camera. To do both, you will need to introduce the First Person Controller object to the script. Since it need only be once, you can just drag and drop it into a variable rather than script it to be found at startup. You may as well do the same for the camera while you're at it.

1. Open the InventoryManager script.

2. Add the following variables:

```
var fPController : GameObject;
var fPCamera : GameObject;
```

3. Save the script.

4. Select the Camera Inventory object.

5. Drag the First Person Controller and the Main Camera onto the appropriate variables in the Inspector.

6. Back in the InventoryManager script, in the ToggleMode function, add the following lines inside the if clause, just below the camera.enabled=false line:

```
fPController.GetComponent(CharacterMotor).enabled = true; // turn on navigation
fPController.GetComponent(FPAdventurerInputController).enabled = true; // turn on navigation
fPController.GetComponent(MouseLookRestricted).enabled = true; // turn on navigation
fPCamera.GetComponent(MouseLookRestricted).enabled = true;
```

7. And in the else clause, under its camera.enabled=true line, add:

```
fPController.GetComponent(CharacterMotor).enabled = false; // turn off navigation
fPController.GetComponent(FPAdventurerInputController).enabled = false; // turn off navigation
fPController.GetComponent(MouseLookRestricted).enabled = false; // turn off navigation
fPCamera.GetComponent(MouseLookRestricted).enabled = false;
```

8. Save the script.

9. Click Play, toggle the inventory panel on and test the functionality.

Next, you need to block mouseovers and picks on anything that is not part of the inventory layer. In the Interactor script, when the OnMouseEnter and OnMouseDown functions are called, you need to find out whether you are in inventory mode by checking with the GameManager and then checking on the layer that the parent object is in.

1. Open the Interactor script.

2. Add the following private var in the //Misc vars section:

private var iMode : **boolean**;

3. In the OnMouseEnter function, below the **if**(processing) **return** line, add the following:

```
iMode = controlCenter.GetComponent(GameManager).iMode; // get current iMode
if (iMode && gameObject.layer != 9) return; // return if the mouse was not over an↵
 inventory object and you are in inventory mode
```

Remember that layers are referred to in the code by their layer number and that the Inventory layer is using number 9. GameObject.layer gets the layer assignment for the object that this script is on. If it returns layer 9 and you are in inventory mode, you exit the OnMouseOver function.

For the mouse pick, OnMouseDown, you already got the updated iMode during the mouseover so you only need the conditional.

4. In the OnMouseDown function, below the **if**(processing) **return** line, add the following:

```
if (iMode  && gameObject.layer != 9) return;
```

5. Save the script.

6. Click Play and test the inventory mode.

Nothing is processed from the 3D scene layer.

Let's add an icon on screen as an alternative means of toggling inventory. It needs to be accessible whether the Inventory layer is invisible or the scene interaction is blocked. Since you are filtering out interaction from both layers at one time or other, your icon either needs to go on a different layer or be a UnityGUI control.

The UnityGUI Button control has a lot of functionality built in, so let's look at it first. Buttons, by their very nature, are conditionals: *if* the button is picked, *do* something. The UnityGUI Button is no exception. The nice thing about having made your ToggleMode function is that it makes testing different modes of access easy.

1. Open the GameManager script.

2. Add the following in the OnGUI function, above the pointer section:

```
if (GUI.Button (Rect(5,Screen.height - 35,32,32),"i")) {
// call the Toggle Mode function when this button is picked
  GameObject.Find("Camera Inventory").SendMessage("ToggleMode");
}
```

3. Save the script.

4. Click Play and test the button, as shown in Figure 11-6.

5. Test a combination of button and keyboard to toggle the inventory screen.

Figure 11-6. *The Unity GUI Button control to access Inventory mode*

The problem with the UnityGUI Button control is that it really doesn't work well as a button, visually. You could change the Button style in your GUISkin, but then when you need to make regular buttons, they would all look like the inventory button. A better solution would be to add another Custom Style variable to create a style just for the inventory icon, using custom textures and behaviors. But that still limits your functionality to that of a GUIButton.

Another solution would be to use a GUITexture object. This will give you control over different aspects. First, the icon should be easy to find, but not intrusive. Second, it should be more apparent when the mouse is over it. Third, it doesn't need a visual click response as the entire inventory screen appears and disappears.

A nice effect would be for it to start semi-transparent, then do a quick fade in to opaque. and fade out with mouseover. This will give you a chance to review the Animation editor and keyframe animation.

1. Comment out the GUI Button script you added to the Game Manager.

2. Save the script.

3. Stop Play mode.

4. Select Camera Inventory and turn off its Camera component.

The Inventory Panel should now be hidden when you are not in Play mode.

522

5. Select the Inventory Icon texture from the Inventory Assets folder in the Project view.

6. In the Inspector, change its Texture Type to GUI and click Apply.

7. From the GameObject menu, Create Other ➤ GUI Texture.

8. Put it in the Pointer layer and make sure the Camera Pointer is turned on.

9. Set the size to 32 × 32 and the X and Y insets to 2 and 2.

10. At the top of the Inspector, set the X Position and Y Position to 0, as shown in Figure 11-7.

Figure 11-7. *The GUI Texture in the lower left corner of the screen*

Next, you will see about adjusting the opacity. It is a bit tricky because Color dialog uses the 0-255 range but the Animation dialog uses 0-1.

1. In the Inspector, open the Color dialog for the InventoryIcon object and set the alpha to about 42, as shown in Figure 11-8.

Figure 11-8. *Opacity reduced*

2. Open the Animation window by pressing CTRL+6.

3. Click the empty selection box to the right of the one with the object's name and select Create New Clip.

4. Navigate to the Animation Clips folder and name it PulseIcon.

5. Click Save.

6. Click the red dot to go into animation mode.

7. Select the Color.a track from the GUITexture drop-down.

Note that your value of 42 is shown as 0.1647.

8. Click the Add Keyframe button.

9. Move the red time line to frame 0:45.

10. Create another key.

11. Move the time line back until it is about halfway between the two keys and create another key.

12. Click to select the key you just created.

13. Change its value to 0.8, as shown in Figure 11-9.

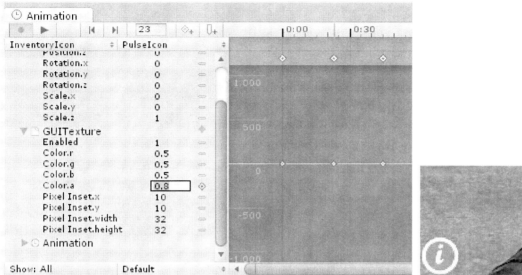

Figure 11-9. *Animating the middle key to increase the opacity*

14. Use the F key to focus in on the keys in the curve window.

15. Select the bottom two keys and right click to bring up the tangents and click Broken.

16. Move both arrows down until they are slightly below horizontal, as shown in Figure 11-10.

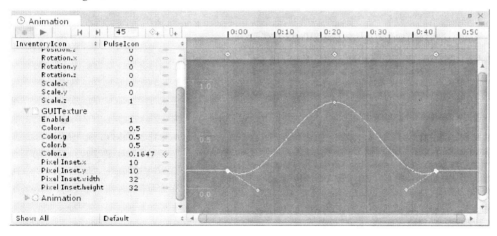

Figure 11-10. *The adjusted opacity curve*

17. Click the Play arrow next to the Animation button to see the results in the Game window.

18. Close the Animation dialog.

19. Close the Animation view.

Now you need to make a simple script to call the functionality. You will create a function to call the PulseIcon animation for later use rather than adding the animation call to the OnMouseEnter function.

1. Create a new JavaScript and put it in the Adventure Scripts folder.

2. Name it InventoryIcon and open it in the script editor.

3. Delete the default Update function and add the following:

```
function OnMouseEnter () {
    PulseIcon();
}

function  OnMouseDown () {
    // call the Toggle Mode function when this button is picked
  GameObject.Find("Camera Inventory").SendMessage("ToggleMode");

}

function PulseIcon () {
    // play the animation
    animation.Play("PulseIcon");
}
```

4. Save the script.

5. Drag the InventoryIcon script onto the InventoryIcon object in the Hierarchy view.

6. Select the InventoryIcon object in the Hierarchy view.

7. In the Inspector, uncheck Play Automatically in the Animation component that was automatically added when you created the animation clip.

8. Click Play and test the new icon by mousing over it.

9. Save your scene and project.

If you wanted it to act more like a regular button, you could create two animation clips and call them on enter and exit. You could also try using a 3D object instead of the GUITexture object. Since the Inventory icon is in its own layer, the Pointer layer, you would need to position it using the Camera Pointer. You could then animate not only its texture's opacity but a small transform as well.

Extending the Lookup Table

Because you are treating cursor and inventory versions of your action objects as *separate* objects, you will need to spare a few moments to go back to the LookUpState script and get it parsing the addition information. Currently you have it checking the first element to see what cursor picked the object, and then it checks the second element to see which state the object goes into. You now need it to evaluate the rest of the elements, if there are any, and send them off to be processed.

In the case of inventory objects, when you pick the mesh object with the default cursor, it needs to be hidden, and the 2D version of it be visible. The metadata for picking the key might look as follows:

- **Key at Rock:**

    State 0: in scene

    State 1: not in scene

- **Iron Key Icon:**

    State 0: not in scene

    State 1: in inventory

    State 2: is cursor

- **Key at Lock:**

    State 0: not in scene

    State 1: inserted into lock

    State 2: turned in lock

    State 3: unavailable

- **Lockplate:**

    State 0: empty

    State 1: key inserted

    State 2: key turned

The metadata in the lookup table for picking up the KeyAtRock object would look as follows:

```
default,1, Iron Key Icon,1
```

Translated, the KeyAtRock object is in state 0 when it is on the ground and visible in the scene. When picked by the default cursor (default), it animates up and fades away, moving to its state 1 (not in scene). At the same time, the Iron Key Icon object, a GUI Texture, is moved from its starting state of 0 (hidden) to 1 (in inventory).

Now you have the Iron Key Icon object in inventory. If you pick it with the default or any other cursor, the other object, the key becomes the new cursor and the other cursor, as long as it is not the default cursor, will go back into inventory. Let's just use the default cursor to pick with for this hypothetical example where the object is in inventory (state 1), is picked by the default cursor, and becomes the cursor (state 2):

```
default,2
```

So now the cursor is using the Iron Key Icon texture. If you pick the Lockplate with the Iron Key Icon texture on the cursor, you would get this:

```
Iron Key Icon,0,Lockplate,1, KeyAtLock,1
```

The Iron Key Icon goes back to state 0 (not in scene), the Lockplate moves to state 1 (key inserted), and the KeyAtLock moves into state 1 (inserted into lock). And so on and so forth…

Let's go ahead and add the code to handle the auxiliary objects.

1. Open the `ObjectLookUp` script.

2. Delete the print statements that you commented out.

```
//~ print ("Object: " + object.name);
//~ print ("State: " + currentState );
//~ print ("Picker: " + picker);
```

Once you've got a match and sent it off to be processed, you will need to see if there are any auxiliary objects. Since you've already processed elements 0 and 1, you need to know how many elements there are in total. If there are more than two, you have auxiliary objects to process, so that will be one of the first things you check for.

3. Below the `object.SendMessage("ProcessObject"` line, add the following:

```
//process auxiliary objects if there are any
var tempLength = (readString.length); //get the length of the current stateArray

if(tempLength > 2){ // that means there are auxiliary objects
    for (var x = 2; x < tempLength; x = x + 2) { // go through the rest of the array by 2s
```

This `for` loop starts at element 2 and goes as long as its counter, x, is less than the total length of the array, incrementing by 2 instead of the usual 1 since you are processing the data in pairs.

4. Next, add the following to remove a leading space if the data got typed in wrong:

```
 //check if the first character is a space, and if so, start the string at the second element
    var tempS = readString[x];
    if (tempS.Substring(0,1) == " ") tempS = tempS.Substring(1);
```

```
//check for special cases here- you will come back to this later
```

You've set a comment to where you will check for special cases, but will fill in that code later. X being the first element in the pair, `tempS` is the name of your auxiliary action object. You need to call the `ProcessObject` function in that object's *own* `ObjectLookUp` script, so you need to reference the actual object, not just its name property, first. To do that, you use the `Find` function.

5. Add the following:

```
    var auxObject = gameObject.Find(tempS);
```

And the auxObject's new state is the x+1 element, the second in the pair, but it needs to be turned into an integer so it can be passed as a number, not a string.

6. Add the following:

```
    var newState = parseInt(readString[x+1]);
```

```
    // process the auxiliary object
    auxObject.SendMessage( "ProcessObject",newState);
```

```
    } // close the for loop
    } // close if clause for the auxiliary objects
    } // close there is a matchSave the script
```

7. Click Play and make sure you have no errors.

Just to check up on your auxiliary object handling code, let's see if you can trigger the ChestLid to open when you click the pedestal in its state 1.

1. Stop Play mode.

2. Select the Pedestal.

3. To its Look Up State 1 array, element 0, add ",ChestLid,2" so it looks like the following:

```
default,2,ChestLid,2
```

4. Click Play and pick the Pedestal into its state 1.

As expected, the ChestLid opens.

5. Now mouseover the ChestLid and try to pick it.

Nothing happens!

Leaving Breadcrumbs

If you have Unity Pro, you could open the Debugger and step through your code line by line until you found out why the ChestLid no longer responds to direct interaction. If you are using the free version, you will need to find the problem the old fashioned way. First, you need to determine whether the ChestLid is still active at all.

1. Pick the Pedestal until it triggers the ChestLid to open again.

This shows that the object still works; it just has no interaction from pick or mouseover.
The next thing to do is inspect the OnMouseDown and see if you can figure out where it goes wrong—or in this case, stops going forward.

2. Open the Interactor script and inspect the OnMouseDown function

The first four bits of code return if their condition is not met. This is a good place to start.

3. Add a print statement above the first for lines and have each print out a different letter or number.

4. Save the script.

5. Click Play and activate the ChestLid via the Pedestal.

6. Clear the Console.

7. Pick the ChestLid.

The results will show that the printouts stop after the if(processing) conditional indicating that that is where the function is exited. You need to find out where the processing flag is turned off and on. Investigation shows you that the processing flag is turned on as soon as you get into the ProcessObject function. You know where it was turned on; now you need to find out where it was turned off. Further investigation (or using Find in the script editor) shows you that the processing flag is turned off in the timer you made in the Update function. Remembering that it also involved telling the GameManager which object started the timer last, you can decide to make the assumption that most auxiliary objects do not need more than a small amount of processing time if any since you are not showing a message for them.

8. At the bottom of the ProcessObject function, add the following:

```
// if the object was activated by another object (no was timer started)
if(timer2 == false) processing = false;
```

9. Save the script.

10. Click Play and test.

Now the ChestLid is still active even after being triggered by the Pedestal.

11. Stop Play mode.

12. Remove or comment out the print statements.

13. Save the scene and the project.

Now that the lookup table has more functionality, you will start to get your inventory icons into the scene.

Adding Inventory Icons

As with the inventory panel, the 2D icons for your game will be GUI Texture objects so you will have something tangible to access in the Hierarchy view. Because they need mouseover events and pick events just like their 3D counterparts, they will need the same metadata and lookup handling as well.

The problem you will run into is that just like your original GUI Texture pointer, these do not have a Mesh Renderer and will throw an error when you add the Interactor script to them and it tries to handle a mouseover color change. Rather than create an Interactor script just for the 2D objects, you will reuse the color change code from the CustomCursor script for color change and write in a condition for which type of color change to use.

Let's add an inventory icon so you will have something to test with.

1. In the Project view, open the Inventory Assets folder and select the Jewel Icon texture.

2. In the Inspector, change its Texture Type to GUI and click Apply.

3. From the CreateObject menu, create a new GUI Texture with the jewel texture.

4. Set its Width and Height to 64.

5. Set the X and Y Pixel Insets to -32.

6. In the Inspector, set its X location to 0.25 so it won't be over any of the 3D action objects, as shown in Figure 11-11.

Figure 11-11. *The Jewel icon in the scene*

7. Add the Interactor and ObjectLookUp scripts to it.

Inventory objects always have the same states. State 0 is not in scene (location 4); state 1 is object is in inventory (location 1); and state 2 is object is cursor (location 2). If an inventory object is combined with another, it becomes a different object so there are no other states. Inventory objects are always shown or hidden immediately.

8. Open the GameNotes text asset from the Adventure Scripts folder.

9. Add the following to it:

   Cursor States:

      0: not in scene

      1: in Inventory

      2: is Cursor

10. Save the text asset.

11. Select the Jewel Icon object.

12. Fill out the Interactor metadata for the icon, unchecking Animates, and giving it three elements for each array including the sound arrays but not the animation arrays, as shown in Figure 11-12.

13. Fill out the name and description for the elements. Use the same name and description for each array's three elements for now, as shown in Figure 11-12.

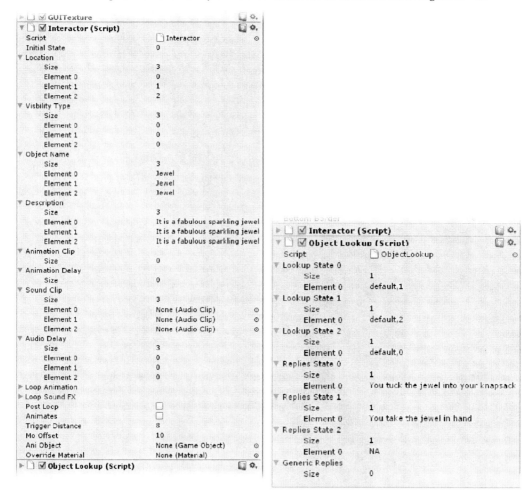

Figure 11-12. *The Jewel icon's metadata and lookup information*

1. In preparation for your mouseover checking, open the Interactor script.

2. And add the following variable somewhere near the top of the //ObjectMetadata section so you will only have to check its type once:

```
var objectIs3D = true; //flag to identify GUI Texture objects
```

3. Save the script.

4. Select the Jewel icon.

5. Uncheck the new Object Is 3d variable.

You will be testing the material change on mouseover, so you will need to turn on that option.

6. In the Inspector on the Control Center's GameManager component, turn on Use MO Material Change.

7. Click Play.

As expected, it throws the error that you see in Figure 11-13: "There is no MeshRenderer attached to the Jewel Icon." Now you need to go through the script and allow for the possibility of 2D and 3D objects. You need to wrap the material handling for the 3D object into an if clause.

MissingComponentException: There is no 'MeshRenderer' attached to the "Jewel Icon" game object, but a script is trying to access it.

Figure 11-13. *Error message*

1. Open the Interactor script.

2. In the Start function, locate the code that stores the original material, originalMaterial = GetComponent.

3. Immediately above it, add the following:

```
//prep for mouse over material change if it is a regular 3D object
if(objectIs3D) { // do the following
```

4. And below the **else** useTexture = false line, add the closing curly bracket so the code now looks as follows:

```
//prep for mouse over material change if it is a regular 3D object
if(objectIs3D) { // do the following
originalMaterial = GetComponent(MeshRenderer).material; // load the material into the var
if (originalMaterial.mainTexture) { // if a texture exists, do…
   aoTexture =  originalMaterial.mainTexture;
   useTexture = true;
   //print (name + ":  " + aoTexture.name);
}
else useTexture = false;
}
```

The icons need to operate like the original GamePointer object. They will have their material's Color tinted by the mouseover color. That means the Interactor script will need to know what color that is.

Near the top of the Start function, under the line that assigns the mouseOverMaterial, add the following code to retrieve the mouseOverColor from the GameManager:

```
mouseOverColor = controlCenter.GetComponent(GameManager).mouseOverColor;
```

And let's remember to declare the mouseOverColor variable for it in the //gain access to section, just under the mouseOverMaterial line:

```
private var mouseOverColor : Color;
```

5. Save the script.

6. Click Play and test.

You no longer get an error message on startup, but you still have no mouseover functionality. If you scan the OnMouseOver function for hints, you may remember that you also get booted out of it if the First Person Controller is not close enough to the camera. As it turns out, the distance check is not valid because the GUI Textures can't be checked for distance. While you are setting up the color change, you will need to disable the distance check.

7. Comment out the if (DistanceFromCamera( ) line.

8. Save the script.

9. Click Play and test.

You no longer get an error message on start up, but now you do get the same "no MeshRenderer" message when mousing over the icon. You've already written code to handle a GUI Texture color change for the CustomCursor script which is no longer being used. You can simplify it for use in the Interactor script.

1. In the OnMouseEnter function, locate the if (useMOMaterialChange) section.

2. Add the objectIs3D conditional and the else clause to handle it so that the block of code now looks as follows:

```
//handle mouseover color changes
if (useMOMaterialChange) {
   if (objectIs3D) {
      //activate the material change
      if (overrideMaterial) renderer.material = overrideMaterial;
      else {
         mouseOverMaterial.mainTexture = aoTexture;
         renderer.material = mouseOverMaterial;
      }
   }
   // else the object is a 2D GUI Texture object, so do this instead
   else if (!objectIs3D) guiTexture.color = mouseOverColor;
}
```

And you will need to change everything back in the OnMouseExit function. Note that the icon's color will return to grey rather than white. Gray is the default color for textures and will allow you to brighten the texture on need.

3. In the OnMouseExit function, change the renderer.material = originalMaterial line to the following:

```
// return the object's material or color to the original
if(useMOMaterialChange) {
   if (objectIs3D) renderer.material = originalMaterial;
   else guiTexture.color = Color.grey;
}
```

4. Save the script.

5. Click Play and test the mouseovers.

The mouseovers now work for both 2D and 3D objects but you had to disable the distance check in the `OnMouseEnter` to get the 2D object working. If you inspect the `OnMouseExit` function, you will realize that two of its conditionals are also checking for distance to camera on the object—a concept that, as you discovered, has no meaning for the 2D GUI objects. While you could exclude *all* GUI Texture objects from the distance check with a `!objectIs3D` clause, you would still get into trouble if you decide to experiment with 3D objects in inventory instead of 2D objects. Regardless of which kind of objects you are using, you will be in inventory mode at the time, and it turns out you already *have* a variable for that, `iMode`.

Let's go ahead and fix the distance from camera conditionals. You can add the and, &&, clause at the end of the existing clause because and, &&, and or, ||, are always evaluated *after* the comparison operators, `>`, `<`, and `==`. You use the *not* symbol, !, so they will skip the rest of the `OnMouseEnter` *and* `OnMouseExit` functions as long as you are not in inventory mode and the distance to camera is not met.

1. In the `OnMouseEnter` function, uncomment the line and add the `&& !iMode` to the line that calls the `DistanceToCamera()` function and reactivate the line:

```
// exit if you are not within range unless you are in Inventory mode
if (DistanceFromCamera() > triggerDistance + moOffset && !iMode) return;
```

2. And fix the two cases in the `OnMouseDown` function:

```
// exit if you are not within range
var tempDistance = DistanceFromCamera();
if (tempDistance > triggerDistance + moOffset && !iMode) return;
```

and

```
// if the player is within mouseover but not picking distance...
if (tempDistance > triggerDistance && !iMode) {
```
And you will also need to restore the icon's original color after being picked.

3. Change the following

```
// turn the object back to original if it is being used
if(useMOMaterialChange) renderer.material = originalMaterial;
```

to

```
// return the object's material or color to the original
if(useMOMaterialChange) {
    if (objectIs3D) renderer.material = originalMaterial;
    else guiTexture.color = Color.grey;
}
```

4. Save the script.

Before you can test, you will need to put the icon into the Inventory layer to bypass the additional distance checks you added.

1. Stop Play mode.

2. Assign the Jewel icon to the Inventory layer.

3. Turn off Maximize on Play.

4. Click Play and go into inventory mode and test the mouseover the jewel.

The first thing you notice is the Jewel icon is behind the InventoryPanel but at least the mouseover is working. It's time to do some testing.

5. Decrease the InventoryPanel's Z Position until it is behind the icon; it needs to be less than 0.

6. Stop Play mode and set the InventoryPanel's Z Position to -1.

■ **Tip**   GUI Texture and GUI Text objects can be draw-ordered using their Z Position in the Inspector.

The icon's mouseover now works, but you may have noticed the jewel does not get the long description text as do the 3D objects.

1. Open the GameManager script.

2. Inspect the OnGUI function to see why the long description is not showing for the icon on mouseover.

You can see that it also needs the inRange flag to be true. This is an easy fix; whenever the mouseover object is 2D, it is automatically in range.

3. Open the Interactor script.

4. In the OnMouseEnter function, change the // automatic bypass flag section to the following:

```
// automatic bypass flag
if(!objectIs3D) controlCenter.GetComponent(GameManager).inRange =true;
else {
    if(DistanceFromCamera() <= triggerDistance) {
        controlCenter.GetComponent(GameManager).inRange =true;}
    else  controlCenter.GetComponent(GameManager).inRange =false;
}
```

5. Save the script.

6. Click Play and test.

The long description now shows for the icon, as you can see in Figure 11-14.

Figure 11-14. *The Jewel Icon with short and long descriptions on mouseover in inventory*

You may decide at this point that the mouseover color is not appropriate for the regular inventory icons. Since all of them should probably work the same way, you can hardcode a color into the code.

So far you have either used the Color type to declare a variable, which then exposes access to the Color editor, or you have used a preset such as Color.white. If you want to use a custom color, you will need to know how to write it.

The Color parameter is generally a four-part value: RGBA, or red, green, blue, and alpha. To refer to it as a value directly, you can use Color(r,g,b,a) where the letters are float numbers from 0 to 1. Unfortunately it doesn't map well to the 256 values many of us are used to, but in this case it should not be an issue.

1. Open the `Interactor` script.

2. In the `OnMouseEnter` function, where you are handling `useMOMaterialChange`, change the `mouseOverColor` as follows:

```
// else the object is a 2D GUI Texture object, so do this instead
else if (!objectIs3D) guiTexture.color = Color(1,1,1,1);
```

3. Save the script.

4. Click Play and test the mouseover.

White is perhaps too much. The default texture color is Color.grey, or Color(0.5,0.5,0.5,1), so if you go half way between, the color brightens just a bit to indicate the mouseover.

5. Change the line to the following:

```
else if (!objectIs3D) guiTexture.color = Color(0.75, 0.75, 0.75,1); // brighten the 2D↵
  icon a little
```

6. Save the script.

7. Click Play and test.

Everything works well, unless you are opting *not* to use the mouseover material change on objects, but would still like to have the 2D objects change. If this is the case, you could simply move the else line out of the useMOMaterialChange block and remove the else. In the spirit of letting the author and eventually the player choose, you can move it out and preface it with another variable.

1. Open the GameManager script.

2. Create a new variable called useIconColorChange:

```
var useIconColorChange = true;
```

3. Save the script.

4. In the Interactor, add it along with the others as a private var in the //gain access section:

```
private var useIconColorChange : boolean;
```

5. Access it along with the others in the Start function:

```
useIconColorChange = controlCenter.GetComponent(GameManager). useIconColorChange;
```

6. In the OnMouseEnter function, cut the following lines from above the closing curly bracket:

```
// else the object is a 2D GUI Texture object, so do this instead
else if (!objectIs3D) guiTexture.color = Color(0.75, 0.75, 0.75,1); // brighten the 2D↵
  icon a little
```

7. Paste them back in below the curly bracket and add the useIconColorChange flag to the conditional:

```
// do the color change for 2D GUI objects if it is being used
if (useIconColorChange && !objectIs3D)guiTexture.color = Color(0.75, 0.75, 0.75,1);
```
The closing curly bracket below it closes the OnMouseEnter function.

8. In the OnMouseExit function, the // return the 2D object's code becomes:

```
// return the 3D object's material to the original
if(useMOMaterialChange && objectIs3D) renderer.material = originalMaterial;

// return the 2D object's color to the original
 if (useIconColorChange && !objectIs3D)guiTexture.color = Color.grey;
```

9. Save the script.

10. Turn off Use MOMaterial Change in the Inspector for the Control Center's Game Manager component.

11. Click play and test mouseovers and picks for 3D objects and 2D objects.

The Inventory Icon retains its mouseover color change and the regular scene objects are no longer affected unless you specifically activate the Use MOMaterial Change in the Inspector.

As long as you are currently focusing on minor details, you may think that the cursor stays away too long when you pick the icon in inventory. Once you finish hooking up the rest of the cursor functionality, when you pick on an icon in inventory, it will either become the cursor and a new one moves into place, a new icon showing the new combination of objects appears, or an empty spot appears, so the timing will probably be fine.

2D Object Handling

Let's forge ahead and handle the visibility of the 2D objects. Unlike the 3D objects, the 2D GUI objects all have the same three states: not in scene, is in inventory and is cursor. As such, the visibility is fairly predictable and should be handled separately from the 3D objects. The key to icon visibility handling is knowing their previous state. This will let you deal with icons in inventory and as cursors at the same time.

The six possible combinations where the states have changed are shown in Table 11-1.

Table 11-1. *State Change Combinations*

States, Previous ➤ Current	Required Action
Not in scene ➤ Is Cursor	Put to Cursor
Not in Scene ➤ In inventory	Add to Inventory Enable GUITexture
Is Cursor ➤ Not in scene	Reset Cursor
Is Cursor ➤ In Inventory	Reset Cursor Add to Inventory Enable GUITexture
In Inventory ➤ Not in scene	Remove from Inventory Disable GUITexture
In Inventory ➤ Is Cursor	Remove from Inventory Disable GUITexture Put to Cursor

To begin with, you need to store the previous state before you update it with the new location. You will also want a variable to store the object's element number when it is in the inventory array, so you will know which one to remove when it is taken out of inventory.

1. Open the Interactor script.

2. In the //State dependent variables section, add the following private variables:

```
private var previousState :int;
private var element = 0; // element number when in inventory
```

3. Inside the `ProcessObject` function, above the `currentState = newState` line, add the following:

```
previousState = currentState; // store the previous state before updating
```
    You will make a function called `Handle2D` to process the 2D objects' visibility.

4. Above the `// process audio` line, add the following:

```
if(!objectIs3D) Handle2D(); // send 2D objects off for processing
```
    You will make some new functions to add and remove objects from inventory as well as manage the cursor. Since the cursor is handled in the `GameManager` script, you will either call a `ResetCursor` function, or change the default cursor's value directly by assigning the action object's texture to it. Since the action object doesn't know what the default cursor on the `GameManager` is, it will need to send a message to a function, `ResetCursor`, to reset the cursor.

5. At the bottom of the `Interactor` script, start the new function and fill in the combinations of previous and current states as conditionals with your future functions to do the work:

```
//handle 2D objects
function Handle2D () {

   // Not in scene -> Is Cursor
   if (previousState == 0 && currentState == 2) {
      controlCenter.GetComponent(GameManager).currentCursor = guiTexture.texture;
   }

   // Not in scene -> In Inventory
   if (previousState == 0 && currentState == 1) {
      controlCenter.SendMessage("AddToInventory", gameObject);
      gameObject.guiTexture.enabled = true;
   }

   // Is Cursor -> Not in scene
   if (previousState == 2 && currentState == 0) {
      controlCenter.SendMessage("ResetCursor");
   }
   // Is Cursor -> In Inventory
   if (previousState == 2 && currentState == 1) {
      controlCenter.SendMessage("AddToInventory", gameObject);
      gameObject.guiTexture.enabled = true;
      controlCenter.SendMessage("ResetCursor");
   }
   // In Inventory -> Not in scene
   if (previousState == 1 && currentState == 0) {
      gameObject.guiTexture.enabled = false;
      controlCenter.SendMessage("RemoveFromInventory", gameObject);
   }

   // In Inventory -> Is Cursor
```

```
  if (previousState == 1 && currentState == 2) {
      gameObject.guiTexture.enabled = false;
      controlCenter.SendMessage("RemoveFromInventory", gameObject);
      controlCenter.GetComponent(GameManager).currentCursor = guiTexture.texture;
  }
}
```

6. Save the script.

7. Open the GameManager script.

8. Add the following function at the bottom of the script to reset the cursor to the default:

```
function ResetCursor() {
   currentCursor = defaultCursor; // reset the cursor to the default
}
```

9. Save the script.

This might be a good time to block in the AddToInventory and RemoveFromInventory functions. Because they need to know what object to remove or add, they will be receiving an argument inside their parentheses.

1. Open the GameManager function again.

2. Add the following below the other functions:

```
function AddToInventory (object : GameObject) {

   print ("adding " + object.name + " to inventory");

}

function RemoveFromInventory (object : GameObject) {

   print ("removing" + object.name + "  from inventory");

}
```

3. Save the script.

Although you have hooked up a lot of functionality, you still have more to do. You can, however, test a small bit. The jewel is currently in state 0, but is showing in the inventory anyway. If you pick it, it will get processed from case 0 to case 1. The cursor will become the jewel and the icon in inventory disappears thanks to your Handle2D function.

4. Select the Jewel icon and set its Initial State to 1 in the Interactor component of the Inspector.

5. Click Play and test the Jewel icon.

If you pick the regular action objects with the new jewel cursor, they will no longer react since interaction with your current 3D objects requires the default cursor. For now, you can replace the print to console line with an action message. Since you have already handled the "You are too far from the…" message in a similar manner, you can borrow its code and adapt it for the "no match" message.

1. Open the ObjectLookup script.

2. In the LookupState function, locate:

```
else print("no match for the " + object.name);
```

When you added the element ++ line, the "no match for the" line was orphaned; it actually belongs below the } // end for loop line, after the current state array has had all of its elements checked for a matching cursor.

3. Delete the **else** print("no match for the " + object.name) line.

4. Below the } // end for loop line, and above the closing curly bracket for the LookUpState function, add the following:

```
// The current cursor, passed in as "picker", was not a match, so did not provoke any
reaction- show a reply
else HandleNoMatchReplies (picker);
```

You will create the HandleNoMatchReplies function next.

5. Start the new function:

```
function HandleNoMatchReplies (picker : String) {
```

6. Inside the new function add:

```
picker = picker.ToLower(); // make it lower case
picker = picker.Substring(0,picker.length - 5); // strip off the icon part of the name
var tempObjectName = this.GetComponent("Interactor").currentObjectName.ToLower();
```

The first thing you do inside the function is reuse the picker variable; it is the name of the current cursor passed into the LookUpState function. Next, convert the name to lower case. Then you use Substring to strip off the " Icon" part of the name. Then you get the currentObjectName from the Interactor component of the object instead of using its object name from the Hierarchy view. Now you are ready to construct a reply and then activate the action message to display it for a couple of seconds.

7. Add the following:

```
var tempMsg = "The " + picker + " does not seem to affect the " + tempObjectName ;
//send the GameManager the action text
controlCenter.GetComponent(GameManager).actionMsg=tempMsg;
//tell the GameManager to show the action text
controlCenter.GetComponent(GameManager).showActionMsg=true;
//wait two seconds then turn off the action text and leave the function
yield new WaitForSeconds(2.0);
controlCenter.GetComponent(GameManager).showActionMsg= false;
return;
}
```

8. Save the script.

9. Click Play.

10. Pick the jewel from inventory, leave inventory and pick the ChestLid.

You get a nice message telling you that it doesn't do anything, as shown in Figure 11-15.

Figure 11-15. *Jewel icon picking the ChestLid*

11. Save the scene and save the project.

Chapter Summary

In this chapter, you got your first look at using Layers to be able to composite multiple camera views together. Armed with this new knowledge, you created a camera and layer to house the Inventory screen as an overlay of the regular scene. Adding a new flag, iMode, you devised a means of toggling your new Inventory mode off and on with both a keyboard and onscreen icon. You also made an executive decision to replace the artist-friendly GUI Texture pointer with a script-only version using the UnityGUI Texture control.

In electing to keep your scene running in the background while accessing inventory, you discovered that you needed to disable navigation and disable mouseover functionality and picks from your 3D action objects yet allow interaction with your 2D inventory. With the introduction of a 2D inventory object, you discovered that by adding a new flag to your action objects, you could make a few changes to your Interactor script and use it for both types of objects. You specified that icon objects would only have three possible states and that enabled you to streamline their processing. Finally, after extending your lookup code to process auxiliary objects, you were able to allow picks on one object to affect multiple objects in preparation for non-default cursors.

In the next chapter, you will add the functionality that will manage the inventory's visual representation on screen and allow for as many objects as you need in your game.

CHAPTER 12

■ ■ ■

Managing the Inventory

Having taken care of most of the preliminary setup for the inventory system, in this chapter you will move on to layout and overflow. The inventory will need to keep an array of all objects it currently contains. For that reason, it makes sense to put inventory-related scripts on the GameManager script.

To start, let's add an internal array to hold the objects. Because it will be constantly growing and shrinking, it needs to be a JavaScript type array.

1. Open the Inventory scene from the book project.

2. Open the GameManager script.

3. Below the existing variables, add the following:

```
//Dynamic array of objects currently in inventory
private var currentInventoryObjects = new Array();
```

Next you will need to define the layout grid for placing the icons. This will fit the panel texture supplied. If you wish to create your own texture, you may need to adjust some of the numbers if you change the size or aspect ratio.

4. Add the following:

```
// inventory layout
private var startPos = 140;
private var iconSize = 90;
```

5. Save the script.

Our inventory grid will show nine items at once and scroll as needed, offering navigation arrows to access overflow. To be able to shift the inventory left and right, you will need to put all inventory objects into a parent gameObject and move it left or right, showing columns of icons as they fall within range of the inventory panel and hiding them when they do not.

1. Make sure you are not in Play mode.

2. Create an empty game object, and name it Inventory Items.

3. Drag the Jewel Icon onto the new game object.

4. Create another empty game object, and name it Inventory Group.

5. Drag the Inventory Items group and the Inventory Panel object into it.

6. In the Transforms, set the X and Y position to **0.0** and the Z to **0.0** for both new game objects.

7. Set the X and Y positions for the Inventory Panel object to **0.5** and **0.5**.

To test the functionality as you go, you will need several items to go into inventory. While developing the inventory system, you will need 11 active icons. If you wish to set up all fourteen from the Inventory Assets folder, simply deactivate the extra three.

8. Open the Inventory Assets folder in the Project view.

9. Go through the contents, changing each texture's Texture Type to GUI.

■ **Tip** The following instructions set up the inventory icons individually. You may prefer to duplicate the existing Jewel Icon object several times over and change its texture and array parameters instead. If you choose this route, be sure to copy and paste the texture names into the inventory object names directly. The inventory object names *must* match the texture names.

---

10. Select each icon texture, and, from the GameObject menu, choose Create Other, and create a GUI Texture object for it.

You can leave the PixelInset information at the default, as both the cursor and the inventory will resize according to their needs.

11. Drag each object into the Inventory Items group.

12. Select the Inventory Group object.

13. Assign it to the Inventory layer, and agree to adding its children as well (see Figure 12-1).

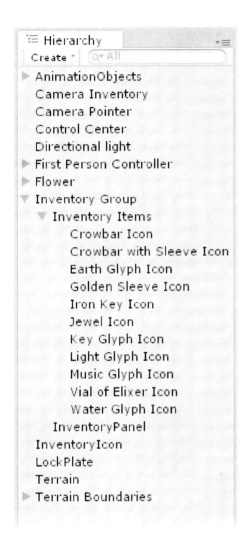

Figure 12-1. *The inventory objects in the Hierarchy view*

To make sure each object gets handled correctly, you need to add the `Interactor` script and fill out the data.

1. Add the `Interactor` script to each object.

2. Give each object one state to begin with, and fill out the metadata for the Object Name and Description (see Figure 12-2).

3. Change the array Size to 3 for Location, Visibility, Object Name, Description, Sound Clip, and Audio Delay.

4. Uncheck Object Is 3D and Animates for each.

5. Set Current State to 1, in inventory, for each object.

Next you need to add the `ObjectLookUp` script.

6. Add the `ObjectLookup` script to each inventory icon object.

7. For the States 0, 1 and 2, create 1 element each.

8. Repeat for the Reply States—remember the number of elements must match the Lookup States.

You do not need to fill out the action replies at this point.

You will eventually want some objects to go directly into inventory for future use. Others, especially when their use is obvious and in the same location as the objects with which they interact, will be better off as cursors immediately. An example of this would be a rock that is launched via physics as ammunition. In this case, with a rock pile nearby, and a limitless supply of rocks, game play is much smoother, avoiding inventory unless expressly entered.

In the first phase of the game, let's have all of the current icons go directly into inventory from state 0 and straight to cursors from state 1.

State 0 (not in scene): default,1

State 1 (in inventory): default,2

State 2 (as cursor): default,1

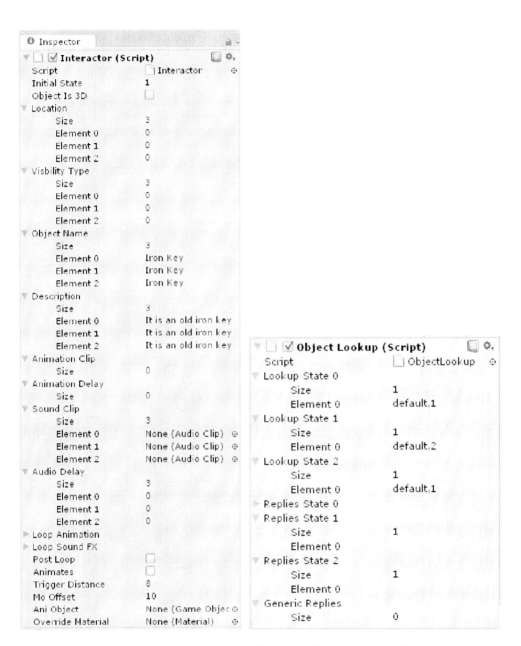

Figure 12-2. *Metadata and object look-up information for the Iron Key Icon object*

The Jewel Icon has already been set up but will need a couple of its parameters changed to match.

9. Change the Jewel Icon to match the others.

10. Click Play and make sure you have no errors. If you do have errors, check to make sure all objects' parameters are filled out correctly.

11. Stop Play mode.

12. Save your scene and save the project.

Before you start arranging the inventory, let's add a bit more functionality to the inventory mode. So far, to get in and out of inventory mode you can either pick the icon or use the keyboard to toggle the mode. It would be nice to be able to pick outside of the inventory panel to exit inventory mode, especially after selecting an inventory item as a cursor. Conversely, if you pick the panel in an empty area, it should "drop" the cursor object back into inventory.

For the latter, you will need to make a script just for the inventory panel. Because you have only one panel, it is perfectly OK to make a script solely for its use.

1. Create a new script, and add it to the Adventure Scripts folder.

2. Rename it `InventoryPanel`.

3. Add it to the `InventoryPanel` object in the Hierarchy view.

4. Open the new script.

5. Change the `Update` function to `OnMouseDown`, and add the temporary `print` statement:

```
function OnMouseDown () {

    print ("I've been hit!");

}
```

6. Save the script.

7. Click Play, go into Inventory mode, and pick the panel.

The message appears on the console's status line.

As long as you have an object to receive a pick, it is fairly easy to add instructions to it. Your challenge then is to make an object *behind* the inventory panel that covers the whole screen. It can, of course, be easily met by creating another GUI Texture object.

1. Stop Play mode.

2. Select the White texture from the Inventory Assets folder.

3. Set its Texture Type to GUI in the Inspector, and click Apply.

4. Create a new GUI Texture object.

5. Rename it `Inventory Screen`.

6. Add it to the `Inventory Group` object.

7. Assign it to the Inventory layer.

8. Set its size to something large, like **2048** Width by **2048** Height.

9. Select the White texture in the project view, increase its Max Size to 2048, and click Apply.

Theoretically, you ought to make the GUI Texture object size itself to the screen size dynamically. Realistically, unless you plan to use an image as a texture, an overly large size will probably work just as well.

1. Select the Inventory Screen object.

2. Set the Pixel Inset to **0** and **0**.

3. Set its X and Y Positions to **0**.

4. Set its Z Position to **-2** to put it back behind the Inventory Panel.

Make sure the Inventory Panel's Z Position is set to **-0**. At this point, the icons should all be at **0.5**, **0.5**, **0**.

5. Click Play, and decide on any changes it needs visually.

6. Stop Play mode and finalize the changes.

At this point, you need to make some executive decisions. You could set the texture's alpha to **0** to make it totally transparent, or you could change its Color and bring down the alpha amount until it is just noticeable enough to remind people they cannot interact with the 3D scene. Let's choose the latter for now, but feel free to change it if you wish.

1. Turn on the Camera Inventory's Camera component to see the inventory layer in the Game view.

2. Select the Inventory Screen object.

3. Adjust the opacity and color of the Inventory Screen's GUItexture component until you are happy with the effect (see Figure 12-3).

Figure 12-3. *The inventory screen with color and opacity adjusted*

4. Turn off the Camera Inventory's Camera component.

5. Create a new script in the Adventure Scripts folder.

6. Name it Inventory Screen.

7. Add it to the Inventory Screen object.

8. Open it in the script editor.

9. Change the Update function to a Start function, add the following to get the screen size, and then set the GUI Texture size:

```
function Start () {

    // set the GUI Texture  to match the screen size on startup
    guiTexture.pixelInset = Rect (0, 0, Screen.width, Screen.height);

}
```

Note that setting the Pixel Inset parameters works just like the UnityGUI controls.

To toggle inventory mode off when when clicking the screen, you will need to access the ToggleMode function over in the InventoryIcon script.

1. In the new InventoryScreen script, create an OnMouseDown function below the Start function:

```
function OnMouseDown () {

    GameObject.Find("Camera Inventory").SendMessage("ToggleMode");
```

}

2.   Save the script.

3.   Turn on Maximize on Play in the Game window.

4.   Click Play and go into Inventory mode.

5.   Click the Inventory Screen (outside of the panel) to exit Inventory mode.

If you did not test the screen in Maximize on Play, you will notice the screen is still the size of the original Game window after resizing. In this case, the window is resized after the Start function was called, so the inventory screen is not updated.

■ **Speed vs. Memory**   You may have noticed that in the foregoing script, you are not defining a variable to hold the camera, finding the camera in the Start function, and accessing its scripts elsewhere in this script. Instead, the script is finding the camera every time it needs to access it. Since it is accessed only once in this script, it shouldn't be a problem. While this method is slower, it doesn't use memory to store the camera. In a classic point and click adventure, speed is rarely an issue, whereas you might wish to spend memory on nice art assets instead.

Let's continue and finish the Inventory Panel's script. As specified, when you click the panel, the current icon, if it is not the default pointer, should go into inventory. So, really, all you need to do is check which texture is on the pointer, and then call the AddToInventory function from the GameManager.

1.   Open the InventoryPanel script.

Since you will need to identify the cursor prior to and during processing the pick, you should use the faster method to "introduce" the Control Center. You need to get the default cursor[texture] only once, so it makes sense to get it in the Start function as well.

2.   Add the following to the top of the script:

```
private var controlCenter : GameObject;
private var defaultCursor : Texture;
private var currentCursor : Texture;

function Start () {

    controlCenter = GameObject.Find("Control Center");
    defaultCursor = controlCenter.GetComponent(GameManager). defaultCursor;

}
```

3.   And now inside the OnMouseDown function, delete the print statement and add the following:

```
// check the current cursor against the default cursor

currentCursor = controlCenter.GetComponent(GameManager). currentCursor;

if (currentCursor == defaultCursor) return; // take no action—it was the default cursor

else { // there is an action icon as cursor, so process it

    // use the cursor texture's name to find the GUI Texture object of the same name
    var addObject = GameObject.Find(currentCursor.name);

    // update the icon's current state to in inventory, 1, in the Interactor script
    addObject.GetComponent(Interactor).currentState = 1;

    //after you store the cursor's texture, reset the cursor to default
    controlCenter.SendMessage("ResetCursor");

    // and add the new object to inventory
    controlCenter.SendMessage("AddToInventory", addObject);

}
```

Since the texture on the current cursor is also the name of the GUI Texture object, you can use its name to locate the object, update its current state, and pass it into the AddToInventory function on the GameManager script.

You should now be able to do a bit more testing. You should be able to go into inventory, click the pile of icons, "drop" the selected one by clicking an empty spot, and then select another. You should not yet be able to pick any object, 2D or 3D, with anything other than the default cursor.

1. Click Play.

2. Pick and drop each of the icons in inventory.

3. Check the console message for each pick.

The console reports the objects going back into inventory, but you have not written the code for it, so they are not yet visible after being dropped.

■ **Tip** If you are getting "out of range" errors, go back and check the inventory objects' Interactor metadata to make sure all of the arrays except the animation-related arrays have three elements. Also check the ObjectLookUp data to make sure both the first three state arrays and the first three reply arrays also have three elements.

If you have other errors, make sure the object names are exactly the same as the texture names (capitalization, spaces, and spelling).

---

4. Save your scene and save your project.

Tags

As you may have guessed, you will eventually need to cycle through the game objects at the start of the game to populate the inventory and put objects into their startup states. In Unity, you can "tag" objects for easier, more efficient processing. Tags are related to layers but are more generic. Let's create a tag for both action objects and inventory items.

1. Click the Layers drop-down at the top right corner of the editor.

2. Select Edit Layers.

3. Click the expand arrow next to Tags at the top of the Inspector.

4. Add ActionObject to element 0.

5. Add InventoryObject to element 1.

The array size increases automatically each time you declare a new tag/element.

6. Select each action object in the scene, and assign the ActionObject tag to it.

7. Select each inventory object, and assign the InventoryObject tag to it (see Figure 12-4).

Figure 12-4. *Adding tags*

Now that you have the objects tagged, you can put them into an array so you will be able to arrange them. You've already declared the currentInventoryObjects array, so now you can go about filling it up.

1. Open the GameManager script.

Inside the Start function, you need to add a local variable to hold the inventory objects as you find them and then go through it and assign them to the inventory array.

2. In the Start function, add the following code:

```
var iObjects = GameObject.FindGameObjectsWithTag ("InventoryObject");

// go through the scene and put the tagged objects in the array
for (var iObject in iObjects) {

    print(iObject.name);
    currentInventoryObjects.Add(iObject); // add the object to the array

}
```

3. Save the script.

4. Click Play.

5. Inspect the console to see the list of objects (see Figure 12-5).

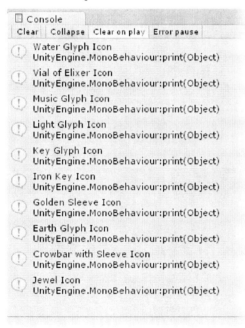

Figure 12-5. *The tagged inventory objects*

6. Stop Play mode.

If you set up all fourteen icons and disabled three, you will notice that the three disabled objects were not found. This is a key concept that you will run into later in the game.

Now that you can generate a list, you need to take it one step further. You need to add *only* the objects whose Current State is 1 (in inventory), as the purpose of the list is to keep track of the current contents of inventory.

1. Change the code as follows:

```
var iObjects = GameObject.FindGameObjectsWithTag ("InventoryObject");

// go through the scene and put the tagged objects in the array
for (var iObject in iObjects) {

    //only if its current state is 1 ( in inventory)
    if(iObject.GetComponent(Interactor).initialState == 1) {
    print (iObject.name);
    currentInventoryObjects.Add(iObject);
    }
}
```

2. Save the script.

3. Select the Crowbar with Sleeve Icon in the Hierarchy view.

4. Set its Initial State to **0**.

5. Click Play, and inspect the console to make sure the Crowbar with Sleeve Icon is no longer included.

6. Comment out the print statement.

7. Save the script.

Not being included in the inventory array does not prevent the object from showing or being drawn in the inventory panel. For that, you need to check its state at startup. In the next chapter, you will deal with visibility in general, but for now you can at least make sure the inventory objects behave at startup.

1. Open the Interactor script.

2. At the bottom of the Start function, add the following line below the currentObjectDescription = description line:

```
//turn off visibility for inventory icons that are not yet in the scene
if (currentState == 0 && !objectIs3D) guiTexture.enabled = false;
```

3. Save the script.

As long as the icons are all piled in the same place, you probably won't be able to tell if the Crowbar with Sleeve Icon is being drawn. Feel free to test visibility with whatever icon is showing at the top of the stack.

4. Stop Play mode.

5. Set all inventory objects back to the Initial State of **1**.

Inventory Layout

Now you can start to arrange the icons. You are going to be arranging them in columns of three, using the layout variables you defined earlier. Since you will need to re-arrange them each time one is added or removed, let's create a function you can call when needed.

1. Open the GameManager script.

2. Create the function for the grid arrangement:

```
// arrange icons in inventory
function InventoryGrid () {


} // close the function
```

You have the starting offset for the icons from the startPos variable. It starts the first icon at the center of the slot, but the icons are actually positioned from their upper left as they are also used as pointer textures. In screen space, 0,0 is at the lower left of the viewport, so the x offset will be a negative direction adjustment of the start position and the y offset will be a positive.

Both x and y start positions are also dependent on the icon size, as is the space between the rows and columns. The first thing to do is adjust those values to fit the icon size.

3. Add the following local variables inside the InventoryGrid function:

```
var xPos = -startPos - iconSize/2;  // adjust column offset start position according to icon
var spacer = startPos - iconSize; // calculate the spacer size
```

When iterating through an array, you always need to know how long it is so you can stop before it throws an *index out of range* error. Because the length may change every time you re-arrange the grid, you will need to define its variable also as local inside the function.

4. Add the following line to get the inventory array's length:

```
var iLength = currentInventoryObjects.length; // length of the array
```

And then you will need to set up the for loop to iterate through the array. As mentioned earlier, you will process the elements in threes, as the position of the rows will always be the same. In this script you will use k as the counter, starting it at element 0, and continuing to increment it by 3 while the k value is less than the array length.

5. Add the for loop:

```
for (var k = 0; k < iLength; k = k + 3) {
```

Since the y position needs to be reset for each new column, it gets adjusted and set inside the for loop.

6. Add the first row's icon's position PixelInset information:

```
//row 1
var yPos = startPos - iconSize/2;
currentInventoryObjects[k].guiTexture.pixelInset = Rect(xPos, yPos, iconSize,iconSize);
```

Because you are incrementing the counter by three, you could conceivably go beyond the array length for the k+1 and k+2 elements; therefore, they need to be checked before the code tries to position a nonexistent element and throws an error.

7. Add the following with its length-checking conditional:

```
//row 2
yPos = yPos - iconSize - spacer;
if (k + 1 < iLength)
    currentInventoryObjects[k+1].guiTexture.pixelInset = Rect(xPos, yPos, iconSize,iconSize);
```

   8.   Add the code for the third row:

```
//row 3
yPos = yPos - iconSize - spacer;
if (k + 2 < iLength)
    currentInventoryObjects[k+2].guiTexture.pixelInset = Rect(xPos, yPos, iconSize,iconSize);
```
      And finally, you will increment the column position for the next group of three icons, add curly brackets to close the for loop, and then close the function.

   9.   Add the following code:

```
xPos = xPos + iconSize + spacer;   // update column position for the next group
```

```
} // close for loop
```
      Before you can test the function, you need to call it from somewhere. The first place will be as soon as the objects have gone into the inventory array in the GameManager's Start function.

   10.   Near the bottom of the GameManager's Start function, add the following to call your new function:

```
InventoryGrid();// arrange the inventory icons
```

   11.   Save the script.

   12.   Set the Crowbar with Sleeve Icon's Initial State back to 1 if you haven't already done so.

   13.   Click Play, and check the inventory to see how the code worked.

   Note the overflow of two of the objects.

▓ **Tip**   If you have more than one object in the center position, check to make sure the Initial state is 1. You have not yet handled visibility for state 0 on start.

   The inventory panel is not symmetrical, so the icons are a bit low. Rather than fuss with the arranging script, you can easily adjust the position of their parent, the Inventory Items game object.

   1.   While still in play mode, with the inventory showing, change the Inventory Items Y Position to about **0.035**.

   2.   Stop Play mode, and enter it again to make it permanent (see Figure 12-6).

Figure 12-6. *Preliminary inventory layout*

3. Save the scene and save the project.

4. Click Play and test the inventory.

Remember that you have not yet hooked up functionality for non-default cursors picking 2D or 3D objects.

▨ **Tip**   If you wish to create your own inventory panel and adjust the spacing of the inventory grid, you can change the icon textures to normal maps to see their true size, or load solid textures and then take a screenshot of the layout into your favorite paint program. If you prefer, you could just do the math and count pixels.

Inventory Overflow

So far the inventory works well for a maximum of nine objects in inventory at any one time. It fails visibly when the number exceeds that, as the fourth column of items falls to the right of the panel, just as you would expect. Concurrent with shifting the Inventory Items gameObject left and right, you will also need to control the visibility of the overflow columns.

Before you tackle visibility, you can go ahead and get the shifting working.

1. Turn on the Camera Inventory's Camera component if it is not already on.

2. Create a `LeftArrow` and `RightArrow` GUI Texture object from the images of the same name in the Inventory Assets folder.

3. Change their Texture Type to GUI, and click Apply.

4. Change their Height and Width to **64**.

5. Add them to the Inventory layer.

6. Move them into the `Inventory Group` gameObject.

7. Set their Y PixelInset to -**245**.

8. Set the left arrow's X PixelInset to -**235**.

9. Set the right arrow's X PixelInset to **166**.

10. Click Play, and go into inventory mode to observe their placement (see Figure 12-7).

Feel free to adjust their position further.

Figure 12-7. *Inventory arrows added*

You will need to make a behavior for mouse-over and the functionality for picking. Let's keep it simple and just increase the Color to a light gray. Remember the default for textures is a middle gray.

1. Create a new script in the Adventure Scripts folder.

2. Name it `ClickArrows`.

3. Change the `Update` function to an `OnMouseEnter`.

4. Add the following line so the function looks as follows:

```
function OnMouseEnter () {

guiTexture .color = Color(0.75,0.75,0.75,1); // brighten the texture

}
```

5. And for its `OnMouseExit` counterpart, add the following:

```
function OnMouseExit () {

guiTexture .color = Color.gray; // return the texture to normal

}
```

6. Save the script.

7. Add it to the `ArrowLeft` and `ArrowRight` objects.

8. Click Play and test the mouse-over.

Next you need to tell the Inventory Items group to move left on mouse-down. You will need to add conditions later, but for now let's just get it started. First you need to introduce the Inventory Items object and the `Control Center` object into the `ClickArrows` script.

1. Add the following private variables at the top of the script:

```
private var inventoryItems : GameObject;
private var controlCenter : GameObject;
private var gridOffset : int; // gridoffset
```

2. Create a `Start` function, and add the following to get access to the grid offset variable and be able to move the grid:

```
function Start () {

    inventoryItems = GameObject.Find("Inventory Items");
    controlCenter = GameObject.Find("Control Center");
    gridOffset = controlCenter.GetComponent(GameManager).startPos;

}
```

As it stands, you are positioning the icons in *pixels*, but must shift the parent game object in *percent of screen*. Fortunately, since you have access to screen width and height, you can do a little math to get the answer in percent. After getting the width of the screen, you can use it to divide the grid offset or start position, startPos, from the `GameManager` script and arrive at the percent of the screen that the Inventory Items group needs to move left or right.

3. Add the following function:

```
function OnMouseDown () {

// convert screen width from percent to pixels for shift amount
 var amount = 1.0 * gridOffset/Screen.width; // divide screen width by the startPos

   if (this.name == "ArrowLeft")  {
      amount = -amount;

   }
   inventoryItems.transform.position.x =  inventoryItems.transform.position.x + amount;

}
```

4.   Save the script.

5.   Click Play and test the arrows (see Figure 12-8).

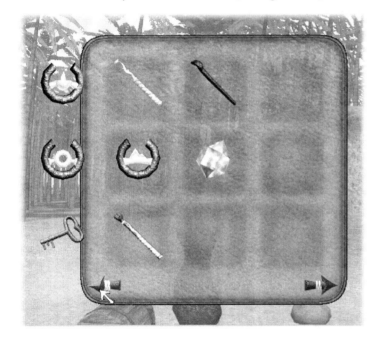

Figure 12-8. *The arrows activated*

Note where you decide which way to move the panel by checking to see what object was picked. Remember that both arrows use the same script.

■ **Tip**   Multiplying the amount by 1.0, a float rather than integer, insures that you will not get 0 when you divide the two integer numbers as they are automatically cast as floats at that point.

Now that the icon grid shifting is working, you need a way to determine which icons are shown. If you consider the default position to be position 0, a left click -1, and a right click +1, you can figure out which columns to hide. Any number less than 0 multiplied by 3 will be the number of elements from the start of the array that need to be hidden. The next nine will be visible, and any after that will be hidden.

Therefore, you need to have a click counter variable that represents the grid's position and sends itself off to the GameManager script where the layout is being handled. The catch is that it needs to be stored and accessed from *only one* location, and you have *two* buttons that use the same script. To solve this, you will put it in the GameManager, as that script needs to have access to it anyway.

1.   Open the ClickArrows script.

2.   Add the following variable to the top of the script to store the updated variable when you get it:

```
private var gridPosition : int;
```

Next you need to get the latest value from the GameManager:

3.   At the top of the OnMouseDown function, add:

```
gridPosition = controlCenter.GetComponent(GameManager).gridPosition; // get latest↵
 gridPosition
```

4.   Inside the if (this.name == "ArrowLeft") clause, add the following below amount = - amount:

```
gridPosition ++; // increment the gridPosition counter by 1
```

5.   And immediately below the if block, add an else for right arrow picks:

```
// else it was the right arrow
else {

   gridPosition --; // decrement the gridPosition counter by 1

}
```

6.   And finally, send the updated gridPosition off to the GameManager by adding the following:

```
controlCenter.GetComponent(GameManager).gridPosition = gridPosition; // send it off
```

7.   Save the script.

Before you can test, you need to add the gridPosition variable to the GameManager.

1.   Open the GameManager script.

2.   Add the variable to the main group of variables at the top of the script:

```
var gridPosition = 0; // the default position of the inventory grid
```

3.   Save the script.

4.   Select the ControlCenter object.

5.   Click Play and test, watching the value of the Grid Position variable in the Inspector (see Figure 12-9).

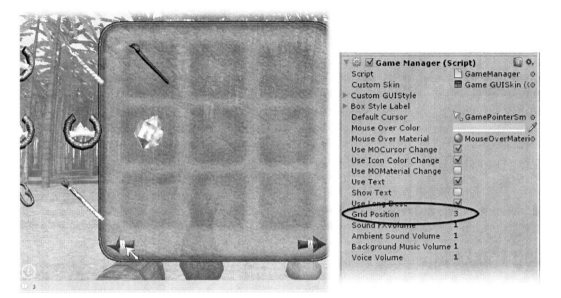

Figure 12-9. *The Inspector reporting the grid position, 3*

The counter works nicely. However, you also need to consider what will happen when a new object is added to the inventory. If the object in question's element number is divisible by three, it is at the top of a *new* column. If it is greater than element 8 (remember arrays start at element 0), its new column will be off the grid. This means that when a new object is added, you should probably shift the grid over to make its column visible—especially if the user drops the object in from a cursor rather than when it goes straight into inventory from a pick event.

The result of this logic is that besides having the grid position sending its updates to the GameManager script, the InventoryGrid function may need to update the position on its own. The conclusion here is that instead of putting the grid shifting functionality in the OnMouseDown function, it should have its own function that is called from the OnMouseDown function. Let's take care of that before you get any further.

1. Change the OnMouseDown function name to ShiftGrid; it will also need to have a direction argument passed to it:

```
function ShiftGrid (shiftDirection: String) {
```

2. Change:

```
if(this.name == "ArrowLeft") {
```

to the following so it will use the argument that will be passed to it:

```
if (shiftDirection == "left")  {
```

■ **Note**   You *could* use a Boolean, true or false, for the variable type to represent left or right because it uses fewer resources, but using a string keeps it more readable. For this script, you will use the more readable option.

---

3. To call the new function, you will make a replacement OnMouseDown function as follows:

```
function OnMouseDown () {

    if (this.name == "ArrowLeft")  var shiftDirection = "left";
    else shiftDirection = "right";

    ShiftGrid (shiftDirection);

}
```

4. Save the script.

5. Click Play, and test to make sure everything still works.

6. Save the scene and save the project.

Setting the Limits

Our inventory grid shifts nicely from left to right with the arrows using your new ShiftArrows function. The next logical step is to limit the use of the arrows according to the number of objects in inventory and the grid's current position. This will need to be done both when the arrows are picked and any time the inventory grid is updated.

To visually indicate an unavailable arrow, you can change its opacity so it appears grayed out. It should also, at that point, no longer react to mouse-overs. Let's start by creating a flag to track its state. Chances are the inventory will have less than ten items on startup, so you can initialize the active state for either arrow to false.

1. Open the ClickArrows script.

2. Add the following private variable near the top of the script:

```
private var isActive : boolean = false; // keeps track of state
```

3. Inside the OnMouseEnter function, above the guiTexture.color line, add the following:

```
if (!isActive) return; // skip the mouse-over functionality if the arrow is not active
```
And to prevent a pick registering, you will need to add the same to the OnMouseDown function.

4. Inside the OnMouseDown function, at the top add the following:

```
if (!isActive) return; // skip the mouse-down functionality if the arrow is not active
```
Because you will need to check the limits when updating the grid *and* picking the arrows, it would be nice to have a function that can be called from either script. You will pass in the new state of the arrow as an argument.

5. Add the following function:

```
function ArrowState (newState) {

    isActive = newState;
    if (isActive) guiTexture.color  = Color(0.5,0.5,0.5,1.0); // full opacity
```

```
    else guiTexture.color = Color(0.5,0.5,0.5,0.2);// half opacity
}
```

If you were to save the script and click play, you would notice that the arrows are not yet grayed out even though you set the starting isActive value to false. The reason is that you have not yet called the function that adjusts the opacity. One logical place to call it will be the Start function so it can be initialized on startup.

6.   Add the following line inside the Start function:

```
ArrowState (isActive); // update the arrow opacity
```

7.   Save the script.

8.   Click Play and test.

Everything works fine until you mouse off the arrows, at which point their opacity reverts to the default color—*including* the alpha value. Take a moment to look at the OnMouseExit function to see why the arrow's transparency gets lost. The last value in the Color variable is 1.0. Because you are *not* using the default color when inactive, you cannot ignore the OnMouseExit function as you have been able to in other scripts. Fortunately this is easily remedied.

1.   Copy and paste the same line you added to the OnMouseEnter to the OnMouseExit function:

```
if (!isActive) return; // skip the mouse exit functionality if the arrow is not active
```

2.   Save the script.

3.   Test the mouse-off functionality again.

Everything works as expected. There is no activity with the arrows.

4.   Change the isActive variable to true, and retest to make sure the arrows still work when active.

You will work out the logic for isActive next, as what state each arrow is in is dependent on the position of the inventory grid as much as the number of objects in inventory.

Inventory Grid Limits

You need to do a few calculations to manage the inventory items' visibility. Let's start with the InventoryGrid function where the items are first laid out. There are only three possibilities for the items. They are either to the left of the grid, on the grid, or to the right of the grid.

To calculate where an item is, you need to know the current grid position. If you multiply the grid position by three (the number of icons in each column), you can get the array element number at the top row of the grid position. Now you can check whether the item is less than the top element, gridPosition * 3, or greater than the top element plus eight, gridPosition * 3 + 8, which puts it off the grid to the right. You need to deal with only top elements, e.g., row one, because all the rest of the rows, two and three, inherit the same visibility as row one.

1. Try the calculations on some random top elements in the following figures (see Figure 12-10).

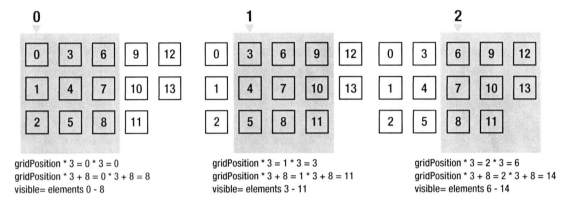

gridPosition * 3 = 0 * 3 = 0
gridPosition * 3 + 8 = 0 * 3 + 8 = 8
visible= elements 0 - 8

gridPosition * 3 = 1 * 3 = 3
gridPosition * 3 + 8 = 1 * 3 + 8 = 11
visible= elements 3 - 11

gridPosition * 3 = 2 * 3 = 6
gridPosition * 3 + 8 = 2 * 3 + 8 = 14
visible= elements 6 - 14

Figure 12-10. *Possible scenarios for inventory grid's current position*

The script for the visibility checking will be only a couple of lines, but it makes more sense to hide the ones that will be hidden *before* they are placed outside the grid, and show the ones that are on the grid *after* they are in place. It will also keep the code cleaner to use functions to handle the actual hiding and showing of the icons. For those reasons, you will use a variable, local to the InventoryGrid function, to represent visibility. You will add the new variable, and then set up the conditional that determines whether it will be true or false for each column of elements. To help check the possibilities quicker, you will also create a variable called iLength to keep track of the length of the inventory array.

2. Open the GameManager script.

3. In the //inventory layout section, add the following variable:

```
private var iLength : int; // length of the array of inventory objects
```
As soon as you fill the array in the Start function, you can get the length.

4. Above the InventoryGrid() line in the Start function, add the following:

```
iLength = currentInventoryObjects.length;
```

5. Near the top of the InventoryGrid function, add the following local variable:

```
var visibility: boolean; // variable for column visibility
```

6. Beneath the for (k = 0; k < iLength; k = k + 3)… statement, add the visibility checker:

```
//calculate the column visibility for the top element, k, using the or, ||
if (k < gridPosition * 3 || k > gridPosition * 3 + 8) visibility = false;
else visibility = true; // else it was on the grid
```
To do the actual hiding and showing of the objects, you will make a couple of functions, one to show and one to hide. You could make a single function for both, but then you would need to pass in both the top element for the column *and* whether the column will need to be shown or hidden.

While that is not an issue when calling the function inside the *same* script, it will prevent you from using the SendMessage command from other scripts as it can take only one argument.

Let's add the show function first. The GameManager script already "knows" all the objects in its currentInventoryObjects array, so you will be enabling their guiTextures.

■ **Tip**   If you wanted to use 3D objects from another camera view, you would need to enable and disable the object's MeshRenderer. You could adapt this script by checking the objects' objectIs3D state and having code for both.

---

7.   Add the following function to the GameManager script:

```
function ShowColumn ( topElement : int) {

    // show the elements in the 3 rows for the top element's column
    currentInventoryObjects[topElement].guiTexture.enabled = true; // row 1 element
    if (topElement + 1 < iLength)
        currentInventoryObjects[topElement + 1].guiTexture.enabled = true; // row 2
    if (topElement + 2 < iLength)
        currentInventoryObjects[topElement + 2].guiTexture.enabled = true; // row 3
}
```

Note that you need to check if the second and third row elements exist before you set their visibility.

8.   Next add the ShowColumn's counterpart, the HideColumn function:

```
function HideColumn ( topElement : int) {

    // hide the elements in the 3 rows for the top element's column
    currentInventoryObjects[topElement].guiTexture.enabled = false; // row 1 element
    if (topElement + 1 < iLength)
        currentInventoryObjects[topElement + 1].guiTexture.enabled = false; // row 2
    if (topElement + 2 < iLength)
        currentInventoryObjects[topElement + 2].guiTexture.enabled = false; // row 3
}
```

And now you can call the functions within the InventoryGrid function.

9.   Below the visibility check conditional you just added and above the //row 1 positioning line, add the following:

```
// if elements need to be hidden, do so before positioning
if (!visibility) HideColumn(k); // send the top row element for processing
```

Below the //row 3 positioning and above the xPos incrementing line, add the show function:

```
// if elements need to be shown, do so after positioning
if (visibility) ShowColumn(k); // send the top row element for processing
```

10.   Save the script.

11.   Click Play and bring up the inventory.

The arrows have not yet been processed, but you should no longer see the overflow icons on startup (see Figure 12-11).

Figure 12-11. *No overflow icons on startup*

To handle the arrow states, you need to check only the grid position and the length of the array. If the grid position is greater than 0, you know there are icons to the left, so you need to activate the right arrow to access them. If there are more elements than grid positions (grid position times 3 plus 8, those on the grid) you need to activate the left arrow to access those. In both cases, if the condition is not met, that arrow will be deactivated.

Since there is no reason to calculate the arrows after each array element, you will process them once the item positioning is finished.

1. Add the following lines to check for items left of the grid just above the closing curly bracket of the InventoryGrid function:

```
//if there are arrows to the left of the grid, activate the right arrow
if (gridPosition > 0) GameObject.Find("ArrowRight").SendMessage("ArrowState", true);
else GameObject.Find("ArrowRight").SendMessage("ArrowState", false);
```

2. And to check the right side overflow, add the following:

```
//if there are arrows to the right of the grid, activate the left arrow
if (iLength > gridPosition * 3 + 9)
  GameObject.Find("ArrowLeft").SendMessage("ArrowState", true);
else GameObject.Find("ArrowLeft").SendMessage("ArrowState", false);
```

▓ **Tip**   Remember, arrays start at element 0, so the length might be 10, but the last element number would be 9.

---

   3.   Save the script.

   4.   Click Play and open the inventory.

The arrow states are correct as long as you don't shift the grid with them.

   5.   Stop Play mode.

   6.   Disable several of the icons at the top of the Inspector so you have less than ten enabled.

   7.   Click Play, and check that both arrows are disabled.

   8.   Enable all of the test icons again.

Arrow Limits

Now that the inventory grid works on update, you will need to get the arrow state and item visibility working when the grid position is changed—in other words, when the player clicks the arrows.

Whereas you iterated through the entire inventory array in the InventoryGrid function, for the arrows, you need to worry about only the columns to the left and to the right of the grid for visibility.

When you click the left arrow, the current grid position column will move right and must be hidden. In the last section, you created a function, HideColumn, to do just that. It wants the top element number to be able to process the elements column. As the column is currently the grid position column, you can multiply it by three and send the resulting top element number off to the hide function. You need to do that before you update the grid position.

   1.   Open the ClickArrows script.

   2.   Inside the ShiftGrid function, inside the (shiftDirection == "left") conditional, below the amount = -amount line, add the following:

```
// hide the column on the left, send its top element
controlCenter.SendMessage("HideColumn", gridPosition *3);
```

   3.   At the bottom of the left conditional, beneath the gridPosition ++ line, you can now tell it to show the new column on the right:

```
// show the new column on the right, send its top element
controlCenter.SendMessage("ShowColumn", gridPosition *3 + 6);
```

And now, the arrows can be managed. By definition, because the left arrow just moved a column to the left of the grid, the right arrow must be activated. However, it was the left arrow whose instance of the script you are processing, so the right arrow must be "found" before it can be activated by calling its ArrowState function and passing it a true argument.

   4.   Add the following line below the ShowColumn line you just added:

```
//activate the right arrow
```

```
GameObject.Find("ArrowRight").SendMessage("ArrowState", true);
```
The left arrow moves the grid to the left, so it needs to know how long the inventory array is in case there are no more columns to the right of the grid and it needs to be deactivated. You need to access the number of inventory items only once in the ClickArrows script, but the line will get rather long, so you will create a local variable for it to make it easier to read.

5. Add the following beneath the lines you just added:

```
// if there are no more columns to the right, disable the left arrow
var iLength = controlCenter.GetComponent(GameManager).currentInventoryObjects.length;
 if(gridPosition *  3 + 9 >= iLength) ArrowState(false); // deactivate the left arrow
```

6. Save the script.

7. Click Play and test the left arrow.

It should stay active until the end of the inventory array and then become inactive.
The right arrow will be slightly easier to process. First you will deal with the visibility.

1. In the else clause for the right arrow, add the following above the gridPosition -- line to hide the far right column as it is shifted right:

```
//hide the column on the right, send its top element
controlCenter.SendMessage("HideColumn", gridPosition *3 +6);
```

2. At the bottom of the else clause, after the gridPosition -- line, add the following to show the new grid position column from the left:

```
//show the column on the left, send its top element
controlCenter.SendMessage("ShowColumn", gridPosition *3);
```
Because you just shifted a row to the right, by definition, the left arrow needs to be activated. Since you are in the right arrow's instance of the script if you are in the else clause, it needs to be "found" before activating.

3. Add the following below the lines you just added:

```
//activate the left arrow
GameObject.Find("ArrowLeft").SendMessage("ArrowState", true);
```
For the right arrow, you need to check only for the grid position. If it is 0, the right arrow needs to be deactivated.

4. Add the following beneath the last line you added:

```
if(gridPosition == 0) ArrowState(false);// deactivate the right arrow
```

5. Save the script.

6. Click Play and test the inventory arrows (see Figure 12-12).

Figure 12-12. *The grid shifted left*

1. This time, visibility and arrow states should all be up and running correctly. If you added the remaining three icons, you may wish to enable them and test for one more column.

2. Save the scene and save the project.

Adding and Removing Objects from Inventory

Now that you've got the mechanics of the extensible inventory working, you can go back and see about adding and removing the icons from inventory. It already hides, shows, and changes the state on the icons. Now you just need to fill out the blocked-in functions.

Let's think about the functionality for a moment. When you remove an object, e.g., pick it with the default cursor, you will need to remove it from the array, and then call the InventoryGrid function to update the grid. That is probably the most straightforward action.

When you add an object, either by picking a scene object, or picking an empty area of the inventory panel, the object will be added to the end of the array. At its simplest, the grid will be updated, but if the inventory is open, one would expect the grid position to be shifted to the end to show the object. This will take a bit more work as it involves shifting the grid, changing arrow states, and other things.

The final scenario is when an object is dropped on another object. Right now, the cursor is dropped as an addition to inventory. Eventually, you need to check if the objects can combine to make a new object. In that case, both objects need to be removed from inventory and scene, and then a new object set in its position in inventory. While this scenario avoids a grid shifting, it will require a bit of work to get everything in the right place. The results, however, will be worth the extra work.

Let's start with what appears to be the simplest—removing an object from inventory.

Removing Objects from Inventory

The quickest way to find the element number of a picked object will be to store it on the object itself. You can assign the number when the object is added to inventory.

1. Open the Interactor script.

2. In the //Gain access to section of the variables, add the following:

```
private var iElement = 0; // will hold the object's element in inventory number
```

3. Save the script.

Now you need to assign the element numbers as you add the objects to inventory in the GameManager's Start function.

4. Open the GameManager script.

5. Above the var iObjects = line, in the Start function, add the following:

```
var element = 0; // initialize a counter
```

6. Inside the for loop, after the currentInventoryObjects.Add line, add the following:

```
iObject.GetComponent(Interactor).iElement = element; // assign the element number to↩
 the current object
element ++; //increment the element
```

7. Save the script.

You ought to make sure the element numbers are getting assigned.

1. Open the Interactor script.

2. Temporarily remove the private from the iElement var.

3. Click Play, and check the inventory objects at runtime for their element numbers (see Figure 12-13).

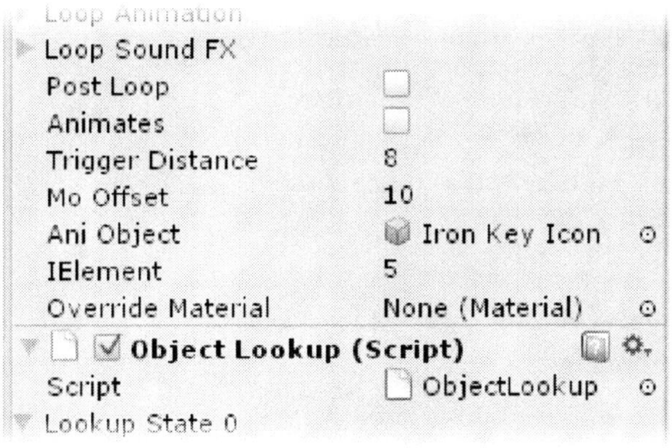

Loop Animation
Loop Sound FX
Post Loop
Animates
Trigger Distance   8
Mo Offset   10
Ani Object   Iron Key Icon   ⊙
IElement   5
Override Material   None (Material)   ⊙
☑ Object Lookup (Script)   ⚙
Script   ObjectLookup   ⊙
Lookup State 0

Figure 12-13. *Inventory element number*

4. Replace the private, and save the Interactor script.

5. Save the scene and save the project.

Next, you will finish the RemoveFromInventory function, also in the GameManager. You will be using RemoveAt() to remove an item from its current position in the array.

■ **Tip**   For more array functionality, search for "array" in the scripting help and look for the available functions at the bottom of the entry.

---

1. Open the GameManager script.

2. Inside the RemoveFromInventory function, below the print statement, add the following:

```
// retrieve its inventory element number
var iElement = object.GetComponent(Interactor).iElement;
//remove that element from the currentInventoryObjects array
currentInventoryObjects.RemoveAt(iElement);
iLength = currentInventoryObjects.length;// update array length
// update the grid
InventoryGrid();
```

3. Delete or comment out the print line.

4. Save the script.

5. Click Play.

6. Pick one of the inventory objects.

7. Stop Play mode.

The object becomes the cursor as before, but this time, the inventory closes the gap and updates itself. There are a couple more things you need to do.

If you start removing objects, you will get an out-of-range error at some point.

1. Adjust the amount of active inventory items you have until they number 13, or 15 (use Ctrl + D to duplicate a few of the icons or enable a couple of the deactivated ones).

2. Click Play and open the inventory.

3. Click the left arrow until you are at the end of the grid.

You should see one icon at the top of the last column.

4. Pick and drop several of the icons.

You should now have at least one empty column.
The console will eventually report an out-of-range error.

5. Open the console, and double-click the error line to see where the problem is.

One possible error is in the HideColumn function. Earlier on, you made the assumption that whenever the grid was shifted, there would at least be an icon at the top of the column. Now that you are removing elements, the assumption is no longer valid. Fortunately, it is an easy fix. You *could* copy the syntax from the row two and three lines using if (topElement < iLength) to bypass the error, but there is really no reason to check the other two when failing the first condition tells you that you are dealing with an empty column. The better solution is to check for the opposite and return if *it* evaluates as true.

6. Add the following at the top of the HideColumn function:

```
if (topElement >= iLength) return; // there are no icons in the column, return
```

7. Add the same line to the top of the ShowColumn function.

8. Save the script.

9. Click Play, and remove only the last icon each time.

This time there is no error, but you still have the empty column to address. You already have a function that will shift the grid. Right now it is being used solely by the arrows, but since you were clever enough to turn it into a function, you can now call it from anywhere you wish. You will, however, need to set the condition to evaluate to true when the top element of the third column doesn't exist, e.g., its number is greater than or equal to (remember elements start at 0) the number of items in inventory.

1. Inside the RemoveFromInventory function, above the InventoryGrid() line, add the following:

```
//if the third column is empty, shift the grid to the right
if(gridPosition * 3 + 6 >= iLength  && iLength>= 9)
GameObject.Find("ArrowRight").SendMessage("ShiftGrid", "right");
```

2. Save the script.

3. Click Play and test.

The grid behaves regardless of where you remove an object, but will throw an error if you remove any but the last in the inventory.

So far, things are looking pretty good—except for one detail that may have not occurred to you as you were working at the end of the grid. If you remove an item from any other position than the last, all of the items *past* the one that was removed now have the wrong element number.

Since removing an element is the only action that will cause the elements to shift like that, you can remedy the problem by iterating through the array from the insertion point and re-assigning the rest of the elements inside the RemoveFromInventory function. As it will not affect the grid updating, you can add it after the call to that function.

4. After the InventoryGrid() line, add the following:

```
//update the element number for items past the removal point
for (var x = iElement; x < iLength; x++){
    currentInventoryObjects[x].GetComponent(Interactor).iElement = x;
}
```

5. Save the script.

6. Click Play and test.

7. Save the scene and save the project.

Adding Objects to Inventory

Let's move on to the AddToInventory function. To start you will just get it adding the object to the end of the array and leaving the grid position as is. You are already passing the picked object into the function, so the first line will use another array function, Add().

1. Open the GameManager script.

2. Delete or comment out the print statement, and add the following to the AddToInventory function:

```
// add the new object to the current inventory array
currentInventoryObjects.Add(object);
```

Once the new object goes into inventory, you need to get its element number and store it in the object's iElement parameter.

3. Add the following to store the object's new element number:

```
// update the object's inventory number
object.GetComponent(Interactor).iElement = currentInventoryObjects.length-1;
```

4. Next, add the update for the iLength variable to reflect the addition to the array:

```
iLength = currentInventoryObjects.length;// update array length
```

5. And finally, call the InventoryGrid function:

```
//Update the grid
InventoryGrid();
```

6. Save the script.

7. Click Play, and try removing and adding objects to the inventory.

So far, so good—the dropped item is returned to the end of the inventory. Let's tackle the grid page next. As usual, you need to consider first the desired functionality and then work out the details and dependencies. When you manually add an item to inventory, that is, take the cursor object into inventory and drop it, you would like the grid to go to the last page so you can see it.

Because you will be using the AddToInventory function to add 3D objects from the scene directly into inventory, you must first check whether the inventory is open by looking at the iMode variable.

8. Add the following conditional below the InventoryGrid() line:

```
if (iMode && iLength > 9) {



}
```

If you are in inventory mode, and there are more than nine items, you need to call the ShiftGrid function until you are at the end. This introduces new functionality in the form of the While function. As long as the expression being evaluated returns true, the instructions will be carried out.

9. Add the following inside the if(iMode… block:

```
// shift the grid to the right until you get to the end where the new object was added
while (gridPosition * 3 + 9 < iLength)
GameObject.Find("ArrowLeft").SendMessage("ShiftGrid", "left");
```

10. Save the script.

11. Click Play and test the functionality.

The grid jumps nicely to the end to reveal the recently added object.

12. Save the scene and save the project.

Combining Items

The next case is what happens when a non-default cursor is used to pick an inventory object. If the two objects can be combined, both the cursor and the inventory object go out of scene and the combination object goes into inventory.

Before you can test, you will need to fill out the Object Look Up table information for the Crowbar Icon and the Golden Sleeve Icon's element 1.

1. Select the Crowbar Icon.

2. In the Interactor component in the Inspector, add an Element 1 to Look Up State 1 by changing the Size to 2.

3. Fill out Element 1as follows:

```
Golden Sleeve Icon,0,Golden Sleeve Icon,0,Crowbar Icon,0,Crowbar with Sleeve Icon,1
```

4. Add a matching element to Replies State 1, and fill it in as follows:

```
You slip the crowbar neatly onto the golden sleeve
```

The Crowbar Icon, when picked by the Golden Sleeve Icon as cursor, goes out of scene, state 0, the Golden Sleeve Icon also goes out of scene, 0, and the combo icon, Crowbar with Sleeve Icon, goes into inventory, 1.

5. Select the Golden Sleeve Icon.

6. In the Interactor component in the Inspector, add an Element 1 to Look Up State 1 by changing the Size to **2**.

7. Fill out Element 1 as follows:

```
Crowbar Icon,0,Crowbar Icon,0,Golden Sleeve Icon,0,Crowbar with Sleeve,1
```

8. Add a matching element to Replies State 1, and fill it in as follows:

```
The golden sleeve slides smoothly over the iron crowbar
```
The Golden Sleeve Icon, when picked by the Crowbar Icon, goes out of scene, 0, the Crowbar Icon also goes out of scene, and then the combo icon, Crowbar with Sleeve Icon, goes into inventory, 1.

░ **Tip**   Type the entries into a text editor, and then copy and paste to put them into the Inspector. Make sure spelling, capitalization, and spaces are correct.

---

9. Select the Crowbar with Sleeve Icon in the Hierarchy view.

10. Change its initial state to 0.

11. Click Play.

12. Open the inventory, and pick the Crowbar.

13. Once the crowbar is the cursor, pick the Golden Sleeve with it.

The cursor disappears, and the crowbar becomes the crowbar with sleeve.

1. Restart the scene, and go into inventory.

2. This time start with the Golden Sleeve, and use it to pick the Crowbar.

The cursor disappears, and the golden sleeve becomes the crowbar with sleeve.

3. Save the scene and save the project.

4. Click Play again.

5. Pick a different inventory object so it becomes the pointer.

6. Click any of the other inventory objects.

While the generic reply works well with the objects in the 3D scene, in inventory you would probably expect the picked object to become the new cursor and the old cursor put back into inventory in anticipation of using the new one.

Wrong Picks

The only thing you have not yet dealt with in the inventory is what happens when the player picks an object in inventory with the wrong cursor. In the Object Look Up, when there is no match and the for loop has finished looking through the options, you will need to put the cursor back into inventory since it was a wrong pick. If it was the default cursor, or the correct cursor, or a cursor with a special message, it was handled and returned, so only "no match found" will get to this next code.

1. Open the ObjectLookUp script.

2. At the bottom of the LookUpState function, change the HandleNoMatchReplies(picker) line as follows:

```
// if the picked object is not an inventory object, build a no match reply for it
if (gameObject.tag != "InventoryObject") HandleNoMatchReplies(picker);
```

3. Below it, just above the closing curly bracket for the LookUpState function, add the following:

```
else if (matchCursor != "default"){  //swap out the cursor with the object it picked


    //put the old cursor in inventory
    GameObject.Find(picker).SendMessage("ProcessObject",1);

    //pick up the new cursor
    SendMessage("ProcessObject",2);


}
```

4. Save the script.

5. Click Play.

6. Select the Jewel Icon.

7. Pick the Vial of Elixir Icon with it.

The Vial of Elixir Icon becomes the cursor, and the Jewel Icon goes into the inventory as the last item.

While this functionality works, it would be nicer if the two would swap places so the cursor took the place in inventory of the object it picked. By doing a bit of creative state management, you can get the results you want. Once you know you are swapping the two, e.g., you are in the else clause, you can assign new states before you process them into their correct states. This will allow you to create a couple of new clauses in the Handle2D function you created earlier.

8. Inside the else clause, above the //put the old cursor in inventory line, add the following:

```
 //change the picked object's state to 10,
GetComponent(Interactor).currentState = 10;
//change the cursor object's state to 11
GameObject.Find(picker).GetComponent(Interactor),currentState = 11;
//store this object's current inventory element number on the GameManager
```

```
controlCenter.GetComponent(GameManager).replaceElement = GetComponent(Interactor).iElement;
```

9. Save the script.

You use a bogus state number for the two objects to remind yourself that it is just temporary.

You also need to store this object's inventory element number somewhere it can be found when the cursor is being processed. Since you are storing the rest of the generic variables on the GameManager script, it makes sense to use that for your replaceElement as well.

1. Open the GameManager script.

2. Add the following in the //inventory layout section:

```
private var replaceElement : int; // var to store the current inventory object's element
```

3. Save the script.

And finally you will add the special case conditionals to the Handle2D function in the Interactor.

1. Open the Interactor script.

At the top of the ProcessObject function, you need to turn your temporary states into the previous states and assign the actual new states.

2. Near the top of the ProcessObject function, just beneath the processing = true line, add the following:

```
//handle replace
if(newState == 10) {
   newState = 1;
   currentState = 10;
}
 if (newState == 11) {
   newState = 2;
   currentState = 11;
}
```

And now you can add the conditions that fit your doctored previousState.

3. Add the following conditional to the Handle2D function to handle the picked object:

```
// In Inventory, will be replaced
if (previousState == 10) {
   //turn off the object
   gameObject.guiTexture.enabled = false;
   //turn it into the cursor
   controlCenter.GetComponent(GameManager).currentCursor = guiTexture.texture;
}
```

4. Add the following conditional to handle the cursor that goes into the picked object's place:

```
//the new object that takes the picked object's position
if (previousState == 11) {
   controlCenter.SendMessage("ResetCursor");
   //set its state to inventory
   currentState = 1;
```

```
      gameObject.guiTexture.enabled = true;
      //get the element number in inventory that it replaces
      iElement = controlCenter.GetComponent(GameManager).replaceElement;
      //insert the new object to inventory at the correct element position
      controlCenter.GetComponent(GameManager).currentInventoryObjects[iElement] =↵
  this.gameObject;
      //update the inventory grid
      controlCenter.GetComponent(GameManager).InventoryGrid();
}
```

     5.   Save the script.

     6.   Click Play and test.

The cursor and inventory object swap out nicely.

The only thing missing is a message text. With a few changes, you can reuse the HandleNoMatchReplies function you are using for the non-inventory replies.

     1.   Open the ObjectLookup script.

     2.   Clone the entire HandleNoMatchReplies function.

     3.   Name it HandleCursorSwapReplies.

     4.   Change its var tempMsg line to the following:

```
var tempMsg = "You exchange the " + picker + " for the " + tempObjectName ;
```
And add the line that calls the function.

     5.   In the ObjectLookupState function, inside the else if (matchCursor !=
           "default") conditional block, just above its closing curly bracket, add the
           following:

```
HandleCursorSwapReplies (picker); // build a reply for the swapped cursor
```

     6.   Save the script.

     7.   Click Play, and test the new message (see Figure 12-14).

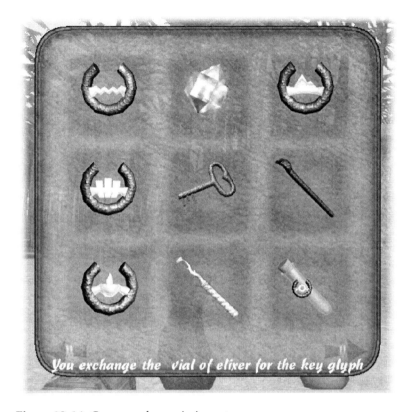

Figure 12-14. *Cursor exchange in inventory*

8. Test the crowbar/golden sleeve combination to make sure it still works.

About now you are probably thinking that the inventory icons are really too small for cursors. Since the mouse-over point is the upper left corner of the GUITexture, it doesn't really matter how big the texture is. You can use a pointer texture with a small arrow positioned up at that corner and increase the pointer size so the icon textures look better as cursors.

1. Locate the GamePointerOffset texture in the Adventure Textures folder.

2. Select the Control Center object.

3. Drag the GamePointerOffset into its Default Cursor field in the Inspector.

4. Open the GameManager script.

5. In the OnGUI function, change the pointer's size to 64 × 64.

```
GUI.DrawTexture (Rect(pos.x, Screen.height - pos.y,64,64), currentCursor);
```

6. Save the script Click Play.

7. Test the new cursor and inventory icon sizes (see Figure 12-15).

Figure 12-15. *The cursor at 64 × 64 using an inventory icon*

8. Deactivate Camera Inventory's Camera component.

9. Save the scene and save the project.

Summary

In this chapter, you implemented the functionality for the inventory system. Starting with a grid system for the layout, you used GUI Texture objects for the inventory icons. With the use of tags, you were able to access all of the objects tagged as InventoryObjects and iterate through them to load the active objects into an array.

Using a bit of math, you were able to design an extensible system to allow any number of inventory items past the visible nine displayed on the panel texture. Using arrows to navigate the inventory grid, you were able to determine visibility according to the grid's position and the current number of items in inventory.

After you got the grid working, you considered the possibilities for interaction with non-default cursors. You were able to see how the metadata system allows you to combine two cursors in inventory to create a new combination object. Continuing non-default cursors, you decided to have a pick with a "wrong" cursor pick up the inventory object and drop the cursor object into inventory in its place.

Being able to dynamically add and remove objects from inventory, you then implemented "custom" generic replies for wrong picks in inventory that differed from the reply for wrong picks in the 3D scene.

By stretching a small semi-transparent texture across the screen, you gave the player a view of the 3D world in action while accessing inventory that also provided a means of intercepting picks outside of the inventory panel.

And finally, you adjusted the cursor size to give a better view of the inventory items when they were used as the current cursor.

In the next chapter, you will deal with object visibility using tags, refine object interaction, and experiment with random replies.

■ ■ ■

CHAPTER 13

Finishing the Basic Functionality

In this chapter, you will finish the basic functionality for action objects, whether they are 2D or 3D. Besides addressing visibility and the means of achieving it, you will be catching other bits of functionality as they crop up.

1. Open the Inventory scene in the Book project.

2. Use Save Scene As to save it as Interaction2 in the Scenes folder.

Handling 3D Object Visibility

In an earlier chapter, you listed the number assignments for your two other states, Location and Visibility, and then added them to your Game Notes text asset. These two will help you to automatically process the data for properties other than keyframed animation.

Location is the final destination. It is a state of sorts, but only pertaining to where the object is in the scene, in inventory, etc. as opposed to an animation state such as open or closed.

Visibility is the method it uses to get there. This includes whether or not it fades in or out and when, in relation to the animation, it does so.

Let's fill in the location and code for the objects from the earlier example. While there are some overlaps, you can see that the information varies. In case you are wondering *why* you are tracking this data, it is because it will allow you to handle it more efficiently for any object in a generic manner. This will be extremely important for handling opacity fade ins and fade outs.

Rather than going through the trouble of duplicating an animation clip on an imported object and animating its material's opacity, you will be able to drop a simple script on it and the code will do the rest.

Table 13-1. *Location and Visibility for the Current Action Objects*

Object/State	Location	Code	Visibility	Code
KeyAtRock				
State 0- On ground	In scene	0	n/a	0
State 1- Not in scene	Not in scene	4	Fade-out at End	0
Iron Key Icon				
State 0- Not in scene	Not in scene	4	Hide at Start	1
State 1- In inventory	In inventory	1	Show at Start	1
State 3- Is cursor	Is cursor	2	Show at Start	1
KeyAtLock				
State 0- Not in scene	Not in scene	4	Fade-out at End	6
State 1- Inserted into lock	In scene	0	Fade-in at Start	2
State 2- Turned in lock	In scene	0	N/A	0
State 3- Unavailable	Inactive	4	N/A	0
LockPlate				
State 0- Empty	In scene	0	N/A	0
State 1- Key inserted	In scene	0	N/A	0
State 2- Key turned	In scene	0	N/A	0

▪ **Tip**   You may want to consult the GameNotes text asset for Location and Visibility to see the code number assignments.

With this information for each state (see Table 13-1), the object knows what its final location will be and what the visibility is at the start and end of the animation.

While you could probably keyframe visibility, it will be less work to script it once rather than duplicate animation clips and keyframe it for each object. In doing so, you will need to make the assumption that *all action objects with transparency shaders will fade in and out of their visibility states.* Because you may occasionally have objects that are never fully opaque, you will also need to store their material's default alpha value at the start. If you are worried about objects that use transparency but do not fade in and out, you will create a variable to check to see if the object should use the fades.

■ **Rule** All action objects with transparency shaders will fade in and out of their visibility states. This will require any action object with a transparency shader to have its own unique material.

Let's set a flag to use to fade the material in and out if the shader is a transparency shader. By keeping the variable public, you will be able to disable the fade manually should the need ever arise. By initializing it to true, you can then go ahead and check internally to see if the material can be faded or not.

1. Open the Interactor script.

2. In the Start function, add the following just under the currentObjectDescription = description[currentState] line:

```
currentLocation = location[currentState];
currentVisibility = visibilityType[currentState];
```

3. In the //Gain access to section, add the following private variables:

```
var useAlpha = true; // flag to fade material during visibility change
private var maxAlpha : float; // maximum alpha value the material can have
```

In the Start function you will need to check first to see if it is a 3D object before querying the material because 2D objects don't have materials and would therefore throw an error. Fortunately, you already have a bit of code that deals with 3D objects' materials, so you can slip your new bit of code right inside it.

4. Inside the Start function, inside the **if**(objectIs3D) block, beneath the originalMaterial= GetComponent line, add the following:

```
maxAlpha = originalMaterial.color.a;// store the alpha value of the original material
```

5. Under that line, temporarily add the following so you can see what gets returned:

```
print (this.name + " " + "Alpha: " + maxAlpha);
print ("Shader: " + renderer.material.shader.name);
```

6. Save the script.

7. Click Play and then look at the results in the Console (see Figure 13-1).

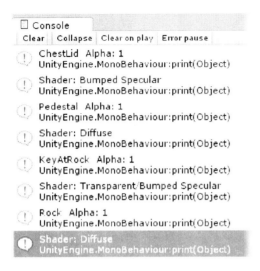

Figure 13-1. *The shader types and alpha values for the action objects' materials*

You should see the Rock, the Pedestal, the two keys, and the ChestLid. With the exception of the KeyAtRock, which already has an opacity animation and transparency shader, each has an alpha of 1 and uses a regular shader. Let's test your code by changing the Rock's Main Color's alpha value to 0.5.

1. Stop Play mode.

2. Select the Rock.

3. At the bottom of the Inspector, open the Color dialog and set the alpha to about 128 (half of 256).

4. Click Play.

Figure 13-2. *Rock with alpha value not showing opacity*

Although the Rock is still solid in the viewport, the console reports the new alpha value (see Figure 13-2). Let's change the shader this time.

1. Stop Play mode.

2. Change the Rock's shader to Transparent ➤ Diffuse.

The alpha value is now apparent on the Rock in the Game view.

3. Click Play.

The console now reports the shader's name as Transparent Diffuse. This means you can use *substring* to check for "Transparent" as the first eleven characters. If you have a match, you set the usesAlpha flag to true. You also need to check to make sure the shader name is long enough to check if "Diffuse," for example, would throw an error if you tried to access its (non-existent) eleventh character.

1. Stop Play mode.

2. Remove the two print statements.

3. Add the following code to replace them:

```
// prep for auto fade of 3D objects unless specified as false
if (useAlpha) { // if it isn't set to false by the author
   useAlpha = false; // set it to false, there will be only one condition to make it true
   var tempShadername = renderer.material.shader.name; // get the shader name
   if (tempShadername.length > 11) { //check for short names- they aren't transparents
      if(tempShadername.Substring (0,11) == "Transparent") useAlpha = true;// set the flag↵
   to uses alpha
   }
}
```

4. Save the script.

This should give you a good start toward automating the opacity fades on objects with Transparency shaders.

Developing Non-Keyframed Fades

You now know whether an object needs to fade, and whether in or out, by the type of shader on its material. The next step is to think about implementing the functionality. Just like your very early experiments in the introduction to scripting, your auto-fade will be managed in the Update function. Given that most of the important events are handled in the Interactor script, this is where you will continue to work.

The fades will work on the material's Main Color alpha component and will go from the maxAlpha value down to near 0 and back up again over time. If an object animates over one second (a typical animate time), the fade should probably be no longer than half a second.

You will need to set a flag to start the fade-in or fade-out and then turn it off when the minimum or maximum value has been reached. You could get clever with the flag and functionality, but for the fades you will try to keep things easier to read and just add a bit more coding. You will set the fade time to 2.0 for now so you will be able to access the functionality easily during setup.

1. Open the Interactor script

2. Add the following private vars below the var useAlpha=true variable declaration:

```
private var fadeIn = false; // flags to control opacity in Update
private var fadeOut = false;
private var fadeTime = 2.0; //default time over which the fades happen
```

3. Inside the Update function, below the timer code, add the following:

```
if(fadeIn) {
    // if the alpha is less than the maxAlpha amount,
    if(renderer.material.color.a < maxAlpha)
        renderer.material.color.a += Time.deltaTime/ fadeTime;// increase the alpha
    // else it is finished , so stop increasing the alpha value
    else fadeIn = false;
}
if(fadeOut) {
    // if the alpha is greater than 0,
    if(renderer.material.color.a > 0.0)
        renderer.material.color.a -= Time.deltaTime/ fadeTime;// decrease the alpha
    // else it is finished , so stop decreasing the alpha value
    else fadeOut = false;
}
```

Note the use of += and -= to increment or decrement the values. As you can see, depending on whether the fadeIn or fadeOut flag is active (true), the material's alpha value will be increased or decreased over two seconds until it reaches the minimum or maximum.

You ought to test the functionality before you move on.

1. Temporarily remove the private from the three fade variables.

2. Save the script.

3. Click Play.

The Rock is currently semi-transparent and will make a good test subject.

4. Select the Rock.

5. In the Inspector, in the Interactor component, toggle the Fade Out parameter on.

The Rock fades out completely and the Fade Out parameter un-checks itself.

6. Turn the Fade In parameter on.

The Rock fades back in to its semi-transparent state.

7. Turn off Play mode and make the Rock fully opaque.

8. Click Play and repeat the previous steps.

The Rock opacity behaves no matter how transparent it starts out. At this point another concern may have occurred to you. What happens if two or more objects share the same material? Will they all share the fade? Let's find out.

9. Create a Sphere next to the Rock.

10. Assign the same material, grndred, to it.

11. Click Play and test the Rock again.

The sphere retains its opacity independently from the Rock. That means you can safely animate material properties on a per object basis during runtime.

12. Delete the sphere.

13. Change FadeTime from 2.0 to 0.5 to cause the fades to happen quicker.

14. Replace the `private` for the three variables.

15. Save the script.

By using a variable for the fade time, you will be able to have it adjust itself according to the length of the animation.

Side Effects of Visibility Changes

Now that you have the mechanics of the visibility change in place, you need to think about other related issues. To begin with, you will need to access the current location and visibility states.

1. Open the `Interactor` script.

2. Inside the `ProcessObject` function, below the lines updating `currentObjectDescription` and `currentLocation`, add the following to update the visibility:

`currentVisibility = visibilityType[currentState];`

You are going to need to handle the various visibility types, but first you need to think about when and where to do that. Several of the scenarios require the object to be hidden or shown at the end. This implies that they are animated and means that you will need to know how long the animation is before they can be initiated. The problem is that you don't get that information until you are in the **if**(animates) block. Furthermore, if you handle the visibility *inside* the block you would miss all the objects that do not animate.

The answer is to make the visibility handling a function so you can call it from *both* inside and outside the **if**(animates) block. The first call to the function is at the start, so you ignore case 4, hide at end, that will get called from inside the animates clause. Keep the GameNotes handy.

1. Open the Interactor script.

2. Inside the ProcessObject function, below the line that sends the 2D objects off for visibility handling, **if**(!objectIs3D) Handle2D(), add the following:

```
// else it is 3d- send it off for handling in case it has a visibility state that is↵
 processed at the start
else if (currentLocation == 0) HandleVisibility();
```

3. Locate the aniLength = currentAnimationClip.length line inside the **if**(animates) block.

At this point you know how long the animation lasts. The line below it sets up a pause until it is finished so it knows when to turn 0. By dividing the time and breaking the pause into two pauses, you can start the fade out at two thirds of the way through the animation.

4. Add a new yield new WaitForSeconds below the aniLength= line:

```
yield new WaitForSeconds(aniLength * 2/3);
```

5. Below it add:

```
if (currentVisibility > 2) {
   if (currentVisibility == 3) currentVisibility =4;// if you're here, the start has been done
   HandleVisibility( );
}
```

6. And below that, change the original yield **new** WaitForSeconds line:

```
yield new WaitForSeconds(aniLength * 1/3);
```

7. Save the script.

You should get two "Unknown identifier: 'HandleVisibility'" errors. If you have more than two errors, check the 'i's in visibility in the variables. You will need to implement more functionality before you return to the visibility handling, but you can block in the function to prevent errors until that time.

8. Add the following function near the bottom of the Interactor script:

```
//handle the various Visibility conditions:
function HandleVisibility() {


}
```

9. Save the script.

You should no longer see any error messages. If you have not yet set up the Visibility Type array Sizes, you will get errors as soon as you click Play.

10. Select each action object and inventory object and set the Visibility Type array Size to match the other arrays in the Interactor component.

Finally, to take care of any objects that did *not* animate but need to go out of scene when picked (currentLocation 4), you need to add a line to send them to the HandleVisibility function.

11. In the ProcessObject function, below the **else** clause of the **if**(animates! block, add the following:

```
if(currentLocation == 4) HandleVisibility(); // goes out of scene
```

12. Save the script.

13. Save the scene and save the project.

Dealing with Colliders

Perhaps the most important issue related to visibility changes has to do with the mesh objects and their colliders. As mentioned several times before, turning off the object's Mesh Renderer component *does not* turn off the collider. In the case of the key on the ground, it doesn't really impact physical game play. But in the case of something large, it could block navigation.

1. Select the Pedestal.

2. Click Play and try to drive into it.

If you watch the area in the Scene window, you can see that the Collider prevents you from going through the object.

3. In the Inspector, from the Mesh Collider component, check Is Trigger.

■ **Tip** Changing Is Trigger during runtime does not always update in the scene. You may need to stop Play mode, change the setting, click Play, and then test.

---

4. Try to drive into it again.

This time you can pass right through it. Therefore, when you disable the Mesh Renderer, you can turn the Is Trigger parameter on to change the collider behavior so it no longer acts as a collision wall or floor. There is only one problem.

5. Disable the Pedestal's Mesh Renderer.

6. Mouse over the hidden object (see Figure 13-3).

Figure 13-3. *The cursor over the invisible Pedestal*

The text and picks still register so this will not be a good enough solution. Unfortunately, there is no way to deactivate the Collider component. The least complicated method would be to deactivate and activate the entire object. In the Inspector, this is easy enough to do.

1. Stop Play mode.

2. Uncheck Is Trigger.

3. Enable the Mesh Renderer.

4. Click Play and test.

5. Deactivate the Pedestal at the top of the Inspector.

6. Try to mouse over, then to move through the Pedestal.

The deactivated object is fully removed from the Game view and is grayed out in the Hierarchy view. Deactivating an object is as easy as gameObject.active = false. The problem comes when you try to activate it. Because it is inactive, it can't be found by referring to it by name using GameObject.Find(). Therefore, you will need to store the objects in an array after they have been added to the game, but before some have been deactivated. This is where the Awake function comes in. As with the inventory array, you will keep the action objects array in the GameManager script.

1. Open the GameManager script.

2. Under the private var currentInventoryObjects =, line, add the following:

```
// array to hold the action objects in case they need to be reactivated
private var actionObjects = new Array();
```

You've seen how to iterate through the scene looking for objects with Tags when you created the active inventory array. As an alternative, you can do the same looking for objects that have a particular script. As it happens, the action objects all share two scripts, the Interactor and the ObjectLookUp. You can use FindObjectOtType() to locate all of the action objects in the scene and then Add them to the array.

3.   Inside the Awake function add the following:

```
//save the action objects into an array for access when deactivated
var aObjects = GameObject.FindObjectsOfType(Interactor);
for (var aObject in aObjects)  actionObjects.Add(aObject);
```

4.   Save the script.

Next you need to update the ObjectLookUp script so it will be able to activate objects in order to use them. As a quick review, the first two objects in the lookup tables are always the cursor that picked the object and the state it goes into. By definition, since the object was picked, it is active, so you need not worry about it. The auxiliary objects are the ones that will typically be turned off and on as a result of the pick so that is where you need to concentrate your next efforts.

The first thing you need to do is head off an error if the named object is not active. You have parsed the array to find the next object and the state it goes into, but you only have the name, which you have stored in the variable tempS, not the actual object.

1.   Open the ObjectLookUp script.

2.   Inside the LookUpState function, locate the **var** auxObject = gameObject.Find(tempS) line.

You will need to use this in a couple of places, so make a function to do the important work. You will pass it the name of the object and have it return the activated object so you can finish processing it.

3.   Change it to the following:

```
var auxObject = CheckForActive(tempS); // check to activate if turned off
```

4.   At the bottom of the script, start a new function to do the work:

```
function CheckForActive(tempS : String) {
   // check to see if the object is active before assigning it to auxObject
   if(gameObject.Find(tempS)) var auxObject = gameObject.Find(tempS);
```

If it can't be found, the next section goes through the array of stored game objects and looks for one whose name matches the one held in the tempS variable. When it finds a match, it activates the object. Once activated, you can then use Find to get the object and store it in the auxObject variable so it can be processed. It sounds like a lot of trouble, but it solves visibility *and* the collider problem for the object and any children it might contain.

5.   Add the following to finish the function:

```
else {
   var actionObjects = controlCenter.GetComponent(GameManager).actionObjects;
   for (var y =0; y < actionObjects.length; y++) { // iterate through the array
      if (actionObjects[y].name == tempS) {  // if there is a match for the name
         actionObjects[y].active = true; // activate the matched object from the array
         auxObject = gameObject.Find(tempS); // assign the newly activated object
   }
}
```

```
      }
      return auxObject;

} // close CheckForActive() function
```

6. Save the script.

7. Test the action object interactivity to make sure it still works.

Now that you have a means of retrieving deactivated objects, you can turn off all of those action objects that should be hidden at the start (the KeyAtLock, for example, once you fill in its metadata).

1. Open the Interactor script.

2. At the bottom of the Start function, add the following:

```
// if the object's location is not in scene, 4, deactivate it after setting its opacity to 0
if (currentLocation == 4) {
   if (useAlpha == true) renderer.material.color.a = 0; // prep for fade in
   gameObject.active = false;
}
```

3. Save the script.

   You will return to your action objects and their visibility a bit later when you have more objects set up. Remember that you added visibility directly to the KeyAtRock so it will not be a good test subject. The KeyAtLock, on the other hand, will give your code a good work out at some point.

Processing No-Match Cursors

Another loose end to tidy up is what happens to a non-default cursor when there is no match found for it in the 3D scene. The only condition not met by the end of the LookUpState function is that of no matching cursor found—in other words, a wrong pick. Currently nothing happens other than a reply that it will do nothing if you pick the wrong action object. You should probably put the cursor object back into inventory, turn off the processing flag, and then show the pointer. To allow for future modifications of your code, you will play it safe and double check to make sure the cursor is not the default cursor.

1. Click Play.

2. In inventory mode, select the key.

3. Exit inventory and pick the Pedestal with the key as cursor.

Other than the wrong pick message, nothing happens when you pick the Pedestal or any other object.

4. Open the ObjectLookUp script.

5. Just above the closing curly bracket for the LookUpState function, add the following:

```
//process non- default cursors that found no match
// get the cursor texture name and put the cursor object back into inventory
```

```
if(matchCursor != "default")gameObject.Find(picker).SendMessage("ProcessObject",1);

//turn on the pointer again
controlCenter.GetComponent(GameManager).showPointer = true;


//turn off the processing flag so the object can be interactive again
this.GetComponent(Interactor).processing = false;
```

6. Save the script.

7. Click Play.

8. In inventory, select the key.

9. Exit inventory and pick the Pedestal with the key as cursor.

The key goes back into inventory and the pointer appears again.

With the `HandleNoMatchReplies` function, you are providing feedback for wrong picks already, but you also have a place to add *specific* replies for wrong picks on an individual object basis: the `genericReplies` array in the `ObjectLookup` function.

Random Replies

Once you have picked an object a few times, you will probably get tired of getting the same message over and over. One of the most entertaining things about the old text adventure games was the variety of often pithy replies one received when repeating certain events. Typically, the first couple of replies were fairly innocuous, but as the player continued to repeat the event, the replies got more entertaining.

When you first set up the `ObjectLookup` function, you defined an array called genericReplies. As of yet, you have not used it. At its simplest, it should provide object-specific replies. If there are no replies listed, it falls back to your semi-generic custom reply. Since the generic replies can be the same for all objects, they should be kept in a central place. You already have the `GameManager` script on the `Control Center` gameObject, but it is more for game styles and settings. Since most of your other scripts access the `Control Center` already, it would make sense to create a new script to hold the really generic replies.

1. Create a new script in the Adventure Scripts folder.

2. Name it `MiscText`.

3. Open it in the script editor.

Right now you just need to store an array of generic replies so you do not need the `Update` function.

4. Delete the `Update` function.

5. Create a variable for the generic replies as follows:

```
// list of really generic replies for wrong picks
var gameGenericReplies : String[];
```

Note that you could have named the variable genericReplies since it is on a different script and a different gameObject than the other genericReplies variable, however, since you will refer to both in the same section of code, this will make it less confusing.

6. Save the script.

7. Stop Play mode.

8. Drop the new script onto the Control Center object.

9. Select the Control Center object.

10. In the Inspector, set the array Size to 5 elements.

11. Add the following values:

> Element 0 Nothing happens
>
> Element 1 There is no response
>
> Element 2 That did nothing
>
> Element 3 Nothing appears to have happened
>
> Element 4 There seems to be no reaction

12. Save the scene.

To retrieve a random reply, you will need to generate a random number between 0 and the length of the array and then send the contents of that element back to whatever script needs the contents. Theoretically, you could easily generate the random number when you ask for the contents of the array at that element. It would look something like this:

```
var reply = controlCenter.GetComponent(MiscText).gameGenericReplies[Random.Range↵
(0,gameGenericReplies.length)];
```

If, on the other hand, you create a function inside the MiscText script to supply the reply, it becomes simpler and will also allow you to prevent two repeat replies in a row. You can also separate the random number generator for easier reading.

13. Add the following function to the MiscText script:

```
function RandomReply () {
   var num = Random.Range(0,gameGenericReplies.length);
   return gameGenericReplies[num]; // send the contents of that element back
}
```

■ **Tip** Look up Random.Range in the Scripting help to see how the numbers are handled. If you use a floating point number, both the minimum and the maximum values are inclusive. If you are using integers, however, the minimum number is inclusive, but the maximum is exclusive. While this may not seem consistent, the benefits become apparent when accessing array elements. For an array with 5 elements, they are numbered 0-4. If you use 0 for the minimum and the array length for the maximum, because the integer version of Random.Range does *not* include the max value, the random number returned will never be 5 and therefore will be a valid element number.

---

14. To test the script, add the following Start function:

```
function Start () {
    print (RandomReply());
}
```

15. Save the script.

16. Click Play.

One of the replies is printed to the Console.

17. In the Console, turn off Clear on play.

18. Stop Play mode and click Play again.

A different reply will probably appear. If you repeat the test several times, you will eventually get a few repeats. You can solve this by retaining the previous number and making sure the new random number is not the same by using a while loop. While loops continue to loop until the condition specified is no longer met.

In your case, you need it to keep retrieving a new random number while the new number is the same as the old number. Because you need to retain the old number each time you leave the function, it needs to be declared outside of the function. Additionally, because it needs a value the first time the function is used, you also must initialize a value. Since an array will never have a negative numbered element, you can initialize the variable to -1.

19. At the top of the MiscText script, add the following:

```
private var oldNum = -1; //var to store the previous random number
```

20. Change the RandomReply function as follows:

```
function RandomReply () {
    var num = Random.Range(0,gameGenericReplies.length);// get a random number
    while (num == oldNum) num = Random.Range(0,gameGenericReplies.length);
    oldNum = num; // store the new random number for next time
    return gameGenericReplies[num]; // send the contents of that element back
}
```

21. Save the script.

You can't test the changes by stopping and starting Play mode because the oldNum variable is cleared each time! Instead, you can write a loop to print out as may calls to the function as you want.

1. Add the following above or in front of the print statement in the Start function:

```
for(i=0; i< 30;i++)
```

The for loop goes until the variable i is no longer less than 30.

2. Save the script.

3. Click Play.

4. Inspect the output of the Console.

The same reply is never used twice in a row.

5. Comment out the contents of the Start function

6.   Turn Clear on play back on in the Console.

7.   Save the script.

Now you can call the function from the ObjectLookUp script when no match has been found for the cursor and no generic reply was supplied for the object.

1.   Open the ObjectLookUp script.

You have already created a function to process wrong picks, HandleNoMatchReplies. When you blocked it in, you had it set the action message to the tempMsg string you created on the fly when there were no replies listed. This time you will have it fetch a random generic reply from the RandomReply function in the MiscText script.

2.   For now, comment out the **var** tempMsg = "The " + picker line.

3.   Add the following below that line:

```
var tempMsg = controlCenter.GetComponent(MiscText).RandomReply();
```

4.   Click Play.

5.   Test the key against the ChestLid.

The random replies appear.

6.   Open the MiscText script.

7.   Delete the Start function.

8.   Copy the contents of the RandomReplies function.

9.   Save the script.

Now that you know how to get a random element from an array, you can re-use the code to pull up random replies from the object's own genericReplies array. The first thing you need to do is check to see if any generic replies were listed for the object. If there were none, you will go ahead and use the Game Generic Replies from the Control Center's Misc Text.

1.   Open the ObjectLookUp script.

2.   Above the **var** tempMsg = controlCenter line that you temporarily commented out in the previous section, add the following:

```
if (genericReplies.length ==0) {
```

3.   Below the **var** tempMsg = controlCenter line, add the closing curly bracket for the new condition:

```
}
```

4.   Below that, add an else:

```
else { // there was at least one generic reply
```

Now you can randomize the replies, if any, for the genericReplies the same way you did with the gameGenericReplies.

5.   Add the following private variable near the top of the ObjectLookUp script:

```
private var oldNum = -1; // keep the previous random number for the generic replies
```

6. Inside the HandleNoMatchReplies function, add the following below the **else** {// there was line, so it looks like the following:

```
else {  // there was at least one generic reply
  if (genericReplies.length >1) {


  }
  else tempMsg = genericReplies[0]; // there was only one
} //close first else
```

7. Paste the contents of the RandomReply function from the MiscText script into the new *if* block and change gameGenericReplies to genericReplies so it looks as follows:

```
if (genericReplies.length >1) {
    var num = Random.Range(0,genericReplies.length);// get a random number
    while (num == oldNum) num = Random.Range(0,genericReplies.length);
    oldNum = num; // store the new random number for next time
    tempMsg= genericReplies[num]; // assign the winner

}
```

8. Save the script.

Before you test the new code, you will need to add a few more generic responses to the Rock. Before you do that, however, you will need to combine a couple of techniques you have already learned to customize the random replies, regardless of their source. By using split characters as you did when you parsed the lookup information, you can reconstruct any of your replies using the current action object (@) and the cursor that picked it (^) as you've already processed them for your original no-match reply.

1. Open the GameNotes text asset.

2. Add the following to it:

> Generic Replies:
>
>> "@" represents the picked object
>>
>> "^" represents the cursor that picked it

3. Save the text asset.

4. Open the ObjectLookup script.

5. In the HandleNoMatchReplies function, under the }//close first else line, add the following:

```
// add a blank character to the end of the string in case the last character is a split
tempMsg = tempMsg + " ";
// split contents into a temp array
var readString : String[] = tempMsg.Split("@".Chars[0]);

if(readString.length > 1) // if there was a "@" in the string
    //rebuild the reply using the object short name at the @
    tempMsg = readString[0] + tempObjectName + readString[1];
```

```
// split contents into a temp array
readString = tempMsg.Split("^".Chars[0]);

if(readString.length > 1) // if there was a "^" in the string
    //rebuild the reply using the cursor name at the ^
    tempMsg = readString[0] + picker + readString[1];
```

Let's reuse your original generic reply and convert it using your split characters. It will look as follows:

```
The ^ does not seem to affect the @
```

6. Make sure you are not in Play mode.

7. Select the Control Center object.

8. Increase the Size of the Game Generic Replies to 6 in the Misc Text component.

9. Add the converted reply.

10. Click Play and test an inventory icon on the action objects.

11. Increase the Size of the Game Generic Replies to 10.

The reply is copied to the new elements.

12. Try non-default cursors on the objects.

The custom generic replies are randomly displayed on wrong picks.

1. Stop Play mode.

2. Replace the duplicate replies with the versions that incorporate the split characters:

```
Using the ^ does nothing to the @
The @ is not affected by the ^
Using the ^ produces no visible affect
The @ shows no response
```

3. Click Play and test to see the new responses (see Figure 13-4).

Figure 13-4. *The custom random game replies*

4.   Stop Play mode.

5.   Select the Rock.

6.   In its Object Lookup component, change the Generic Replies array Size to 3.

7.   Add the following three replies:

```
The ^ has no affect on something as hard as a rock
Despite your efforts, the ^ does not produce sparks as it hits the rock
Rocks of this size are immune to being struck with a ^
```

8.   Click Play.

9.   Test the Rock several times with any of the inventory items (see Figure 13-5).

Figure 13-5. *The Rock after picking with the Crowbar Icon*

Movies (Disney movies, in particular) rely heavily on the wise-cracking sidekick to add comic relief or spice up bland hero/heroine action. While a few adventure games have tried using a similar character as a guide or mentor, it is hard to keep it from ruining the game play for many players. Keeping the wise-cracks text-based allows the player to "hear" the kind of voice they imagine.

Dropping Cursors in the 3D Scene

You may remember that when you click on the Inventory Panel with a non-default cursor, it goes into inventory. If you click outside the Inventory Panel, the inventory closes and you have the object as cursor in the 3D scene. You may be wondering what happens if you decide you no longer want the object as cursor. To have to open the inventory and drop it in is a lot of trouble for something that minor.

You already have the cursor handled if it picks an action object, but so far, it does nothing if the object was not an action object. This would be the perfect opportunity to put the cursor back into inventory. The only problem is that unless the object has a collider, it will not even register a pick—the sky being one big example. You would also rather not have to put a script on every other object in the scene for when it was picked. The answer lies in casting a ray into the scene whenever the left mouse button is used.

Ray casting is used regularly when shooting projectiles. The hit object is queried for type or tag, and if matched, a message is sent to set off a series of events. You will need to check to see if the hit object is an action object, and if not, send the cursor back to inventory. Since the ray is associated with a camera's GUILayer, you get the added benefit that other camera layers, such as inventory, will be ignored.

1.   Open the `GameManager` script.

The first thing you need to add is a means of knowing when the mouse button is pressed. Because it has nothing to do with an object, where you have been using `OnMouseDown`, you will need to always be checking the input for that event, so you add it to the `Update` function.

2.   Add the following inside the Update function:

```
// handle dropped cursors
if (Input.GetMouseButtonDown(0)) { // if the left button, 0, is pressed


} // close handle dropped cursors
```

Next you will need to make a few local variables with some new variable types so you can use the raycast.

3.   Add the following inside the Input.GetMouseButtonDown block:

```
var ray : Ray = Camera.main.ScreenPointToRay(Input.mousePosition);
var hit : RaycastHit;
var didHit : boolean = Physics.Raycast(ray,hit); // did it hit anything?
var cursor = GameObject.Find(currentCursor.name); // get the cursor object

if (didHit) { // you did hit something
    if (hit.transform.tag == "ActionObject") print ("Action Object : " + hit.transform.name);
    else {
    print ("nothing of note... " + hit.transform.name);
    // drop cursor here
    }
}
else  { // you hit nothing
    print ("air...");
    // drop cursor here
  }
```

You do not yet have it resetting the cursor, but you will now be able to see what the cursor was over when you pressed the left mouse button.

4.   Save the script.

5.   Click Play and test picking around the scene and in inventory.

The console reports what you have hit (see Figure 13-6).

Figure 13-6. *Results of the raycast from a mouse pick in the scene*

Since you are in the GameManager script where the cursor is controlled, it will be easy to change the code to add the desired functionality.

6.   Remove the print statements and rewrite the **if**(didHit) block as follows:

```
if (didHit) { // you did hit something
```

```
    if (hit.transform.tag == "ActionObject")  return; // do nothing
    else {
        AddToInventory(cursor); //add the current cursor
        ResetCursor();  // reset to default
        cursor.GetComponent(Interactor).currentState = 1; // update current state
    }
}
else  { // you hit nothing
        AddToInventory( cursor); //add the current cursor
        ResetCursor();  // reset to default
        cursor.GetComponent(Interactor).currentState = 1; // update current state
}
```

    7.   Save the script.

And to prevent it adding the default cursor to inventory by mistake, or even processing the pick if the current cursor is the default cursor, you need to have it return before it even checks for a mouse button down.

To give you an object to collect without going into inventory first, yo can finish adding metadata to the KeyAtRock so the Iron Key Icon appears as a cursor after it is picked.

    1.   Make sure Play mode is turned off.

    2.   Select KeyAtRock from the Hierarchy view.

    3.   Change its LookupState 0, Element 0 to:

```
default,1,Iron Key Icon,2
```

    4.   Select the Iron Key Icon object.

    5.   Set its Initial State to 0 in the Interactor component.

    6.   Open the GameManager script.

    7.   Directly above the Input.GetMouseButtonDown line, add the following:

```
if (currentCursor == defaultCursor ) return;
```

    8.   Save the script.

    9.   Click play and experiment with dropping cursors.

░ **Tip**   You will need to use the keyboard toggle 'i' to leave inventory with you cursor.

---

   10.   Be sure to check that they have gone into inventory.

If you were thorough in your testing, you probably noticed that the cursor resets when you press the i icon to get into inventory. While this might seem like a bonus, it would be annoying if you were planning on using the cursor on an existing inventory object.

The problem is that the Inventory Icon is *not* on the main camera layer, *so it never gets seen/hit.* You do, however, know when you are in inventory mode—you have the iMode variable that tracks its state. By expanding the last return statement with the or,||, you should be able to prevent the drop cursor functionality from happening.

11. Add to the last statement so it reads as follows:

```
if (currentCursor == defaultCursor || iMode == true) return;
```

12. Save the script and test again.

Now you can once again bring non-default cursors into inventory.

In the spirit of being thorough in your testing, you need to check one more case. You need to see if you can leave inventory with a non-default cursor.

1. Pick one of the inventory objects and try to remove it from inventory.

The cursor reverts to the default cursor and the object is back in inventory. The problem arises because the iMode flag is apparently being toggled off slightly before the mouse down is evaluated. You should be able to prevent this by adding a small delay to the state change when leaving inventory. The inventory is managed in the InventoryManager script so you can easily make the addition.

2. Open the InventoryManager script.

3. Locate the ToggleMode function.

4. Just above the iMode = false line in the **if** block, add the following:

```
yield new WaitForSeconds(0.5); // delay changing the iMode flag
```

5. Save the script.

6. Click Play and try removing an inventory item.

This time all behaves as desired.

A last nice touch for the inventory would be to pulse the icon when an object goes into inventory. This gives you a visual clue that it got added. This will be a fairly easy addition as you already have a function that you can call.

1. Open the GameManager script.

2. Inside the AddToInventory function, the top, add the following:

```
GameObject.Find("InventoryIcon").SendMessage("PulseIcon");
```

3. Save the script.

4. Test a cursor drop in the scene.

The icon pulses when an object is added to the inventor.

You may also wish to add a non-invasive sound effect to the PulseIcon function.

1. Stop Play mode.

2. Select the InventoryIcon object from the Hierarchy view.

3. From the Component menu, add an Audio Source.

4. Load a sound such as Ding into the Audio Clip.

5. Uncheck Play On Awake.

Play On Awake is useful for objects that are instantiated or created during runtime such as explosions or other ordnance. This sound is needed throughout the game.

1. Open the InventoryIcon script.

2. Add the following line to the PulseIcon function:

```
audio.Play();
```

3. Save the script.

4. Click Play and test.

5. Stop Play mode.

The sound does not play. As a default in Unity, sounds are imported as 3D. Since your icon is a GUI Texture object that is attached to a camera layer at an unknown position, you are probably not within its range. The most logical thing to do is to duplicate it and convert the new sound to a 2D sound.

1. Select the Ding sound asset in the Test Sounds folder.

2. Duplicate it and rename it Ding2D.

3. In the Inspector, uncheck 3D Sound.

4. Click Apply.

5. Select the InventoryIcon object and assign the new object to its Audio Source.

6. Click Play and test.

7. Adjust the volume as necessary.

After a few test runs with inventory objects, you're probably ready to get rid of the sound effect altogether. The pulsing icon is one thing. but to hear a ding every time you click the icon, mouseover it, or anything else that triggers it is probably overkill. Let's limit it to the times when the cursor is dropped into inventory.

1. Delete the audio.Play() from the PulseIcon() function and create a function to hold it:

```
function DingIcon () {

    audio.Play();

}
```

2. Save the script.

3. Open the GameManager script.

4. In the AddToInventory function, below the line that calls the PulseIcon line, add the following:

```
GameObject.Find("InventoryIcon").SendMessage("DingIcon");
```

5. Save the script and test cursor dropping.

The ding on drop only is a welcome refinement.

6. Save the scene and save the project.

Building the Visibility Function

You have dealt with the various issues associated with making the object visible and invisible so you should get to work on the `HandleVisibililty` function—the function that will direct the action objects to the right behavior according to their location and visibility type.

For the function, you will introduce the Switch command as a means of checking several conditions with the same variable, in this case, the `currentVisibililty`. The syntax is a bit different than you are used to, but it is a nice way to organize condition checking when possible.

Let's create a function to do the visibility processing. You will start by blocking it in, and then fill out each condition one at a time. You may want to refer to your States notes for the Visibility path or revisit Table 13-1.

1. Open the `Interactor` script.

2. Add the following content to the currently empty `HandleVisibility` function:

```
switch (currentVisibility) {


}
```

You can set the animation fade time for both fade in and fade out by getting the animation clip's length- providing the object animates. However, since not every state must have an animation when `animates` is set to true, you need to make sure there is a clip before asking for its length. You will need to use the and, `&&`, in the conditional along with the `animates`.

3. Add the following above the switch statement:

```
// adjust the fade time for the ani length if there is a clip for this state
if(animates && currentAnimationClip != null)
    fadeTime = fadeTime = currentAnimationClip.length * 1/3;
  else fadeTime = 0.5; //set it back to default
  if (!useAlpha && !animates) fadeTime = 0.0; // set it to 0 if the object doesn't fade
```

Since the function is called at the start or the end of the animation, your visibility handling is simplified to hide or show the object allowing for fades before deactivating.

Here is what happens for each case: VisibilityType 0 indicates that the object does not need to have its visibility changed with fades. If, however, you have an object that goes into Location 4, not in scene, and have neglected to specify how it leaves, you should automatically deactivate it. If the object has just been activated, Location 0, but does not have any animation, you will also need to turn off its action message. The two at Start cases are the easiest as they require no adjustments for animation. The object is already activated, or you wouldn't be in its `Interactor` script, processing it. The specific details of each case follow.

Case 0: No fades, but object will be turned off if Location is 4

Case 1: Show at Start

Fade the object in if it uses alpha

Case 2: Hide at Start

Fade the object out if it uses alpha

Deactivate the object

Case 3: Show at Start … Hide at End

This is actually a special case. You want the Case 1 when the function is called *before* the animation, but would then like to switch to the Case 4 once inside the animation. The solution is doable if you combine Cases 1 and 3, Show at Start, and change the Case 3 to a Case 4 once inside the animation clause (which you have already done).

Case 4: Hide at End

Fade the object out if it uses alpha

Wait the fade time, then deactivate the object

4. Add the following case statements inside the switch clause:

```
case 0 : // no fades
    if(currentLocation == 4 ) gameObject.active = false; // deactivate the object
    break;

case 1: // currentVisibilityis 1 show
    if (useAlpha) fadeIn = true;
    break;

case 2 :  // currentVisibilityis 2 hide
    if (useAlpha) fadeOut = true; // start fade out if it gets used
    yield new WaitForSeconds(fadeTime); // allow fade time
    gameObject.active = false; // deactivate the object
    break;

case 3: // currentVisibility3 show
    if (useAlpha) fadeIn = true;
    break;

case 4 :  // currentVisibilityis 4 hide
    if (useAlpha) fadeOut = true; // start fade out if it gets used
    yield new WaitForSeconds(fadeTime); // allow fade time before deactivating
    gameObject.active = false; // deactivate the object
    break;
```

The break statements break out of the condition statements as soon as a match is found and the instructions are carried out. In a switch statement with a lot of cases to check, this is much more efficient than having to check each one as you would do with the regular if clauses. Since two of the cases are actually duplicates, you could just as well have used a couple of conditions but this was a good time to try switch.

5. Save the script.

> ■ **Tip** When trying to decide how an object should leave the scene, a rule of thumb could be if the object goes directly into inventory, have it fade out. If it becomes a cursor, have it go out of scene immediately.

You will now need a test subject to see if it works. The KeyAtRock already has an animation to fade, but the Rock will suit your purposes, especially as you left a Transparent shader on it earlier. The Location tells it whether and when to be in the scene, and the Visibility Type tells it whether and when to fade in or out.

1. Select the Rock.

2. Set its Element 1 Visibility Type to 4.

3. Set its Element 1 Location to 4.

4. Click Play and pick the Rock.

The Rock fades away nicely and is deactivated, but because it is deactivated, it never has a chance to turn off the action message. You could add a yield statement before deactivating the Rock, but you will be better off to redesign the action message functionality to cover future gotchas as you develop more customizations.

5. Save the scene and save the project.

Action Message Revisited

Originally, you used the ProcessObject function to do most of the processing work after getting the instruction from the ObjectLookup's LookupState function. The contents of the action message were sent off to the GameManager and the GameManager was told to show the message, and then later, told not to show it. One of the nice features was calculating the read time to extend the processing time to force the player to wait for an animation to play out and also have enough time to read longer action messages. With a bit of thought, you can streamline your existing action message and allow for extra read time and even give your players the chance to adjust it as well.

Let's start by creating a function in the GameManager as that is where the text is displayed. If you pass the action message into the function, you know two things. You can get the length of it and figure out how long to show it, and you also know that it needs to be shown. You have already found that using a yield statement is not always safe since it can't be canceled, so you will create a timer in the GameManager to keep track of the action message for you. This solves the problem of deactivating an object only to leave its action message unattended.

1. Open the GameManager script.

2. Add the following variables to set up for your timer:

```
//Timer variables
private var timer1 : boolean = false; // timer 1 on or off
private var timeLimit1 : float; // amount of time the timer runs for
var readTime = 2.5; // minimum time to read messages
```

3. Create the ShowActionMessage function as follows:

```
function ShowActionMessage (message : String) { //pass in action message

   actionMsg = message; // load the message that was passed in
   var stringLength : int  =  actionMsg.length;
   timeLimit1 = stringLength / 25.0 -1.75; //calculate the amount of time to add
   if (timeLimit1 < readTime) timeLimit1 = readTime; // minimum read time
   timeLimit1 = Time.time + timeLimit1; // add the current time
   showActionMsg = true; // turn it on
   // start a timer to turn off the message when the time has elapsed
   timer1 = true;
}
```

4. Add the following at the top of the Update function to turn off the action message:

```
// timer 1 - turn off action message
   if(timer1 && Time.time > timeLimit1){
   showActionMsg= false;
   timer1 = false;
}
```

░ **Tip**   If you tried to add the timer code to the bottom of the Update function, it might never be reached due to the return statements in the handle dropped cursors section.

Now you can look through the other two functions to remove or replace the old code. To begin, you can remove anything that tells the showActionMsg to be false.

1. Open the Interactor script.

2. From the Search menu, search for showActionMsg = false.

3. In the Update function it finds the following:

```
if (controlCenter.GetComponent(GameManager).actionObject  == this.name) {
   //tell the GameManager to hide the action text
   controlCenter.GetComponent(GameManager).showActionMsg=false;
}
```

Since your new method removes the timing of the action message from the individual objects, you can remove the entire **if** clause.

4. Remove the **if** clause

5. Search for showActionMsg = true.

6. In the OnMouseDown function, replace

```
//send the GameManager the action text
controlCenter.SendMessage("ShowActionMessage", tempMsg);
controlCenter.GetComponent(GameManager).actionMsg=tempMsg;
//tell the GameManager to show the action text
```

613

```
controlCenter.GetComponent(GameManager).showActionMsg=true;
//wait two seconds then turn off the action text and leave the function
yield new WaitForSeconds(2.0);
controlCenter.GetComponent(GameManager).showActionMsg= false;
return;
```

with the following

```
//send the GameManager the action text for processing
controlCenter.SendMessage("ShowActionMessage", tempMsg);
return;
```

7. Continue the search.

8. In the ProcessObject function, remove the following lines:

```
//tell the GameManager to show the action text
controlCenter.GetComponent(GameManager).showActionMsg=true;
```

9. Save the script.

10. Click Play and make sure you have no typographical errors.

11. Stop Play mode.

And now you will send the message off from the ObjectLookup script.

12. Open the ObjectLookup script.

13. In the LookUpState function, replace this line

```
controlCenter.GetComponent(GameManager).actionMsg= actionMsg;
```

with this line

```
controlCenter.SendMessage("ShowActionMessage", actionMsg);
```

Because you have separated the action message from the processing time allowed for the animations, you can now delete the timeAdjuster line and its function.

14. Delete the following line:

```
timeAdjuster(actionMsg); //send the message off to adjust processing time
```

15. And delete this function:

```
// function to calculate extra processing time to read action message
function timeAdjuster(actionMsg : String) {

   var stringLength: int  =  actionMsg.length;
   var addTime = stringLength / 25.0 -1.75; //calculate the amount of time to add
   if (addTime >= 0) GetComponent("Interactor").timeLimit2 =↵
 GetComponent("Interactor").timeLimit2 + addTime;

}
```

16. Save the script.

17. Click Play and make sure you have no typographical errors.

18. Stop Play mode.

Because it was accessing the `timeLimit2` variable in the Interactor, you need to go back and check on it there.

1. Open the Interactor script.

2. Use Find to locate `timeLimit2` in the script.

It appears as a variable, is used in the `timer2` section in the `Update` function and in a section in `OnMouseDown`. The section in `OnMouseDown` looks as follows:

```
// start a timer to turn off processing
timeLimit2 = Time.time + 2.0;
timer2 = true;
//tell the GameManager which object just started the timer2
controlCenter.GetComponent(GameManager).actionObject = this.name;
```

Since the `timeLimit2` variable is controlling processing time to allow the animation play out, you can leave it as is. The last two lines, however, are no longer needed since you moved the action message time management to the `GameManager`. If you think back a bit, you will remember that the `actionObject` variable was created as a means of preventing the previous object's timer from turning off the message when another had already started using it.

3. Delete the last two lines.

4. Save the script.

Having worked with the project for some time now, you may be tempted to speed up the processing time. Typically, you will end up being so familiar with the project that your tendency is to minimize the time allotted for things. When a person who has not seen the game or application before tries it for the first time, they will probably complain that things happen too quickly.

The processing time prevents mouseover text from overrunning action text during animations. Animations generally last about a second but you probably do not want to allow mouseovers for at least 1.5 seconds.

1. Change the `timeLimit2 = Time.time + 2.0` line to the following if you feel you need to:

```
timeLimit2 = Time.time + 1.5;
```

2. Save the script.

So far, the system holds up well for interactions with animations. Objects that go directly into inventory or other states or locations leave the user without a visible cursor for the whole read time. You can add an `else` clause to the `if animates` section to turn the cursor back on while allowing the text to be read as usual.

1. Open the Interactor script.

2. Beneath the closing curly bracket for the if(animates **&&** animationClip[currentState] != null) block in the ProcessObject function, add the following:

```
//if it doesn't animate, show the pointer again after a brief pause
else {
   yield new WaitForSeconds(0.25);
   controlCenter.GetComponent(GameManager).showPointer = true;
}
```

3. Save the script.

As a final bit of housekeeping, you can remove the actionObject variable from the GameManager since you are no longer using it.

1. Open the GameManager script.

2. Delete the following line:

```
private var actionObject : String; // the name of the latest action object to turn on↩
 the actionMsg
```

3. Save the script.

4. Click Play and make sure things still work smoothly.

Back to Fades

1. Click Play and pick the Rock (yes, the action that instigated the last several pages of spring cleaning).

This time you have enough time to read the message before the object is deactivated. The action message is well behaved and ready for future modifications you may want to implement in your functionality.

Let's test a fade in next. The KeyAtLock needs to fade in, but first you need to make sure it is off at scene start up, and then you will activate it by picking another object.

2. Stop Play mode.

3. Select the KeyAtLock.

4. Add the Interactor and ObjectLookup scripts to it.

5. For now, fill out the two states as shown in Figure 13-7.

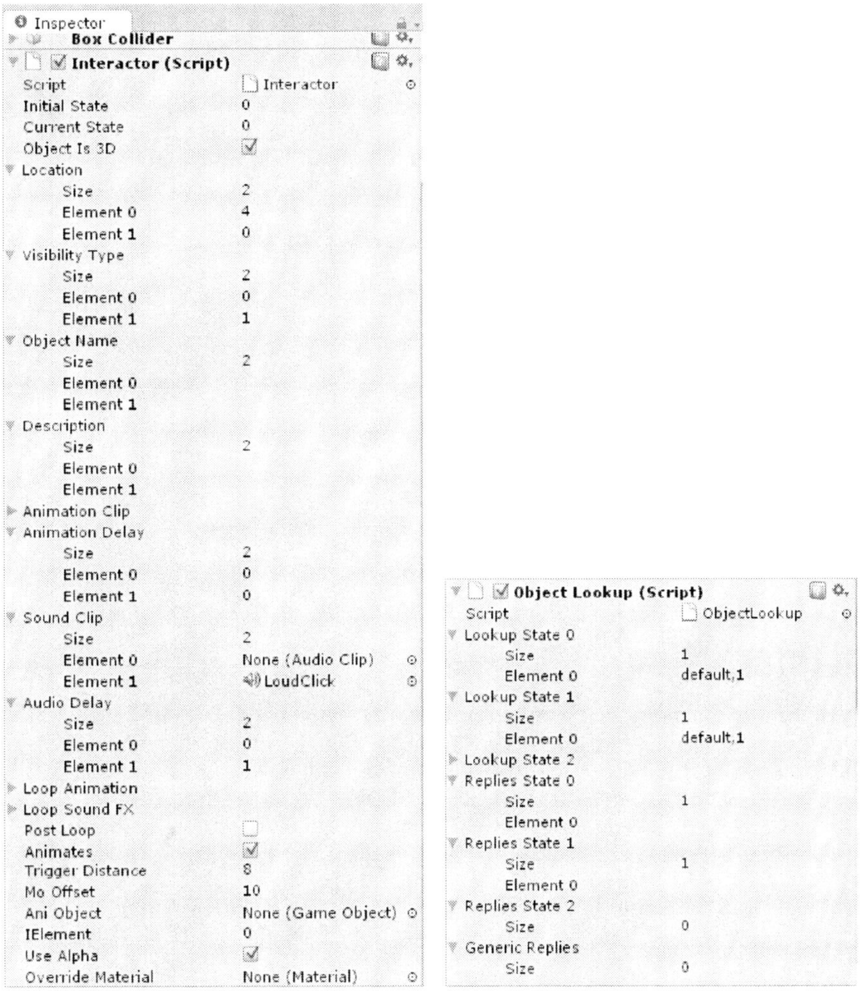

Figure 13-7. *Metadata and state information for the KeyAtLock*

6. Click Play.

The KeyAtLock disappears on start up as expected since its Location is 4, not in scene. To activate it, you will trigger it to appear when you pick a different object.

1. Stop Play mode.

2. Select the ChestLid.

3. Change its Initial State to 0.

4. In the Object Lookup component, change its Lookup State 0, Element 0 to the following:

```
default,0,KeyAtLock,1
```

5. Click Play and pick the ChestLid.

You get a message saying that an animation clip has not been assigned. You switched the ChestLid to state 0, a state that does not yet have an animation. Its other states, however do, so your check for the `animates` value breaks. There are several possible solutions, but the easiest right now is to add a check for a null animation clip.

6. Stop Play mode.

7. Open the Interactor script.

8. In the `ProcessObject` function, change the `if`(`animates`) line to the following:

```
if(animates && animationClip[currentState] != null) {
```

9. Save the script.

10. Click Play and test.

Location and Visibility Type should be under control now.

11. Save the scene and save the project.

Object to Object Interaction

So far, you have concentrated on functionality that involves only one 3D object at a time. In a classic interactive adventure game, the challenge is often about figuring out how to combine objects to make something that is crucial to moving the game forward. In your game, you will need to combine the Golden Sleeve with the Crowbar to use on a couple of other action objects. You have their cursor counterparts combining correctly in inventory so now it would be nice to have the option to combine them in the 3D scene. Most of the pieces of the puzzle should be in place now to test this kind of functionality.

Let's load a few more objects into the scene so you will be able to test your progress better.

1. Set all of the inventory icon objects' Initial States to 0.

2. Copy the ActionObjects folder from the BookAssets folder into the Assets folder of the project.

3. Adjust the import Scale Factor to 0.0025.

4. Click Apply.

5. Drag the action objects and Jewel into the scene near the existing items.

6. Add the key material from the Materials folder in the Animation Tests to the plain crowbar.

For the Golden Sleeve and Crowbar With Sleeve, do the following:

1. Duplicate the Crowbar With Sleeve and SleeveGold textures in the Action Objects folder and append their names with Bmp or Nrml so you can recognize them easily.

2. Turn the copies into normal maps in the Inspector.

3. Set their bumpiness to about 0.05.

4. Select the individual objects in the Hierarchy view and modify their materials.

5. Change the shaders to Bumped Specular and add the normal maps.

6. Set their Main Color to a yellowish color, about 255,220.125.

7. Set their Specular Color to a stronger yellowish gold, about 255,195,60.

8. Adjust their Shininess sliders so they are almost to the far left so the Specular Color is fairly bright.

For the Vial of Elixir:

1. Select the Vial of Elixir.

2. Lighten the Cork material's Main Color.

3. For the glassref material, choose the Reflective > Specular shader.

4. Set the Main Color to a strong turquoise, 0,130,225.

5. Set the Specular Color to a mid pink, 250,105,255.

6. Adjust the Shininess slider to about 5 percent.

7. Leave the Reflection Cubemap empty.

For the Message:

1. Change the shader to a Specular shader.

2. Add a Box Collider.

For the JewelLoose:

1. Drag the Jewel into the scene from the Project view near the other objects.

2. Set the Scale Factor to about 0.008 for now.

3. You already have a Jewel object inside the flower hierarchy, so rename this one to JewelLoose.

4. Open the Jewel Folder and select the Jewel material; it will be a violent magenta.

5. Assign the FX/Diamond shader to it.

6. Drag the light reflection cubemap into its Reflection Texture.

7. Drag the refractions texture into its Refraction Texture (see Figure 13-8).

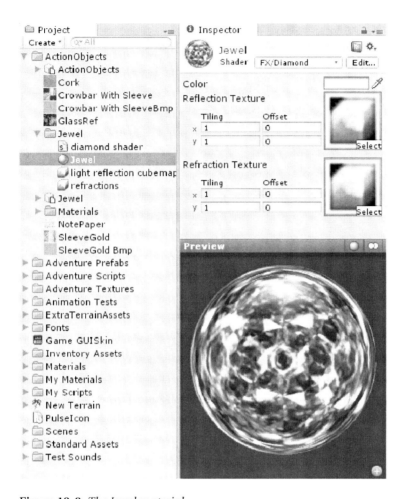

Figure 13-8. *The Jewel material*

⬛**Note**   The Diamond shader and the light reflection cubemap and refractions textures are from the Unity Gem Pack, available from www.unity3d.com/support/resources/assets/gem-shader.html

8. Apply the Jewel material to the JewelLoose in the scene.

9. Add a Sphere Collider to the JewelLoose.

You should now have a crowbar, a golden sleeve, a crowbar with a golden sleeve, a piece of paper with a note on it and a small vial of elixir, as shown in Figure 13-9.

Figure 13-9. *The new action objects*

10. Add the Interactor and LookUpState scripts to the Crowbar, the Golden Sleeve, and the Crowbar With Sleeve objects.

11. Fill out their metadata as shown in Figures 13-10, 13-11, and 13-12.

Figure 13-10. *The Crowbar*

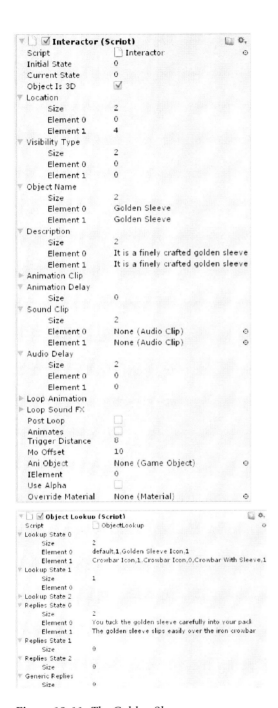

Figure 13-11. *The Golden Sleeve*

Figure 13-12. *The Crowbar With Sleeve*

Be sure to fill out the arrays as before, being careful to have the same number of elements for the LookUp States and their corresponding Replies States.

12. Set each object's Tag to ActionObjects.

13. Add a Capsule Collider to each and adjust its size and orientation (direction) to fit.

14. Save your scene and save your project.

15. Click Play.

16. Try adding the Crowbar and Golden Sleeve together in both the scene and in inventory.

░ **Tip**   Whenever you are creating combination objects that will replace the component parts in the 3D scene, you must make sure each of the objects uses the same pivot point or the positioning will be off when the substitution is made.

Positioning Objects in the Scene

You will have noticed that when you pick up the Golden Sleeve and add it to the Crowbar in the scene, or start with the Crowbar and add it to the Golden Sleeve, the new object (the Crowbar With Sleeve combination object) appears to jump to a different location.

With objects that animate, such as the key, you used duplicates. With an object that doesn't animate, at least when combined, or objects that need to appear in different locations depending on state, you will need a means of positioning them. If they have animations, they will automatically jump to the position defined by the keyframes, but those that do not have animations will need a different solution.

With an object that needs to be combined with another to make a third object, you will not know ahead of time where the new object needs to be put. At present, your use-case for this is the Crowbar and Golden Sleeve. Either one could be the cursor or the picked object. What you can do is create an empty game object that will hold the picked object's transform providing it is a 3D object. Once you have that, you will be able to use it to position the new object.

1. Create an empty gameObject.

2. Name it HoldTransform.

Now you need to add a bit of code to transfer the picked object's transform information to the holder object.

3. Open the ObjectLookup script.

4. Inside the LookupState function, just below the **else** matchCursor = picker; line (near the top), add the following:

```
// store the picked object's position on the holder object
var holder = GameObject.Find("HoldTransform"); // get the holder object
```

```
// store the current object's position on the holder object
   holder.transform.position= this.transform.position;
   holder.transform.rotation= this.transform.rotation;
```

5. Save the script.

6. Click Play.

7. Select the HoldTransform object in the Hierarchy view.

8. Pick various objects in the Game view.

In the Scene view, you will see the HoldTransform's transform gizmo move to the various picked objects (see Figure 13-13).

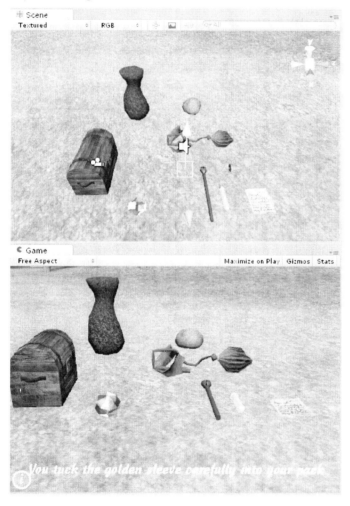

Figure 13-13. *The HoldTransform object moving to the picked object's transform*

Since the object may need to move to a static location, you ought to allow for another target position. This may be an actual object in the scene, or, like the HoldTransform object, it may be a simple place holder to match to. Next you will need to make an array to hold these objects and a variable to tell you what type of drop object it is.

1. Open the Interactor script.

2. In the //object metadata section, add the following:

```
var transformTo : GameObject[];  // move to another object's transforms array
var dropType : int = 0; // 0 is not dropable, 1 is dropable , 2 is a drop location
```

3. Open the GameNotes text asset and add the following:

```
Drop Type:
0 - Not droppable
1 - Droppable
2 - Is a drop location
```

Since most objects will *not* need to be transformed, you will not bother to make a currentTransformTo variable, but instead will check the dropType variable to see what to do. If there are no elements in the array and the object is droppable, you will use the holder object's location. If there are elements, you will need to see if the element for the current state has a valid entry, and then process accordingly.

4. In the ProcessObject function, beneath the //load new states' metadata section, add the following:

```
if (dropType == 1) {

    var holder = GameObject.Find("HoldTransform"); // get the holder object

    // if there are any elements in the array
    if (transformTo.length > 0 && transformTo[currentState] != null) {
        print ("moving to " + transformTo[currentState].name);
        holder.transform.position= transformTo [currentState].transform.position;
        holder.transform.rotation= transformTo [currentState].transform.rotation;
    }
    transform.position = holder.transform.position;
    transform.rotation = holder.transform.rotation;
}
```

5. Save the script.

As with the other metadata arrays, if they are used, they must have an element for each state whether or not it contains any data.

6. Turn off Play mode.

7. Select the Crowbar With Sleeve.

8. Set its Drop Type to 1.

9. Click Play and test for Crowbar picking Golden Sleeve and vice versa.

To assure yourselves that it works well, you can rotate one of the objects and see what happens.

10. Click Play.

11. In the Scene window, rotate the Crowbar.

12. In the Game window, pick the Golden Sleeve, fetch it from inventory, and pick the Crowbar (see Figure 13-14).

Figure 13-14. *The target object transform rotated*

The Crowbar With Sleeve appears in the correct place. Let's try the code with some other location as the target.

1. Create an empty gameObject, name it SomeOtherPlace.

2. Move to a place apart from the action objects (make sure it is not below the terrain).

3. Select the Crowbar With Sleeve.

4. Set its Transform To array Size to 2 (to match the rest of its arrays).

5. Drag the SomeOtherPlace object into its Element 1 (remember it is not in scene in state 0).

6. Click Play and test.

The Crowbar With Sleeve object appears at the auxiliary location once the component parts are combined, as shown in Figure 13-15.

Figure 13-15. *Using an auxiliary target*

7. Stop Play mode.

8. Set the Transform To array Size back to 0.

9. Save your scene and save your project.

Special Cases

Before you can finish filling out the metadata and getting the final game sequences up and running, you need to add a last important block of code to the LookUpState script. This bit of code is like a wild card that will enable you to extend the functionality of some of the action objects without disturbing the generic nature of the Interactor and LookUpState scripts.

As they stand, the concept is for an object to animate into the new state. The problem with this is that if there are dependencies, you will need to make extra states to be able to go into a particular state either by animating, or in some cases, not animating. The Rock was one example of this. The ChestLid is another.

The ChestLid would require four states. If the lid is closed, it is either unlocked or locked. Neither of these states require animation. It starts out closed and locked, state 0. The key moves it to state 1, closed and unlocked, with no animation. It can be opened into state 2. From state 2, it must go to state 3, also closed and unlocked, but animating to get into the state. And from state 3, closed, it can animate back to state 2, open. From state 3, closed and unlocked, it can also be moved back to the locked state, 0, by turning the key, there again with no animation.

If you had a way to tag the lookup information, you could easily skip the animation and sound effects and avoid having to calculate dependencies and extra non-animating states. The one thing you do know is that it will always be the auxiliary object processing that will need to change object's states without animation.

Much in the same way as you have developed numbers to stand for various states, you can preface the lookup information with special characters to tell it to handle all types of scenarios that differ from the stock setup. The system will allow you to add cases as needed in the future as well. You will start with the need for skipping animations for now, and will later expand it to cover special effect, special scripts, and other things.

Extensible Code

For special cases in the auxiliary objects, you will preface the regular object name with a three character code. The first is the case identifier, the second is an "extra information needed" flag, and the third is an underscore that identifies the data as needing special processing.

1. Open the ObjectLookUp script.

2. In the LookUpState function, under the //check for special cases here line, add the following:

```
//check for special tags according to first 3 characters; first is the case, second is↵
 optional
//info for processing, third is the tag "_"  for special case, example: s0_SomeObjectName
if (tempS.Substring(2,1) == "_") { // if there is a special case
   var s = tempS.Substring(0,1);
   var s2 = parseInt(tempS.Substring(1,1)); // convert the second character to an integer
   var auxObject = CheckForActive(tempS .Substring(3)); // find the object of that name and↵
   activate

   // look for the matching case
   switch (s) {
      case "a":  // trigger animation only on the auxiliary object
         auxObject.animation.Play(GetComponent(Interactor).animationClip[s2].name);
         var bypass = true; // skip the regular processing
         break;
      case "s": // send a message to a script on the auxiliary object to the "DoTheJob"
function
         auxObject.SendMessage("DoTheJob");
         if (s2 == 1) bypass = true; // skip the regular processing
         break;
      case "b": // change the state on the object only- no animations
         auxObject.GetComponent(Interactor).currentState= parseInt(readString[x+1]);
         bypass = true; // skip the regular processing
         break;
      case "p": // instantiate a prefab
         // some code here
         bypass = true; // skip the regular processing
         break;
   } // close switch
```

```
} // close if
```

3. Change the auxObject = CheckForActive(tempS) line to an **else** so the tempS will get processed if it was not a special case:

```
else auxObject = CheckForActive(tempS);
```

And then you check for the bypass and process the object into its new state.

4. After the var newState = parseInt(readString[x+1]) line, add the condition so the next line reads as follows:

```
 // process the object as long as it is not marked to bypass
if (nextState >= 0 && !bypass) auxObject.SendMessage( "ProcessObject",newState);
// -1 is bypass
```

5. Save the script.

6. Test existing functionality to make sure it still works.

7. Add the special cases to the GameNotes text asset as follows:

    case "a": trigger animation only on the auxiliary object

    case "s": send a message to a script on this object to the "DoTheJob" function

    case "b": change the state on the object only- no animations

    case "p": instantiate a prefab

8. Save the GameNotes changes.

Reply, No State Change

Specialty clauses will work well on the auxiliary objects, but you could still use an option to reuse a state without playing the animation that got it into that state in the first place. A prime example would be the Rock. It has two states, original position and moved. When it goes from state 0 to state 1, it animates to get there. Once there, however, you are no longer allowing the user to pick it. In classic point and click adventure games, "used" objects often continue to evoke entertaining or even helpful responses. Since the action message goes with the current state, if you could bypass the ProcessObject function, you could avoid having to fill out an extra state.

One option to solve this is to set up a very simple flag that does not even need to be declared. Your states are all greater than or equal to 0. If you specify -1 as the new state, you can reinterpret that to mean "skip the ProcessObject and just display the action message."

Let's go ahead and set up the Rock as a test subject. To start, you will removing the fade from the Rock.

1. Stop Play mode.

2. Select the Rock.

3. In the Interactor component in the Inspector, change both Location and Visibility Type for Element 1 from 4 to 0.

4. Add a Lookup State 1 and a Replies State 1.

5. Fill them in as follows:

Lookup State 1 - `default,1`

Replies State 1 - `The rock seems tightly wedged`

6. Click Play and test.

The Rock goes back to its original position, and then animates back into to state 1
Same state, message only, new state -1

1. Open the `ObjectLookup` script.

2. Near the top of the `LookUpState` function, change the
`SendMessage("ProcessObject", nextState)` line to the following:

```
if (nextState >= 0) SendMessage("ProcessObject", nextState); // no bypass flag so process it
```

3. Save the script.

4. Stop Play mode.

5. Change the Rock's Lookup State 1 to:

```
default,-1
```

6. Click Play and test.

The Rock stays put and the message appears.

7. Stop Play mode.

8. Open the GameNotes text asset.

9. Add the following:

```
Setting the new state to -1 in the Lookup information flags an object to remain in its↵
 current state, but display an action message
```

10. Save the GameNotes changes.

Activating the Treasure Chest Sequence

With most of the regular scripting in place, you can get the treasure chest sequence set up and
functional. The ideal sequence of events is as follows:

1. With the key as cursor, select the LockPlate – key goes into lock.

2. With the key in the lock, turn it, the ChestLid is unlocked.

3. With the lid unlocked, open it.

4. Take the piece of Paper, it goes into inventory or is read immediately.

5. Or read the Paper from inventory; it gives a hint about leaving the Crowbar.

6. Select the Crowbar.

7. Drop the Crowbar into the chest.

8. Close the ChestLid.

   9. Lock the key.

   10. Remove the key.

Now that you have a means of changing states without having to process an object, you can set up a more complex key-lock-chest lid sequence. To start, let's clean up a few objects that you used as test subjects.

   1. Select the Pedestal.

   2. Remove the ChestLid from its Lookup State 1, Element 0 so it is as follows:

`default,2`

   3. Select the KeyAtRock.

   4. Change its Lookup State 0, Element 0 as follows:

`default,1,Iron Key Icon,1`

The LockPlate has three states, described in Table 13-2.

Table 13-2. *LockPlate States*

State	Description	Animation	Cursor	New State	Aux Objects, New State
0	Empty	None	default	0	
0		None	Iron Key Icon	1	Iron Key Icon,0,KeyAtLock,1
1	Key in lock, locked	None	default	0	Iron Key Icon,1,KeyAtLock,0
2	Key in lock, unlocked	None	default	2	

The KeyAtLock has five states, described in Table 13-3.

Table 13-3. *KeyAtLock States*

State	Description	Animation	Cursor (triggered by)	New State	Aux Objects, New State
0	Not in scene	key insert	(LockPlate)	1	
1	Inserted, locked	key unlock	default	2	b0_ChestLid,1,LockPlate,2
2	Inserted, unlocked	key lock	default	3	b0_ChestLid,0,LockPlate,1
3	Inserted, locked	Key unlock	default	2	LockPlate,2,b0_ChestLid,1
4	unlocked, lid open	None	default	4,(-1)	

The ChestLid has three states, described in Table 13-4.

Table 13-4. *ChestLid States*

State	Description	Animation	Cursor (triggered by)	New State	Aux Objects, New State
0	Locked	lid rattle (bypass)	default (KeyAtLock)	0 1	
1	closed, unlocked	chest open	default	2	b0_KeyAtLock,4,b0_LockPlate,3
2	open, unlocked	chest close	default	1	b0_KeyAtLock,2

The Message has two states, described in Table 13-5.

Table 13-5. *Message States*

State	Description	Animation	Cursor (triggered by)	New State	Aux Objects, New State
0	In scene	None	default	1	MessageView,1
1	Not in scene	None			

The MessageView has two states, described in Table 13-6.

Table 13-6. *MessageView States*

State	Description	Animation	Cursor (triggered by)	New State	Aux Objects, New State
0	Not in scene	None	(Message)	1	Message,1
1	At Camera	None	default	0	Message Icon,1

The ChestInside has two states, described in Table 13-7.

Table 13-7. *ChestInside States*

State	Description	Animation	Cursor (triggered by)	New State	Aux Objects, New State
0	Empty	None	default Crowbar Icon	−1 1	Crowbar,0,Crowbar Icon,0
1	Has crowbar	None	default	0	Message Icon,1

Now you can set up the LockPlate for more functionality. It will start out empty (and locked), as state 0, have the key inserted (still locked), as state 1, and as state 2, the key turned (unlocked). In its unlocked state, the player can not remove the key.

1. Activate the LockPlate.

2. Add the `Interactor` script (it should already have the `ObjectLookup`).

3. Fill out the metadata for three states- empty, key in, key unlocked (see Figure 13-16).

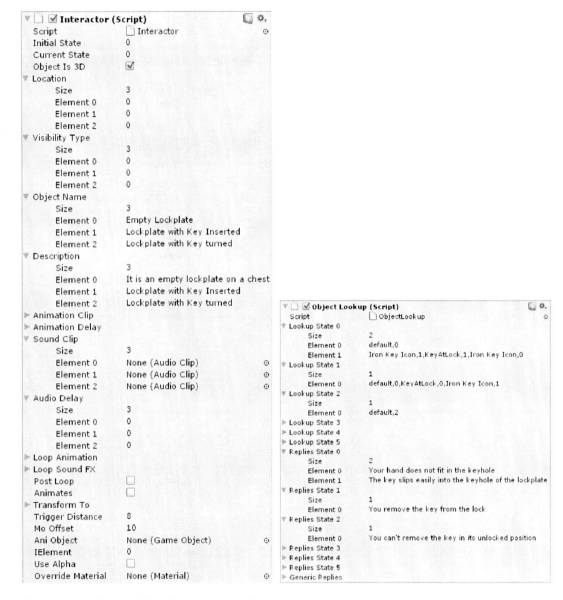

Figure 13-16. *The LockPlate's metadata and lookup information*

4. Click Play.

You get a "missing MeshRenderer" error message (see Figure 13-17).

MissingComponentException: There is no 'MeshRenderer' attached to the 'LockPlate' game object, but a script is trying to access it.

Figure 13-17. *The error message*

Although the LockPlate is an empty gameObject with a Collider, you can still add a Mesh Renderer and avoid the error message.

1. Stop Play mode.

2. Add Mesh Renderer to it from the Component/Mesh menu.

3. Disable the Mesh Renderer component.

4. Click Play.

The error message disappears.

5. Test the LockPlate with the default cursor.

6. Test it with key cursor.

The key appears and is inserted in the LockPlate. You need to break the KeyAtLock's animation into four splits instead of two. Since you now have a means of automatically fading in the key, you can use the original imported animations.

1. Stop Play mode.

2. Select the KeyAtLock in the Project view from the Animation Tests/Animation Objects folder.

3. In the FBX Importer, add two more splits and change key animation splits to:

    key insert, 31-45

    key unlock, 46-59

    key lock, 121-135

    key remove, 136-150

4. Click Apply.

Because you lost the prefab when you added the scripts, you will need to load the new clips manually.

5. Select the KeyAtLock in the Hierarchy view.

6. In the Animation component, increase the size of the Animations array to 8.

7. Select the existing key clips in the array.

Note that they are all in the first group of duplicates.

8. Load the new key lock and key unlock from the first set of new duplicates.

9. Load the key lock clip in the Animation parameter as the default.

10. Check Play Automatically.

11. Set the Element 0 Location to 0 instead of 4.

12. Click Play and watch the key in the Scene view to make sure you have the correct clip.

13. Test with the three other newly added clips.

14. Stop Play mode.

15. Set the Element 0 Location back to 4.

16. Uncheck Play Automatically.

The KeyAtLock will need four states and you presently have only allowed for three in the ObjectLookup script.

1. Open the ObjectLookup script.

2. Increase the lookupStates and repliesStates variable to six each.

```
var lookupState0 : String[];  //declare an array of string type content
var lookupState1 : String[];  //declare an array of string type content
var lookupState2 : String[];  //declare an array of string type content
var lookupState3 : String[];  //declare an array of string type content
var lookupState4 : String[];  //declare an array of string type content
var lookupState5 : String[];  //declare an array of string type content
var repliesState0 : String[];
var repliesState1 : String[];
var repliesState2 : String[];
var repliesState3 : String[];
var repliesState4 : String[];
var repliesState5 : String[];
```

3. Change these lines to 6 instead of 3:

```
// make a regular array holding 6 elements to process the selected element's contents
private var stateArray = new Array [6];
// make a regular array holding 6 elements to hold the replies for each state
private var replyArray = new Array [6];
```

4. In the Start function, increase those to match as well:

```
// load the Unity string arrays into the JavaScript array elements
stateArray[0] = lookupState0;
stateArray[1] = lookupState1;
stateArray[2] = lookupState2;
stateArray[3] = lookupState3;
stateArray[4] = lookupState4;
stateArray[5] = lookupState5;
// load the Unity string arrays into the JavaScript array elements
replyArray[0] = repliesState0;
replyArray[1] = repliesState1;
replyArray[2] = repliesState2;
replyArray[3] = repliesState3;
replyArray[4] = repliesState4;
replyArray[5] = repliesState5;
```

5. Save the script.

6. Fill out the metadata and lookup information for the KeyAtLock (see Figure 13-18).

Figure 13-18. *The KeyAtLock's metadata and lookup information*

Note the addition of an extra state for not available when the key is in the lock and the chest lid open.

The ChestLid will need a short rattle animation for when the lid is locked.

1. Select the ChestLid.

2. Open the Animation view, Ctrl+6.

3. Add a new animation clip in the Animation Clips folder.

4. Name the new clip lid rattle.

The new animation clip appears in the ChestLid's Animations array.

1. Select the Rotation.z track and turn on the Record button.

2. Add a key at frame 0.

3. Move the indicator to frame 5.

Note that the native animation shows 60 frames per second.

4. Set the value to 178.

5. Move the indicator to frame 10.

6. Set the value to 180.

7. Repeat a few times.

8. Click the Play button next to the Record button to see how the animation looks.

9. Close the Animation view.

10. Fill out the ChestLid's metadata and lookup information (see Figure 13-19).

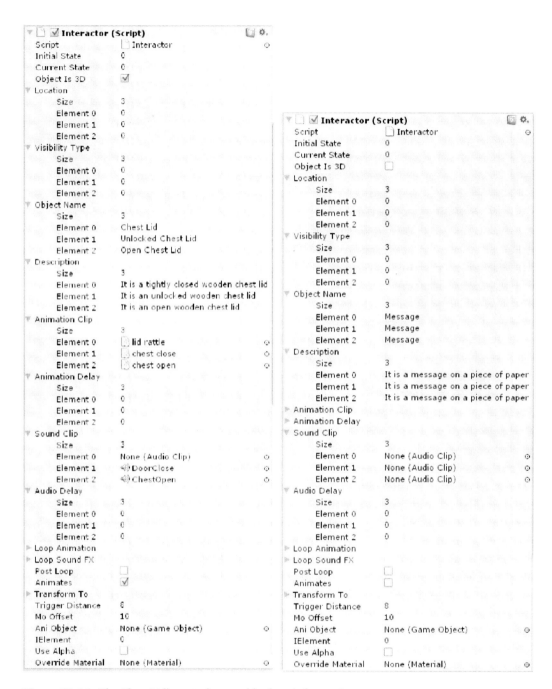

Figure 13-19. *The ChestLid's metadata and lookup information*

With the addition of the KeyAtLock and ChestLid, you should be able to test using the following procedure:

1. Pick Rock.

2. Take key.

3. Take key from inventory.

4. Insert key into LockPlate (pick LockPlate).

5. Turn key.

6. Open ChestLid.

7. Try to turn key.

8. Try to remove key (pick LockPlate).

9. Close Lid.

10. Turn key.

11. Remove key (goes into inventory).

■ **Tip**   Feel free to change inventory/cursor assignments so you do not need to go into inventory to fetch items while you are testing.

---

12. Click Play and test the procedure.

13. Save the scene and save the project.

Reading Material

A mainstay of the adventure genre is the existence of objects such as books, notes, and letters that provide the player with clues to the story or necessary game play. While giving written clues and other information may seem a bit too obvious, it does provide a nice variation from the other action objects. Clues, of course, can be blatant to obscure. In your game, you will use a bitmap with the writing already on it, but you might also use an empty page object and use the Unity GUI to provide the actual text. That method would make changing languages or hint levels more economical.

You will need three objects for your text message; the message on the ground, Message, the Message Icon in inventory, and a message in front of the camera, MessageView. Let's start with the easy ones.

1. Select the Message Icon.

2. Add the Interactor and ObjectLookup scripts to it.

3. Fill them out as in Figure 13-20).

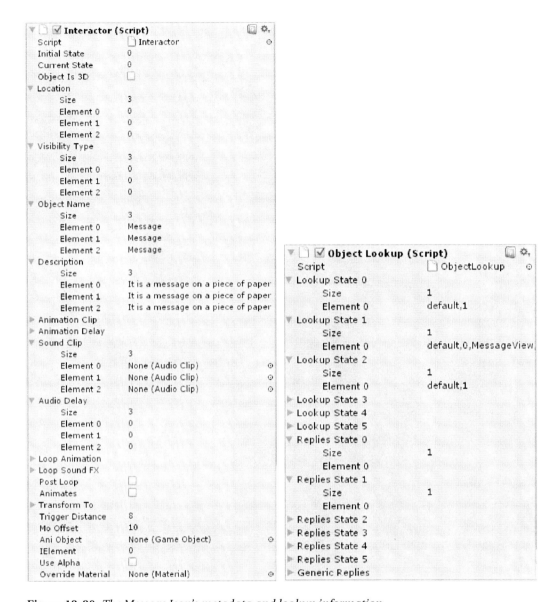

Figure 13-20. *The Message Icon's metadata and lookup information*

4.   Select the Message from the ActionObjects group.

5.   Add the Interactor and ObjectLookup scripts to it.

6.   Fill them out as in Figure 13-21).

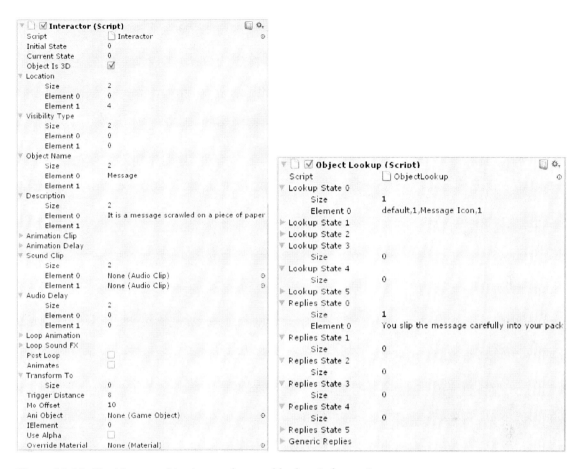

Figure 13-21. *The Message object's metadata and lookup information*

7.   Tag it as an ActionObject.

To allow your players to read the Message, you will create a copy and put it in front of the camera. The trick here is to remember that you will also need to read it from inventory where you have turned off your Main Camera layer and are using the inventory camera. Fortunately, you have a camera layer that always renders on top of both layers, the Camera Pointer.

1.   Duplicate the Message object and name it MessageView.

2.   Add the new object to the Pointer layer.

3.   Select Camera Pointer and Align View to Selected.

4.   Select the MessageView object.

5.   Use Align With View and Move to View.

6.   Change the Scene view to a top view.

7. Adjust the MessageView object's distance to the camera until it fills the Game window nicely.

8. In the Inspector, rotate the object on the X axis until the MessageView object is aligned with the Game view.

9. Rotate the object on the Y axis until the paper is in the light.

10. Select the Camera Pointer and Align With View (see Figure 13-22).

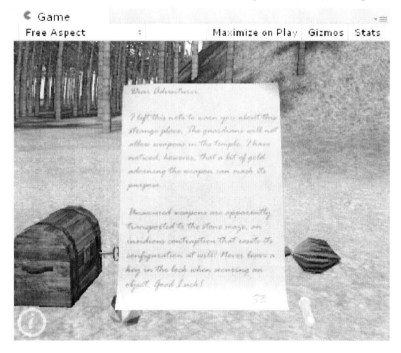

Figure 13-22. *The MessageView object in the game window*

11. Select the MessageView object.

12. Change its metadata and object lookup data (see Figure 13-23).

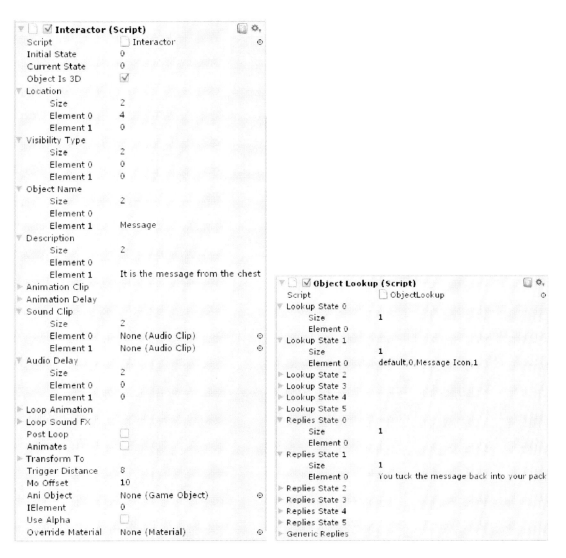

Figure 13-23. *The MessageView object's metadata and lookup information*

13. Save the scene and save the project.

14. Click Play and test the message on the ground and in inventory.

Unlike GUI based objects, your 3D mesh scales to match the viewport whatever its size. Everything works until you try to close the message to put it back in inventory. The pick is not processed because you have a return if you are in iMode and the layer is not 9, the inventory camera's layer. The Pointer camera's layer is 8, so it is a quick fix to process picks to it from the Interactor script for objects in the Pointer layer.

1. Open the Interactor script.

2. in the OnMouseDown function, change the **if** (iMode **&&** gameObject.layer !=
    9) line as follows:

```
// allow picks from layers 8 and 9 in inventory mode
```

if (iMode **&&** gameObject.layer < 8) **return**;

3. Save the script.

4. Pick the MessageView.

The message now goes back into inventory as expected. The filtering for layers only happens in
inventory mode, but it is still good practice to see if there are any problems if the MessageView is
displayed immediately instead of going into inventory.

5. Stop Play mode.

6. Select the Message object.

7. In its Object Lookup component, change the Lookup state 1, Element 0 to:

```
default,1,MessageView,1
```

8. Click Play and test.

The MessageView object is not being processed. This time, the culprit is the distance to camera,
specifically, the distance to the Main Camera. There are several different ways you could handle the
issue. You could add more conditions to the return statements, setting flags or using a negative distance
as an ignore flag, or you could simply override the distance to camera returned if the object's layer is 8.
Let's try the latter. To begin with, you will need to create a local variable that will hold the distance from
camera so it can be overridden.

1. Open the Interactor script.

2. In the OnMouseDown function, locate the two lines that check for distance to
    camera and replace DistanceFromCamera() with tempDistance:

3. In the OnMouseDown function, beneath the **if** (iMode **&&** gameObject.layer line,
    add the following:

```
//store the distance from camera in a variable
var tempDistance: float = DistanceFromCamera();
```

4. Beneath the **var** tempDistance = DistanceFromCamera() line, add the
    following:

```
//override the distance check if the object is in layer 8
if(gameObject.layer == 8) tempDistance = 1;
```

5. Save the script.

6. Click Play and test.

The message is now pickable (see Figure 13-2).

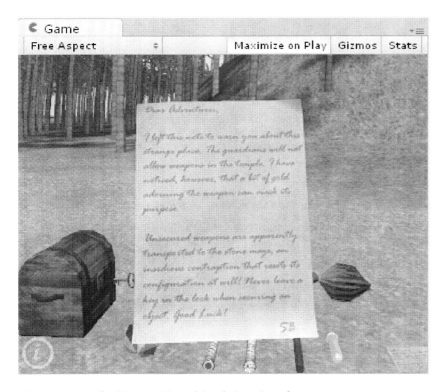

Figure 13-42. *The MessageView object being viewed*

You can force inventory mode to turn off when you are reading the MessageView by using your special case tag. The script that toggles inventory mode is found on the Camera Inventory, so you need to include it in the instructions for the Message icon. A quick peek at the GameNotes tells you the 's' flag calls a function named DoTheJob on any script that contains a function of that name on the specified object.

1. Stop Play mode.

2. Select the Message Icon object.

3. Change its Lookup State 1, Element 0 to:

default,0,MessageView,1,s1_Camera Inventory,0

4. Open the InventoryManager script.

5. Add the following function to it:

```
function DoTheJob () {

   if(iMode) ToggleMode ();

}
```

6. Save the script.

7. Click Play and test.

8. Stop Play mode.

Now the MessageView is read with the inventory hidden. The only problem is that the player can navigate the scene with it in front of the scene. If you consider that bonus functionality, you still need to have the message go back into inventory if the player picks anywhere else other than the object. In inventory mode, you had another object that covers the scene to catch picks, but it is associated with the Inventory layer. Rather than create another object and write code for it, you can just increase the size of the MessageView's collider to cover the screen.

1. Select the MessageView object,

2. In the Game window, turn on Gizmos (next to the Maximize on Play toggle).

3. Increase the MessageView's collider's size until it is covering the screen at the appropriate aspect ratio.

4. Turn off Gizmos in the Game window.

5. Click Play and test by clicking somewhere other than the MessageView object to close it.

At this point, you may opt to have the message being read immediately when picked from the scene or only after it has first gone into inventory.

1. Stop Play mode.

2. Select the Message object.

3. If you wish to have the MessageView being read immediately, change the Replies State 0, Element 0 to the following:

You carefully lift the message for inspection.

4. If you wish to have the message go into inventory first, change the Lookup State 0, Element 0 to the following:

default,1,Message Icon,1

As a last bit of functionality, you may want to hide the message during regular editing. Unfortunately, if you deactivate it during edit mode, it will not be found when the game starts up. You could turn off its Mesh Renderer and write code to turn it on in the Awake function, before it gets deactivated into its state 0, or you could just turn the Camera Pointer off during editing and turn it on Start. Both options are probably the same amount of work, but the latter is more generic should you add more objects that need to be read.

Because the Pointer camera has no scripts of its own, you will need to create a script to specifically implement the functionality, or you could find the camera from another object's script. The most logical place to turn the camera on is in the GameManager script where you are already managing most of the game's generic functionality.

1. Select the Camera Pointer.

2. Deactivate its Camera component.

3. Open the GameManager script.

4. Add the following near the top of the Start function:

```
GameObject.Find("Camera Pointer").GetComponent(Camera).enabled = true;
```

5. Save the script.

6. Click Play and test the message.

7. Stop Play mode.

The message remains hidden during edit mode.

Tip While the Camera Pointer layer is not drawn in the Game window, it *does* show up in the Scene window directly in front of its camera. You could, if you wished, move the camera and MessageView object to a less intrusive position as long as they are moved as one. Moving the objects may require an additional light with limited range to keep it properly lit.

Hiding the Message

1. Select the ChestLid and turn off its Mesh Renderer.

2. Select the Message object and move it into the bottom of the chest, scaling it to fit inside.

3. Turn on the ChestLid's Mesh Renderer.

4. Turn on Maximize on Play in the Game window.

5. Click Play and test (see Figure 13-25).

6. Save the scene and save the project.

With the addition of the message inside the chest, you can see how the player must navigate to the chest to look inside it. While experienced gamers will have no trouble with this, neophytes may find it frustrating. In the next chapter, you will devise a means of positioning the player in the ideal place to interact with objects.

Figure 13-25. *The Message in the Chest*

In an expanded version of the game, the player may need to hide the Crowbar in the chest to keep it safe while he enters the temple. You could duplicate the Crowbar and use it as an in-chest version much as you have two keys, but in the next chapter you will create a system that will let the player stash qualified objects in different locations.

Chapter Summary

In this chapter, you finished up the basic functionality for the action objects by dealing with Location and Visibility to script automated fade ins and outs of action objects. Along the way you discovered that "invisible" did not affect collisions, mouseovers, or picking of objects, so you learned how to activate and deactivate objects during runtime.

Returning to cursors, you added the functionality to recognize scene object types that were not action objects. Utilizing ray casting, you were able to know when to drop cursor objects back into inventory when incorrect picks were registered. This functionality gave you the opportunity to experiment with random replies that were automatically customized for the objects involved in the interaction.

As a side effect of activating and deactivating 3D objects in the scene as their 2D counterparts go in and out of inventory, you discovered that pending actions such as turning text off required a different means of deactivation. By setting timers in the Update functions of persistent scripts such as the GameManager, you were able to keep things moving smoothly as objects were removed from the scene.

After adding more action objects to the scene, you got a chance to combine objects by replacing one of the component objects with the combo version regardless of its position in the scene.

Finally, you completed the "Special Cases" section of the LookupState function, enabling you to make good progress toward your most complicated sequence, the treasure chest scenario. As a bonus, you created the means to use papers or other reading material as action objects.

In the next chapter, you will put the final touches on the treasure chest sequence, bring in your final game assets and create a small final scene.

■ ■ ■

Getting Down to Game

In this chapter you will finish up the treasure chest sequence, revive the flower so you can get the jewel, import most of the rest of the necessary assets for your game, enhance the temple and make sure the magic happens, and tidy up a few more loose ends.

1. Open the project.

2. Save the current scene, Inventory, as **Interaction2**.

Drop Box

The last bit of functionality to finish up for the treasure chest sequence is the ability to drop an object into the chest. You already have the framework for this functionality from the crowbar sequence. At minimum, you need to be able to drop the crowbar into the chest. You could make another crowbar for that position, but it would entail setting up all of the metadata and information. You could also set up another state for the crowbar and create a helper object for that particular location. A third possibility is to simply transform the object to that location much as we transformed the Crowbar with Sleeve object to the location of the Crowbar or Golden Sleeve objects. Since this is a more flexible solution, let's add it to the game's functionality.

Let's start by creating an action object for the *inside* of the box. Since the action object represented by the icon will move to the pivot point of the box's action object, it will need to be centered at the point the other objects should be positioned. This also means that any objects you choose to drop into the chest (or other places) need to have their pivot points centered and at their base.

1. Disable the ChestLid from the top of the Inspector.

2. Focus in on the ChestBase.

3. Create an Empty GameObject and name it **DropGroup**.

4. Create a Cube.

5. Name it **ChestInside**.

6. Drag ChestInside into the DropGroup.

7. Scale the cube to fit inside the box on the X and Z axes.

8. Using a side view, scale and position the cube so that its center is slightly above the floor of the ChestBase and it is slightly lower than the inside lip, (see Figure 14-1).

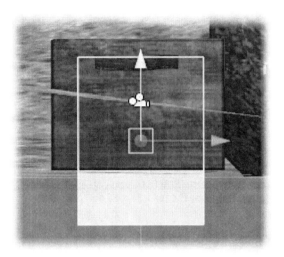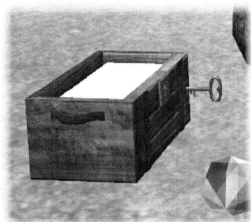

Figure 14-1. *The ChestInside object scaled and positioned for receiving picks*

     9.   Change its Box Collider component to Is Trigger.

The ChestInside object will have two states. State 0 is in scene and active so an object can be placed in the chest. State 1 is in use and deactivated. You will need to add each of the allowed objects to the ChestInside's lookup data as well.

    1.   Set its Tag to **ActionObject**.

    2.   Add the Interactor and ObjectLookup scripts.

    3.   Fill them out as shown in Figure 14-2.

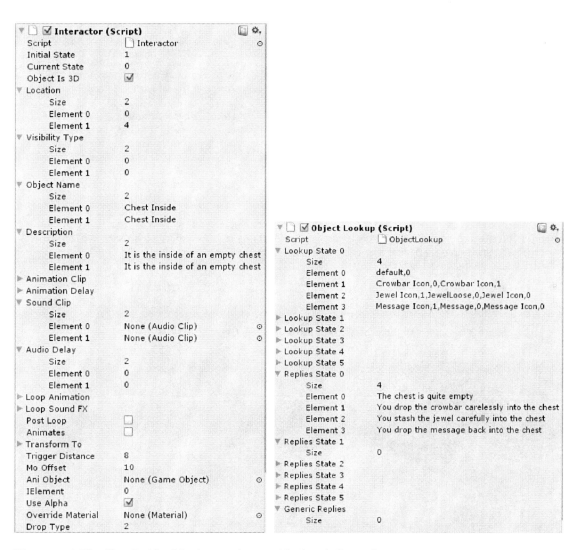

Figure 14-2. *The ChestInside object's metadata and lookup information*

4. Change the Drop Type for the crowbar and golden sleeve to **1** (can be dropped).

5. Click Play and turn off the ChestInside's Mesh Renderer so you can see what happens.

6. Test the crowbar or golden sleeve.

The dropped object moves nicely into the chest and the ChestInside object is deactivated. There are a few issues with size and orientation, but you can address those later.

7. Click Play again.

8. Drop the crowbar into the chest, then pick it with the Golden Sleeve as icon.

The tricky part of our solution is reactivating the ChestInside object. As you may have found, the objects inside the chest can be picked again and put into inventory, but the ChestInside object needs to be reactivated when the chest is left empty.

It would seem you need to let each object be aware of its location, or the drop box object it turned off, so the object can be turned back on when the picked object is "removed." While you might think this should be an easy logic sequence to figure out, you hit a snag when you realize the possibility of putting an auxiliary object into the chest, such as when the Crowbar with Golden Sleeve is substituted for either of its component parts. Because ChestInside is not active when the swap is made, there is no easy, generic way to know to turn it back on. You could write custom code to check for the location of the picked object and then compare it with a list to see if anything needs to be turned back on, but that would require too much specialized code.

Instead, you can use a simple physical test on the volume occupied by the dropped objects. The only time you need to perform the test is when an object or any of its auxiliary objects have been picked and have had time to be processed into their new state, specifically, if they have been deactivated. The test should also be designed to check any locations that can contain dropped objects.

1. Duplicate the ChestInside object.

2. Name it ChestChecker and remove the `Interactor` and `ObjectLookup` scripts.

3. Move it up so it's slightly lower than the top of the ChestBase, (see Figure 14-3).

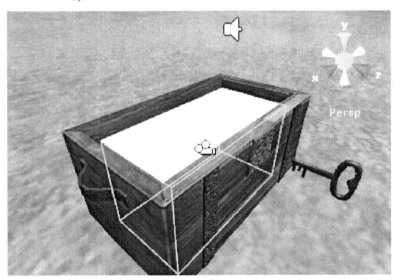

Figure 14-3. *The ChestChecker object*

4. Create a new script.

5. Name it DropBox.

Since this is going to be a generic script, the checker object it will be put on needs to know which object's volume it is checking so it can turn it on if there are no intersecting action objects found. And as long as you're checking for an action object intersection, you may as well store the contents in a variable as well.

6. Open the script and remove the Update function.

7. Add the following code:

```
var dropBox : GameObject; // the location/object this box is checking
var contents : GameObject; // the object currently found in the dropBox

function OnTriggerEnter (other : Collider) {

    print(other.gameObject.name);

}
```

8. Save the script.

9. Drop it on the ChestChecker object.

10. Drag the ChestInside object onto the Drop Box parameter.

Thinking back to our early experiments with the moving platform, you may realize that at least one of the objects will need a rigidbody component before intersection can be recognized and the intersecting object returned.

1. Add a Rigidbody component to the ChestChecker.

2. Uncheck Use Gravity.

Since the function is OnTriggerEnter, you need to animate the checker moving into the space. You can "backward engineer" the animation.

1. With the checker object selected, open the Animation window using Ctrl + 6.

2. Create a New Clip in the Animation Clips folder and name it **CheckLocation**. Select the Position.y track.

3. Turn on the record button and move the marker to frame 25.

4. Add a keyframe.

5. Move the marker back to frame 0 and add another keyframe.

6. Set the value to about 5 units less than its current amount—about -6.0; this should drop the checker well below the terrain.

7. Go to frame 50, create a keyframe, and set it to the same value as the one at frame 0 (see Figure 14-4).

CHAPTER 14 ■ GETTING DOWN TO GAME

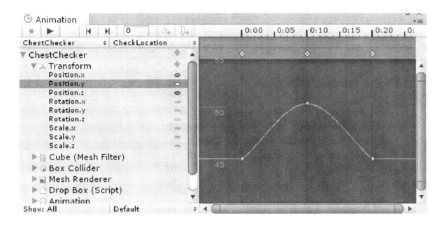

Figure 14-4. *The checker's animation curve*

8. With the cursor in the graph area, press the F key to zoom the curve.

9. Drag the time indicator and watch the checker move to intersect the chest inside.

10. Close the Animation window.

11. In the Inspector, set the Y Position to match the starting position from the animation.

12. Click Play.

When you added the Animation Clip, an Animation component was automatically added and the default was set to Play Automatically on start up.

The Console reports the intersections shown in Figure 14-5.

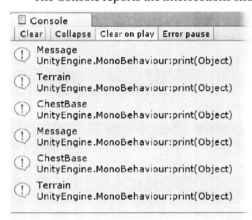

Figure 14-5. *Intersections found by the checker object*

Since the only intersections you are concerned with are action objects, filter out for just the objects you want to check. You also need to ignore the presence of the drop box you are checking for.

1. Open the DropBox script.

2. Change the contents of the OnTriggerEnter function to look like this:

```
function OnTriggerEnter (other : Collider) {

    if (other.name ==  dropBox.name) return;

    if (other.gameObject.tag == "ActionObject" ) {
        print(other.gameObject.name);
    }
}
```

3. Save the script.

4. Click Play and test.

This time the Message is the only object reported.
If the conditions are met, you need to activate the drop box and set its current state to 1.

■ **Tip**   Note that all drop box objects will need to use 0 as "on" or empty and 1 as "off" or in use for their states in the Interactor script.

---

5. Add the following beneath the print line to update the state of the drop box:

```
dropBox.GetComponent(Interactor).currentState = 1;
dropBox.active = false;
```
And now you can store the found action object as the contents.

6. Change the print line to the following:

```
contents = other.gameObject; // store the found action object
```
Since you will want to trigger the animation clip whenever an object is processed, let's go ahead and create a function you can call from the appropriate place. Because you'll be checking for the existence of an action object to *disable* the drop box, you need to *enable* it first in the event an action object was just removed from the location in question. You'll call the function by contacting *all* objects with the DropBox script on them, so you can have as many drop locations in your scene as you want.

7. Add the following function:

```
function CheckState () {

    yield new WaitForSeconds(0.5); // allow auxiliary objects to finish processing

    //turn on the drop box
    dropBox.active = true;
    contents = null; // clear the contents before the next check
    dropBox.GetComponent(Interactor).currentState = 0;
```

```
    animation.Play(); // do the intersection check
}
```

8. Save the script.

If you click Play now, you will see the ChestInside object disappear and the Contents parameter of the Drop Box component show the Message object.

9. Open the ObjectLookup script.

10. In the LookupState function, locate the return statement just above the curly bracket that closes the **if**(readString[0] == matchCursor) block.

11. Immediately above that **return** statement, add the following:

```
// Find any game objects with the DropBox script and call their CheckState function
var checker : DropBox[] = FindObjectsOfType(DropBox) as DropBox[];
for (var box : DropBox in checker){
    box.CheckState();
}
```

12. Save the script.

13. Stop Play mode.

14. Select the ChestChecker object.

15. Click Play and click the Message from the ChestInside.

The ChestInside object appears and you can now drop other allowed objects onto it. Once you see that it works, you can turn off the Mesh Renderer components.

1. Deactivate the ChestInside's Mesh Renderer component.

2. Deactivate the ChestChecker's Mesh Renderer component.

3. Enable the ChestLid.

You should now be able to perform the full chest sequence:

1. Find key.

2. Unlock chest.

3. Take and read message.

4. Drop crowbar in chest.

5. Lock and remove key.

6. Find Golden Sleeve.

7. Unlock and open chest.

8. Add sleeve to crowbar.

9. Take the newly adorned Crowbar with Sleeve.

1. Select the ChestChecker in the Hierarchy view.

2. Click Play and test the sequence.

3. Watch the Contents parameter as you put different objects into the box.

4. In the DropBox script, change the contents var to a private var.

5. Save the script.

Other than the crowbar poking out the ends, all seems to work fairly well as long as the objects' orientations are compatible with the drop box's orientation. With a few extra lines of code, you can skip the orientation part of the positioning instructions if the picked object was a drop box. Rather than add one more variable to identify the location as a drop box, you can conscript the scale component of the HoldTransform object and use it to store information about its current location. When you align the HoldTransform object, you check the picked object's dropType variable. If it is 2 (a drop box), you set the scale of the HoldTransform object to **0,0,0**; otherwise you set it to 1,1,1.

1. Open the ObjectLookup script.

2. In the LookupState function near the top, under the holder.transform.rotation= this.transform.rotation line, add the following:

```
if (object.GetComponent(Interactor).dropType == 2)
   holder.transform.localScale= Vector3(0,0,0);// flag for skipping rotation on alignment
else holder.transform.localScale= Vector3(1,1,1); // flag to match rotation
```

3. Save the script.

To implement the instructions according to the flag, you need to change a few more lines.

1. Open the Interactor script.

2. In the ProcessObject function, inside the **if**(dropType == 1) section, delete the following line:

```
 transform.rotation = holder.transform.rotation;
```

3. Replace it with the following:

```
// rotate only if matching an object instead of a dropbox location
if (holder.transform.localScale == Vector3(1,1,1))
   transform.rotation = holder.transform.rotation;
```

4. Save the script.

5. Click Play.

6. Rotate the crowbar 90 degrees in the Scene window.

7. Work through the chest sequence.

The crowbar is now rotated in the chest, as is the Crowbar with Sleeve when you make the combination object. Unfortunately, it is still a bit too large to fit in the small wooden chest. Luckily, when you bring in your final assets for the game, you'll have a stone chest of sufficient size to protect your unadorned crowbar from being transformed in the maze. That being the case, you'll need to inform the player that the crowbar does not quite fit in the wooden chest, thereby giving him a clue that he is on the right track.

8. Stop Play mode.

9. Select the ChestInside object.

10. In the Inspector, change the Object Lookup data as follows:

```
Lookup State 0, Element 1:
Crowbar Icon,0,Crowbar Icon,1

Replies State 0, Element 1:
The crowbar doesn't quite fit in the wooden chest
```

11. Save the scene and save the project.

12. Click Play and test the functionality.

Reviving the Flower

To obtain the jewel that provides the entry price to the temple, you need to revive the plant. You can rescale the plant and move it to a better location once you've imported the final assets, but for now, you can go ahead and set up the functionality.

To revive the plant, you'll need to use the Vial of Elixir.

1. Select the Vial of Elixir.

2. Add the Interactor and ObjectLookup scripts to it.

3. Tag it as an ActionObject.

4. Fill out the metadata and lookup information, as shown in Figure 14-6.

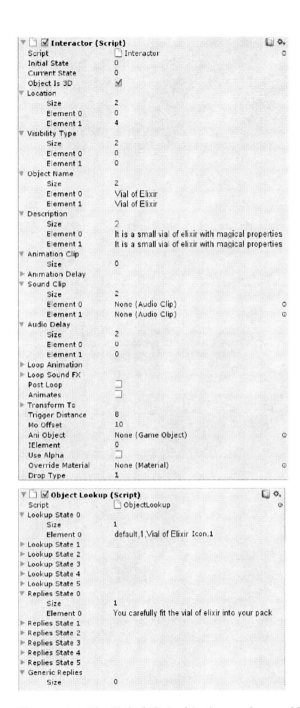

Figure 14-6. *The Vial of Elixir object's metadata and lookup information*

You have already added the Vial of Elixir Icon so you should be ready to test.

5. Click Play.

6. Mouse over and then pick the Vial of Elixir.

7. Stop Play mode.

The Flower object, as you'll remember, is one of the most complicated object types you'll encounter. In an earlier chapter, you found you needed to put the activating scripts on the mesh object you want the player to pick.

1. Holding down the Alt key, expand the Flower hierarchy in the Hierarchy view.

2. Add the Interactor and ObjectLookup scripts to the Stem.

3. In the Interactor component, drag the Flower into the Stem's AniObject parameter.

4. Add a Box Collider and check Is Trigger.

Its size should cover the wilted plant nicely. Because the plant can only be picked in its wilted stage and it will be installed in one of the shrines, you don't need to worry about collision in its revived state.

5. Tag the Stem as an ActionObject.

6. Remove the Box Collider and Audio Source components from the parent, Flower.

7. Fill out the metadata and lookup information, as shown in Figure 14-7.

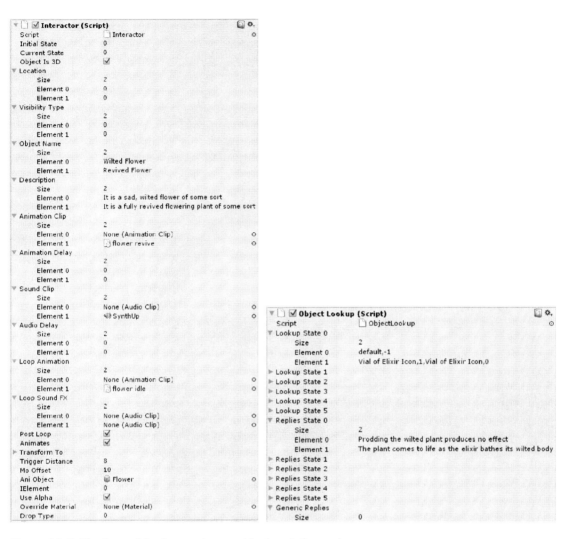

Figure 14-7. *The Stem object's metadata and lookup information*

8. Click Play.

An error about a missing Mesh Renderer is reported in the console, as shown in Figure 14-8.

ⓘ MissingComponentException: There is no 'MeshRenderer' attached to the "Stem" game object, but a script is trying to access it.

Figure 14-8. *Error message for the Stem*

Closer inspection of the Stem object in the Inspector reveals that the stem has a "Skinned Mesh Renderer" instead of the usual Mesh Renderer. You'll need to allow for the possibility of objects animated with bone systems in your Interactor script.

9. Open the Interactor script.

10. In the Start function, beneath the if(objectIs3D) line, change the originalMaterial = GetComponent(MeshRenderer).material line to the following:

```
// load the material into the var
if(GetComponent(MeshRenderer))
   originalMaterial = GetComponent(MeshRenderer).material;
if(GetComponent(SkinnedMeshRenderer))
   originalMaterial = GetComponent(SkinnedMeshRenderer).material;
```

11. Save the script.

12. Click Play and test by clicking the Stem with the Vial of Elixir Icon.

The Flower opens and the Jewel is revealed, but there's an error.

13. Select the Jewel object from the Flower hierarchy.

14. Remove the AniTest script component.

15. Add the Interactor and ObjectLookup scripts.

16. Tag the object as an ActionObject.

17. Fill out the metadata and lookup information (see Figure 14-9).

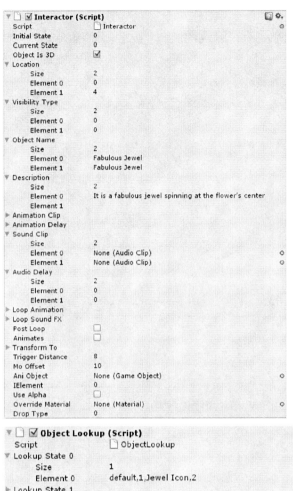

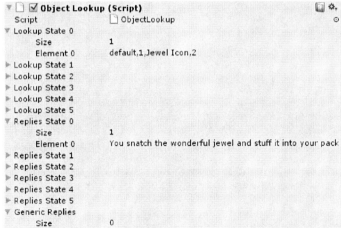

Figure 14-9. *The Jewel object's metadata and lookup information*

18. Click Play.

The Console reports that the material used on the Jewel does not have a '_Color' property (see Figure 14-10).

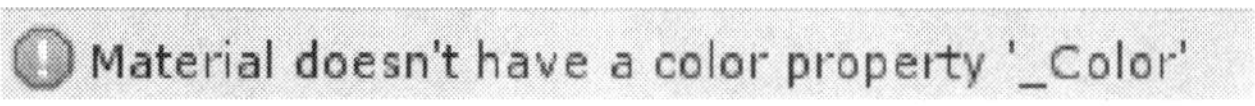

Material doesn't have a color property '_Color'

Figure 14-10. *The Jewel object's error message*

If you were going to use multiple shaders with no color properties, it might be worth scripting to avoid the error. In this case, you've already created a material for the loose jewel, so in the spirit of continuity, you can use the same material on the flower's jewel.

1. Stop Play mode.

2. In the Jewel's Mesh Renderer component, load the Jewel material into the Materials array's Element 0 to replace pods.

3. Click Play and test again.

This time you can play through the sequence and get the flower's jewel into inventory.

Although you have access to the jewel from the Flower, having access to the JewelLoose object will be useful at times for testing so you don't have to go through the entire sequence to get the jewel into inventory.

1. Stop Play mode.

2. Select the JewelLoose object.

3. Add the Interactor and ObjectLookup scripts to it.

4. Using the same metadata and lookup information from the original Jewel, shown in Figure 14-9, fill out the JewelLoose's Interactor and ObjectLookup components.

5. Click Play and test the functionality.

6. Save the scene and save the project.

Frustum Culling

An issue sometimes encountered in real-time engines has to do with frustum culling. When an object's bounding box moves out of the screen viewing area (or frustum), it is culled, or no longer drawn in the scene. In the case of our flower at its current scale, as soon as we move too close or look up at the jewel, the bounding box of the object in its original configuration is no longer in the viewing frustum and the stem and leaves are no longer drawn. Since constantly updating the bounding box during a skinned object's animation would take unnecessary resources for most objects, we need to find a workaround for this extreme example.

The trick is to have something that forces a mesh to have a taller bounding box. A quick and dirty workaround is to duplicate a single face from the mesh skin as an element, move the timeline to the plant's upright configuration, then move the orphaned face until the object's bounding box is high enough so it will not be out of the viewing frustum when the player is close to the jewel. Once the bounding box is high enough, the single face is scaled so small it will not be seen (see Figure 14-11).

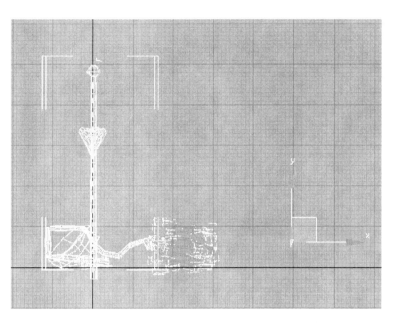

Figure 14-11. *The orphaned face positioned to increase the height of the Stem's bounding box*

In the Book Assets folder, in the Fixed Flower folder, you'll find the fixed version of the `Flower.fbx` file. By overwriting the one currently in your project folder via Windows Explorer (or the Finder on the Mac), the substitution should be seamless.

▨ **Tip**   While renaming or moving files in Explorer or the Finder generally causes associations in your project to break, overwriting existing files with updated versions is not only safe, it is part of the standard workflow in game development. Do be aware that renaming an object within an existing file will cause the object to be brought in as an entirely different object.

---

1. Replace the current `Flower.fbx` asset in the Animation Tests folder with the file of the same name from the Fixed Flower folder (from the BookAssets folder , which you'll find on the book's page on the Apress Web site).

The replacement fixes the problem without having to change anything else (see Figure 14-12).

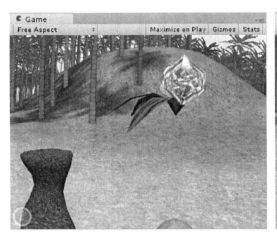

Figure 14-12. *The bounding boxes of the flower meshes original (left) and adjusted (right)*

■ **Tip**   If you know ahead of time that frustum culling could be an issue with your animated object, consider creating an orphaned face that is not controlled by any of the bones before adding the skin modifier.

---

2. Save the scene and save the project.

Pouring the Elixir

While the animation of the plant reviving is interesting, it would be even more so if you could see the vial pouring its magic onto the plant. We have an animated version of the vial for that express purpose. Let's bring it into the scene.

1. Select the ActionObjects folder in the Project view.

2. From the Assets menu, select Import New Asset and import the AnimatedVial.fbx file from the Fixed Flower folder.

3. Set the Scale Factor to **0.0025** to match the other action objects.

4. Create an empty GameObject in the scene at 0,0,0.

5. Name it Vial Group.

6. Drag the AnimatedVial from the Project view into the Hierarchy view and drop it directly into the new group.

7. Use Move to View to position the Vial Group near the flower in the Scene window.

8. Click Play and observe the Vial's animation (see Figure 14-13).

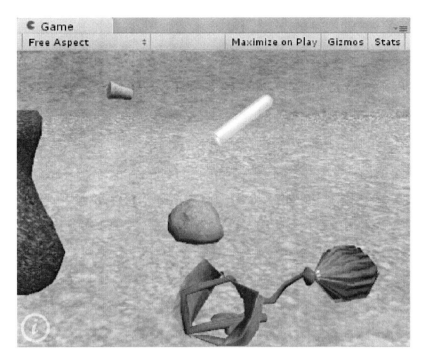

Figure 14-13. *The animated vial*

The vial group should appear only after the flower is picked with the vial icon and then should disappear when it has finished its job. You could set it up as a regular action object, but since it will never get picked, you can do something different. You'll need to fade the Vial group out at the end, and so you'll need to duplicate the imported Animation Clip, Take 001.

1. Select the Take 001 animation clip in the Project view.

2. Use Ctrl + D to duplicate it.

3. Name the new clip **vial** and put it into the Animation Clips folder.

4. Select the AnimatedVial object in the Hierarchy view.

5. Load the new clip in as the Element 1 animation in the Animations array.

6. Set the default Animation to it as well.

7. Open the Animation view and select the vial clip.

8. Turn on record.

9. Locate the Cork material's Color.a track.

10. Create a key at frame **0**; its value should be **1**.

11. Create a key at frame **40**; its value should be **1**.

673

12. Create a key at frame **55** and set its value to **0**.

13. Change the keys to Free Smooth and use Constant tangents to flatten the center section.

14. Adjust the handles to get a nice ease in/ease out on the rest of the curve (see Figure 14-14).

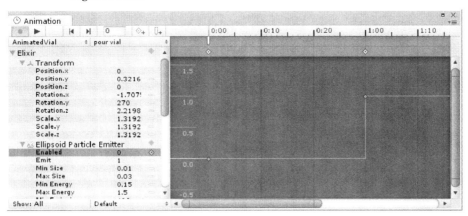

Figure 14-14. *The Cork material's fade animation*

Before you can see the visual results of the animation, you need to change to a transparent shader.

15. Change the cork material to a Transparent Diffuse shader.

16. Select the AnimatedVial again and drag the time indicator to watch the cork fade out.

Solving the Vial Visibility

Part of good game design is learning to design around your tools whenever possible. At present, Unity's free version does not ship with a good "glass" shader—that is, a shader that uses a cube map for reflection *and* allows for transparency, preferably with a Fresnel falloff option for the transparency.

░ **Note**   The Fresnel Effect (pronounced "fre-nel" with a silent s) was first documented by French physicist Augustin-Jean Fresnel. It concerns the difference in reflectivity according the viewing angle. If you picture yourself standing at the edge of a lake in about a foot of water, you can look down and see your feet with very little reflection on surface of the water. Looking across the water to the far side of the lake, where the glancing angle approaches parallel instead of perpendicular, refelection and specularity obsure the transparency. Shaders using the effect for both opacity and reflection appear more realistic but the effect does take longer to calculate than a simpler shader.

Since the vial is not using a transparent shader it will make sense to come up with a different means to visually remove the vial from the scene after it has done its animation. Since you've already created a duplicate animation clip, you can scale the object quickly down to nothing and then remove it from the scene.

1. In the Animation view, turn on the record button.

2. Select the AnimatedVial's three scale tracks and create a key at frame **0**.

3. Move the time indicator to frame **70** and create another key (use the corner arrows to reach that part of the timeline).

4. Move the indicator to frame **75**.

5. In the Scene view, scale the vial down until it disappears.

6. In the Animation view, manually set the three scale values to **0**.

7. Click the Animation view's Play button and watch the results.

8. Close the Animation view.

Making the Magic Happen

At this point, it becomes apparent that we need something to pour from the vial as it is tipped. We will create a particle system to do the job.

1. Focus or find the AnimatedVial in the Scene view.

2. From Create Other on the GameObject menu, select Particle System (see Figure 14-15).

3. Name it **Elixir**.

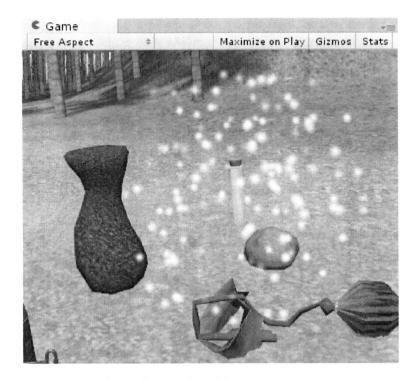

Figure 14-15. *The newly created particle system*

■ **Tip** The particles will animate when selected in edit mode, so you can set them up independently of Play mode. Once they're set up, you can temporarily turn off the Particle Renderer component if they are too distracting.

The particle system consists of three components; the Ellipsoid Particle Emitter, the Particle Animator, and the Particle Renderer. The Ellipsoid emitter generates particles in an ellipsoid-shaped volume, as you may have guessed. You will need to do quite a bit of adjusting. Let's start by parenting the particle system to the vial.

1. Move the Elixir up to the top of the vial's mouth in the Scene view.

2. Expand the Animated Vial group.

3. Drag the Elixir object onto the Vial object, and allow the prefab connection to be lost.

4. Select the Elixir again.

5. In the Ellipsoid Particle Emitter component, set the Elipsoid X, Y, and Z values to **0.01** each to decrease the size of the emitter volume.

6. In the Particle Animator component, set the Y Force to **-1.5** so the particles drop instead of float.

You should now see a steady stream of particles flowing down from the vial.

7. Set the color of the particles in the Color Animation array to different colors.

Element 0 is the color and opacity at the beginning of each particle's life and element 4 is at its end. You are probably only seeing the first color in the array.

8. Rotate the Scene view until you can see underneath the terrain.

The particles are traveling quite a ways below the terrain but you should now be able to see the different-age colors if you look beneath the ground (see Figure 14-16).

Figure 14-16. *The particles under the terrain*

As with any particle system, you want it to be as efficient as possible. Let's shorten the life of the particles so they are almost always visible.

9. Back in the Ellipsoid Particle Emitter component, set the Min energy to **0.15** and the Max Energy to **1.5**.

10. Set the Min Emission to **200** and the Max Emission to **400** to increase the number of particles.

Next, let's adjust the spread of the particles as they fall and increase the size as they age.

11. Set the Rnd Velocity to **0.08** for each of the *X, Y* and *Z* parameters to spread the particles a bit (see Figure 14-17).

Figure 14-17. *The particles with a bit of spread*

12. Click Play and see the results in action.

The particle size is too big at the mouth of the vial to look like a pouring liquid.

1. Stop Play mode.

2. Set the Min Size to **0.01** and the Max Size to **0.03**.

The particles now look like sprinkles.

3. In the Particle Animator component, set the Size Grow to **2** so particles increase in size with age.

4. Click Play and watch the results (see Figure 14-18).

Figure 14-18. *The pouring particles*

    5.   Stop Play mode.

Since shadows for this particle system would probably be a waste of resources, you can turn them off.

    6.   In the Particle Renderer, turn off Cast Shadows and Receive Shadows.

    7.   Save the scene and save the project.

The next task is to turn both the AnimatedVial and the particle system on at the appropriate time. Since you want a pause to allow the vial to tip before the particles start up, you can animate one of its parameters. One of the advantages of parenting the particle system to the AnimatedVial is that it is part of the clip you are already using. Emit would act to destroy the particle system completely, so use Enabled instead.

    1.   Select the AnimatedVial and open the Animation view.

    2.   Locate the Elixir's Ellipsoid Particle Emitter and select its Enabled track (see Figure 14-19).

    3.   Turn on Record and set the indicator to frame **30**.

    4.   Create a key.

    5.   Move the indicator back to frame **0**.

    6.   Set a key and manually set the value to **0**.

7. Set both keys to Flat and all tangents to Constant.

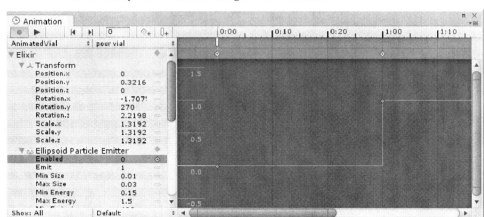

Figure 14-19. *The Emitter enabled after a short pause*

To turn the particles off, let's destroy them with the Emit parameter as removing them from the scene is more efficient.

1. Select the Emit track.

2. Create a key at frame **0**.

3. Move the indicator to frame **75**.

4. Create a key and manually set the value to **0**.

5. Change the keys to Flat and set the tangents to Constant.

6. Close the Animation view.

7. Save the scene and save the project.

8. Click Play and watch the Hierarchy view as the animation plays out.

The Elixir object is removed from the scene.

Destroying the GameObjects

If you examine the possible tracks for the AnimatedVial, you won't find a track for the active parameter so you can take advantage of another feature of the Animation view. You can create an Event to call functions during the timeline. Markers are the equivalent of the SendMessage function; they will call a function, if it exists, in any script that resides on the object. Let's create a function to destroy or remove the vial group once it has finished animating.

1. Create a new script.

2. Name it Destructor.

3. Open it in the editor and set it as follows:

```
var parentObject : GameObject;
function DestroyObject () {

   //Kills the game object's parent
   Destroy (parentObject;

}
```

4. Save the script.

5. Add the script to the AnimatedVial object.

6. Drag its parent, Vial Group, onto the Parent Object parameter in the Inspector.

7. Back in the Animation view, move the indicator to frame **85**.

8. Click the Add Event button (next to the Add Keyframe button).

9. Click on the new marker and select the `DestroyObject ()` function.

10. Turn off the record button.

11. Click Play in the editor to watch the results.

The entire AnimatedVial object is removed from the Hierarchy view, but the particle system may disappear before the particles have died a natural death.

12. Stop Play mode and select the AnimatedVial object when it reappears.

13. In the Animation view, turn on record and move the Event marker out to about 4:00 seconds to allow the particles to finish before the object is destroyed.

14. Close the Animation view.

15. Click Play and test.

⬛ **Tip**   If you get an error message about an event that does not have a function, move the event marker to make sure there is not an empty marker beneath it.

The vial sequence plays out nicely.

Next you need a way to start the sequence. To do this, you need to make a prefab that gets instantiated at runtime. This method is used extensively with armaments as they are created and destroyed many times over. In our game, the vial sequence only gets used once, but the technique is worth knowing about so let's incorporate it into the scene.

1. In the Adventure Prefabs folder, create a new Prefab.

2. Name it VialPrefab.

3. Drag the Vial Group object into it from the Hierarchy view.

4. Delete the original from the Hierarchy view and drag a new one in from the Project view.

5. Click Play to see that it behaves exactly as the original.

6. Save the scene and save the project.

Activating the Prefab

Now you need a way to instantiate your new prefab at runtime. Thinking back to the special cases you allowed for in the `ObjectLookup` script, you remember you already blocked in the possibility for instantiating prefabs.

The code to instantiate an object is simple, but like any object that is not already active in the Hierarchy, it needs to be "introduced" before you can insert it into the scene.

To allow for the possibility that different prefabs (usually particle systems, lights, and so forth) may need to be instantiated for different object states, you should create an array to hold them. As long as you'll be calling them by name, there's no need to create an array for each state. You can create one array that will hold as many elements as you need.

1. Open the `ObjectLookup` script.

2. Beneath the `genericReplies` variable declaration, add a new variable as follows:

```
var prefabs : GameObject[]; // holder for prefab objects
```

Since you won't be doing anything other than getting an element from the array, you don't need to load the Unity array into a JavaScript array as with the others.

Next you need to finish the code for instantiating prefabs in the special cases section.

3. In the `LookupState` function, in the `switch(s)` section, change **case** "p" as follows:

```
case "p": // instantiate a prefab
    // use the s2 number to specify which element of the prefabs array to instantiate
    Instantiate (prefabs[s2]);
    bypass = true; // skip the regular processing
    break;
```

4. Save the script.

And, finally, hook up the vial sequence to play when the Stem is picked with the Vial of Elixir Icon.

1. Select the Stem object.

2. Set the Size of its Prefabs array to **1**.

3. Drag the VialPrefab into the Element 0.

4. Change the LookupState 0, Element 1 to read as follows:

```
Vial of Elixir Icon,1,Vial of Elixir Icon,0,p0_Stem,0
```

The p tells us to instantiate an object and the 0 tells us its array element number. The object and state are ignored.

5. Delete the VialPrefab object that is currently in the Hierarchy view.

6. Click Play and use the Vial of Elixir on the plant.

The Flower animation could stand to wait for the vial animation to finish.

1. Stop Play mode.

2. Select the Stem object again.

3. Set the Animation Delay, Element 1 to about **2.2**.

4. Set the Element 1 Audio Delay to **5**.

5. Click Play and test again.

The delays and the animations are well-synchronized.

Once you import all of the final assets, you will scale and position both the plant and vial objects correctly.

1. Stop Play mode.

2. Open the GameNotes text asset.

3. Change the line that says `case "p": instantiate a prefab` to:

```
case "p": instantiate a prefab-
    the prefab is put in the Prefabs array at the bottom of the Object Lookup component, its
element number is the is s2 number that follows the p, example: p2_Some Object, instantiates
the prefab at element 2 on the object that was picked.
```

4. Save the GameNotes.

5. Delete the pedestal from the scene.

6. Save the scene and save the project.

Camera Focus

Having sorted out the take and drop functionality for the chest and the reviving of the flower, we now need to navigate to the chest to be able to look inside and examine the contents or look up to watch the animation of the flower play out. One of the beauties of 3D games is the ability to go almost anywhere. The downside is the need to reposition to see newly discovered action objects or to watch a complicated animation sequence play out. Also worth considering is the level of player. In addition to the regular audience, classic adventure games are well-known for drawing in people who normally don't play games on a regular basis, especially shooter type games.

With this in mind, it would seem we need to add one more piece of generic functionality. For several of the objects, we need to force a camera match to a predefined location. The camera will then need to stay at that position a predefined amount of time and in some cases ay need to return to the player's former position. While this is happening, navigation and mouse functionality should be disabled.

You can use a set time for the camera match and automatically delay the action by this amount. The time to watch could be calculated from the animation length and the flag to use a camera match could tell whether to use it at all, **0**, match to camera, **1**, or match and return, **2**.

The next design decision becomes the handling of the target camera position. You could create a separate camera for each object to match to, but the downside of that would be cluttering the scene view with numerous camera icons. All you really need is the position of the match camera location. You can control the orientation the same way enemies are controlled in a shooter style game—by adding a look-at target. And then you can use a lerp (linear interpolation) function to get to the target location and rotation. You can use the scene view to find the target position, create an empty GameObject and move it to that location, then assign that object's transform as the *match-to* location. While the animating object might make a good look-at target, you'll get more flexibility if you add a variable that lets you specify a particular object as the target.

Before creating the scripts for the camera match, let's create a couple of target locations. It's probably easier to find the correct position in Play mode because you can also use the mouse look to help with the positioning. In the scripts, you'll match the First Person Controller's *position* to the target GameObject's position, but use the Main Camera to *look at* the specified target. As mentioned earlier, the look-at target does not have to be an action object.

To create a position for the chest, first go into Play mode.

1. Zero any rotations you may have put on the First Person Controller (except the Y Rotation) and Main Camera.

2. Disable the chest lid so you can see the contents.

3. Turn off Maximize on Play if it was on.

4. Click Play.

5. Navigate to the chest and look down until you have a nice view of the contents, as shown in Figure 14-20.

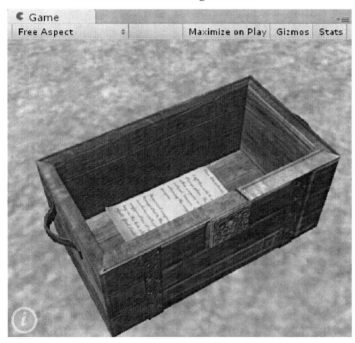

Figure 14-20. *A good view of the chest contents*

6. Select the First Person Controller in the Hierarchy view.

7. From the GameObject menu, choose Align View to Selected.

8. Stop Play mode.

9. Create a new Empty GameObject.

10. Name it Target Chest.

11. From the GameObject menu, choose Align With View.

We now have a target object for the chest.
Next we might want a good view of the plant reviving as well.

1. Click Play.

2. Complete the sequence to bring the plant to life.

3. Navigate to a good vantage point, remembering that the vial is above the plant when it pours, (see Figure 14-21).

Figure 14-21. *A good view for the plant revival*

4. Select the First Person Controller again.

5. From the GameObject menu, choose Align View to Selected.

6. Stop Play mode.

7.   Create a new Empty GameObject.

8.   Name it **Target Jewel**.

9.   From the GameObject menu, choose Align With View.

We now have a target object for the jewel.

 Tip   Because the camera match can happen from any direction, you may want to provide natural barriers to prevent awkward position matches.

Camera Match Metadata

The camera match is performed on two different objects. The location and side-to-side look-at is matched by the First Person Controller. The up/down look-at is handled by the Main Camera.

The number of variables you'll need to make sure the camera match goes to the right place, over the right amount of time, and possibly returns, seem to be at least six target position, look-at target, delay time, animate time, original position for return and a different return position, and time before return. If you constructed your data arrays to fit in with the existing metadata, it would be a lot slower and add more clutter to the `Interactor` script. Instead, you can break with tradition and create a special script, just for camera matches. This way you can add all the variables you need to just the action objects that require the camera control.

1.   Create a new script in the Adventure Scripts folder.

2.   Rename it `CameraMatchData`.

3.   Open it in the script editor.

4.   Add the following variables:

```
// camera match metadata - resides on action objects
var targetPos : Transform; // where it ends up
var targetLook : Transform; // what object it looks at
var matchDelay = 0.0; // any delay time needed before the match
var matchTime = 1.0 ; //  the time the camera match animates over
var matchReturn = false;// whether the player needs to be put back after the action
var animationTime = 0.0; // time after the match before control is returned to the player
private var returnPos : Transform; // position to reset player at if the match returns
```

5.   You will need access to the Control Center to turn navigation and mouse functionality off and on, so add the following:

```
private var controlCenter : GameObject;
```

And you'll need to put the mechanism for the camera match on the Main Camera itself, so you'll need to find it as well.

6.   Add the following:

```
private var fPCamera: GameObject; //
```

And since the script that does the actual animation for the match will be on the First Person Controller object, you will need access to it.

7. Add the following:

```
private var fPController: GameObject; //
```

And, as usual, you will load the objects in the Start function.

8. Change the Update function into a Start function and assign the private variables' values:

```
function Start () {

    // gain access to these objects
    controlCenter = GameObject.Find("Control Center");
    fPCamera = GameObject.Find("Main Camera");
    fPController = GameObject.Find("First Person Controller");

}
```

Since you need to trigger everything involved with the camera match from one place, create a function called DoTheJob as specified by the s special case section we completed earlier in the ObjectLookUp script.

9. Block in the following function:

```
function DoTheJob () {

    // disable cursor visibility and mouse functionality
controlCenter.GetComponent(GameManager).camMatch = true;//disable mouse functions

    //send off position and look-at values to First Person Controller


    // Wait for the delay


    // trigger the camera match



}
```

Let's start by sending all of this object's variable values to the camera object so they can be used to perform the camera match. We will create a script named CameraMatch for this as soon as we have finished the CameraMatchData script.

10. In the // send off section, add the following:

```
fPController.GetComponent(CameraMatch).targetPos = targetPos; // the position target
fPController.GetComponent(CameraMatch).targetLook = targetLook; // the lookAt target
fPController.GetComponent(CameraMatch).matchTime = matchTime; // the match time
fPController.GetComponent(CameraMatch).animationTime = animationTime; // extra observation
time
```

Before we actually trigger the camera match to start, we may need to wait. This is the matchDelay. As a default, it is set to 0.0 in case there is no delay.

11. Add the following in the // wait for delay section:

```
yield new WaitForSeconds(matchDelay);
```

And after the values are in place and the delay served, we will trigger the match with a call to the function in the CameraMatch script that will start the match.

12. Add the following in the // trigger the camera match section:

```
fPController.SendMessage("Match"); // start the match
```

The CameraMatch script will use a flag called watch in its Update function to tell the match to be active. When the time is finished, the camera match will shut itself off but control will not be returned to the player until any extra observation time, the animationTime parameter, has passed. This allows time for auxiliary animations to play out while the player is still a captive audience, insuring that crucial visual clues will not be missed.

13. Save the script.

You should get three error messages concerning the nonexistent CameraMatch script.

Scripting the Camera Match

Now that we have enough of the script finished for preliminary tests, let's build the CameraMatch script so we can see if everything works so far.

1. Create a new script in the Adventure Scripts folder.

2. Rename it CameraMatch.

3. Open it in the editor.

4. Add the following comments at the top of the script:

```
// Purpose: to move an object towards a target location while looking at a target object.
//The idea is to move the player character to a good spot to see an animation play out.
//
// Resides on the 'player' object.
// the camera used in the scene is assume to be "Main Camera."
//
```

5. Add the following variables to the script:

```
var targetLook : Transform; // target to look at
var targetPos : Transform ; // destination to look from

private var source : Vector3 ; // original First person controller position

var animationTime: float = 0.0; // time after the match for some other animation to play /
finish playing

private var startTime : float;

private var start : Transform; // starting position/transform
private var end : Transform; // ending position/transform

private var endTime : float = 0.0 ;
```

```
var matchTime = float 1.0 ; // seconds duration of the camera match
private var isLookAtSmooth  = true ; // Smooth look at when matching.

var fPCamera : GameObject; // main camera.
private var camRotX : float ; // store the camera rotation when starting

private var matching: boolean = false ; // so you don't get interrupted once started
private var justMatched : boolean = false ; // so you know when we are finished

private var camMouseScript : MouseLookRestricted ;
```

In the Start function, we introduce the camera

6. Add the Start function as follows:

```
function Start () {

    fPCamera = GameObject.Find("Main Camera");
    camMouseScript = fPCamera.GetComponent("MouseLookRestricted") ;

    endTime = animationTime* -2 ; // fudge factor: turns off cam control at first
}
```

The first condition in the Update function checks to see if a camera match is being performed. If it is not, leave the function.

1. Inside the Update function, add the following conditional:

```
if (!matching) return;
```

Under that, set up a conditional that checks to see if the time allotted for the match has finished yet.

2. Start the following conditional:

```
if ( Time.time < endTime ) {
```

Next we handle the movement with the help of some serious math. Note the call to the Wavelike function—this provides the essential (at least to any artist's eye) ease-in and ease-out speed adjustments for the movement.

3. Add the following:

```
// Do movement

var t = ( Time.time - endTime + matchTime ) / matchTime; // Goes from 0 to 1
WaveLike ( t, 9 ) ; // make movement start and end slower- ease-in/ease-out
var toPos = Vector3 ( targetPos.position.x, source.y, targetPos.position.z ) ;
 transform.position = Vector3.Lerp ( source, toPos , t ) ;
```

The rotation match is a bit more complicated as it controls an axis of the First Person Controller and an axis of the Main Camera.

4. Add the following:

```
// Do rotation
if ( isLookAtSmooth ) {
  // Separate horizontal & vertical movement, apply to player & cam objects, respectively

  // Horizontal
```

```
   var playerAngle = Mathf.Atan2 ( targetLook.position.x - transform.position.x,↩
     targetLook.position.z - transform.position.z ) * Mathf.Rad2Deg ;
   var playerRot = Quaternion.AngleAxis ( playerAngle, Vector3.up ) ;
   transform.rotation = Quaternion.Slerp ( transform.rotation, playerRot, t ) ;

   // Vertical , rotate camera towards target
   var targetPoint = targetLook.position;
   var targetRotation = Quaternion.LookRotation (targetPoint -  fPCamera.transform.position,
Vector3.up);

//get distance away from target so you can adjust speed of match
var dist = Vector3.Distance(targetPos.position, transform.position);
   fPCamera.transform.rotation = Quaternion.Slerp(fPCamera.transform.rotation,↩
targetRotation, Time.deltaTime * (10-dist));

} // close isLookAtSmooth

   justMatched = true ;
```

You will also need to block all input while the camera match is happening. The Input.ResetInputAxes stops keyboard input for navigation.

> 5. Add the following:

```
// Disable player navigation input while this script controls player position
Input.ResetInputAxes() ;

} // close the original conditional
```

If the match time *has* completed, and there's still some observation time left…

> 6. Add:

```
else {
   if ( justMatched )    {

      // Keep player input disabled
      Input.ResetInputAxes() ;
     //report the new rotation back to the mouselook script- very important!
      camMouseScript.ResetRotationY ( -1 * fPCamera.transform.rotation.eulerAngles.x ) ;

      toPos = Vector3 ( targetPos.position.x, source.y, targetPos.position.z ) ;
      transform.position = toPos ;

      justMatched = false ;
   }

if ( Time.time < ( endTime + animationTime ) ) { // if there are other animations to watch

   // Keep player input disabled
   Input.ResetInputAxes() ;
}
```

And finally, if the observation time is also finished …

7. Add the following:

```
else {
  // Done with match. Reset for next time
   matching = false;

  // enable mouse again
  Screen.lockCursor = false;

 // flag for cursor visibility and mouse functions-
 gameObject.Find("Control Center").GetComponent(GameManager).camMatch = false;

 }

} // end else

} // end Update function
```

8. And now add the WaveLike function called earlier that calculates the ease in/ease out:

```
static function WaveLike ( tStep, iterations ) {

   for ( var i = 0 ; i < iterations ; i++ ) {
      tStep = ( 1 - Mathf.Cos ( tStep * Mathf.PI ) ) / 2 ;
   }
   return tStep ;

}
```

And, finally, add the Match function that sets the whole thing in motion:

```
function Match() {

   endTime = Time.time + matchTime ;

   source = transform.position ;

   // get current camera x
   camRotX = fPCamera.transform.rotation.x ;

   // disable mouse- this forces the cursor position to the center of the screen
   Screen.lockCursor = true;

   matching = true; // start the camera match
}
```

9. Save the script.

You get an error because you are calling a function in the MouseLookRestricted.cs script to update the Y rotation so when the player takes control back, the First Person Controller and Main Camera know where the camera match left them. As it turns out, you have not yet created that function.

1. From Standard Assets ➤ Character Controllers ➤ Scripts, open the `MouseLookRestricted.cs` script.

The syntax in this C# script is a bit different than in the JavaScripts we've been working with, but we can add the missing function easily. One of the differences is the way this script wraps all of the code we are used to seeing in a class. We will need to put our function inside the class's curly brackets.

2. Above the closing curly bracket for the entire `MouseLookRestricted` class, add the following function:

```
public void ResetRotationY(float newRotY)
{
   rotationY = newRotY ;
}
```

3. Save the script.

The error generated by the `CameraMatch` script goes away.

4. Add the `CameraMatch` script to the First Person Controller object.

The `Target Look` and `Target Pos` parameters have been left public in case we want to watch and see where the camera match is taking the player. Let's test the plant first since it is a quicker sequence to carry out.

5. Select the Stem object.

6. Drag the `CameraMatchData` script onto it.

7. Drag the Target Flower object into its Target Pos parameter.

8. Drag the Jewel (the one in the Flower hierarchy) into the Target Look parameter.

9. Change the Stem object's `LookupState 0, Element 1` to read as follows:

```
Vial of Elixir Icon,1,Vial of Elixir Icon,0,p0_Stem,0,s1_Stem,0
```

10. Click Play and test.

11. Change the location of the position target if you wish.

The Jewel's pivot point is at its base, making the camera look a bit low. In its final position in the game, we should probably make a target to look at instead of using the jewel.

▧ **Note** The code does not check for the First Person Controller's distance above the ground, so you may need to adjust the target position Y position to prevent a bump at the end of the camera match as the First Person Controller readjusts to ground level.

Before testing the camera match, you will need to need to finish the code that hides the cursor and disables the mouse functionality during the camera match. The GameManager will need the camMatch variable to store the current state of any ongoing camera matching and the Interactor script will need to access it before allowing mouseovers and mouse picks.

1. Open the GameManager script.

2. Add the following variable:

private var camMatch : boolean = false; // flag to hide mouse during camera match

3. In the OnGUI function, change if (showPointer && !navigating){ to:

if (showPointer && !navigating && !camMatch) {

4. Save the script.

Even with the cursor locked to the center of the game screen and hidden, mouseover and mouse pick functionality is still possible. Adding another condition to the Interactor is fairly easy and will prevent mishaps.

5. Open the Interactor script.

6. In the OnMouseEnter function, above the if(DistanceFromCamera line, add the following:

// if there is an active camera match in process, exit the function now
if (controlCenter.GetComponent(GameManager).camMatch) return;

7. In the OnMouseDown function, below the if (iMode && gameObject.layer line, add the following:

// if there is an active camera match in process, exit the function now
if (controlCenter.GetComponent(GameManager).camMatch) return;

8. Save the script.

▨ **Tip**   When deciding where to add new conditionals that will exit the function when evaluated to true, try to order them to cause the least amount of evaluation time. If the condition is common and uses a variable local to the script, check it near the top of the list. If it is less likely to evaluate as true and requires calculation time (as with the distance checks), put it near the bottom of the list.

And now you can finally test the chest.

1. Select the ChestLid object.

2. Drag the CameraMatchData script onto it.

3. Drag the Target Chest object into its Target Pos parameter.

4. Drag the ChestInside into the Target Look parameter.

5. Change the LookupState 1, Element 0 to read as follows:

default,2,b0_KeyAtLock,4,b0_LockPlate,3,s1_ChestLid,0

6. Click Play and test.

7. Make any necessary adjustments.

8. Save the scene and save the project.

Importing the Final Assets

To provide an environment in which to put all of our hard-earned functionality into play, let's import the rest of the 3D art assets that are included with the book. They include:

- The temple of Tizzleblat with its attendant guardian beasts.

- Six stelae or standing stones representing the six natural elements of the Tizzleblat pantheon.

- Six glyphs representing the elements that can act as keys to activate things.

- Six shrines, each dedicated to one of the elements, scattered about the environment.

- A small cave system with tunnels.

We will be using only a small number of the assets to finish the book project, but you may continue to experiment and create more functionality to challenge the end player.

Most objects come with lightmaps in case you are using Unity free and prefer a GI (Global Illumination) solution. The temple comes in as two parts. The inner temple has a lightmap that should not be rebaked—unless you want lots of practice with lighting and Beast in Unity Pro.

Bringing in the Structures

The remaining assets for the environment will be brought in as a Unity package, so you won't need to set up materials for every object.

1. From the Assets menu, choose Import Package ➤ Custom Package.

2. From the BookAssets folder, select and import FinalAssets.unitypackage.

3. In the dialog, choose Import and import all.

The package adds a Structures folder and Structures prefab, a prefab with materials already set up on most of the objects.

4. Drag the Structures prefab into the scene into a large flat area.

5. Adjust it further in the top view so that most of the objects can be easily accessed.

Because we prepared lightmaps for the main objects, a new directional light was included with the package. At this point, you need to make a decision. If you have Unity Pro and want to bake your own maps with Beast, feel free to delete the Sun for Lightmaps directional light and rotate the individual objects at will.

For the book, we will go ahead and use the provided lightmaps and light source so if you wish to change the orientation, *you must rotate the entire prefab* if you want the lighting to be consistent.

6. Delete or deactivate the original directional light unless you plan to rebake the lightmaps.

7. In a perspective view, lower the prefab until the shrines and the stone steles (monoliths) contact the ground.

The temple and cave system will be partially underground.

8. Open the prefab in the Hierarchy view but don't expand it all the way.

While you are setting up the last bits of functionality and special effects, you will want to keep the objects fairly close to each other. Move only the objects or groups at this level of the prefab's hierarchy (see Figure 14-21).

Figure 14-22. *The Structures prefab in the Hierarchy view*

9. Rearrange, but do not rotate, the GameObjects so they are all visible on the terrain.

The Dome, the stelae, and the Group Earth require no set up and can be left as is for now (see Figure 14-23).

Figure 14-23. *The new assets in the scene*

10. Click Play and investigate the new assets, (see Figures 14-24 and 14-25).

Figure 14-24. *The Temple of Tizzleblat guarded by Gertrude and Harvey*

Figure 14-25. *One of the shrines*

11. Save the scene as MainLevel.

12. Save the project.

Materials and Lightmapping

Before going inside the temple, let's take a moment to look at the material options included in the package. For most objects with lightmaps, you have a choice of two different materials. The first material uses a standard Unity legacy lightmap shader. The second, appended with a **1**, contains a custom shader created with the Strumpy Shader Editor, a free visual shader editor that can be found on the Unity forum's Showcase area or downloaded from the Unity Asset Store. Feel free to use whichever material you prefer.

As with almost anything in a real-time engine, you need to balance the cost in frames per second with the visual gain. In this type of genre, where the visual richness of the environment is a large part of the experience, you are more likely to go for more expensive shaders. Let's do a bit of research into the lightmapping and materials available.

1. Select the Temple Outer object from the Scene view.

2. Observe its material in the Inspector.

The Temple Outer object uses the Temple Outside 1 material with a custom shader that can add some specular highlight from the actual scene. While this helps remove the chalky look of a traditional fully emissive shader that ignores scene lights, it does use more resources when computing the lighting solution. The standard material, Temple Outside, uses the Unity Legacy Lightmap shader.

■ **Note**   Because the Unity game engine is constantly evolving and the Strumpy Shader Editor is a third-party add-on, there is a chance the custom shaders will occasionally need updating to be compatible with the newer versions of Unity. If the structures appear a violent shade of magenta, you will need to use the standard shader versions of the materials—the ones that are not appended with a '1'. Be sure to check this book's web page for updated assets.

---

3. In its Mesh Renderer component, click on its Element 0 material to locate it quickly in the Project view.

4. Select the Temple Outside material (see Figure 14-26).

5. Drag it onto the temple in the Scene view or directly into the Element 0 slot.

6. Adjust its Main Color until it looks good.

7. Repeat the process for any magenta-colored objects in your scene if necessary, or use the Structures prefab Standard instead.

Figure 14-26. *The custom shader vs. the legacy shader*

Note   If you wish to try your hand at creating your own custom shaders with the Strumpy Shader Editor, be sure to check out Appendix A to see the SSE graph for the BetterLightmap shader and the LedgeFringe material's two shader options. The Strumpy Shader Editor is a flow-graph style editor that lets you add nodes to create shaders with feature combinations not found in Unity's standard shaders.

Typically, if you are using lightmaps on objects along with the traditional shader, you would create a layer called Lightmapped and exclude its objects from being lit by lights in the scene.

To see the effect without setting up a new layer, you can turn off the scene light, (see Figure 14-27).

8.   Select the Sun for Lightmaps light object inside the Structures prefab, just above the Temple Group.

9.   Deactivate the light component.

10.   Select the Temple Outer again and adjust its shader's Main Color component (see Figure 14-27).

If you haven't yet baked light into your terrain, it will appear dark as in Figure 14-27. If you have baked lighting into the terrain, it will appear self-illuminated along with the temple. You can open Lightmapping from the Window menu and turn off Use Lightmaps to see the same effect.

Figure 14-27. *The scene light turned off*

11. Reactivate the scene light.

To see what baked light from Beast looks like without GI, you can test the Temple Outside object.

1. From the Structures ➤ Materials folder, select the stonetexture material.

2. Change it to a Bumped Specular shader.

3. Add StoneBumpTextureMed to the Normalmap slot.

4. Apply the material to the Temple Outside and adjust the Shininess.

5. Set the Shininess to a very low amount and the Specular Color to a dark Gray (see Figure 14-28)

Figure 14-28. *The Bumped Specular texture*

6. Select the Temple Outside object.

7. Make sure the temple is marked as Static.

8. From the Window menu, open Lightmapping.

9. In the Bake section, select Low Quality and set it to Single Lightmaps.

10. Click Bake Selected (see Figure 14-29).

Figure 14-29. *Lightmap baked in Unity, no GI*

The terrain is rebaked and the new lightmap added internally. With the use of Unity-generated lightmaps, you no longer need to generate a material for each different object using the same texture. The downside is that the specular is no longer calculated for the object in the scene so the bump map is not used either. The object also does not receive any of the bounced light and color it would receive with GI, so it never quite looks like it is part of the scene.

1. Select the stonetexture material again.

2. Try adjusting the Specular Color and the Shininess.

Nothing happens.

Of interest is what happens with the generated alpha channel. When you used the legacy Lightmap shader, you had to adjust the main color to a darkish mid-gray to get the right look. When a lightmap is generated in Unity, that color adjustment is added to the copy of the map in its alpha channel. To view the generated lightmap, you need to look in the folder created to hold lightmaps for the scene.

1. From the Scenes folder, open the newly added MainLevel folder.

2. Select the LightmapFar-1 (or element 0 if 1 is the terrain lightmap).

3. In the Inspector, toggle the alpha/diffuse button to see the dark shade added to the alpha, a shown in Figure 14-30.

Figures 14-30. *The lightmap and its alpha channel*

To take advantage of Beast's GI feature in Unity Pro, you use Dual Lightmaps. The Far version contains both GI and regular shadows. The Near version contains only GI, and the real-time shadows are added inside the Shadow Distance. Feel free to use whichever material or lightmapping method you wish on the various objects.

Once you have added a lightmap to the lightmap array, the object's regular shader will be overwritten. To disable Unity's lightmap, you need to delete the lightmap and set the Lightmap Index number back to 255 in the Lightmapping editor.

1. Open the Lightmapping view.

2. Select the Temple Outside.

3. On the Object tab, select Atlas and set the Lightmap Index to **255.**

4. Delete the map in the Scene folder's lightmap folder if you don't plan to use it, and reassign the Temple Outside or Temple Outside 1 material to the temple.

■ **Tip**   You may wish to experiment with combining the two lightmaps in your favorite paint program.

Underground

Currently, Unity's terrain-generation system doesn't allow you to cut holes in the terrain. You can turn off the Terrain component once you're inside a building, but since you can't easily disable the Terrain Collider and then enable it again, you can't get below the surface. The other problem is the time it takes to regenerate the terrain when you turned it back on. If you have very little vegetation, it will regenerate almost immediately; if you have a lot, there will be an annoying pause when the controls seem to lag. There are several workarounds—from using shaders and forcing draw order, to stitching multiple terrain maps together and leaving the hole where they do not meet. If the building is large and important, you might even have a separate level or scene for it. Our solution will be to lower the ground out of the way when we are in the temple.

Before you can look inside, let's address a small detail you may have noticed during your forays into the temple. Unless you are coming at them at an angle, the stairs are difficult to climb as they have been designed on a scale to make the humble pilgrims feel small and insignificant. To make game play better, you may wish to adjust the Character Controller components Step offset. Another option, especially useful for architectural walkthroughs, is to create a collider that acts as a ramp so the player moves smoothly up the incline. The easiest approach is to start with a cube, adjust the placement, then remove or turn off its mesh Renderer.

1. Create a cube.

2. Rename it **Easy Access**.

3. Using both Local and Global coordinate systems, adjust its scale, position, and orientation so it matches the stairs (see Figure 14-31).

Figure 14-31. *The ramp over the stairs for smoother navigation*

4. Turn off the ramp's Mesh Renderer.

To get a good look inside the temple; you can start by creating a simple toggle to turn the terrain off and on—until we devise our permanent solution.

1. Create a new script.

2. Name it Deactivate and open it in the script editor.

3. Add the following:

```
var object : GameObject;

function OnMouseDown () {

    if (object.active == false) object.active =true;
    else object.active = false;

}
```

4. Save the script.

5. Create a cube and position it on the steps up to the temple.

6. Add the Deactivate script to it.

7. Drag the Terrain object into the Object field.

8. Click Play.

9. Explore the inside of the temple.

You are quickly stopped by the terrain.

10. Out on the temple steps, pick the cube.

The terrain disappears.

11. Explore the inside of the temple (see Figure 14-32).

Figure 14-32. *The temple's lower passageway is uncovered when the terrain is removed.*

12. Pick the cube again to reactivate the terrain.

13. Stop Play mode.

14. Delete the cube.

For the scene, you need to go in and out of the building at will, so you need a solution that is easy to script, but effective. Let's move the terrain up and down as it is the least problematic of the various options. It now becomes a design problem to keep the player from seeing the terrain inside the temple before you hide it and not seeing it outside when he is in the temple. The floor plan of the temple is such that with careful placement, you could get away with the temple as is. To make it more fun, let's help hide the deception with the addition of a couple of hanging cloths at the opening.

1. From the GameObject menu, create a Cloth object.

2. Name it **Entry Cloth**.

3. Set its Scale to X, **0.25**; Y, **0.65**; and Z, **0.5**.

4. Set its Rotation to X, **90**; Y, **180** and Z; **180**.

5. Set its Bending Stiffness to **0.5**.

6. Move it to the temple opening on the right and align it with the entrance shadow.

7. In the Cloth Renderer component, assign the GoldFringeSolid material to its Element 0.

8. Click Play and watch the Scene view.

The cloth crumples to a heap, as shown in Figure 14-33.

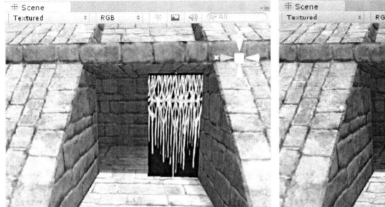

Figure 14-33. *The cloth before and during Play*

Creating hangers for cloth in Unity is extremely easy.

1. Create an Empty GameObject.

2. Name It **Entry Hanger**.

3. Add a Box Collider to it.

4. Position it at the top of the doorway so that it intersects the cloth and set its X Size to **5.4** to span the doorway.

5. Set its Y Size to **0.8** and its Z Size to **0.5**.

6. Select the cloth.

7. Set its Attached Colliders array Size to **1**.

8. Drag the Entry Hanger object into its Element 0 Collider slot.

9. Click Play.

This time the cloth twitches a couple of times and then moves gently on its own

10. While in Play mode, try adjusting its External Acceleration Z value.

11. Set the amounts back to 0 and try moving through the cloth in the Game window.

12. Turn and view the cloth from the back side.

The cloth object is apparently single-sided.

A check of the standard Unity shaders shows that the only shaders that are two-sided are for particle systems and tree foliage, neither of which is appropriate for our temple entryway.

Although the Unity shaders that ship with the editor have already been compiled, you can download the original source code from www.Unity3d/support/resources/assets/built-in-shaders. By comparing the two-sided shaders with the regular shaders and checking the shaderlab help, you can see that all you need to do is add two words to make your shader double-sided: "cull off".

1. Locate the DS BumpSpec shader in the Structures ➤ Custom Shaders folder.

2. Open the shader (it also uses the UniScite editor).

3. After the Tags { "RenderType"="Opaque" } line, add the following:

   Cull Off

4. Save the shader.

5. Select the GoldFringeSolid material.

6. Select the new double-sided shader for it.

7. Click Play and test the cloth again.

This time the cloth can be seen from the back side (see Figure 14-34).

Figure 14-34. *The double-sided cloth*

Before you clone the cloth, let's adjust the UVs on the texture.

1. Duplicate the GoldFringeSolid material and name it GoldFringeRight.

2. Set the x Tiling to **0.5**, the x Offset to **0.25** and the y Offset to **0.02**.

3. Apply the new material to the cloth.

4. Duplicate the cloth and move the new cloth to the left of the original.

5. Duplicate the GoldFringeRight material and name it GoldFringeLeft.

6. Set its x Offset to 0 and apply this to the left cloth.

7. Drag the two cloth objects and their hanger into the Temple Group.

8. Click Continue at the Losing prefab warning.

9. Save the scene and save the project.

■ **Note**   You could just rotate the cloth 180 degrees, but because the shader uses a cube map for the reflection on the gold parts, it would not match up properly with the other cloth.

Into the Temple

Before setting up the terrain-managing trigger colliders, you can carefully push the terrain down a bit inside the temple.

1. Select the Temple Outside and disable it.

2. Change the Scene view to Top and zoom in on the temple inside (Temple of Tizzleblat object).

3. Select the Terrain object and use the Paint Height tool to carefully drop the terrain only along the main passage ways—the outer walls should provide enough coverage to hide the change (see Figure 14-35).

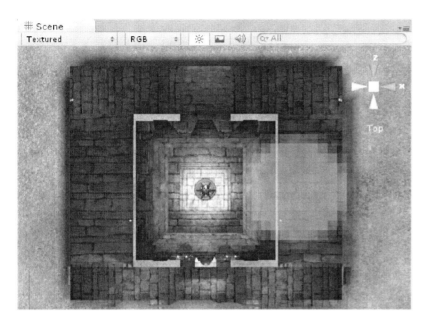

Figure 14-35. *Lowering the terrain in the main part of the temple*

While the outer temple is turned off, you can create and position your trigger objects. Let's start with cubes in order to see the positioning more easily. Since you'll need four triggers, you can design the script accordingly and create a prefab.

1. Create a Cube and name it **Terrain Trigger On**.

2. Set its Scale to X, **0.3**; Y, **6**; and Z, **6.5**.

You want to minimize the possibility of the player seeing the terrain being turned off and on, so you should add the trigger in the corner area.

3. Rotate and position the cube as shown in Figure 14-36.

4. Move it down until it is close to touching the passage floor so the First Person Controller will have to go through it.

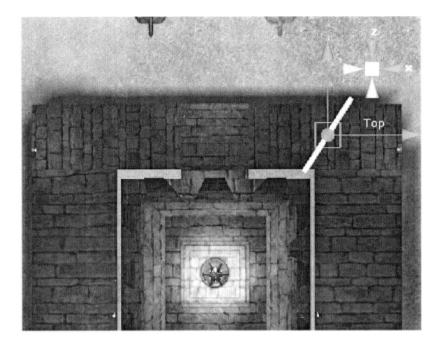

Figure 14-36. *Terrain Trigger On's position in the passageway*

To avoid running into the terrain as you are bumping around the temple's lower rooms and exploring the great cavern beneath it, you'll simply lower the terrain while in the temple. Since the cavern isn't as deep underground as you'd expect, you can also shift its Y position as needed. The terrain-managing script will be implemented so that it will raise and lower the two objects as needed. Because the script will be used for both the on and off triggers, you'll need a variable for using On or Off. You will also need to recognize the Terrain and the Cavern.

Because the TerrainManager script will be on several objects, you can't move the cavern down in its Start function or it would get moved for each object the TerrainManager will be assigned to. Instead, you will need to create a small script to move the cavern down on start up so it records its original position before being moved down. The TerrainManager script will access the new script to get the Cavern Group's original position.

1. Create a new script.

2. Name it CavernPosition.

3. Open it in the editor.

4. Add the following to it:

```
var cavernPosY : float; //starting position of cavern

function Awake () {
  cavernPosY = transform.position.y; // save original cavern y position
}
```

```
function Start () {
    transform.position.y = cavernPosY - 100; // drop the cavern 100 units
}
```

5. Save the script.

6. Add it to the Cavern Group object.

7. Click Play and check to see that the cavern is dropped below the terrain.

8. Stop Play mode.

And now you can build the TerrainManager script that will move the terrain and cavern objects up and down as needed.

1. Create a new script.

2. Name it TerrainManager.

3. Open it in the editor.

4. Add the following variables to the new script:

```
var showTerrain = true; // true means show on enter, false means hide on enter

private var terrain : GameObject;
private var cavern : GameObject;

private var terrainPosY : float;
private var cavernPosY : float;
```

In the Start function, let's assign the starting positions of the objects that will be shifted.

5. Add the following Start function:

```
function Start () {

    terrain = GameObject.Find("Terrain");
    cavern = GameObject.Find("Cavern");

    cavernPosY = cavern.GetComponent(CavernPosition).cavernPosY; // get cavern's original
position
    terrainPosY = terrain.transform.position.y ; // get terrain y pos
}
```

Because you'll need to pass *through* the trigger object, the functionality will be in an OnTriggerEnter function.

6. Add the following:

```
 function OnTriggerEnter () {

    if (showTerrain) {
        terrain.transform.position.y = terrainPosY; // restore the terrain
        cavern.transform.position.y = cavernPosY - 100;  // drop the cavern    }
```

```
    else {
        terrain.transform.position.y = terrainPosY - 100; // drop the terrain
        cavern.transform.position.y = cavernPosY ;  // restore the cavern    }
}
```

If you are wondering about the layout of the triggers, think about the sequence of events. The first trigger usually tells the terrain to go into a state that it's already in so the instruction is ignored. The second trigger changes state as the player is closer to needing the change. The logic holds for approaching in either direction.

7. Save the script.

Before going any further, let's finish the trigger object and turn it into a prefab.

1. Drag the new script onto the Terrain Trigger On object.

2. In the Project view, in the Adventure Prefabs folder, create a new prefab.

3. Name it **TriggerToggler**.

4. Drag the TerrainTriggerOn script onto it.

The prefab icon should turn blue.

5. Drag three prefabs into the scene (or clone the existing one) and position them all at the corners of the passageway (see Figure 14-37).

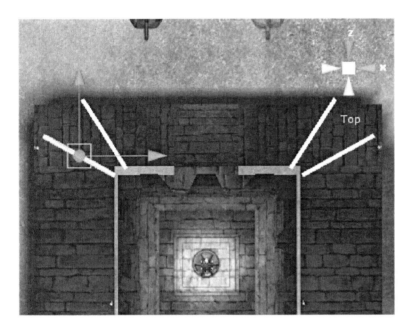

Figure 14-37. *The trigger colliders in the temple*

6. Name the two outer triggers Terrain Trigger Off.

7. In the Inspector, set their Show Terrain parameters to false.

Before you can test, you need to tidy up the prefab by turning off the collision and hiding the cubes.

1. Switch to a Perspective view to make sure the objects are all at the correct height.

2. Select the prefab in the Project view.

3. Check Is Trigger.

4. Turn off the Mesh Renderer.

5. Save the scene.

6. Turn on the Temple Outside.

7. Click Play.

8. Test the triggers and watch the Scene view as you test.

9. Create a new Empty GameObject and name it Trigger Group.

10. Drag the trigger objects into it.

11. Drag the Trigger Group into the Temple Group.

The terrain turns off and on depending on your travels through the temple. Feel free to adjust the position of the trigger objects if necessary.

Holograph Image

Once the player is inside the temple, he should get some clues regarding the quest. Let's "hang" an image of the blasted tree over the smoky brazier in the main temple chamber. Rather than using cloth, you can use another useful Unity object, the Line Renderer. This object is similar to a particle system in that it always faces the player. You can give it as many segments as you want, but in this case, let's keep it simple.

1. Select the Bowl object in the center of the main chamber and focus it in the Scene view.

2. Create a new Empty GameObject and name it **Hologram**.

3. Drag it into the Temple Group.

4. From Components ➤ Miscellaneous, add a Line Renderer.

5. In the Inspector, uncheck Use World Space.

6. In the Parameters section, set the Start and End Width to **2**.

7. In the Positions section, set the Element 1 Y to **4**.

8. Assign the Hologram material to it.

9. Adjust the height of the object so it "floats" over the bowl, a shown in Figure 14-389.

Figure 14-38. *The Line Renderer hologram*

10. Orbit the view and see that the hologram faces the viewer.

For a quick fake volumetric light effect, we can duplicate the hologram and apply a different material.

1. Duplicate the Hologram object.

2. Name it Volume Light Effect.

3. Move it up so its pivot point is at the Topi Fruit Lamp object.

4. Change its Element 1 Z to -8.

5. Set its Start Width to **0.5** and its End Width to **3.75**.

6. Add the Fairy Dust material and adjust its Alpha value in the Tint color.

Because the Line Renderer currently has only two faces, the mapping is rather skewed. Let's add a couple more segments.

7. Set its Positions array Size to **5**.

8. Change the Y values for the elements to **0**, **-2**, **-4**, **-6**, and **-8**.

The mapping looks better, but the texture isn't right.

1. Select the material in Element 0 to find it quickly in the Project view.

2. Duplicate the standard material and name it **VolumeRay**.

3. Move the new material to one of the game material folders.

4. Load the new material into the object.

5. Change the Particle Texture to LightRayGradient.

6. Adjust the opacity and tint it slightly golden, as shown in Figure 14-39).

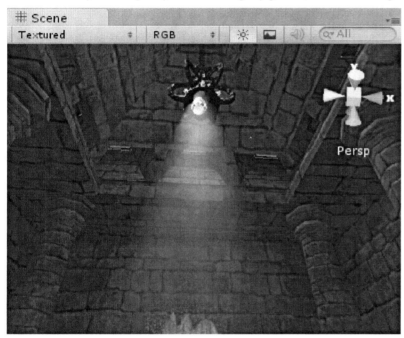

Figure 14-39. *The fake volume light using the Line Renderer*

The hologram looks rather static on its own. Let's add a bit of smoke to make it look more mystic. Fortunately, Unity has some nice special effects prefabs that you can cannibalize.

1. From the Standard Assets folder ➤ Particles ➤ Fire, add the Flame preset to your scene, aligned with the bowl (see Figure 14-40).

The effect is a bit over the top for our hologram, but will be useful elsewhere in the environment.

2. Drag the Smoke object out of it and add it to the temple group.

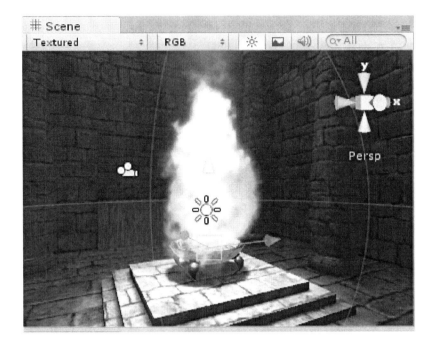

Figure 14-40. *The Flame prefab*

3.   Delete the remainder of the Flame.

4.   Select the Smoke object.

5.   Set the Min and Max Energy to **2** to shorten the life of the particles.

6.   Adjust the opacity of the particles and the color until the smoke looks good (see Figure 14-41).

Figure 14-41. *The smoke and the hologram*

The effect is better, but the hologram still looks quite static. Let's create a small script that will cycle an object up and down a bit.

1. Create a new script.

2. Name it V_PositionCycler.

3. Open it in the editor.

4. Add the following variables:

```
var upRange : float =1.0;
var downRange : float =1.0;
var speed : float = 0.2;

private var yPos : float;
private var upPos : float;
private var downPos : float;
```

The Start function provides the current Y position of the object.

5. Add the Start function:

```
function Start () {

  yPos = transform.position.y;
```

}
    The FixedUpdate function (used so the speed will be the same on any system), uses a cosine curve to go between the two minimum and maximum positions. Mathematical functions like this can be found in many sample tutorials for moving platforms up and down, or for many other purposes.

6.   Add the following:

```
function FixedUpdate () {

    upPos = yPos +upRange;
    downPos = yPos - downRange;
    var weight = Mathf.Cos((Time.time) * speed * 2 * Mathf.PI) * 0.5 + 0.5;
    transform.position.y = upPos * weight        + downPos * (1-weight);

}
```

7.   Save the script.

8.   Drop it onto the Hologram.

9.   Set the up and down range to about **0.1**.

10.   Click Play and watch the results.

11.   Save the scene and save the project.

The Balcony

To access the balcony, you'll need to open one of the secret passageway doors for the player. Once up there, the player will find the jewel (no longer accessible) and the Golden Sleeve.

1.   Select Door Upper in the Hierarchy and double-click to focus in on it in the Scene view.

2.   Set its Z Value to 78.

■ **Note**   The Z value is still up for the door since it was created in 3ds Max and imported with Z up.

---

3.   Click Play and make your way up to the balcony via the secret passage (see Figure 14-42).

Figure 14-42. *The bowl on the ledge of the balcony*

    4.   Stop Play mode.

Now you need to create a light as the source of the bluish glow and what better visual source than the Jewel that was given to the temple in order to gain access. Since it doesn't need to be interactive anymore, you can make a simple clone of one of the existing jewels.

1.   Select the Small Bowl 1 in the Temple Group and Focus in on it.

2.   Select the Golden Sleeve and place it in the bowl using Move to View.

3.   Select the Jewel Loose and duplicate it.

4.   Name it **Jewel Temple**.

5.   Delete the Interactor and Object Lookup scripts as well as the collider from the new jewel if you had set it up as an action object.

6.   Create a new Empty GameObject at the new Jewel's position.

7.   Name it **Floating Jewel**.

8.   Create a Point Light at the same position.

9.   Name it **Glow**.

10. Add the light and the jewel to the new GameObject.

11. Move the Floating Jewel object above the bowl in the temple.

12. Select the light and set its Range to about **0.7**.

13. Set its Color to a blue-green to blend between the jewel color and the blue of the ledge.

14. Set its Intensity to **0.5** and check Draw Halo.

15. Duplicate the light and uncheck Draw Halo.

16. Name it **Glow Light**.

17. Set its Intensity to **6.7**, its Range to **1.4**, and make its Color more bluish to match the ledge.

18. Move it down so it lights the bowl.

19. Click Play and travel up to the ledge.

After watching the dynamic hologram, the new construction looks rather boring. Let's add the cycler script to it and, because it would also be useful, let's add rotate functionality to the script.

1. Stop Play mode.

2. Add the V_PositionCycler to the Floating Jewel group and set the Up Range to **0** and the Down Range to **0.5**.

3. Open the V_PositionCycler script.

4. Add the following variables to the script:

```
var rotate = false; // rotation option
var degrees = 30; // rotation degrees per second
```
You can borrow the rotation from one of the scripts you created near the start of the book.

5. Add the following inside the FixedUpdate function:

```
if (rotate) transform.Rotate(0, degrees * Time.deltaTime, 0);
```

6. Save the script.

7. Check Rotate in the Inspector.

8. Click Play and test.

The result is much more interesting and dynamic.

10. Move the Floating Jewel Group into the Temple Group.

9. Save the scene and save the project.

Getting the Topi Fruit

Before activating the temple bouncer, let's go ahead and get the Topi fruit working. The Topi Fruit is hidden in the sack down in one of the storage rooms. The GrainSack, the GrainSackOpen, Door Lower, and the Topi Fruit Sack all need to be set up.

1. Add the Interactor and ObjectLookup scripts to each of the four objects.

2. Tag each as an Action Object.

When the player takes the golden topi fruit from the grain sack, you need to open the other secret door to give access to the subterranean cavern. If you check your special cases notes in the Game Notes text object, you'll see that you've allowed for triggering an action object's animation only. Since you need to keep track of the door's state, you can make it an action object, but set its states to 3—in the scene but not pickable.

3. Select the Door Lower.

4. From the Components menu, select Miscellaneous and then add an Animation component.

▨ **Tip** Because the door has a parent, you need to add an Animation component to it manually or the Animation would go on the parent if you allowed it to be automatically applied while creating a new clip.

---

5. Uncheck Play Automatically.

6. Open the Animation view.

7. Create a New Clip in the Animation Clips folder.

8. Name it **open passage**.

9. Select the Rotate.z track.

10. Click Record and create a key at frame 0.

11. At frame 30 create a key and rotate the door to **-78**.

12. Close the Animation view.

13. In the Inspector, set the Animation to **open passage**.

14. Set up the door as shown in Figure 14-43.

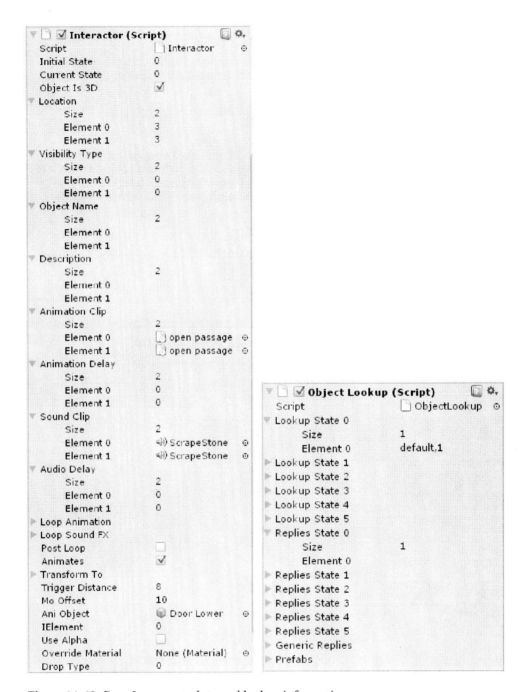

Figure 14-43. *Door Lower metadata and lookup information*

The GrainSack only has two states—it gets swapped out of the scene instead of animating the sack ripping open.

15. Set it up as shown in Figure 14-44.

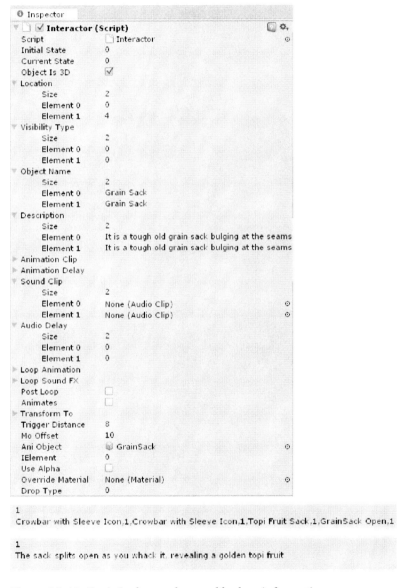

1
Crowbar with Sleeve Icon,1,Crowbar with Sleeve Icon,1,Topi Fruit Sack,1,GrainSack Open,1

1
The sack splits open as you whack it, revealing a golden topi fruit

Figure 14-44. *GrainSack metadata and lookup information*

The *GrainSackOpen* has two states—out of scene and in scene.

16. Set it up as shown in Figure 14-45.

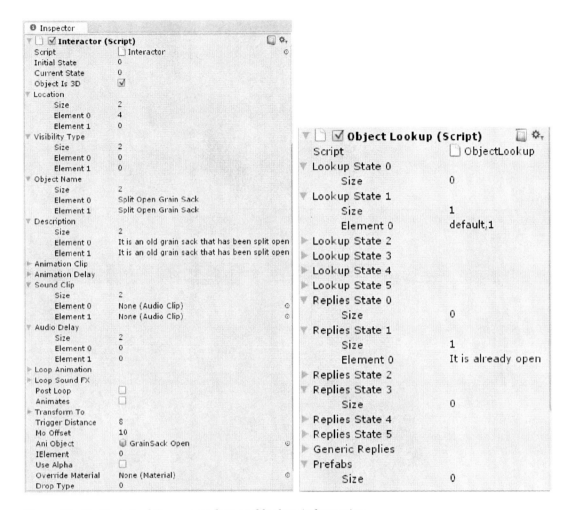

Figure 14-45. *GrainSackOpen metadata and lookup information*

The *Topi Fruit Sack* has two states—as is and out of scene.

17. Set it up as shown in Figure 14-46.

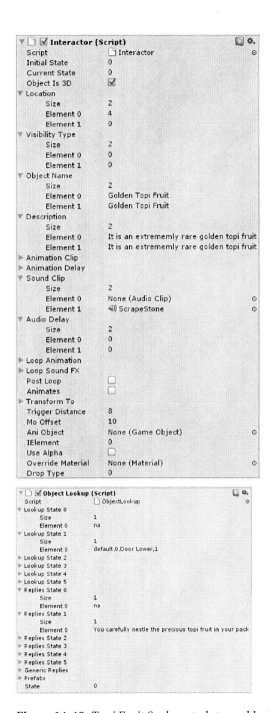

Figure 14-46. *Topi Fruit Sack metadata and lookup information*

You'll also need to set up an inventory icon for the Topi Fruit if you haven't already done so.

1. Select one of the existing icons and duplicate it.

2. Name it **Topi Fruit Icon**.

3. Change its texture to the Topi Fruit Icon texture.

4. Set it up as shown in Figure 14-47.

Figure 14-47. *Topi Fruit Icon metadata and lookup information*

The player should now have access to the cavern. You can finish that area when you create the final level in the next chapter.

Let's finish moving the other action objects to their correct locations. The plant needs to be moved to the Shrine Flora. You can move the shrine and plant to your chosen final location later.

1. Select the Flower object.

2. Move it to the Shrine Flora and position it on the center pedestal.

3. Select the Flower in the Project view.

4. Change its import Scale Factor to **0.0075** and click Apply.

5. Open the Animation view, turn on the record button, and scrub through the read-only animation to make sure the flower is not too large when revived.

6. Close the Animation view.

7. Move the Target Jewel object (for the camera match) to the new location.

8. Click Play, then pick up the vial and test the new location (see Figure 14-48).

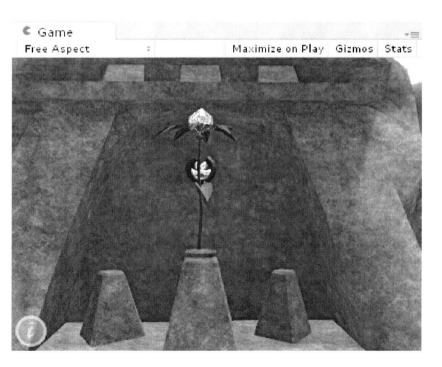

Figure 14-48. *The Flower revived in its new location*

The flower works as expected, but the animated Vial of Elixir that you turned into a prefab is still animating in its original position, because you haven't allowed for a moved location. To update it, let's put it back into the scene and then drag it back to the prefab.

727

1. Focus in on the Flower in the Scene view.

2. From the AnimatedObjects folder in Project view, drag the VialPrefab into the scene and align it to the Flower's base, as shown in Figure 14-49.

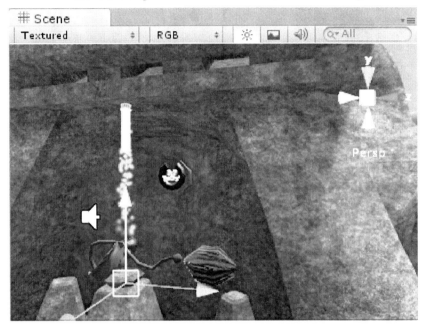

Figure 14-49. *The VialPrefab relocated*

3. Drag it back onto the VialPrefab in the Project view to update the position.

4. Delete the scene VialPrefab.

5. Click Play and test.

The vial now pours over the flower as it did previously.

The Vial of Elixir should go into the Stone Chest in the Shrine Safekeep. The stone chest can be set up exactly like the wooden chest, but for now, let's just go for the simpler unlocked scenario.

1. Select the Stone Chest Lid from the Structures prefab, Shrine Safekeep, and focus in on it.

2. Turn it off.

3. Move the Vial of Elixir to inside the stone chest in the Shrine Safekeep.

4. Select the Stone Chest Lid and activate it again.

5. Add the Interactor and ObjectLookup scripts onto the Stone Chest Lid.

6. Tag it as an ActionObject.

7. Add an Animation component to the lid.

8. Uncheck Play Automatically.

9. Create a New Clip and name it **stone lid open**.

10. Animate it opening to **-110** degrees on the Rotation.x over **60** frames.

11. Create a second clip and name it.

12. Animate it closing from **-110** degrees on the Rotation.x over **30** frames back to **0**.

13. Close the Animation view and load the open animation in the Animation parameter of the Animation component.

14. Set the lid up as shown in Figure 14-50.

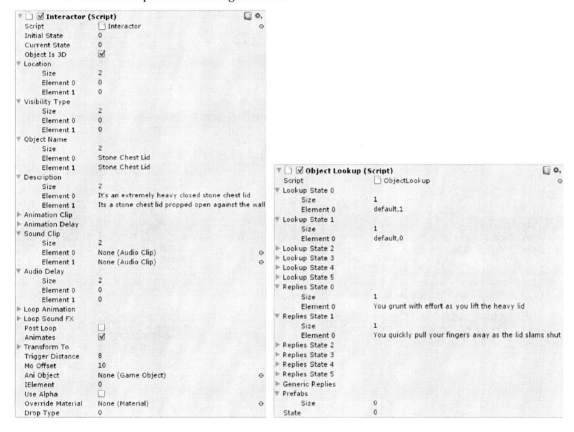

Figure 14-50. *The Stone Chest Lid metadata and lookup information*

15. Click Play and test the lid (see Figure 14-51).

Figure 14-51. *The stone chest*

It seems a bit difficult to look inside the chest. Rather than redo the models, you can add a collider to provide an invisible ramp up to a better vantage point. Since the shrine already has a step, the player will not notice the difference.

1. Select the chest base.

2. Add a Box Collider in addition to the Mesh Collider.

3. Adjust its Size and Center to improve the view inside the chest, as shown in Figure 14-52.

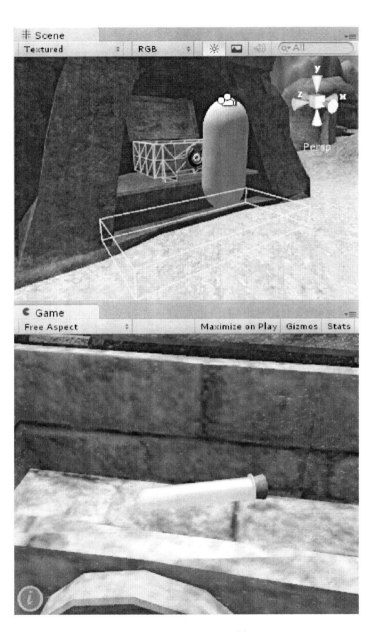

Figure 14-52. *The Box collider as an invisible step*

4. Click Play and test

The play is improved without remaking assets.

▪ **Tip**   A Sphere Collider will give smoother access, but is more difficult to set up.

---

5. Save the scene and save the project.

The Elements

A couple of shrines don't have any action objects associated with them, but you can still make them interesting for the player should you want to extend the game at a later date.

1. Select the Shrine Light and focus in on its Small Bowl.

2. Drag the Flame prefab from the standard assets and place it in the bowl.

3. Adjust the two particle systems, as shown in Figure 14-53.

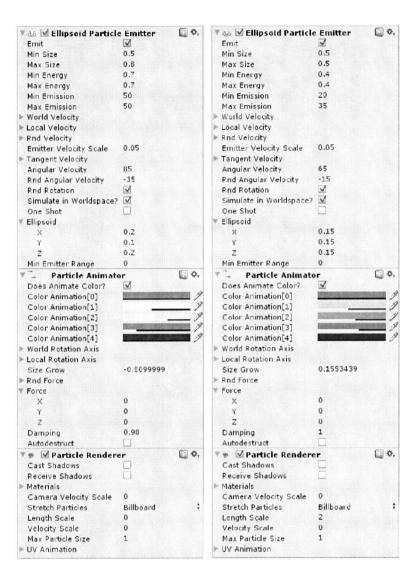

Figure 14-53. *The Flame particle parameters*

To make the flame more interesting, let's create a little script to flicker the light's intensity by adding a random amount to the minimum value of the light.

1. Create a new script.

2. Name it **Flicker**.

3. Open it in the script editor.

4. Add the following:

```
var timer : float; // light update interval to slow down flicker
var baseIntensity = 0.4;
var maxOffset = 0.2;

function Start () {

    timer =  Time.time + 0.15; // update interval

}

function Update () {

    if (Time.time > timer ) {
        light.intensity =  baseIntensity + Random.Range (0.0, maxOffset) ;
        timer = Time.time + 0.15;
    }

}
```

5. Save the script.

6. Drop it onto the Flame prefab's Lightsource light.

7. Select Continue at the losing prefab warning.

8. Click Play and watch the flame flickering (see Figure 14-54).

Figure 14-54. *The Flame in the Shrine Light*

The Waterfall

Unity comes with two very useful particle systems for creating waterfalls. Combining these with animating the UVs on the mesh objects, you can create quite respectable waterfalls in the free version of Unity .

1. Position the water shrine group where you'd like it, remembering not to rotate it unless you plan on rebaking the lightmaps.

2. With the Terrain tools, create a mountain backing for the rock face and a hole for the water basin.

3. Focus in on the Shrine Water, a shown in Figure 14-55.

Figure 14-55. *Terrain prepared for water shrine group*

Take a moment to inspect the materials used for the rocky cliff and the waterfalls and water surfaces. The waterfalls use a variation of the water surface texture with an alpha edge.

While the water texture looks okay in a still shot, it needs some animation to bring it to life. For that, let's create a useful little script that accesses the Shader UV Tiling settings. One trick used to make a water surface interesting without a reflection (if you are using the free version of Unity), is to animate the Diffuse or main color at a slightly different speed or direction from the bump. Our script will provide parameters for both, as well as speed adjustments.

1. Select the two large waterfalls and make sure they do not have colliders.

2. Create a new script.

3. Name it UVAnimator.

4. Open it in the script editor.

5. Add the following variables:

```
// Scroll main texture based on time
var materialIndex : int = 0;

var animateUV = true;
var scrollSpeedU1 = 0.0;
var scrollSpeedV1 = 0.0;
```

```
var animateBump = true;
var scrollSpeedU2 = 0.0;
var scrollSpeedV2 = 0.0;
```

6. To experiment with accessing other shader properties, you may want to include the following:

```
function Start () {

   //print ("shininess " + renderer.materials[materialIndex].HasProperty("_Shininess"));
   //print ("parallax " + renderer.materials[materialIndex].HasProperty("_Parallax"));

}
```

To animate the Offset for the main texture and bump maps, let's use Time.time and the speed to control the Offset.

7. Add the following:

```
function FixedUpdate () {

   var offsetU1 = Time.time  * -scrollSpeedU1;
   var offsetV1 = Time.time  * -scrollSpeedV1;

   var offsetU2 = Time.time  * -scrollSpeedU2;
   var offsetV2 = Time.time  * -scrollSpeedV2;

   if (animateUV) {
       renderer.materials[materialIndex].SetTextureOffset ("_MainTex",
Vector2(offsetU1,offsetV1));
   }

   if (animateBump) {
       renderer.materials[materialIndex].SetTextureOffset ("_BumpMap",
Vector2(offsetU2,offsetV2));
   }

}
```

8. Save the script.

9. Apply it to the three waterfall objects in the group as well as the Water Basin and the Water Hole.

10. Set up the parameters as shown in Table 14-1.

Table 14-1. *Water Parameters*

Object	Scroll Speed U1	Scroll Speed U1	Scroll Speed U1	Scroll Speed U1
Large waterfall	1	0	1.5	0
Mini waterfall	1	0	0.5	0
Water Basin	-0.03	0.05	0.05	0.03
Water Hole	-0.03	0.05	0.05	0.03

11. Click Play and observe the result.

12. Zoom in close to see the effect of the slightly different speeds and directions.

13. Stop Play mode.

■ **Tip**   You could adapt this script to animate a shininess or glossiness texture on a rock wall by having the UV 2 channel mapped to "flow" downhill. Our rock is already using the UV 2 channel for the lightmap, but it is an interesting effect to consider.

Now we need to add some particles to liven things up.

1. From Standard Assets ➤ Particles ➤ Water, drag the Water Surface Splash to the base of the large waterfall.

2. Drag it into the scene below the falls.

3. Adjust the height of the particle system so it generates its particles slightly on top of the Water Hole's surface.

4. Change its Max Size to **1.5**, Min Emission to **60** and the Max Emission to **80**.

5. Set Size Grow to **2** and uncheck Cast and Receive Shadows.

6. Drag it into the Group Water GameObject.

For the waterfall spray, let's use the Waterfall prefab, again from the Standard Assets.

7. Drag the Waterfall prefab near the top of the large waterfall.

8. Change its orientation in the Transforms to match the waterfall mesh.

9. Add it to the Group Water GameObject,

10. Deselect it and click Play to see it in action in the Scene view.

It will take quite a bit of adjustment to match the mesh waterfall.

11. Set its parameters as shown in Figure 14-56.

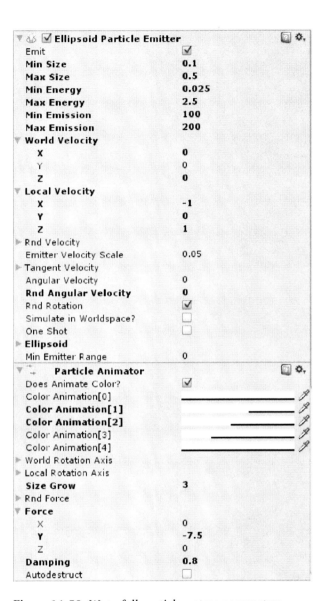

Figure 14-56. *Waterfall particle system parameters*

12. Click Play and travel to the waterfall to see the full effect (see Figures 14-57 and 14-58).

Figure 14-57. *The finished waterfall*

Figure 14-58. *Waterfall at player level*

13. Stop Play mode.

14. Save the scene and save the project.

The Shrine's Guardian

Now that we've had a break from game functionality, let's get back to the bouncer at the temple.

The bouncer will consist of several objects: a collider to trigger the visual effect on when the player is within range; a collider to check the player's inventory for offerings or weapons; and a collider to prevent the player from entering. Let's start with the collider at the entry that does the checking. It will be the parent GameObject for the bouncer entity.

1. Focus in on the front of the temple.

2. Create a new Empty GameObject.

3. Name it **Temple Bouncer**.

4. Add a Capsule Collider to it.

5. Set its Radius to **8** and its Height to **25**.

6. Check Is Trigger.

You can be sure that at least some of the players will try to sneak in by scaling the walls to get behind the "bouncer," so the blocker collider needs to fill the space well.

1. Create another Empty GameObject and name it **Temple Blocker**.

2. Drag Temple Blocker into Temple Bouncer.

3. Add a Box Collider component to Temple Blocker and position it to fill the entryway.

4. Set its Size to X, **6**; Y, **10**; and Z, **8** (see Figure 14-59).

5. Align the front of the collider with the guardian beasts' pedestal fronts.

Figure 14-59. *The TempleBlocker's collider*

■ **Caution**   Make sure the Box Collider does not intersect the Cloth objects or they will be ripped from their moorings when you click Play.

The third collider needs to be range-based and set to Is Trigger so when the player enters or exits it, you can manage the particle system.

1. Create another Empty GameObject.

2. Name it **FX Range**.

3. Add it to the Temple Bouncer.

4. Add a Capsule Collider to the FX Range object (see Figure 14-60).

5. Set its Radius to **30** and its Height to **60**.

6. Check Is Trigger.

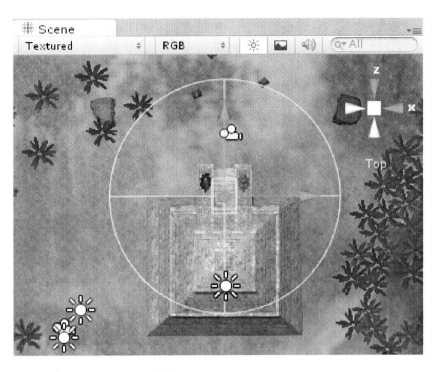

Figure 14-60. *The range collider*

7. Select the Temple Bouncer.

8. Nudge its collider's X or Z Center value until it is slightly in front of the Temple Blocker so the player will intersect it before hitting the blocker.

For the particle system, let's create an Aurora Borealis effect.

1. From the GameObject menu, create a Particle System.

2. Name it **BouncerFX**.

3. Set it up using some nice blues, greens and magentas for the particle colors, as shown in Figures 14-61 and 14-62.

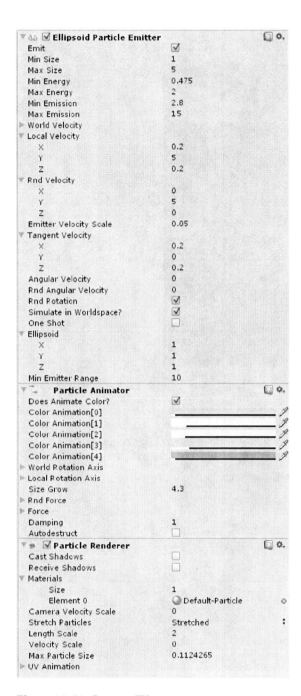

Figure 14-61. *BouncerFX parameters*

Figure 14-62. *The BouncerFX at the temple entrance*

Because you will need to instantiate and destroy the particle system as the play goes in and out of the range collider, you need to make a prefab.

1. Create a new Prefab in the Adventure Prefabs folder.

2. Name it **BouncerFX**.

3. Drag the current BouncerFX onto it from the Hierarchy view.

4. Delete the object in the Hierarchy view.

5. Save the scene and save the project.

Next you'll need a script to control the bouncer and its effects. Because this one is rather different from the rest of the action objects, we will depart from our usual mantra of making reusable scripts and write just what is needed.

1. Create a new script and name it BouncerFXManager.

2. Open it in the script editor.

3. Add the following to create the BouncerFX functionality:

```
var fxParticles: GameObject; // the bouncer's particle system
```

```
private var fx : GameObject; // the one we will be creating

function OnTriggerEnter () {

    fx = Instantiate (fxParticles);

}

function OnTriggerExit () {

    KillEffect ();
}


//so we can turn off the particles from any event
function KillEffect () {

    yield;
    Destroy(fx, 5);

}
```

By putting the kill functionality in its own function, you will be able to turn off the particles once the player has gained entry into the temple.

4. Save the script.

5. Add it to the FX Range object.

6. Assign the BouncerFX prefab to the Fx field.

7. Click Play and test the functionality.

The particles appear and disappear according to range.

The Bouncer

Now you need a script that allows the player to go inside the temple, take the jewel, and remove any weapons (in our case, the crowbar). You will need a few arrays to hold the weapons to be checked, in icon format, along with their mesh counterparts. Rather than try to hook up the replies to the regular text handling, let's use a disembodied voice to give the player feedback. Since waiting for voice audio to play out can be time-consuming, you can also include text replies for quicker testing.

While you could create an array of *possible* offerings, it would require a lot more thought to deal with the accompanying issues. If the item the player offered is needed elsewhere in the game, you would need to allow him to get it back at a later time from inside the temple. Some sort of checking and consequence mechanism would be needed to allow the substitution or, as an Indiana Jones-type sequence of events, indicate that it was a wrong choice. An alternative would be to sprinkle multiple offering candidates about the environment. The problem with that is that it would litter the game with objects that never get used, something that is generally avoided in classic adventure games. The best solution for our project is to limit the offering to a single object, the jewel.

1. Create a new script.

2. Name it BouncerManager.

3. Open it in the script editor.

4. Add the following variables:

```
var offeringIcon : GameObject; // this will be the Jewel Icon

var weapons : GameObject[];
var weaponsIcons : GameObject[];
var weaponsNewState : int[]; // state the object goes to when found

var controlCenter : GameObject; // where the current cursor texture can be found
var reply : String[]; // temp way to check the replies quickly before adding the audio
var audioReply : AudioClip[]; // reply according to action needed
private var templeState : int; // 0, no entry, 1 can enter, 2, passage open
private var response : int; // array element for response

var dropPoint : Transform; // the place weapons get located to
//response codes:
//0- no cursor, needs offering in hand
//1- has offering, but not accepted
//2- offering accepted, entry granted
//3- offering accepted, entry granted, weapons relocated
//4-weapons relocated
//5- no response
```

1. Save the script.

2. Add the script to the Temple Bouncer object.

3. Drag the Jewel Icon onto its Offering Icon parameter.

4. Drag the Control Center object onto the matching parameter.

5. Set the three weapons array Sizes to **1**.

6. Drag the Crowbar and Crowbar Icon onto the appropriate parameters.

7. Set the new state for the crowbar to **0** so it stays in scene.

8. Set the Reply array's Size to **6**.

9. Fill out the replies using the notes in the script, as shown in Figure 14-63.

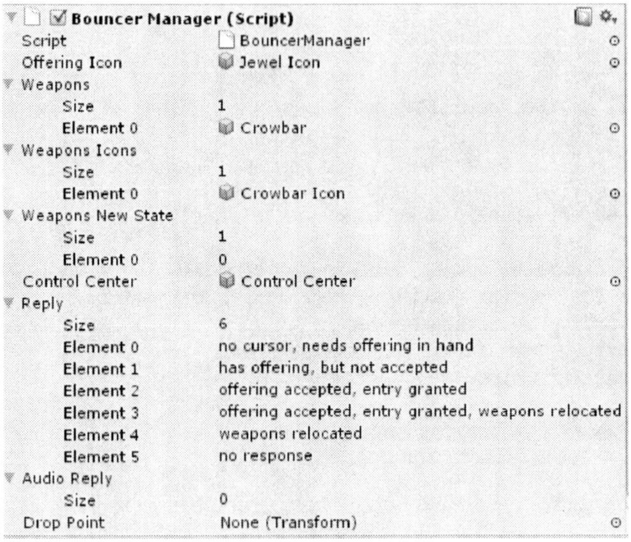

Figure 14-63. *The loaded objects*

The first check should be whether or not the player has made the offering and been given permission to enter. If the temple state is 0, the cursor will be checked and the player will be admitted or refused accordingly. Rather than going to the trouble of parsing the currentInventoryObjects array from the GameManager to look for the jewel, let's simplify the process by requiring the jewel to be "in hand" or the current cursor. Audio replies will indicate this so the player can figure it out. This functionality is a bit different from the regular interaction in that it will be use the OnTriggerEnter function rather than an OnMouseDown function since there isn't anything concrete for the player to pick. If you had a lot of this type of interaction, you might consider a means of triggering the usual object look-up and process-object functions. Since we only have this one, it will be good practice to have it as a standalone script.

10. Add the following:

```
function OnTriggerEnter () {

response = 5; // no response

    //get access to the cursor to see if player is holding anything
    var cursorName = controlCenter.GetComponent(GameManager).currentCursor.name;
    var defaultCursor = controlCenter.GetComponent(GameManager).defaultCursor.name;
    var empty = true; // clear cursor flag
    if (cursorName != defaultCursor) empty = false; // holding something- need to check
    // see if there are currently any items in inventory
    var iCount : int =
(controlCenter.GetComponent(GameManager).currentInventoryObjects.length);

    // load the current inventory objects if there are any - they will need to be check for
weapons
```

```
    if (iCount > 0) var iObjects =
controlCenter.GetComponent(GameManager).currentInventoryObjects;
```

Now you can check the cursor to see if it is the correct offering. You will eventually create a function to do the processing if a match is made and to handle replies.

11. Add the following:

```
//Check for the jewel
if (templeState == 0 ) { //no admittance yet, so first look for offering
    response =0; // assume no offering
    // check cursor
    if (cursorName == offeringIcon.name) {
        ProcessOffering();
        response = 2; // player has correct offering
    }
  else if (cursorName != defaultCursor)  response = 1; // wrong offering


    if (response < 2) { // no admittance
        HandleReply();
        return;
    }

}
```

Once the temple state has been upgraded to allow the player to enter, the cursor and the player inventory must be checked for weapons. If weapons are found, they will be processed into the provided state and their icon counterparts set to state 0.

Both the cursor and the inventory must be checked for weapons. As with the offering, let's create a function to process the weapons once identified.

12. Add the following:

```
// player has access so strip out weapons

    // see if cursor is a weapon
    for (i = 0; i < weaponsIcons.length; i++) {
        if (weaponsIcons[i].name == cursorName) { // a match was found
            ProcessWeapons(i);
            response = 4;
        }
    }
```

Now go through the current inventory if there is anything in it and check for weapons. This requires a nested for loop as each item in inventory must be checked against each item in the list of weapons.

13. Add the following:

```
//check current inventory (if any) items against weapons list
    if (iCount > 0) {
        for (i = 0; i < weaponsIcons.length; i++) { // check the list
            //update the inventory count in case you just removed one on the last pass
            iCount = (controlCenter.GetComponent(GameManager).currentInventoryObjects.length);
            for (var  k = 0; k < iCount; k++) { // with the contents
                if (weaponsIcons[i] == iObjects[k]) {// looking for a match
```

```
                    ProcessWeapons(i); // got one, send it off to be processed
                    k = iCount; //force end of loop so we don't get an error changing iCount
                    if (response == 2) response = 3;
                    else response = 4;
                }
            }
        }
    }
```

And, finally, call the reply and close the `OnTriggerEnter` function.

14. Add the following:

```
HandleReply ();

}
```

15. Save the script.

Now you need to add the processing functions. Let's start with processing the offering. You will need to reset the cursor, update the temple's state, and turn off the temple blocker.

1. Add the following function:

```
function ProcessOffering () {

    // take icon out of inventory
    gameObject.Find(offeringIcon.name).SendMessage("ProcessObject",0);
    templeState = 1; // upgrade temple state
    gameObject.Find("Temple Blocker").active = false; //disable the blocker
    gameObject.Find("FX Range").SendMessage("KillEffect");
    yield new WaitForSeconds(6); // wait for the particles to fade
    gameObject.Find("FX Range").active = false; //disable the fx checker
}
```

For the weapons processing, it is the icon version of the weapon that needs to be processed, whether it was the cursor or it was in inventory. You are passing in the index number of the weapons array element that matched an inventory object. Its mesh counterpart then needs to be reactivated and moved to a different location. The easiest way to move the object to the correct position is to unparent it first so you don't have to calculate offsets from the parent.

2. Add the following function:

```
function ProcessWeapons (index : int) {

    // take icon out of inventory or cursor
    gameObject.Find(weaponsIcons[index].name).SendMessage("ProcessObject",0);

    // find, activate and process mesh object into scene
    var actionObjects = controlCenter.GetComponent(GameManager).actionObjects;
    for (var y =0; y < actionObjects.length; y++) { // iterate through the array
        if (actionObjects[y].name == weapons[index].name) {  // if there is a match for the
object

            actionObjects[y].active = true; // activate the matched object from the array
            actionObjects[y].SendMessage("ProcessObject",weaponsNewState[index]);
        }
```

```
}

//un-parent the object, then move weapon to new location
var pos : Vector3 = dropPoint.transform.position;
var rot : Vector3 = dropPoint.transform.localEulerAngles;
//if the object has a parent, remove it from the parent first
if (weapons[index].transform.IsChildOf(weapons[index].transform))
    weapons[index].transform.parent = null; // detach from parent
weapons[index].transform.localPosition = pos;
;
   weapons[index].transform.localEulerAngles = rot;

}
```

And, finally, a simple function to play the audio response. A function makes it easier to add code to display a text response in the console or even implement a text response using the GUI controls in the GameManager script. Let's leave the audio reply commented out until we populate the audio clips array.

3.   Add the following function:

```
function HandleReply () {

if (response == 5) return;
print (reply[response]); // this is temporary until we load the audio files
// audio.PlayOneShot(audioReply[response]);

}
```

4.   Save the script.

Before you test, you will need to assign an object as the drop point. In the next chapter we will get serious with the drop point, but for now, let's simply use a static drop point.

1.   Create an Empty GameObject and name it **DropPoint**.

2.   Move it somewhere in the scene where you want the crowbar to be relocated.

3.   Drag the DropPoint object into the Temple Bouncer's Drop Point parameter.

4.   Click Play and test the bouncer functionality.

░ **Tip**   You may wish to use the JewelLoose to test with instead of repeating the full sequence each time.

The bouncer will let the player in if the jewel is being carried (as the cursor). The crowbar will be confiscated and left at the drop point. You should be able to retrieve the crowbar after you have taken the Golden Sleeve from the temple balcony.

5.   Save the scene and save the project

6.   When you are happy with the functionality, locate the Voice Assets folder in the Game Assets folder and listen to the three "voices" provided for the temple bouncer/guardian.

7. Choose your favorite and add the sound files to your project.

8. Set the Audio Reply array Size to **6**.

9. Load the appropriate audio clip for each.

10. Leave Element 5 as None.

Summary

In this chapter you finished bringing in most of the game's assets and filling out their metadata and lookup information. You completed the treasure chest sequence with a system that checks for the contents of the chest no matter how an object was placed inside it, and later discovered a possible issue with skinned meshed and frustum cull as you finished the flower functionality. Using a particle system, you spiced up the animation of the vial of elixir and learned about instantiating and destroying particle systems.

With animations that could easily happen beyond the player's view, you added a camera matching script that let you help the player by taking over navigation for visually challenged sequences.

After importing the final assets, you experimented with shaders and lightmaps to gain insight into the various options with respect to the Indie version. You later compared results with the same object with light baked into Unity Pro's full featured version of Beast.

You enhanced the imported temple with Unity's Cloth object and Line Renderer to provide a dynamic entryway that also helped disguise the implemented workaround for gaining access to the temple's lower floors—turning off the terrain while inside the temple. With the addition of cloth hanging in an open doorway, you discovered the need to alter a standard shader to show on both sides of a single-sided mesh (the cloth mesh).

Inside the temple, you made use of the Flame prefab s, a quick way to get some smoke for the brazier, and then created a handy script to make an object look as if it were floating. The Line Renderer component proved useful for both the floating hologram and the fake volumetric light in the inner chamber.

Outside, you enhanced the Flame prefab with a `flicker` script in the Light shrine, and later learned how to access and animate shader parameters to make a respectable waterfall and water basin using only Unity Indie. Unity's built-in Waterfall and Water Splash prefabs completed the Water shrine using a custom shader created in the Strumpy Shader Editor, a shareware visual shader editor available through Unity's Showcase forum.

Your final task was to create the bouncer logic to restrict user and weapon access to the temple. Although most of the scripts involved were specific to the project game, you did create a range-based means of turning objects off and on.

By the end of the chapter, you were able to complete most of the game play. In the next chapter, you will create a simple final level as well as a bonus feature—a classic dynamic maze implemented in 3D.

■ ■ ■

CHAPTER 15

A Maze and the Final Level

The maze has always been a mainstay of adventure games. In the early days of text adventures as well as modern-day, restricted camera type navigation, the game was free to pop up exits or treasure trove areas according to any criteria. In first-person games, however, the maze needs to be based on a physical reality. Moreover, at the very least, it should change every time the game runs, or, better yet, change in-game when specific events are triggered.

In our scenario, when the player enters the temple, with the crowbar in hand or in inventory, it will be randomly relocated to the maze. To encourage the player to find a better solution than having to find the crowbar from within the maze, let's have the maze regenerate each time the temple is entered.

Maze Geometry

To create the maze, you will be taking advantage of Unity's snap functionality. Since you need to be able to generate a new configuration of the maze at any time, the pieces should all be the same dimension. However, rather than have all maze pieces exactly the same, let's use seven variations throughout the maze to make things more economical. To start, the imported asset will contain placeholders to help you position the prefabs. You will need an area of approximately eighty square meters near the temple for the maze.

1. Locate and select the MazeWalls object in the Structures folder.

2. Make sure Generate Colliders is checked.

3. For Animations, select Generate and set it to Don't Import.

4. Make sure the Scale Factor matches the temple, **0.32**.

5. Click Apply after making the changes.

6. Drag the MazeWalls object into the scene.

7. Move it until it is near the temple.

8. Adjust its Y Position until it is sitting on the ground.

9. Select the Outer Wall object.

10. Remove it from the MazeWalls group.

11. Click Continue at the Losing Prefab warning.

12. Make note of its Y Position.

13. Drag it back into the MazeWalls group.

14. Adjust the terrain height beneath the maze to create a large flat area for it to sit on, using the Paint Height tool and setting the Height parameter to the Outer Wall's unparented Y Position value.

15. Remove any stray trees and other terrain objects from the maze area.

16. Select the MazeWalls group and do the final height adjustments on it.

17. Mark *only* the Outer Wall as static and rebake the terrain lightmap now if you wish (see Figure 15-1).

Figure 15-1. *The Maze*

18. Open the MazeWall group in the Hierarchy view.

There are thirty DropPoint objects, seven MazeWall objects, and thirty-five MazeWallProxy objects. The DropPoint objects are simple gameObjects that consist of their transforms and little else. They will be used as possible locations to drop the Crowbar object. To view the DropPoint objects in the scene view, you'll need to activate the Move button and select the DropPoint object.

1. Focus the view on the MazeWalls group.

2. Change to the Top view.

3. Select the Move button.

4. Try selecting the various DropPoint objects in the Hierarchy view to see their locations, as shown in Figure 15-2.

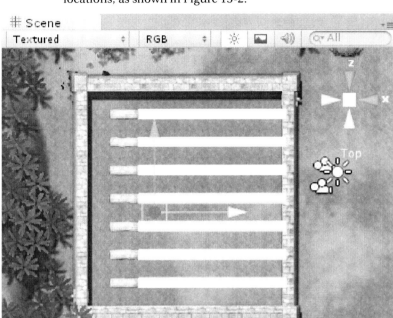

Figure 15-2. *A DropPoint selected*

As noted earlier, you will use seven variations of the wall throughout the maze. Following Unity best practices, when you need several duplicates of an object, make prefabs.

1. In the Adventure Prefabs folder, right-click and create a new Prefab.

2. Name it **WallMaze01**.

3. Duplicate it until you have one for each of the seven WallMaze objects.

4. Drag and drop the existing WallMaze01 from the Hierarchy view, onto the new prefab.

5. Repeat for the other six maze wall objects.

The names in the Hierarchy view will turn blue, as will the cube icon for the prefabs in the Project view.

Take a moment to look at the new prefabs in the Inspector. Note that the collider that was automatically generated for the wall sections was a Mesh Collider. Other than the geometry that gives the wall sections some variation and character, the walls are simple box volumes. If this was a shooter type game, where a projectile could bounce off the uneven surface to give varied results, it would make sense to leave the Mesh Colliders in place, but our needs are very basic. By changing each to a Box Collider, you can improve the framerate slightly.

6. Select each of the new prefabs in the Project view and change the Mesh Collider to a Box Collider, choosing Replace in the dialog.

Before making duplicates of the prefab to finish populating the maze, you may be curious to see how the walls will work. If you select the Rotate tool with the Pivot set to Center, the wall will appear to rotate from its center, but that is not the case.

1. Select one of the walls and focus in on it in the Scene view.

2. Select the Rotate tool.

3. Try to rotate the wall—it pivots from its center.

4. Undo the rotation.

5. In the Inspector, rotate the wall on its Z Rotation; it rotates from its actual pivot point (see Figure 15-3).

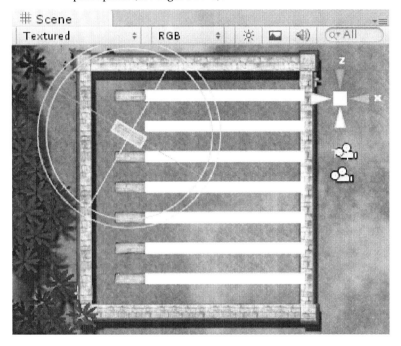

Figure 15-3. *The wall rotating from its pivot point*

6. Above the Scene view, toggle the coordinate button from Center to Pivot to see the correct pivot location in the viewport.

7. Zoom back out to see the entire maze.

8. Change the Scene view to Wireframe and hide the Terrain, as shown in Figure 15-4.

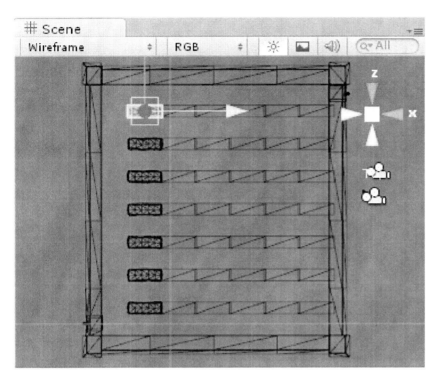

Figure 15-4. *The View set for easy positioning of the maze walls*

9. Duplicate the prefabs and replace the proxy walls with the prefab of your choice.

■ **Tip** You can use the Snap feature to help your placement. Open the Snap dialog from the bottom of the Edit menu and hold Ctrl (Cmd on the Mac) down as you drag the walls.

---

10. Delete the proxy wall objects when you have finished populating the maze.

11. Adjust the overlaps if needed to ensure a small, even overlap between the columns of walls.

12. Check to make sure that you have forty-two walls and delete any extras (see Figure 15-5).

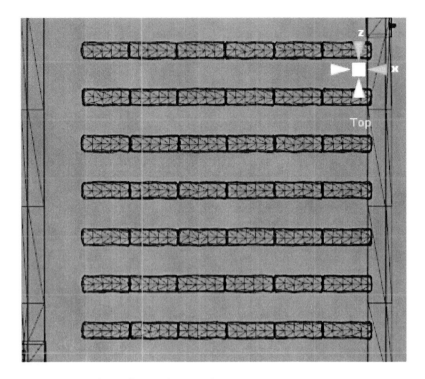

Figure 15-5. *The walls evenly spaced*

    13.   Change the view back to Textured and turn the terrain back on.

    14.   Save your scene and save your project.

Managing the Maze

Next you need to create a couple of scripts to manage the maze. The functionality is fairly simple. The script will turn each wall 0, 90, 180, or 270 degrees on its Z axis. The number of degrees rotated will be randomly selected from the available choices. To make the configuration slightly more interesting, let's decrease the odds of a zero rotation by doubling each of the others in the array you'll create to store the options.

    1.   Create a new script in the Adventure Scripts folder.

    2.   Name it `MazeWalls`.

    3.   Open it in the script editor.

    4.   At the top of the script, define and populate the array as follows:

```
private var rotAngles = new Array (0,90,90,180,180,270,270);
```
    Since you'll need to call this function periodically throughout the game, it makes sense to create a function to do the work for you.

5.   Change the Update function to Scramble so it looks like the following:

```
function Scramble () {
   // get a random element number in the array's range
   var element = Random.Range(0, 6); //remember arrays start at element 0
   //rotate the object on its local Z the number of degrees represented by that element
   transform.localEulerAngles.z = rotAngles[element];
}
```

The maze will always need to be set at scene start, so you'll need to call the new function from the Start function.

6.   Add the following Start function to your script:

```
function Start () {
   Scramble();
}
```

7.   Save the script.

8.   Add it to each of the wall prefabs in the Project View.

9.   Click Play.

The walls rotate into a random configuration, creating a simple maze as shown in Figure 15-6.

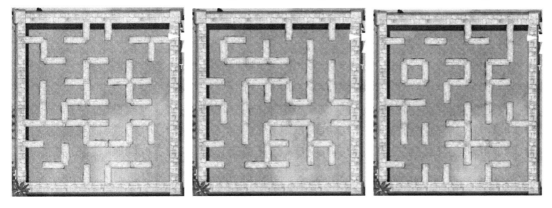

Figure 15-6. *A few maze configurations on startup*

The maze now sets itself up as soon as you click the Play button, but at various times during the game, it will need to be reset to a new configuration. You'll need a new script to handle the event. This script will be in charge of contacting each wall object and triggering its Scramble function. As with many scripts, the trick is often deciding on which object the script should reside.

You will obviously need to use some sort of SendMessage to trigger the Scramble function, but the trouble with SendMessage is that it sends the message to all components of the gameObject on which it resides. The problem is how to contact the forty-two GameObject walls. If you search the scripting help for SendMessage, you will notice a related option, GameObject.BroadcastMessage.

"Calls the method named methodName on every MonoBehaviour in this game object or any of its children."

This is the perfect solution. You can put a script with the broadcast message on the parent of all the maze walls, the MazeWalls group or gameObject.

1. Create a new script in the Adventure Scripts folder.

2. Name it MazeManager.

3. Open it in the script editor.

4. Change the Update function to the following:

```
function ResetMaze () {
    // trigger the wall rotations on all of the children
    gameObject.BroadcastMessage("Scramble");
}
```

5. Save the script.

6. Add the new script to the MazeWalls object in the Hierarchy view.

With the script in place, there should be a simple way to test it without having to hook it up to an actual event at this time. One possible solution is to create a texture object and use it to trigger the event. Once you are satisfied with the maze and related functionality, you can deactivate or delete the texture object.

1. Make sure you are not in Play mode.

2. From the GameObject menu, create a GUI Texture object.

This object uses the UnityWatermark image and is named after the image.

3. Change the X and Y Pixel Inset values in the Inspector to move the object off to the side of the game window if you wish.

If you look in the old MyScripts folder, you'll find a script named MousePick.

4. Drag and drop the MousePick script onto the GUI Texture object

5. Open the script in the editor.

6. Change the contents of the OnMouseDown function to the following:

```
GameObject.Find("MazeWalls").SendMessage("ResetMaze");
```

7. Comment out the var line.

8. Save the script.

9. Click Play and try picking the GUI Texture object several times.

The maze resets nicely.

If you reset the maze enough times, you will notice an occasional closed block of four walls. If it were just a matter of traveling through the maze, you could safely ignore this, but in the next section, you will be dealing with positioning the crowbar and you'll need a way to make sure it is accessible from any drop point.

Drop Points

As you have seen, a drop point is nothing more than an empty gameObject with a transform and a name. You could also consider them to be simple waypoints—objects that help in the calculation of pathfinding algorithms and NPCs (non-player characters such as enemies). When used for simple AI (artificial intelligence), you generally add a collider to define a target zone. The object is oriented in the direction of the target waypoint, and upon entering the zone, an OnTriggerEnter function is called, giving it its next waypoint goal. In the maze scenario, you need only the drop point's position, so there is no need to add colliders.

Now that you have the maze working, you need to select a drop point for the crowbar. Once the maze has been reset, a random number between 1 and 30 can be generated. That number is then cast to a character string and added to the base name, DropPoint. You will get the X and Z coordinates from DropPoint and use a previously stored Z position for the terrain height under the maze, then check to see if the position is accessible.

Unity does not currently come with AI or path finding, so you'll be using a simplified method to check to see if the chosen position is trapped or not. This will provide a chance to revisit the Raycast functionality.

In shooter type games, ray casting is used extensively to predict where projectiles will hit and trigger sounds and special effects at the point of intersection, tailored to the specific object that was hit.

In our less demanding adventure game, you will cast rays in the Cartesian directions and check for walls. If the distance to the wall that is being checked is less than half the cell size, and all four wall checks return that result, the position is trapped and the maze must be reset.

Less likely is when three walls are close, but the next open direction is trapped as well.

And rare, but within reasonable probability, is when three cells in a row are closed, as shown in Figure 15-7.

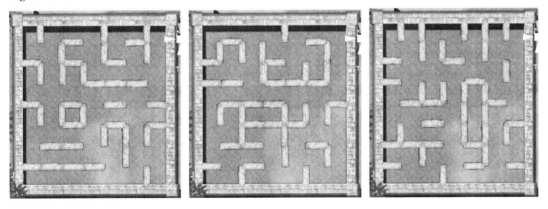

Figure 15-7. *Three configurations that will prevent player access to the relocated weapon: a common single, a double, and very rare triple trap.*

So the logic behind the checking can be as follows:

- If four walls are close, the position is inaccessible, so reset the maze and test again.

- If only one wall is close, it is safe, return.

- If two walls are close, test the position in each direction. If each direction is closed off in the three other directions, the cell is inaccessible, so reset the maze and test again; else if there was at least one other opening, it is probably safe.

- If three walls are close, move to the next position and test again. If only one new direction is open in the new position, move to it and test again. If there is at least one new open direction, let's assume it is accessible; else reset the maze and test again.

Let's start with the easy part of the script, generating a random position from the drop points.

Since the object drop point needs to be calculated every time the maze is reset, it makes sense to add the new code to the MazeManager script where you reset the maze. Since the code is likely to get complex, you can create another function to handle the drop point and call it right after you tell the walls to reset or Scramble.

1. Open the MazeManager script.

2. In the ResetMaze function, after the BroadcastMessage line, add the following:

```
yield new WaitForSeconds(0.05); //make sure the walls are finished configuring
FindDropPoint(); // generate and check a drop point for the new maze
```

3. Next, block in the FindDropPoint function:

```
function FindDropPoint() {
   //randomly generate the name of one of the 30 drop points
   var num = Random.Range(1,30);
   var name = "DropPoint"+ parseInt(num); // parseInt changes the integer to a string
   print (name);
}
```

4. Save the script.

5. Click Play.

6. Pick the GUI Texture object.

Nothing is reported in the Console until you pick the GUI Texture object. If you remember, the MazeWalls script on each of the walls initializes in a Start function. In order to generate the drop point at the start of the scene, you need to remove the Start function from that script and add one to the MazeManager script.

1. Open the MazeWalls script.

2. Delete the Start function.

3. Save the script.

4. Open the MazeManager script.

5. Copy the ResetMaze function and paste it above the original.

6. Rename the function Start.

7. It will look as follows:

```
function Start () {

    // trigger the wall rotations on all of the children
    gameObject.BroadcastMessage ("Scramble");
    yield new WaitForSeconds(0.05); //make sure the walls are finished configuring
    FindDropPoint(); // generate and check a drop point for the new maze

}
```

8.   Save the script.

9.   Click Play.

The console reports the randomly chosen drop point each time the maze is reset after giving the walls enough time to reconfigure themselves.

A DropPoint is generated as soon as the first maze is set up.

Now that you have the name of a DropPoint, you can get its location and move an object to it.

To do this, you can make a variable and drag and drop an object into it in the Inspector. Because the crowbar is too small to see from a bird's eye view, let's test using a sphere.

1.   At the top of the MazeManager script, add the following variable:

```
var dropObject : GameObject; // object to move to the drop point
```

2.   Save the script.

3.   Make sure you are not in Play mode.

4.   Create a new Sphere object.

5.   Scale it up to about three meters so you will be able to see it in the top viewport.

6.   Select the MazeWalls group.

7.   In the Inspector, drag and drop the new sphere onto the DropObject variable.

Now you need to get the X and Z position from the drop point so you can pass it on to the drop object.

8.   Add the following to the FindDropPoint function:

```
var dropPoint = GameObject.Find(name);
print (dropPoint.transform.position.x);
print (dropPoint.transform.position.z);
```

9.   Save the script.

10. Click Play.

If the number generated was less than ten, you will get an error message because the object names/numbers contain 0s. You could rename the objects, but this is a typical problem when dealing with cloned objects so let's adjust the script to account for it.

11. In the FindDropPoint function, change the **var** name = "DropPoint" + parseInt(num) line to the following:

```
// parseInt changes the integer to a string
```

```
    if (num > 9) var name = "DropPoint" + parseInt(num);
  else  name = "DropPoint0" + parseInt(num);
```

12. Save the script.

13. Click Play again.

14. Select the generated DropPoint.

15. Compare the reported X and Z to the values in the Inspector.

You have probably noticed that they don't match. Remember, though, that the values in the Inspector show the *offset* from the parent's position. Let's go ahead and feed the numbers into the drop object's transform and see what happens.

16. Delete the two print statements and add the following:

```
dropObject.transform.position.x = dropPoint.transform.position.x;
dropObject.transform.position.y = dropPoint.transform.position.y;
dropObject.transform.position.z = dropPoint.transform.position.z;
```

17. Save the script.

18. Click Play.

19. Pick the GUI Texture object and watch the sphere get positioned.

20. Locate the reported drop point and see that they are in the same place.

21. Reset the maze several times.

Eventually the sphere will land in a trapped position. Let's add a bit of code to prevent the most common trap.

Checking for Traps

To check for a trapped drop object, you need to cast rays in four directions. If you look in the Script Reference for Physics.Raycast, you'll see that it needs several bits of information. The first is the position of the object you are casting from. In this case, it will be the dropPoint object.

The second piece of information is the direction, encoded as a Vector3 type. A search for Vector3 shows us that the forward direction for the object, Vector3(0,0,1), can also be written as Vector3.forward. The right direction can be written as Vector3(1,0,0) or Vector3.right. For the opposite directions, you add a minus in front of the direction. So backward is –Vector3.forward, and left is –Vector3.right.

Third, you need to create a variable of type RaycastHit to store the hit object. With that, you can then get the distance from the source object to the hit object.

To hit an object, it must have a collider. On the off chance that your raycast might escape out the entrance of the maze and manage to miss all colliders in the scene, you should put the entire operation inside a conditional statement.

And lastly, because you need to perform the same operation for each of the four directions, you may as well create a little function that returns the distance if you pass it the source object's position and the direction.

> ■ **Note** At some point, you will need to move the source forward into the single open direction and check again. To this end, if you allow for locations other than the current drop point, you can continue to use the raycasting function.

Let's get started.

When you start checking for traps, you will want to be able to identify the walls that are hit by a raycast, so you need to give each wall a unique number to make sure the code works properly.

1. Renumber the walls so each has a unique number.

2. Open the `MazeManager` script.

3. Inside the `FindDropPoint` function, after you set the drop object into place, add the following to get the distances to the walls in each of the four directions:

```
// get distances to surrounding walls clockwise from 12 o'clock
var dForward = DistToWall(dropObject.transform .position, Vector3.forward);
var dRight = DistToWall(dropObject.transform .position, Vector3.right);
var dBackward = DistToWall(dropObject.transform .position,-Vector3.forward);
var dLeft = DistToWall(dropObject.transform .position,-Vector3.right);
```

Each call to the `DistToWall` function returns the distance that is immediately assigned to the local variables. While you are setting this up, it is also useful to know which drop point was selected.

4. Add a variable to store the total, and then print out the results:

```
var total = dForward + dRight + dBackward + dLeft;
print (name + " " + dForward + " " + dRight + " " + dBackward + " " + dLeft +↵
" " + total);
```

Before you can test the code, you need to create the `DistToWall` function. `DistToWall` receives the arguments passed to it from the lines that call it for each direction. On the off chance there wasn't a hit in that direction, you can assign it a large number on the assumption that the ray went out one of the doorways in the outer wall.

5. Below the `FindDropPoint` function, create the `DistToWall` function:

```
function DistToWall (origin: Vector3, direction : Vector3) {
    // pass the source/origin and direction in to be checked
    // do raycasting
    var hit : RaycastHit; // create a variable to hold the collider that was hit
    if (Physics.Raycast(origin, direction, hit)) {
        print (hit.transform.name);
        return hit.distance;
    }
    else return 1000.0; // didn't hit anything, so assign a large number
}
```

6. Save the script.

7. Click Play and test the results.

To check the results of the ray casting, you can check the total distances for the most common trap. The drop points are about 8.4 meters apart, with walls that are 3 meters thick. Halving the remaining distance, you arrive at about 2.7 meters to the closest walls, depending on how accurately you replaced the proxy wall with the prefabs. At the average range of 2.7 meters, a total of 10.8 should tell you that there is a wall on each of the four sides. It follows, then, that if there were only three close walls and the fourth is only a single square away, the next total should be 19.2. Realistically, you can safely assume that anything less than a well-padded 14 or 15 means the drop point is trapped.

Having determined that any total less than 14 means the drop point is enclosed within a single square, you can tell the maze to reset. To prove this to yourself visually, you can create a template cube to test with.

1. Create a cube in the Hierarchy.

2. Set its scale to 7x7x7.

3. Click Play.

4. In the Scene view, Top, move the cube into one of the squares.

It should overlap the walls, assuring you that the number is good for a valid test.

5. Delete the cube.

6. In the DistToWall function, comment out the print (hit.transform.name) line.

7. In the FindDropPoint function, comment out the print (name + " " + dForward line:

```
//print (name + "  " + dForward + "  " + dRight +  "  " +  dBackward +  "  " + dLeft +⏎
"  " + total);
```

8. Below it, add the following to perform the single square check:

```
// check for single square trap
if (total < 12) {
   print ("trapped");
}
```

Once you know it is trapped, you can get a new drop point and check again.

9. Beneath the print ("trapped") line, add the following:

```
FindDropPoint (); // get a new drop point
```

10. Save the script.

11. Click Play.

12. Test the maze several times, watching to see if the drop point is ever trapped.

Now you should see the message, but never the trapped sphere.

13. Save the scene and save the project.

Confiscated Weapons

Now that you have a means of positioning an object in the maze, you can go ahead and use it to relocate the confiscated weapons in the BouncerManager script.

The first thing to address is the actual height of the drop point. Currently, you are using the DropPoint object's local Z position, which was purposely set high enough to insure collision with the walls when raycasting. You have also been using a temporary sphere object so you could easily see the results of your scripting. Moreover, you already have a positioning object, DropPoint, that you made for the BouncerManager script to use when relocating the weapons.

Because you designed the "movable" action objects with their pivot points near their bases, you can set the DropPoint object slightly above the terrain inside the maze and use that as the height for any objects you need to relocate. Since the DropPoint has no mesh, you can use the sphere to get the position correct and then move the DropPoint object to it.

1. Select the Sphere.

2. Position its center point height slightly above the ground, as in Figure 15-8.

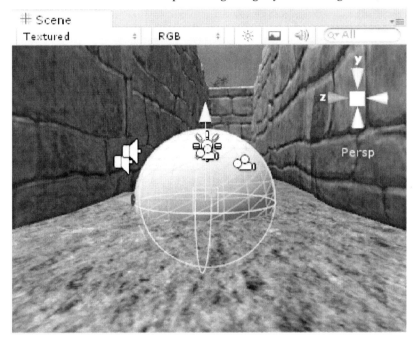

Figure 15-8. *The Sphere in position near ground level*

3. Use the F key to focus in on the sphere.

4. Select the DropPoint object.

5. Use Move To View to align it to the sphere.

6. Delete the sphere.

After deleting the sphere, you will need to need to assign the DropPoint object to the MazeManager.

1. Select the MazeWalls object.

2. Drag the DropPoint object into its Drop Object parameter..

Since you'll be calling the FindDropPoint function from the BouncerManager whenever you need to relocate a weapon, you no longer need to call it after each maze reset.

3. Open the MazeManager script.

4. Remove the following from both the Start function and the ResetMaze function:

```
yield new WaitForSeconds(0.05); //make sure the walls are finished
FindDropPoint(); // generate and check a drop point for the new maze
```

5. In the FindDropPoint function, delete the following line:

```
dropObject.transform.position.y = dropPoint.transform.position.y;
```
The easiest way to relocate the confiscated weapon is probably going to be just passing it into the FindDropPoint function as an argument and letting it get moved from there after the drop point location has been checked.

6. Change the function FindDropPoint() { line to the following:

```
function FindDropPoint (weapon : GameObject) {
```
When you call the function again if the location is "trapped," you need to pass the weapon object back into the function.

7. Inside the **if** (total < 12) { conditional, change the **FindDropPoint()** line to the following:

```
  FindDropPoint(weapon); // get a new drop point
```
Once you are relatively sure it is accessible, you can move the weapon to the drop point.

8. At the bottom of the FindDropPoint function, just above its closing curly bracket, add the following:

```
//relocate the weapon
weapon.transform.position.x = dropObject.transform.position.x;
weapon.transform.position.y = dropObject.transform.position.y;
weapon.transform.position.z = dropObject.transform.position.z;
```

9. Save the script.

And, finally, you need to change the BouncerManager script to utilize the new functionality.

1. Open the BouncerManager script.

2. Inside the ProcessWeapons function, remove the following lines:

```
var pos : Vector3 = dropPoint.transform.position;
var rot : Vector3 = dropPoint.transform.localEulerAngles;
```

3. Also remove the following lines:

```
weapons[index].transform.localPosition = pos;
```

```
weapons[index].transform.localEulerAngles = rot;
```

4. Replace them with:

```
gameObject.Find("MazeWalls").SendMessage("FindDropPoint",weapons[index]);
```

5. Save the script.

6. Click Play, grab the crowbar and the jewel, and enter the temple.

7. Exit the temple, enter the maze, and see if you can find the crowbar, as shown
    in Figure 15-9.

▨ **Tip**   If you are having trouble finding it, feel free to cheat and locate it in the Scene view. You can also watch
the First Person Controller's position in the maze to help you get to that position.

Figure 15-9. *The crowbar discovered in the maze after being relocated by the temple's bouncer*

8. Select the UnityWatermark-small object and disable it for now.

9. Save the scene and save the project.

Playing the Odds

There is a small chance that the maze configuration will produce a closed two-square block and an even smaller chance that the drop point will be inside it. Therefore, at this point, you need to make an executive decision on the maze. The two most logical options are to perform more sophisticated trap-checking or to allow the player to reset the maze himself if he can't find the dropped object.

User Reset

The most artist-friendly option is to allow the player to reset the maze. Obviously, you shouldn't allow the player to stand at the entrance and click a button until a configuration appears with the object in clear sight. It follows that you'll need to place the button at some distance from the maze to discourage that unsporting behavior.

But if the mechanism to reset the maze is not near the maze entrance, you will face the problem of association. A button on the trunk of a palm tree a hundred meters away is not likely to provide much of a clue to its function. Therefore, you'll need to devise a way to provide a clue, subtle or blatant, to the operation of the maze-resetting mechanism. You can do this in several ways.

A very subtle way would be to trigger a tune or chord to play every time the player passed into the maze. You can associate the music key to the sound by placing the key in one of the shrines and having it play the same sound when the layer activates it. If you wish to make the association easier, you can place the music stele near the entrance to the maze.

By locating the key in one of the shrines, you can also encourage another association. You may have noticed the stone "drawer" mechanism in the lower passage of the temple. While you will not be setting it up as part of the book project, you can give clues to the use of the drawer to lower the water level in the flooded passageway—an optional addition to the game. In the temple, the drawer is almost closed, requiring the player to open it before using the water key with it. In the shrine, you could leave the drawer open and the key glyph at hand. When the user sets the key glyph into the matching pattern in the stone drawer, it closes, the notes play, and the mechanism resets. You can set the drawer up ready for use.

Let's start by creating a collider for the entry passages into the maze in order to help the player with some special effects as hints.

1. Change the Scene view to a top view and focus in on the entrance closest to the temple.

Let's use the simplest collider, the Box Collider, to trigger an eerie musical chord.

2. Create an empty GameObject and name it **MazeFX**.

3. From the Components menu, add a Box Collider.

4. Check Is Trigger.

5. Set the collider's Y size to **8**.

6. Increase the X and Z sizes until they are partway through the wall (see Figure 15-10).

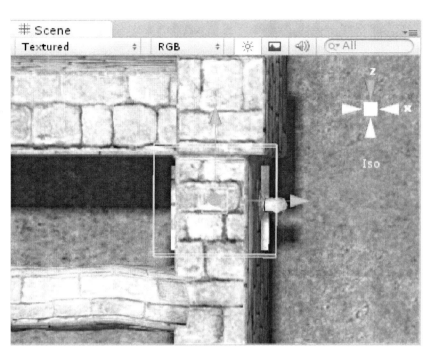

Figure 15-10. *The MazeFX collider*

7. Change the view to Perspective and adjust the Y position to make sure the collider will be at the right height.

Now let's add some sound effects.

1. From the Components menu, add an Audio Source.

2. For the Audio Clip, choose MazeChord.

3. Check Loop.

4. Click Play and go into the maze.

The looping sound gives the maze an eerie feel, but you'll need to trigger the sound on and off when you enter and exit the collider.

5. Uncheck Play on Awake.

6. In the Adventure Scripts folder, create a new script.

7. Name it MazeFX.

8. Open it in the editor.

9. Remove the Update function and replace it with the following:

```
function OnTriggerEnter () {
    audio.Play(); // start the sound
```

```
}

function OnTriggerExit() {
    audio.Stop(); // stop the sound
}
```

10. Save the script.

11. Drag the script onto the MazeFX object.

12. Click Play and travel into the maze and out.

13. Stop Play mode.

The sound is nice, but not eerie enough. Let's add a reverb zone to improve it.

14. With the MazeFX object selected, add an Audio Reverb Zone component from the Audio section of the Component menu.

15. Click Play.

16. Test some of the presets and then choose Auditorium.

17. Stop Play mode and make the change permanent.

Activating the Drawer

Whether or not you decide to make the music key an action object, the drawer and its stunt double, Music Key in Drawer, will need their own animation and script to trigger the drawer group. Let's set it up now to trigger on pick; later, if you wish, you can make adjustments.

1. From Group Music in the Structures prefab, select the DrawerMusic object.

You should see the MusicGlyph in DrawerMusic as its child (see Figure 15-11).

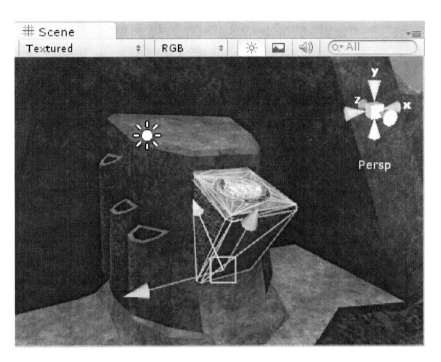

Figure 15-11. *The music drawer and its child, the music key gylph*

2. From the Component menu, select Miscellaneous and add an Animation component to the DrawerMusic.

3. Turn off Play Automatically in the Inspector.

4. Change the coordinate system to Local and Pivot above the Scene view.

5. Open the Animation view.

6. Click Record and create a new clip named **music drawer** in the Animation Clips folder.

7. Select the Rotation.x track.

8. Click Add Keyframe at time 0:00.

9. Move the time marker to frame a time 3:00 by using the arrows in the lower right corner and create another key.

10. Move the time marker to 1:00 and rotate the drawer in the Scene view until it is nearly closed, a value of **-2.5** degrees.

11. Add a keyframe.

12. Move the time indicator to 2:00 and set the rotation to **-2.5** as well.

13. With the cursor in the graph area, press the F key to zoom the extents of the curve view.

14. Set each of the key's tangents to Free Smooth and adjust the handles so they are horizontal.

15. Select the key at 1:00 and change its Right Tangent to Linear.

16. Select the key at 2:00 and change its Left Tangent to Linear (Figure 15-12).

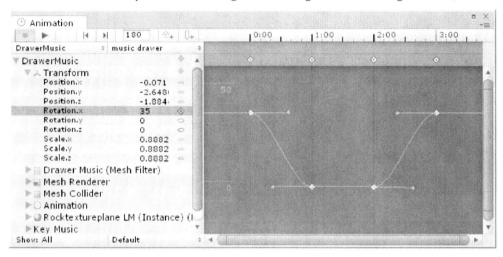

Figure 15-12. *The drawer's curve*

17. Click the Play button in the Animation view and observe the result.

18. Close the Animation view.

19. Assign the music drawer animation clip as the default Animation parameter.

Now let's add a sound effect to go along with the animation.

1. Add an Audio Source component to the drawer.

2. Set its Audio Clip to MazeChord.

3. Uncheck Play on Awake.

4. Save the scene.

5. Create a new script in the Adventure Scripts folder.

6. Name it `TriggerMusicDrawer`.

7. Open it in the editor.

8. Replace the `Update` function with the following:

```
function OnMouseDown () {
```

```
    CloseDrawer();
}
function CloseDrawer() {
    animation.Play();
    yield new WaitForSeconds(1.75);
    audio.Play();
}
```

9. Save the script.

10. Add it to the DrawerMusic object.

11. Click Play and test the drawer.

12. Adjust the Volume if necessary.

13. Add an Audio Reverb and choose a preset.

Next let's add a point light to spice up the effect.

1. Create a new Point Light in the scene and name it Point Light FX

2. Position it directly over the Music Key glyph in the Drawer object.

3. Set its Range to about **8.3**.

4. Set its color to a bluish-green tint.

5. Experiment with its Intensity to check its low and high ranges, as shown in Figure 15-13.

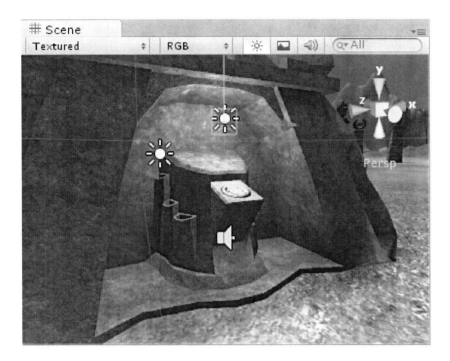

Figure 15-13. *The light at 2.5 Intensity*

Let's leave it at 0 Intensity as the default, then animate it up to about 2.5.

6. Set the Intensity to **0**.

7. Add an Animation component to it and open the Animation view.

8. Click the Record button and navigate to the Animation Clips folder.

9. Name the new clip **flash light**.

10. Close the Transform tracks and open the Light tracks.

11. Select the Intensity track and create a key at frame **0**.

12. Move the time marker to **0:30** and set the Intensity up to **2.5**.

13. At time **1:0**, set the Intensity back to **0**.

14. Press the F key to zoom in on the new curve.

15. Change the tangents to free and adjust the curve for a better ease in/ease out (see Figure 15-14).

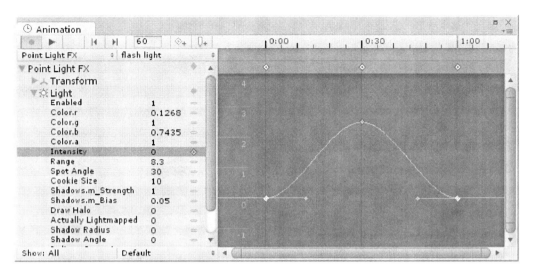

Figure 15-14. *The light's Intensity curve*

16. Close the Animation view.

17. Assign the newly created animation to the Animation component.

18. Uncheck Play Automatically.

19. Open the `TriggerMusicDrawer` script.

20. Add the following line below the `yield` line:

```
GameObject.Find("Point Light FX").animation.Play();
```

21. Save the script.

22. Click Play and test the drawer.

23. Stop Play mode.

As long as you've gone to all the trouble of making an animated light, it would be nice to be able to reuse it at the maze entrances to insure that the player makes the connection. In the case of the maze entrances, the player could miss the effect entirely if he moves through too quickly, so rather than use a statically placed light for each position, let's parent the light to the First Person Controller. That way it will be handy wherever you choose to use it.

1. Open the `MazeFX` script.

2. Add the following line to both the `OnTriggerEnter` and `OnTriggerExit` functions:

```
GameObject.Find("Point Light FX").animation.Play();
```

3. Save the script.

4. Focus in on the First Person Controller and move the light to it.

5. Drag the light onto the First Person Controller in the Hierarchy view.

6. Position it in the middle of the Capsule mesh.

7. Click Play and travel into the maze.

8. Stop Play mode.

The drawer works nicely to provide clues to the maze. Now we need to have it change the maze as well.

1. Open the `TriggerMusicDrawer` script again.

2. Add the following line after the `audio.Play()` line:

```
GameObject.Find("MazeWalls").SendMessage("ResetMaze");// reset the maze
```

3. Save the script.

4. Focus the Top viewport on the maze.

5. Click Play and test the drawer, watching the maze as you do so.

6. Stop Play mode.

To prevent the player from repicking the drawer before the animation is finished, you need to add a bit more code. You could set a flag and start a timer with `yield`, but there's a method you can use that's simpler since it involves an animation clip. You need only check to see if the animation is playing. If so, a simple return will prevent a repick.

7. Add the following inside the `OnMouseDown` function, above the `CloseDrawer()` line:

```
if(animation.isPlaying) return;
```

8. Save the script.

9. Click Play and test.

Extra drawer picks are ignored while the animation is playing.

10. Save the scene and save the project.

Finally, as you have trained the player to expect action objects to react to cursor mouseovers, you ought to set the drawer up as an action object.

1. Add the `Interactor` and `ObjectLookup` scripts to the `DrawerMusic`.

2. Tag it as an ActionObject.

Set it up as if the player needs to add the Music Key glyph before it can be activated, but start it in the state that tells you the key is in place. Since you are using a script to call all of the media effects, the drawer is not marked as animating.

3. Set the metadata and lookup information as shown in Figure 15-15.

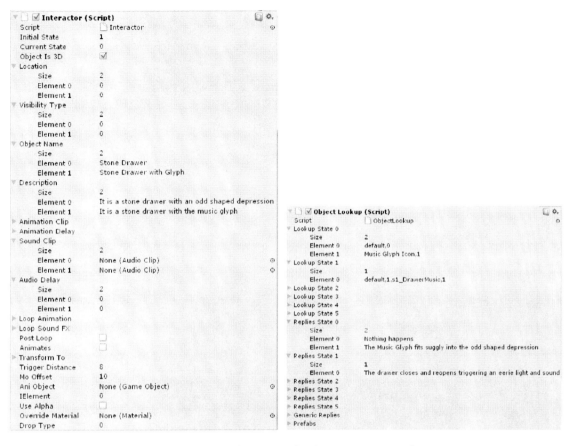

Figure 15-15. *The metadata and lookup information for the DrawerMusic object*

Having rerouted the drawer's functionality to an action object, you need to do a couple of things. Since all of the action is set up in the CloseDoor function, you can trigger it as a special case using the s1_ prefix.

1. Open the TriggerMusicDrawer script.

2. Delete the OnMouseDown function.

3. Rename the CloseDrawer function to DoTheJob.

4. Save the script.

5. Click Play and make sure the functionality still works.

6. Save the scene and save the project.

Easter Egg

With Unity Pro, you can render a camera view to a texture, which lets you create surveillance cameras that update the materials on monitors in your scene in real time. In your scene however, it would be fun to add a bit of bonus functionality in the form of a "minimap" of the maze. Since you are not putting it on a mesh object in the scene, you can achieve this without using the Pro Render Texture feature, and create a camera that will render to a portion of the screen when a secret keyboard key is toggled.

1. Create a new camera.

2. Name it **Camera MazeView** and delete its Audio Listener.

3. Position it so it is centered over the maze.

4. Set its Rotation to **90, 300, 300**.

5. et Culling Mask to Nothing, then to Default.

6. Move the camera up until you can see the entire maze in the preview window, as shown in Figure 15-16.

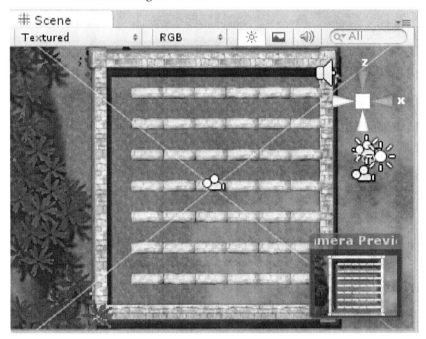

Figure 15-16. *The new camera with the maze in view*

7. Set Clear Flags to Depth Only.

8. Set the Projection to Orthographic.

9. Set its Near Clipping Plane to **10** and its Far Clipping plane to **25**.

10. Adjust the camera's Y Position until the maze and the terrain both show in the preview again.

11. Set the Size to about **34** or until the maze fills the preview.

Unlike GUI Textures and Unity GUI scripted 2D screen-space objects, cameras use normalized screen space instead of pixel size. That is, the camera will use a percent of the screen size for both location and rectangle draw size. Normalized values are between 0 and 1.

12. Set the Game window to Standalone instead of Free Aspect.

13. Set the X and Y Normalized Rect Viewport values to **0.75** each.

14. Set the W and H values to **0.18** and **0.25**.

Adjust the Game view to see the effect on different aspect ratios. Since this is just a little bonus feature, we won't bother with a bunch of math to constrain it, but you could use `Screen.Width` and `Screen.height` in the `Start` function of the script if you wish.

15. Click Play.

The minimap disappears.

16. Try clicking the camera component off and on.

The maze reappears. Since you don't want it on at the start, it will probably be okay if you toggle it on later though a script.

1. Create a new script in the Adventure Scripts folder.

2. Name it `ToggleMiniMap`.

3. Open it in the editor.

4. Add a `Start` function and change the `Update` function as follows:

```
function Start () {
   //add adjustments to compensate for aspect ratio here
}

function Update () {
   if (Input.GetKeyDown("m")) { // check for m keyboard key press
      if(camera.enabled == false) camera.enabled = true;
      else camera.enabled = false;
   }
}
```

5. Save the script.

6. Add the script to the Camera MazeView.

7. Turn off the Camera component.

8. Click play and test the "m" key.

The cheat key toggles the maze minimap off and on.

9. Delete the UnityWatermark-small object.

10. Save the scene and save the project.

■ **Note**   If you do try to use Render Texture to generate your minimap, you will notice that the terrain object is treated as transparent when applied to a GUI Texture or to Unity GUI object. You could work around this with the addition of another camera. Another interesting characteristic of Render Texture is that when you set the camera to Don't Clear, it will leave a trail as the First Person Controller moves through the maze.

The Cavern Portal

Once the player has gained access to the topi fruit from the old grain sack, the door to the lower passage opens and he can make his way down the passage to the great cavern. Upon entering the cavern, the player will see the topi stele as a beacon to move towards. About halfway there, as the water starts to get deep, the player will be transported to the final level, a new scene.

Let's finish up the main level with a few additions to the cavern. You need to make sure the player knows which way to go, so let's make the center goal more obvious with a spotlight.

■ **Tip**   Hide the Terrain while working on the Cavern section.

---

1. Click on the Cavern Group in the Structures prefab to see its children.

1. Focus in on the Stele Topi object.

2. Create a Spot Light above it.

3. Name the light **Cavern Spot**.

4. Drag it into the Cavern Group.

5. Set its X Rotation to **90**.

6. Set its Range to **100** and the Spot Angle to about **75**.

7. Set its Color to a light gold and its Intensity to **8** (see Figure 15-17).

Figure 15-17. *The Cavern Spot as a beacon for the player*

You already have a fake volumetric effect you can use to make the center point even more alluring.

8. Select the Volume Light Effect object from inside the Temple Group and duplicate it.

9. Name it Volume Light Effect Cavern and move it into the Cavern Group.

10. Position it above the Stele Topi and its Y Scale to about **3** and its End Width to about **20**.

11. Change its Start and End Colors to a light gold color.

To complete the cavern, let's add some knee-deep water.

12. Focus on the Stele Topi again.

13. Create a Sphere.

14. Move it into the Cavern Group.

15. Name it **Cavern Water**.

16. Set its Scale to *X,* **120**; *Y,* **0.01**; and *Z,* **120**.

17. Position it in the cavern so that it is slightly lower than the mud or darker area of the floor.

18. Apply the Simple Water Still material to it.

19. Add the UVAnimator script to it.

20. Set the Scroll Speed V1 to -0.05, the Scroll Speed U2 to 0.01, and the Scroll Speed V2 to -0.02. The result is shown in Figure 15-18.

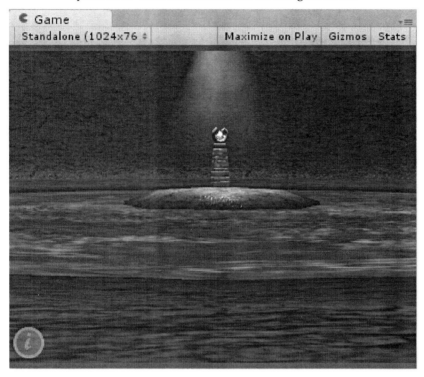

Figure 15-18. *The finished Cavern*

21. Remove the Sphere Collider component.

22. Click Play and work through the game to get to the cavern.

Because of the Sphere's mapping, the water appears to flow out toward the shore.

If the water is too deep, adjust its Y Position and note the changes you will need to make back in Edit mode.

Before we start on the final level, we need a collider to trigger the level change.

1. Stop Play mode.

2. Focus on the Stele Topi once again.

3. Create an Empty GameObject and name it **WinLevelTrigger.**

4. Add a Capsule collider to it.

5. Drag it into the Cavern Group.

6. Set the Collider's Radius to **25** and its Height to **60** (Figure 15-19).

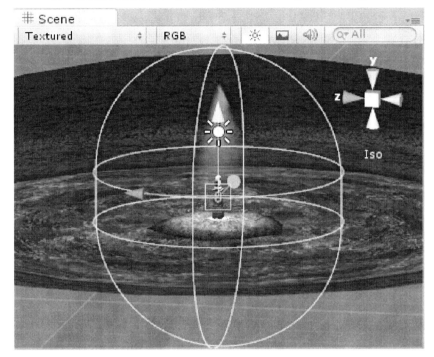

Figure 15-19. *The level trigger's collider*

7. Check Is Trigger.

8. Save the scene and save the project.

The Final Level

Let's keep the final level short and quick, as the only new functionality is the script to change levels. We will, however, make use of a couple more Unity features for our final scene.

Tree Generator

New to Unity 3.0 is the Tree Generator. You can create trees for use in the terrain editor, or to use as individuals. We will create a small tree to use in the end sequence of our game.

1. From the GameObject menu ➤ Create Other, choose Tree.

2. Name the tree **Tree of Life**.

3. Focus in on it in the Scene view.

A tree trunk is created at 0,0,0 in the scene. It consists of a Tree Root Node and a Branch Group.

4. In the Inspector, open the Tree component.

5. Make sure the Inspector panel is wide enough to see the parameter sliders.

6. Click to select the Branch group from the tree hierarchy view window.

7. Open the Distribution section.

8. Change the Frequency to see multiple trunks, then set it back to 1.

9. From the Geometry section, assign the BigTree bark material to the branches and the trunk.

Tip   If you assign a non-tree material to a node, the tree generator will offer to convert it for you.

---

10. From the icons at the bottom of the Tree Hierarchy view, press the Add Branch Group button.

11. A lone Branch is added to the trunk.

12. In Distribution, change its Frequency until you have about 6 or 8 branches.

13. Adjust the Growth Angle until the branches tilt up a bit more.

14. In the Shape section, adjust the Length at both ends of its slider adjustor so the branches are not so long.

15. Adjust the Crinklyness to give the tree a more gnarled appearance.

16. Give it a little Seek Sun to tip the branches a bit more.

17. To move the branches' starting position higher on the trunk, select the curve to the far right of the Distribution parameter in the Distribution rollout.

18. Move the left point down and watch the branches move higher up the tree trunk (see Figure 15-20).

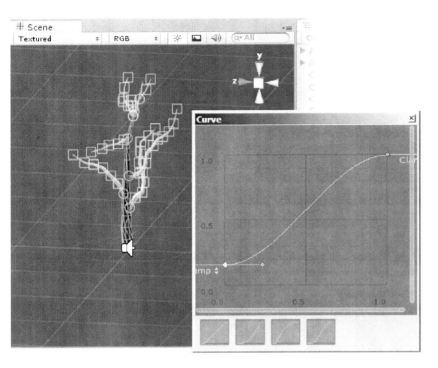

Figure 15-20. *Adjusting the Branch Group placement*

19. From the Geometry section, assign the bark material to the branches.

20. With the second Branch Group selected, press the Add Leaf Group button.

21. Adjust the Frequency in Distribution to about **24**.

22. Adjust the Size in Shape.

■ **Tip**   If the leaf planes do not appear, deselect the tree in the Hierarchy view, and then reselect it.

---

23. From the Geometry section, assign the Big Tree branches material to the leaves.

24. In Distribution, adjust the GrowthScale to see how the branches are scaled in relation to their position on the tree.

Now let's take a look at the poly count for the tree. It Shows Tris (triangles) at about 600-800 depending on the settings so it is a fairly economical tree so far. As with terrain trees, you should probably try not to exceed about 2,000 faces or tris.

25. Adjust the Frequency in Distribution until your tree has about 1000 tris.

26. Save the scene as FinalLevel and save the project.

The Standing Stones

Any respectable Tree of Life ought to have a fancy place to grow and ours is no exception. In this game, however, the quest will soon become apparent—the Tree is blasted and dead and the player must bring a new seed (the topi fruit) to replace it.

Let's bring in the geometry for the final location.

1. Focus in on the tree.

2. From the Structures folder, drag the StandingStones into the Hierarchy view.

3. Set their X and Z Positions to **0** but leave the Y as is.

4. Change the materials to the standard versions if necessary.

The final group needs to be raised slightly so let's move the tree to match the Standing Stones prefab group. The stones do a pretty good job at blocking the view, so you will need to turn them off for a few minutes.

5. Open the StandingStones group.

6. Turn off the Standing Stones.

7. Select the tree.

8. Select the Move transform button.

Note that there is no transform gizmo for the tree. To move the tree with the transform gizmo in the scene, you must first select the root node.

9. Move the tree up or down so it aligns with the Trunk Blasted.

10. Adjust the Trunk's height (Shape/Length) and Radius to make it match the blasted trunk, more or less, as shown in Figure 15-21.

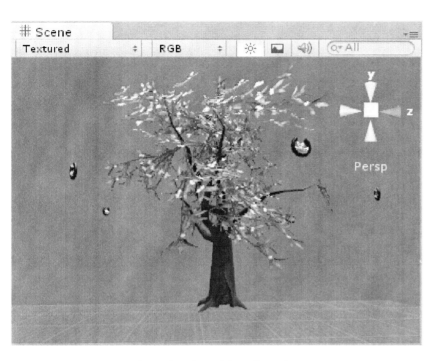

Figure 15-21. *The tree aligned with the blasted trunk*

11. Turn the StandingStones back on when you are happy with the tree (see Figure 15-22).

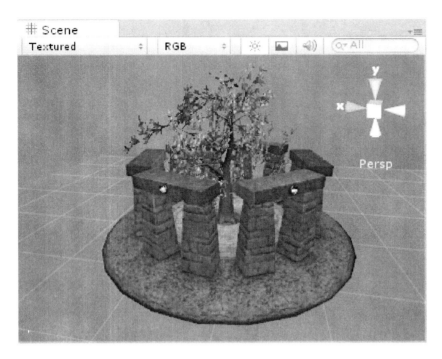

Figure 15-22. *The tree and standing stones*

    12.   Save the scene and save the project.

The Prize

Even though our intrepid adventurer is bringing the last known topi fruit to regrow the Tree of Life, it's a good idea to create some more golden topi fruit in case you want to enhance the game later by requiring the player to stash a new fruit back on the main level. Let's instantiate a new fruit high in the tree top and let physics bring it to earth.

    1.   Disable the Tree of Life.

    2.   Select the Topi Fruit Trunk from the Standing Stones group.

    3.   Add a Capsule collider component to it.

    4.   Adjust the Radius, Height, and Alignment of the collider.

    5.   Duplicate it and name the clone **Topi Fruit Hanging**.

    6.   Add Rigidbody component to the object.

    7.   Move the object up and to the right, well into the tree branches as shown in Figure 15-23 (turn the tree back on to check if you need to).

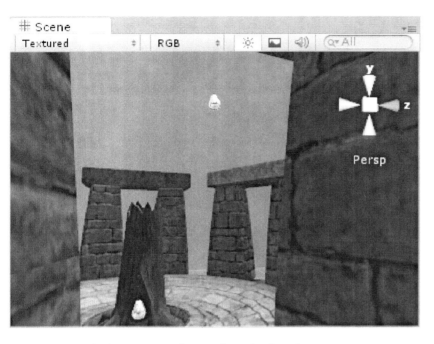

Figure 15-23. *The hanging topi fruit in dropping location*

No terrain.

8. In the Adventure Prefabs folder, create a new Prefab.

9. Name it **Hanging Topi Fruit**.

10. Drag the Topi Fruit Hanging object onto it from the Hierarchy view.

11. The white cube icon of the prefab turns light blue.

You can return to make the new prefab more interesting later on.

In an adventure type game, physics is useful for generic events rather than actions that require a specific outcome. In this case, the fruit will drop and roll away from the player, but because there is not much else around, as long as the player knows the fruit was dropped, you can expect him to find it.

A Touch of Wind

For the final sequence, you are going to animate a WindZone to reincarnate the tree. For now, let's just see what it will look like.

1. Reactivate the tree and focus in on it.

2. From the bottom of the Tree component or from the GameObject menu, select Create Other and choose WindZone from the bottom of the list.

3. Select the WindZone.

4. Set the WindZone's Mode to Spherical.

5. Click Play and watch the action.

The topi fruit falls off the tree and the tree branches sway in the wind (see Figure 15-24).

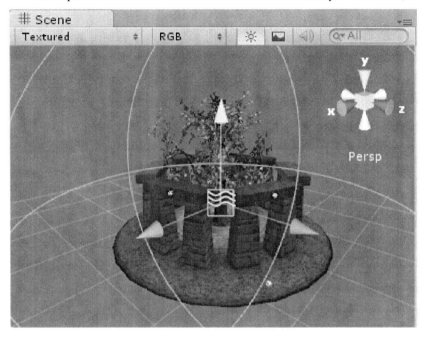

Figure 15-24. *Wind and gravity—the tree sways and the fruit drops*

6. Stop Play mode and disable the WindZone component.

7. Set its Wind Main and Wind Turbulence parameters to **0**.

8. Create an Empty GameObject and name it Final Group.

9. Move the Tree of Life, Standing Stones prefab, and WindZone into it.

10. Save the Scene and save the project.

The Final Terrain

A few more steps and our final scene will be ready to activate.

1. Drag the Sun for Structures light out of the Structures Prefab group.

2. Rename it Directional Light.

3. Delete the terrain, Camera MazeView, Structures prefab, Shrine groups, Maze Walls, and associated special effects and non-inventory or action objects.

Your Hierarchy view should now look like what's shown in Figure 15-25.

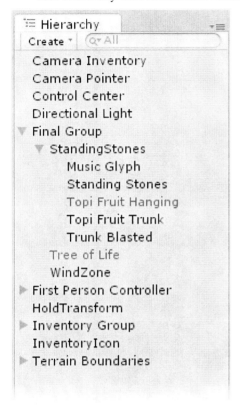

Figure 15-25. *The remaining objects*

4. Save the scene.

Since you deleted the terrain from the final scene, you'll need to replace it. This time, let's just add a flat plane and use fog to lend an air of mystery to the level. You can set the boundary colliders so that the fog hides the edge of the terrain.

1. Create a new Terrain object from the Terrain menu.

2. Open the Set Resolution dialog.

3. Set the Terrain Width and Length to **500**.

4. Set the Terrain Height to **10**.

5. Open Flatten Heightmap and set that to **2**.

6. Duplicate the Terrain Boundaries group and rename it **Terrain Barriers Final**.

7. Delete the original group.

8. Move the terrain and boundaries so that the Final Group is in the terrain center, and about 3 units above the terrain.

9. Move the barriers to give access to the center area while keeping them inset from the edges of the terrain by about a quarter. See Figure 15-26.

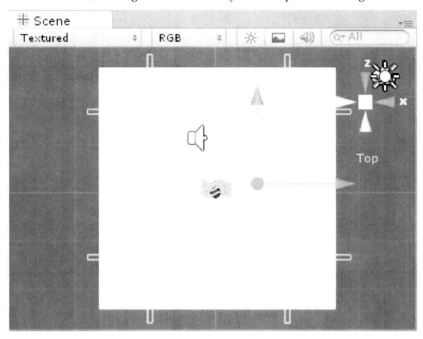

Figure 15-26. *The boundaries and the new terrain with Final Group in center*

10. Move the First Person Controller so that you have a view of the terrain and Standing Stones in the Game window—this will be the starting position for the final level, as shown in Figure 15-27.

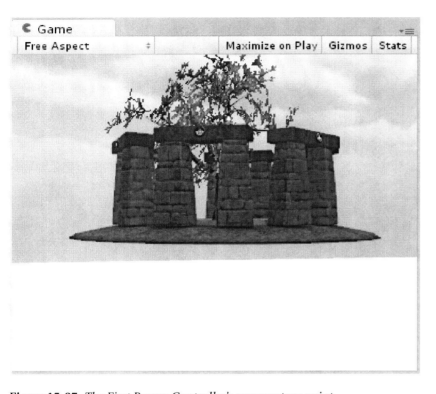

Figure 15-27. *The First Person Controller's new vantage point*

Next, let's put some preliminary textures on the terrain.

11. In the Terrain's Paint Texture tool, use Edit Textures to load a new texture, Grass & Rock, for the terrain.

Use the Raise/Lower tool to raise a low mound in the center of the terrain where the tree will be.

12. Select the Paint Height tool.

13. Set the Brush Size to **100** and the Opacity to **7**.

14. Choose the softest brush and paint a mound beneath the Standing Stones.

15. Use the Smooth Height to soften the mound's edge area, as shown in Figure 15-28.

Figure 15-28. *The standing stones on a mound*

16. Select the Final Group.

17. Move it up or down until the Final Group is the right height for the terrain.

Be sure the terrain does not poke through the center of the group.

18. Select the Terrain again.

19. In the editor, choose Paint Textures, add the Rocky Shale Twilight texture, and set its tiling to **4** and **4**.

20. Paint the mound around the standing stones with the texture.

21. Paint other textures lightly with a spotty brush to make the ground more interesting, as in Figure 15-29.

Figure 15-29. *Improved terrain*

Now you need to add some fog to the new scene—but you'll run into a problem with the skybox. Because the skybox is a shader, the fog does not affect it. Luckily, if it's foggy, you wouldn't see the sky anyway, so you can leave off the skybox and set the background color to match the fog.

1. Select the Main Camera from the First Person Controller.

2. Set Clear Flags to Solid Color.

3. Adjust the Background color to a mid grayish-blue (43,60,84).

4. From the Edit menu, select the Render Settings.

5. Turn on Fog.

6. Set the Fog Color to match the background using the eyedropper in the color selector.

7. Adjust the Density to **0.02**.

The scene starts out in a sort of twilight. Let's add a couple of point lights to the standing stones to draw the player's eye to it.

1. Turn off the tree.

2. Turn off the Topi Fruit Trunk and the Topi Fruit Hanging.

3. Select the Directional Light and set its Intensity to about **0.1**.

4. *4.* Drag it into the Final Group.

The scene is fairly dark now.

5. If you are using Unity Pro, set the Shadow Type to Soft and the Strength to about **0.25**.

6. Focus in on the standing stones.

7. Create a Point light and name it **Point Standing Stones Blue**.

8. Set its Range to **12**, its Intensity to **3.5** and its Color to a medium blue (about 50,100,255).

9. Center it over the standing stones and move it up about even with their top height, a shown in Figure 15-30.

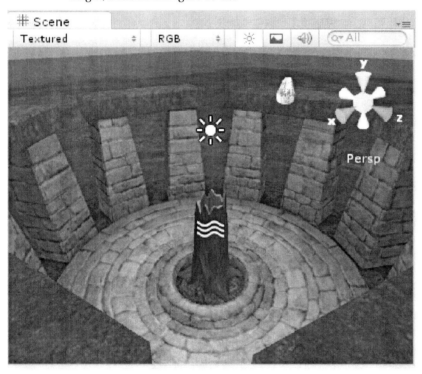

Figure 15-30. *The stones lit from the blue light*

10. Duplicate the point light and name it **Point Trunk Blue**.

11. Set its Range to **4**, its Intensity to **2.6** and its Color to a medium blue.

12. Position it in front of the opening at the base of the trunk to highlight the opening (see Figure 15-31).

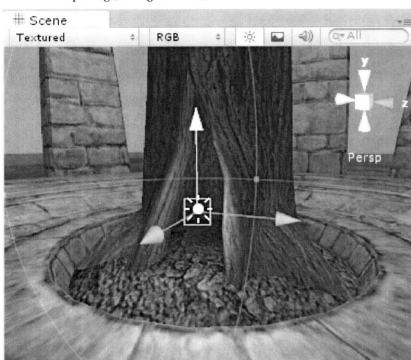

Figure 15-31. *The opening revealed*

13. Move both point lights into the Final Group.

14. Save the scene and save the project.

The Final Sequence

The scene is now set for the player to complete the game. The final sequence plays out as follows:

1. The player makes his way up to the standing stones.

2. He puts the Golden Topi fruit into opening in the blasted tree trunk.

3. There is a blinding light, thunderclap, wind, and so forth.

4. The new tree appears, the old trunk and topi fruit disappear, and the lighting and materials change on the standing stones.

5. A disembodied voice instructs the player to tap the tree to receive the new seed that must be hidden against the next time of great need.

6. The player taps the tree with the crowbar with the golden sleeve, the hanging topi fruit drops.

7. When the player takes the dropped fruit, he has finished the game.

The first interaction will be placing the topi fruit in the opening. This requires an object to mouseover and receive a pick.

1. Focus in on the Topi Fruit Trunk.

2. Create an Empty GameObject.

3. Name it **Trunk Opening**.

4. Drag it into the StandingStones prefab object.

5. Add a Sphere collider and set its Radius to **0.75**.

6. Add Interactor and ObjectLookup scripts to it.

7. Tag it as an ActionObject.

8. Set the metadata and lookup information as in Figure 15-32.

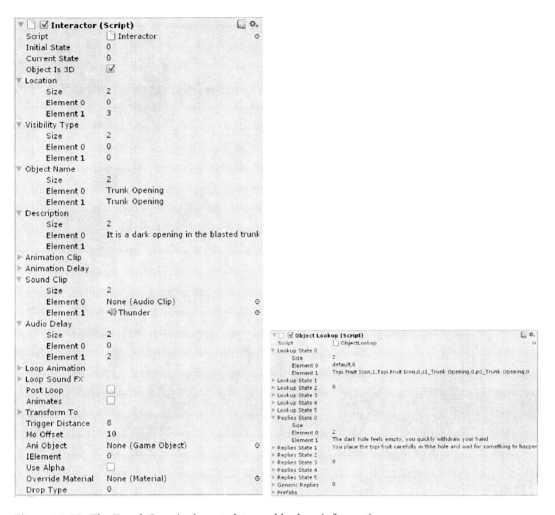

Figure 15-32. *The Trunk Opening's metadata and lookup information*

9.   Add a Mesh Renderer component to prevent it from throwing errors.

For the Final level, let's allow the player to have two inventory items with him—the topi fruit and the crowbar with the golden sleeve. Since this is in a different level or scene, you need to set their Initial states to 1 in inventory.

10.   Select the Topi Fruit Icon and set its Initial State to **1**.

11.   Select the Crowbar With Sleeve Icon and set its Initial State to **1**.

You also need to set up the topi fruit. The fruit in the trunk just appears and then disappears; so you never interacted with it, much like the animated Vial of Elixir. Even so, it still needs a few things done to it.

    12. Select the Topi Fruit Trunk.

    13. Disable it if you haven't already done so.

    14. Remove its collider.

The hanging topi fruit needs to be put into inventory, so it needs the action object scripts.

    15. Select the Topi Fruit Hanging.

    16. Add `Interactor` and `ObjectLookup` scripts to it (it will lose the prefab connection).

    17. Tag it as an ActionObject.

    18. Set the metadata and lookup information as in Figure 15-33.

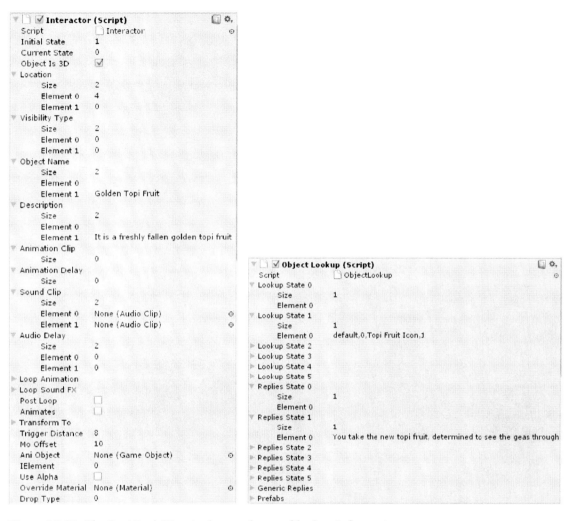

Figure 15-33. *The Topi Fruit Hanging's metadata and lookup information*

Since this one is a prefab and needs to get instantiated at runtime, you need to update the prefab.

19. Drag the Topi Fruit Hanging back onto its prefab in the Project view.

The tree will be an action object as well. When tapped with the Crowbar With Sleeve, it will shake and drop the final topi fruit.

20. Select the Tree of Life.

21. Enable it.

22. Add Interactor and ObjectLookup scripts to it (it will lose the prefab connection).

23. Tag it as an ActionObject.

24. Turn the leaf node off (the eye on the icon) so you can see the trunk.

25. Add a Capsule collider and adjust the size and center position to fit the trunk.

26. Set the metadata and lookup information as in Figure 15-34.

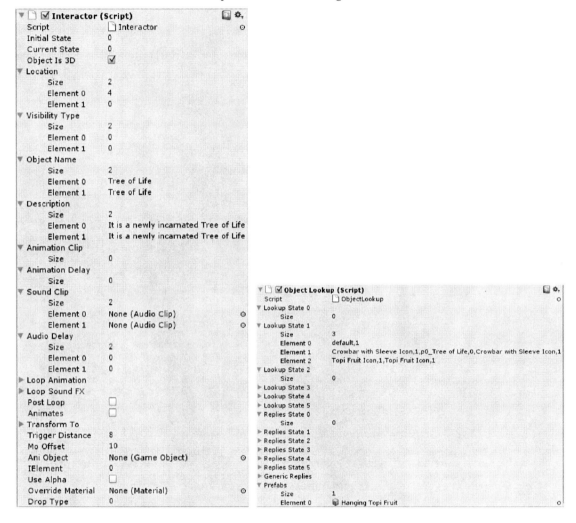

Figure 15-34. *The Tree of Life's metadata and lookup information*

27. Turn the leaf nodes back on.

28. Assign the Hanging Topi Fruit prefab to its Prefab, Element 0.

29. Delete the Topi Fruit Hanging object from the Hierarchy.

30. Disable the tree again.

31. Enable the Trunk Blasted.

Environmental Effects

You can leave the fog in place, but you'll need to animate several objects and their parameters. Since you will need to swap out the blasted trunk with the new Tree of Life, you'll need to have a bit of a screen blackout or whiteout to cover the transition. One way to do that is with a GUI Texture object. You already have one handy, so you can duplicate it and make a few changes.

1. Select the Inventory Screen from the Inventory Group.

2. Duplicate it and remove the Inventory Screen script.

3. Rename the new object Blackout and drag it into the Final Group.

4. Change its Layer to Default and set its Color to Black and its Opacity to **0**.

With imported action objects, objects that came in as a group required more care when triggering their animation clips as individuals. This time you can use the group effect to your advantage as you animate several objects in the Final group with a single animation clip.

The final timeline, in seconds, will be as follows:

0: User drops topi fruit into trunk opening.

0-3: Point Trunk Blue animates to yellow and moves inside trunk where topi fruit is.

4-5: Blackout flickers in and hides all for about half a second.

At this time the materials on the Standing Stones change, the trunk is deactivated and the tree appears. These events are called, not animated.

1. Select the Final Group.

2. Add an Animation component to it.

3. Uncheck Play Automatically.

4. Open the Animation view.

5. Create a New Clip in the Animation Clips folder and name it **end game**.

6. Turn on Record.

7. Select the Point Light Blue.

8. Add a keyframe at 0 for its Intensity, Position x, y, and z and its Color r, g, and b tracks.

9. At 30 frames, move the light inside the tree's center.

10. At 3 seconds, frame 180, change the light's color to a mid golden yellow using the color dialog to make the changes.

11. Change the Intensity to **8**.

12. At frame 195, change the Intensity to **0**.

13. Change the tangents to Linear prevent the interpolation from blowing out the intensity (see Figure 15-35).

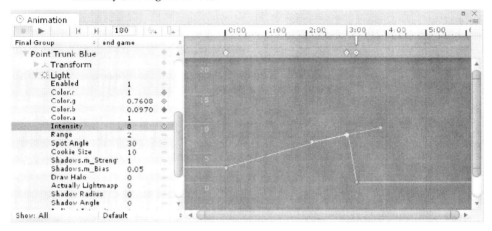

Figure 15-35. *The point light's Intensity curve*

14. Scrub the time marker to see the result.

The other light can come on during the blackout.

15. Select Point Standing Stones Blue.

16. Select its Intensity, Color r, g, and b tracks.

17. At frame 195, create a keyframe.

18. At frame 205, change its Color to a pale golden and its Intensity to **2**.

19. Select the Directional Light.

20. Animate the Directional Light's Intensity from its current **0.1** to **0.5,** from frame 195 to frame 205.

Next we will animate the Blackout.

1. Select the Blackout object and set a key at frame 180 for its GUI Texture's Color.a.

2. Between frames 180 and 190, use the color dialog or track value to animate the opacity flickering on and off several times.

3. At frame 190, set the opacity to **1** and again at frame 200.

4. At frame 275, set its opacity back to **0**.

The curves have played havoc with the interpolation.

5. Select all of the keys and set them to Both Tangents to Linear (Figure 15-36).

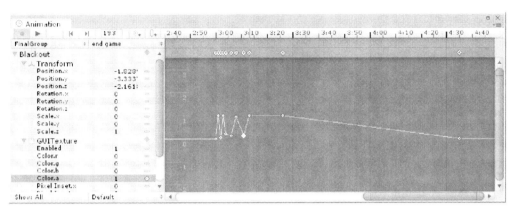

Figure 15-36. *The Blackout flicker*

The tree will appear at frame 195, so you'll need to ramp up the wind.

6. Select the Wind Zone.

7. At frame 195, set a keyframe for Wind Main and Wind Turbulence.

8. At frame 200, set both their values to **1**.

9. At frame 250, set both their values to **1**.

10. At frame 260, set both values down to **0.2**.

11. Focus in on the curve and change all key tangents to Flat and Linear, as in Figure 15-37.

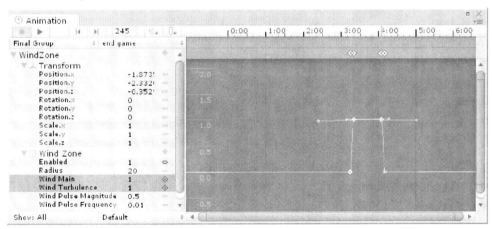

Figure 15-37. *The WindZone tracks*

The effects of the wind will die down slowly, so you don't need a ramping down period for the two values.

12. Close the Animation view.

13. Turn off the tree.

Most of the effects will happen several seconds after the player has placed the topi fruit in the opening, so let's make a single script to handle the sequence and call it via the special cases s1_. Let's also make use of the Animation view's Event functionality to handle the non-animated changes.

1. Create a new script and name it TreeEffects.

2. Open it in the editor.

3. Add the DoTheJob function:

```
var animationTarget : GameObject; // object with the animations

function DoTheJob () {

    animationTarget.animation.Play("end game");

}
```

4. Save the script.

5. Add the script to the Trunk Opening object.

6. Select the Trunk Opening object.

7. Drag the Final Group into the Animation Target parameter.

There's one more object unaccounted for—the topi fruit that appears briefly inside the tree opening. Since the idea was to control it manually, the TreeEffects script is as good a place as any to do that.

1. Add a variable to find the topi fruit object:

```
var topiFruit : GameObject; // load the topi fruit trunk object here
```

2. Add a Start function to hide it at the start:

```
function Start () {
        // hide trunk topi
        topiFruit.active = false;
}
```

3. In the DoTheJob function, above the animationTarget.animation.Play("end game") line, add the following:

```
topiFruit.active = true;
yield new WaitForSeconds(3); // pause before starting
```

4. Save the script.

5. Select the Trunk Opening.

6. Assign the Topi Fruit Trunk object to the new Topi Fruit parameter.

7. Save the scene and save the project.

Animation Events

The extra tasks need to be done while the Blackout GUI Texture is opaque at the end of its animation. Let's create a function that you can call from the end game animation clip by using an event. The function needs to be on the same object as the animation clip, so let's create another script to hold it.

1. Create a new script and name it ExtraTasks.

2. Open it in the editor.

3. Add the following variable to hold the final standing stones material:

```
var lightMaterial : Material; // standing stone material for light
var tree : GameObject; // the tree
```

Next, let's create a function that takes care of the things that don't get animated. You could animate the enabled property for some of the objects, but since you need to swap out a material and need a function for that, you may as well take the easier way out and turn them off with scripting.

4. Add the following function:

```
function ExtraTasks () {

    // hide trunk topi
    GameObject.Find("Topi Fruit Trunk").active = false;

    // hide blasted trunk
    GameObject.Find("Trunk Blasted").active = false;

    // turn on tree
    tree.active = true;
    tree.GetComponent(Interactor).SendMessage("ProcessObject",1);

    //Change the material on the Standing Stones' element 0 material
    GameObject.Find ("Standing Stones").renderer.materials[0] = lightMaterial;

    //Play the voice audio message
    tree.audio.Play();

}
```

5. Save the script.

6. Add it to the Final Group.

As part of the extra tasks, you need to trigger the last voice message from the tree.

1. Add an Audio Source component to the tree.

2. Assign the OneTaskRemaining audio clip to it.

3. Do *not* turn off Play On Awake

4. Add an Audio Reverb component and choose an appropriate preset.

5. Select the Final Group again.

6. Drag the Standing Stone Lt 1 material onto the Light Material parameter.

Now you can trigger ExtraTasks from the Final Group's animation clip with an event. The event works like SendMessage but is triggered in an animation clip's timeline.

1. Select the Final Group.

2. Open the Animation view and turn on Record.

3. Scrub the time marker to frame 195.

4. Click the Add Event button (next to the Add Keyframe button).

An Event marker appears just beneath the time line. If you mouse over the marker, it reports "(No Function Selected)."

5. Click on the marker.

The function selection dialog appears.

6. Click the drop-down and select the only function available on the Final Group object, the ExtraTasks function, as shown in Figure 15-38.

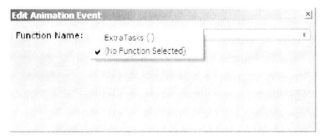

Figure 15-38. The function selection dialog

7. When the animation reaches that point in the timeline, the function will be called or triggered.

8. Close the Animation view.

Add Some Sparkles

Because a Tree of Life should never come to life without a few sparkly particles, let's commandeer a prefab from the Standard Assets ➤ Particles ➤ Sparkles folder. A few changes and it will be ready to go.

1. Focus in on the Standing Stones.

2. Drag the Sparkle Rising particles prefab into the Hierarchy view.

3. In the Scene view, move them up until they are even with the top of the tree.

4. In both particle systems, set Y World Velocity to -**1** and X and Z Ellipsoid size to **5**.

5. In both particle systems, set Max Energy to **15**.

6. In the SparkleParticles, set Min Emission to **10** and Max Emission to **20**.

7. Create a new Prefab in the Adventure Prefabs folder and name it **SparklesFalling**.

8. Drag the altered version of Sparkles Rising into it from the Hierarchy view.

9. Delete the version in the Hierarchy view.

10. Select the Trunk Opening object.

11. At the bottom of its `ObjectLookup` component, set the Prefab array Size to **1** and add the SparklesFalling prefab to it.

Since the particles will take a while to drift down, you can start them when the Trunk Opening is picked. The special case p tells the code which prefab to instantiate, p0_Trunk Opening, where the second character is the element number in the Prefab array in the `ObjectLookup` component.

We should now be ready to play through the final sequence.

1. Turn on the WindZone and turn on the Topi Fruit Trunk objects.

2. Save the scene and save the project.

3. Click Play.

4. Put the topi fruit into the trunk opening and move to see the best view of the action.

While you have a good vantage point for watching the tree sequence play out, you should go ahead and create a position GameObject.

1. Select the First Person Controller.

2. Use Align View To Selected in the Scene view.

3. When the sequence is finished, stop Play mode and create an Empty GameObject.

4. Name it **TargetTrunkOpening** and use Align With View to set it where the First Person Controller was during Play mode.

This is a good time to add the camera match. You have already sent out the message to `DoTheJob` on any of the objects' scripts, so the setup will be quick.

1. Select the Trunk Opening object.

2. Add the `CameraMatchData` script to it.

3. Drag the TargetTrunkOpening onto the Target Pos parameter.

4. Drag the Topi Fruit Trunk object onto the Target Look parameter.

5. Set the Match Time to **3** and the Animation Time to **6**

6. Click Play and test the sequence.

The player is moved to the best vantage point to watch the sequence, as shown in Figure 15-39.

Figure 15-39. *Part of the tree sequence*

7. Continue the game and tap the tree with the Crowbar With Sleeve.

Tip   If your topi fruit falls through the ground at the base of the tree, try moving it around until it hits a better part of the mesh—the stone curb around the tree makes a good landing spot as the fruits will roll off into different directions.

Multiple Topis

The sequence plays out and you can knock several topi fruit from the tree, as shown in Figure 15-40. You could move the tree to another state to prevent more topi fruit from being knocked off, but watching them fall and be handled by physics has good entertainment value. Instead, you can set the topi prefab to destroy itself after a few seconds on the ground.

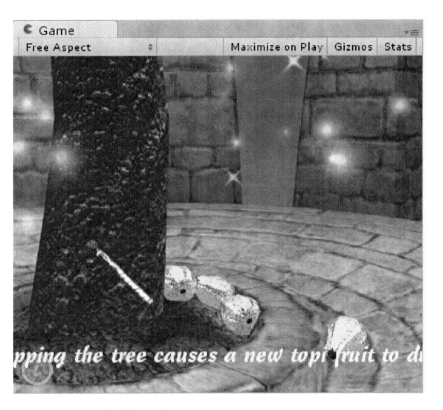

Figure 15-40. *Multiple topi fruit*

1. Stop Play mode.

2. Drag a new Hanging Topi Fruit into the hierarchy.

3. Open the Animation view and accept loosing the prefab.

4. Uncheck Play Automatically.

5. Create an animation clip and name it **shrink topi**.

6. Select the Scale tracks and create a key at frame 0.

7. At frame 5, scale the object down to **0.01**.

8. Close the Animation view.

9. In the Animation component, be sure to assign the clip as the default Animation.

A popping sound will be useful when the dropping fruit collides with other objects.

1. Add an Audio Source component and load the smplop sound effect.

2. Uncheck Play on Awake.

A puff of smoke would be a good addition as the fruit winks out of existence.

1. From the Standard Assets folder, locate the Dust Storm particle prefab.

2. Drag it into the scene and rename it **Poof**.

3. Set its Min Size 1, Max Size 2, Min and Max Energy to 1.

4. Check One Shot and set all the Ellipsoid sizes to **0.1**.

5. In the Particle Animator component, check Autodestruct.

6. Change the colors to golden yellows.

The particles now create a puff.

1. Uncheck Emit.

2. Align the particle system with the hanging topi.

3. Drag the Poof object onto the Hanging Topi Fruit object so it becomes a child of the topi fruit object.

To set off the events, you need a small script that triggers the animation and particle system after a short delay.

1. Create a new script and name it TopiDropper.

2. Open it in the editor.

3. Add the following:

```
function Awake () {

    PoofTopi ();

}

function OnCollisionEnter () {

    audio.Play(); // play the default  hit sound

}

function PoofTopi () {

    yield new WaitForSeconds(5);
    GameObject.Find("Poof").GetComponent(ParticleEmitter).emit = true;
    animation.Play(); // shrink the topi

    yield new WaitForSeconds(1);
    Destroy (gameObject); // destroys the gameobject and its children

}
```

Because the script uses yield to delay the commands, you have to create a function that contains them and call it from the Awake function when the prefab first gets instantiated.

1. Save the script.

2. Drag it onto the Hanging Topi Fruit.

3. Drag the Hanging Topi Fruit onto the Hanging Topi Fruit prefab in the Project view to update it.

4. Agree to replace the existing contents.

5. Delete the version in the Hierarchy.

6. Save the scene and save the project.

7. Click Play and test.

8. Delete the Hanging Topi Fruit in the Hierarchy view.

The topi fruit drops and pops out indefinitely so you'll need to set an end to the game once the player finally takes one of the fruits. For now, let's stop player input and zoom out to a good place to fade to a credits scene or level.

1. Select the Main Camera.

2. Create an Animation Clip for it and name it **pull back**.

3. In the Animation view, add a keyframe at frame 60 to the Field of View track.

4. At frame 180, set the Field of View to **90**.

5. Change the tangents to Free Smooth and make the curve fast in/ slow out, as in Figure 15-41.

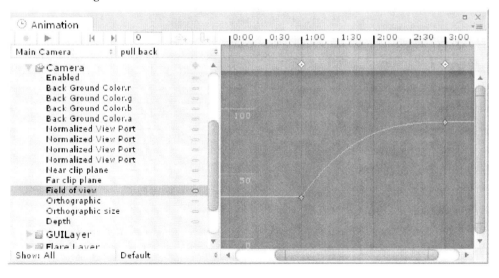

Figure 15-41. *The camera's Field of View animation*

6. Close the Animation view.

7. Turn off Play Automatically.

8. Load the new clip in as the default Animation.

You need to trigger the camera's Field of View change, play the final instructions audio clip and prevent user input. You can do all of this in a custom script.

1. Create a new script and name it **FinalTask**.

2. Open it in the editor.

3. Add the following:

```
var audioSource : GameObject; // object with the final voice message
private var cam : GameObject; // the main camera
private var end = false; // flag to block user input

function Start () {

   cam = GameObject.Find("Main Camera");

}

function Update () {

    // Keep player input disabled
    if (end) Input.ResetInputAxes() ;

}

function DoTheJob () {

   //block the user input
   end = true; // turn on the flag

   //give player three seconds to read take message
   yield new WaitForSeconds(3);

   //hide the inventory icon
   GameObject.Find("Camera Pointer").active = false;


   //Play the Field of view Change
   cam.animation.Play("pull back");

   //trigger the audio clip
   audioSource.audio.Play();

   //go to credits level
   //yield new WaitForSeconds(5);
   //Application.LoadLevel ("Credits");
```

}

4. Save the script,

5. Drag the script onto the Main Camera in the Hierarchy view.

6. Assign the Point Trunk Blue to its Audio Source parameter.

Next you need a place for the audio in order to get the full 3D effect. The tree already has its Audio Source component and several of the other objects at that location will have been deactivated, so you are left with the light that illuminates the inside of the trunk.

1. Select the Point Trunk Blue light.

2. Add an Audio Source component.

3. Load the FinalMessage audio clip.

4. Turn off Play on Awake.

Next you need to update the Hanging Topi Fruit's ObjectLookup metadata to include the new animation.

1. Change its metadata to call the camera's DoTheJob function (Figure 15-42).

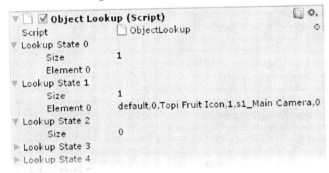

Figure 15-42. *The Hanging Topi Fruit's metadata changes*

2. Save the scene and save the project.

3. Click Play and test the final scene, which is shown in Figure 15-43.

Figure 15-43. *End view*

User keyboard entry is blocked until the camera match is finished, but the mouse still functions. We will deal with those issues in the next chapter when we roll credits.

Load Level

Now that the final scene is pretty much finished, let's go back to the Main level and hook up the level change. You already have the trigger in place so you just need to create a script to do the level change.

1. Open the MainLevel from the Scenes folder.

2. Turn the Terrain on.

3. Create a new script and name it **LoadFinalLevel**.

4. Open it in the editor.

5. Add the following:

```
function OnTriggerEnter () {

Application.LoadLevel ("FinalLevel");

}
```

6. Save the script.

7. Add it to the WinLevelTrigger object in the Cavern Group inside the Temple Group.

8. Save the scene and save the project.

Before you can test the level change, you'll need to add it to the Build.

9. From the File menu, select Build Settings

10. Uncheck whatever scenes are checked and click Add Current.

The MainLevel is added.

11. Click Build and give the build a temporary name.

12. Close the Build Settings.

13. Back in the editor, load the FinalScene and add it to the build as well, as shown in Figure 15-44.

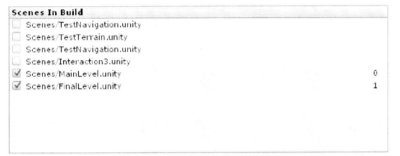

Figure 15-44. *The two levels loaded*

14. Note the level numbers to the far right—Unity will start with level 0.

15. Close the Build Settings.

16. Reload the MainLevel.

17. Click Play and run through the game.

Summary

In this chapter you were introduced to a classic adventure game element—the maze. In 3D form, you added the functionality to randomly reset its configuration. As the maze serves as a place to relocate confiscated weapons, you had to devise a means of ensuring that the weapon would always be accessible.

After scripting a check for the most common trap in the maze, you allowed the player to reset the maze on his own. This involved giving the player clues and functionality attached to one of the shrines in the scene. As an "Easter Egg," a hidden bonus feature, you created a minimap for viewing the maze while in game.

In the underground cavern, the place where you wanted to trigger a level change, you provided a visual stimulus to get the player to head toward the center stele.

For the Final Level, you experimented with the Tree Generator to create the goal for the player. As the player was required to instigate the regeneration of the Tree of Life, you added several special effects to mark the occasion, including a fade to black, a Wind Zone for the tree, particles systems, and more. The final action, instructed by the tree entity, was enhanced with the use of physics to drop the replacement topi fruits.

You added the two new levels to the Build Settings and were then able to play through the game from start to finish.

In the next chapter you will add GUI functionality to the game.

■ ■ ■

CHAPTER 16

Menus and Levels

So far you have been working on your game's basic functionality and are now able to play through the entire game. Having gotten this far, it is time to start thinking about the graphical user interface (GUI) and menus for your game.

With the advent of 3D and especially real-time 3D environments, you usually strive to keep non-environmental GUI objects hidden from the player so as not to break the "suspension of disbelief." You can accomplish this with the use of key-activated or position-activated menus that will bring up stand-alone scenes or levels.

Following your current workflow of addressing issues as they appear, we will tackle the menus and their access from within your game as it stands now.

■ **Tip** If you have the luxury of a team with someone dedicated to menu asset creation, you probably would have set them to work on the menus needed in a more linear fashion, e.g., Start menu, Main menu, secondary menus, and finally credits. If you are working alone, however, it makes more sense to make sure you have a playable game before you think about enhancing it with player options and informational content.

Menu Access: The Mini-Menu

The first thing you will need for your quick access mini-menu is a list of *possible* contents:

- New Game

- Navigation/Instructions

- Play/Resume

- Settings

- Load/Save

- Credits

- Quit

Typically, in Unity, one creates an entire level to hold a menu. In part, this avoids navigation and game play conflicts, many of which you have already solved for your inventory system, but it also has the added benefit of breaking functionality down into bite-sized pieces so it is less overwhelming. The downside is load time to get back to the main game level. With that in mind, you will make use of both types of menus. Your Start menu will be a separate level or scene, and your other menus will be contained within your game.

You can prune down the original list for your in-game mini-menu by shifting some of them off to a regular main menu:

- Main Menu button (a variation of the Start menu, instructions, credits)

- Settings button (where the player can adjust speed, volume, text, etc.)

- Save button (quick save)

- Resume button (back to the game)

- Quit button (with Save? prompt)

With your previous GUI elements, you have manually placed them into screen-space position. Because at most you would see only two elements at a time, the object name and its description, that was an acceptable solution. As soon as you start organizing several elements together, however, it will make sense to introduce the concept of a *GUI group*. This will allow for easier setup as well as the possibility of sliding the menu into view.

To start, you will create a new script to hold the GUI code for a generic menu. Once you are happy with its functionality, you could move the sub-menu parts in with the rest of the GameManager's GUI section so the correct draw order is maintained *or*, conversely, you could reload the GameManager script so that it follows the menu script.

1. Open the MainLevel scene.

2. Create a new script.

3. Name it MenuManager.

4. Open it in the editor.

5. Add the following variables:

```
private var groupWidth = 300;  // width of the group
private var buttnRect  = Rect (0,140,150,30); // default button size, x,y location, width↩
 and height
```

```
private var miniMenu = false; // flag to turn menu off and on
private var mainMenu = false; // flag for main menu
private var settingsMenu = false; // flag for settings
private var confirmDialog = false; // flag for yes/no on quit dialog
private var creditsScreen = false; // flag for credits menu
```

The first and second variables establish a default button size so you can start to automate your button layout and the width of the menu. As usual you will need to create conditionals in the OnGUI function to tell it when to draw the elements. You have several variables you will use as flags to turn various menus off and on.

If you wish to experiment with the button dimensions, you can temporarily change the private var to var for the buttnRect variable. This will allow you to change the values during runtime to see the results since you are using the variable in the OnGUI function to set their size. Be sure to replace the private and add the new values to the script when you are finished. Block in the OnGUI function as follows:

```
function OnGUI () {

    // *****  mini menu  ******
    if(miniMenu) {

        // Make a group on the center of the screen
        GUI.BeginGroup (Rect (Screen.width / 2 - 150, Screen.height / 2 - 160, 300, 280));
        // all rectangles are now adjusted to the group
        // (0,0) is the top left corner of the group

        // make a box so we can see where the group is on-screen.
        GUI.Box (Rect (25,0,250,280), "Options");


        // control elements


        // End the group we started above. This is very important to remember!
        GUI.EndGroup ();

    } // end the mini-menu if

} // end the OnGui function
```

To start, you will set up your mini-menu to toggle off and on with the F1 key.

1. Add the following inside the Update function:

```
//toggle the minimenu off and on
if (Input.GetKeyDown("f1")) {
    if(miniMenu) miniMenu = false;
    else miniMenu = true;
}
```

2. Save the script.

3. Add it to the Control Center object in the Hierarchy view.

4. Click Play, and test the menu by pressing the F1 key.

The GUI Box appears in the middle of the game window. The cursor appears behind the menu, as the GameManager's GUI is drawn first.

5. In the OnGUI function, under the // control elements line, add the following:

```
//this is a local variable that gets changed after each button is added
var buttnRectTemp = Rect (groupWidth/2 - buttnRect .width/2,50,buttnRect .width,buttnRect↵
 .height);

    if (GUI.Button (buttnRectTemp, "Main Menu")) {
        // go to main menu
        miniMenu = false;
        mainMenu= true;
    }
```

```
// move the next control down a bit to avoid overlapping
buttnRectTemp.y += 40;

if (GUI.Button (buttnRectTemp, "Settings")) {
    // go to settings menu
    miniMenu = false;
    settingsMenu = true;
}

// move the next control down a bit to avoid overlapping
buttnRectTemp.y += 40;

if (GUI.Button (buttnRectTemp, "Save")) {
    // save the current game
    miniMenu = false;
  // SaveGame(true);
}

// move the next control down a bit to avoid overlapping
buttnRectTemp.y += 40;


if (GUI.Button (buttnRectTemp, "Resume")) {
    // turn off the menu
    miniMenu = false;
}

// move the next control down a bit to avoid overlapping
buttnRectTemp.y += 40;

if (GUI.Button (buttnRectTemp, "Quit")) {
    // turn off the menu
    miniMenu = false;
  //set flag for yes/no pop-up
    confirmDialog = true;
  }
```

6.   Save the script and test.

The buttons appear evenly spaced in the GUI Box (see Figure 16-1).

Figure 16-1. *Auto-placed buttons*

If you wish to adjust the dimensions of the box at this time, feel free, but you will eventually introduce a GUI Style and texture for the box and controls.

Confirm Dialog

Next you will need to create another group to hold the Yes/No confirmation buttons if the player chooses Quit. Application.Quit() does not stop the application in the editor or web player, so you will add a few print statements just to keep tabs on where you are.

1. Below the } // end the minimenu if line for the its conditional, add the following:

```
// *******   confirmDialog dialog   *******
if (confirmDialog) {

  // Make a group on the center of the screen
  GUI.BeginGroup (Rect (Screen.width / 2 - 100, Screen.height / 2 - 75, 200, 150));

  // make a box so we can see where the group is on-screen.
  GUI.Box (Rect (0,0,200,380), "Do you really want to quit?");

  // reset the  buttnRectTemp.y value
  buttnRectTemp = Rect (25,30,150,buttnRect .height);

  if (GUI.Button (buttnRectTemp, "No, resume game")) {
```

```
        // turn off the menu
        confirmDialog = false;
    }

    buttnRectTemp.y += 40;

    if (GUI.Button (buttnRectTemp, " Yes, quit without saving")) {
        // quit the game without saving
        confirmDialog = false;
        print ("closing");
        Application.Quit();
    }


    buttnRectTemp.y += 40;

    if (GUI.Button (buttnRectTemp, " Yes, but Save first")) {
        // turn off the menu, save the game, then quit
        confirmDialog = false;
        //SaveGame(true); // quit after saving
    }

        // End the confirmDialog group we started above. This is very important to remember!
        GUI.EndGroup ();

} // end confirm
```

2. Save the script.

3. Press the F1 key, select the Quit option, and observe the results (see Figure 16-2).

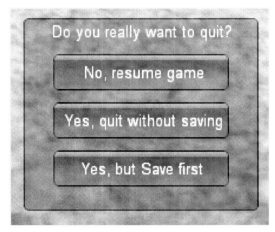

Figure 16-2. *Confirm dialog*

Since you now have a yes/no menu for quitting the game, you can add the escape key to the Update function.

1. Add the following to the Update function:

```
// brings up the yes/no menu when the player hits the escape key to quit
 if (Input.GetKey ("escape")) {
 confirmDialog = true; // flag to bring up yes/no menu
}
```

Before you save the changes, you need to set up a place holder for the SaveGame function you will eventually write. Note that it will take an argument, quitAfter, so it will know whether to resume the game or quit, regardless of where it has been called from.

2. Add the following function:

```
function SaveGame (quitAfter : boolean) {

    print ("saving");

    yield new WaitForSeconds(3);

    if (quitAfter) Application.Quit();

    print ("closing");

}
```

3. Uncomment the SaveGame(true); // quit after saving lines in both the Confirm and the miniMenu sections of the OnGUI function.

4. Save the script.

5. Click Play and test.

An alternative method to bring up the mini-menu is to track the position of the cursor and bring up the menu if the cursor is in the top section of the screen.

6. Add the following inside the Update function:

```
var pos = Input.mousePosition; //get the location of the cursor
print (pos);
```

7. Save the script.

8. Click Play, and move the cursor toward the top and bottom of the Game view.

9. Resize the game view, and repeat.

The Input.mousePosition considers 0 at the bottom of the screen and Screen.height at the top of its y element. Set up the position check so that it will work while you are in edit mode.

10. Replace the print line with the following:

```
if (pos.y > Screen.height - 5.0) miniMenu = true;
```

11. Save the script.

12. Test by moving the cursor up to the top of the Game view.

13. Repeat the test in Maximize on Play mode.

Since the mouse is always beyond the location when you click the Play button, the menu will always turn up at the start. Another option is to use one side of the screen, say the last five pixels, as an activation area. This could be a problem with players who prefer to mouse-turn rather than arrow-turn. A good compromise might be to bring the menu up when the cursor is in the top left corner of the screen. It is quick to get to and will not interfere with navigation or the Play button.

14. Change the line as follows:

```
if (pos.y > Screen.height - 5.0 && pos.x <  5.0 ) {
   miniMenu = true;
  }
```

15. Save the scene, and save the project.

Tracking Menu Mode

While your menu pops up on cue now, your player is still free to wander around. The menu functionality is basically the same as inventory mode. The player should not be able to navigate the scene, and mouse-overs and picks outside the menu layer should be ignored.

Since you are likely to discover other things that need to be included in your menu mode, you will make a function to toggle secondary functionality off and on.

1. Open the MenuManager script.

2. Add a new variable to tell you if a menu is open:

```
private var menuMode = false; // no menus are open
```

This gives you a means of preventing the mini-menu from being opened on top of a sub-menu.

3. In the Update function, change the if (Input.GetKeyDown("f1")) block as follows:

```
//toggle the minimenu off and on
if (Input.GetKeyDown("f1")) {
    if(miniMenu) {
        miniMenu = false;
        MenuMode(false);
    }
     else if (!menuMode ) { // if no other menus are open, open it
        miniMenu = true;
        MenuMode(true);
     }
}
```

Before you can test it, you need to block in your MenuMode function. You will be passing in the state you want to be in as a Boolean (true/false) argument.

1. Create the following function:

```
function MenuMode (state : boolean) {

   if (state) { // go into menuMode
   menuMode = true;
```

```
}

    else { // return from menuMode
    menuMode = false;

    }
}
```

Next you need to turn on menuMode from the sub-menus as soon as they are called. Currently the confirmDialog is your only working sub-menu.

2.   Below the `confirmDialog = true` lines in the `OnGUI` and `Update` functions, add the following:

```
MenuMode(true);
```

Whenever you turn off a menu and are not turning on another, you need to turn off menuMode as well.

1.   Add the following line to the `Save` and `Resume` sections, beneath their `miniMenu = false` lines:

```
MenuMode(false);
```

All three of the options in the `confirmDialog` conditional leave no menus showing, so you will need to add the same line to each.

2.   Add the following under each of the three `confirmDialog = false` lines:

```
MenuMode(false);
```

Having set your menuMode flag off and on for the various buttons, you can now add the condition that menuMode is off before you allow the "F1" keypress, the "escape" keypress, or the cursor position trigger to open the miniMenu or confirmDialog.

1.   Change `if (Input.GetKeyDown("f1")) {` to the following:

```
if (Input.GetKeyDown("f1") && !menuMode) {
```

2.   Change `if (Input.GetKey ("escape")) {` to the following:

```
if (Input.GetKey ("escape") && !menuMode) {
```

3.   Change `if (pos.y > Screen.height - 5.0 && pos.x < 5.0) {` to the following:

```
if (pos.y > Screen.height - 5.0  && pos.x <  5.0 && !menuMode) {
   miniMenu = true;
   MenuMode(true);
 }
```

4.   Save the script.

5.   Click Play and test.

The Main Menu

All but the Main Menu and Settings buttons work well. Block them in now. The Main Menu will need the following components:

- Instructions (how to interact with objects, etc.)
- Navigation instructions (keys, options)
- New Game button (load the first game level)
- Load Game button (load the previously saved game)
- Settings Menu button (same as before)
- Resume button (in case the player changed his mind)
- Credits screen button (because you need to show who created your game)

You can reuse a couple of the buttons, but you will need a few new controls. For the navigation and instructions, you will need to add GUI Labels to hold some text. The Load Game will need a function similar to the SaveGame function you blocked in earlier, and the New Game is simply an Application.LoadLevel like you used to load the FinalLevel.

Instead of keeping a lot of text inside the OnGUI function, you will create variables to hold it. Note the use of /n to force a carriage return (line feed) in a GUI label. This keeps you from needing to create extra GUILabels if you want to break the text.

1. Add the following variables to the script:

```
// misc menu text
private var introText = "Welcome to the Mystery of Tizzleblat...\n a simple world with↵
 a solvable problem.";
private var infoText = "Interactive objects- cursor changes color on \nmouse over, click to↵
 activate\nInventory- i key or pick on icon at lower left to \naccess\nGeneral- objects can↵
 be combined in scene or \nin inventory";
private var navText = "Navigation:\nUP/Down, W/S to move forward/Backward\n A/D to strafe↵
 left and right\nLeft and Right arrow keys to turn/look around, or <shift> or right mouse↵
 button and move mouse to turn and look around";
```

■ **Tip** If you wish to experiment with your own text, you will need to restart the game each time the text is changed since you are storing it in variables that get read in only at startup.

---

2. Add the following *beneath* the closing curly bracket of the confirmDialog conditional:

```
// ********  main menu  *************
 if(mainMenu) {

// Make a group on the center of the screen
```

```
GUI.BeginGroup (Rect (Screen.width / 2 - 150 , Screen.height  / 2 - 250, 300, 500));
 // all rectangles are now adjusted to the group
 // (0,0) is the top left corner of the group

 // control elements

 // make a box so we can see where the group is on-screen.
 GUI.Box (Rect (0,0,300,110), "Main Menu");

 // make a box so we can see where the group is on-screen.
 GUI.Box (Rect (0,120,300,200), "General Information and Navigation");

 // make a box so we can see where the group is on-screen.
 GUI.Box (Rect (0,330,300,150), "");

 //this is a local variable that gets changed after each button is added
 buttnRectTemp = Rect (groupWidth/2 - buttnRect.width +5,50,buttnRect.width-10,↵
 buttnRect.height);

 //Game Intro
 GUI.Label( Rect (20,20,250,100), introText);

 //General Info
 GUI.Label( Rect (10,150,300,80), infoText);

 //Navigation Instructions
 GUI.Label( Rect (10,230,300,130), navText);


 // start the buttons down a bit to avoid overlapping
 buttnRectTemp.y += 300;

 if (GUI.Button (buttnRectTemp, "New Game")) {
     // Start the Main Level
     Application.LoadLevel("MainLevel");
 }

 buttnRectTemp.x = groupWidth/2 +5;

 if (GUI.Button (buttnRectTemp, "Settings")) {
    // go to settings menu
    mainMenu = false;
    settingsMenu = true;
 }

 // move the next control down a bit to avoid overlapping
 buttnRectTemp.y += 40;
 buttnRectTemp.x = groupWidth/2 - buttnRect.width +5;

 if (GUI.Button (buttnRectTemp, "Load Game")) {
    // load the previous game
    mainMenu = false;
```

```
    LoadGame();
    MenuMode(false);
}

buttnRectTemp.x = groupWidth/2 +5;

 if (GUI.Button (buttnRectTemp, "Credits")) {
 // go to settings menu
    mainMenu = false;
    creditsScreen = true;
}

// move the next control down a bit to avoid overlapping
buttnRectTemp.y += 40;
buttnRectTemp.x = groupWidth/2 - buttnRect.width /2;

if (GUI.Button (buttnRectTemp, "Resume")) {
    // turn off the menu
    mainMenu = false;
    MenuMode(false);
}


 // End the main menu group we started above. This is very important to remember!
 GUI.EndGroup ();

} // end the main menu conditional
```

Before you test the code, make a quick place holder function for the LoadGame function.

    1.   Create a LoadGame function as follows:

```
function LoadGame () {

    print ("loading");

    yield new WaitForSeconds(3);
}
```

    2.   Save the script.

    3.   Click Play, and check out the Main Menu.

The main menu is blocked in with all pertinent information (see Figure 16-3). Don't worry about refining the layout at this point—as soon as you add the final font, things will need adjusting again.

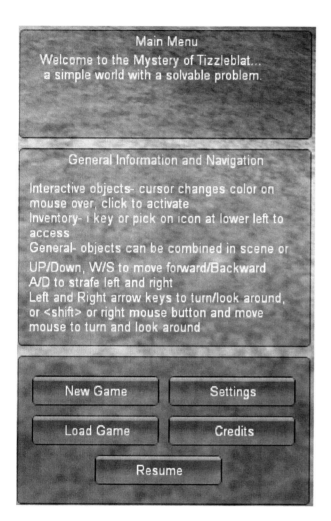

Figure 16-3. *Main Menu, blocked in*

The Credits screen can be very simple at this stage. It will consist of at least one GUI Label. To return to the game from the credits menu, however, you will try something new, the "anyKey" input.

Beneath the closing curly bracket of the `mainMenu` conditional, add the following:

```
// ********  credits screen  *************
if(creditsScreen) {

    // Make a group on the center of the screen
    GUI.BeginGroup (Rect (Screen.width / 2 - 150 , Screen.height  / 2 - 200, 300, 400));
    // all rectangles are now adjusted to the group
    // (0,0) is the top left corner of the group

    // make a box so we can see where the group is on-screen.
```

```
GUI.Box (Rect (0,0,300,400), "Credits");

// move the next control down a bit to avoid overlapping
buttnRectTemp.y += 40;

// add labels here
GUI.Label( Rect (20,20,250,100), "Your name here in lights!");

// End the main menu group we started above. This is very important to remember!
GUI.EndGroup ();

} // end the credits screen conditional
```

Because the "anyKey" also includes mouse buttons, pretty much any input from the player will take him back to the game, making a text prompt unnecessary.

4. In the Update function, add the following:

```
if(creditsScreen && Input.anyKeyDown) {
    creditsScreen = false;
    MenuMode(false);
}
```

5. Save the script, and test the new main menu and Credits screen.

The Settings Menu

Your final in-game menu is the Settings menu. This is where you will let the player have some control over the visual and audio presentation of the game. Unlike the previous menus that consisted mainly of buttons and labels, your Settings menu will give you a chance to see how a few of the other more interactive GUI controls work.

As before, you need to have a list of what you need so you will be using variables you set up early in the project.

- Navigation:
  - Walk Speed, slider
  - Turning speed, slider
- Text:
  - Use Text, Check Box
  - Object Description, Check Box
- Audio:
  - Sound FX Volume, Slider
  - Ambient Sound Volume, Slider
  - Music Volume, Slider
  - Voice Volume, Slider

- Cursor:
    - Use Mouseover color change, CheckBox
    - Cursor Color on Mouseover, Slider, Hue
- Menu:
    - Resume button
    - Main Menu button

Before you start punching in numbers, it would make sense to have a rough layout in mind (see Figure 16-4).

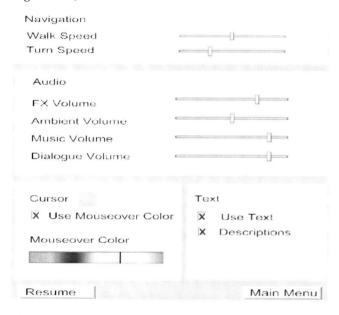

Figure 16-4. *Rough layout for Settings menu*

Unlike the previous menu's buttons, most of the controls in the Settings menu return values other than just `true` or `false`. To utilize those values, you will need to assign them to variables so they can be processed.

Another peculiarity of these controls is that you are better off checking for user changes in the GUI before you process changes rather than processing the values of all of the controls every frame. You will also try something a bit different for the Settings menu by creating a function to draw its contents and calling that function from the `OnGUI` function.

Let's get started.

1. Open the `MenuManager` script.

2. Below the closing curly bracket for the credits section, add the following:

```
//******* Settings menu  ********
```

```
if (settingsMenu) Settings(); // let the setting function process all of its own content
```
And now you will start in on the Settings function. You will start by creating the overall group and sub-group areas and then fill in the various sections one by one.

3. Start the function as follows:

```
function Settings () {

    // Make a group on the center of the screen for  the settings menu
    GUI.BeginGroup (Rect (Screen.width / 2 - 300 , Screen.height  / 2 - 250, 600, 500));
    // all rectangles are now adjusted to the group


    //****  guts group    *****
    GUI.BeginGroup (Rect (0,10, 600, 500));

    // navigation
    var navBox = Rect (10,20,580,80);
    GUI.Box (navBox, "Navigation");




    // text
    var textBox = Rect (300,270,290,150);
    GUI.Box (textBox, "Text");




    // audio
    var audioBox = Rect (10,110,580,150);
    GUI.Box (audioBox, "Audio");




    // cursor
    var cursorBox = Rect (10,270,280,150);
    GUI.Box (cursorBox, "Cursor");




    // button
    var buttonBox = Rect (10,430,580,50);
    GUI.Box (buttonBox, "");
```

```
    // End the groups we started above. This is very important to remember!
    GUI.EndGroup ();
    GUI.EndGroup ();

}
```

4. Save the script.

5. Click Play, and go to the Settings menu to see the results.

Player Settings

Before you start adding the controls to your Settings menu, you will need to create variables to hold their values.

1. Near the top of the MenuManager script, add the following:

```
//player settings variables
private var walkSpeed : float;
private var turnSpeed : float;
private var useText : boolean;
private var objectDescriptions : boolean;
private var fXVolume : float;
private var ambVolume : float;
private var musicVolume : float;
private var voiceVolume : float;
private var useMOCursor : boolean;
private var cursorColorChange : float;
```

Since the starting values are already defined in other scripts, you will need access to the Control Center object so you can load them into your MenuManager script at startup.

2. Add the following:

```
//Gain access to
private var controlCenter : GameObject;
```

3. "Find" the Control Center in the Start menu:

```
function Start () {

    controlCenter  = GameObject.Find("Control Center");

}
```

Thinking ahead, you will probably realize that you will need to get and set the player settings every time the player changes them and also when loading and saving the game. It would make handling them a lot easier if you could store them in an array and pass the array back and forth. You will assume your array will contain your settings in the order in which you have declared the variables.

4. Comment each of the variables with their prospect element number as per the example:

```
//Settings menu variables
private var walkSpeed : float; // element 0
```

```
private var turnSpeed : float; // element 1
```
To hold the player settings, you will define an array.

   5. Add the following below the settings variables section:

```
private var playerSettings = new Array (); // player settings array
```

   6. Create a function to load the values after getting them from the GameManager:

```
function LoadPlayerSettings () {

    //load in the array of current settings for the parameters exposed to the player
    playerSettings = controlCenter.GetComponent(GameManager).playerSettings;

    walkSpeed = playerSettings[0];
    turnSpeed = playerSettings[1];
    objectNames = playerSettings[2];
    objectDescriptions = playerSettings[3];
    fXVolume= playerSettings[4];
    ambVolume = playerSettings[5];
    musicVolume = playerSettings[6];
    voiceVolume = playerSettings[7];
    useMOCursor = playerSettings[8];
    //cursorColorChange

}
```

The cursor color change is commented out at present because you are passing it an RGB value and you will need to convert it so you can use its hue only.

   7. Add the following line to the Start function to call the function and load the values:

```
LoadPlayerSettings(); // load the player settings values
```

   8. Save the script.

Back in the GameManager, you will need to create the function to store the values in the array that your LoadPlayerSettings function needs to load. Note that you have pulled in the two navigation values from the First Person Controller's CharacterMotor script as well. Because this is a JavaScript array, not a built-in Unity array, you can load all different types of data into it.

   1. Open the GameManager script.

   2. Add the following variable to define your array:

```
private var playerSettings = new Array (); // player settings array
```
And to load the values, you will create a function.

   3. Add the following function:

```
// load the various settings into an array for easier management
function StorePlayerSettings() {

var fpController = GameObject.Find("First Person Controller");

    playerSettings[0] = fpController.GetComponent(CharacterMotor).movement.maxForwardSpeed;
```

```
playerSettings[1] = fpController.GetComponent(FPAdventurerInputController).rotationSpeed;
playerSettings[2] = useText;
playerSettings[3] = useLongDesc;
playerSettings[4] = soundFXVolume;
playerSettings[5] = ambientSoundVolume;
playerSettings[6] = backgroundMusicVolume;
playerSettings[7] = voiceVolume;
playerSettings[8] = useMOCursorChange;
playerSettings[9] = mouseOverColor;

}
```

The tricky part about your array is that the values need to be loaded into it *before* the function in the MenuManager script tries to access them. To ensure that they are loaded beforehand, you will call the function from the Awake function rather than the Start function.

1. Add the following to the Awake function in the GameManager script:

```
StorePlayerSettings();// load the player accessible settings into an array
```

2. Save the script.

3. Click Play, and make sure you have no errors.

Filling in the Controls

Now that most of your settings have been initialized, you can start adding the GUI controls.

1. Open the MenuManager script.

2. In the Settings function, in the //navigation section, add the following:

```
GUI.Label (Rect (25, 35, 100, 30), "Walk Speed");
walkSpeed = GUI.HorizontalSlider (Rect (150, 40, 100, 20), walkSpeed, 0.0, 20.0);
```

For the Horizontal Slider, the last two numbers are its start and end values. The third from the last value is the sliding knob's value. It was set originally when you loaded the player settings values but can now be changed using the slider knob. Since your preset forward speed is 10, you will set the maximum value of the slider to 20.0 so that the knob sits at halfway.

1. Add the following for the Left/Right arrow turn speed:

```
GUI.Label (Rect (25, 60, 100, 30), "Turn Speed");
turnSpeed = GUI.HorizontalSlider (Rect (150,65, 100, 20), turnSpeed, 0.0, 40.0);
```

The default turn speed is 20, so you can set its slider's max value to 40.

2. Save the script.

3. Click Play, and test the sliders in the Settings menu.

Now that you can adjust the sliders, you need to send the final value back to the appropriate script to update the parameter. To do this, you will check to see if the GUI was changed.

4. Add the following above the //button section:

```
// track changes
if (GUI.changed) {
```

```
print (walkSpeed + " " + turnSpeed);
```

```
}
```

Changing any GUI components *above* the check will trigger it. Since the buttons will have their own conditional and do not change any of the settings, you will keep the GUI.changed check above them.

5. Save the script.

6. Click Play, and test the sliders, noting the output in the console.

The new values are reported as soon as you stop moving the knobs.

Now you need to update the values. Unfortunately, the GUI.changed does not report *which* control was changed, so you will update them all. Theoretically, you could keep track of the old values and update only the changed value, but speed is not enough of an issue for your few settings.

1. Change the print statement to the following:

```
UpdateSettings(); // process the changes
```

2. Create the following function:

```
function UpdateSettings() {

    playerSettings[0] = walkSpeed;
    playerSettings[1] = turnSpeed;
    playerSettings[2] = useText;
    playerSettings[3] = objectDescriptions;
    playerSettings[4] = fXVolume;
    playerSettings[5] = ambVolume;
    playerSettings[6] = musicVolume;
    playerSettings[7] = voiceVolume;
    playerSettings[8] = useMOCursor;
    // cursorColorChange

    // send the updated settings off to the GameManager
    controlCenter.SendMessage("NewSettings", playerSettings);

}
```

3. Save the script.

And now you can create the NewSettings function back in the GameManager to receive and update the changes made in the Settings menu.

1. Open the GameManager script.

2. Add the following function:

```
function NewSettings(newSettings : Array) {

    var fpController = GameObject.Find("First Person Controller");

    //update the array
    playerSettings = newSettings;
```

```
    //assign the individual vars
    fpController.GetComponent(CharacterMotor).movement.maxForwardSpeed = playerSettings [0];
    fpController.GetComponent(FPAdventurerInputController).rotationSpeed =    playerSettings⏎
[1];
    useText = playerSettings [2];
    useLongDesc = playerSettings [3];
    soundFXVolume = playerSettings [4];
    ambientSoundVolume = playerSettings [5];
    backgroundMusicVolume = playerSettings [6];
    voiceVolume = playerSettings [7];
    useMOCursorChange = playerSettings [8];
    // mouseOverColor = playerSettings [9];
}
```

3. Save the script.

4. Click Play, change the walk and turn speeds in the settings menu, and watch the values update in the Inspector.

Add the rest of the controls into the Settings menu.

1. Open the MenuManager script.

2. Add the following to the Audio section:

```
audioBox.y += 30;
GUI.Label (Rect (25, audioBox.y, 100, 30), "FX Volume");
audioBox.y += 10;
fXVolume = GUI.HorizontalSlider (Rect (150, audioBox.y, 100, 20), fXVolume, 0.0, 1.0);
audioBox.y += 14;
GUI.Label (Rect (25, audioBox.y, 100, 30), "Ambient Volume");
audioBox.y += 10;
ambVolume = GUI.HorizontalSlider (Rect (150,audioBox.y, 100, 20), ambVolume, 0.0, 1.0);
audioBox.y += 14;
GUI.Label (Rect (25, audioBox.y, 100, 30), "Music Volume");
audioBox.y += 10;
musicVolume = GUI.HorizontalSlider (Rect (150, audioBox.y, 100, 20), musicVolume, 0.0, 1.0);
audioBox.y += 14;
GUI.Label (Rect (25, audioBox.y, 100, 30), "Dialog Volume");
audioBox.y += 10;
voiceVolume = GUI.HorizontalSlider (Rect (150,audioBox.y, 100, 20), voiceVolume, 0.0, 1.0);
```

3. Save the script, and test the new sliders.

You will hook up the volume functionality later when you revisit the sound in your game.

1. Add the following to the text section:

```
useText = GUI.Toggle (Rect (320, 300, 120, 30), useText, "Use Text");
objectDescriptions = GUI.Toggle (Rect (320,330, 120, 30), objectDescriptions, "Use⏎
Descriptions");
```

2. Save the script.

3. Test the text check boxes, and observe the results in the Inspector.

Because the text variables act in the GameManager's OnGUI function, they work immediately. To get the full effect, you need to add the buttons to be able to leave the Settings menu.

1. Add the following to the MenuManager's Settings function, in the //buttons section:

```
if (GUI.Button (Rect (20,440,150,30), "Main Menu")) {
    // turn off the menu
    settingsMenu = false;
    mainMenu = true;
}
if (GUI.Button (Rect (430,440,150,30), "Resume")) {
    // turn off the menu
    settingsMenu = false;
    MenuMode(false);
}
```

2. Save the script.

3. Click Play, and test both the buttons and the text options.

Buttons and text options should work as expected.

Color Selector

For the color selector that allows players to select their own mouse-over color, you will need to add a few extra variables to be able to override whatever GUISkin you eventually assign to your menus.

Some of the GUI controls, such as the box and buttons, allow you to override the texture assigned to them in the GUISkin. You, however, will need to use the horizontal slider control, which has no such option. This means you will need to add a couple of GUI Styles to locally override your regular GUISkin. You will also need a simple white texture that can be tinted to match the color picker's selection as well as a variable to hold your slider's value converted to RGB so it can be used tint the color swatch and send the new color to the GameManager.

1. Select the Control Center object.

2. Open the MenuManager script.

3. Add the following variables for your color bar functionality:

```
// color bar variables
var colorBar : GUIStyle; // color picker slider
var pickerThumb : GUIStyle; // color picker slider
var colorSwatch : Texture;
var moColor : Color; // mouseover color
```

4. Save the script.

The new GUI Styles appear in the Inspector.

1. Make sure Play mode is off.

2. Open the Color Bar GUIStyle in the Menu Manager component.

3. Under Normal, load the ColorBar texture into the Background parameter.

This will be the slider's background color.

The thumb/indicator is a bit trickier. It needs a custom background image too, but will need further adjustments.

1. Open the Picker Thumb GUIStyle.

2. Under Normal, load the ColorThumb texture into the Background parameter.

3. Under Hover, add the ColorThumbMO texture into the Background parameter.

4. Set Fixed Width to **10** and Fixed Height to **20**.

5. In the Overflow section, set Top to **-6** and Bottom to **14**.

These numbers allow you to make the thumb/indicator overlap the color bar to mimic Unity's color bar functionality. You may need to make further adjustments once your control is in place.

1. Collapse/close both GUIStyles, and load the White texture into the third of your added variables, the Color Swatch.

2. For the Mo Color, use the eyedropper to the right of the color bar and sample the GameManager's Mouse Over Color.

Since you will be using this one on a box control that allows you to override a texture, you do not need to make a full GUIStyle.

The moColor will be loaded and maintained dynamically, so you can leave it as is for now.

Add the slider and other controls to the script.

1. In the MenuManager, Settings function, add the following to the //cursor section:

```
cursorBox.y += 40;
useMOCursor = GUI.Toggle (Rect (20, cursorBox.y , 180, 30), useMOCursor, "Use Mouseover↵
 Color");
cursorBox.y += 30;
GUI.Label (Rect (20, cursorBox.y , 120, 30),  "Mouseover Color");
cursorBox.y += 20;
cursorColorChange = GUI.HorizontalSlider(Rect (20, cursorBox.y , 200,
40),cursorColorChange,0.0,1536.0,colorBar,pickerThumb);
```

Note the use of both the colorBar and pickerThumb GUIStyles in the slider line.

For the color swatch, you will use GUI.contentColor to tint the color swatch, and then revert the tint back to white immediately after drawing the swatch.

2. In the same section, add the following to handle the color swatch:

```
GUI.contentColor = moColor;
GUI.Box (Rect (180, 312 , 40, 40), colorSwatch);
GUI.contentColor = Color.white;
```

Note the use of the colorSwatch texture to override the regular GUISkin's Background texture.

3. Save the script.

4. Click Play, and check out the Cursor section of the Settings menu (see Figure 16-5).

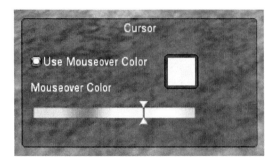

Figure 16-5. *The Color Bar in the Cursor section*

The Use Mouseover Color check box works already because its variable is sent to the `GameManager` with the rest of the settings. Now you need to work out how to convert the slider position representing Hue to an RGB value that can be used to tint the color swatch and the cursor itself.

If you do a bit of research on RGB to HSV color conversion, you will probably be overwhelmed by angles and other convoluted formulas. Fortunately, your functionality does not need to be extremely accurate, so you can evaluate what happens and work out the functionality from your own observations and get a workable solution.

Let's start with some observations.

1. Select the Control Center object.

2. While in Play mode, open the Mo Color color dialog in the Inspector.

3. Make sure the Hue bar is vertical on the right and the lower sliders are using RGBA (see Figure 16-6).

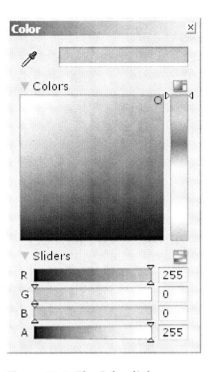

Figure 16-6. *The Color dialog*

4. With the color fully saturated, and the Hue at the top, red, slowly drag the hue marker down to the bottom red, watching the RGB values change.

Only *one* of the components is active *at any one time*. It can be charted as shown in Table 16-1.

Table 16-1. *RGB Color Value Changes*

	Red	Magenta	Blue	Cyan	Green	Yellow	Red
R	255	255 ➤	0	0	0 ➤	255	255
G	0	0	0 ➤	255	255	255 ➤	0
B	0 ➤	255	255	255 ➤	0	0	0
div	0	1	2	3	4	5	6

With six "zones," you get a total of 1536 (6 * 256) as the maximum value for your slider. Once you have a value from the slider, you can divide it by 256 to find its "zone." You can do that by converting it to an integer so you lose the remainder. Then you can add or subtract the remainder (we can get that using the modulo/modulus operator, %) from the appropriate component, and finally convert the values to decimal for use in Unity's Color variable type since it expects values from 0 to 1.

1. Open the MenuManager script.

2. Add the following function to convert the Hue to RGB:

```
function ProcessHue (value :float) {

    var zone = parseInt(value / 256);
    var mod = parseInt(value % 256);

    print (value + "  " + zone + "  " + mod);

    var r : int;
    var g : int;
    var b : int;

    switch (zone) {

    case 0 :
        //red
        r = 255;
        g = 0;
        b = 0 + mod;
        break;

    case 1 :
        //magenta
        r = 255 - mod;
        g = 0;
        b = 255;
        break;

    case 2 :
        //blue
        r = 0;
        g = 0 + mod;
        b = 255;
        break;

    case 3 :
        //cyan
        r = 0;
        g = 255;
        b = 255 - mod;
        break;

    case 4 :
        //green
        r = 0 + mod;
        g = 255;
```

```
          b = 0;
          break;

    case 5 :
          //yellow
          r = 255;
          g = 255 - mod;
          b = 0;
          break;

    case 6 :
          //red
          r = 255;
          g = 0;
          b = 0;
          break;

    }

    //change fractions to decimal & assign to the variable
    moColor = Color(r/255.0,g/255.0,b/255.0);


}
```

Note the use of the float value, 255.0, to make sure you get a fraction back rather than rounding off to the integers, 0 or 1.

Now you can go back and add in the color change code in the various places it is needed.

3. In the LoadPlayerSettings function, add the following beneath the //cursorColorChange line:

```
moColor = playerSettings[9]; // the rgb color
cursorColorChange = playerSettings[10];
```

The loaded RGB color is used to tint the color swatch. You could try to derive a Hue number to position your slider's marker to match the swatch, but it really needs to be read in only when a new scene is loaded. That being the case, it is probably not worth all the code that would be required to pull the hue from the RGB. By reading the values sent out to the console by your print statements, you can manually set the value to match the default mouse-over color you have chosen for the new scenes. When saving a scene, you can save the value directly.

4. In the UpdateSettings function, add the following beneath the //cursorColorChange line:

```
ProcessHue(cursorColorChange); // convert Hue/slider value to rgb
playerSettings[9] =  moColor;
playerSettings[10] = cursorColorChange; // send back the slider value
```

Now when the GUI change is detected, the color bar is read for hue, converted, and sent to the GameManager, and the tint of the color swatch is automatically updated.

5. Save the script.

6. Click Play, and change the cursor mouse-over color using the color slider in the Settings menu.

7.   Exit the Settings menu, and test the mouse-over to make sure the color has been changed.

8.   Open the Settings menu again, and adjust the slider to the color you want it to start with.

9.   Make note of the slider value for your color, as shown in the console's print-out.

10. Open the `GameManager` script.

11. At the top of the script, add a new variable for the slider value using the value you noted earlier:

```
private var colorSliderValue = 1030.0; // element 10, set this one manually for the⏎
 default mouseover color
```

12. Uncomment the `// mouseOverColor = newSettings[9]` line in the `NewSettings` function, and add the slider value line:

```
colorSliderValue = playerSettings[10];
```

13. In the `StorePlayerSettings` function, add the following:

```
playerSettings[10] = colorSliderValue;
```

14. Save the script.

15. Stop Play mode.

16. Comment out the `print` line in the `ProcessHue` function.

17. Save the script.

18. Save the scene, and save the project.

The Settings menu is quite functional (see Figure 16-7).

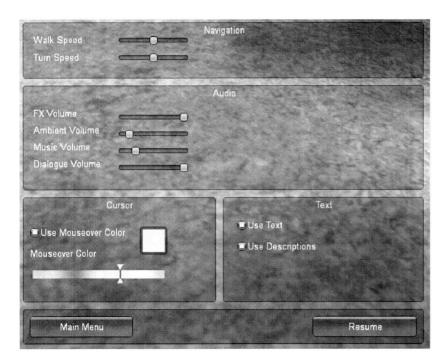

Figure 16-7. *Preliminary Settings menu*

Finishing Audio

To implement the volume changes you blocked out in the Settings menu, you will need to devise a means of identifying each audio type. Because you have no way of tagging an audio component, you will need to devise a set of conventions.

Sound FX

The sound effects used by the action objects are already set up to use volume control. You need only to figure out how to tell them all to update. While this may sound easy, you will discover a minor issue that needs to be dealt with.

    1.   Open the Interactor script.

In the Start function, you can see that you have already read in the volume from the GameManager into a variable called soundFXVolume that is used with the AudioSource.PlayClipAtPoint calls.

For immediate results, you will need to tell any object tagged as an ActionObject to update that variable. The main setting in the GameManager script is already automatically updated with the playerSetting array, but you will need to tell each of the individual action objects to update their settings.

    2.   Open the MenuManager script.

3. In the UpdateSettings function, below the controlCenter.SendMessage line, add the following:

```
//Update Audio volumes
var gos = GameObject.FindGameObjectsWithTag ("ActionObject");
for (var go in gos) {
    print(go.name); // use until we get no errors
    go.GetComponent(Interactor).soundFXVolume = fXVolume;
}
```

Tip   If you get any error messages, make sure all action objects have the Interactor script. The Temple Jewel, for example, was duplicated and its scripts removed. If you neglected to set it to Untagged, it will throw an error.

The FindGameObjectsWithTag command creates an array of all of the objects it finds with the ActionObject tag. You then iterate through the array, changing the volume variable.

4. Save the script.

5. Click Play, and make an adjustment in the Settings menu.

The console reports an error.

6. Open the console, and see which object is causing the problem.

The error turns up after it tries to process an object named Iron Sphere. The Iron Sphere came in with the Temple Group and can be found in the storage room opposite the grain sacks' room. At some point, you may wish to use the Iron Sphere an action object that activates the hologram so the player needs to search for its clue.

7. Stop Play mode.

8. Set the Iron Sphere's Tag to Untagged until you make use of it.

9. Click Play, and make an adjustment in the Settings menu.

10. Fix any remaining action object problems, and then comment out the print statement.

11. Save the script.

12. Test the sound effects adjustment using the Chest Lid or other action object that has a sound effect assigned to it.

As long as the object is active in the scene, its sound is adjusted. The Key At Lock, however, may not have been active when the volume was changed. Because any number of action objects may be inactive at any one time, you should make sure their volume is adjusted when they are activated in the ObjectLookUp script. You will update the volume setting any time you reactivate an action object.

1. Open the ObjectLookUp script.

2. In the `CheckForActive` function near the bottom of the script, add the following immediately after the `auxObject = gameObject.Find(tempS)` line:

```
//update the fx volume
auxObject.GetComponent(Interactor).soundFXVolume =↵
 controlCenter.GetComponent(GameManager).soundFXVolume;
```

3. Save the script.

4. Click Play, and test the Key At Lock.

This time its volume reflects the changes made while it was inactive.

5. Save the scene, and save the project.

Ambient Sound

Before you can adjust the volume on ambient sounds, you need to add at least one. The nice thing about the ambient sound is that it can go on its own GameObject, and you can create a Tag with which to access it.

1. Create an empty GameObject.

2. Name it Ambient Jungle.

3. From the Tag drop-down in the Inspector, choose Add Tag.

4. Create a new Tag named Ambient.

5. Assign the Ambient tag to the new GameObject.

6. Add an Audio Source component to it.

7. Load the Birds audio clip into it.

8. Check Loop.

░ **Tip**   The birds in the clip are decidedly North American. If you have access to the Island demo that shipped with Unity 2.5, you may prefer to use the *jungle* clip.

---

9. Focus in on an object in the scene.

10. Use Move to View to bring the Ambient Jungle object to that position.

11. From the top view, move the GameObject to a densely foliated area where you can easily test the 3D sound parameters.

12. Click Play, and navigate to the area to test the sound.

13. Change the Rolloff Mode to Linear to get a more ambient effect.

14. Experiment with the Max Distance.

15. Stop Play mode, and make the changes permanent.

You can reuse the ambient sound elsewhere in the scene after you turn it into a prefab.

1. In the Adventure Prefabs folder, create a new prefab.

2. Name it Ambient Sounds.

3. Drag the Ambient Jungle object into it.

4. Drag new Ambient Sounds into the scene, and arrange them to suit.

5. Drag one of the new prefabs over to the waterfall.

6. Name it Ambient Falls, and position it at the waterfall.

7. Load the Waterfall audio clip from the Bootcamp demo into it.

8. Because the waterfall is a very localized sound, change the Rolloff Mode to Logarithmic Rolloff.

By now you are probably more than ready to be able to adjust the ambient sound. With a few small changes, you should be able to reuse the FX code.

1. Open the MenuManager script.

2. In the //Update Audio volumes section of the UpdateSettings function, add the following:

```
gos = GameObject.FindGameObjectsWithTag ("Ambient");
for (go in gos) go.GetComponent(AudioSource).volume = ambVolume;
```

■ **Tip**   You are reusing the variables for the different volume adjustments, so you do not need to declare them more than once in the UpdateSettings function.

---

3. Save the script, and test the ambient volume.

Because you can hear it in the background, the instant feedback is quite useful.

Music

You do not yet have any music in the scene, but you can easily add some using the same methods as before. In a more sophisticated system, you might want to attach the sound to the player and have it fade out and load different sound clips according to location, but the following method will provide you with similar results for a lot less work.

1. Open the MenuManager script.

2. In the //Update Audio volumes section of the UpdateSettings function, add the following:

```
gos = GameObject.FindGameObjectsWithTag ("Music");
```

```
for (go in gos) go.GetComponent(AudioSource).volume = musicVolume;
```

3. Save the script.

4. Create an empty GameObject.

5. Name it Music Temple.

6. From the Tag drop-down in the Inspector, choose Add Tag.

7. Create a new Tag named Music.

8. Assign the Music tag to the new GameObject.

9. Add an Audio Source component to it.

10. Load the Temple audio clip into it.

11. Check Loop.

■ **Note**   The music is a variation on a sample learning project found in the Garage Band app.

---

12. Focus in on the temple in the scene.

13. Use Move to View to bring the Music Temple object to that position.

14. Click Play, and navigate around the temple to test the sound.

There is a noticeable amount of distortion on the sound clip.

15. Set the Doppler Level to **0**.

The distortion goes away.

16. Set the Max Distance to **50** and the Rolloff Mode to Custom.

The keys for the Rolloff curve behave like the Animation keys. You can delete unwanted keys by hovering over them and using the right-click menu.

17. Adjust the roll-off so that the volume is fairly even while you are in the temple (see Figure 16-8).

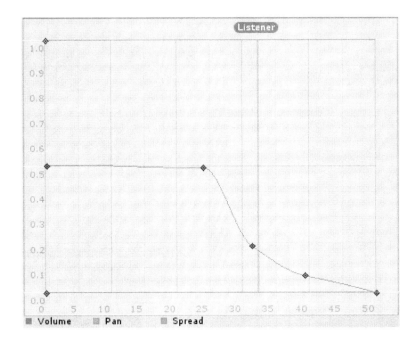

Figure 16-8. *The temple music roll-off curve*

18. Adjust any other settings you wish in the Audio Source.

19. Stop Play Mode.

20. Make the changes permanent.

21. Create a new Prefab, and name it Music.

22. Drag the Music Temple onto it in the Project view.

Having tested the music in the scene and probably decided it needed to be turned down quite a bit, you should probably update the default value for the music in the GameManager and its component on the Control Center object in the Inspector.

1. Select the Control Center.

2. Lower the default volume for the music.

3. Click Play.

The volume was not affected by the changes. If you think back, the action objects consult the GameManager for their default game settings. Your new objects, however, have no connection with it. Fortunately, you have just written code that searches the scene and updates the volume for ambient and music.

1. Open the GameManager script.

2. Add the following lines to the Start function to initialize the default volumes on your non-Action item GameObjects:

```
//initialize Audio volumes
var gos = GameObject.FindGameObjectsWithTag ("ActionObject");
for (var go in gos) {
   go.GetComponent(Interactor).soundFXVolume = soundFXVolume;

}
gos = GameObject.FindGameObjectsWithTag ("Ambient");
for (go in gos) go.GetComponent(AudioSource).volume = ambientSoundVolume;
gos = GameObject.FindGameObjectsWithTag ("Music");
for (go in gos) go.GetComponent(AudioSource).volume = backgroundMusicVolume;
```

3. Save the script.

4. Click Play, and make sure the music volume is now correct from the start.

5. Save the scene, and save the project.

Voice or Dialog Volume

You have only a couple of voice/dialogs sets in your game. The Temple Bouncer holds one such set. It has an Audio Source, and the files are loaded according to need (as with a dialog tree) so it could also be tagged. The other Voice file resides on an action object in the final scene where it is used in conjunction with the FX clip. Since that is also a valid setup, go ahead and account for it when you go through the action objects. Additionally, there is an audio clip that is on a light object's Audio Source component in the final scene that will fall under the voice category.

Since there could be other objects with sound effects that are not directly on action objects, you should include that in your final volume control. Because the setup of the audio is achieved through the conventions you have developed, you will need to update your GameNotes text file to note the "rules" for all of the audio you have set up.

1. Open the GameNotes text asset.

2. Add the following:

```
Audio:
Sound effects on objects tagged as "ActionObjects" are played via PlayClipAtPoint
Sound effects on non-action objects must be tagged as "FX"
Audio Source components on "ActionObjects" are reserved for voice/dialogue
Non-ActionObjects with Audio Sources for voice/dialogue must be tagged as "Voice"
Objects with Audio Source components for ambient sounds must be tagged as "Ambient"
Objects with Audio Source components for music must be tagged as "Music"
```

3. Create two new tags, FX and Voice.

4. In the MainLevel, select the Temple Bouncer and tag it as Voice.

5. Save the scene.

6. Open the FinalLevel scene.

7. In the FinalLevel, select the Point Trunk Blue, and tag it as FX.

With the final audio conventions recorded, you can update the code in the two scripts.

1. Open the `MenuManager` script.

2. In the `UpdateSettings` function, under the `go.GetComponent(Interactor).soundFXVolume` line, add the following:

```
//check for audio source & update Voice if found
if (go.GetComponent(AudioSource)) go.GetComponent(AudioSource).volume = voiceVolume;
```

3. To catch the two new tags, add the following to the `//Update Audio` volumes as well:

```
gos = GameObject.FindGameObjectsWithTag ("FX");
for (go in gos) go.GetComponent(AudioSource).volume = fXVolume;
gos = GameObject.FindGameObjectsWithTag ("Voice");
for (go in gos) go.GetComponent(AudioSource).volume = voiceVolume;
```

4. Save the script.

And finally, you will update the `GameManager`'s `Start` function to match.

1. Open the `GameManager` script.

2. In the `Start` function, under the `go.GetComponent(Interactor).soundFXVolume` line, add the following:

```
//check for audio source & update Voice if found
if (go.GetComponent(AudioSource)) go.GetComponent(AudioSource).volume = voiceVolume;
```

3. To catch the two new tags, add the following to the `//Initialize Audio` volumes section as well:

```
gos = GameObject.FindGameObjectsWithTag ("FX");
for (go in gos) go.GetComponent(AudioSource).volume = soundFXVolume;
gos = GameObject.FindGameObjectsWithTag ("Voice");
for (go in gos) go.GetComponent(AudioSource).volume = voiceVolume;
```

4. Save the script.

5. Save the scene, and save the project.

Custom Skin for Menus

Just as you originally created a GUISkin for your regular game UI, you will need one especially for your menus. In the game, you have a motif of hammered wrought iron and shiny gold. Your menu skin will make use of it as well to visually tie everything together.

1. Open the MainLevel scene.

2. From the right-click menu or the Assets menu, at the bottom of the Create sub-menu, select GUI Skin.

3. Name the new skin Menu GUISkin.

4. Change its font to BOOMERAN.

5. Select the font in the Fonts folder in the Project view, and change its Font Size to **24**.

6. Press Apply.

7. Select the Menu GUISkin again.

8. For the Box preset, load the TbBox texture into the Normal/Background.

9. Set the Text Color to a silver/gray.

10. For the Button preset, load the buttonDarkIron into the Normal/Background.

11. Set the Text Color to R, **255**, G, **193**, B, **53** for a nice gold color.

12. For Hover and Active, load the buttonDarkIronOver texture into the Normal/Background.

13. For Hover, set the Text Color to R, **0**, G, **255**, B, **180** to match your mystic blue/green.

14. For Active, set the Text Color to R, **206**, G, **255**, B, **240** as a lighter version of the blue/green.

15. For the Label preset, set the Normal text to the gold color, R, **255**, G, **193**, B, **53**.

16. Set its text Alignment to MiddleCenter.

17. For the Horizontal Slider preset, select the Band texture.

18. For the Horizontal Slider Thumb, load the TbInvBox texture into the Normal and Hover Backgrounds.

19. For the Active parameter's Background, load TbInvBoxActive.

As before with the regular GUI, you need to create a variable where you can load the new skin, then declare it in the `OnGUI` function.

1. Open the `MenuManager` script.

2. Add the following variable near the top:

var menuSkin : GUISkin; // custom skin for the menus

3. Save the script.

4. Stop Play mode.

5. Select the Control Center object in the Hierarchy.

6. Drag the new Menu GUISkin object into the Menu Skin parameter.

7. At the top of the `OnGUI` function, add the following line:

GUI.skin = menuSkin;

8. Save the script.

9. Click Play, and inspect the menus with their new skin (see Figure 16-9).

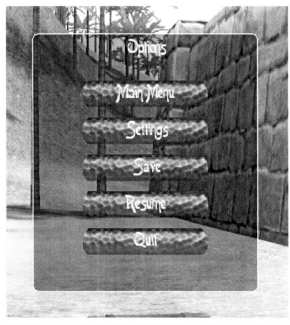

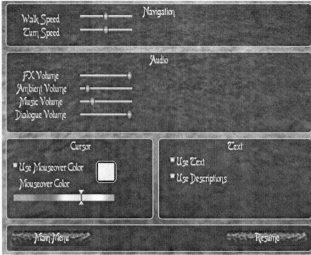

Figure 16-9. *The new skin*

The only menu that seems to have suffered is the Main Menu where the navigation text is displayed. Aside from the size being too large, the Boomerang font is more suited to labels and buttons. To make the instructions easier to read, you need to override the new skin with a simpler GUIStyle for the label text.

1. Open the MenuManager script.

2. Add the following variable:

```
var simpleText : GUIStyle; // text for nav and info
```

3. Save the script.

4. Stop Play mode.

5. Select the Control Center object in the Hierarchy.

6. Change the Simple Text, Normal Text Color to the R, **255**, G, **193**, B, **53** gold.

7. Change the Font to Arial.

8. Set the Alignment to UpperLeft.

9. Set the Font Size to **13** and the Font Style to Italic.

10. Open the MenuManager script.

11. In the Main Menu section of the OnGui function, add the simpleText style override to the infoText and navText lines:

```
//General Info
GUI.Label( Rect (10,150,300,80), infoText,simpleText);

//Navigation Instructions
GUI.Label( Rect (10,230,300,130), navText,simpleText);
```

12. Save the script.

13. Click Play, and open the main Menu.

Everything fits nicely and is easy to read (see Figure 16-10).

Figure 16-10. *The overridden style in the Main Menu*

With the controls all working properly, it is time to prevent player navigation and interaction conflicts with the scene, inventory, and menus.

Suspending Navigation and Scene Interaction Finishing Menus

The first task is to prevent conflicts with the Inventory screen and the menus. Since the OnGUI checks every frame, you need to make sure the MenuManager is informed of changes in iMode so it will not have to check for itself every frame. To do this, you will need to add a couple of lines to the InventoryManager's mastermind, the ToggleMode function. The MenuManager resides on the Control Center object, so you do not need to make any new "introductions."

1. Open the InventoryManager script.

2. In the ToggleMode function, duplicate the
   controlCenter.GetComponent(GameManager).iMode = false line in the if
   clause, and change the copy as follows:

```
controlCenter.GetComponent(MenuManager).iMode = false; // inform the menu manager
```

3. Repeat for the same line in the else clause:

```
controlCenter.GetComponent(MenuManager).iMode = true; // inform the menu manager
```

4. Save the script.

If the inventory screen is active, you will not process any menus.

5. Open the MenuManager script.

6. Add the following variable:

```
private var iMode = false; // track inventory mode
```

7. At the top of the Update function, add the following:

```
if (iMode) return; // the inventory screen is open
```

8. Add it to the top of the OnGUI function as well:

```
if (iMode) return; // the inventory screen is open
```

9. Save the script.

10. Click Play, and test to make sure the menu will not appear if the inventory
    screen is up either from the F1 keypress or the cursor position.

The menus are not drawn when the inventory screen is active, and they automatically go away if inventory is opened, then return when it is closed. You need to prevent inventory from being opened if menuMode is true.

11. Open the InventoryManager script.

12. Add the following to the top of the ToggleMode function:

```
// if there is a menu open, inventory is not allowed
if(controlCenter.GetComponent(MenuManager).menuMode) return;
```
Next you need to prevent navigation and mouse-overs and picks on action objects. You can copy the same code you used with the inventory mode to do much of the work. You already have a means of tracking when the menus are up via the menuMode variable that is updated in the MenuMode function.

First you need to add a few more variables. You will need to disable the mouse look on the main camera, so it needs to be accessed.

1. Add the following variables to the MenuManager under the /gain access to section:

```
private var fPCamera : GameObject;
private var fPController: GameObject;
```

2. Find the camera and First Person Controller in the Start function:

```
fPCamera= GameObject.Find("Main Camera");
fPController  = GameObject.Find("First Person Controller");
```

3. In the MenuMode function, under the menuMode = true line, add the following:

```
fPController.GetComponent(CharacterMotor).enabled = false; // turn off navigation
fPController.GetComponent(FPAdventurerInputController).enabled = false; // turn off navigation
fPController.GetComponent(MouseLookRestricted).enabled = false; // turn off navigation
fPCamera.GetComponent(MouseLookRestricted).enabled = false;
```

4. In the MenuMode function, under the menuMode = false line, add the following:

```
fPController.GetComponent(CharacterMotor).enabled = true; // turn on navigation
fPController.GetComponent(FPAdventurerInputController).enabled = true; // turn on navigation
fPController.GetComponent(MouseLookRestricted).enabled = true; // turn on navigation
fPCamera.GetComponent(MouseLookRestricted).enabled = true;
```

5. Save the script.

6. Click Play and test.

Navigation is disabled, but mouse-overs and picks are still allowed. In the Interactor, you check for inventory mode, iMode. You will check for menuMode in the same way.

1. Open the Interactor script.

2. Add the menuMode variable:

```
private var menuMode : boolean; // menu mode flag
```

3. In the OnMouseEnter function, below the if (processing) return line, add the following:

```
menuMode = controlCenter.GetComponent(MenuManager).menuMode; // check for active menus
if (menuMode) return;
```

4. In the OnMouseDown function, below the if (processing) return line, add the following:

```
if (menuMode) return;
```

5. Save the script.

6. Click.

7. Play and test.

Mouse-over and picks are disabled when the menus are up.

Real-Time Backgrounds

Along with the 2D GUI, you have the option of using part of your dynamic 3D scene as the background of your menus. Currently, you are using the current player's view of the scene when you bring up the menus. This is a good choice for the easy-access mini-menu, but if the player commits to one of the sub-menus, it would be nice to have a different view.

To this end, you will provide the option to use a specified camera as the background image for some of your menus. You will create an array to hold the various cameras and then specify which to use by its element number. You will need an array to hold the different cameras and a single variable to hold the current choice.

In some levels, you may not want to use a 3D background at all. In that case, you will create an array of images that can be used for various levels as well. Most importantly, each menu needs to know *which camera view or which 2D texture to use on the basis of which level* you are in.

1. Open the GameNotes text asset.

2. Add the following:

```
Menu Backgrounds:
Menu backgrounds can be 2D or 3D
The menuCameras and menuBackgrounds arrays hold the available assets
For cameras, element 0 is the default player or main camera
For texture backgrounds, a plain black texture is default, element 0, background 100
If a menu ever uses more than the default main camera, it must have an array containing↵
 the assignments for each level by element number
Level 0 = Start menu
Level 1 = MainLevel
Level 3 = FinalLevel
Texture backgrounds will be the texture's element number + 100
Example: the array for the settings menu might look as follows: (0,2,101),
where in the mainLevel, it uses the camera in element 2 of the menuCameras array and in the
FinalLevel, it uses the texture in element 1 of the menuBackgrounds array
```

3. Save the text asset.

4. Open the MenuManager script.

5. Create the following variables:

```
 //background handling
var menuCameras : Camera[];
var menuBackgrounds : Texture[];//var backgroundImage : GameObject;private var menuCamera↵
 = 0; // the Camera for the current menu
private var menuBackground : int; // the current  background texture
private var overRide = false; // emergency override if cam change is bad idea
```

6. Save the script.

7. Turn off Play mode.

8. Add a new Layer to the project, and name it Menus.

By adding a layer that will be seen *only* by your menu cameras, you will be able to add objects that cannot be seen in the regular scene to dress up the menu backgrounds.

1. Select the Control Center object.

2. In the Inspector, set the Menu Cameras array Size to **3**.

3. Drag the Main Camera into the Element **0** field.

4. Change the Game view from Free Aspect to StandAlone so the aspect ratio is the same as the game will be.

5. Travel around the scene, and choose a nice vista for one of the sub-menus.

6. Select the Main Camera, and use Align View to Selected to get the same view in the Scene window.

7. Stop Play mode.

8. Create a new Camera.

9. Use Align with View to get the shot you wanted.

10. Name it to match the vista.

11. Set its Culling Mask to Default and Menus.

■ **Tip** If you have added a Lightmapped layer, you may need to add that to the new camera as well.

---

12. Set its Depth to 5 so it will be drawn on top of all other cameras.

13. Remove its Audio Listener component.

14. Click Play.

The new Camera is drawn on top of the main camera.

15. Bring up the menus.

Because they are on a GUI Layer, they are drawn over the new camera.

16. Turn off the new camera's Camera component.

The main Camera takes over once again.

17. Repeat to create one more menu camera.

18. Turn their Camera components off.

Assign your two new cameras to the camera array you made for the MenuManager.

1. Select the Control Center object.

2. Drag the two new cameras into elements 1 and 2.

3. Save the scene, and save the project.

While you are there, assign a couple of textures as well.

1. Set the array Size to 2.

2. Select the Black texture for Element 0.

3. Select TizzleblatScreen for Element 1.

4. Save the scene, and save the project.

The main menu and credits menu now show a different location or image instead of the current player position, see Figure 16-11.

Figure 16-11. *Custom camera and custom image for menu backgrounds*

Start Menu/Level

Before you can make the background assignments, you need a start screen as your first menu/level or your array elements will be off.

1. From the File menu, create a New Scene.

2. Save it as StartScene.

3. From the File menu, add it to Build Settings with Add Current.

4. Move it up so it becomes level 0 (see Figure 16-12).

Figure 16-12. *StartScene in Build Settings, as Level 0*

5. Close the Build Settings dialog.

6. Drag the StartScene prefab into the Hierarchy view.

7. Focus in on the new objects in the Scene window.

8. Select the camera, and use Align with View to get a preliminary view (see Figure 16-13).

9. Fix the materials on the stele if necessary.

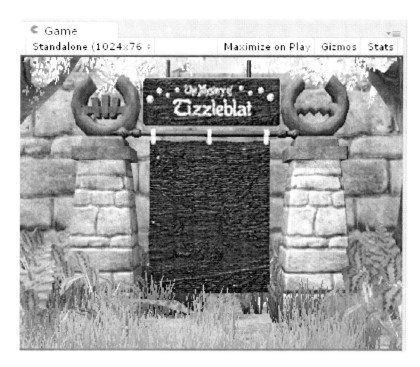

Figure 16-13. *The StartScene prefab*

You will return to set up the menu in the StartScene level later.

10. Save the scene, and save the project.

11. Open the MainLevel.

Now that you have your level numbers finalized, you can make the background assignments for the menus that need them. You will specify custom backgrounds for the MainMenu, the Settings menu, and the Credits menu. The arrays hold information for levels 0, 1 and 2.

1. Open the MenuManager script.

2. Add the following variables:

```
// Menu background assignments, 0= default cam, 100 = default texture
// numbers less than 100 are cameras, more than 100 are texture (element + 100)
private var mainMenuBG = Array(0,1,100);
private var settingsMenuBG = Array (0,2,100);
private var creditsMenuBG = Array (0,101,0);

private var level = 0; // will tell us which element to use
```

You will find out the level number in the Start function.

3. Add the following to the Start function:

```
level = Application.loadedLevel; // get the current level's id
```

Because you are not carrying anything from level to level via a DontDestroyOnLoad command, the MenuManager in the FinalLevel will identify itself as level 2 in its Start function when the level is loaded.

4. Save the script.

Managing the Backgrounds

You will need a function to manage the backgrounds. As a bit of housekeeping, you will also want to turn off the pointer and maze cameras. Additionally, you need to prevent the maze camera from being toggled on when in menu mode. Take care of these side issues before you write the background handler.

1. Open the MenuManager script.

2. In the MenuMode function, under the menuMode = true line, add the following:

```
// handle other cameras
GameObject.Find("Camera Pointer").GetComponent(Camera).enabled = false;
if (level == 1) GameObject.Find("Camera MazeView").GetComponent(Camera).enabled = false;
```
Note the conditional to check for the level before looking up the maze camera. In the FinalLevel, it does not exist, so you would get an error here.

▧ **Caution**   When accessing objects from generic scripts that may not exist in all levels using the script, be sure to add a level check to avoid errors.

When you leave menu mode, you need only to turn the Camera Pointer back on.

3. In the MenuMode function, under the menuMode = false line, add the following:

```
GameObject.Find("Camera Pointer").GetComponent(Camera).enabled = true;
```

4. Save the script.

You also need to tell the maze cam not to toggle on if you are in menu mode.

5. Open the ToggleMiniMap script.

6. Change the Update function as follows:

```
function Update () {
    if (Input.GetKeyDown("m")) { // check for m keyboard keypress
        if (gameObject.Find("Control Center").GetComponent(MenuManager).menuMode) return;
        if(camera.enabled == false) camera.enabled = true;
        else camera.enabled = false;
    }
}
```

7. Save the script.

8. Click Play and test.

The scene is much better behaved.

Start the background manager function now. It will need to turn 2D and 3D backgrounds off or on depending on the message you send to it. You already know that if the number passed to it is greater than 99, you are passing a texture. You can expand your numbering system further. When you pass it a -1, it will mean you have gone out of menu mode and to turn off the current menu camera or background image.

Rather than fussing with yet another GUI Style and GUI Box for your menu's background, you will just create a GUI Texture to hold an image for any of the menus you choose a 2D rather an a 3D background for. Since the scripted GUI Elements are always drawn on top of everything else, it makes it an easy choice. You will control visibility and texture through its GUI Texture properties.

1. Create a new GUI Texture object.

2. Name it MenuBackground.

3. Set its X, Y, and Z Positions to **0**.

4. For its Pixel Inset, set its Width to **1024** and its Height to **768**.

5. Deactivate its GUITexture component.

You should make sure it is off at startup.

1. Open the `MenuManager` script.

2. Uncomment the `//var backgroundImage : GameObject` line in the `//background handling` section.

3. Add the following line to the `Start` function, above the `level = Application.loadedLevel` line:

```
backgroundImage.guiTexture.enabled = false; // turn off the background texture
```

And now you are ready to create the function to control your various backgrounds.

1. Add the following function to manage the menu backgrounds:

```
function Background (newBG : int) {

  //menu mode is finished
  if (newBG == -1) {
      //turn off current camera unless it was 0, the main camera if it one was on
      if (menuCamera > 0) menuCameras[menuCamera].enabled = false;
      backgroundImage.guiTexture.enabled = false; // turn off the background texture
  }

//emergency override of cameras
  if (overRide) {
      menuBackground = 0;
      return;
  }

  // is a 3D background
  if (newBG >= 0 && newBG <100) {
      //turn off current camera unless it was 0, the main camera if it one was on
      if (menuCamera > 0) menuCameras[menuCamera].enabled = false;
      backgroundImage.guiTexture.enabled = false; // turn off the texture
```

```
    //turn on new camera
    menuCameras[newBG].enabled = true;
    menuCamera = newBG; // assign the new camera number
}

//is a 2D background
if (newBG > 99) {
    //turn off current camera unless it was 0, the main camera if it one was on
    if (menuCamera > 0) menuCameras[menuCamera].enabled = false;
  // assign the texture using the true element number and activate the background
  menuBackground = newBG;
  backgroundImage.guiTexture.texture = menuBackgrounds[menuBackground-100];
  backgroundImage.guiTexture.enabled = true;
  }

}// end background function
```

To make use of the new code, you will need to call the Background function for the menus that can use a background.

2. In the miniMenu section of the OnGUI function, insert the call to the Background function in the Main Menu button conditional:

```
if (GUI.Button (buttnRectTemp, "Main Menu")) {
    // go to main menu
    miniMenu = false;
    Background(mainMenuBG[level]); // custom background
    mainMenu= true;
}
```

3. Insert the call to the Background function in the Settings button conditional:

```
if (GUI.Button (buttnRectTemp, "Settings")) {
    // go to settings menu
    miniMenu = false;
    Background(settingsMenuBG[level]); // custom background
    settingsMenu = true;
}
```

4. In the mainMenu section, insert the call to the Background function in the Settings button conditional :

```
if (GUI.Button (buttnRectTemp, "Settings")) {
    // go to settings menu
    mainMenu = false;
    Background(settingsMenuBG[level]); // custom background
    settingsMenu = true;
}
```

5. Insert the call to the Background function in the Credits button conditional:

```
if (GUI.Button (buttnRectTemp, "Credits")) {
    // go to settings menu
    mainMenu = false;
    Background(creditsMenuBG[level]); // custom background
```

```
    creditsScreen = true;
}
```

6. In the Settings function, insert the call to the Background function in the Main Menu button conditional:

```
if (GUI.Button (Rect (20,440,150,30), "Main Menu")) {
    // turn off the menu
    settingsMenu = false;
    Background(mainMenuBG[level]); // custom background
    mainMenu = true;
}
```

7. Save the script.

8. Select the Control Center object, and drag the MenuBackground object into its Background Image parameter.

9. Click Play, and test the menus,

Now you need to turn off the background any time you exit menuMode. Since your Background function is already set up to take care of that when you pass it a -1, it is an easy addition to the MenuMode function.

10. In the MenuMode function's else clause, add the following line after the GameObject.Find("Camera Pointer").GetComponent(Camera).enabled = true line:

```
Background(-1); // turn off the background
```

11. Save the script.

Everything works well until you try to access a menu from inside the temple. The menus that use scene locations are missing the terrain, since you relocated it when you entered the temple. This will be a perfect time to use the emergency overRide.

You move the terrain in the TerrainManager script so it will be fairly straightforward to have it turn the override variable off and on.

1. Open the TerrainManager script.

2. Add the following to the if(showTerrain) section:

```
GameObject.Find("Control Center").GetComponent(MenuManager).overRide = false;
```

3. Add the following to the else section:

```
GameObject.Find("Control Center").GetComponent(MenuManager).overRide = true;
```

4. Save the script.

While you are there, it might be nice to turn off the ambient sounds (chirping birds) while you are inside the temple. You could turn off all ambient sounds via their Ambient tag, but in some cases you may wish to add an ambient sound or two to the temple, so it is best in this case to specify the actual objects. Rather than hardcode the functionality into the TerrainManager script, you will have it call a function to enable or disable the sounds on another script in case you want to do the same elsewhere.

5. Add the following to the if(showTerrain) section:

```
this.SendMessage("Switcher", true); // turn on various sounds
```

6. Add the following to the else section:

```
this.SendMessage("Switcher", false); // turn off various sounds
```

The little function will turn the sounds in its array off and on. While it would be nice to fade them in and out, you have allowed your player to change the volumes so it would not be able to use animations to do the job.

1. Create a new script.

2. Name it SoundSwitch.

3. Add the following to it:

```
var outsideSounds : GameObject[]; // the sound prefabs we want to control

function Switcher (state : boolean) {
    for (var s in outsideSounds) {
        if(state) s.GetComponent(AudioSource).enabled = true;
        else s.GetComponent(AudioSource).enabled = false;
    }
}
```

4. Save the script.

5. Add it to the TriggerToggler prefab in the Adventure Prefabs folder.

For each of the Trigger Toggler objects in the temple, do the following:

6. Set the Outside Sounds array Size to 1.

7. Drag the Ambient Jungle object into its Element 0.

8. Feel free to add any other sound-related prefabs you have created into the array.

9. Save the scene, and save the project.

With the menus sorted out, you can take care of one last related task. You need to get the cursor back on top of the controls. To do this, rather than add the contents of the MenuManager to the GameManager, you will change the order of the components.

Since there is no obvious way to re-arrange the order of the components, you will need to write down a few of your customizations before you remove the existing GameManager script.

1. Select the Control Center object.

2. Add a new GameManager script.

3. Copy the settings you need from the original Game Manager component onto the new one.

4. Delete the original Game Manager component.

5. Save the scene, and save the project.

6. Click Play, and test the menus.

The cursor is back on top as it should be.

Changing Levels

If you have played all the way through the game lately, you will have noticed another related problem. The Control Center in the FinalLevel does not have your MenuManager script. If you add it, you are back to the problem of the pointer not being on top. Since you have just finished fixing your Control Center object, you may as well create a prefab of it and replace the current one in the FinalScene.

1. Create a new Prefab.

2. Name it Control Center.

3. Drag the existing Control Center object onto it from the Hierarchy view.

4. Save the scene, and save the project.

5. Create a prefab for the MenuBackground object as well.

▓ **Tip** Be very careful about naming when making prefabs that are accessed by name, e.g., GameObject.Find("Control Center").

You will still need to make a few changes, but it also makes it easier to add it to additional levels.

1. Load the FinalLevel scene.

2. Delete the existing Control Center object from the Hierarchy view.

3. Drag the prefab version of it into the Hierarchy view.

4. Set the Menu Camera and Menu Background array Sizes to **1**.

5. Load the Main Camera and Black texture into them.

6. Open the MenuManager script.

7. Check the element 2 values for the mainMenuBG, settingsMenuBG, and creditsMenuBG arrays to make sure they are valid for the FinalLevel.

8. Drag the MenuBackground prefab into the scene.

9. Select the Control Center.

10. Drag the MenuBackground into the Background Image field of the MenuManager component.

11. Save the scene, and save the project.

Save/Restore

Saving games can be quite involved, depending on platform and purpose. Once again your classic adventure game will prove to be a good place to start. Generally, the quality of the graphics and scene assets in general will suggest that the game be downloaded and played from the desktop as opposed to hosting it through a web browser. This bypasses the need to worry about saving to remote servers and all that entails. You will save your game in the same directory the application is being run from.

The next consideration is how and in what format to save the data. As usual, there are many options, with different pros and cons. A nice feature of adventure-type games is that the saved games need not be secure against the player breaking in and changing values. Unlike a first-person shooter, where the player is amassing points toward bragging rights, your player is more concerned with seeing and experiencing everything the game has to offer while he pits his intellect and powers of observation and problem solving against the game's end goal. He is more likely to go online to find vague hints when he is stuck and tries not to learn any more than he has to so as to move forward in the game. With this in mind, you will write your saved values out to a simple text file, giving the file a cryptic name and extension if you feel it is necessary.

The means of saving the data is another topic. While serious coders may use special classes to serialize and save their data in its native format, you will stick with simple text strings and convert when necessary on save and load.

With a couple of exceptions, the data you need to save is already ready for you. You have an array of Action Objects that you can parse to get the current states. The states are simple integer values. Your player's settings from the menus are already nicely organized in an array you can access from the GameManager as well.

This leaves you with current level, player location and orientation, and a couple of miscellaneous states, such as the temple bouncer, to organize.

Start by testing read/write functionality. You call the save and load functions from the MenuManager, but if you use SendMessage, it will allow you to keep the two functions on their own script.

1. Open the MainLevel scene.

2. Create a new script.

3. Name it SaveLoad, and open it in the editor.

4. Delete the Update function, and add the following code:

```
import System.IO;
private var filePath : String;
private var filename= "SavedGame";
private var extension = ".txt";


function Start () {

    filePath = Application.dataPath + "/";

    print (filePath + filename+ extension);

}
```

5. Save the script.

The SystemIO gives you access to functions and variable types specific to the system's input and output. As usual, you need to specify a path, along with a name for your file. `Application.dataPath` returns the path that is being used by your project while you are authoring and the application's data folder after you have published the game. In case you are not sure where this path is, you will have the `Start` function print it out to the console as soon as it gets it.

1. Create an empty GameObject.

2. Name it SystemIO.

3. Drag the new SaveLoad script onto it.

4. Save the scene, and save the project.

5. Click Play.

The console reports the path and name of the file you will be creating.

6. Add the following to write (and create if it does not yet exist) your text file:

```
function WriteFile(fileName : String) {

    var sWrite: StreamWriter = new StreamWriter(filePath + filename + extension);
    sWrite.WriteLine("This is a test");
    sWrite.WriteLine("We are in level " + Application.loadedLevel);
    sWrite.WriteLine("This will be some data");
    sWrite.Flush();
    sWrite.Close();
}
```

In your game, you will be saving and loading only one file, but breaking the path, file name, and extension apart allows for easy modification if you wanted to increment save games by appending the name with sequential numbers or allow the players to name the files themselves.

7. Save the script.

Call the function from the `MenuManager`.

1. Open the `MenuManager` script.

2. In the `SaveGame` function, above the `yield` line, add the following:

```
GameObject.Find("SystemIO").SendMessage( "WriteFile", "MyNewSavedGame");
```

`SendMessage` passes the name of the file as an argument to the `WriteFile` function in the `SystemIO` object's `LoadSave` function.

3. Save the script.

4. Click Play.

5. Open the mini-menu, and click the Save button.

6. Find and open the newly created text file from the location shown in the console.

7. Close the text file after you check it.

The contents of the file are exactly as you specified.

It is always useful to know if the game is actually saving—especially if the file is small and the save is fast. Create another GUI element to let your player know what is happening.

1. In the SaveGame function, change the yield line as follows:

```
saving = true;
yield new WaitForSeconds(2);
saving = false;
```

2. Delete or comment out the print ("saving") line.

3. Add the new variable to the script:

```
private var saving = false; // flag for message for save function
```

4. And just above the closing curly bracket for the OnGui function line, add the following:

```
    // saving message
if (saving) GUI.Label( Rect (20,20,250,100), "Saving game");
```

5. Save the script.

6. Open the LoadSave script.

7. Change some of the text to make sure the file is updated the next time you save.

8. Save the script.

9. Click Play.

10. Open the mini-menu, and click the Save button.

11. Look for the saving message in the upper left corner of the screen.

12. Open the text file again to make sure it has updated the content.

13. Close the text file after you check it.

The save function is working nicely—it creates a text file if one does not exist and updates it if it already exists. Let's see about reading content back out of the file.

1. Open the LoadSave script.

2. Add the following function:

```
function ReadFile(fileName : String) {

    var sRead = new File.OpenText(filePath + fileName + extension);

    var input = ""; //
    while (true) {
            input = sRead.ReadLine();
            if (input == null) break;
            print ("Content: "+ input);
    }
    sRead.Close();
```

```
}
```

3. Save the file.

The `ReadFile` function is a bit more cryptic. It reads in lines of data until the input variable comes back as `null` or empty, then breaks out of the `while` loop. Because it checks for `null`, the input variable must be initialized as `""`, which is a string with no characters, as opposed to a `null` value.

Call the function from `MenuManager`.

1. Open the `MenuManager` script.

2. In the `LoadGame` function, replace the `print ("loading")` line with the following:

```
GameObject.Find("SystemIO").SendMessage( "ReadFile", "SavedGame");
```

3. Delete the `yield` line.

4. Save the file.

5. Click Play.

6. Open the mini-menu, go to the Main Menu, and click Load Game.

7. Open the console to see the content that was printed from the text file.

8. Open the `LoadSave` script.

9. For fun, change the extension name to `.gme`.

10. Change the content of the first line to a float number:

```
sWrite.WriteLine( 1.05);
```

11. Save the script.

12. Click Play, and save and load the game.

13. Check the console.

The new extension was handled the same as the original `.txt` extension, and the float number was automatically converted to a string when written to the text file.

Saving the Game Data

When organizing the game data, you will be relying on the order of the data when you read it back in after it has been saved. For that reason, you will save the Action Object data last, as it could vary according to level.

1. Open the `LoadSave` script.

2. Delete the three `sWrite.WriteLine` lines and replace them with the following:

```
// level
var level = Application.loadedLevel;
sWrite.WriteLine(level);

//First Person Controller transforms
```

```
var fpc = GameObject.Find("First Person Controller");
sWrite.WriteLine(fpc.transform.position.x);
sWrite.WriteLine(fpc.transform.position.y);
sWrite.WriteLine(fpc.transform.position.z);
// saving rotation as localEulerAngles to match inspector
sWrite.WriteLine(fpc.transform.localEulerAngles.y);

//Player Settings
var ps = GameObject.Find("Control Center").GetComponent(GameManager).playerSettings;
sWrite.WriteLine(ps[0]); //walkSpeed
sWrite.WriteLine(ps[1]); //turnSpeed
sWrite.WriteLine(ps[2]); // useText
sWrite.WriteLine(ps[3]); //objectDescriptions
sWrite.WriteLine(ps[4]); //fXVolume
sWrite.WriteLine(ps[5]); //ambVolume
sWrite.WriteLine(ps[6]); //musicVolume
sWrite.WriteLine(ps[7]); // voiceVolume
sWrite.WriteLine(ps[8]); //useMOCursor
var c = ps[9]; // mouse over color
sWrite.WriteLine(c[0]); //  moColor r
sWrite.WriteLine(c[1]); //  moColor g
sWrite.WriteLine(c[2]); //  moColor b
sWrite.WriteLine(c[3]); //  moColor a
sWrite.WriteLine(ps[10]); //  cursorColorChange/slider value
```

```
//Action Objects- get the list generated by the GameManager on Awake
var ao = GameObject.Find("Control Center").GetComponent(GameManager).actionObjects;
```

Before you load in the action objects, you need to think about how you are going to get the current state of the action objects that are temporarily disabled. You will need to identify the objects via the array, check to see if they are active, save the current state or activate, save the state, and then deactivate the object.

3. Add the following:

```
for (var x =0; x < ao.length; x++) { // iterate through the array of action objects
   // save its current state
   if (ao[x].active == true) sWrite.WriteLine(ao[x]. currentState);
   else { // if inactive, wake it up long enough to save its current state
      ao[x].active = true; // activate it
      sWrite.WriteLine(ao[x]. currentState);
      ao[x].active = false; // deactivate it
   }
   // if it is an object that can be moved, store its current location/orientation
   if (ao[x].dropType == 1) {
    sWrite.WriteLine(ao[x].transform.position.x);
    sWrite.WriteLine(ao[x].transform.position.y);
    sWrite.WriteLine(ao[x].transform.position.z);
    sWrite.WriteLine(ao[x].transform.localEulerAngles.x);
    sWrite.WriteLine(ao[x].transform.localEulerAngles.y);
    sWrite.WriteLine(ao[x].transform.localEulerAngles.z);
   }
}
```

You will need to catch a few miscellaneous objects that are not covered as action objects. These objects will not have standardized state variables, so you will create a GenericStateTracker script to hold the generic state variable and a LoadState function that can be customized for each. By using SendMessage, you can put the function on any script on the object and have it update the state variable on the script. To identify the objects, you will search for the GenericStateTracker script. You will assume these objects will not be disabled.

4. Add the following:

```
//Misc object states - check for Misc tag
var mos = GameObject.FindObjectsOfType(GenericStateTracker);
for (var mo in mos) {
        mo.SendMessage("UpdateStateVar");
        sWrite.WriteLine(mo.GetComponent(GenericStateTracker).state);
}
```

5. Save the script.

Because you have just set a new convention, you will need to open the GameNotes text asset and update it.

1. Open the GameNotes text asset.

2. Add the following:

```
Non-Action Objects with states:
Objects whose states need to be tracked for load/save must have the GenericStateTracker script
The object must contain a function called "UpdateStateVar" that updates the object's current↵
 state into the GenericStateTracker
The object must contain a function named "LoadState" that receives the new state as an↵
 argument and processes the object and its dependencies appropriately
The LoadState function may be in any of its scripts
```

3. Save the GameNotes text asset.

Create the GenericStateTracker script.

1. Create a new script.

2. Name it GenericStateTracker.

3. It needs to contain one line:

```
private var state = 0; // var to hold the state of the object for saving
```

4. Save the script.

Since the Temple Bouncer qualifies as an object whose state needs tracking, you will set it up now.

1. Drag the GenericStateTracker script onto it.

2. Open its BouncerManager script.

3. Add the following function:

```
function UpdateStateVar () {

    //send the object's state value to the GenericStateTracker script
```

```
    GetComponent(GenericStateTracker).currentState = templeState;

}
```
For `LoadState`, if you search the script for `templeState`, you see that it has only two states: 0, its default on startup, and 1, after the offering has been accepted. If its saved state is 0, you can just return from the function. If it is 1, any action objects involved have already been processed, so you need only to take care of the remainder of the tasks in the `ProcessOffering` function.

4.   Add the following function:

```
function LoadState (newState : int) {

    if(newState > 0) {
        gameObject.Find("TempleBlocker").active = false; //disable the blocker
        gameObject.Find("FX Range").SendMessage("KillEffect");
        gameObject.Find("FX Range").active = false; //disable the fx checker
    }
    else return;
}
```

5.   Save the script.

6.   Click Play, and do a few things in the scene.

7.   Save the game, and open the text file to see how everything is saved.

Before you go as far as checking the FinalLevel game saves, you will need to add the SystemIO to that scene.

1.   Create a new prefab.

2.   Name it SystemIO, and drop the original SystemIO onto it.

3.   Save the scene, and save the project.

4.   Open the FinalLevel.

5.   Drag the SystemIO prefab into the Hierarchy view.

6.   Save the scene.

7.   Click Play, and try saving the game.

8.   Open the text file, and check out the differences (see Figure 16-14).

```
2
5.709489
8.477639
0.951738
260.6933
10
20
True
True
1
0.8
0.2
1
True
0
1
0
1
1030
1
1
0
0
0
0
0
0
0
0
0
0
1
0
0
```

Figure 16-14. *Part of the text file with the saved data*

9. Save the scene, and save the project.

Loading the Saved Data

As you read the saved text file back into the scene, you will need to convert the data to the right type and re-assign it back to its original variables. Because you stored only the variable and not the object or variable type, you will have to be careful about keeping the read order exactly the same as the write order. Once again you will start with the level, as that will dictate some of the other processes.

1. Open the MainLevel scene.

2. Open the LoadSave script.

3. Beneath the var sRead = new File.OpenText(filePath + fileName + extension) line, add the following:

```
// level, if the level is different than the present level, load it
var level = parseInt( sRead.ReadLine());
if (level != Application.loadedLevel) Application.LoadLevel(level);
```
You can assign the transforms directly to the First Person Controller.

4. Process the First Person Controller transforms next:

```
// First Person Controller transforms
var fpc = GameObject.Find("First Person Controller");
fpc.transform.position.x  = parseFloat(sRead.ReadLine());
fpc.transform.position.y  = parseFloat(sRead.ReadLine());
fpc.transform.position.z  = parseFloat(sRead.ReadLine());
// using localEulerAngles to match saved rotation
fpc.transform.localEulerAngles.y  = parseFloat(sRead.ReadLine());
```
You are converting the strings from the text file to integers and floats with parseInt and parseFloat. You will also need to convert the True and False to Booleans once again. You will need to make a little function to do so. Note the capital P in parse since you are creating your own function.

5. Create the following function near the bottom of the script:

```
function ParseBool (value : String) {
    if (value  == "True") return true;
    else return false;
}
```
For the player settings, you will assign the settings into an array and then send the array off to both the MenuManager and GameManager scripts to be processed through their own functions.

6. Back in the ReadFile function, below the transforms section, add the following:

```
//player settings
var ps = Array();
ps[0] = parseFloat(sRead.ReadLine());//walkSpeed
ps[1] = parseFloat(sRead.ReadLine());//turnSpeed
ps[2] = ParseBool(sRead.ReadLine());// useText
ps[3] = ParseBool(sRead.ReadLine());//objectDescriptions
ps[4] = parseFloat(sRead.ReadLine());//fXVolume
ps[5] = parseFloat(sRead.ReadLine());//ambVolume
ps[6] = parseFloat(sRead.ReadLine());//musicVolume
ps[7] = parseFloat(sRead.ReadLine());// voiceVolume
ps[8] = ParseBool(sRead.ReadLine());//useMOCursor
// mouse over color
ps[9] = Array (sRead.ReadLine(),sRead.ReadLine(),sRead.ReadLine(),sRead.ReadLine());
ps[10] = parseFloat(sRead.ReadLine());//cursorColorChange
```

7. Save the script.

Now you need to read in the action objects and process them into their saved states. Once again you will need to get the list of action objects before you start processing them. For a quick test, you will reuse the ProcessObject function from the action object's Interactor script, and then assess the results.

8. Add the following:

```
//Process action objects- get the list generated by the GameManager on Awake
var ao = GameObject.Find("Control Center").GetComponent(GameManager).actionObjects;
for (var x =0; x < ao.length; x++) { // iterate through the array of action objects
   // process it into the save's state
   ao[x].active = true; // activate it
   ao[x].SendMessage("ProcessObject",parseInt(sRead.ReadLine()));
   // if it is an object that can be moved, restore its current location/orientation
   if (ao[x].dropType == 1) {
     ao[x].transform.position.x = parseFloat(sRead.ReadLine());
     ao[x].transform.position.y = parseFloat(sRead.ReadLine());
     ao[x].transform.position.z = parseFloat(sRead.ReadLine());
     ao[x].transform.localEulerAngles.x = parseFloat(sRead.ReadLine());
     ao[x].transform.localEulerAngles.y = parseFloat(sRead.ReadLine());
     ao[x].transform.localEulerAngles.z = parseFloat(sRead.ReadLine());
   }
}
```

9. Save the script.

10. Click Play.

11. Play through far enough to get the crowbar removed to the maze (note its location), and save the game in front of the stone chest with its lid open.

12. Start a new game.

13. Load the previous saved game.

A few things are apparent:

- The message appears briefly.

- The stone lid opens.

- You may be able to hear the sound effect of the flower reviving.

- The crowbar is safely at its saved location in the maze.

Tackle the message first. Most of the objects will not be in front of the camera when they are temporarily activated to change their state. Messages, books, or anything else you are placing in front of the player's face will show briefly. Fortunately, you have an easy solution. Since those objects have been assigned to the Camera Pointer layer, you can simply turn the camera off before reading in the data and off after you are finished.

1. Add the following line near the top of the ReadFile function:

```
gameObject.Find("Camera Pointer").camera.enabled = false;
```

2. Add the following line just above the closing curly bracket for the ReadFile function:

```
//allow processing time before reactivating the camera again
yield new WaitForSeconds (1);
gameObject.Find("Camera Pointer").camera.enabled = true;
```

3. Save the script.

4. Click Play and test.

The message no longer appears on load.

To solve the next two issues, you will want to skip the audio playback and tell the animation to skip to the end. An investigation of animation in the scripting reference shows you that `normalizedTime` will allow you to jump to the end of the animation when set to 1. You will need to reset the value after you have played the animation, of course.

Rather than recreating a stripped-down version of the `Interactor`'s `ProcessObject` function, you will just insert a couple of flags to alter its functionality when you are using it to load states.

1. In the `readFile` function, above the `ao[x].SendMessage("ProcessObject"` line, add the following:

```
ao[x].loading = true; // turn on the loading flag
```

2. Save the script.

3. Open the `Interactor` script.

4. Add the new variable to the `//Misc vars` section:

```
private var loading = false; // flag for alternate processing of object state
```

5. In the `ProcessObject` function, in the `//process audio` section, change the `if(currentSound)` to the following:

```
if(currentSound && !loading)  { // if there is a sound and the state is not being loaded
```

6. At the bottom of the `ProcessObject` function, just above its closing curly bracket, turn off the loading flag:

```
loading = false;
```

7. Save the script.

8. Click Play and test.

The sound effects of the flower reviving no longer play.

1. In the `if(animates` section, just below the `currentAnimationDelay = animationDelay[currentState]` line, add the following:

```
if (loading && aniObject != null) {
    // set the animate time to 0, play the animation, then set it back to normal
    aniObject.animation[currentAnimationClip.name].normalizedTime = 0.0;
    aniObject.animation.Play(currentAnimationClip.name);
    aniObject.animation[currentAnimationClip.name].normalizedTime = 1.0;
    if(postLoop) aniObject.animation.Play(loopAnimation[currentState].name);
}

else { // else it is not loading so process as usual
```

2. Close the `else` by adding a closing curly bracket, just above the closing curly bracket for the entire `if(animates` conditional:

```
    } // close if (aniObject != null)
  }// close else
} // close if(animates)
```

3. Save the script.

4. Click Play, and test by leaving a chest lid open, saving, closing it, and then loading; watch to make sure the lid opens instantly.

The final task for the loader is to handle the objects with the GenericStateTracker script.

1. Open the SaveLoad script.

2. In the ReadFile function, beneath the //Process action objects section, add the following:

```
// process generic state objects
var mos = GameObject.FindObjectsOfType(GenericStateTracker);
for (var mo in mos) {
   mo.SendMessage("LoadState",parseInt(sRead.ReadLine()));
}
```

And finally, you can delete the original code that read through the contents and printed them out to the console.

3. Delete the following from the ReadFile function:

```
var input = ""; //
while (true) {
   input = sRead.ReadLine();
   if (input == null) break;
   print ("Content: "+ input);
}
```

Make sure you leave the sRead.Close() line.

4. Save the script.

5. Click Play and test.

Tidy Up

Having finished your menu functionality, you can go back and tie up a few loose ends, the first of which is the credits at the end of the game. You could turn on the credits menu at the end of the game with the settingsMenu variable, but it would be more interesting to let them roll in as if you had a long list of people to credit.

1. Open the MenuManager script.

2. Add the following variables:

```
//moving menu
private var rollCredits = true;
private var vPos =  0.0;
private var base = 1000.0;
private var end = false;  //end sequence
```

3. In the OnGUI function, just below the GUI.skin = menuSkin line, add the following:

```
// ************* Roll Credits   ******************
```

```
if (rollCredits) {

    //Make a group on the center of the screen
   GUI.BeginGroup (Rect (Screen.width / 2 - 200 , vPos, 400, 600));

    GUI.Box (Rect (0,20,400,500), "The End");

    GUI.Label( Rect (20,40,200,100), "Credits listed here");

    // add labels here


    GUI.EndGroup ();
```

The rollCredits group is animated using `Mathf.SmoothStep`. The start position is 600, and 100 is the stop position. The speed is 1.0.

4. Add the following:

```
// update the credits menu position if time is not up
vPos =  Mathf.SmoothStep(800.0, 100.0, (Time.time - base)  *  0.05);

} // end roll credits
```

The base variable is what sets the timer starting. You need to initialize it to `Time.time` in the `Start` function to test it.

1. Add the following to the `Start` function:

```
base = Time.time;
```

2. Turn on Maximize on Play.

3. Save the script, and click Play.

The credits scroll up and slow to a stop.

4. Set the speed to **0.05** and restart.

5. Set the `rollCredits` variable to false.

6. Save the script.

7. Save the scene, and save the project.

Now you can change the variable and set the time when the final scene plays out.

1. Load the FinalLevel.

2. Open the `FinalTask` script.

3. At the top of the `DoTheJob` function, add the following:

```
GameObject.Find("Control Center").GetComponent(MenuManager).end = true;
GameObject.Find("Control Center").GetComponent(MenuManager).menuMode = true; //skips
Interactor
GameObject.Find("Control Center").GetComponent(GameManager).end = true;// cursor off
```

4. Add the following to the bottom of the DoTheJob function:

```
//roll credits
yield new WaitForSeconds(2);
GameObject.Find("Control Center").GetComponent(MenuManager).base = Time.time;
GameObject.Find("Control Center").GetComponent(MenuManager).rollCredits = true;
```

5. Save the script.

To prevent mouseovers and mouse picks once the end sequence has been initiated, you will use the menuMode flag. This will prevent the player from picking more topi fruit.

1. Open the Interactor script.

2. Add the following variable near the top of the script:

```
private var menuMode : boolean; // menu mode flag
```

3. In the OnMouseEnter function, below the if(processing) line, add the following:

```
menuMode = controlCenter.GetComponent(MenuManager).menuMode; // check for active menus
if (menuMode) return;
```

4. In the OnMouseDown function, below the if(processing) line, add the following:

```
if (menuMode) return;
```

5. Save the script.

To prevent any of the regular game GUI text from appearing once you are in the final sequence, you can use the end flag in the GameManager's OnGUI function. This also prevents the cursor from being drawn.

1. Open the GameManager script.

2. Add the following variable near the top of the script:

```
private var end : boolean; // menu mode flag
```

3. At the top of the OnGUI function, add the following:

```
if (end) return; // no more game gui needed;
```

4. Save the script.

You will also need to prevent the player from bringing up the mini-menu once the end sequence has been initiated. For that functionality you can add the rollCredits flag to the if(miniMenu) conditional.

5. Open the MenuManager script.

6. In the OnGUI function, change the if(miniMenu) line to the following:

```
// ****** mini menu *******,
if(miniMenu && !end) {
```

You should also prevent the menu from appearing if the player presses the Esc key to close the application at that point.

7. In the Update function, below the if (Input.GetKey ("escape") line, add the following:

```
if (end) Application.Quit();
```

8. Save the script.

9. Click Play.

10. Play through to the end.

The credits roll in on cue (see Figure 16-15).

Figure 16-15. *The final credits rolling in*

A bit of music might be nice at the end. You already have a line that calls an audio clip to play in the FinalTask script for a sound effect. Add another for some music.

The FinalTask script is on the main camera. You can easily add an Audio Source to it.

1. Open the FinalTask script.

2. Move the existing voiceSource.audio.Play() line so it is above the first yield.

3. Add an Audio Source component to the Main Camera.

4. Load the Temple music clip into it.

5. Uncheck Play On Awake.

6. Set the Volume down to about **0.1**.

7. Add the following below the animation.Play line:

```
//trigger the music clip
AudioSource.PlayClipAtPoint(music,Vector3(0,0,0),0.5);
```

8. And the following variable to the FinalTask script:

```
var music : AudioClip;
```

9. Select the Main Camera.

10. Drag the Point Trunk Blue onto the Voice Source parameter.

11. Load the Temple music into the Music parameter.

12. Save the script.

13. Click Play and test the end sequence.

Depending on where the player ends up after picking the fallen topi fruit, the final camera position may be less than optimal. By adding one last camera match and re-using the targets from a previous match you can make sure the final shot of the scene will be the same for everyone. Since the camera match contains its own data, it doesn't matter which object contains the data script. Let's put it on the Point Trunk Blue object since it will also be used as the look at target. It will be triggered when the player picks one of the fallen topi fruits.

1. Stop Play mode.

2. Select the Point Trunk Blue object.

3. Add the CameraMatchData script to it.

4. Load the TargetTrunkOpening into the Target Pos parameter.

5. Load the Point Trunk Blue into the Target Look parameter.

6. Set the Match Time to 3.

7. Select the Hanging Topi Fruit prefab in the Project view.

8. Change its Lookup State 0, Element 0 to the following:

```
default,1,Topi Fruit Icon,1,s1_Main Camera,0,s1_Point Trunk Blue,0
```

9. Click Play, and test the end sequence.

10. Adjust the Match Time on the Point Trunk Blue object until you are happy with the transition to the camera pull back animation.

11. Save the scene, and save the project.

Finally, Back to the Start

So far you have not tried your game from the very start. You briefly added a Start scene as a place holder, but have not yet added its GUI.

Once again, you need to list the contents:

- Game Title

- Instructions/Background Story

- New Game

- Load Game

- Quit

You will skip Settings, as they are in-game settings rather than general settings such as key mapping. The game title is already on the 3D geometry in the scene, so you will need three buttons and a couple of text labels.

1. Load the StartScene level.

2. Select the Main Camera.

3. Use Align View to Selected to see the scene in the Scene view.

4. Create a new script.

5. Name it StartMenu.

Your start menu GUI Skin will be similar to the regular game menu's skin, but you will drop the "button" look for your buttons.

6. Select the Boomerang font in the Project view.

7. Duplicate it, and name the copy Boomerang Lg.

8. Change its Font Size to **32**, and click Apply.

9. Select the Menu GUISkin from the Project view.

10. Duplicate it, and name the copy StartMenu GUISkin.

11. Change the font to Boomerang Lg.

12. Change the Button preset's Normal Background to the buttonShadow texture.

13. Change its Hover and Active Backgrounds to the buttonHighlight texture.

14. Change the Label preset's Normal Background to the buttonShadow texture.

15. Save the scene, and save the project.

If you were starting with an empty scene, the most logical object to hold the script is the Main Camera—the only object in the scene. While you do have objects from the prefab, you will add your menu script to the camera anyway.

1. Add the StartMenu script to the Main Camera.

2. Open the StartMenu script in the editor.

3. Add the following variables:

```
var startSkin : GUISkin; // custom skin for the start menu
var simpleText : GUIStyle; //simple font/style for navigation text
var hoverOver : GUIStyle; // override for manual mouseover on label
```

```
// misc menu text
private var introText = "Welcome to the Mystery of Tizzleblat...\n a simple world with↵
 a solvable problem.";



private var infoText = "Interactive objects- cursor changes color on mouseover, click to↵
 activate-objects can be combined in scene or in inventory\nInventory- i key or pick on↵
 icon at lower left to access\nMenu access, F1 or mouseover upper left corner of view ";
private var storyText = "Deep in the tropical forest of the equatorial realm, an ancient↵
 temple sits. It is said the priests of the early days hid a golden topi fruit against times↵
 of need. Should the tree of life fail it contains the seed to re-grow the precious tree.↵
 That time is now...";
private var navText = "Interactive objects- cursor changes color on mouseover, click to↵
 activate\nInventory- i key or pick on icon at lower left to access\nGeneral- objects can↵
 be combined in scene or in inventory ";
private var show = 1; //flag for which text to show- 1= story, 2 = info, 3 = navigation

private var groupWidth = 300;  // width of the group
private var buttnRect  = Rect (0,0,140,50); // default button size, x,y location, width↵
 and height
```

4. Block in the OnGUI function as follows:

```
function OnGUI () {

GUI.skin = startSkin;

  //alternate text here

  // Make a group on the center of the screen
  GUI.BeginGroup (Rect (Screen.width / 2 - 150, Screen.height  / 2 - 210, 300, 500));
  // all rectangles are now adjusted to the group
  // (0,0) is the top left corner of the group


  // make a box so we can see where the group is on-screen.
  GUI.Box (Rect (0,60,300,350), "");

 // control elements
  //this is a local variable that gets changed after each button is added
  buttnRectTemp = Rect (groupWidth/2 - buttnRect.width/2,40,buttnRect.width,buttnRect↵
.height);

  //Game Intro
  GUI.Label( Rect (20,40,250,100), introText);
```
As you have quite a bit of text to display, you need to make a decision about how you will manage it. Rather than create new menus, since your story, info, and navigation instructions are all about the same length, you will show the story text as default and then swap it out for the other text on mouse-over. The show flag will tell the OnGUI which text to display. As you did with the navigation instructions in the main menu, you also need an override for the style for a smaller, easier-to-read text, simpleText.

5.   Add the following:

```
//background story
if(show == 1) GUI.Label( Rect (15,130,280,140), storyText,simpleText);

//Navigation Instructions
if (show == 2) GUI.Label( Rect (15,130, 280,140), infoText,simpleText);

//Navigation Instructions
if (show == 3) GUI.Label( Rect (15,130, 280,140), navText,simpleText);
```
Your three buttons are fairly easy to set up, so you will leave that section to be filled in later.

6.   Add the following:

```
//Content goes here



// End the main menu group we started above. This is very important to remember!
GUI.EndGroup ();

} // end the OnGui function
```

7.   Save the script.

8.   Select the Main Camera.

9.   Drag the StartMenu GUISkin onto the Start Skin parameter in the Inspector.

The Simple Text style parameters need to be filled out next.

10.   Change the Simple Text, Normal Text Color to the R, **255**, G, **193**, B, **53** gold.

11.   Change the Font to Arial.

12.   Check Word Wrap.

13.   Set the Alignment to UpperLeft.

14.   Set the Font Size to **13** and the Font Style to Italic.

15.   Save the scene.

Before you add the buttons, you need to consider a rather important issue. For the New Scene button functionality, you can simply use LoadLevel to load the MainLevel. The problem comes when you need to load the stored game. Besides the LoadSave script, it would need the entire Control Center object to handle the settings. If it had the Control Center, a lot of functionality would start throwing errors because of a myriad of missing scripts and objects. The solution will be to send a flag to the MainLevel to open the saved game on startup. The problem with that, of course, is that it does not yet exist.

Enter the DontDestroyOnLoad function. This function prevents the object it resides on, and all of its children, from being destroyed when a new level or scene is loaded. You will use it to receive the flag for loading a saved scene and then pass it on when the MainLevel loads. The DontDestroyOnLoad function is usually added to the Awake function.

1.   Create a new script.

    2.   Name it `PreLoader`.

    3.   Create an empty GameObject.

    4.   Name it Starter.

    5.   Apply the `PreLoader` script to the Starter object.

    6.   Open the script in the editor.

    7.   Add the following:

```
function Awake () {

    DontDestroyOnLoad (transform.gameObject);

}
```

Next you need a little function to process the code. You cannot put it in a `Start` function because the script was started with StartScene and already exists when the MainLevel is being loaded. It will get called right before the new scene is loaded, which is too early to access any scripts or data, so you need to add a `yield` statement to delay it slightly.

    1.   Add the following function:

```
function ProcessLoad () {

    yield new WaitForSeconds(0.2); //make sure everything is loaded

    GameObject.Find("SystemIO").SendMessage( "ReadFile", "SavedGame");

}
```

    2.   Save the script.

    3.   Create a new empty GameObject.

    4.   Name it Starter.

    5.   Drag the `PreLoader` script onto it.

With the logic taken care of, you can add the button code to the `StartMenu` script.

    1.   Open the `StartMenu` script.

    2.   Add the following below the `//Content goes here` section:

```
// start the buttons down a bit to avoid overlapping
buttnRectTemp.y += 200;

if (GUI.Button (buttnRectTemp, "New Game")) {
    // Start the Main Level
     Application.LoadLevel("MainLevel");
}

// move the next control down a bit to avoid overlapping
buttnRectTemp.y += 50;
```

Next, the Load Game button initiates the game loading process right before loading the main level.

3. Add the following:

```
if (GUI.Button (buttnRectTemp, "Load Game")) {
  // load the previous game
    starter.SendMessage("ProcessLoad"); // start the loading process
    Application.LoadLevel("MainLevel");
}
```

4. Add the following variable to the top of the script to identify the object:

```
var starter : GameObject;
```

5. Save the script.

6. Select the Main Camera in the Hierarchy view.

7. Drag the Starter object into the Starter parameter in the Inspector.

8. Back in the StartMenu script, add the following below the load game section:

```
// move the next control down a bit to avoid overlapping
buttnRectTemp.y += 50;

if (GUI.Button (buttnRectTemp, "Quit")) {
    // turn off the game
    Application.Quit();
}
```

9. Save the script.

10. Save the scene, and save the project.

11. Click Play.

Unless you get extremely lucky when you set up the preliminary camera position, you can see you will need to fine-tune its transforms to get it to match up with your 2D GUI. Since it needs to be in Maximize on Play, you could tweak for hours to get it right. The camera's Field of View needs to be adjusted before you can even start.

12. Select the Main Camera.

13. Set its Field of View to 36.

14. Set its X, Y, and Z Positions to **84**, **9.88**, and **133.4**, respectively.

15. Set its X, Y, and Z Rotations to **0**, **180**, and **0**, respectively.

16. Save the scene, and save the project.

17. Click Play, and test the buttons.

The text handling functionality presents you with a conundrum. Your aim is to swap out the text on a mouse-over. The problem is that the UnityGUI system does not provide for capturing mouse-over events. Mouse-over text and background changes are handled internally, so you have no way of adding extra functionality, including sound effects, if you want something else to be triggered. Coupled with the fact that UnityGUI elements are not caught in GUI ray casting, you will need to come up with a different means of invoking your text change.

You could resort to using GUI Text and Texture objects, but then the positioning uses a different coordinate system and the look might be different as well. A third option, available to you because you do not allow user scene navigation in the menu, is to check for mouse-over on 3D objects' colliders. This will allow you to use the UnityGUI elements and still get a mouse-over event to process.

It would be easy if you could use the Button control, as it has built-in functionality to change the text and texture. Unfortunately, it also blocks mouse-over inside the 3D scene. The control that does not "block" the 3D scene is the Label. It, unfortunately, does not change text or background on mouse-over. Nor does it allow for overwriting its texture if you wish to use text. You can, however, use an override *style* to fake your mouse-over "button" change. It means one more style to fill out in the Inspector, but the rest of the work is fairly simple to get your desired effect.

Fill out the Hover Over style in the Inspector as follows:

1. Turn off Play mode.

2. Select the Main Camera object.

3. Set the Normal Background to the buttonHighlight texture.

4. Set the Text Color to your blue/green, **0, 255, 180**.

5. Set the Font to BOOMERAN.

6. Set Alignment to MiddleCenter.

7. Set FontSize to **34**.

8. Back in the StartMenu script, in the OnGUI function, under the //alternate text here section, add the following:

```
//Game Intructions
if (show == 2) GUI.Label( Rect (Screen.width / 2 - 390 ,218,160,60),↵
"Instructions",hoverOver);
else GUI.Label( Rect (Screen.width / 2 - 390 ,218,160,60), "Instructions");

//Game Navigation
if (show == 3) GUI.Label( Rect (Screen.width / 2 +215,218,160,60), "Navigation",hoverOver);
else GUI.Label( Rect (Screen.width / 2 +215,218,160,60), "Navigation");
```

9. Save the script.

10. Click Play.

The two new labels should be positioned over the capstones of the two steles (see Figure 16-16).

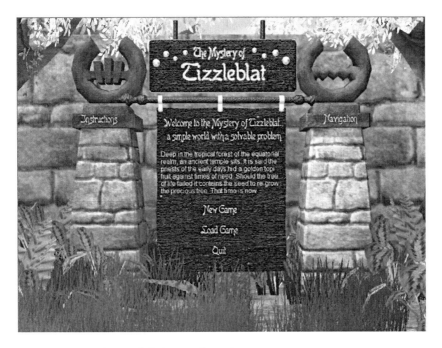

Figure 16-16. *The new labels over the stele*

As long as you are writing in code for the mouse-over event, you may as well add a small sound effect.

1. Select the Main Camera.

2. Add an Audio Source component to it.

3. Load the Tick sound clip into it.

4. Reduce the Volume to make it subtle.

5. Uncheck Play On Awake.

The StartScene prefab already has colliders in place on the stele to receive the mouse-overs (see Figure 16-17), so you now need to make a script that will send back the correct value to the show variable.

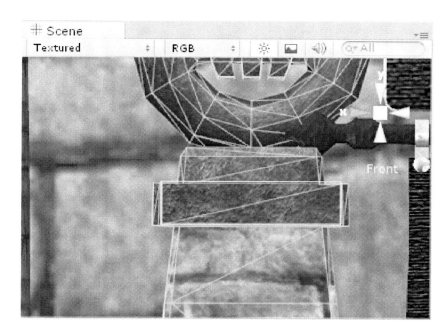

Figure 16-17. *The stele's collider*

1. Create a new script.
2. Name it MouseOverGUI.
3. Open it in the editor.
4. Add the following:

```
var showThis: int; // flag for menu display
var menuObject : GameObject;


function OnMouseEnter () {

    menuObject.GetComponent("StartMenu").show = showThis;
    menuObject.GetComponent(AudioSource).Play();

}

function OnMouseExit () {

    menuObject.GetComponent("StartMenu").show = 1;

}
```

5. Save the script.
6. Drag it onto both of the stele objects.

7. On the Stele Music, set the Show This value to 2.

8. On the Stele Water, set the Show This value to 3.

9. Drag the Main Camera object onto the Menu object for both.

10. Save the scene, and save the project.

11. Click Play, and test the text swapping functionality (see Figure 16-18).

Figure 16-18. *The instruction text on mouse-over*

You should now have a fully playable game from start to finish. Test it as thoroughly as possible, and then pass it on to any fresh beta testers if possible. Make a list of any small issues that crop up.

Is It Done Yet?

At this point in your project, you are probably wondering if there is anything left to do. The game is looking quite presentable and behaving relatively well (see Figure 16-19).

Figure 16-19. *The new starting position*

The hardest part of creating any work of art is *knowing when it is finished*. A game is no different. There are always art assets that could be improved, special effects and sound effects that could be added, story that could be extended, and even scripting that could be made more efficient. In industry, time deadlines or budgets will normally dictate when the game needs to be ready to be released. When time and money are not part of the mix, the decision becomes more difficult. If the project is a portfolio piece, or one done for personal enjoyment, it may never be "finished" to the degree you envision.

The approach taken to create the project for this book was decidedly non-linear. If you think about how the project came together, you can see that it could have been considered "finished" at several different points along the way. The importance of this concept cannot be emphasized enough. Thinking back, you can see how basic functionality was blocked in for the most crucial components first, and then revisited from time to time to make improvements and refinements. While it may have felt that you were jumping back and forth a lot, it served to create the project by building it up gradually and evenly. There were very few times when you did not have a working game.

The best way to think about the process is the way an artist approaches figure painting. To start, preliminary rough sketches are made to decide upon the pose, view, and general content. This is similar to deciding what basic genre your game will belong to and then what subset of that genre you plan to pursue. Once committed, the artist will block in the figure with gesture lines, volumes, or other very preliminary means. Your equivalent would be early tests with proxy objects to show proof of concept. Like the artist's first rough outlines that will be covered over with subsequent layers, you retain the scripting that you have developed, but not the art assets. From this point, the artist's painting progresses in generalities—broad areas of color are laid down, and detail is added in levels, until the painting is far enough along to start refining. Your game process follows the same technique. As the painting reaches higher and higher levels of refinement, the changes become less and less noticeable. Most artists will admit at some point that the majority of their audience will not be able to see the difference.

So get back to the original question. Is your game "finished"? You need to define "finished" to start with. Can you play through to the end? Yes. Are there any issues that are "show stoppers" that will crash the game or prevent the player from completing the game? You would probably say no at this point, but this is where you need to enlist the help of fresh beta testers. What may seem totally illogical to us as authors can be counted on to be tried (with glee) by players. The next question is "could anything be improved?" The answer to this, of course, will always be yes. "Feature creep" is a phenomenon that can be deadly to a project, so you need to consider the question carefully. Let's be more specific. Is there anything that could be improved quickly and easily for high gain? This requires serious assessment of the game as it stands.

1. Save the game, and save the project.

2. Build an .exe of the game.

3. Close the editor.

4. Play through the game, and make notes of things that could be improved.

Sound effects: Obviously, adding more or better sound effects will be on the list unless you have been doing that along the way.

Special effects: Animation always enhances game play. If it requires the original imported mesh to be reanimated, it may not be worth the trouble. If the addition of a particle system or two will enhance it greatly, then it would be worth considering.

Transitions: You have only one transition from level to level (if you do not count the start menu). Since the FinalLevel does not contain much, it loads almost instantly. The jump between levels is visually abrupt, however. Creating a simple fade-in and fade-out object would give you a good gain visually and a useful reusable asset. Go ahead and add this one last feature.

5. Load the FinalLevel.

6. Select the Inventory Screen object.

7. Duplicate it, and drag it out of the Inventory Group.

8. Name it Fade.

9. Set its Layer to Default.

10. Change its color to fully opaque black.

11. Remove its Inventory Screen component.

12. Open the Animation view.

13. Create a new clip called fade-out.

14. Select the GUI Texture's Color.a track.

15. Animate it going from **1** to **0** over one second.

16. Create another new clip, and name it fade-in.

17. Animate the `Color.a`, going from **0** to **1** over one second.

18. Close the Animation view.

The Animation component is set to Play Automatically. Since you will be instantiating the fades when needed, you will need to write a small script to kill the objects off once their animation is finished.

1. Create a new script.

2. Name it `TimedDestructor`.

3. Delete the `Update` function.

4. Add the following line:

```
Destroy (gameObject,1.5); //destroy object after 1.5 seconds
```

5. Save the script.

6. Drag it onto the Fade object.

7. Create a new Prefab.

8. Name it Fade Out from Black.

9. Select the Fade object, and make sure its default animation clip is fade-out.

10. Drag the Fade object from the Hierarchy view to the prefab in the Project view.

11. Duplicate the prefab.

12. Name it Fade In to Black.

13. Change its default animation to fade-in.

14. Save the scene, and save the project.

15. Click Play.

The scene fades in nicely from black, and the Fade object is destroyed shortly thereafter.

1. Save the scene, and save the project.

2. Open the MainLevel.

The level change is triggered by intersection with the collider in the cavern.

3. Select the WinLevelTrigger object.

4. Open its `LoadFinalLevel` script.

5. Add the following variable:

```
var fade : GameObject; // fade out prefab
```

6. Inside its `OnTriggerEnter` function, above the line, add the following:

```
Instantiate(fade);
```

```
yield new WaitForSeconds(1);
```

7. Save the script.

8. Assign the Fade In to Black object to the Fade parameter.

9. Save the scene, and save the project.

10. Click play and test.

11. Drag a Fade Out from Black into the MainLevel.

If you were being diligent in your testing, you may have noticed one more annoying thing. If you saved a game from the final scene and tried to load it from the start menu, there is a brief image of the sky during transition. Process of elimination pinpoints the sky belonging to the main level. And, because you are now using a fade-in, the offending sky must be from the main level as it is being closed out. To fix this problem, you can change the Clear Flags to Solid Color right before loading the new level.

1. Open the SaveLoad script.

2. In the ReadFile function, change the if (level != Application.loadedLevel) line to the following:

```
if (level != Application.loadedLevel) {
    GameObject.Find("Main Camera").camera.clearFlags= CameraClearFlags.SolidColor;
    Application.LoadLevel(level);
}
```

3. Save the script.

4. Save the scene, and save the project.

5. Load the MainLevel.

6. Select the Main Camera from within the First Person Controller.

7. Change the Background color to black.

8. Save the scene, and save the project.

Final Tasks

While you are now able to play through your game with all of the functionality in place, there are a few more things to do. First you will need to finalize object placement and make any terrain adjustments you feel are necessary. Once those issues have been addressed, you will need to take care of a few publishing related details before doing your final game build.

Finalizing the Layout at this point, if you kept all of the action objects within reach while you developed the game, you will need to move them to their final locations around the environment. Do not forget to move the objects that came in with animations on the parent group together (the Animation Objects).

The Chest sequence, for example, requires the following objects to be moved together:

- Animation Objects (contains ChestLid, ChestBase, KeyAtLock, KeyAtRock, and Rock)

- LockPlate

- Message

- Target Chest (for the camera match)

- DropGroup (contains Chest Checker, the object that scans the contents, and ChestInside, pick object for the chest contents)

Test the game after doing any re-arranging.

When you have finalized the locations and the terrain, bake the terrain shadows one last time.

Publishing

Assuming you are calling the game "finished" now, there are a couple of things yet to do. While you have been doing some organization of assets along the way, feel free to organize further. For example, you now have three GUI Skins, so it would be useful to put them in a folder of their own.

Before you remove old, unused levels and assets, you will probably want to make a copy of the entire project folder elsewhere on your machine and give it an appropriate name. You will need to turn off Unity while doing this.

One last thing you need to do is disable the Player settings so the player will not be able to change the screen size or make other changes that would mean extra work for you.

1. Go to Edit ➤ Project Settings ➤ Player.

2. Under Standalone Player Settings, set Display Resolution Dialog to Disabled.

To select the game icons, do the following.

3. Load the Key Glyph Icon as the Default Icon (at the top of the Inspector).

4. Open the Icon section.

An icon of each required size has been generated (see Figure 16-20).

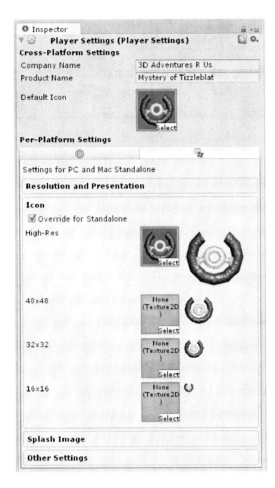

Figure 16-20. *Game Icon*

    5.   Save the scene, and save the project.

Publishing

You have already published several executables along the way. If you wish to distribute your game for Windows deployment, consider zipping both the .exe and the data folder together along with instruction that the two must reside in the same location.

    While you have created this project as a desktop stand-alone application, it might be worth a few notes on stand-alone vs. web browser–based.

    To publish for browser-based delivery, you will need to change the Platform to Web Player in the Build Settings dialog. Select Offline Deployment, and select the Build button. After compiling the build, you can find your game in a folder named Web Player. It contains three files: UnityObject.js, WebPlayer.html, and WebPlayer.unity3d (see Figure 16-21).

Figure 16-21. *Web Player*

By its size, you can recognize your game as the last file. The first file contains instructions to check if the Unity player is installed. The middle file contains the code to add your game to a web page. If you run the HTML file, the first thing you notice is that, despite your instructions to set the size to 1024 × 768, the window is too small for your text. It is correct on full screen, however.

If you open the HTML file in the script editor (or any HTML editor), you can see where the window size is set.

```
if (typeof unityObject != "undefined") {
   unityObject.embedUnity("unityPlayer", "WebPlayer.unity3d", 600, 450);
}
```

Change the window size to 1024 × 768 and save.

The other issue is that many browsers "sandbox" the application they are running to prevent the application from executing malicious code on the player's machine. This means the Load and Save functionality may not work in the web player.

A third consideration is that the current version of your game may not play in the next version of Unity. If the game is a small, casual game with a short shelf life, that may not be a worry. If you would like your game to be playable for some time into the future, the stand-alone executable ensures that future changes in the software will not affect your finished game. Even if you want to release your game with only web deployment, it is wise to save an .exe so you can see what it used to work like when updating functionality in new versions of Unity.

If you *are* interested in web delivery, the Unity manual has a good section on web player streaming and web player deployment.

Summary

In this chapter, you created menus and delved deeper into the UnityGUI system. After learning how to use GUI groups and automating some of the button layout, you set up the mini-menu so that it could be accessed by both keyboard and cursor position, allowing you to preserve "suspension of disbelief." In your menu script, you used flags to control the visibility of the various menus, including the menu you relegated to its own function.

In the Settings menu, you went beyond GUIButtons and GUILabels and added toggles and sliders to control navigation speeds, audio volumes, and even cursor color with the help of GUI.changed. With the color selector, you learned that it wasn't always necessary to use "correct" algorithms and complicated formulas when a close, easy-to-derive calculation would suffice. When implementing the volume changes for audio, you discovered the need for conventions in order to differentiate between your four types of audio. As usual, you recorded your audio management system in the GameNotes text file.

Because you opted to keep the menu GUI in a separate script from your regular text and pointer, you needed an economical means of passing the settings back and forth between the menu script and the game's main brain, the GameManager. By using a JavaScript array, you were able to store each of the settings, regardless of type, into a single easily accessed array. When it came time to implement the Load and Save functionality, the array was easily parsed and added to the simple text file along with the First Person Controller transform, the current level, and the current state of each of the action objects. Along with including the SystemIO class in your load/save script, you learned how to access the game's data path and add it to a file name and extension in case you wanted to implement multiple saved games at a later date.

With the menu functionality complete, you went back and refined your menus with their own GUI Skin to match your game's color scheme and wrought iron and gold motif. Your menus were further enhanced with the creation of a system to assign either a still image or an actual game location as the background.

With the addition of the new StartScene level, you learned how to order your scenes in the Build Settings so the game would start with the correct scene when you created an executable. In the StartScene, you weighed the pros and cons of several different methods to achieve control of a mouse-over event. With the menu set, you discovered the use of DontDestroyOnLoad to allow an object to persist when new levels were loaded.

Finally, with a fully working game to show for your tenacity, you considered the concept of "finished" and discovered that you could have called the game "finished" at several times during its development, with each new version just a richer, more feature-laden implementation of the last. After a short discussion about "feature creep," you made one final addition to your game, deeming it a quick addition for large visual gain.

Wrapping it up, you limited player choices by disabling the application settings menu at the start of the game since you had already decided on a set resolution and navigation keys. Having originally set the game settings to "Fantastic" quality, you are assuming that visual quality is more important than fast frame rate for this genre. You will rely on Unity's built-in degradation to automatically control quality settings on older or lower-end machines.

Although you designed this game with the intent of creating a desktop stand-alone executable, you looked briefly at a few considerations for deploying via web players in browsers. Aside from the default window size, you discovered that loading and saving to the player's hard drive could be unrealistic.

■ ■ ■

CHAPTER 17

Beyond the Basics

This is the final chapter, and here you'll take a look at the logical progressions for your game. There are always more features you could include to make it more interesting or more fun to play. You're not actually going to add them, but let's discuss possible means of doing so. You will also assess the changes you would need to implement to take your game from first person to third person format. Since a good portion of your first person functionality carries over into a third person format, it's well worth discussing. Another topic of interest is porting to mobile platforms. As you may have guessed, there are a lot of technical restrictions as concessions must be made to be able to run everything on smaller devices. Finally, having made it through the process of creating a game utilizing several features beyond basic Unity functionality, you'll have a go at putting your game into a simple design document.

Additional Features

As you found when investigating the concept of "finished," there are always more features that could be added to enhance your game. Some would be fairly easy to add, but others would take a bit more effort. Assuming that you will want to go ahead and add some of them, let's look into what that might entail.

HUD Score/Rating

In the early days of the classic text adventure, one earned points as various goals were met. At its simplest, when an object was collected, a point would be added to the total score. In your game, that would mean adding another variable to the Interactor script for each object's value and displaying the current total on screen. While that sounds easy at first, you need to consider the different types of action objects that your game offers. Some can be collected and put into inventory, but others are strictly for interaction. The problems become apparent when you consider that some items, such as the Crowbar, can go in and out of inventory several times. Interactive objects such as the Stone Drawer in the music shrine can be opened and closed repeatedly as well.

One solution for preventing multiple points from the same object would be to have a current value that starts out as the assigned value for the object and is set to zero after the first time the object is collected or accessed. Conversely, you could have, instead of a current value variable, a Boolean type variable to tell you if the point value has been used.

The other problem you need to think about is in what state the score gets added. Some of your action objects have several states. For the stone drawer in the music shrine, you could give points for when the player first inserts the glyph into the matching depression in the drawer to take the drawer from state 0 to state 1. The problem is that until he or she picks the drawer again, nothing really happens. If, on the other hand, the player has discovered the Easter Egg mini-map of the maze, they may close the drawer several times to watch the changing maze configuration.

Logically, it would make the most sense to have an array with point values for when the action object goes into each state. Most would be zero, but in the case of the stone drawer, it allows for a few points for putting the glyph in the right slot and more points for when the player figures out how to close the drawer. A matching array of Boolean type, not exposed to the Inspector, to track whether the points have been used yet for each state would prevent the points from being added more than once.

Another benefit of a state-based point system is that you could remove points if the player loses an item such as the crowbar. The point value for taking it from state 0 might be 10, but moving to state 0 could hold a value of -10. You would, of course, need to make sure it didn't remove points when starting or restoring the game.

Health or strength could also be tracked and used in a similar manner. When early text adventures progressed from a lamp that ran out of oil or batteries, one often had to remember to eat and drink to gain strength. While some of us thought this made the game tedious rather than more fun, you could use the idea on a more limited basis to make your game more challenging. Too many trips through a noxious yellow fog (a particle system with a large box collider) could reduce the player's health to the point where he could no longer move. A timer could be set on each entrance into the toxic zone and health points could be restored when the accumulated amount of time has passed.

Conversely, if a player goes through a power zone, similar to the temple bouncer, you could temporarily increase the First Person Controller's jump height, allowing the player to be able to get to a ledge or other inaccessible area. The effect could be controlled by a timer so that it wears off after a period of time. Another possibility would be the presence of a strength-enhancing action object in the player's inventory. While he has it, he is capable of extraordinary strength or other abilities.

To add yet more functionality to the Interactor script to check for health for every interaction would probably not be worth the complication when there might only be one or two scenarios that made use of it. In this case, it might make more sense to put the conditionals in their own script. A single checkbox (Boolean variable) in the Interactor component could tell the OnMouseDown function to SendMessage to a player health or strength script that housed the variable and the conditions to be met before the action could be initiated. If the conditions were not met (a true value returned), a return would be carried out.

While this type of functionality strays a bit from traditional adventure games, there is nothing wrong with hybrid functionality. Genres were defined after the games were created to help with marketing, not vice versa.

Hints/Difficulty

Hints are another feature that appears fairly straightforward at first glance. The hints related to each task obviously need to be stored or identified so that the proper version, according the level, appears. The tricky part about hints is when and where they should appear.

The simplest mechanism would be to create a new text element to display hints when an object was picked. If hints were turned off or there were no hints associated with the action, no text would be displayed; otherwise, the hint for the current level of difficulty would be shown. The problem with this method is that it is quite obvious when the player is being given a hint because the hint follows the action reply text.

A better version would be an array of action text replies for each state where the correct difficulty level (element number) reply would be used.

You are probably cringing at the thought of adding more verbose text strings in the Inspector but are not quite desperate enough to consider learning how to manage all of your text strings in a database. When you started the project, you began by using Unity built-in arrays. This gave you several advantages. You could see the arrays in the Inspector, which was less scary than looking at the scripts directly. Additionally, you could dynamically change both the size and contents of the arrays in the

Inspector. Inside the `ObjectLookup` script, in the `Start` function, the text strings you added to the arrays in the Inspector were loaded into regular JavaScript arrays.

Now that you are hopefully more comfortable with scripting, you may want to consider creating a script that holds all of the verbose text strings for an object. It could store object descriptions for the `Interactor` script as well as action replies for the `ObjectLookup` script. With the Load and Save functionality, you were introduced to passing the contents of an array between scripts, so a few changes to the `Start` functions to load the strings from a separate script should be well within your capabilities.

Aside from managing the hints, you could conceivably have them pop up independently from the action replies, or even in addition to those hints. When the player enters an area defined by a collider, a hint related to some object or possible action in the area could be displayed. The problem with this idea is that unless the player is constrained by geometry to be facing the correct direction as he enters the area, he may not see the relevant object to make the connection. To be an effective hint, you need to make sure the player is facing the correct direction before displaying the hint. If you think about it, this is a typical condition for first person shooter type action. Enemies are activated when the player gets within range, but they do not shoot unless they are facing the direction of the player. This is a perfect example of how investigating tutorials and examples from a completely different genre pays off. By using `Physics.Raycast` to see if the player is facing the correct direction, you can ensure that a hint will be seen in its correct context.

To implement, you would need to check for four things before displaying the hint. The raycast is put in the `Update` function but you really don't want it doing all of its calculations throughout the entire game. By setting a flag when the player enters the area but a hint has not yet been given, you can activate the raycast script and deactivate it upon exit. If the raycast returns a hit on your target, you will need to check which hint should be displayed and finally display it while disabling the raycast at least until the player exits the area. To add complexity, you could allow a hint to be displayed three times or repeated after a certain amount of time has passed, or you could show a random hint of the proper level.

As with most features, you need to have a very clear idea of the functionality before you start to script it. This is even more important if someone else is going to be helping out with the scripting. Write down the feature requirements. Prioritize them into "must have" and "nice to have." Do early prototyping to work out the technical bits and then design the system depending on whether time or future enhancements will take precedence

Multiple Saves

Although the framework allows the user to save multiple games, you went no farther than using and overwriting a single saved game. To allow multiple saves, you will need to create a new menu to display the saved games. This would allow the player to choose a game to overwrite as well. Another option would be to let the user name the saved game. This doesn't necessarily mean the file is saved with that name. Ideally, you would want to add one more WriteLine command at the top that stores the player's name for the saved game. When the files are listed in the menu, the first entry, the saved game's name, is shown next to the filename's number.

Currently, you are using the constructed string with the variables *filepath* + *filename* + *extension* to access the file. Remembering that if you try to open a file that does not exist, one is created, so you can change the string to *filepath* + *filename* + *filenumber.ToString()* + *extension* where *filenumber* is an integer that gets converted to a string. You can then use a `while` loop to iterate through the files, adding 1 to the value and checking the first line for the player's file name. When you open a file and the first ReadLine returns null, you know you have the next available file number to use. The Load/Save menu should load the saved files' names each time it is opened so the player can see what files have been saved and are available to open.

To allow the player to type in text, you will need to use the GUI.Textfield. There are some nice examples of how it works in the Help ➤ Reference Manual ➤ GUI Scripting Guide. Since it is constantly updated, you will need a means of telling it when to save the file. Since the OnGUI function doesn't know (or care) which TextFields are changed, the existing file names will need to be dynamically created as controls that look like labels (so they can't be changed) and the empty file drawn as a TextField. This would probably be best handled as a user defined function outside of the OnGUI function where you can use a variable an array to keep track of the saved games and generate the GUI elements.

Consider drawing the existing saved games as a SelectionGrid type element where if the user selects an existing game and clicks either the Load or Save button, the correct name/file number can be processed. Better yet, the TextField could only appear if the last SelectionGrid element is active to avoid ambiguity.

If your game is large enough to need an unlimited number of saves, you will need to implement a scrolling system as with the inventory items so any of the saved games can be accessed.

Physics and Projectiles

Many adventure games feature the use of some sort of projectile, based more or less on physics, to move the game forward at some point. As well as providing a bit of a break from brain teasing logic sequences, physics-based cause and effect can provide an entertaining way for the player to gain access to a new area or reveal a new action object. The key with adventure games is to make sure the odds are stacked in favor of the player being successful within about three to five tries. If the result of misses is just as entertaining as hits, you could, of course, get away with tougher odds.

To avoid the need to include the challenge in the regular action object category, you could keep the goals restricted to access-related things like blowing up a beaver dam to drain a lake in order to get to a subterranean cavern or causing an avalanche to fill a deadly crevasse to allow passage to the other side. If you would like to include a monster or two in your game but don't want to have to script full-blown combat sequences, a variety of unexpected projectiles could prove to be the poor creature's undoing. Randomly chosen behaviors (animation clips) could prevail until a projectile with the correct tag hits him.

In your game, you used physics and rigidbodies only briefly at the end of the game to drop the topi fruit. Just as with the topi fruit, projectiles are instantiated when fired and then generally destroyed when they hit something. The direction they hit the object from is returned with the collision information, allowing a particle system to instantiate spewing sparks, smoke, or other effects in the correct direction.

As there are numerous scripts and tutorials readily available concerning this topic online, you concentrated on other features for the framework of your game. You are, however, encouraged to try a bit of wanton destruction on your own. A good place to start is the FPS Tutorial on the Unity web site. It provides an excellent introduction to weapons as well as a waypoint system for a very basic AI system.

Retaining Data

In your game, you had one main level and a very short end level. When you moved the player into the final level, you specified that he would start it with two inventory items. Since he had to take the topi fruit to cause the secret passageway to open and had no way to get rid of it, you know he had it in inventory in the final level. Likewise, the player needed the crowbar to open the sack to access the topi fruit. If the player found the music glyph or used it and took it back from the stone drawer, it could have been in the player's inventory as he moved to the final level. Since it wasn't necessary for winning the game and might even have confused him, you didn't bother to see if he had it and opted not to bring it forward.

In the bonus version of the game with its extra functionality, the player could have taken the crowbar back out of the temple and put it into the stone chest and then gone down into the underground cavern and on to the final level, only to find out he had no way to finish the game or find his way back. You could have provided a portal back to the main level or maybe just offered an alternate object with which to whack the tree. Either way would have allowed the game to progress.

In a traditional adventure game, the player is usually allowed to move freely between worlds or levels. Most, in fact, require the player to acquire crucial objects from different levels to solve the puzzles and tasks throughout the game. One means of dragging objects from one level to the next is with a DontDestroyOnLoad function.

In order for objects to retain their current settings and variable values when different scenes are loaded and unloaded, you would need to tell the engine to not destroy your meshes, scripts, and their current variable values when loading new scenes. You can do this via a DontDestroyOnLoad function in the Awake function. Any object that needs to remain intact between levels will need this. By adding it to the parent object, all of its children will be kept as well.

```
function Awake () {

    DontDestroyOnLoad (transform.gameObject);

}
```

■ **Tip**   DontDestroyOnLoad is generally added to the Awake function.

In your game, you would need to add DontDestroyOnLoad to the Inventory Items gameObject. The problem is that it does not contain any scripts. A possible solution would be to make a stand-alone script that could be used on any object you wish to retain between levels. Just for fun, you may wish to try adding the DontDestroyOnLoad to a few of your scripts. Since the inventory icon objects would need to be carried forward, you would need to add it to the Interactor or ObjectLookup script. Unfortunately, all of the action objects also have the same scripts so you would probably discover them littered around the final level in some very odd places.

In your game, it would make a lot more sense to utilize your mechanism for saving games. A simple test to see if you were saving a game or moving between levels could save the data to a file of a different name. On starting the level, the alternate data file could be parsed and the appropriate objects loaded into inventory.

Additional Content

You may be wondering why there are several objects in the game environment that you did not use. By providing several extra assets, you have the opportunity to practice using the system without having to spend time creating new meshes. A few have already been implemented in the extended version of the game. Here are some more ideas:

- The passage leading down to the cavern under the temple is flooded. The player must retrieve the water glyph from the shrine behind the waterfall to activate the stone drawer at the landing above the water in the passage. The stone drawer is subtly colored so the player will have to locate it, open it, and put the water glyph in it. When activated, the closing drawer with the glyph causes the water level to drop, giving the player access to the cavern.

- The dirt in the earth temple sparkles with gold, but it falls through the player's hands as he tries to collect some of it. The tunnel system beneath the rock dome contains a small shovel left by some long forgotten adventurer. Unfortunately, the tunnels are in darkness. The player will need to find a torch or light source to find his way around.

From First Person to Third Person

While first person adventure games rely heavily on the environment, mechanical gizmos, and special effects to engage the player, third person adventure games invest a large part of their creativity in character development. One could easily devote an entire book to moving your current project into a third person adventure format. The nice part is that you have already laid down a good foundation with the current functionality as most of the features, state management, inventory, player settings, and load/save can be used as-is. If you *do* want to take the next step, you will need to make changes in the camera and add your main character plus any supporting characters with whom he will interact.

Characters

Importing characters is similar to the way you imported the flower asset. One object serves as the parent or root, and the behaviors are segments of time or frames out of the total animation. As with the flower, the character and its animations are in a file of their own. Store in Root is specified in the FBX Importer so that the root object controls all of the animations of the children. Clips are defined just as you did with your regular action objects. Additionally, you can split the character animation clips into separate fbx files where the file name is appended with an @, followed by the clip name or *model name@animation name.fbx*. While this will certainly make the setup process quicker, there will be more files to handle and continuity may be more difficult to achieve as you are animating the character for the various behaviors.

You already have a means of moving the First Person Controller to a better vantage point for watching an animation sequence play out. Since the main difference between first person and third person is camera placement, your current system should work just as well to move the character as it does with the first person representation of an unseen character. For the look target, instead of rotating the camera, you could adjust the head rotation if you were getting fancy; alternatively, you could just use the height of the target to tell your character to look up, straight ahead, or look down. Your existing script also could provide a means of true point-and-click navigation by having a mouse pick on the terrain to return its X,Y,Z position and feed that into the script.

Calling non-navigation animations should be fairly straightforward. When you pick on an action object in the scene, not only does your character need to move to the object's action position and orientation, but you need to trigger the appropriate behavior for the object and its current state. As you have probably guessed, there are a number of behaviors that are generic enough to reuse in many situations. A gather and stash behavior, for instance, could be used with any number of small objects that go directly into inventory. Once again, you could create an array—this time for the character animation clips associated with the action object's state. The current system could be used to instantiate the object into the character's hand as he takes it before stashing it via the special instruction flags, but it might make more sense to create an array specifically for the purpose of handling inventory objects along with the behaviors that go with them.

Character control could well be the trickiest part of bringing a character to life. If you have experimented with the 3rd Person Controller that ships with Unity, the construction worker, you will have discovered a few interesting shortcomings. The first is that it requires idle, walk, run and jump behaviors, yet it was apparently adapted from the script used in the Lerpz tutorial where the Lerpz character walks a few seconds then automatically goes into a jog behavior as his speed increases. Because your script does not call for a jog behavior, the only thing changing at the end of the specified seconds is the character's speed. This means that either he will be moonwalking in the slow section or skating in the fast section. If you reduce the amount of walk before jog seconds to zero, you miss out on the smoother start. Obviously, you could spend time tweaking the settings to arrive at a reasonable compromise; the point is that there is no out-of-the-box character controller that you can easily commandeer to make the task of controlling an animated character a no-brainer.

Unity provides the functionality to blend one animation or behavior into another over time with CrossFade. This is how a character moves smoothly from any part of an idle cycle into a walk or run cycle or between the same behaviors into a jump or other play-once animation. While this produces superior results visually, it all has to be scripted. As you might imagine, character control scripts tend to get complicated quickly. Add in the ability to jump and now the script not only needs to check to see when the character is in contact with the ground, but the correct animation for the action needs to be triggered and then blended back to the current stride type.

The interesting thing about the 3rd Person Controller is that rather than triggering both the movement and the corresponding animation from a key press, the movement is triggered, and then the correct animation is triggered in response to the speed. To test this, try making a platform that cycles up and down. If you walk the character up onto the platform and then just watch him, he walks in place even when you are no longer pressing the keys. This means that theoretically, if you move the character from one place to the other with your existing script, the 3rd person controller should automatically initiate the walk or run behavior as he lerps (linear interpolation) between his current and target positions. The same mechanism is often used to animate enemies as they patrol their designated areas, moving between pre-assigned waypoints.

Aside from the actual mechanics of the character control, another decision that must be made is how the controls actually work. The two most obvious schemes use world coordinates and local coordinates. World coordinates are quite commonly used in side scrolling platform jumpers. The left arrow always moves the character to the left direction of the screen and the right arrow to the right. In the next section on cameras, you will see how this could work well in a limited area of a third person adventure game. If, however, you need the character to move easily in any direction, it's often less confusing for the player if the keys move the character in its local coordinate system. That is, the up arrow always moves the character forward, left turns or strafes him to the left, right arrow turns or strafes him to the right *regardless of his current orientation*.

Cameras

The biggest difference between third person and first person, aside from seeing and controlling a character in the scene, is the camera manipulation. With your first person project, the camera is roughly where the character's head would be. With third person, it can range from somewhere behind the character where you never see the front of the character to a full side-scroller where the camera moves to keep the character within range, as in a classic platform jumper.

With the 3rd Person Controller that currently ships with Unity, the camera starts out above and behind the character but is allowed to get out of position if the player changes the character's position. So if you start to move the character forward or away from you with the up arrow, then press the down arrow, the character flips around to face you and heads towards you. As soon as you release the key, the camera attempts to get back behind the character. At this point, if you press the up key while the camera is enroute to position itself behind again, the character will not move in the direction the character is facing, but will move in the direction the camera is facing, making for a thoroughly confusing and frustrating user experience. The speed in which the camera attempts to regain its position can be increased, but then you are left with dizzying camera swings as the keyboard controls flip the character in the directions specified by the player's input.

Another problem with third person cameras in general is their collision detection. If the character is standing alongside a wall or a steep bit of terrain, as soon as the character turns to face away from the wall or terrain, the camera will either go through the mesh so the player is treated to a view that was never meant to be seen, or the camera loses sight of the character completely if there's geometry on the other side of the faces in question. Various games have handled the issue in different ways. In a town situation, they may set the cameras near clipping range to avoid drawing the geometry directly behind the character. In close quarters, such as inside a room, the camera's range may be decreased so it is quite close to the character's head. Alternatively, the third person camera may be switched for a fixed camera that merely watches, or stays oriented towards, the character as he is maneuvered around the room.

One camera management technique used successfully in third person adventure games is a variation of a side-scroller camera used in conjunction with full directional character control. TellTales' Tales of Monkey Island is an excellent example of this method. The camera is closer to the character than a traditional side-scroller, but just as its predecessor, it is constrained to a particular range. The camera moves left and right as if on a short track in an orthogonal direction while the character is moved about the scene. Obviously the design and layout of the scene is extremely important; the character must always be well within view. By using invisible colliders set as triggers, the view is switched from camera to camera as the character is moved around the game environment. When an action object is picked and the character moved into the action position, a camera match can be performed between the view camera and the ideal position in which to watch the sequence play out.

In third person adventures, the clues are often revealed to the character through dialog with other characters. If you think of other characters as action objects themselves, you can see that the camera positions required to watch the conversations are exactly the same as watching any regular sequence play out. There will be a target position for the character as well as the camera.

For more insight into constrained cameras for a third person adventure, consult the 2D Gameplay tutorial on the Unity3D web site. It is a 3D platform jumper constrained to 2D space, which has a well designed camera system.

Character Dialog

In the old days of text adventure games when dialog between the player and the game entity was the essence of the game, players were expected to type in their requests, commands, or questions to move the game forward. The player's input was parsed; nouns, verbs, adjectives and conjunctions identified; and the results run through dialog trees that output the response that corresponded to the input. The seemingly infinite possibilities for conversational direction were part of the challenge as well as the reward for the clever adventurer.

With the advent of the graphic adventure game, text was distilled into a few simple verbs and nouns limited to inventory items. Dialog between characters and player became a matter of multiple choice. In witty, irreverent games, you had to click on each possible question or reply to find out if there was anything entertaining, even if you had already received the clue you were searching for. In games driven by strong story lines, you were forced to tediously click through each dialog tree to make sure you didn't miss any vague or obscure hints. In one solution, when clicking on an NPC (non-player character) for the first time, a player should receive the full topic information as if from a chatty neighbor. When she has finished blathering on, the conversation topics can be offered and the player can get a refresher on the one he wants rather than having to prompt her for all of her canned responses one at a time.

Often, the topics offered for a particular character are dynamically changed when the player has gained access to a particular object or location, making the dialog state dependent with respect to certain objects. If a player has not yet discovered a key object or at least become aware of its existence, he should obviously not be given a chance to ask the character about it.

914

For us, as developers, restricting dialog choices makes the task far simpler but much less creative. As a result, you need to carefully plan how the conversation will play out.

Dialog Trees

Dialog trees can use a similar mechanism as your `ObjectLookup` script to initiate a sequence of replies instead of animated events. When the player enters a character's conversation area or the player picks the NPC, the player's choice for questions or conversation topics is listed on screen. The topics or questions are presented using GUI Buttons so the chosen line can be processed to play the appropriate NPC response and generate the next bunch of choices. Each topic, therefore, needs to know, or contain, the reply to initialize and the topics that go with it.

The following are some possible replies:

replyBlue[0] = ""

replyBlue[1] = "Hi, I'm the Blue Sphere. I know everything that happens around here."

replyBlue[2] = "Well, uhm…I don't know. You should ask the cube."

replyBlue[3] = "Yes, perfect weather for spheres. It's too hot for cubes, of course."

replyBlue[4] = "Which cube? The red cube or the green cube?"

replyBlue[5] = "We used to have a green cube, but he left the valley a long time ago."

replyBlue[6] = "He lives over on the other side of the valley."

Conversation zero, shown in Figure 17-1, could look something like the following:

A- "Hi." ➤ replyBlue[1],c[0]

B- "Is there a way out of the valley?" ➤ replyBlue[2],c[1]

C- "Lovely weather we're having, isn't it?" ➤ replyBlue[3],c[0]

D- "Gotta go. See ya." ➤ replyBlue[0](exit dialog mode)

A and C display replyBlue elements 1 and 2, respectively, of a reply array, then re-display conversation one. D exits the dialog mode completely. C, however, displays a different topic list, conversation two, after playing or displaying its reply.

Conversation one:

A- "Where do I find the cube?" ➤ replyBlue[4], c[2]

B- "Never mind." ➤ replyBlue[0], c[0]

Conversation two:

A- "Where do I find the green cube?" ➤ replyBlue[5], c[0]

B- "Where do I find the red cube?" ➤ replyBlue[6], c[0]

C- "Never mind." ➤ replyBlue[0], c[0]

Figure 17-1. *Blue conversation*

By now, you probably realize that instead of introducing new conversations that keep the player pursuing the current topic, you could just add the new questions or topics to the original conversation. Far from being a simple solution, it raises a couple of new issues. You would need to check to see if the topic or question is already showing, and at some point, you would probably need to implement a scrolling system when you had too many topics to display nicely at once.

A third possibility for displaying the conversation would be to dynamically build the topic list each time. That way you don't need to store multiple conversations, just the possible topics, referenced by element number.

The topic array could look as follows:

topic[0] = "Hi."

topic[1] = "Is there a way out of the valley?"

topic[2] = "Lovely weather we're having, isn't it?"

topic[3] = "Where do I find the cube?"

topic[4] = "Where do I find the green cube?"

topic[5] = "Where do I find the red cube?"

topic[6] = "Gotta go. See ya."

topic[7] = "Never mind."

Now the conversation array is not an element number, but an array of topic element numbers. Conversation zero:

A- "Hi." ➤ replyBlue[1],c(0,1,2,6)

B- "Is there a way out of the valley?" ➤ replyBlue[2],c(3,7)

C- "Lovely weather we're having, isn't it?" ➤ replyBlue[3],c(0,1,2,6)

D- "Gotta go. See ya." ➤ replyBlue[0](exit dialog mode)

Conversation one:

    A- "Where do I find the cube?" ➤ replyBlue[4], c(4,5,7)

    B- "Never mind." ➤ replyBlue[0], c(0,1,2,6)

Conversation two:

    A- "Where do I find the green cube?" ➤ replyBlue[5], c(0,1,2,6)

    B- "Where do I find the red cube?" ➤ replyBlue[6], c(0,1,2,6)

    C- "Never mind." ➤ replyBlue[0], c(0,1,2,6)

By creating an array of the conversation arrays, as long as nothing ever changes, you can use an element number to retrieve all the information you need. If the array element is 20 (or some other chosen number), you exit the dialog before trying to process the non-existent element. Another number could be an automatic return to the original conversation elements.

    conv[0] = (0,1,2,6)

    conv[1] = (3,7)

    conv[2] = (4,5,7)

    conv[3] = (0,1,2,6)

    conv[4] = (4,5,7)

    conv[5] = (0,1,2,6)

    conv[6] = (0,1,2,6)

    conv[7] = (100)

Conversation zero:

    A- 1

    B- 2

    C- 3

    D- 100

Conversation one:

    A- 4

    B- 0

Conversation two:

    A- 5

    B- 6

    C- 0

So now, using the element number, you can load the topic text into the buttons' text variables, and when picked, display the reply of the same element number, and finally, load the next batch of topics. While this simplifies processing the conversation, it could get challenging to make sure the reply is the correct element number. If you had several topics that resulted in the same reply, you would need to make several duplicates.

To extend the system, you could decide that the first element number in the topic array is the element number of the reply. This would allow you to designate whatever reply you wanted, avoiding the need to have reply elements match the topic numbers. It also would give you an easy way to reuse the topics with different characters. Although you could put the character replies all in a single array, it would probably be easier to keep track of them if they each had their own reply array.

Red cube's replies (see Figure 17-2) consist of the following:

replyRed[0] = "";

replyRed[1] = "Go away.";

replyRed[2] = "The tunnel, of course.";

replyRed[3] = "No, it's too hot.";

replyRed[4] = "No idea, I'm not exactly mobile here.";

replyRed[5] = "Yeah, he talks too much.";

replyRed[6] = "No. There's never been a green cube in the valley. Blue just says that to keep people talking to him.";

Figure 17-2. *Red conversation*

Additional topics (red specific):

topics[6] = "Where is the tunnel?"

topics[7] = " Know anything about the blue sphere?"

If you decide topic 20 is "Gotta go. See ya." you can tell the processor function to exit the dialog. You could then say that anything larger than element 20 will return you to the starting conversation for that particular character.

Reserved topics:

topics[20] = "Gotta go. See ya."

topics[22] = "Okay, thanks."

topics[21] = "Never mind."

The system works fairly smoothly until circumstances change. When you finally find out from the red cube that there is a tunnel, you need to go back and ask the blue sphere about it. Rather than creating a new set of conversations for every possible condition, it might make more sense to let each reply know whether it is active or not. That way, you could use the same topic list even if the conditions change.

Another helpful feature is the ability to randomly choose from several possible replies for a particular topic. Grouchy red cube may have three different replies when you say "Hi." to him. If you consider a hint type system, you may also want the replies for a particular topic to get more explicit each time the player chooses the topic.

To store the instructions for each topic's reply on a per NPC basis, you could use a couple of new arrays to hold the status and the treatment (random or sequential) of each reply; an array of strings to hold the reply text, the status, and the treatment; or (since you may have more than one reply) a combination of any of the three. You might even consider a single string for the information you require, parsing it into it component parts when needed.

The goal here is to be able to change the information easily as well as merely access it. It matters less how you store and access it and more about the information you need to process the dialog. If you are conversant with databases, you are probably thinking how much easier it would be to manage the data with one.

Character Alternatives

With character conversation, you also need to think about how or even whether to lip sync to audio clips. Currently, Unity does not support vertex animation, so facial animation needs to be done with a bone system. If you're feeling adventurous, search the Unity forum for blendshapes. There are a few people working on coding that functionality on their own.

Facial animation to match phonemes could be a lot of work, even with the help of plug-ins for your favorite 3D authoring program. If the task seems daunting, consider giving the character generic mouth movement. The audio clip used for the dialog can be checked for its length and the mouth movement looped and timed accordingly. This method also provides the benefit of allowing your characters to be multi-lingual for different markets.

Perhaps the most logical way to start out with character dialogs is to consider using non-humanoid characters. This could greatly simplify the character animation required. Distilled down to the simplest form, you could have your character talk to an inanimate machine such as a two-way radio. If your character was also a robotic construction or a nebulous alien entity, it would allow you to experiment with the dialog tree itself before worrying about animating characters to match.

When you are ready to tackle lip syncing, consider animating a ghostly disembodied head or perhaps a face embedded in a static object such as a tree trunk or stone surface. This would allow you to concentrate on facial animation.

Design Considerations for Mobile Platforms

Creating your game for a desktop platform simplified many of your choices: you were able to use the free version of the engine; your input for user interaction and navigation was all conventional; and because the genre generally does not need smoking fast frame rates, you did not need to keep strict account of your art assets' poly count and texture size. With mobile platforms, however, all of the previously mentioned issues become crucial as the hardware takes a step or two back in time. Many a developer has broken quickly into the mobile phone market by reworking games that were cutting edge a decade earlier.

As little as a year ago, the word "mobile" was synonymous with mobile phones. Today, however, the iPhone's larger cousin, the iPad, and its Android-based counterparts are redefining the casual gaming experience. While making games for mobile platforms is beyond the scope of this book, let's take a quick look at some basic considerations for mobile game development and the necessary changes required to a project like yours to allow it to go mobile.

In general, as artists or designers, you were able to manage to script the functionality you needed as best you could for desktop deployment. In mobile deployment, the available resources put a lot more technical restrictions on what you produce. Code, art assets, and general game play must always be designed around the technical limitations of the hardware, with efficiency at the core of all.

The three main considerations when developing for mobile platforms are additional hardware and software needs, input limitations and unique differences for mobile devices, and finally, art asset restrictions and best practices. While the first is likely to be a matter of available funds, the second can provide exciting challenges for designers, and the third is the logical next step in the learning process. Even if you do not have an immediate need or desire to develop for mobile platforms, once you have learned the basics, the next step is to learn how to make things more efficient, whether it concerns polygon modeling, texture layout and size, or environmental design able to hide large amounts of geometry at any one time.

License, Hardware, and Setup

Of primary concern for those on limited budgets is the need to pay extra for a mobile license in addition to the base Unity or Unity Pro version you already have. Theoretically, if you consider the time you will rack up developing your game, the cost of the license for the desired mobile platform is probably ridiculously small—even if you set your hourly worth to minimum wage. On the other hand, coming up with the cost of the license could be a difficult hurdle.

Another requirement is the extra hardware you will need. Besides the actual hardware (iPhone, iPad, or Android device), Windows developers will need a Mac of some sort to create a build. You can't publish for iPhone or iPad from a Windows environment.

Along with the hardware, you will need to install the appropriate SDK (software developer's kit) for the platform. With Android, you will need not only the Android SDK but the Java JDK, too, as the Android platform is written in Java (not to be confused with JavaScript). Even though the SDKs are free, they do require what can sometimes be a complicated setup. The iOs requires its equivalent SDK.

Unity provides a Unity Remote for both iOS and Android that allows you to plug your deployment device into your computer via USB port, use it for input, and observe your application in the editor. This allows you to test your game using the accelerometer or touch inputs without the need for making builds and loading them on the device throughout the development process.

To publish your app and make it available to the public, you will need to be a registered developer. The additional fee to export to iPhone or iPad and sell your app on the Apple store costs about $99 per year. The corresponding Android account will cost you about $24. In return for your fees, the stores will provide filtering to help your customers make sure your game will run on their device and check to see if their device has purchased the game or app. If not, it is up to you to script what should be done. Marketing will be up to you. The Apple AppStore does have favorites, top sellers, and other such marketing aids, but with the number of apps available at the time of this writing somewhere around 300,000, some kind of marketing strategy will probably be necessary. Android also has an app store, but at this point it offers only barebones functionality. Another outlet for Android apps is through carrier stores where the game is sold by specific device manufacturers.

Unlike iPhone, Android is not standardized because of the different manufacturers that use the OS on their devices, so you will need to choose carefully as you make design decisions for your game. With the growing consumer acceptance of the iPad, even authoring for iOS now requires executive decisions. As specifications for mobile devices change regularly, you may want to check out www.apple.com/iphone/specs.html for the latest specifications on Apple devices. The following are the current resolutions for each device, see Figure 17-3:

- iPhone: 480×320
- Retina: 960×640
- iPad: 1024×768
- Nexus One: 480×800
- Droid X: 854×480
- Evo 4G: 800×480

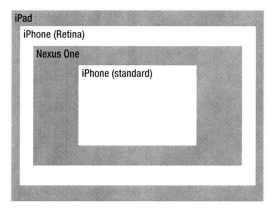

Figure 17-3. *In mobile resolutions, pixels per inch vary and will affect actual screen size*

The Unity documentation sections "Getting Started with Android" and "Getting Started with iOS" are well worth reading. The iOS section provides a good breakdown of hardware as well.

Scripting

In keeping with Unity's "build once" mantra, the scripting for iOS and Android is handled mostly through the Input class where you will find Input.touches, Input.acceleration, Input.deviceOrientation, and a host of other related class functions and variables. A few device functions such as GPS are only available for the iOS. iPhoneInput.lastLocation gets the last measured device geographical location. Additionally, in some cases, such as the device's virtual keyboard, Unity Android reuses the iOS API to display a system keyboard.

For general scripting purposes, as mentioned earlier in the project, mobile platforms do not allow dynamic typing, where, if you use

```
var someVar = 4;
```

it will assume you are creating a variable of type Int and assigning the value 4 to it. For mobile you *must* declare the type, like so:

```
var someVar : Int = 4;
```

If you find yourself in the position where you need get serious about typing your variables, you can use the following at the top of each script:

```
#pragma strict
```
This line acts like the typing police and will force the compiler to report dynamic typing as errors, allowing you to quickly find and correct any infractions.

Not surprisingly, mouse functions like OnMouseDown and OnMouseOver are not supported in mobile devices.

Navigation and Input

Perhaps the most important design consideration when developing for mobile platforms is that of user input and navigation. Without keyboards, mice, or gamepad type input devices, player interaction with your game will be quite different. The additional functionality of multitouch and accelerometer orientation and tracking (and in some cases, even GPS) opens the door to several new possibilities. The challenge is not to merely port a desktop game to a mobile device but to be innovative in how the player interacts with objects inside the game.

For instance, take your first person adventure game. You can see that its current game play is greatly dependent on having a mouse for interaction and keyboard keys for navigation. You currently use the mouse to identify action objects through your scene by hovering over promising looking objects. With mobile, your fingertip in place of the cursor could obscure the objects you are looking for and even hide a color changing object. Screen real estate is severely limited in mobile phones, so text descriptions may need to be less verbose.

Obviously, some major design changes would make the port to mobile more feasible. Without the arrow keys to navigate the scene, you could consider using the accelerometer to navigate the scene. On both iPhone and Android, the three axes of rotation could be used to move the player through the scene. As a device is moved, its accelerometer hardware reports linear acceleration changes along the three primary axes in three-dimensional space. This means you can detect both the current orientation of the device (relative to the ground) and any immediate changes to that orientation. If you think of the player or a character in the scene as a ball rolling on a flat surface, you can picture how navigation could be implemented.

Used in conjunction with additional touch contact, you could design navigation so it only happens when the lower corner or corners of the screen are being touched while the device is being tipped, giving the device a gamepad-like feel. If no corner touch is detected, a crosshair or hot spot could appear in the center of the screen to detect "mouseovers" as the player looks around via the accelerometer while tipping the device. Or, using a script similar to your camera match script, you could simply have the player tap the screen and, using waypoints for simple AI, let the game take him to that point with minimal effort and skill required on his part.

You could also use a small icon that behaves as a virtual joystick. The player touches the icon on the screen and moves his finger in the direction he wants the character (first person or third) to go. As you can see, there are several navigation systems that get the job done.

Touch input is quite sophisticated; iOS and Android devices are capable of tracking multiple fingers touching the screen simultaneously. Touches are tracked for time since first touch, so it's possible to tell if the player's finger or fingers have tapped once or multiple times or have moved past a minimum distance since the touch began. Most users are already familiar with moving fingers closer together to zoom out and further apart to zoom in, even if you have not yet employed that type of functionality.

Just as the focal point got closer when the entertainment industry shifted from movie theaters to the small screen of the early televisions, so too can you adjust the visual expectations of your adventure game. Once identified as an action object, a quick finger tap on the object could bring it into Examine mode by zooming in on it and disabling regular navigation. Using familiar touch screen functionality, the player could spin the object or zoom in and out before triggering its response. By utilizing camera layers, you could choose to mask the background during the mode as well.

Unity documentation on touch and accelerometer is quite good. Unity's Mobile Devices Input API is based on Apple's iOS API, so you may wish to learn more about the native API to better understand Unity's Input API. To find links to the Apple input documentation, check the Unity help documents at Unity Manual ➤ User Guide ➤ Creating Gameplay ➤ Input under Further Reading.

On the off chance you occasionally need a keyboard interface for user input, both iPhone and Android make use of the iOS API. There are a few features that are not supported on the Android, so be sure to read the documentation before trying to implement the feature.

For more information on mobile platform navigation, be sure to check out the Penelope tutorial for iPhone on the Unity web site. About a third of the tutorial is devoted to developing three different types of navigation controls for the third person character, Penelope.

Shaders and Textures

For mobile platforms, you will most certainly need to put some thought into both the size and format of the textures needed for the game assets. Lights and shaders also play a part in optimizing your game for maximum performance as you await the next jump in mobile hardware capabilities.

One of the most common concerns of artists is how big to make the textures. The answer will depend on the target platform and how the object or objects using them will appear in the scene. Before you can make an informed decision, you need know how big they will appear on screen. Currently, mobile phones range from a resolution of about 320×480 for iPhone to 800×480 for an Android Nexus One. As new models are constantly increasing in resolution, you will need to be aware of your target platform. If you specify 320×480 for your screen size and the object in question will never be seen taking up more than 100-150 pixels of the screen at any time, you would be probably be wasting memory if the texture used on the object was bigger than 128×128.

As artists, you probably like to use big textures with lots of detail. If the game is destined for more than just mobile platforms, consider have two version of the texture: a low resolution version for mobile and the regular version. While you can tell Unity to constrain a texture to a maximum size, allowing any application, be it your favorite image editor or game engine, to shrink a large image using some sort of formula does not insure a useful result. For this same reason, a good rule of thumb is to author the image no more than one size larger than the finished image needs to be. This way, the compression will be less likely to harm the integrity of the original image, and you won't be tempted to spend time on details that will be obliterated in the final resolution. In the smaller version, the brightness and contrast will need to be higher because some small details will need to be exaggerated.

For texture size on mobile platforms, a good rule of thumb is currently 256×256 or smaller. The most important rule here is to follow the base 2 size rule: images should be 8×8, 16×16, 32×32, 128×128, 256×256, and in some cases, 512×512 if the hardware permits and the object is justified. You would, of course, use a more detailed and larger texture on a main character than a filler object with little importance in the game.

Realtime shadows, expensive even on cutting edge desktop systems, are not supported on mobile platforms yet so you would need to bake lighting into your textures whenever possible for static objects. Consider baking ambient occlusion into dynamic objects so the nooks and crannies will be darker, thereby defining shapes better. Remember to mark static objects as Static for better internal processing.

Lights, in general, are expensive: each light has to be calculated and added to each vertex in the scene. While pixel shaders are supported on newer phones, vertex shaders and vertex lights use fewer resources. Blob shadows, as created with projectors, should be avoided as they require extra lighting passes.

Using alpha channels is also expensive and may not necessarily be supported, depending on platform. Be sure to read the documentation thoroughly and do plenty of experiments to make sure your ideas can be implemented before spending masses of time on unusable assets.

Another good practice is to share materials, not just textures, between objects. Using the same brick material on several structures is obvious, but combining multiple objects for unwrapping on a single texture sheet has several benefits. The more pieces to be unwrapped, the more likely you will get a more efficient packing of the pieces. When painting the texture map, the colors and style will be more likely to have better continuity, and finally, using the same texture on multiple objects is always more efficient in game.

Texture compression is another issue faced in mobile games. As a default, Unity compresses images to an appropriate version of DXT, as can be seen in the preview window in the Inspector when the texture is selected. For iOS, Unity recommends that you use the PVRTC format; for Android, you should use ETC. DXT may be supported, but if it isn't, textures will be decompressed to RGBA format at runtime, taking much more memory. Note that non- square textures are not supported by the ETC format on Android. The main thing to keep an eye on here is that textures used for the GUI may be too lossy and that they will need to be set to a different format to retain their integrity.

Poly Count

Poly count (the number of vertices or triangles in the scene) is usually one of the first questions artists ask about. While you *do* need to be aware of the entire scene's poly count for memory usage, what is of immediate importance is how many polygons are drawn on screen at any one time. This directly impacts frame rate.

Also note that in the Unity documentation, guidelines are given in vertex count instead of triangle or face count. The same object that is smoothed or sharing vertices will take less time to render than its hard-edged counterpart. In realtime engines, to achieve a hard edge, the vertex normals where faces meet will each have a different value and are shown as separate vertices, hence the use of vertex count rather than triangle or face count.

Be aware that, as in real time, *everything* in your scene affects frame rate, be it physics, textures, shaders, animations, or special effects. Compromises can be made when you decide one feature is more important than another. If you really must use a fancier shader on a mesh, consider lowering the poly count in the rest of the scene to make up the frame rate and vice versa.

You may have heard of the 7,000 polygon limit on screen or in the viewing frustum at any one time. Even though the previously mentioned factors also play a part and it is considered to be more of a myth, you can still use poly count as a starting place when designing the models for your scene.

Keeping in mind that hardware is constantly changing, Unity has suggested the following guidelines for iOS:

- With the first and second generations of iPhone, 7-10,000 vertices, 5,000 skinned vertices, and 40-100 objects on screen were the suggested guidelines.
- Newer devices, such as the third and fourth generation iPad, iPhone 3 and iPhone 4G are considerably more robust with 30-40,000 regular vertex count, 15,000 for skinned vertices, and 70-200 objects on screen at any one time, thereby illustrating the jump in hardware improvement.
- Thirty or less bones per character is still recommended for characters, but the amount of vertices they control has almost tripled.

Although the fragmentation in Android devices as far as standardization goes makes it difficult to safely predict performance across devices, Unity suggests that the iOS guidelines are valid for them as well.

Batching

For better performance, Unity automatically combines or batches small meshes (less than 300 triangles) using the same texture sheet. This means that up to 20 objects could be batched into one draw call if they all use the same material. This dynamic batching of individual objects is more efficient than combining meshes, either with actual geometry or through scripting (such as the Combine Children script), when the objects are spread across the scene because it is done after frustum culling.

As an example, a row of 20 corral fence posts, all using the same material and less than 300 triangles each, could either be batched or combined. Let's say only three are visible on screen (Figure 17-4, right). If combined, the engine checks and sees that the bounding box of the fence posts is at least partially inside the viewing frustum. While it is a single draw call, it still must now go through each triangle for all twenty fence posts to see if each needs to be drawn. With batching, the bounding boxes of the twenty fence posts are checked first and only the faces of the three in the viewing frustum are checked before drawing.

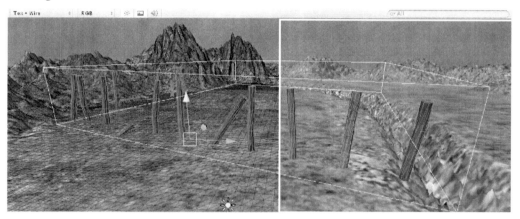

Figure 17-4. *The fence posts as a single mesh. All faces must be checked, even if only the three on the right are inside the viewing frustum.*

Conversely, a lot of small objects in close proximity are better off combined (see Figure 17-5) as it is less likely they will not all be on screen at the same time, making it more efficient to check a single bounding box. Draw calls are calculated on a per material basis for them, so you are assuming they share the same texture sheet or image.

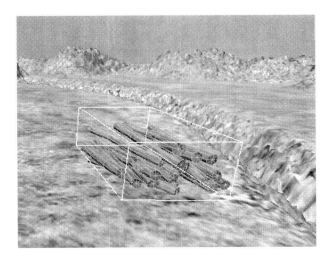

Figure 17-5. *The same posts in a pile—a good candidate to be combined as a single mesh*

For large objects that will rarely be seen fully within the viewing frustum at any one time, such as large buildings, combine meshes when possible (1500-4000 is apparently the sweet spot) if they can use one material but keep logical sectors separate for occlusion culling.

Another important way to take advantage of batching is to bake the textures for several different objects into the same image or texture sheet. Since they all use the same material, they can be batched, even though they have different meshes, thereby saving draw calls. In Figure 17-6, the sign, cow skull, and lunch sack have been unwrapped, while the odd looking fungi use simple mapping for both stem and cap textures. The unwrapped textures and flat textures are all combined and arranged on the same texture sheet so they can all use the same material.

Figure 17-6. *Six objects sharing the same texture sheet*

Colliders

As with any scene, you will want to simplify colliders for meshes that are too complex to use primitives because of design functionality. Create low poly stand-ins along with the regular objects in your DCC program. Once imported, you can remove or turn off the Mesh Renderer for them and use Mesh Colliders. Because terrains generated inside Unity are not supported in the current mobile platforms, you will need to create meshes for your terrains. Consider creating lower polygon versions of these as well. The performance gain may be worth the slight visual abnormalities of a character's feet being a bit above or below the terrain's surface, especially on the smaller screens of mobile phones.

Menus and GUI

Menus and GUI elements present special challenges. On mobile phones, the controls, whether buttons or navigation icons, need to be big enough and far enough apart so that the player interacts with only one at a time. With limited screen real estate, this may also mean that menus should scroll, as you have come to expect on mobile phones. HUD (heads up displays), on the other hand, can easily hog enough screen space to become unwanted distractions.

The bottom line with menus and GUI elements is that you should probably invest a bit of time testing existing games to see how well other developers have met the challenge. While investigating various ideas can be rewarding, there are enough apps out these days that you need not re-invent the wheel unless the uniqueness of your game requires it.

Whatever scheme you decide upon for your menus and GUI elements, it is strongly recommended that you use a percent of screen rather than pixel position to arrange the components. This is especially true if you are going to publish to Android where the resolutions vary enough to make your GUI visually different, but not enough to justify the substitution of different sized controls through coding. Another thing to be aware of is that wildly different screen resolutions may actually be nearly the same size in actual measurement upon the actual devices. What will be a perfect button-sized resolution on one device could be totally wrong on another.

Miscellaneous

Among the features that are not supported on the mobile devices are the tree generator, the terrain generator, and dynamic shadows. Use skyboxes to fake distant geometry and camera clipping planes to further cull distant geometry. Supported, but not recommended until the hardware gets more powerful, are fog and blob shadows and other projector type effects that cause more draw calls.

Several features are only supported in the Pro version. Occlusion culling, Asset Bundles, static batching, and video playback are a few of the features that are only available with Unity Pro.

Occlusion culling can be done manually with good design, allowing you to turn off large chunks of geometry not visible at various locations. Backface culling, where triangles facing away from the camera are not rendered, is automatic. Overdraw is where triangles facing the camera are drawn; when occluded by other objects, they are no longer visible but were drawn just the same. With the iOS, overdraw is handled later in the rendering process and is more efficient. While best practice is to reduce overdraw by turning off entire blocks of objects, remember that parallax is by definition going to cause overdraw, but it's also what gives the player a feeling of being in 3D space.

Asset bundles allow the game to load and unload assets dynamically during the game but require the extra assets to be managed from a remote server. This is quickly becoming a favorite feature for Android developers due to the stringent size restrictions placed on apps by the app store. If your interest lies in this direction, you will need to invest in Unity Pro at some point. If your game is small, asset-wise, you may not require this feature.

Be sure to consult the documentation for a full list of supported features on mobile platforms if you want to pursue the mobile market.

Design Doc

Finally, now that you have a much better idea of what is involved in making a game, you can put together a simple design doc. Although this may seem more than a bit backwards, it actually makes a lot of sense for a few different reasons.

The primary reason to create the document at this stage, especially if it is your first project, is that it will serve as a review of the game building process while things are still relatively fresh in your mind. As you write out the story, you may think of features that required a change in story to improve game play or avoid unnecessary workarounds. You are far more likely to still recall the reasons behind the mechanics of navigation, interaction, and feature behavior; you remember the problems that arose and the solutions that were developed. It is also a nice way to have quick access to design ideas and implementation should you wish to continue with a sequel where continuity is important; or perhaps you want to create a new game and you want to make sure you are *not* repeating something you have already done. It can also serve a quick means to see what assets were used and possibly available for other projects long after the files have been archived.

The second reason to get some practice with a design document is if you ever plan to work with a team. As an indie developer, you probably kept lists of assets needed, tasks to be completed, story line considerations, and game play ideas. This may be sufficient for small teams working in a single location where communication is good and ongoing, but in today's world where it is quite conceivable to have team members spread across the globe, a more formal roadmap of the project and its goals is crucial. If you are in charge and paying the team members, it will help keep your costs down by minimizing changes as the project progresses. If you are in charge and your team consists of all volunteers, it can help minimize the frustration of needing assets redone by forcing you to define things more clearly from the start. If the specifications exist, a preliminary discussion can reduce a lot of wasted time and hurt feelings. Free help is more likely to stick with a project when they know they are appreciated and can see that the game will actually be completed at some point.

As a last scenario, you have taken your project as far as you can, but you feel that it deserves more time and money to put the final polish on it. As an artist or designer, your next step after completing your proof of concept game may be to look for funding, programmers skilled in optimization, people skilled in marketing, or other help in bringing it to market. While the game as-is goes a long way towards establishing your credibility, there's nothing like a formal design document to let people know you have the discipline and communication skills to be able to work with collaborators to see the project to the next level.

Here, then, is your book project in useful generic design document form. Your design document could contain images from the game since it is that far along; for games that are not yet underway, be sure to use only top quality concept art to illustrate where necessary. Because this is an adventure game, the detailed description of your game becomes a general walkthrough.

The Story/Game in Its Briefest Form

You are an adventurer exploring ruins in a tropical jungle. You will need to figure out how to use the objects at hand to gain entry into the temple and solve its mystery.

The Story/Game in More Detail

You start near a clearing with an old wooden chest. There is an old iron crowbar nearby. You take it. Checking the lid, you find that the chest is locked. Noticing a rock that looks a bit out of place, you lift it to find an old iron key that can only belong to the chest. After unlocking the chest, you discover a note left by an earlier adventurer. It warns of needing to adorn iron weapons or have them confiscated and removed to a maze. It also goes on about the maze being evil and able to reconfigure itself, which you promptly dismiss as poppycock.

Wandering on through the area, you discover a small shrine with an odd looking stone representation that is reminiscent of a pipe organ. Where the keyboard would have been, this has a stone drawer that appears to hinge from the bottom edge like a laundry chute door. Nothing happens when you click it until, after perusing the lump of stone from which the shrine is carved, you discover a glyph with the exact shape of the indentation. Upon inserting the glyph and clicking on the drawer, it closes and then opens again to the accompaniment of an eerie greenish light and the sound of the breathy chords of a pan pipe.

Shaking your head in puzzlement, you head over to inspect the massive stone walls of a structure that seems to dominate a good portion of the area. Upon reaching the corner, you discover the entrance to what must be the "evil" maze. Chuckling to yourself, you enter the maze only to be greeted by the same weird light and eerie sound you heard back at the little shrine. After the hairs on the back of your neck settle back down, you take a quick wander through the maze, noting that it is more imposing than difficult to navigate through.

Finding your way back out, you head for the next large structure, a stone temple guarded by two large jaguar statues. As you get closer, you decide it is not just your imagination—a play of light resembling, oddly enough, a miniature aurora borealis comes to life as you approach. You cautiously draw near the temple steps and nearly drop your backpack when a voice out of nowhere tells you that you must bring an offering before you will be admitted to the temple. Quickly retreating, you decide to explore the area, wondering where you will find something that will serve as a suitable offering now that you are determined to explore the inside of the temple.

A short distance from the temple you discover a beautiful waterfall and the small shrine carved into the rock behind it. You keep thinking there ought to be a corresponding water glyph somewhere nearby, but you surmise that someone else must have beat you to it.

Adjacent to the waterfall is a huge domed rock formation. Eventually, you discover that you can scale the beast by starting from the milder slope of its backside. In a moment of carelessness, you fall down a hole in the top of the dome, landing in a small circular chamber where you are now picturing your bones crumbling into dust. Before you can contemplate the company that is sure to join you over the millennia, you spot a dark passageway off in the shadows. With a fatalistic shrug, you drop down once more, this time into a narrow tunnel. Bumping around for a bit, you arrive with great relief to a low ledge overlooking the temple and surrounding jungle.

Back on your feet again, you decide to investigate several other shrines in the immediate area that you noticed from the ledge. There is a shrine with a mountain glyph half buried in the rich forest soil and a shrine with a flame burning from an apparently empty bowl. As neither shrine offer any immediate means of interacting, you look to the next shrine.

This next shrine contains a stone chest with glyph containing an open circle. You have the brief flash of the open symbol used in electronics. Trying the chest's lid, you discover you are not able to budge it. In a flash of insight, you decide the glyph must be the key and the stone mechanism the chest's lock. Rotating the mechanism, you once again try the lid to find that with a bit of straining, you can open it. Revealed inside is a strange vial of some sort of elixir.

Stashing the vial carefully in your pack, you head off to the next shrine, the one that features what looks to be a couple of sprouting leaves. Oddly, the plant that seems to be the centerpiece of the shrine is wilted and drooping off of its pedestal. In a moment of pity, you use the vial of elixir to revive the plant, regretting your impulse until you spot the fabulous jewel spinning at the center of the now robust flower.

Recognizing the jewel as the means to enter the temple, you rush off to test your theory. With the jewel in hand, you are allowed to enter the temple through the distinctive gold and black tapestries. In your haste to enter the intriguing edifice, you ignore the second half of the guardian entity's message to you.

Spotting an open stone door at the bottom of the temple's outside passage, you make your way up to the balcony you noticed when you first turned the corner of the passageway. In an opening that looks over the inner chamber, you spot your former offering floating above a bowl containing a strange golden tube-shaped object with a trailing floral device. Grabbing the object, you head back down to investigate the inner chamber.

The inner chamber sports a large bowl filled with fire that doesn't seem to do anything so you cross the room and head downward to investigate the two storage rooms at the bottom of the ramp. In the room on the right, you notice a small iron sphere on the floor. When you try to pick it up, it sputters to life to display a hologram of a blasted tree trunk with something golden in its bole.

In the opposite room, you find a couple of musty old grain sacks. Curiosity getting the best of you, you try to rip one open, only to find the material much tougher than you had imaged. In a moment of inspiration, you riffle through your pack to find the crowbar, thinking it will be able to rip through the sack. Unable to find the crowbar, you suddenly remember the warning about weapons being relocated to the maze. Heading back up through the inner chamber, you notice a couple of beautiful black and gold tapestries on the far wall. They depict the stylized jaguars holding a large gourd-like object. You briefly wonder if it was the same thing that was in the tree bole in the hologram.

Outside, you make your way to the maze again and, after a bit of searching, find your crowbar. As the weird lights are no longer blocking the entrance into the temple, you run up the steps only to find that your crowbar has been taken again. Back in the maze, you realize that not only has the maze shifted configuration, the crowbar is not in the same place either! When you finally locate the pesky thing, you pause for a moment to puzzle out how you will get the crowbar into the temple. Checking the meager contents of your backpack, you are struck by the shape and size of the gold tube thing—it looks as if it will easily slip right over the crowbar. Testing your theory, you discover you are correct; the sleeve slips easily onto the crowbar, leaving you with what appears to resemble some ceremonial device instead of a simple crowbar.

As expected, this time you enter the temple unchallenged and head down to the storeroom with anticipation. Taking the crowbar with golden sleeve out of your pack, you give the old grain sack a mighty whack. The grain spills out, revealing a golden fruit-like object that is obviously the same as in the tapestries and hologram. As you take the fruit, you feel a rumble and here the scraping of stone on stone. The word "topi" comes to mind as you put your hands around the strange fruit.

Keeping alert, you slowly head back up, looking for a change in your surroundings. As you exit the inner chamber, your excitement grows as you spot the newly opened door opposite the one leading up to the balcony. The new passage, however, leads downward, getting increasingly damper as you go.

Finally, after going through a tiny side room, you find yourself in a large cavern whose main feature is a large shallow lake. On a small island in the middle of the lake is a stele topped with a topi fruit glyph and bathed in golden. Unable to stop yourself, you head toward the beacon, hoping the water is shallow all the way to the island. As you get near the island, everything suddenly goes black.

When the darkness clears, you find yourself in a strange twilight world heading toward a ring of standing stones. Since the rest of the place is shrouded in fog and pretty much featureless, you head toward the stones. On entering them, you see the blasted trunk from the hologram, but there is nothing in the hole. The task now seems obvious. You take the topi fruit from your pack and put it in the hole.

In a few seconds, it begins to glow; in a clap of thunder and a brief flash of darkness, a new live tree replaces the dead tree trunk. A voice tells you that you must secure a new seed (fruit) against future need by tapping the tree.

Touching the tree only gives you a feeling of awe so you decide to try something stronger. You find the ceremonial crowbar and use it to tap the tree; a golden topi fruit falls to the ground. Unfortunately, while you stand there gawking in wonderment at the whole situation, the fruit disappears in a puff of smoke. Panicking, you tap the trunk several more times and are relieved to find there seems to be an endless supply of the fruits. Finally getting your timing right, you manage to grab one before it can disappear.

Game over, roll credits.

Who Is the Game For?

This game is for lovers of the classic first person adventure where mechanical puzzles mix with magic to challenge the player with intriguing tasks and unexpected events.

What is the Target Platform?

Mac OS X and Windows on a desktop.

Uniqueness and Marketability

There aren't many classic first person adventure games around anymore where the player can wander around the environment, take in the beauty of the scenery, and use everything that is not nailed down in order to divine the use and combinations to move the story along. This genre is an armchair substitution for those whose desire for world travel and cultural discovery, combined with a sprinkling of fantasy is not attainable in their everyday lives.

Controls and Navigation

The player navigates about the scene using the arrow keys to move forward and backward and to turn left and right. The A and D keys allow the player to strafe left and right while the W and S key mimic the up and down arrow keys. The spacebar allows the player to jump, but that action is not an integral feature of the game and is implemented to ease the player through difficult navigation rather than as a requirement to reach certain areas.

Since most of the action object interaction is done while the player is not moving, mouse-look requires either the Shift key or the right mouse button to be held down while moving the mouse to enable the player to look up and down. The cursor or pointer, the essential means for identifying and interacting with action objects, is suppressed during navigation. It also changes color when over action objects.

The player is allowed to customize the cursor mouseover color as well as suppress mouseover and text functionality through a Settings menu. Audio levels for the various asset types can also be adjusted through the menu. The player cannot remap the navigation keys.

To make navigation easier, when the player picks an object, the First Person Controller can be automatically moved and oriented to the ideal place to watch the resultant animation.

Game Mechanics

The primary means of interaction in the game consists of the player clicking on objects to either take the object or cause something to happen. To identify action objects, the cursor changes color on mouseover and the object's name and a short description is displayed. At a certain distance away from the object, the description is suppressed; if the player tries to click on the object, he is told he is too far away from it for interaction. Cursor and mouseover functionality is suppressed while the player is navigating the scene. When stopped, the player may use the mouse to scan the scene for action objects with the cursor. To look up and down, he is required to use the Shift key or right mouse button. This system ensures that the scene does not spin wildly as the player looks for action objects.

Once identified, the player will be required to click on the action objects to initiate a response. An action message will be displayed, describing the result or offering further clues. Picking the objects may do one of three things. The action message may inform the player that something else is needed to produce a reaction, thereby offering a clue and confirming that the player is on the right track. Or picking the object may initiate a sequence of animations and special effects on that object as well as any number of auxiliary objects.

The third possibility is that the object will be taken into the player's inventory, a virtual backpack of unlimited space. In inventory mode, objects are represented by square 2D texture icons and can be either in inventory or as a cursor. To enter inventory, the player presses the i key on the keyboard or picks the inventory icon in the lower left corner of the screen. Both methods act as toggles for inventory mode.

The inventory screen is a camera overlay of the existing scene where objects can be taken or dropped at will. If the cursor is the default cursor and an object is picked, it is removed from the grid and becomes the current cursor. If the cursor is an inventory object and a blank spot is clicked on the panel, the object is added to the end of the grid. If the cursor is an inventory object and the player picks an object on the grid, the two are swapped—the cursor takes the place of the other object and the other object becomes the new cursor. If the two objects can be combined, the grid object is removed, causing the grid layout to be updated, and the new combination object becomes the cursor. The order of picking is not relevant.

The inventory panel holds places for nine objects to be viewed at any one time. If there are more than nine objects currently in inventory, the appropriate panel navigation arrows are activated. Inventory mode can be exited by picking outside of the inventory panel. Cursors that are inventory objects will be retained on returning to the scene.

When the cursor is an inventory object in the regular scene, it can be used to pick action objects. If there is no benefit in using that cursor with the picked action object, the cursor object will be returned to inventory and the action message will confirm that it was of no use. If the cursor was indeed required to precipitate an action sequence, the sequence will be triggered and the cursor will either go back into inventory, be removed from the scene altogether, or in the case of objects that can be combined, produce a new object in the scene. As with combination items in inventory, the two component objects are replaced in the scene with a third object.

Reading material, as an inventory object, is brought to the front of the camera for perusal. On clicking, it is returned to inventory. This allows for papers, books, etc. to contain diagrams, story background, and clues necessary for the game.

While most interaction is pick-based, the temple bouncer, an invisible entity represented by a particle system, is managed by colliders. The outmost collider serves as a distance range to display the particle system. The next collider area manages interaction and voice response to the player's presence. The third serves a regular collision wall to prevent entry into the temple. The managing collider checks to see if an offering of sufficient value is being carried as a cursor. If so, the player is allowed to enter the temple and the object is taken. Once allowed in, the bouncer entity goes through the player's inventory looking for objects defined as weapons. If any are found, they are removed to a random position in the maze. A weapon can have its true purpose masked with the addition of gold ornamentation.

The maze is a construction of forty-nine interior walls that are rotated a random direction and random degrees (90 degree increments) at startup. It is checked for one-cell and two-cell closed configurations and will regenerate itself if any are found, as this could cause the transformed weapon to be inaccessible by the player. Because the odds of more than two cells being enclosed are very high and the math involved in checking those configurations increasingly complicated, there is a mechanism that allows the player to reset the maze in game. When the music glyph is added to the stone drawer in the music shrine, the user can operate the drawer, which will cause the maze to be reset. The eerie light and sound effect produced along with the action is repeated whenever the player enters or exits the maze to clue the player in to the connection. As an Easter egg, if the player presses the M key on the keyboard, a mini-map of the maze appears in the top right corner of the screen, allowing him to witness the resetting of the maze. Unfortunately, the weapon will be too small to locate in this way, but it may help him find his way out once he has located the weapon.

In the final level, physics are used to drop topi fruit from atop the Tree of Life where they are instantiated one at a time and then destroyed in a puff of dust after a short interval.

Cloth objects are used at the temple entrance to help hide the transition from inside to outside where the terrain is turned off and the cavern turned onto allow the game to continue underground. The mechanism for turning appropriated objects off and on is a set of colliders using on trigger.

The game can be saved and loaded to a single file retaining the state of all action items, inventory items, the player's location and orientation as well as his preferences. Non-action objects' states can be saved with the addition of an extra script or two.

The camera match used to move the First Person Controller to watch a sequence play out is optional. When used, it will require a position target and a look at target. When completed, navigation control is returned to the player.

Assessment, Scoring, and Winning

As with most adventure games, assessment is tied directly with the accomplishment of tasks or problem solving that allows the player to move the game along so a score system is not necessary. The goal of the game is slowly revealed as the player goes about the process of collecting an odd assortment of objects and tries to figure out what their purpose will be in moving the game forward. The game is completed when the player completes the final task, restoring a new incarnation of the tree of life and securing a new topi fruit to hide for the next time the tree needs to be renewed.

Level Design

The game prototype consists of three levels. The first level contains the Start menu and sets the mood and style for the game through the use of several elements borrowed from the main level.

In the main level, the player finds seven stone stele, seven small shrines (one for each of the Tizzleblat glyphs), a large stone maze, the temple, and a large stone dome complete with a small tunnel system. Most features are within close range of each other so the player can concentrate on making connections and solving tasks as opposed to traveling long distances to locate clues and action objects. The majority of game play happens in the main level where the terrain adds visual interest but not physical obstacles for the player.

The final level is concerned with the player performing the two remaining tasks and consists of a large plain swathed in fog and a small rise where the standing stones can be seen to draw the player for the win sequence.

Visual Style

The style is realistic with slightly over-saturated colors. The main theme is hammered black iron adorned with gold—this is found not only on the glyphs, but is used throughout the man-made artifacts. Structures superficially reflect the Mayan pyramid in form but generally contain a ledge part way up the structure to break the sloping lines of the walls. This can be seen in the temple, the stele, and the shrines. The Jaguar, less stylized than its Mayan counterpart, is a common theme and is normally depicted in a rather rough hewn form as the Tizzleblatians believed that too much realism would draw live big cats to the vicinity. The most prevalent motif is that of an open torus, open side up, containing one of the seven symbols represented in the Tizzleblat religion. In their smaller form, the glyphs are constructed with the hammered iron for the torus and high karat gold for the contained symbol. The feel is of an era of masonry mastery with a touch of the mystical. Engineering prowess is apparent with the ease of movement shown by the dynamic tendencies of various stone elements throughout the environment.

User Interface

The GUI consists of game text displayed on mouseover so the player can recognize action objects by their name and short description. Picking the object will cause an action message to be displayed, either describing the resultant action or offering hints or comments relevant to the object and its state.

Game menus are brought up by moving the cursor to the upper left corner of the screen or pressing the F1 key to toggle the main menu. Menus overlay the current level with the use of camera layers so there is no lag when moving back and forth. They feature different locations throughout the environment as backgrounds.

Characters and Action Objects

- **Wooden Chest** must be unlocked before the lid can be opened.

- **Iron Crowbar** is considered a weapon. If you attempt to take it into the temple, it will be relocated to a random location inside the maze.

- **Rock** on the ground must be moved to reveal the key to the chest.

- **Iron Key** is found under the rock and must be inserted, then turned before the player can open the chest lid. It can't be removed or turned when the lid is open.

- **Message**, hand written on an old sheet of paper, is locked inside the chest. It contains hints about combining gold with iron to mask a weapon's purpose and an evil maze that resets its configuration.

- **Drawer** is part of the pipes in the music shrine and it has an indentation where the music glyph fits. With the glyph in place, the drawer closes then opens to an eerie chord and spooky greenish light. Unseen, the maze reconfigures itself when the drawer is operated.

- **Music Glyph** can be found on the left side of the music shrine. When inserted in the drawer's indentation, the drawer can be activated.

- **Stone Chest** is found in safekeeping shrine, its glyph is already in place. You will still need to turn the "key" (the section holding its glyph) to unlock the chest before you can open the lid.

- **Vial of Elixir** is found safely tucked away inside the stone chest.

- **Flower** is found in the flora shrine. You must use the vial of elixir to revive the plant from its wilted state.

- **Jewel** is revealed when the plant is revived. You will need it as an offering to gain entrance in the temple.

- **Temple Guardian** is also known as the Temple Bouncer. This non-mesh entity, represented by a particle system resembling a miniature aurora borealis, controls access to the temple entrance. You will need to be carrying the jewel before it will grant you access.

- **Golden Sleeve** is found at the upper balcony inside the temple. You will need it to slip over the iron crowbar in order to disguise its purpose.

- **Iron Sphere** is located in on the floor of one of the storage rooms at the bottom of the temple, touching the sphere activates a hologram that shows a golden object inside the bole of a blasted tree trunk.

- **Grain Sack** is located in the opposite storage room. You will need to whack it with the crowbar with golden sleeve to open it and reveal a golden topi fruit.

- **Crowbar with Sleeve** needs to take the golden sleeve back out of the temple and locate the crowbar and combine the two either in inventory or in the scene to create the combination object that is allowed inside the temple

- **Topi Fruit** is first revealed when the old grain sack is breached. In the final scene, it must be used to precipitate the final sequence; after that, it becomes the last action object as it is the new seed that must be taken and hidden (implied) for the next time the Tree of Life needs to be reincarnated.

- **Trunk Bole** is where you place the topi fruit in the final level; it will cause the tree to become reincarnated.

- **Tree of Life,** once reincarnated, must be tapped by the crowbar and golden sleeve. Whenever it is tapped, the tree will drop a new topi fruit. If you don't take it quickly, it disappears in a puff of smoke. Picking one of the dropped topi fruit ends the game.

Environmental and Non-Interactive Assets

Architectural assets include the Temple of Tizzleblat, a large stone temple reminiscent of the Mayan temples of Mesoamerica. A stone walled maze of heroic proportion that dynamically resets itself dominates much of the landscape. There are seven stone stele, consisting of a lower pillar of the common grey stone blocks and topped by the various mystic symbols of the followers of Tizzleblat, cunningly crafted in the brown stone local to the area. Several small wayside shrines carved from the brown stone are themed and dedicated to each of the symbols; their corresponding elements can be found scattered throughout the jungle. The water shrine is carved directly into a mountain side where it is hidden by a spectacular waterfall that empties into a medium sized waterhole. The strangest feature is a large rock dome filled with a small tunnel system. It can only be reached by dropping down an access hole on the top of the formation.

The final level contains a Stonehenge-type ring of standing stones with a blasted tree trunk at its center. Upon completion of the final task, a new revitalized Tree of Life takes its place. Structural assets include the following:

- Temple of Tizzleblat

- Underground cavern

- Stone stele

- Shrines

- Maze

- Dome rock with tunnel system

Sound F/X

Bird/jungle sounds, various sound FX for the action objects.

Music

The music for the temple and final win sequence is of a pan-pipe type theme to go with the structures and environment.

Voice

Voice messages are used for the temple guardian messages and also at the final sequence.

Chapter Summary

In your final chapter you took a brief look at possible features that could be added to your game. You discussed issues related to HUD for score tracking or health tracking in adventure games. Another feature not implemented in your game was a hint system; you looked at a number of implementation scenarios. Entertaining the thought of extending your load/save system, you discovered that other than an addition menu, it probably wouldn't require too much extra scripting for the functionality.

You also took a look at the possibility of adding projectiles and more physics to your game and found that there are many existing examples and tutorials available on the topic. Thinking about extending the game led to the concept of retaining data across multiple levels as the player solved tasks and collected objects. With the extra assets provided with the project, you formulated a few more ideas that could be carried out to embellish the existing base game.

Since the next logical direction to go with a first person adventure game is a third person adventure game, you investigated a few of the additional features that would entail. Although beyond the scope of this book, you looked briefly at character animation. In addition to character development and animation, you looked at camera control scenarios and discovered that your camera match script could offer a way to move the character into position, but the camera itself would need to be handled differently than most third person scenarios.

Dialog trees presented an intriguing challenge as you sketched a simple conversation, then played with adding a second character. You thought about increasing the functionality to generate alternate versions of the topics and later allowing for conditions to affect the possible topics. In the end, you decided the data you needed to track was more important than your means of processing or storing it; several different paths would lead to the same results. As a visual progression from dialog trees, you formulated simple or alternative ways to integrate dialog and characters for your first tests.

Mobile platforms being a popular format for today's casual games, you had a look at some basic requirements for moving to mobile platforms. Besides additional hardware, software, and licensing concerns, you discovered that, not surprisingly, a good portion of development for mobile platform centers around optimization. Texture and mesh guidelines were discussed for iOS and Android, keeping in mind how frequently hardware can change.

The most intriguing topic from a design viewpoint was the differences in user input and navigation. With no mouse or keyboard to rely upon, you realized that porting a game to a mobile platform was far more involved than finding workarounds for traditional input. You discovered that mobile offers multitouch and accelerometer functionality on a surprisingly sophisticated level. Combined with Unity's policy of "build once" to deliver to different platforms and devices, you learned that much of the scripting would work for multiple devices.

Finally, to finish off the book's project of creating your own adventure game, you ended the journey with some practice in writing a design document with your game as the topic. Although many indie developers never bother with a formal document for their games, you found it was a good way to summarize the design problems you learned to analyze and overcome. Not only a recap of the design and development process, this document could serve as a means to interest others in your game should you decide to develop it further.

APPENDIX A

■ ■ ■

SSE Shader Graphs

The Strumpy Shader Editor (SSE) is a flow graph-style editor for making shaders in Unity. It is currently free and can be found in the Unity Asset Store. You can connect directly to the Asset Store from the Window menu inside your Unity project. You can also find different versions of the SSE in the Showcase section of the Unity forum in case you are not using the current Unity build.

The SSE BetterLightmap Shader Graph

The BetterLightmap shader allows you to blend in just the right amount of emissive with the lightmap and lets you have glossiness and specular for a more realistic lightmapped solution. Figure A-1 shows how the Diffuse component combines diffuse color, a lightmap, and a regular texture. Note the use of the MeshUV node to specify the UV2 mapping channel. This shader can be used on the temple and other main structural objects by selecting their material version appended with a 1. In other words, the Temple Outer material uses a Legacy Lightmap shader while Temple Outer 1 uses the BetterLightmap shader. Both materials use the same lightmap and texture map

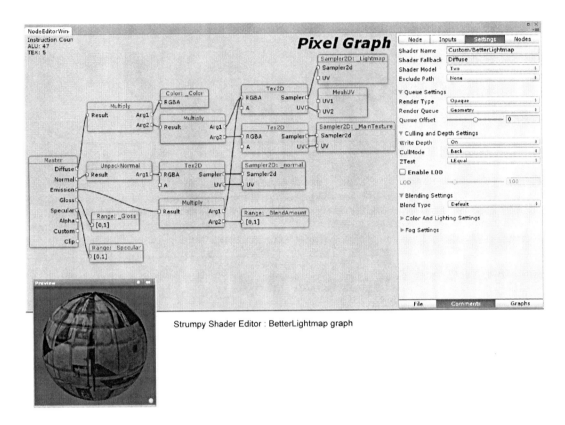

Strumpy Shader Editor : BetterLightmap graph

Figure A-1. *The SSE BetterLightmap shader graph*

The SSE ReflectiveAlpha Shader Graph

The ReflectiveAlpha shader (Figure A-2) allows you to combine a normal map, alpha channel, and a cube map for reflection. Note the use of the Advanced Shadow Pass to incorporate the opacity information into shadows. This shader is used in the Ledge Fringe object's material inside the temple.

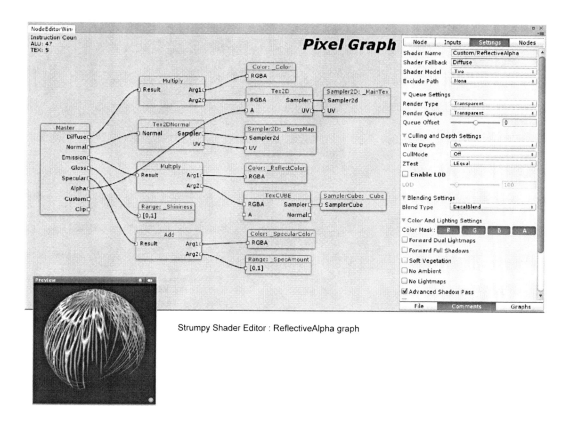

Figure A-2. *The SSE ReflectiveAlpha shader graph*

The SSE ReflectiveCutout Shader Graph

The ReflectiveCutout shader (Figure A-3) also allows you to combine a normal map, alpha channel, and a cube map for reflection. By subtracting the value of the range node, 0 to 1, from the texture's alpha channel value, 0 to 1 (black to white), the resulting value will be anywhere from -1 to 1. In the Clip component, any value below 0 is shown as fully transparent. Anything above is fully opaque. In this shader, the outline of the alpha part will be crisper and will appear to sparkle since it doesn't anti-alias like the alpha blended version. It has the advantage of being rendered in the Geometry pass and is written to the Z buffer. It also needs the Advanced Shadow Pass to incorporate the opacity information into shadows. This shader can be used as an alternative in the Ledge Fringe object's material inside the temple. Try adjusting the Clamp range to change the clipping amount.

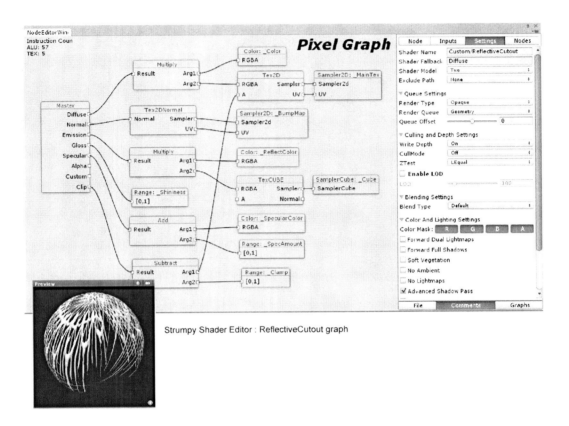

Figure A-3. *The SSE ReflectiveCutout shader graph*

APPENDIX B

Key Codes

Key codes returned by Event.keyCode. These map directly to a physical key on the keyboard.
    Use lower case: Input.GetKeyDown("i"), Input.GetKey ("escape"), Input.GetKeyDown("f1")

Values	
None	Not assigned (never pressed)
Backspace	Backspace key
Delete	Forward delete key
Tab	Tab keyrt
Clear	Clear key
Return	Return key
Pause	Pause on PC machines
Escape	Escape key
Space	Space key
Keypad0	Numeric keypad 0
Keypad1	Numeric keypad 1
Keypad2	Numeric keypad 2
Keypad3	Numeric keypad 3
Keypad4	Numeric keypad 4
Keypad5	Numeric keypad 5
Keypad6	Numeric keypad 6
Keypad7	Numeric keypad 7
Keypad8	Numeric keypad 8
Keypad9	Numeric keypad 9
KeypadPeriod	Numeric keypad .
KeypadDivide	Numeric keypad /
KeypadMultiply	Numeric keypad *

Values

KeypadMinus	Numeric keypad -
KeypadPlus	Numeric keypad +
KeypadEnter	Numeric keypad enter
KeypadEquals	Numeric keypad =
UpArrow	Up arrow key
DownArrow	Down arrow key
RightArrow	Right arrow key
LeftArrow	Left arrow key
Insert	Insert key key
Home	Home key
End	End key
PageUp	Page up key
PageDown	Page down key
F1	F1 function key
F2	F2 function key
F3	F3 function key
F4	F4 function key
F5	F5 function key
F6	F6 function key
F7	F7 function key
F8	F8 function key
F9	F9 function key
F10	F10 function key
F11	F11 function key
F12	F12 function key
F13	F13 function key
F14	F14 function key
F15	F15 function key
Alpha0	The 0 key on the top of the alphanumeric keyboard.
Alpha1	The 1 key on the top of the alphanumeric keyboard.
Alpha2	The 2 key on the top of the alphanumeric keyboard.

Values

Alpha3	The 3 key on the top of the alphanumeric keyboard.
Alpha4	The 4 key on the top of the alphanumeric keyboard.
Alpha5	The 5 key on the top of the alphanumeric keyboard.
Alpha6	The 6 key on the top of the alphanumeric keyboard.
Alpha7	The 7 key on the top of the alphanumeric keyboard.
Alpha8	The 8 key on the top of the alphanumeric keyboard.
Alpha9	The 9 key on the top of the alphanumeric keyboard.
Exclaim	Exclaim key
DoubleQuote	Double quote key
Hash	Hash key
Dollar	Dollar sign key
Ampersand	Ampersand key
Quote	Quote key
LeftParen	Left Parent key
RightParen	Right Parent key
Asterisk	Asterisk key
Plus	Plus key
Comma	Comma key (,)
Minus	Minus key (-)
Period	Period key (.)
Slash	Slash key (/)
Colon	Colon key (,)
Semicolon	Semicolon key (;)
Less	Less key (<)
Equals	Equals key (=)
Greater	Greater key (>)
Question	Question mark key (?)
At	At key
LeftBracket	Left bracket key
Backslash	Backslash key
RightBracket	Backslash key

Values

Caret	Caret key
Underscore	Underscore key (_)
BackQuote	Back quote key
A	a key
B	b key
C	c key
D	d key
E	e key
F	f key
G	g key
H	h key
I	i key
J	j key
K	k key
L	l key
M	m key
N	n key
O	o key
P	p key
Q	q key
R	r key
S	s key
T	t key
U	u key
V	v key
W	w key
X	x key
Y	y key
Z	z key
Numlock	Numlock key
CapsLock	Capslock key

Values

ScrollLock	Scroll lock key
RightShift	Right Shift key
LeftShift	Left shift key
RightControl	Right Control key
LeftControl	Left Control key
RightAlt	Right Alt key
LeftAlt	Left Alt key
LeftApple	Left Apple key
LeftWindows	Left Windows key
RightApple	Right Apple key
RightWindows	Right Windows key
AltGr	Alt Gr key
Help	Help key
Print	Print key
SysReq	Sys Req key
Break	Break key
Menu	Menu key
Mouse0	First (primary) mouse button
Mouse1	Second (secondary) mouse button
Mouse2	Third mouse button
Mouse3	Fourth mouse button
Mouse4	Fifth mouse button
Mouse5	Sixth mouse button
Mouse6	Seventh mouse button

APPENDIX C

■ ■ ■

Final Sequence

1: Player picks TrunkOpening with Topi Fruit Icon

- Metadata:
    - Thunder audio
    - SparklesFalling prefab
- Calls DoTheJob() in:
    - TreeEffects.js
        - triggers Final Group's *end game* animation:
            o Animate windZone
            o Point Trunk Blue position, Intensity and color
            o Point Standing Stones Intensity and color
            o Directional light intensity
            o Blackout opacity animation
            o Calls ExtraTasks() event from Final Group's TreeTasks.js
                - Hide/show tree trunk and topi fruit
                - Activate tree and process metadata, OneTaskRemaining
    - CameraMatchData.js
        - Sends new targets
        - Triggers camera match

2: Player picks Tree of Life with Crowbar with Sleeve Icon, new Hanging Topi Fruit prefab appears
3: Pick Hanging Topi Fruit with default cursor:

- Metadata
- Calls DoTheJob() on:

- CameraMatchData.js (on Point Trunk Blue)– uses Point Trunk Blue as Target Look and TargetTrunkOpening as Target Pos
- FinalTask.js on Main Camera:
  - Set 'end' flag to true (prevent mouseover, etc)
  - Turn off pointer layer for inventory icon
  - Trigger win sound clip from fXSource (this will be Point Trunk Blue)
  - Point Trunk Blue holds SynthUp
  - Play camera's Field of view Change animation, pull back
  - Play the camera's audio clip, Temple

Roll credits

Index

CPSIA information can be obtained at www.ICGtesting.com

232651LV00004B/1/P